Using Excel 3
for Windows™

Special Edition

Ron Person

que®

Using Excel 3 for Windows,™ Special Edition.

Library of Congress Catalog No.: 90-64389

ISBN 0-88022-685-4

94 93 92 91   4 3 2 1

Interpretation of the printing code: the rightmost double-digit number is the year of the book's printing; the rightmost single-digit number, the number of the book's printing. For example, a printing code of 91-1 shows that the first printing of the book occurred in 1991.

This book is based on Microsoft® Excel Version 3.0.

Publisher: Lloyd J. Short

Associate Publisher: Karen A. Bluestein

Acquisitions Manager: Terrie Lynn Solomon

Product Development Manager: Mary Bednarek

Managing Editor: Paul Boger

Book Designer: Scott Cook

Production Team: Hilary Adams, Claudia Bell, Scott Boucher, Martin Coleman, Sandy Grieshop, Denny Hager, Betty Kish, Bob LaRoche, Kimberly Leslie, Howard Peirce, Cindy L. Phipps, Tad Ringo, Bruce Steed, Johnna VanHoose

Product Director
Shelley O'Hara

Production Editor
Pamela Wampler

Editors
Mary Bednarek
Sandra Blackthorn
Fran Blauw
Kelly Currie
Robin Drake
Jeannine McDonel
Diane L. Steele
Laura Wirthlin

Technical Editors
Sharel McVey
Bob Voss

Editorial Assistants
Dorothy Aylward
Patricia J. Brooks

*Composed in Garamond and Macmillan
by Que Corporation*

Ron Person

Ron Person has written more than 12 books for Que Corporation, including *Using Microsoft Windows 3,* 2nd Edition; *Excel Tips, Tricks, and Traps*; *Using Word for Windows*; and *Using 1-2-3 Release 3*. Ron is the principal consultant for Ron Person & Co. He has an M.S. in physics from The Ohio State University and an M.B.A. from Hardin-Simmons University.

Ron Person & Co., based in San Francisco, is one of 14 firms that has attained Microsoft's highest rating for Excel consultants—Microsoft Consulting Partner. The firm is also a Microsoft Registered Developer for Excel and Word for Windows. The firm's experience includes financial, marketing, and executive information systems based in Excel, and office automation systems based in Word for Windows. The firm converts Lotus 1-2-3 based systems to Excel. In addition to consulting, Ron Person & Co. delivers training and licenses training materials to corporate clients in Windows, Excel, and Word for Windows. Courses range from introductory to developer levels.

For more information about consulting, training, or training materials, contact Ron Person & Co. at:

Ron Person & Co.
P.O. Box 5647
Santa Rosa, CA 95402
707-539-1525

TRADEMARK ACKNOWLEDGMENTS

Que Corporation has made every effort to supply trademark information about company names, products, and services mentioned in this book. Trademarks indicated below were derived from various sources. Que Corporation cannot attest to the accuracy of this information.

1-2-3 and Ami Pro are registered trademarks of Lotus Development Corporation.

3Com EtherSeries is a trademark of 3Com Corporation.

Access is a trademark of Digital Research Inc.

BrainCel is a registered trademark of Promised Land Technologies, Inc.

COMPAQ Deskpro 386 is a registered trademark of COMPAQ Computer Corporation.

CompuServe Information Service is a registered trademark of CompuServe Incorporated and H&R Block, Inc.

CorelDRAW! is a registered copyright of Corel Systems Corporation.

Crosstalk is a registered trademark and IRMA is a trademark of Digital Communications Associates, Inc.

dBASE, dBASE II, dBASE III, and dBASE IV are registered trademarks of Ashton-Tate Corporation.

DynaComm is a trademark of Future Soft Engineering, Inc.

EXTRA! for Windows is a trademark of Attachmate Corporation.

FAXit! for Windows is a trademark of Alien Computing.

IBM and IBM Personal System/2 are registered trademarks and SQL/DS is a trademark of International Business Machines Corporation.

LaserJet is a registered trademark of Hewlett-Packard Co.

Macintosh is a registered trademark of Apple Computer, Inc.

Micrografx Designer is a trademark of Micrografx, Inc.

Microsoft Excel, Microsoft Paintbrush, Microsoft Windows, Microsoft Word for Windows, MS-DOS, Multiplan, and PowerPoint are registered trademarks of Microsoft Corporation.

Net/One Personal Connection is a registered trademark of Ungermann-Bass, Inc.

NetWare is a registered trademark of Novell, Inc.

PackRat is a trademark of Polaris Software.

PageMaker is a registered trademark of Aldus Corporation.

Paradox is a registered trademark and ObjectVision for Windows is a trademark of Borland International, Inc.

PostScript is a registered trademark of Adobe Systems Incorporated.

Q+E is a registered trademark of Pioneer Software.

Quicken is a registered trademark of Intuit.

Rumba is a trademark of Wall Data, Inc.

Ungermann-Bass is a registered trademark of Ungermann-Bass Inc.

Windowlinks is a trademark of Digital Communications Associates, Inc.

WordPerfect is a registered trademark of WordPerfect Corporation.

Trademarks of other products mentioned in this book are held by the companies producing them.

ACKNOWLEDGMENTS

Using Excel 3 for Windows, Special Edition, was created through the work and contributions of many professionals. I want to thank the people who helped make this book possible:

Thanks to everyone at Microsoft for their energy and clear vision. Working with you is exciting and stimulating. You make a major difference in people's lives.

Mike Conte and Dan Williams provided continued support; they developed a vehicle for Excel consultants to learn and better support their clients.

Tanya van Dam and Christy Gersich provided information and software coordination with Microsoft. They kept us up-to-date and informed.

Thanks to the Microsoft product managers, sales people, analysts, and technical support specialists for their assistance and support.

Thanks to everyone at Que Corporation for their professional attitudes and high energy. You're a great group of people who produce the best computer books on the market. From our vantage point behind the desks on the business battlefront, we see how much people depend on Que books to get their work done. Thank you from them and from us.

Thanks to Dave Ewing and Lloyd Short, Publishers, and Terrie Lynn Solomon, Acquisitions Manager, for standing by us through a suite of Windows books and guiding us through the meteoric rush of deadlines. Thanks for your support and understanding.

Thanks to Shelley O'Hara, Senior Product Development Specialist; Mary Bednarek, Product Development Manager; and Paul Boger, Managing Editor, for guiding us down the path to the printing presses.

Thanks to Production Editor Pamela Wampler for her daily management of manuscripts, deadlines, edits, and production schedules.

Thanks to Editors Jeannine McDonel, Kelley Currie, and Laura Wirthlin for their literacy and Que style.

Thanks to the people who keep our consulting and training business running smoothly.

Thanks to Sharel McVey and Bob Voss for their excellent technical edits. You've added confidence and value to the book.

Thanks to Wilma Thompson for keeping us organized and on schedule.

CONTENTS AT A GLANCE

TABLE OF CONTENTS ▼

II   Excel Worksheets

III   Excel Charts

V   Excel Macros

Introduction

On May 22, 1990, the introduction of Windows 3 revolutionized the world of personal computers. Windows 3 created almost as much change as the introduction of IBM's first personal computer. Within seven months, two million copies of Windows 3 were sold.

January 9, 1991, marked a second major change in personal computers: the introduction of Excel 3. The press and many consultants had already proclaimed Excel 2 the most simple-to-use, yet the most powerful worksheet. With the introduction of version 3, Excel has once again proven itself as the most capable and easiest-to-use worksheet.

Now, the "bleeding edge" of the revolution has passed. Because of the proliferation and adaptability of Windows programs, companies selecting software no longer have to sacrifice power for safety or convenience. You can take advantage of Excel's capabilities without making any sacrifices. If you still are hesitant to use Excel, consider the following facts:

- Nearly every business computer sold now runs Windows 3 and Windows application software.

- Windows programs such as Excel 3, Word for Windows, Amí Pro, and Aldus PageMaker coexist with existing software in the office, so you don't have to upgrade all personal computers at once.

- Excel 3's new Lotus 1-2-3 instruction and demonstration features enable you to learn Excel while you continue to work with 1-2-3 keystrokes.

Converting from Lotus 1-2-3

You needn't worry about converting from Lotus 1-2-3 to Excel—it's easy. Excel 3 reads and writes all versions of Lotus 1-2-3 worksheets. Excel 3 even brings in Lotus worksheet charts so that you can enhance them with Excel's greater charting ability. Chapter 5, "Making the Switch from 1-2-3 to Excel," covers this topic.

You can set up Excel to accept your Lotus 1-2-3 keystrokes or menu choices. Once you have entered a 1-2-3 command, Excel demonstrates how to execute the equivalent command. By using your 1-2-3 knowledge with your new Excel worksheets, you can continue to do productive work and learn Excel at the same time.

Operating from the Tool Bar

Excel is distinguished as the easiest-to-use worksheet, as well as the most capable. This paradox is possible because of Excel's tool bar, which appears under the menu bar at the top of the screen. When you use a mouse with the tool bar, you have quick access to the most frequently used commands in a worksheet. The Bold tool, for example, a letter B under the Options menu, enables you to bold whatever cell is selected. The Auto-SUM tool, a capital sigma (Σ), automatically enters a SUM function in the active cell and totals the adjacent row or column of numbers. Other tools enable you to align cell contents, draw shapes on worksheets, create charts, display worksheet outlines, or capture pictures of cells for use in other programs.

Formatting Like a Publisher

Excel 3 is easily the leader in worksheet publishing capabilities. The templates and cell styles available in Excel will really help you if you need to create a frequently used worksheet or a worksheet that presents a standardized appearance. Templates act like "master documents" that contain worksheet layouts, text, formulas, cell styles, custom menus, and macros. When opened, a template gives you a new worksheet that contains everything in the template. You must save the document to a new name, thus preserving the template as a master.

Styles are a powerful feature found in professional-level word processors. With a style, you can name a collection of formatting commands and apply all the formats by selecting that style name. For example, a style named Total might contain the formats Helvetica 12 point, bold, right align, currency with two decimal places, and a double-line upper border. Changing the definition of a style changes all cells that are formatted by that style.

Excel enables you to use the full capability of your printer. On a laser printer, for example, Excel can print up to 256 different fonts on a worksheet or chart, use up to 18 shades of grey, use a custom palette of 16 colors, and use numerous line and underline combinations.

If you need a numeric or date format that isn't on the list of formats, you can design your own format. You even can add text in a format so that numbers include abbreviations, such as 5.678 Kph. You also can design formats so that numbers or dates within different ranges appear in different colors.

Excel 3's printing preview capabilities show you how print will be positioned on the page. You can zoom in to see the detail of character and drawing positions. You also can drag column and margin markers while in the preview to reposition columns and change print margins.

Drawing on Worksheets

You can do many types of drawings on Excel worksheets. Using the drawing tools at the left side of the tool bar, you can draw lines, arrows, rectangles, ovals, circles, and arcs. You also can create text boxes that can be positioned anywhere on the page. All the colors in your custom color palette and many shades of grey are available for emphasis.

You can embed charts or cell pictures in a worksheet. When you change data, the embedded charts or cell pictures are updated. Embedding a chart in a worksheet is simple: you select the data on the worksheet, click on the Chart tool in the tool bar, and then drag across the worksheet to mark where you want the chart to appear. All charts and drawings print with the worksheet.

Linking and Consolidating with Flexibility

Excel is flexible enough to adapt to many business situations. Within Excel, you can link worksheets to fit the way you work. You can link cells or ranges of cells between open worksheets or worksheets on disk.

When you need to gather data from multiple divisions or times into a single worksheet, use Excel's consolidation feature. Excel can consolidate data from Excel or Lotus 1-2-3 worksheets. Using one method, you can link worksheets according to the contents of cells at a specific location. For example, all cells at the top left corner of a range add together. This method is not very flexible because it requires all worksheets to be laid out in exactly the same manner—a rare occurrence in the real world.

Excel's more flexible method uses the row and column labels to the left of and above the areas you want to consolidate. Excel examines the row and column name of each item in all the worksheets and works with those items that are the same. If some items are unique, they are given their own unique position in the consolidation. This flexibility is helpful when some divisions or departments have different budget line items or have different products.

Creating Charts

Excel 3 has 68 predefined chart formats. Once you choose a predefined format, you can customize the chart. You can drag the legend anywhere on the chart, orient text in any direction, use up to 256 different fonts, link numbers and text boxes back to worksheet cells, and more. Excel's charting capability rivals that of dedicated charting programs.

Excel even enables you to solve worksheet problems, using a chart as the data-entry device. In line, bar, and column charts, you can drag a chart marker (line symbol or top of bar or column) to a new location. If that marker reflects the result of a formula in a worksheet, Excel asks you which cell to manipulate to accomplish the chart result you asked for. This feature provides a way to back into solutions, using the chart to specify your final answer.

Using Excel's Built-In Database

A database is like a card-file system that stores information. Excel has built-in database capabilities because so many worksheet problems involve a collection of historical sales, marketing, engineering, or scientific information. To enter and find information in a database, you only need to know two commands: **Data Set Database** and **Data Form**.

If you need more database features or the ability to analyze database contents, Excel still can help you. Excel enables you to statistically analyze database contents; for example, you can find the average amount owed in all accounts receivable that are more than 30 days overdue and less than 90 days overdue.

When you need to work with extremely large databases or databases stored on a mainframe computer or a local area network server, you will want to use Q+E, a program that comes with Excel. Q+E adds commands to Excel that enable you to link worksheets to large databases external to the worksheet.

Outlining To Expand and Condense Reports

Excel contains an outliner—a feature that will be dear to anyone who has to create extensive reports. The outliner enables you to quickly expand and collapse databases and worksheets so you see only the level of information you need to print or display.

Using Excel's Advanced Capabilities

Excel has an extensive built-in programming language so that experienced users can customize Excel's menus and dialog boxes, link Excel to other Windows programs, control other Windows programs, automate processes, and download and upload mainframe information automatically.

If you are not experienced with programming, you can use Excel's macro recorder to create automated procedures to save time. To run these procedures, you press a shortcut key, choose the macro name from a list, or click on a "hot-button" on the worksheet.

For more advanced users, Excel comes with two of the many add-in products available: Solver and Q+E. Solver enables you to find the optimal or best solution to linear and nonlinear problems. If you want to link Excel to databases on disk or on a mainframe, you will want to use Q+E. Q+E is a database query and edit program that runs as a stand-alone Windows program or as an intermediary that passes database information to Excel worksheets.

Because Excel is a Windows program, Excel can work with many other programs. You can manually copy data, charts, and graphics between Excel and other Windows programs; or you can link programs so that they automatically pass data when it changes. Some of these programs are listed in the Appendix.

Using This Book

Using Excel 3 for Windows, Special Edition, contains six parts. Four parts begin with Quick Starts—short but important tutorials that will guide you through the most important concepts in that part. Using Quick Starts is the quickest way to become productive. Each Quick Start is followed by related chapters that discuss in detail the topics in the Quick Start.

Part I, "Excel Installation," shows you how to install and run Excel. The chapters in this section introduce concepts that apply to all Windows programs.

Part II, "Excel Worksheets," shows you how to create, edit, format, and print worksheets. The chapters in this section include beginning topics, such as data entry, as well as intermediate chapters on the many worksheet functions available in Excel. Chapter 5 is dedicated to helping 1-2-3 users learn Excel.

Part III, "Excel Charts," shows you how to create, format, and manipulate charts. The chapters in this section cover topics ranging from basic charts, to charts embedded in worksheets, to advanced charting tricks.

Part IV, "Excel Databases," shows you how to create and maintain a database. The chapters in this section teach you how to enter, edit, sort, find, and extract information from a database. An advanced chapter discusses how to analyze database contents.

Part V, "Excel Macros," shows you how to record simple macros and modify them so that they request data and check it. Other chapters explain how to build custom menus and dialog boxes and how to do more advanced programming. A directory lists all of the commands in Excel's extensive macro language.

Part VI, "Advanced Techniques," shows you how to use Excel with other software, both DOS applications—such as Lotus 1-2-3 and WordPerfect—and Windows applications—such as Word for Windows and CorelDRAW!. The final chapter describes how to customize many of the features in Excel and Windows.

The Appendix, "Excel Support and Add-Ins," shows you how to find other products that work well with with Excel. The Appendix lists sources of additional books, templates, and training and consulting services.

Conventions Used in This Book

Certain conventions are used in this edition to help you more easily understand the concepts. The conventions are explained again at appropriate places in the book.

Special Typefaces and Representations

Uppercase letters are used to distinguish DOS commands and file names, and Excel functions. In most cases, the keys on the keyboard are represented as they appear on your keyboard, with the exception of the arrow keys. Terms such as "up arrow" or "down arrow" have been used instead.

Shift +End indicates that you press the Shift key and hold it down while you press also the End key. Other key combinations, such as Ctrl +Break or Shift +F4, are performed in the same manner.

The following special typefaces and command representations are used in *Using Excel 3 for Windows,* Special Edition.

Typeface	Meaning
italic type	This font is used for words or phrases defined for the first time, and for optional items in the function format examples.
boldface type	This font is used for user input—what the user types, such as commands and functions. It is also used for mandatory items in the function format examples.
`special font`	This font is used to represent system and screen messages and on-screen results of functions.

Icons and Asides

Throughout *Using Excel 3 for Windows*, Special Edition, you will find the following special icons used to identify certain text.

Icon	Meaning
	This icon identifies a feature new with Excel 3, or a feature that has been changed significantly from its capabilities in previous Excel versions. When the icon appears at the beginning of a chapter or section, all features covered in that chapter or section are features new or enhanced with Excel 3.
	This icon identifies a method of accessing Excel commands by using the mouse.
	This icon identifies a method of accessing Excel commands through keyboard keystrokes.

Shaded Notes and Tips

Certain discussions in *Using Excel 3 for Windows* are expanded by the use of tips and notes. A note provides brief, additional information relating to the topic in the surrounding text. Such information can serve as a reminder or clarify a point. A tip is an insight that can help you more fully realize and benefit from the features of Excel. The text for tips and notes is enclosed in a shaded box.

From Here...

Consider this book a resource. You can consult the book when you need to look up advanced features, solve a unique situation, or troubleshoot a problem. Most of the learning, however, will take place at the computer. When you come to a Quick Start chapter, reach for the mouse and keyboard!

If you want to quickly become an adept user of Excel, set aside about an hour to work through each Quick Start. The Quick Starts, which are like built-in tutors, have been used to train many students; readers have praised the Quick Starts for efficiently presenting the most important Excel concepts.

When you begin using Excel, the most important topics are those in the Worksheet Quick Start and the chapter on printing. Once you are familiar with entering formulas and editing, you can become more productive by learning how to record and make simple modifications to macros.

Next, depending on the type of work that you do, you might work through either the Database Quick Start or the Chart Quick Start. If you like to eat your dessert first, you may want to do the Chart Quick Start as soon as possible.

Part I

Excel Installation

Includes

Installing and Running Excel

Operating Windows

Windows applications, like Excel, all operate with the same concepts and procedures, and often, Windows applications have similar commands. When you learn one Windows application, you are well on your way to learning another. Procedures like making selections from a menu or choosing options from a dialog box work the same in different Windows applications.

This similarity between Windows applications means that you can often learn one Windows application, and then immediately begin productive work with a different application that you have never used before. The common procedures among Windows applications provides an immense savings in time and frustration.

Part I contains two chapters that help you install Excel and learn some of the fundamental commands necessary to use Windows applications effectively. The commands and concepts you will learn can be transferred to most Windows applications.

The installation process for Excel is easy. Chapter 1 guides you through the installation process. You also learn how to create an Excel icon in any group window of the Program Manager that will start Excel and load an Excel document.

Chapter 2 goes into detail about operating Windows—how to start and stop Windows, how to use the menus, commands, and dialog boxes, and how to manipulate windows.

If you are a Lotus 1-2-3 user, you will find it helpful at this point to skip forward to Chapter 5, "Making the Switch from 1-2- 3 to Excel." Chapter 5 is designed to help people familiar with Lotus 1-2-3 understand Excel's compatibility, differences, and enhancements.

1

Installing and Running Excel

E xcel is one of the new generation of software that runs under Windows 3 or with OS/2 Presentation Manager. In this chapter, you learn how to install and run Excel on a Windows or an OS/2 system. In addition, you will see how to create special icons that start Excel with specific worksheets. The last section of this chapter helps you decide how to use the rest of the book most effectively, as you learn about Excel's features.

Reviewing Hardware Requirements

To provide optimum performance for Excel, your computer should meet or exceed the following requirements:

- IBM Personal System/2, AT, COMPAQ 386 Deskpro, or compatible. Computers with 8088 or 8086 processors do not normally have sufficient computing power for Excel to operate efficiently. A Windows 3 compatible system using an 80286 processor running at 12 MHz or better is recommended.

- IBM VGA, Extended Graphics Adapter, or other graphics cards and monitors that are compatible with Windows 3 or later. The quality of display and the performance of Excel may vary significantly with the graphics card.

13

- A minimum of 1 megabyte of random access memory for Excel for Windows and 2.5 megabytes minimum for OS/2.

- A hard disk with at least 2.5 megabytes of available storage. To install all options, a minimum of 5.1 megabytes is required.

- At least one 360K, 1.2M, or 1.44M floppy-disk drive.

- DOS 3.1 or later with Windows 3 or later, and OS/2 1.2 or later.

In addition, Excel supports the following:

- A wide range of printers and plotters, including the Hewlett-Packard LaserJet and PostScript-compatible laser printers.

- A mouse.

- Extended memory, for increased memory and performance.

- Math coprocessors (Intel 80287 and 80387), to decrease math recalculation time.

- Major personal computer networks, such as IBM PC Network, IBM Token Ring Network, AT&T STARLAN, Novell Netware, 3Com 3+, 3Com EtherSeries, Ungermann-Bass/One, and networks supporting Windows 3 or later.

If you are unfamiliar with the equipment you have, check your equipment manuals or the sales receipt. You also can consult the dealer or your corporate MIS hot line.

Installing Excel

Before you install Excel, you should have Windows 3 installed and running. To learn how to install, operate, and enhance Windows 3, refer to the Que book, *Using Microsoft Windows 3,* 2nd Edition.

Before you begin Excel installation, know the disk drive and directory name where Windows is installed and decide where you want to put Excel.

To install Excel, follow these steps:

1. Protect your original disks from accidental change. On 5 1/4-inch disks, place a write-protect tab over the square-cut notch on the edge. On 3 1/2-inch disks, slide the write-protect notch so that it is open.

2. Start Windows 3 by typing WIN at the DOS prompt.

3. Insert the Setup disk into drive A and close the drive door.

4. Bring up the Main group window within the Program Manager. To do this, place the tip of the mouse pointer on the Main window and click the mouse button. If Main is an icon at the bottom of the screen, place the pointer tip on the icon and click twice quickly. To select the Main window from the keyboard, press Ctrl+Tab either until the Main window appears or until the title of the Main icon is highlighted. Press Enter to expand the icon into a window.

5. With the Main group as the topmost window, as the window in figure 1.1 shows, place the tip of the mouse pointer on the File Manager icon and click the button twice quickly. If you are using a keyboard, press the arrow keys until the title of the File Manager is highlighted, and then press Enter.

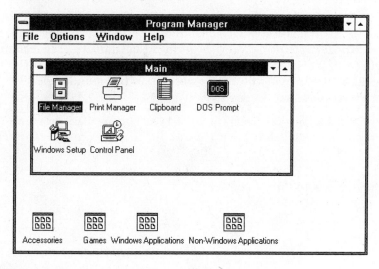

Fig. 1.1. The Main group window with File Manager selected.

6. Choose the File Run command by clicking on the File menu, and then select the Run command with the mouse pointer or by pressing Alt, F, and then R.

7. When the Run dialog box appears (see fig. 1.2), type the following command:

    a:setup

Fig. 1.2. The File Run dialog box.

8. Press Enter.

9. Read and follow the directions that appear on-screen. As you go through the installation process, you have the opportunity to make corrections or to quit and start over. You can select to install all the files or only those files absolutely necessary to run Excel.

During installation, you have the opportunity to read files that contain additional information about installation and performance enhancements. If you do not elect to read these files during installation, you can read them later by using the Notepad program found in the Accessories group window. These README files end with a TXT extension and are found in the directory in which you installed Windows.

During installation, you can choose the Excel and ancillary programs that you want to install. Following is a list of the programs you can choose to install:

Excel and Ancillary Programs

Microsoft Excel	Worksheet, database, charts, and macros
Microsoft Excel Tutorial	Guided Excel tutorial
Dialog Editor	Custom dialog box drawing program used for macro programming
Macro Translator	Converts Lotus 1-2-3 macros
Macro Library Files	Add-in programs, sample files, and macros put into a LIBRARY directory
Microsoft Excel Solver	Linear and nonlinear programming application that finds the optimal solution to worksheet problems
Q+E	Enables Excel worksheets to link to disk-based and some mainframe files

If you choose to install Q+E, you can "hot-link" Excel worksheets to data on disk-based files or you can query databases from within Excel by using SQL (Structured Query Language). You can choose to link Excel with disk-based Excel databases, an SQL Server (Microsoft Server/ORACLE), dBASE II, III, IV, and ASCII files. You can also elect to start Q+E when Excel starts and limit Q+E so that it can query and extract from files but not update files.

Before you install all Excel and ancillary programs, make sure that you have enough available disk space for the selected programs. To do this, look at the bottom of the dialog box for the required disk space; compare that space to the reported disk space. If there is not enough space available, you have several options: select fewer Excel programs to install, change the Excel directory to a disk with more space, or exit the installation and erase files from the current disk. If you are installing Excel on the same disk as the Windows directory, make sure that there are a few megabytes free after installation for use by Windows' temporary swap files and the Print Manager.

When the installation is complete, the File Manager reappears. A new group window is created in the Program Manager. This new window contains Excel and its related programs. Chapter 2 describes how to start and exit Excel after it is installed.

Adding an Excel Program Item Icon to a Work Group

You can create your own group window in which to place an icon that starts Excel. In fact, you also can create an icon that starts Excel and immediately loads a worksheet, chart, or macro sheet. This enables you to have icons that match the specific jobs that you do.

If you are unfamiliar with how to choose commands and select options from dialog boxes, read Chapter 2 before creating your own group windows and program item icons.

Follow these steps to create a new group window in the Program Manager:

1. Activate the Program Manager window by clicking on it or by pressing Alt+Tab until it is the topmost window.

2. Choose the File menu and select the New command.

3. Select the Program Group option.

4. Choose OK or press Enter. The Program Group Properties dialog box appears (see fig. 1.3).

5. Select the Description box and type the title you want for this group window. The title will appear in the bar at the top of the window.

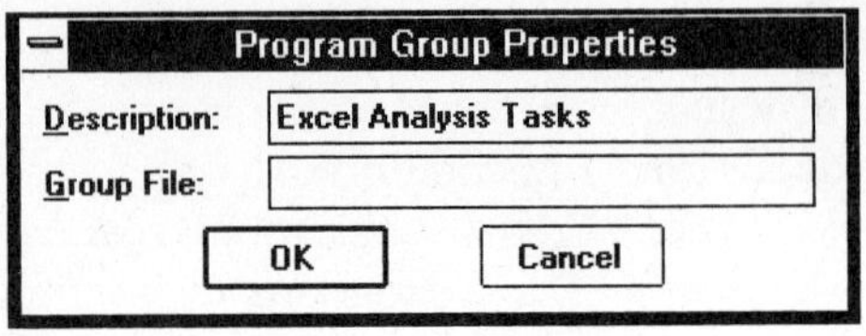

Fig. 1.3. *The Program Group Properties dialog box.*

6. Choose OK or press Enter.

To add a program item icon to the group window that will start Excel or another program of your choice, follow these steps:

1. Activate the group window in which you want to add the icon by clicking on it or by pressing Ctrl+F6 or Ctrl+Tab.

2. Choose the File menu and select the New command.

3. Select the Program Item option from the New Program Object dialog box.

4. Choose OK or press Enter. The Program Item Properties dialog box appears (see fig. 1.4).

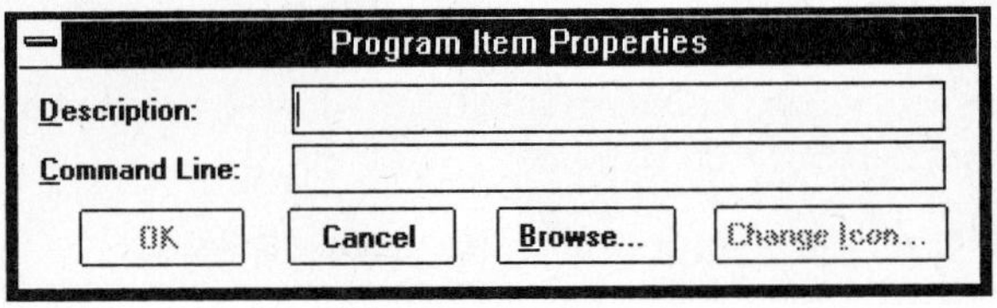

Fig. 1.4. *The Program Item Properties dialog box.*

5. From the Program Item Properties dialog box, select the Description text box and type the title you want to appear under the program item icon.

6. Select the Command Line text box.

7. Choose the Browse button to display the Browse dialog box (see fig. 1.5), from which you can choose a program name.

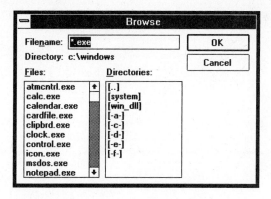

Fig. 1.5. The Browse dialog box.

8. From the **D**irectories list, select the drive and directory in which the program is located, and then choose OK or press Enter.

9. Select from the **F**iles list the file name of the program that you want the icon to start. Choose OK or press Enter.

10. If you want a document (such as a worksheet, chart, macro sheet, or workspace) to open when Excel starts, type a space, followed by the drive, path name, and file name of the document. You cannot select the file name from the Browse box. If you include a file name, your Program Item Properties dialog box will now include a description, program name, and file name. Figure 1.6 shows a file that will be loaded with Excel, but remember that specifying a file name is optional.

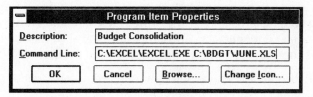

Fig. 1.6. The Program Item Properties dialog box filled out to start Excel with a worksheet.

11. Choose OK or press Enter.

Your new group window and the program item icon, as shown in figure 1.7, will now appear on-screen. You can add more icons to any of the group windows. Chapter 2 explains how to start Excel; Chapter 11, "Building Systems and Managing Multiple Windows," explains how to load multiple documents automatically when Excel starts.

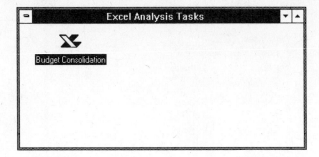

Fig. 1.7. *A group window with an Excel icon for a special task.*

From Here ...

After you install Excel, you may want to read Chapter 2 to learn techniques for operating Windows and then complete the Worksheet Quick Start in Chapter 3. If you are a Lotus 1-2-3 user, you will definitely want to read Chapter 5, "Making the Switch from 1-2-3 to Excel." From there, you can skip to any of the other Quick Starts.

When you complete a Quick Start for a section, you will be knowledgeable enough to scan through the detailed chapters that follow the Quick Start.

If you want to learn Excel as quickly as possible, follow these steps:

1. If you are a former Lotus 1-2-3 user, learn how to use the Help Lotus command that guides you through correct procedures. The Help command enables you to enter the commands you would use in 1-2-3, and then it accomplishes the task in slow motion using Excel commands so that you can see how to use Excel.

2. Work through the Quick Starts that precede each section. Keep the completed Quick Start on-screen.

3. Skim through the chapters following the Quick Start so that you are familiar with the available features. As you go through the chapters, experiment in your completed Quick Start worksheet, chart, or macro sheet with the features you see.

4. Every few weeks, glance through the Table of Contents and the Index. Use the Index if you know the specific word that describes what you want. Use the Table of Contents to find general ideas.

2

Operating
Windows

This chapter is the place to start if you are not familiar with Microsoft Windows. You will use the ideas and concepts that you learn here in all your Excel operations. In fact, what you learn in your first Windows program will carry over to other Windows programs.

You will learn how to control not only Excel's menus and dialog boxes but also the windows that contain Excel and its worksheets, charts, and macro documents. By the end of this chapter, you should be able to choose commands from menus, select options from dialog boxes, and manipulate windows on-screen. Of course, you need to know how to choose from menus and to select options in dialog boxes in order to run the program. Beyond these basic tasks, you should be able to organize windows so that you can access and use multiple worksheets at once or "to clear away your desktop" so that you can concentrate on a single job.

Starting Windows and Excel

To start Excel, follow these steps:

1. Start Windows by typing **WIN** and pressing Enter.

2. Activate the group window that contains Excel. This will be either the Microsoft Excel 3 group or a group in which an Excel program item icon has been created. Figure 2.1 shows the Microsoft Excel 3 group window and the Excel 3 program item icon within.

21

Click on the group window or double-click on the icon that contains the Excel program item icon.

 Press Ctrl+Tab until the desired group window is active or until the title of the group icon is highlighted. Press Enter to maximize the selected icon into a window.

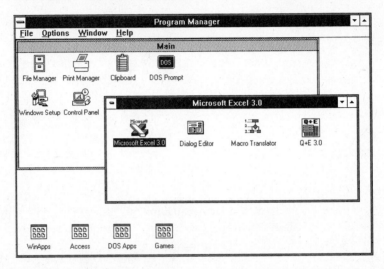

Fig. 2.1. The open Microsoft Excel 3 group window with Excel 3 selected.

3. Start the Excel 3 program:

 Double-click on the Excel 3 program item icon.

 Press the arrow keys until the title of the Excel 3 program item icon is highlighted, and then press Enter.

If you want Excel to open files when it starts, refer to Chapter 11's discussion of the startup directory and loading files on startup.

You also can start Excel by choosing a worksheet, chart, or macro file from the File Manager. To do this, double-click on the file name for an Excel document, or select the file name and press Enter. This starts Excel and loads the document. If this does not work, check to see whether the PATH command in the AUTOEXEC.BAT file gives the directory where the EXCEL.EXE file is located. If this procedure still does not work, you may need to *associate* Excel files with Excel. The association process is described in the Windows 3 manual and in *Using Microsoft Windows 3,* 2nd Ed., from Que.

Understanding a Windows Screen

One advantage of Windows programs is the capability to run several programs and display them on-screen simultaneously. Chapters 33 and 34 describe how you can run Excel and other Windows or DOS programs together and transfer on-screen information among them. This capability can save you time when you transfer numbers into or out of Excel, transfer charts to graphics programs for further enhancements, or create automatically updated links between Excel worksheets and certain Windows programs.

Each Windows program, such as Excel, runs in its own program window. Some program windows can contain multiple document windows, so that you can work simultaneously with more than one worksheet, chart, or macro sheet. Figure 2.2 shows the Excel program window with a worksheet and a chart document window inside.

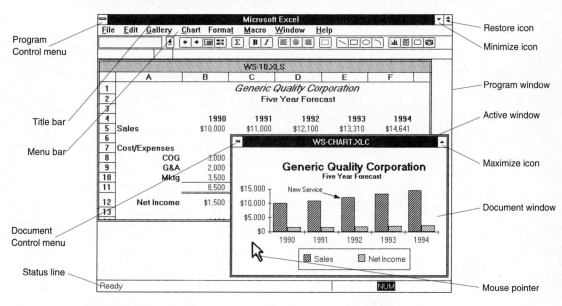

Fig. 2.2. *Excel screen with multiple document windows displayed.*

Table 2.1 lists and describes the parts of an Excel screen.

Table 2.1
Parts of an Excel Screen

Part	Description
Program window	The window within which Excel runs.
Program icon	Icon of a running program.
Document window	The window within which worksheets, macro sheets, and charts are displayed.
Program Control menu	The menu that enables you to manipulate the program window.
Document Control menu	The menu that enables you to manipulate the active (top) document window.
Active window	The window that accepts entries and commands; this window is shown with a solid title bar and is normally the top window.
Mouse pointer	The on-screen arrow, cross, or I-beam that indicates the current mouse location.
Title bar	The bar at the top of a program or document window.
Menu bar	A list of menu names displayed below the title bar of a program.
Menu	A pull-down list of commands.
Command	A function or procedure chosen from a pull-down menu.
Minimize icon	A down arrowhead at the right of a title bar that stores a program as a program icon at the bottom of the screen; equivalent to the program Control Minimize command.
Maximize icon	An up arrowhead at the right of a title bar that fills available space with the document or program; equivalent to the Control Maximize command.
Restore icon	A double arrowhead at the right of a title bar that restores a program or

Part	Description
	document into a sizable window; equivalent to the Control **R**estore command.
Scroll bar	A gray horizontal and vertical bar that enables the mouse to scroll the screen; a scroll box in the bar shows the current display's position relative to the entire document.
Split window icons	Dark bars at the end of the scroll bar that can be dragged across the scroll bar to split a window into two views of the same document.
Status bar	A bar at the bottom of the screen that explains the selected command or prompts you with guidance.

Using the Mouse

The mouse is an optional piece of hardware that attaches to your PC and enables you to move the on-screen pointer as you move the mouse with your hand. In Excel, you can control the program either with mouse movements or with keystrokes. Each approach works well; the choice depends on your personal preference and the task at hand. For example, windows are easier to size and move with the mouse. You will find that combining mouse actions, touch-typing, and shortcut keys is the most productive way to work.

Moving the Mouse

The mouse, shown in figure 2.3, is a small hand-held device that lies on your desktop and fits comfortably under your palm. As you move the mouse across your desk, the *mouse pointer*—a shape on the screen—moves in the same relative direction across the screen. You will find that using the mouse to *point* at an item on the screen with the mouse pointer becomes a natural process. The mouse is especially useful for selecting large cell areas, copying and pasting cells, exploring menus, changing the sizes and locations of windows, and moving objects on charts.

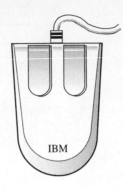

Fig. 2.3. The mouse.

When you hold the mouse, the wire should project forward, away from your arm, so that the buttons are under your fingers. A mouse may have two or three buttons; Excel, however, uses only the left button.

> **Tip:** *For Left-Handed Operators Controlling Right-Handed Mice*
> If you are left-handed, you should run the Mouse program and switch the mouse-button control from the left button to the right. To find the Mouse program, start the Control Panel from the Main group window of the Program Manager.

As you move the mouse pointer on-screen, the mouse may run out of clear space on your desk. This does not mean that you need a larger desk or that you need to shovel away the work that has stacked up. Instead, when the mouse collides with something, just pick up the mouse, move it to a clear area, put it down, and continue the motion. Usually, about one square foot of clear desk space gives you enough room to control the mouse.

Understanding the Changing Mouse Pointer

The mouse pointer changes appearance depending on its location. You usually see the mouse pointer as an arrow when it is in the menus, or as a cross when it is in the worksheet. When seen over an editable area of text, the pointer appears as an I-beam. Each shape signals to you what you can do at that location. The different shapes of the pointer are shown and explained in table 2.2.

Table 2.2
Mouse Pointer Shapes

Pointer Shape	Locations	Use
↖	Menu, scroll bar, tool bar	Select by moving the tip of the arrow onto a name or icon and then clicking the mouse button.
I	Text boxes, formula bar	Repositions the flashing cursor (insertion point) within editable text. To move the insertion point location, move the I-beam to the location and then click.
+	Appears during placement or resizing of objects	Choose object placement command and drag across sheet, or move to square handle on object and drag to resize.
↔	Appears between column headings or on window edge	Drag to change column width or position of window edge.
↕	Appears between row headings or on window edge	Drag to change row height or position of window edge.
⬂	Window corners	Drag to reposition two window edges at one time.
✛	Inside worksheet	Click to select cells in worksheet.
⬅	Split bar at ends of scroll bar	Drag to split window into two views.
Q	Print Preview	Select document area for closer view.
☞	Help window	Select items for more information.
⧖	Any screen location	Means "Please wait."

Understanding Actions Used in Windows and Excel

All Windows programs, including Excel, require the same keyboard and mouse actions to select what is changed on-screen or to give commands. By learning the actions named in table 2.3, you will learn how to operate menus and to select items within any Windows program.

Table 2.3
Windows and Excel Actions

Action	Description
Select	Highlight or mark a menu name, command, dialog box option, cell location, or graphical object either with the keyboard or mouse actions.
Choose	Execute and complete a command.

Mouse Actions

Mouse techniques are simple to learn and remember. These techniques make using Excel much easier. In fact, for such work as charting, the mouse is nearly indispensable. Table 2.4 describes the mouse actions that you use in carrying out Excel operations.

> **Tip: *Using the Mouse with Shift and Ctrl for Additional Features***
> Some mouse actions have a different effect when you hold down the Shift or Ctrl key as you click, double-click, or drag with the mouse. As a general rule, holding down the Shift key as you click selects text or cells between the current location and the location where you Shift+Click. Holding down the Ctrl key as you drag across nonadjacent areas enables you to select areas that are not contiguous. With this method, you can format multiple areas with a single command.

Table 2.4
Mouse Actions

Action	Description
Click	Put the tip of the mouse pointer or the lower portion of the I-beam pointer at the desired location and then quickly press the left mouse button *once*. This action selects a menu, command, cell, or graphical object so that you can work with it; this action also places the insertion point in text boxes and formula bars.
Double-click	Put the tip of the mouse pointer or the lower portion of the I-beam pointer at the desired location and then quickly press the left mouse button *twice*. This action is usually a shortcut for selecting and changing the item you click on.
Drag	Put the tip of the mouse pointer or the lower portion of the I-beam on an item; then hold down the left mouse button as you move the mouse pointer. This action selects multiple text characters or moves graphical objects.

Keyboard Actions

The keyboard is most useful for entering text and numbers, performing fast operations with shortcut keys, and operating with portable or laptop computers that don't have a mouse. But don't forget that the best way of operating Excel and other Windows programs is through the combined use of mouse and keyboard. Table 2.5 lists and describes the keyboard actions that you will use in Excel.

Table 2.5
Keyboard Actions

Action	Description
Type	Type, but do not press the Enter key.
Enter	Type and then press the Enter key.
Alt	Press the Alt key.

continues

Table 2.5 (*continued*)

Action	Description
Alt, *letter*	Press the Alt key, release it, and then press the underlined letter or number shown. In this book, the active letters that appear underlined on-screen appear in bold print.
Letter	Press only the underlined letter shown in the menu, command, or option.
Alt+*letter*	Hold down the Alt key as you press the underlined letter.
Alt, hyphen	Press the Alt key, release it, and then press the hyphen key.
Alt, space bar	Press the Alt key, release it, and then press the space bar.
Tab	Press the Tab key.
Esc	Press the Esc key.

Throughout this book, you see combinations of keys indicated with a plus sign (+), such as Alt+F. This combination means that you must hold down the Alt key while you press F. After pressing F, release both keys. (Although this book shows capital letters, as with the F, you don't need to hold down the Shift key unless indicated.)

Keystrokes that appear separated by commas should be pressed in sequence. For example, Alt, space bar, is accomplished by pressing and releasing Alt and then pressing the space bar.

If you have a mouse, try using both mouse actions and keystrokes to perform commands and tasks. The exercises in this Quick Start provide instructions for using both options. You soon will find that the keyboard works well for some commands and features and that the mouse works well for others. A combination of both mouse and keyboard usually is the most efficient.

The keyboard is also useful for many shortcut keys. These shortcut keys are listed in the appropriate areas throughout this book.

The 12 function keys give you a shortcut method of choosing commands that you normally choose from a menu. Some function keys use other keys in combination. When two or more keys are listed with a plus sign, hold down the first key(s) as you press the last key. The function keys and their equivalent menu commands are as follows:

Excel Program Window

Alt+F4	Close

Excel Document Window

Ctrl+F4	Close
Ctrl+F5	Restore
Ctrl+F6	Next Document Window
Ctrl+F7	Move
Ctrl+F8	Size
Ctrl+F10	Maximize

Excel Menu Command — Equivalents

F1	Help
Shift+F1	Context Choosing Help
F2	Activate Formula Bar
Shift+F2	Formula Note
Ctrl+F2	Window Show Info
F3	Formula Paste Name
Shift+F3	Formula Paste Function
Ctrl+F3	Formula Define Name
Ctrl+Shift+F3	Formula Create Names
F4	Formula Reference
Ctrl+F4	Control Close (document window)
Alt+F4	File Exit
F5	Formula Goto
Shift+F5	Formula Find (cell contents)
Ctrl+F5	Control Restore (document window)
F6	Next Pane
Shift+F6	Previous Pane
Ctrl+F6	Control Next Window
Ctrl+Shift+F6	Previous Document Window
F7	Formula Find (next cell)
Shift+F7	Formula Find (previous cell)
Ctrl+F7	Control Move (document window)
F8	Extend Mode (toggles on/off)
Shift+F8	Add Mode (toggles on/off)
Ctrl+F8	Control Size (document window)

Excel Menu Command	Equivalents
F9	Options Calculate Now
Shift+F9	Options Calculate Document
F10	Activate Menu Bar
Ctrl+F10	Control Maximize (document window)
F11	File New (chart)
Shift+F11	File New (worksheet)
Ctrl+F11	File New (macro sheet)
F12	File Save As
Shift+F12	File Save
Ctrl+F12	File Open
Ctrl+Shift+F12	File Print

You will notice that key combinations are listed on the right side of some pull-down menus. These key combinations execute the command immediately, without going through the menu and menu item. For example, instead of choosing the **Edit Clear** command, you can press Del to clear a cell or group of cells.

If you are working in Excel and forget a function key or shortcut key combination, choose the **Help Keyboard** command to see a listing.

Choosing Commands from Menus

Excel uses the same menu-selection methods used by all Windows programs. The various methods you can use to choose commands from Excel menus illustrate the program's versatility. You can control commands with the mouse, keystrokes, cursor keys, or shortcut keys. With Excel, you can learn easier methods first and then graduate to methods that best fit your work style and the function you want to perform. In many cases, you can mix your methods of menu selection, starting with one method and finishing with another. However, you cannot use a shortcut key while a menu is pulled down or a dialog box is displayed.

When choosing a command by mouse or keyboard, you first pull down the menu and then choose the command. Figure 2.4 shows a menu pulled down.

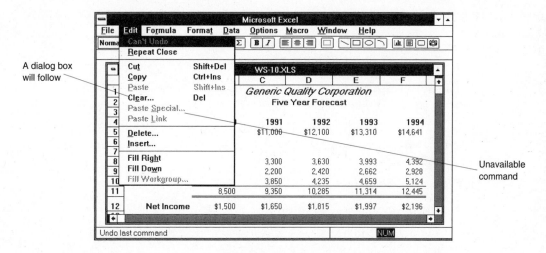

Fig. 2.4. *A partial screen of a menu pulled down with gray commands and ellipses.*

Notice that some commands in a menu may be gray. These commands are unavailable at that current point in Excel operation. Commands that are grayed may be inappropriate for the current situation or may require that another procedure be accomplished first. For example, you need to perform **Edit C**ut or **Edit C**opy before **Edit P**aste becomes available.

Commands in the menu that are followed by ellipses (...) need more information from you before they execute. These commands display dialog boxes that ask you for more information.

> **Note:** *Backing Out of Menus*
> In some programs, you cannot explore new territory and then escape easily when you need to. But in Excel, you can. You can back out of any pull-down menu or dialog box by pressing Esc. If you are using a mouse, you can back out by clicking on the menu name a second time or by clicking on the Cancel button in a dialog box.

Choosing Commands with the Mouse

Most people prefer to learn Windows programs with the mouse. As your familiarity and confidence increase, you can add or replace mouse operations with keyboard operations.

Follow these two steps if you know the command that you want to execute:

1. Click on the menu name.

2. Click on the command name.

You do not have to hold down the mouse button to keep the menu pulled down. It stays down by itself.

If you are unfamiliar with a menu or command, you can see a prompt that describes what the command does. To see a description of a command, follow these steps:

1. Click on the menu name.

2. Hold down the mouse button.

3. Continue holding down the button as you drag down to a command.

4. Continue holding down the button as you read the command's description in the status bar at the bottom of the screen.

5. If you want to complete the command, release the mouse button while the pointer tip is on the command. If you do not want to use the command, slide the pointer off the menu and then release the mouse button.

To read through menus, click on one menu name, hold down the mouse button, and drag across to other menu names. This enables you to read adjacent menus without selecting a command. Click a second time on a menu name to remove the pull-down menu.

Choosing Commands with the Keyboard

If you are not familiar with the Excel menu structure, you will want to choose commands by looking for them and reading an explanation about them. Follow these steps:

1. Press Alt to select the menu bar.

2. Press the right or left arrow to highlight the menu name. Notice that the status bar at the bottom of the screen explains the menu's function.

3. Press Enter to display the selected menu.

4. Press the up or down arrow to select (highlight) a command. Read the status bar at the bottom of the screen for an explanation of each command.

5. Press the right or left arrow to move from one menu to another.

6. Select the command that you want and then press Enter; or you can press Esc to back out without selecting.

When you become more familiar with the Excel menus, you can touch-type commands as follows:

1. Press Alt to select the menu bar.

2. Press the underlined letter in the menu name you want. For example, you press F for File. The menu then pulls down.

3. Press the underlined letter in the command that you want to execute, as with O for Open.

You do not need to wait for the menu to appear when touch-typing commands.

Selecting Options from Dialog Boxes

One reason that Windows programs are easier to operate than most DOS programs is that Windows programs do not have ten or twelve layers of menus. Menus and commands are a single layer deep. If more information is needed after a command is chosen, a dialog box appears. Dialog boxes enable you to select options, enter data, and control how a command operates.

A dialog box displays all available options in one view. Both beginners and advanced users have an opportunity to see what features are available.

In the pull-down menus, commands that require additional information are followed by ellipses (...). Choosing one of these commands displays a dialog box in which you enter needed information. For example, the Format Alignment... command results in the dialog box shown in figure 2.5.

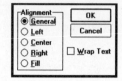

Fig. 2.5. *The Format Alignment dialog box.*

Dialog boxes contain different types of items. These items are described later in more detail. To familiarize yourself with these items, read the following list:

Excel Dialog Box Items

Text box	A box in which you can type and edit text or numbers.
Option button	A round button that gives you one choice from the available options.
Check box	A square box that can be turned on or off.
List boxes	A list or pull-down list that scrolls to display available alternatives.
Command buttons	Buttons that complete or cancel the command; some buttons give you access to additional options.

To select options in a dialog box, follow these steps:

 Move the pointer tip onto the option button, check box, text box, or item in a scrolling list; then click.

 Press Alt+*letter,* where *letter* is the underlined letter in the name of the option or group of options you want. Move to the selection in a list or move between round option buttons by pressing an arrow key.

To complete a command from a dialog box, follow these steps:

 Click on the OK command button or double-click on the item that you want in a list box.

Press Enter or Tab until a dashed line appears around OK, and then press the space bar.

To back out of a dialog box, follow these steps:

 Click on the Cancel button.

 Press the Esc key.

Option Buttons and Check Boxes

Figure 2.6 shows text boxes and a group of option buttons. You can select only one option button from within a group, but you can select one or more check boxes.

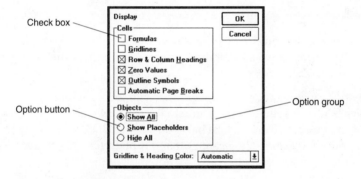

Fig. 2.6. *A dialog box with option buttons and check boxes.*

To change an option button with the mouse, click on the button. To turn off an option button, you must click on another in the same group. A dot within the option indicates that the option is on. Remember, you can select only one button in a group.

To change an option button from the keyboard, hold down the Alt key and then press the underlined letter or number of the option you want. Or you can press Tab until an option in the group is enclosed by dashed lines; then press the arrow keys to select the option button that you want.

Check boxes are square boxes that you can turn on or off and can use in combination with other check boxes. A check box is on when an X appears in the box.

To select or deselect a check box, click on the check box that you want changed. From the keyboard, press Alt+*letter* where *letter* is the underlined letter in the name of the check box.

> **Tip: *Using the Tab or Shift+Tab To Move within a Dialog Box***
> If you are making a succession of changes in a dialog box, you may find that pressing the Tab key is the easiest way to move between items in the box. (Shift+Tab moves in the reverse direction.) The active item is enclosed in a dashed line or contains the flashing insertion point for text editing. To change a check box that is enclosed by the dashed line, press the space bar. To change an option button in a group enclosed by the dashed line, press the arrow keys.

Text Boxes

Text boxes enable you to type information, such as file names and numbers, into a dialog box. You can edit the text within a text box the same way you edit text elsewhere in Excel.

When the mouse pointer is over a text box, it appears in the shape of a capital I, which is known as an I-beam. The actual location where typing will appear is indicated by a flashing vertical bar. You can use the Formula Replace text box, shown in figure 2.7, to search for and replace text or parts of formulas throughout the worksheet.

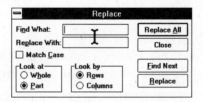

Fig. 2.7. The Formula Replace text box.

Follow these instructions to select a text box:

Move the pointer over the box and notice that it changes to an I-beam. Position the I-beam where you want the insertion point (cursor) to appear in the text and then click.

Press the Alt+*letter* combination for the text box, or press Tab until the text box is selected. Type to replace all the selected (high-lighted) text. Or you can press the left- or right-arrow keys to move the flashing vertical cursor and then type the text you want to insert.

Delete characters to the right of the flashing insertion point by pressing the Del key. Delete characters to the left of the insertion point by pressing the Backspace key.

To select multiple characters so that you can delete or replace them by typing, perform these actions:

Select	Keyboard Action
Multiple letters	Shift+arrow
Words	Shift+Ctrl+arrow
To the beginning	Shift+Home
To the end	Shift+End

Select	Mouse Action
Multiple letters	Drag across letters
Word	Double-click on word
Words	Double-click on word; then drag

List Boxes

In some cases, Excel has multiple alternatives from which to choose. For example, the Forma**t** **F**ont dialog box (see fig. 2.8) shows you lists of typefaces and sizes.

Some list boxes show only the current selection in what appears to be a text box. To see the entire list of alternatives, you must pull down the list. Figures 2.9 and 2.10 show the Forma**t** **P**atterns dialog box before and after the Patterns list has been pulled down.

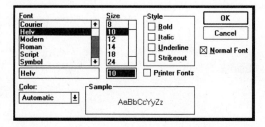

Fig. 2.8. Format Font list boxes.

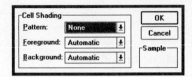

Fig. 2.9. The Patterns dialog box with the Pattern list up.

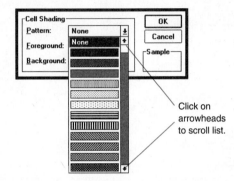

Click on
arrowheads
to scroll list.

Fig. 2.10. The Patterns dialog box with the Pattern list down.

Follow these steps to select an item from a list box:

1. If the list is not displayed, click on the down arrow to the side of the list.

2. When the list is displayed, click on the arrowheads in the scroll bar to scroll to the name you want.

3. Click on the name in the list that you want.

4. Click on OK if you are in a dialog box.

1. Activate the list box by pressing Alt +*underlined letter*.

2. If the box is a pull-down list box, press Alt +down arrow.

3. Scroll to the name you want by pressing the up arrow, down arrow, Home key, End key, or the first letter of the name.

4. Press Enter to complete the command.

In most dialog boxes, you can double-click on a name in a list box to select the name and choose OK in one operation.

Note: *Before Selecting a Command Button*
Before you select a command button such as OK, make sure that the name you want to select from the list box is selected (highlighted), not just surrounded by a dashed line.

Tip: *Saving Time in List Boxes*
You can find names quickly in a list box because they appear in alphabetical order. Select the box by clicking in it once or by pressing the down arrow. Then press the first letter of the name you are searching for. The list will scroll to the first name beginning with that letter. You also can scroll with the up- and down-arrow keys and with the Home, End, or PgUp and PgDn keys.

Command Buttons

Command buttons usually appear at the upper right corner of dialog boxes. These buttons enable you either to execute or cancel the command. Occasionally, as you can see in figure 2.11, command buttons let you expand a dialog box or "tunnel through" to the dialog box for another related command. For example, choosing the **Gallery 3-D Column** command displays a dialog box that shows predefined 3-D column charts. The box also contains buttons that let you tunnel through to other types of predefined charts.

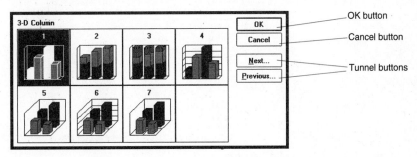

Fig. 2.11. The Gallery 3-D dialog box.

The right side of the dialog box in figure 2.11 contains the command buttons OK, Cancel, Next, and Previous. OK always executes the command and closes the dialog box. Cancel removes the dialog box without executing the command.

With the mouse, you can choose a command button by clicking on it. From the keyboard, you can choose a command button using a couple of methods. If the command button contains an underlined letter, press Alt+*underlined letter*. If a button is bold, press Enter to choose the button. Choose Cancel by pressing Esc. You can select any command button by pressing Tab until the button name is enclosed in dashed lines and then pressing Enter.

Getting Help

Windows and Excel have Help information to guide you through new commands and procedures. Excel's Help files are quite extensive, explaining topics that range from parts of the screen to commands, dialog boxes, and business procedures.

To get help in Excel or a Windows program, choose a command from the **H**elp menu or press F1. The **Help Index** command or F1 will display the window shown in figure 2.12. From this window you can learn how to use Help, or you can see the index of topics. Notice that Help has three different ways by which you can access or control help information. You can use the menus at the top of the Help window, or you can use the buttons under the menus for quick browsing through Help information or for jumping forward or backward through related topics.

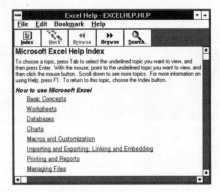

Fig. 2.12. The Help Index window.

The following list describes the menu commands available in Help:

Command	*Action*
File Open	Opens a Help file to another program.
File Print Topic	Prints the current Help topic to the current printer.
File Printer Setup	Sets up a printer.
File Exit	Exits the Help program.
Edit Copy	Copies the active Help window's text contents into the clipboard so that you can paste this information into other documents.
Edit Annotate	Displays a notepad in which you can type your own notes to attach to the current Help topic. Topics with custom notes show a paper-clip icon at the top to remind you that these topics have annotations.
Bookmark Define	Creates a bookmark name that attaches to the current Help topic. You can quickly return to this topic by selecting the name from the list in the Bookmark Define list or by choosing the name from under the Bookmark menu. (Bookmarks are like range names in Excel.)
Bookmark *# name*	Lists the available bookmarks so that you can choose one and quickly go to the topic where that bookmark is located. (*# name* is not a visible command until bookmarks have been created.)
Help Using Help	Shows you information about how to use Help.
Help About	Shows the copyright and version of your Help file.

Tip: *Using the Bookmark and Annotate Commands To Customize Help*
By marking the location of interesting topics and annotating those topics with notes, you can customize Help to fit your work.

Command buttons are located under the menu and help you move through the Help topics. Choose a button by clicking on it or by pressing Alt+*letter*. The following command buttons help you move through information:

Button	*Action*
Index	Shows the **Help Index**.
Back	Returns to the previous Help topic. With this button, you can retrace the topics you have viewed back to the initial Help Index.
Browse <<	Shows the previous related topic. If no previous topics are present, the button dims.
Browse >>	Shows the next related topic. If no more related topics exist, the button dims.
Search	Displays a list of key words from which you can choose a topic. The Search dialog box enables you to search for topics within the Help file.

The Search dialog box enables you to find topics related to the subject you need help with. To use Search, choose the **S**earch button; the dialog box shown in figure 2.13 will appear.

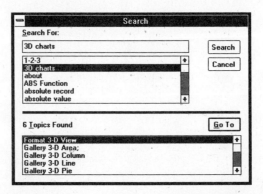

Fig. 2.13. The Search dialog box enables you to search for help by topic.

If you are using a mouse, scroll through the Search For list and click on a topic. Click on the Search button. The lower box, Topics Found, will fill in with related topics. Scroll through these topics, click on the topic you want more information about, and then click on the Go To button. The Help window for that topic will appear.

 If you are using the keyboard, press Alt+S to choose the Search For list. Type a topic in the text box. As you type, the list scrolls to topics that start with the letters you type. If you want to scroll through the list, press Tab until a topic in the list is enclosed with dashes, and then press the up or down arrow. Press Enter, and the Go To list will fill with related topics. Press the up or down arrow to select a topic and then press Enter.

"Hot" words or phrases appear within the actual Help text. These words or phrases have a solid or dashed underline, meaning that the word or phrase is linked to additional information.

To jump to the topic related to a solid underlined word, click on the word or press Tab until the word is selected; then press Enter. To see the definition of a word with a dashed underline, hold down the mouse button on the word, or tab to the word and hold down the Enter key.

You can get help for any dialog box or error message that appears in Excel. Figure 2.14 shows the error box that appears when you attempt to enter a formula containing an error. When such a dialog box or error message appears, press F1 to get help about the error. Figure 2.15 shows the Help message that appears when there is an error in the formula bar and after you press F1.

Fig. 2.14. The Error dialog box for a formula that contains an error.

To learn what a command does or how a portion of the screen works, press Shift+F1 and then choose the command or portion of the screen by clicking on it. Notice that the mouse pointer changes to a question mark that overlays the pointer. Pressing Shift+F1 enables you to ask a question about the item you click on.

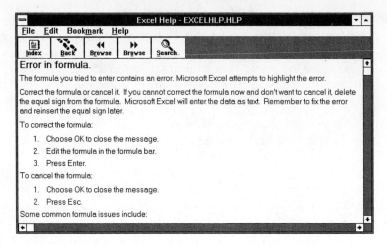

Fig. 2.15. The Help box for an error in the formula bar.

Help is an actual program, so you need to close its window when you are done. To remove the Help window, double-click on the Control menu icon to the left of the Help title bar; or press Alt, space bar, and then C for Close (Alt+F4).

Manipulating Windows

When you use Excel with Windows, you can display and run more than one program in Windows or have multiple worksheets, charts, and macros in Excel. Seeing that much information on your screen can be confusing unless you keep your windows organized. Just as you organize folders and papers on your desk, you can organize your Windows programs and Excel documents.

You will see two types of windows on the screen. A program window contains a program such as the Program Manager, Excel, or Microsoft Word for Windows. Excel can also have multiple document windows within the Excel window.

Selecting the Active Window

You can work in a program or document only when its window is active. The active window has a solid title bar. Notice the difference between the title bars in figure 2.16. In most cases, the active window is also the window on top; however, in some instances, such as during the process of linking worksheets together, the active window may not be on top.

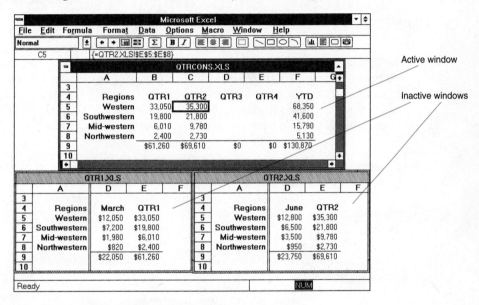

Fig. 2.16. The active window is where your actions take place.

If you are running Excel with other Windows or non-Windows programs, you can switch between programs. Press Ctrl+Esc to display the Task List and then select the program that you want to activate. You can also cycle between programs by pressing Alt+Tab.

Because Excel makes working with several worksheets and charts easy, you frequently have more than one document window on-screen. However, you can affect only the active document. From within the Excel window, if you can see the document, you can make it active by clicking on the document with the mouse pointer. If you cannot see the document, move the other windows so that you can see it, or use the mouse to select the same commands you would use with the keyboard method.

To switch to another window from the keyboard, choose the **W**indow menu and then press the number of the document window that you want to activate. Each document appears in the menu with a name. You can cycle between documents by pressing Ctrl+F6.

Shrinking, Expanding, and Restoring Windows

You soon will find that your computer desktop can become as cluttered as your real desktop. To gain more space, you can store programs by minimizing them so that they become small symbols (icons) at the bottom of the screen. (Document windows containing worksheets, macros, or charts cannot be minimized to icons. You can, however, hide them by using the **W**indow **H**ide command.)

When you need one of the programs that has been minimized, you can restore the icon to its former program window at the original location and size. When you want a window to fill the entire available screen area, you will then maximize it. The icons for minimizing and maximizing space are shown in figure 2.17.

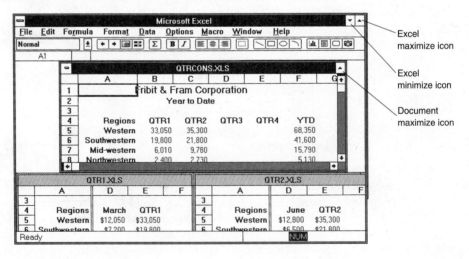

Fig. 2.17. *The minimize and maximize icons.*

To maximize a program or document window with the mouse, click on the maximize icon for the active window or double-click in the title bar of the window. To maximize a program or document window from the keyboard, press Alt, hyphen to display the document Control menu, or press Alt, space bar to display the program Control menu. Press X for the Maximize command.

You can shrink program windows so that they are temporarily stored at the bottom of the screen. To do this, click on the minimize icon. From the keyboard, press Alt, space bar to display the program Control menu. Then press N to choose Minimize.

Excel and document windows can always be restored from their maximized or minimized sizes into their previous window size. If Excel is an icon at the bottom of the screen, double-click on it. If Excel or a document window is maximized, click on the double-headed icon to the right of the Excel or document title bar. With a keyboard, select the document Control menu with Alt, hyphen, or select the Excel Control menu with Alt, space bar; then choose **Restore** (see fig. 2.18).

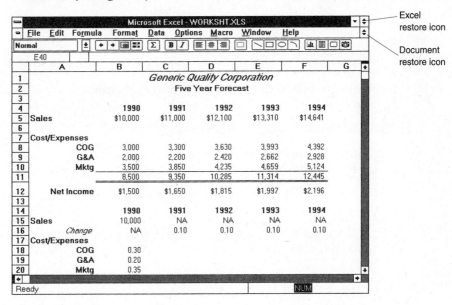

Fig. 2.18. The restore icon.

Moving a Window

With multiple programs or multiple Excel documents on-screen, you will want to move windows for the same reason that you shuffle papers on your desk. You can move a window with either the mouse or the keyboard by following these steps:

 First activate the window that you want to move. Drag the title bar until the shadow border is where you want the window. Then release the mouse button to fix the window in its new location.

 Select the program or document Control menu by pressing Alt, space bar for the program Control menu, or Alt, hyphen for the document Control menu. Press M to select **M**ove. A four-headed arrow now appears in the title bar. Press an arrow key to move the shadowed outline of the window. Press Enter to fix the window in its new location, or press Esc to retain the original location.

Sizing a Window

You frequently will want to see only part of a program or document window. You can do this by changing the size of the window. Follow these steps:

1. Click on the window to activate it.

2. Move the pointer over the edge or corner that you want to resize; the pointer changes to a two-headed arrow.

3. Drag the two-headed arrow in the direction that you want that edge or corner to move.

4. When the shadow edge is in the correct location, release the mouse button.

1. Activate the window and move it so that you can see the edge you want to resize. Press Alt +Tab until Excel is active, or press Ctrl +F6 until the document you want is active.

2. Choose the Control menu by pressing Alt, space bar for the program Control menu, or Alt, hyphen for the document Control menu.

3. Press M for **M**ove.

4. Press the arrow key that points to the edge you want to move.

5. Press the arrow keys to move that edge.

6. Press Enter to fix the edge in its new location, or press Esc to cancel.

Closing a Document Window

When you finish with the program, worksheet, or chart, you should close the window to remove it from the screen and to free memory. If you made a change since the last time you saved the document, Excel displays an alert dialog box, as shown in figure 2.19, asking whether you want to save your work before closing.

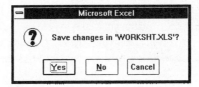

Fig. 2.19. The Save dialog box.

To close the active document window, follow these steps:

1. Close the window.

 Double-click on the document Control menu icon on the left side of the document's title bar. The window closes if no changes were made.

 Choose the document Control menu. Press C for Close. The window closes if no changes were made. If you have more than one window opened onto the same file, you can close the file and all of its windows by choosing File Close.

2. If changes were made to the document, you are asked to confirm whether you want to save your changes.

 In the dialog box, click on the No command button if you don't want to save the changed version of the file, or click on the Yes command button to save your changes.

In the dialog box, press Alt+N to choose the No command button, or press Enter to choose the Yes command button and save your changes.

3. If you chose Yes, enter a new file name.

 Enter the new name in the Save Worksheet dialog box that appears, and then click on the OK command button.

 Enter the new name in the Save Worksheet dialog box that appears and press Enter.

> **Tip: *Saving Your Work***
>
> You can avoid frustration and lost work if you save different versions of your work. When you save your document using the same file name, your previous work is replaced by the current work, and you cannot go back to old files.
>
> Instead of using the same file name over and over, reserve two characters at the end of each file name for a version number—for example, BUDGET07, BUDGET08, and so on. If you do this, you can return to your previous work. (Don't retype the entire name; just press the left arrow or Backspace to edit the old name.) When you get too many files of the same type, erase the old ones with the **File Delete** command.

Quitting Windows and Excel

Close or quit Excel when you are finished working for the day or when you need to free memory for other programs. To quit Excel, follow these steps:

1. Quit Excel.

 Double-click on the program Control menu icon, which is on the left of the Excel title bar. Excel quits immediately if you made no changes since the last time you saved your documents.

 Press Alt, space bar to display the program Control menu. Press C to choose the Close command or press Alt+F4.

2. Confirm whether you want to save your changes.

If you made changes to any document, Excel displays an alert box asking whether you want to save your current work. Click on the Yes command button to save your work, or click on the No command button to quit without saving.

If you made changes to any document, Excel displays an alert box asking whether you want to save your work since the last file save. Press Enter to choose Yes and save your work, or press N to choose No and abandon your changes.

3. Repeat steps 1 and 2 for each document name displayed in an alert box. The alert box appears for each document you have on-screen that has been changed.

> **Tip:** *Saving All Your Work Just As It Is*
> To save all the documents and their window arrangements that you are currently working with, use the File Save Workspace command, described in Chapter 11.

From Here...

You should work through the Worksheet Quick Start in Chapter 3. This Quick Start will take you step-by-step through a small practice worksheet. If you are familiar with Lotus 1-2-3, you should read Chapter 5, "Making the Switch from 1-2-3 to Excel," to learn about Excel's improvements over Lotus 1-2-3 and the differences between Excel and 1-2-3.

After you go through the Worksheet Quick Start in Chapter 3, you may want to skim through the worksheet chapters and look for features or examples that relate to the work you do. Experiment with a few small test worksheets and basic features, such as formatting and editing, before you attempt to build a large worksheet.

Part II

Excel Worksheets

Includes

Worksheet Quick Start

Designing Worksheets

Making the Switch from 1-2-3 to Excel

Creating Worksheets

Entering and Editing Worksheet Data

Formatting Worksheets

Drawing and Placing Graphics in Worksheets

Using Functions

Building Systems and Managing Multiple Windows

Linking and Consolidating Worksheets

Building Extensive Worksheets

Using the Solver

Using Excel's Add-In Macros

Printing Worksheets

The worksheet is the heart of Excel. It is like a giant sheet of columnar paper as wide as two big cars and as tall as a thirty-story building. On this paper you can place text, numbers, and formulas. What makes the worksheet indispensable to business is that when you change a number, all formulas that depend on that number automatically recalculate and display new results. In your work, this automatic recalculation means that budgets, forecasts, cost estimates, and other number-intensive jobs suddenly become easier and more accurate. Jobs that you used to have to calculate each time from scratch now only need to be calculated once. You can recalculate changes to a job by entering just the changed number. Excel does all the recalculation.

The Worksheet Quick Start in Chapter 3 is a good place to start learning about Excel because it gives you a quick hands-on overview of the worksheet's features and commands. The Quick Start guides you through exercises that build a forecasting worksheet. You get a quick look and feel at how Excel operates. When you finish the Quick Start, you can read other chapters in this part to learn specific features or commands in detail.

Other chapters in Part II provide in-depth discussions about designing and operating worksheets, entering and editing worksheet data, formatting worksheets, drawing or inserting graphics, using functions (pre-built formulas), linking and consolidating worksheets, and printing. This part includes chapters to help you build more advanced worksheets and to help you run the Solver and Goal Seek programs that find worksheet solutions for you.

3

Worksheet Quick Start

Whether you are new to electronic worksheets or you are an experienced user, you will find the Quick Start for worksheets a good introduction to Excel. Even if you are familiar with Excel, you should work through this Quick Start. You will discover some new features and shortcuts available in Excel. The Quick Start is an introduction; the chapters that follow discuss extensive details and include many practical examples.

This Quick Start will give you enough information to begin building simple worksheets on your own. Because you may not have enough time to work through the entire Quick Start at one sitting, a midway section describes how to save your work so you can restart later.

Creating a Forecasting Worksheet

The two most frequent uses for worksheets are budgeting and forecasting. The following example prepares a simple forecast of sales and expenses as a percentage of sales. In the example, the Global Quality Corporation has a single source of revenue and only three expense items. The three cost and expense items will be entered as a percentage of each year's sales.

Figures 3.1 and 3.2 represent the kind of forecast worksheet you might create. The upper rows of the worksheet, in figure 3.1, show the calculated results of the forecast. These rows contain only text and formulas. The lower rows, in figure 3.2, contain an area to enter data. When you change the numbers in figure 3.2, you immediately will see the recalculated results in figure 3.1. The two portions are kept separate to reduce the chance of typing a number over a formula—the single largest cause of errors in worksheets.

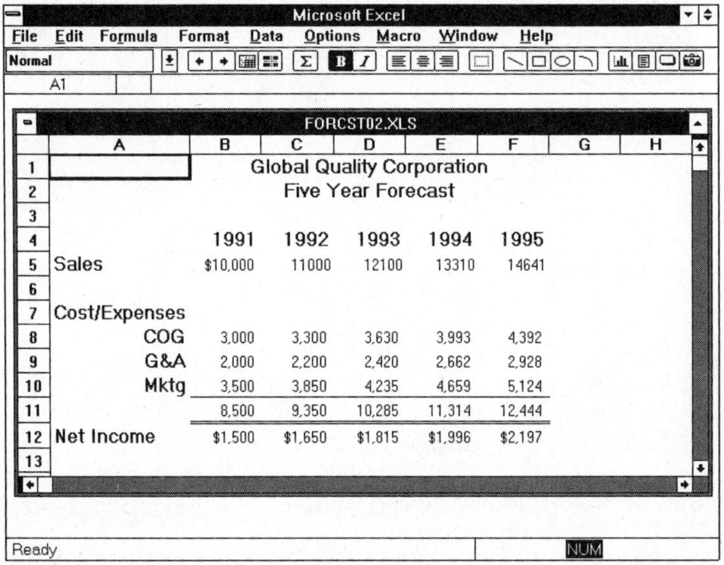

Fig. 3.1. The calculated forecast portion of the worksheet.

If you haven't yet started Excel, do so before you continue. For instructions on starting the program, see Chapter 1, "Installing and Running Excel." If you are not familiar with working in a Windows environment and operating menus and dialog boxes, you will want to experiment with Windows as you read Chapter 2, "Operating Windows."

Reviewing the Worksheet

Excel opens with a blank worksheet titled *Sheet1*. Sheet1 appears in its own document window. Figure 3.3 points out important parts of the Excel and document window.

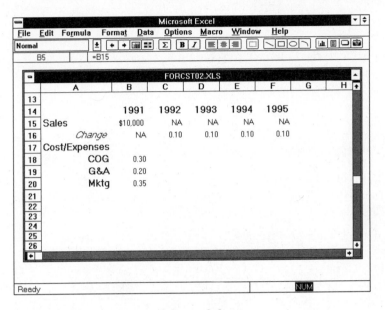

Fig. 3.2. *The data-entry portion of the worksheet.*

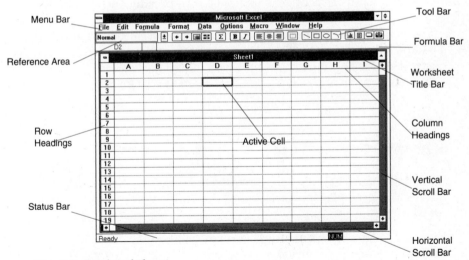

Fig. 3.3. *Excel and Sheet1.*

The worksheet contains 256 columns with alphabetic headings and 16,384 numbered rows. Each intersection of row and column is a unique *cell* that can be referenced by its row and column; for example, the cell where row D intersects with column 1 is named cell D1. In each cell, you can type a number, text, or a formula.

Moving around in the Worksheet

In figure 3.3, cell D2 is the *active cell*. The active cell has a border around it. This is the cell affected if you type or give a command. If you cannot see the active cell, its *cell reference* will show in the Reference Area.

From the keyboard, you can select a different cell by pressing arrow keys or page movement keys, such as PgUp or PgDn. To select cells an entire screen to the left or right, press Ctrl+PgDn or Ctrl+PgUp. Press Ctrl+Home to move to the A1 cell. You can press F5 to display a Goto dialog box in which you can type a cell or range you want to select. Many movement and selection keys are listed in Chapter 6, "Creating Worksheets."

With a mouse, you can activate a different cell by clicking once on it. If the cell is not visible, move the window by clicking on the scroll bar arrowhead that points in the direction you want to move. You can click in the gray area of a scroll bar to move a screen at a time, or you can drag the scroll box in the scroll bar for large moves. After you have moved the window so that you can see the cell you want, click once on the cell to activate it.

Preparing the Worksheet

Before beginning the Quick Start, you will want to customize some of Excel's features. For example, you can turn off the gridlines that display on the worksheet.

To choose a menu using a mouse, click on the menu name. When the menu appears, click on the command name. When a dialog box appears, click on the button or check box for the option you want to select (turn on) or deselect (turn off). Selected options appear either with a darkened dot (buttons) or an X (check boxes). Click on the button or check box a second time to deselect the option. Complete the selection by choosing (clicking on) the OK button. Back out of a selection by choosing the Cancel button.

To choose a menu using the keyboard, press the Alt key, release, then press the letter underlined in the name of the menu you want. The Quick Start shows these keystrokes as Alt, *letter*. Select the command from the pull-down menu by pressing the letter underlined in the command. If a dialog box appears, select or deselect option buttons or check boxes by holding down the Alt key as you press the underlined letter. The Quick Start shows these keystrokes as Alt+*letter*. Selected options display a darkened center (buttons) or an X (check boxes). Deselect an option by selecting it a second time. Complete the selection by pressing Enter or back out by pressing Esc.

To turn off the gridlines, follow these steps:

1. Choose the Options Display command.

 Click on Options, then click on Display.

 Press Alt, O, then D.

2. Deselect the Gridlines check box so that the feature is turned off.

 Click on the Gridlines check box.

 Press Alt+G. (Hold down the Alt key as you press G.)

3. Choose OK by clicking on it, or press Enter.

Selecting Short or Full Menus

Excel provides you with two degrees of menus. One shows the full set of commands; the other shows a shortened set of commands. To make sure that you can see the full set of commands, follow these steps:

1. Choose the Options menu.

 Click on the Option menu name.

 Press Alt, O.

2. If you see the command Full Menus, choose it by clicking on Full Menus or press the M key to change to full menus. If you see the command Short Menus, Excel is already displaying full menus, so press Esc to back out of the menu.

Displaying the Tool Bar

If you are using a mouse with Excel, you can save time by using the tool bar. The tool bar gives you quick access to many commands, but it can only be used with the mouse. To display the tool bar, follow these steps:

1. Choose the Options Workspace command.

 Click on Options, then on Workspace.

 Press Alt, O, then W.

2. Select the Tool Bar check box in the Display group.

 Click on the Tool Bar check box so that it displays an X.

 Press Alt+T.

3. Choose OK by clicking on it, or press Enter.

Checking Text Fonts

Before you begin entering text in the worksheet, set Excel to use only the text fonts that your printer is capable of printing. If you do not do this, your text on-screen will appear different than the text when printed. To ensure that the on-screen characters match the printed characters, follow these steps:

1. Choose the Format Font command.

 Click on Format, then on Font.

 Press Alt, T, then F.

2. Select the Printer Fonts check box and notice that the Font list will change to match your currently selected printer.

 Click on the Printer Fonts check box.

 Press Alt+R.

3. Choose OK by clicking on it or press Enter.

Building a Text Skeleton

Worksheets are much easier to build when you have a text skeleton, or outline, as a guide for entering data and formulas. To build a text skeleton, move the active cell to the cell you want to enter data in and then type.

Entering Text

To change a cell or its contents, you must select the cell first. Follow these steps to select cells for the text entries in your sample worksheet:

1. Select cell A1.

 Click on the scroll bar arrowheads until A1 is visible. Click on A1 to make it active.

 Press Ctrl+Home to make A1 active.

2. Select cell D1.

 Click on cell D1.

 Press the right-arrow key to move the active cell to D1.

Notice that the reference for the active cell, D1, appears in the Reference Area to the left of the formula bar.

3. Type the following title: Global Quality Corporation. Your text will appear in the formula bar, as shown in figure 3.4.

4. Enter the title in cell D1.

 Click on the check box to the left of the formula bar. (Clicking on the Cancel box [X] cancels your text.)

 Press Enter. (Pressing Esc cancels your text.)

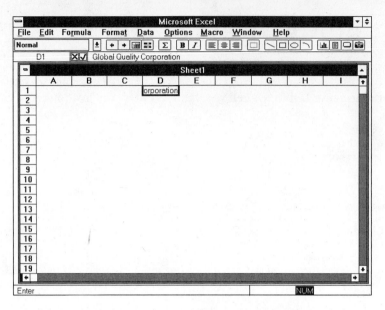

Fig. 3.4. Text appears in the formula bar before it is entered in a cell.

5. Select D2 and type the title **Five Year Forecast**; then press Enter.

6. Select both cells D1 and D2 so that the worksheet looks like figure 3.5.

 Click on cell D1. Hold down the left mouse button and drag the mouse pointer from D1 to D2 so that both cells are highlighted. Release the mouse button.

 Move to cell D1. Press Shift+down arrow to highlight both cells.

Notice that cell D1 is still active, but cell D2 is also selected. To return to having a single cell active, select any cell outside the selected cells.

If you make a mistake or enter something incorrectly during the Quick Start, you can erase a cell's format or contents easily. Select the cell(s) you want to correct, and then press the Delete key, Del. A dialog box with option buttons appears. Press the arrow keys to select whether you want formulas (contents), formats, or everything in the cell erased and then press Enter.

To edit the contents of a cell, press the Edit key, F2. The contents then shows in the formula bar. You can use the left- or right-arrow keys to move, the Delete and Backspace keys to erase, and the typing keys to insert characters. Press Enter to reenter the cell contents.

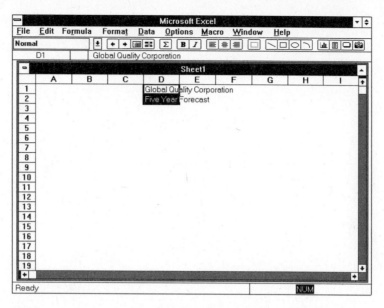

Fig. 3.5. *You can select and change more than one cell at a time.*

Changing Text Style and Alignment

You now can use the following steps to change the text alignments and style of the selected cells, D1 and D2, at the same time. If you are using a mouse, the tool bar, shown in figure 3.6, will make the most frequently used commands readily available.

If you are using a mouse and the tool bar is visible, click on the Center Alignment icon to center the selected text. If you are using a keyboard or the tool bar is not visible, follow these steps:

1. Make sure that cells D1 and D2 are still selected.

2. Choose the Format menu.

   The Format menu shown in figure 3.7 appears underneath Format. Notice that ellipses (. . .) follow the Font command on the menu. Ellipses indicate that a dialog box requesting more information will follow the command.

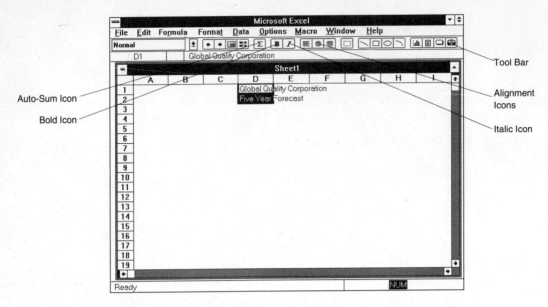

Fig. 3.6. The Alignment icons align contents left, center, or right in a cell.

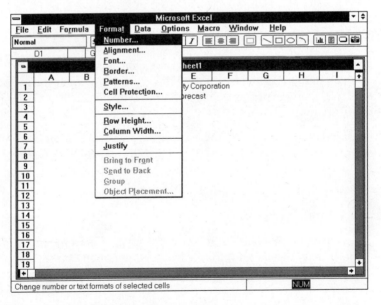

Fig. 3.7. The Format menu.

3. Select the **A**lignment command.

Click on the **A**lignment command.

Press A for the **A**lignment command.

The Alignment dialog box appears, displaying an option button for each type of text, number, or date alignment (see fig. 3.8).

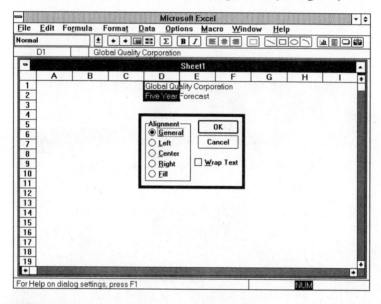

Fig. 3.8. The Alignment dialog box.

4. Select the **C**enter option.

Click on the **C**enter button.

Press Alt+C.

5. Choose the OK button or press Enter.

6. Do not move or select other cells. You will continue formatting cells D1 and D2.

Both titles center on column D, the cells containing the text.

Because both cells remain selected, you can continue to choose commands to change the appearance of the text. Follow these steps to change the font and style of the headings. If you are using a mouse and the tool bar is visible, click on the bold icon, **B**, to bold the selected text. If you are using a keyboard or you are using a mouse and the tool bar is not visible, follow these steps:

1. Choose the Format Font command.

 Click on Format, and then click on Font.

 Press Alt, T, and then F.

Figure 3.9 shows the Font dialog box.

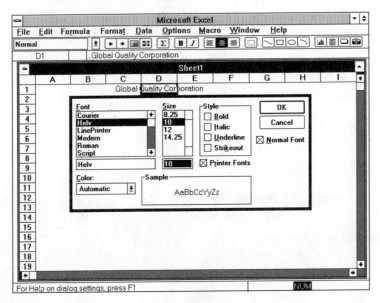

***Fig. 3.9.** The font dialog box.*

The fonts you have available in your printer may be different than the ones shown. Normally, you should select the Printer Fonts check box to ensure that the Font list shows only fonts available in your printer. If you want to use the Helv fonts shown, deselect the Printer Fonts check box within the Fonts dialog box. Because Helvetica fonts may not be available in your printer, the worksheet may print differently than it appears on-screen.

2. Select the Helv font from the Font list.

Click on the scroll arrows to the right of the Font list until you see Helv; then click on Helv.

Press Alt+F; then press the up or down arrow until Helv is selected.

3. Select 12 point from the Size list.

Click on the scroll arrows to the right of the Size list until you see 12; then click on 12.

Press Alt+S; then press the up or down arrow until 12 is selected.

4. Select the Bold style.

Click on the Bold check box.

Press Alt+B.

5. Choose OK or press Enter.

Complete the text skeleton as shown in figures 3.10 and 3.11. To enter the text, select the cell you want to enter text in, type the entry, and then press Enter. *Do not* put spaces in front of the entries COG, G&A, or Mktg. Type the years as numbers.

After entering the text, you may want to format the cells containing headings so that the headings appear as shown in figures 3.10 and 3.11. Use 12-point Helvetica in bold or italic style.

Widening a Column

After entering the text, you probably noticed that some of the text is wider than the default column width. To widen column A with a mouse, follow these steps:

1. Move the cell pointer over the line that separates the A and B headings at the top of the column.

2. When the pointer changes to a two-headed arrow, drag the pointer right by holding down the left mouse button and moving the mouse right.

3. Release the mouse button.

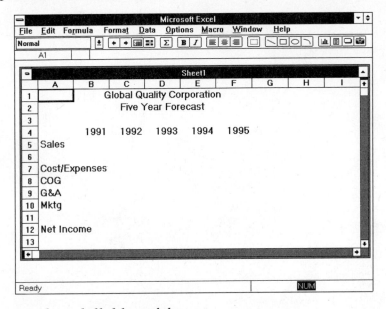

Fig. 3.10. The top half of the worksheet.

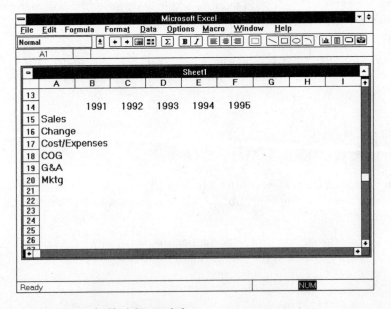

Fig. 3.11. The lower half of the worksheet.

To widen column A by keyboard or to widen the column so that the widest contents fit well follow these steps:

1. Select any cell in column A.

2. Choose the Format Column Width command.

   In the dialog box that appears, notice that the Column Width text box is selected. Although you can type a number for the width of the column, there is a faster method.

3. Select the Best Fit button so that Excel widens the column to fit the widest cell content in the column.

> **Tip: *Automatically Adjusting a Column***
> Automatically adjust a column to the best fit width by double-clicking on the line that separates A and B in the headings.

After column A is widened, you can see that Excel normally aligns text against the left edge of the column. Numbers and dates align against the right edge.

Aligning Items

To make the worksheet clearer, you can align the three expense items—COG, G&A, and Mktg—against the right column edge. Follow these steps to align the contents:

1. Select the cells containing COG, G&A, and Mktg.

 Click on cell A8, hold down the mouse button, drag down to A10, and then release.

 Move to cell A8 and hold down the Shift key as you press the down arrow until cells A8 through A10 are selected.

2. If you are using a mouse and the tool bar is visible, click on the Right Alignment icon in the tool bar. Alignment is completed.

   Or

   If you are not using the tool bar, choose the Format Alignment command.

Click on **Format**; then click on **Alignment**.

 Press Alt, T, and then A.

3. Select the **Right** option.

 Click on the **Right** option button.

 Press Alt+R.

4. Choose the OK button or press Enter.

Align the cells A16 and A18 through A20, using the same method. In Excel, a selection of multiple cells is called a range. The range in which A18 is one corner and A20 is the opposite corner is noted as range A18:A20.

Saving Your Worksheet

As you work, you should save your file, especially before taking breaks. Saving your work enables you to come back at a later time and open your work at the point where you left it. Worksheets that are not saved are lost when the worksheet is closed, Excel is closed, or the power is lost. To save your partially completed worksheet, follow these steps:

1. Choose the **File Save As** command (see fig. 3.12).

2. Type the name **FORCST01** (it will replace the name Sheet1 in the **Save Worksheet as:** text box).

3. Choose the OK button or press Enter.

Notice that the worksheet name in the worksheet title bar has changed from Sheet1 to FORCST01.XLS, the name you specified. XLS is the file extension for an Excel worksheet.

If you decide to exit Excel at this point, follow the instructions for exiting provided at the end of this Quick Start. When you want to return to the Quick Start, start Excel again and begin with the following topic on opening saved worksheets.

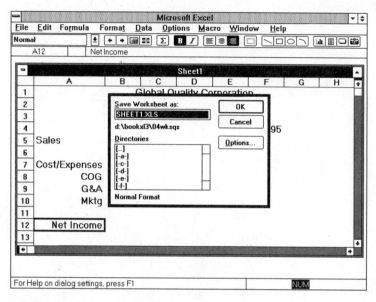

Fig. 3.12. *The Save As dialog box.*

Opening Your Saved Worksheet

You can reopen worksheets that are on a disk or diskette. If you saved the FORCST01 worksheet and exited Excel, you can reopen the worksheet with the following steps:

1. Choose the **File Open** command (see fig. 3.13).

2. Scroll through the **Files** list box.

 Click on the scroll arrows beside the box until you see the name FORCST01.XLS. Click on the name.

 Press Alt+F; then type F to scroll to names beginning with F in the list. Continue pressing F or the down arrow key until you select the name FORCST01.XLS.

3. Choose the **OK** button or press Enter.

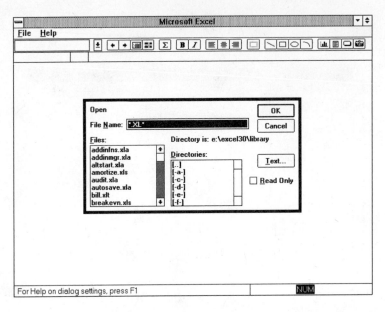

Fig. 3.13. The Open dialog box.

Entering Simple Data

Entering simple data is easier when you are typing into a text skeleton. If you next enter simple data before entering formulas, you will be able to see the results of a formula as soon as you enter the formula. This technique can help you pinpoint problems. If you use simple data, you can immediately tell whether a solution is realistic.

Whenever Excel recognizes a numeric, date, or time format, Excel stores the corresponding numbers and automatically formats the cell so that any number entered in that cell will appear with that numeric, date, or time format. Follow these steps to enter an item with a numeric format:

1. Select B15.

2. Type $10,000 and press Enter.

Notice that Excel accepts the number and retains the currency format with no decimal places. Only the number without formatting appears in the formula bar.

Enter the rest of the numeric data shown in figure 3.2. To enter a number, select the cell, type the number, and then press Enter or Tab. You can change Excel so that the active cell automatically moves down or stays on the same cell after you enter data. You can also make the numeric pad automatically enter a decimal point like a ten-key machine. Excel has a number of data-entry and data-formatting shortcuts described in Chapter 7, "Entering and Editing Worksheet Data," and in Chapter 23, "Entering and Sorting Data."

Enter the following data:

1991 Sales	B15 $10,000	Change	C16	0.1
COG	B18 0.3		D16	0.1
G&A	B19 0.2		E16	0.1
Mktg	B20 0.35		F16	0.1

Sometimes Excel doesn't recognize how you want a number or date formatted. To use one of Excel's predefined formats to format numbers with two decimal places, follow these steps:

1. Select cells C16:F16.

2. Choose the Format Number command (see fig. 3.14).

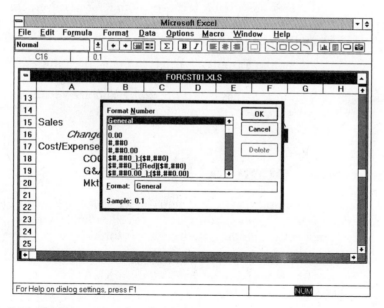

Fig. 3.14. The Format Number dialog box.

3. Select the 0.00 format.

 Click on the 0.00 format in the list.

 Because the Format **Number** is already selected, just press the down-arrow key until 0.00 is highlighted.

4. Choose the OK button or press Enter.

The Change numbers will now show leading zeros with two decimal places. Now repeat this same procedure, but select the cells B18:B20 and format them with 0.00.

The simple data portion of your worksheet should now look like figure 3.2 near the beginning of this chapter.

Entering Formulas

Electronic worksheets are useful because of the formulas entered in worksheet cells. These formulas produce new answers whenever the data used by the formulas changes.

Cells may contain simple formulas that refer only to the value stored in another cell, or they may contain complex formulas that include text manipulation, built-in formulas called *functions*, and array mathematics. All formulas begin with an equal sign (=).

Entering Formulas by Typing

A text skeleton and simple sample data help you see which cells are involved in a formula. To enter a formula, you will select a cell, enter the formula, and then press Enter or click on the Enter box in the formula bar.

One way to enter a formula is to type it. Use the following steps to enter a simple formula that reads the value $10,000 from cell B15 to cell B5:

1. Select B5.

2. Type the formula =B15.

3. Choose the Enter box in the formula bar or press Enter.

The number 10000 from B15 will appear in B5. Because cell B5 is not formatted, however, no dollar signs or commas will appear.

Entering Formulas by Pointing

In addition to typing a formula, you can enter it by "pointing" to the cells used in the formula. The pointing method reduces typographical errors, and you can use the method with either a mouse or keyboard.

The formula you will enter in cell C5 takes the value in B5 and adds to it the amount of sales increase according to the percentage in cell C16. The formula is =B5+B5*C16.

Follow these steps to enter the formula, using the pointing method:

1. Select C5.

2. Type an equal sign (=) to let Excel know that you are entering a formula.

3. Select B5 to add B5 to the formula (see fig. 3.15).

Click on cell B5.

Press the left-arrow key.

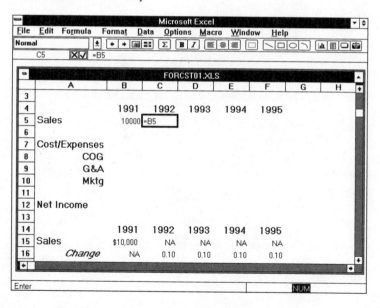

Fig. 3.15. *Cell references appear in formulas whether you type them or point to them.*

4. Type the next operator—the plus sign (+).

   The formula now should look like =B5+. Entering a math operator tells Excel to freeze the cell you pointed at (B5) so that you can point to the next cell reference to include in the formula.

5. Select B5 again by clicking on it or pressing the left arrow. The formula should look like =B5+B5.

6. Type the multiplication operator (*).

7. Select cell C16 (the last cell reference in the formula).

 Click on cell C16.

 Press the down-arrow key until you have selected cell C16.

8. If the formula bar displays =B5+B5*C16, enter the formula by pressing Enter or clicking on the Enter box. If the formula is not displayed correctly, press Esc or click on the X box, and then recreate the formula.

You can see that the result of the formula in cell C5 is 11000. Because you expected a ten percent increase over 1990's value of 10000, the result appears to be correct.

Copying and Pasting Formulas

If you had to go through the process of typing or pointing to enter every formula, building a worksheet would take a long time. Instead, you can copy formulas into other cells. The cell references in the formulas automatically adjust to their new locations. To copy a formula, follow these steps:

1. Select C5, the cell containing the formula you want to copy.

2. Choose the Edit Copy command.

   Notice that the status bar at the bottom of the screen gives you hints on what to do next. The status bar will guide you or give you hints with many commands.

3. Select cells D5:F5 (see fig. 3.16) as the location for the copied formula.

Drag from D5 to F5 by clicking on D5, holding down the mouse button and dragging to F5, and then releasing.

Move to cell D5. Hold down the Shift key and press the right-arrow key until cells D5 to F5 are selected.

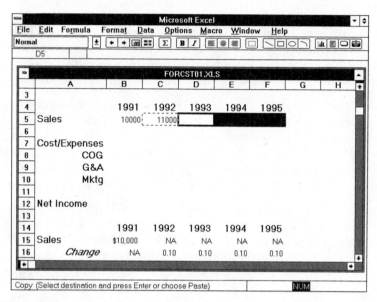

Fig. 3.16. Selected cells in which you will paste the copied formula.

4. Choose the Edit Paste command.

The Edit Copy command copies the contents of cell C5 into temporary memory called the *clipboard*. The Edit Paste command transfers the contents of the clipboard into the selected cells, D5 through F5. Press Esc to remove the dashed marquee encircling C5, if you want.

Using Absolute and Relative Cell References

When Excel pastes an existing formula from one cell into a new location, each formula adjusts to fit its new location. Move to each of the copied formulas in cells C5 through F5 and notice the difference between the original formula and the copies.

Cell		
C5	=B5+B5*C16	Original Formula
D5	=C5+C5*D16	Duplicate Formula
E5	=D5+D5*E16	Duplicate Formula
F5	=E5+E5*F16	Duplicate Formula

Cell references that adjust to their new location when copied are known as *relative references*. Excel normally enters cell references in a formula using a relative reference. The formula actually refers to a cell's location by its position *relative* to the formula, such as two rows up and one column left.

In some cases, you will *not* want Excel to change a cell reference when the formula is copied and pasted into a new location. This is the case for the formula in cell B8 for the Cost of Goods (COG), =B5*B18. Copying this formula from B8 and pasting it into C8 results in the adjusted formula =C5*C18; this formula is incorrect because no number exists in cell C18. If Excel adjusted the relative reference, the formula was no longer valid.

Instead, you want the B18 cell reference to stay the same no matter where the formula is copied. References that stay the same are known as *absolute references*. (The reference stays "absolutely" the same wherever it is copied.) To copy the contents of B18 as an absolute reference, put a dollar sign in front of the row and column address: $B$18. The following Excel shortcut enters a formula using both relative and absolute references:

1. Select B8.

2. Create the formula =B5*B18 using either pointing or typing. ***Do not press Enter.***

3. While the flashing insertion point is touching B18 in the formula bar, press F4 (the Reference key) so that B18 changes to $B$18.

4. Press Enter or click the check mark to enter the formula =B5*$B$18.

The result, 3000, in cell B8 appears reasonable because COG was 30% of the 10000 in first year sales.

Use the previous steps to enter the following formulas and check for a reasonable answer:

Cell	Formula	Result
B8	=B5*$B$18	3000
B9	=B5*$B$19	2000
B10	=B5*$B$20	3500

Do not enter other formulas across these rows. You can fill the rows in later with a single command.

Summing a Column of Numbers

The sample worksheet needs to display in cell B11 a total of the expenses in cells B8:B10. You could enter a formula in B11, such as =B8+B9+B10, but then the total would not include new expense items inserted into new rows. A much better method for writing this formula uses Excel's SUM( ) function. Functions are predefined formulas built into Excel. SUM( ) totals all the values that are within the range of cells you specify. To enter the formula for the total in cell B11, follow these steps:

1. Select B11.

2. If you are using a mouse and the tool bar, quickly click twice on the Auto-Sum icon. This automatically enters the Auto-Sum formula and totals the range B8:B10. (Figure 3.6 shows the Auto-Sum icon.)

   Or

   Press Alt+=.

   Or

   Type the formula **=SUM(B8:B11)**, and then press Enter.

The result, 8500, appears to be the correct total. You also can enter the SUM formula with the pointing method by typing **=SUM(**, then selecting the cells from B8 to B10, typing the closing parenthesis, **)**, and then pressing Enter.

Finish the calculations for column B by typing the formula for Net Income, which is Sales minus the total Cost/Expenses. Type the formula **=B5–B11** in cell B12. The result should be 1500.

Entering Single and Double Underlines

Make your worksheets look more professional by using underlines to set off columns of numbers from their subtotals or totals. Use a solid single line for subtotals and a double line for final totals. To draw a line at the bottom of cells, follow these steps:

1. Select cell B10.

2. Choose the Format Border command (see fig. 3.17).

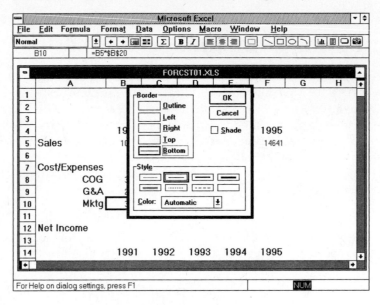

***Fig. 3.17.** The Format Border dialog box.*

3. Select the Bottom check box.

4. Select the single-underline style.

 Click on the single-underline box.

 Press Alt+E, then use the arrow keys to select the single-underline box.

5. Choose the OK button or press Enter.

The underline in the cell may not be visible until you select another cell.

Add a double underline to the bottom of cell B11 by selecting B11 and repeating the preceding steps. In step 4, select the double-underline box. The result of your nearly completed worksheet appears in figure 3.18.

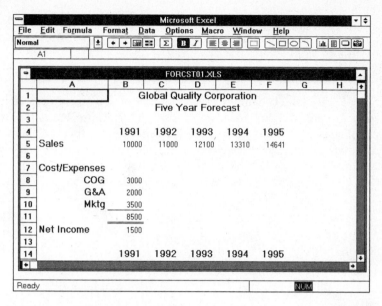

Fig. 3.18. *The worksheet after underlines are added.*

Formatting Formula Results

Formulas in cells that have the default numeric format of General do not display the number in a format. You will need to add the currency format to the formula cells. In the process, you will learn how easy it is to create custom numeric formats.

To format cells B5:F5 and cell B12 as currency, follow these steps:

1. Select B5:F5.

2. Choose the Format Number command.

3. Select the $#,##0_);($#,##0) format from the list box.

 Click on the $#,##0_);($#,##0) format.

 Press the down arrow until you highlight the $#,##0_);($#,##0) format.

4. Choose OK or press Enter.

The characters _) at the end of the positive-number format adjust the position of positive numbers so that they align with negative numbers in parentheses, ( ).

Repeat the procedure in steps 1-4 to format cell B12 with a currency format.

To format cells B8:B11 with commas, you will need to create a custom numeric format. The custom format is needed because Excel's existing comma format does not align with the currency format that uses a trailing parenthesis. The difference between one format having a trailing parenthesis and the other not causes the data to be misaligned in a column. To format the cells and create a custom format for better alignment, follow these steps:

1. Select B8:B11.

Drag from B8 through B11.

Select B8. Press Shift +down arrow to highlight from B8 through B11.

2. Choose the Format Number command.

3. Select the same format you selected before, $#,##0_);($#,##0).

4. Delete the $ signs from the format shown in the Format text box. Figure 3.19 shows the edited format.

Click in the Format text box; then use the left- and right-arrow keys and the Backspace or Delete key to remove the $ signs.

Press Alt +F to select the Format text box; then use the left- and right-arrow keys and the Backspace or Delete key to remove the $ signs.

5. Choose the OK button or press Enter.

You have created a custom numeric format. This format will remain at the bottom of the Format Number list, so you can use it anywhere on the worksheet. Chapter 8, "Formatting Worksheets," describes how flexible custom numeric and date formatting can be.

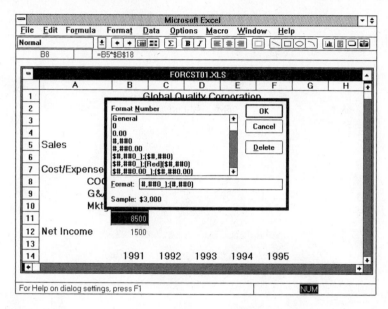

Fig. 3.19. *Create custom numeric formats by typing or editing.*

Filling Adjacent Cells with Formulas and Formats

Another useful method of duplicating formulas, besides copying and pasting, is filling a formula into an adjacent area. The following procedure will fill the remainder of the worksheet with the formulas and formats in column B. To fill in the worksheet, follow these steps:

1. Select B8:F12 so that the cells to be copied are on the left edge of the selection, as shown in figure 3.20.

 Click on B8, and hold down the mouse button as you drag to F12.

 Select B8, and hold down Shift as you use the arrow keys to move to F12.

2. Choose the Edit Fill Right command.

The formulas and formats from the left column fill the cells to the right. The upper portion of your worksheet now should look like figure 3.21.

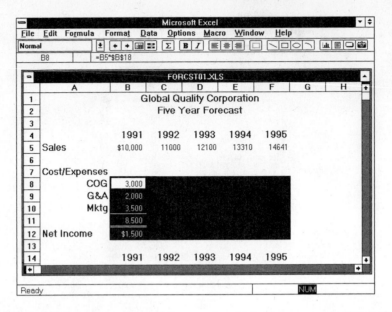

Fig. 3.20. Select the formulas and the area in which you want to duplicate the formulas.

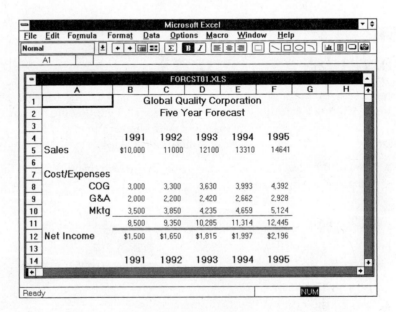

Fig. 3.21. A worksheet isn't complete until it's tested for accuracy.

Notice that the numbers in F8, F9, and F10 do not appear to total the result in F11. The displayed numbers have been rounded by formatting; however, calculated results use the full number. In other electronic spreadsheets, this discrepancy is difficult to fix; in Excel, the discrepancy is resolved with one command.

Choose the **O**ptions **C**alculation command. When the dialog box appears, select the **P**recision as Displayed check box and press Enter. When the alert appears, choose OK. The alert warns you that Excel will round constant numbers that have more decimal places than their formatting allows. The forecast worksheet now uses the numbers displayed to perform its calculations.

Saving Your Worksheet

Before testing your worksheet, save it. You will use it again in Chapter 17, "Chart Quick Start." Follow these steps to save the worksheet:

1. Choose the **F**ile **S**ave **A**s command so that you will have a chance to rename the file. (Use **F**ile **S**ave to save with the same name.)

2. Type the file name **FORCST02**.

3. Choose OK or press Enter.

These steps save your worksheet to the hard-disk directory shown in the upper left corner of the dialog box.

Testing Your Worksheet

Test your worksheet by entering new numbers into the data-entry area in the lower portion of the worksheet. Notice how Excel immediately recalculates formula results as you enter new data.

Although Excel is fast when recalculating, extremely large worksheets may take some time. With Excel, you can continue entering data and making changes as the recalculation continues.

Exiting Excel

To exit Excel, follow these steps:

1. Choose the File Exit command.

   If you have made changes to the worksheet since the last time you saved it, an alert box will ask whether you want to save the worksheet (see fig. 3.22).

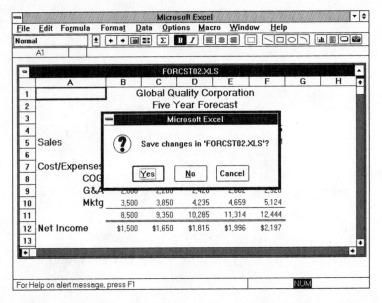

Fig. 3.22. You will be asked to save any changed worksheets before closing Excel.

2. Choose Yes if you want to save the worksheet or No if you do not.

3. If you chose Yes in step 2, Excel will save the file with its current name or give you a chance to name a new worksheet.

You will return to the Windows desktop.

From Here...

This Quick Start covers only a few of Excel's basic capabilities. Excel has many more features and functions. Other chapters will show you how to import graphics and draw on the worksheet, how to use multiple worksheets or split a single worksheet into multiple views, how to link and consolidate data between worksheets, and how to use the numerous add-in programs that come free with Excel.

As you read through the following chapters, you may want to experiment with the worksheet you have created. Experimenting will give you more hands-on experience. Save an unchanged copy of this worksheet for use with the Chart Quick Start (Chapter 17). Other Quick Starts in this book show you how to use Excel's database and Excel's charting and macro features. Try them out. The Quick Starts will help you quickly learn the many ways Excel can assist you.

4

Designing Worksheets

You have two options when you start a new worksheet. You can spend a little time planning ahead in the beginning, or you can spend a great amount of time repairing and restructuring the worksheet later on. For small, one- or two-screen worksheets, planning and design methods are helpful. For anything larger, planning and building the worksheet in the correct order is essential to save you time and effort. Moreover, planning will increase the flexibility of the system if you need to change it.

Designing a good worksheet involves at least 14 steps. These worksheet design and construction steps save time, increase your alternatives if you need to change the completed worksheet, and reduce the likelihood of errors. To design a good worksheet, follow these steps:

1. Understand the problem and the desired solution.

2. Make thumbnail sketches.

3. Build a text skeleton.

4. Enter simple sample data.

5. Enter formulas.

6. Check for reasonable results.

7. Apply formatting and styles.

8. Cross-check for accurate results.

9. Add graphics and explanatory text boxes.

91

10. Link the worksheet to other sheets in the system.

11. Automate the system.

12. Cross-check your system.

13. Document the worksheets and system.

14. Archive your system and documentation.

This chapter discusses these steps. To read more about a specific step, find its section heading.

Understanding the Problem and the Desired Solution

You must understand the problem and the desired solution before you start to create a worksheet or larger system. Whether you are creating a worksheet for yourself or for someone else, you must know what the finished system needs to accomplish and how users expect to use it. One way to prevent miscommunication is to create prototype data-entry screens and reports. Create sample data-entry screens and report output in Excel. From these examples, the users can tell you what changes are needed before you get too far into the project.

Many questions need to be answered before you design a worksheet:

- What solution are you seeking?

- What input do you need in order to find that solution?

- What is the best design for entering data?

- How do you want the output to look? Will you use the worksheet in a larger system? Should you build the system on one worksheet or on many worksheets linked together?

Making Thumbnail Sketches

Every great artist from Michelangelo and Leonardo da Vinci to Picasso has made thumbnail sketches, or small practice exercises, and sample drawings before starting a major work. You will find that thumbnail sketches are helpful when designing worksheets as well.

An excellent idea is to test smaller versions of your worksheet before attempting to establish a final version. Drawing charts of the data flow and maps of the worksheet layout, such as the one shown in figure 4.1, can be very helpful. These flowcharts and maps often pinpoint problems before you have committed yourself to a specific design. You can even draw the flowchart on an Excel worksheet.

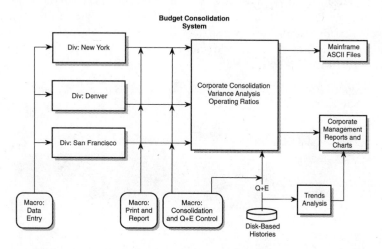

Fig 4.1. *A flowchart drawing done on an Excel worksheet.*

Remember to design the layout so that you can modify it easily in the future. Few worksheets ever remain the same. Before laying out a worksheet, read through the discussions in this book on conserving memory, linking multiple worksheets, and improving performance. Your worksheet map should show blocks that indicate the data-entry areas, calculation areas, the database, the database extract areas for printed reports, and other major parts of the worksheet.

Keep data-entry cells separate from calculation areas. This practice reduces the chance of errors and allows room for instructions and entry-checking formulas. You should try to make the data-entry screen appear like a paper form. Keep values that might change, such as growth rates, outside of the formulas. Formulas should refer to the cell that contains the value so that such assumptions as growth rate are easy to change and less prone to error.

Building a Text Skeleton

One of the easiest ways to design a worksheet is to create a framework on which you can build (see fig. 4.2). Your framework will be the text that shows where data will be entered, where formula results will appear, and so on. Text skeletons make it easier to enter sample data in the correct locations and to select the correct cells for use in a formula. If you later decide that you don't like your original layout, Excel's editing commands make moving cell contents easy. When you move the cells used in formulas, Excel automatically adjusts the formulas so that they continue to work correctly.

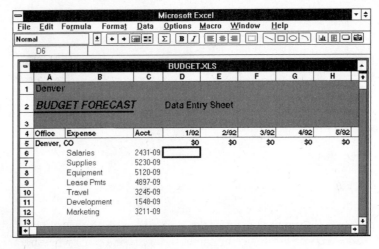

Fig. 4.2. *A data-entry text skeleton for the Denver office.*

Entering Simple Sample Data

The text skeleton will show you where to enter simple data that you use as sample data. Use simple data, such as .1 and 200, so that you can immediately recognize whether the results of formulas are correct. Figure 4.3 shows the simple data used to build a budget worksheet. If you enter this type of data before entering formulas, you can tell as soon as you enter the formula whether the result is reasonable and correct. Using easily understood sample data increases the odds that you will immediately detect an error and also makes it easier to select the correct cells for a formula by making the data and its text label visible.

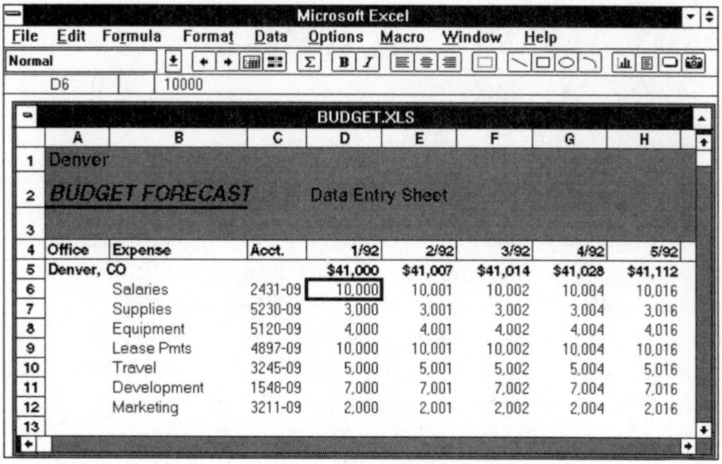

Fig. 4.3. *Simple data in worksheet entered as a sample.*

Entering Formulas

When you enter formulas, start with the simple ones and work toward the more complex formulas that depend on the results of other formulas. Never enter numbers that can change, such as an interest rate, directly in a formula. Enter such numbers in a cell, and then use the cell address in the formula. By keeping variables out of the formulas, you increase the reliability of your worksheet and reduce the need for corrections later. In this way, you can update variables by typing a new number in one cell, rather than editing formulas throughout the worksheet. Entering and editing formulas is described in Chapter 7, "Entering and Editing Worksheet Data."

Checking for Reasonable Results

Because you entered sample data first, most of your formulas produce a result as soon as you enter them. And because the data is simple, you should be able to judge whether the formula is correct. Ask yourself if the answer seems reasonable so that you can catch obvious mistakes as soon as you enter the formula.

Applying Formatting and Styles

One of Excel's powerful features is its capability to create a polished printed or on-screen result. At this point you will want to apply formatting that you have not already used. You can save time by selecting all the cells and ranges requiring the same format and then formatting them with one command. The selected cells do not need to be adjacent. Define styles for formats that you use repeatedly. Styles contain a combination of formats that you define. When you change the definition of a style, all cells using the style change to reflect the new definition.

If you need a numeric or date format that doesn't exist, create the format by using custom numeric or date formatting. Keep in mind that formatting rounds off the displayed number, but not the number used in Excel's internal calculations. To make the calculated numbers match the display, choose the **O**ptions **C**alculations command and select the **P**recision as Displayed option.

Use borders, shading, and color formats to create a pleasant and more readable screen. Change the worksheet and window display appearance with the **O**ptions **D**isplay and **O**ptions **W**orkspace commands. Formatting and styles are covered in Chapter 8.

Cross-Checking for Accurate Results

Use real data and compare the worksheet results against more than one hand-calculated answer from previously solved problems. Never trust a new worksheet. Add data-entry checking formulas such as those described in Chapter 13.

Adding Graphics and Explanatory Text Boxes

You can create worksheets that include your company's logo, include explanatory text boxes, display charts next to the worksheet, and add graphics to make your worksheet look polished and professional. You can use the drawing and text tools in Excel, or you can bring in graphics and charts drawn in other programs. Your Excel charts can even use pictures or logos as markers where bars or columns would normally appear. Chapter 9 describes how to draw on your worksheet, add text boxes, and import graphics from other Windows programs.

Linking the Worksheet to Other Sheets in the System

After verifying that individual worksheets work correctly, you may need to link multiple worksheets together to form a larger system. The power of linking is described in Chapter 12. Remember that you must also verify that your worksheet works correctly as part of a larger system.

If the worksheet you created will be used as a master from which other sheets will be created, you may want to save the worksheet as a template. Templates act as partially completed worksheets from which other worksheets can be built and include all the data, text, formulas, styles, outlines, and macros of the original. Building systems involving multiple worksheets or templates is covered in Chapter 11.

Automating the System

Add features to the system that make operation easier or automated. You may want to add macros, outlines, named printing ranges, custom menus, custom dialog boxes, and even custom help files. Building systems is covered in Chapter 11. Automating systems with the use of macros is treated in Chapters 28–32.

Cross-Checking Your System

Just as editing your own writing is difficult, so is verifying your own worksheets. Run your system, just as the actual operators would, using real numbers, and compare the results against manual calculations. Have operators run the completed system during a trial period to check for errors in calculations and operating procedures. Have these operators keep log books of errors and how they occurred. If the system is critical to your business, operate parallel business functions by operating both manual and

Excel systems until you are sure that the Excel system works correctly. Solve problems or verify operations with the worksheet audit and macro debugging features built into Excel or included free in the Library directory.

Documenting the Worksheets and System

Enter a date and version number in a corner of the completed worksheets along with the creator's initials and the initials of the audit team. You also may want to write a macro that automatically enters the version number into the page footer when the worksheet is printed. Document macros by using the three-column method of writing macros, which is described in Chapter 28.

Use the Formula Note command to attach notes to cells. In these notes, you can explain formulas and assumptions as well as add instructions. Notes can help you and others remember how your worksheet works, why you used certain numbers, or how a formula was derived.

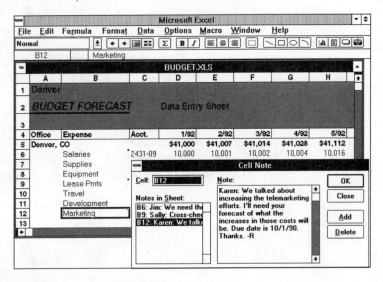

Fig. 4.4. A note window used for documentation.

Archiving Your System and Documentation

To coin a new computer maxim: There are those who back up their work and those who wish they had backed up their work. Save copies of your worksheets about every 15 minutes as you build them. Use different version numbers for each worksheet so that you can refer to previous versions, as in the sequence FORCST12, FORCST13, FORCST14, and so on. You later can erase outdated versions with the File Delete command.

If your worksheets and data are important, store copies in physically separate locations. If the building burns or if a thief steals the computer and disks, you will not lose both your original and backup disks.

From Here...

This short chapter gave you a few general guidelines for building worksheets and databases. If you haven't gone through the Worksheet Quick Start in Chapter 3, do so before you explore Chapters 6–16. These chapters describe in detail the many features available in Exel worksheets.

5

Making the Switch from 1-2-3 to Excel

If you used Lotus 1-2-3 in the past, you can make the transition to Excel smoothly, continue to use your 1-2-3 knowledge, and gain the increased power available from Excel and the other Windows programs Excel works with so well.

 Excel's new Help features let you enter the 1-2-3 keystrokes and commands you are familiar with. Excel then demonstrates in your worksheet how to perform the same commands using Excel. This approach enables you to use your 1-2-3 experience to learn Excel. Within a few weeks, you will progress beyond the best level you achieved with Lotus 1-2-3. You will find that even though Excel is more flexible and powerful than other spreadsheets, it is more accessible, so you can use more of its features with less effort.

Reviewing Excel Features

The following list shows some of the features and functions available in Excel.

Entering Data

- Automatically format cells when Excel recognizes a numeric or date/time format in the entered data. For example:

Entering	Displays
Sep 9, 91	9-Sep-91
$3,500	$3,500

- Automatically enter a decimal just as you would with a ten-key calculator through the **Options Workspace** command and **Fixed Decimal** option.

- Move the active cell down when you press Enter. (This option can be turned off.)

- Enter multiple numbers at one time by selecting the cells before typing, entering the number, and then pressing Ctrl+Enter.

Editing Formulas or Text

- Enter cell references or ranges by clicking or dragging with the mouse during formula creation or editing.

- Paste worksheet functions and their arguments into formulas with the **Formula Paste Function**, so you do not have to remember the correct syntax.

- Paste names into formulas with **Formula Paste Names**.

- Enter a large range of formulas as a single array formula to save memory.

- Undo typing, editing mistakes, and commands with **Edit Undo**.

- Search and replace values or terms in formulas with **Formula Replace**.

Calculating

- Recalculate only formulas that need to be recalculated.

- Recalculate tables automatically or on command.

- Calculate multiple data tables per worksheet.

- Calculate large worksheets in the background (as you continue to work in the worksheet, on other worksheets, or in other Windows programs).

Formatting

- Create custom numeric and date/time formats that include special characters, symbols, decimal precision, and colors.

 - Specify different custom numeric and date/time formats for different ranges of numeric or date/time formats.

- Create worksheet ranges, text boxes, graphics, and pictures and charts on the same page.

- Draw on the worksheet using Excel's drawing tools.

- Paste high-quality drawings, logos, or artwork on worksheets.

- Format a cell's contents with a unique font, size, style, and color.

- Use up to 256 fonts per worksheet.

- Add color formats, shades of grey, and patterns to the worksheet.

- Add eight different types of cell borders including double-underlining.

- Change row height or column width.

 - Double-click on column heading border to adjust column-width to best fit.

- Hide worksheets, rows, columns, or cells.

- Align numbers, dates, or text.

- Switch number, currency, and date formats to many international styles.

Using Worksheet Functions

 - Use Excel's 146 built-in functions for math, finance, and science.

- Use advanced functions such as WEEKDAY, MIRR (Modified Internal Rate of Return), and many array and text functions.

- Name formulas and values so that you can refer to them by English names rather than by nontext names.

- Create custom macro functions for formulas you use that work the same as built-in functions.

Printing

 - Preview documents on-screen to see exactly how they will appear on paper.

- Change margins within the preview document.

- Print vertically or horizontally.

- Print worksheet ranges, text boxes, graphics, and pictures and charts on the same page.

Database

- Automatically generate a data-entry, edit, and search form using the **Data Form** command.

- Use Excel database features the same way as in Lotus 1-2-3.

- Link worksheets to disk-based databases or to selected SQL query databases, using the Q+E program that comes with Excel.

- Analyze database contents using data functions and the Data Table command.

- Analyze database contents with array math, using minimum worksheet area and memory.

Charts

- Choose from six types of two-dimensional charts, combination charts, and four types of 3-D charts.

- Select from 68 different predefined chart formats.

- Customize charts with colors, patterns, shading, fonts, overlay charts, hi-lo points, floating text, scaling, arrows, and more.

- Create picture charts using pictures in place of bars or columns.

- Move a bar or column in a chart and cause the corresponding value in a worksheet change.

- Rotate and change the perspective on 3-D charts.

Linked and Consolidated Worksheets

- Link worksheets, databases, and charts so that changing data in one passes the change to another.

- Link to sheets on-screen or on disk.

- Consolidate data between worksheets that have the same layout.

- Consolidate data between worksheets according to row and column heading names.

- Link Excel data to other Windows applications via Dynamic Data Exchange (DDE).

- Link data from other applications to Excel via Dynamic Data Exchange (DDE).

Worksheet Features and Add-in Programs

- Use the Solver to find optimal solutions for worksheet problems.

- Use the What-If add-in to find the data-entry value needed to solve for a specific solution.

- Add more features using the many free add-ins included with Excel. Add-ins include a worksheet auditor for troubleshooting, a macro debugger, a slide show program, and many other features.

Debugging and Documenting

- Use the free Audit and Debug add-in programs to find and trouble-shoot errors in worksheets and macros.

- Tag notes on cells with Formula Note.

- Find formulas, terms, or errors with Formula Find or Formula Select Special.

- Find cells that feed into or out of a formula with Formula Select Special.

- Easily understand error messages with more specific error types: #N/A, #VALUE!, #DIV/0!, #NAME?, #NULL!, #NUM!, and #REF!

Windowing

- Display multiple programs and multiple data documents on one screen.

- Split windows into four panes showing different views of the same sheet.

- Open multiple windows onto the same sheet.

Macros

- Record macros using keystrokes, shortcut keys, or mouse actions.

- Create custom worksheet functions with function macros.

- Write or modify macros using over 277 macro commands that you can combine with 146 worksheet functions.

- Keep macros independent of documents so that you can use them with other documents.

- Create buttons on worksheets that run macros.

- Link pictures to macros so that selecting a picture runs a macro.

- Create custom menus and full-featured dialog boxes.

- Operate other Windows programs under Excel control. For example, an Excel macro can control the time when a communication program begins printing.

Windows Environment

- Copy and paste data with standard DOS or Windows programs.

- Link data to other Windows programs.

Using Your 1-2-3 Knowledge To Learn Excel

If you are familiar with Lotus 1-2-3, you can learn Excel quickly with the new Excel Help features. You can use your Lotus 1-2-3 knowledge and skills to do the same work you did in Lotus. As you learn Excel, you can use its more accessible and greater power to do even more than you could in Lotus.

❖ Using 1-2-3 Commands To Learn and Operate Excel

Excel will accept your Lotus 1-2-3 commands and either paste a temporary list of instructions on your worksheet or show you how to perform the equivalent operation in Excel. As Excel demonstrates the equivalent operation, it acts on your worksheet to produce the result you wanted. You can work and learn at the same time. As you gain more knowledge of Excel, you can use its accessible features and enhancements directly from Excel menus.

To set up Excel to paste instructions or to demonstrate Lotus equivalent procedures, follow these steps:

1. Choose the Options Workspace command to display the following dialog box (see fig. 5.1).

2. Select the Alternate Menu or Help Key by pressing Alt+A and typing the / (slash), if a slash is not already there.

3. Select the Lotus 1-2-3 Help option by pressing Alt+L. The option is selected when the circle is darkened.

Fig. 5.1. *Change the settings in the Workspace dialog box for help learning Excel.*

4. Press Enter to choose the OK button.

Now when you press the / (slash) key, the Lotus 1-2-3 Help dialog box shown in figure 5.2 is displayed.

If you want to temporarily paste instructions on your worksheet, follow these steps:

1. Press the / (slash) key. The Help for Lotus 1-2-3 Users dialog box shown in figure 5.2 is displayed.

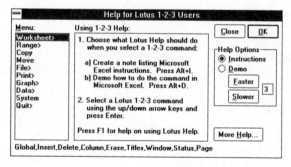

Fig. 5.2. *Select the Instructions option to temporarily paste Help on your worksheet.*

2. Check to make sure that the Instructions option is selected (darkened). Press Alt+I if you need to select the Instructions option.

3. Select 1-2-3 commands from the Menu list by pressing the same keystrokes you use in Lotus 1-2-3. Touch-type with the first letters or press arrow keys to select a Lotus 1-2-3 command; then press Enter. With a mouse, double-click on a command. Press Esc to back up to previous menu options.

4. Type the final command or select it, and then press Enter.

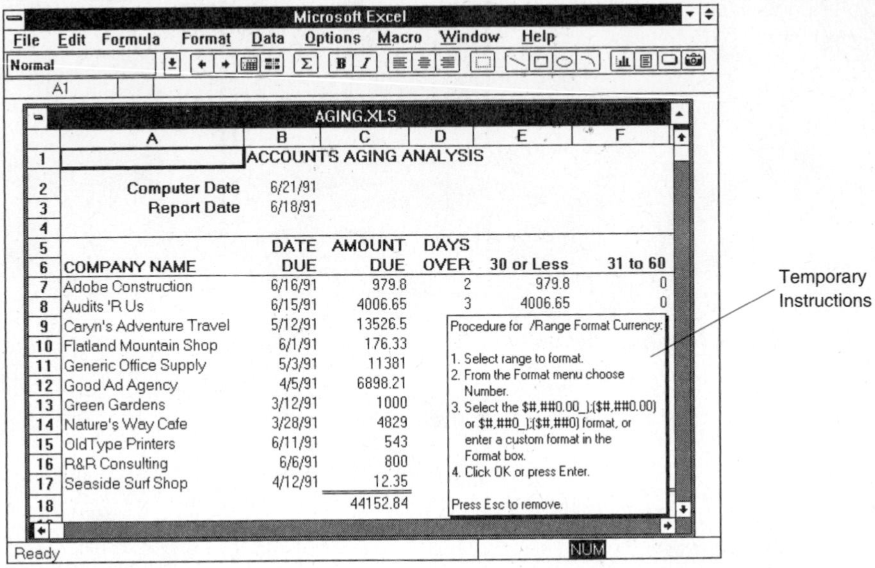

Fig. 5.3. Excel temporarily pastes instructions over the worksheet.

Excel pastes a list of instructions over your worksheet, as shown in the lower right corner of the worksheet in figure 5.3. You can move this list by dragging it to a new location with a mouse as you would drag any graphical object on an Excel worksheet. You can select and copy the list to make a permanent copy. To remove the temporary instruction list when you are done, press Esc.

If you want Excel to accept your Lotus 1-2-3 keystrokes and demonstrate how to do the equivalent Excel keystrokes, follow these steps:

1. Press the / (slash) key. The Help for Lotus 1-2-3 Users dialog box shown in figure 5.4 is displayed.

2. Check to make sure that the Demo option is selected (darkened). Press Alt+D if you need to select the Demo option.

3. Choose the Faster (Alt+F) or Slower (Alt+S) buttons to change the speed of the demonstration or change the speed number to any number from 1–5.

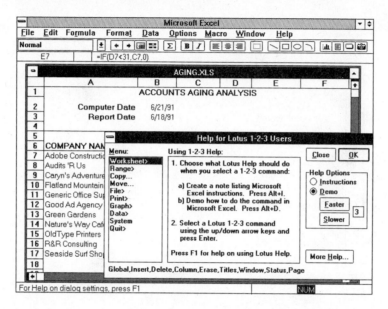

Fig. 5.4. *Select the Demo option for Excel to demonstrate the equivalent of your 1-2-3 commands.*

4. Select 1-2-3 commands from the Menu list by pressing the same keystrokes you use in Lotus 1-2-3. Touch-type with the first letters or press arrow keys to select a Lotus 1-2-3 command; then press Enter. With a mouse, click on a command. Press Esc to back up in the Lotus 1-2-3 menu.

   If more information is required, Excel displays a 1-2-3 Help bar across the top of the screen after you select a 1-2-3 command, as shown in figure 5.5. The bar in the figure is for the Lotus /Copy command. In your 1-2-3 Help bar, enter the necessary cell ranges or data required to complete the command.

5. Press Tab to move between text boxes and buttons in the 1-2-3 Help bar. Enter data, such as the number of decimals in a format, by selecting the text box and typing. Select a range of cells to be affected, using either Lotus or Excel techniques.

   To select a cell range using Lotus techniques, type the range. Press Enter or Tab to move to a second text or cell reference box, if required. Press the period (.) key to fix a cell reference as the corner of a range. Press Esc to remove the period and unanchor a cell reference or to back up the previous text or cell reference.

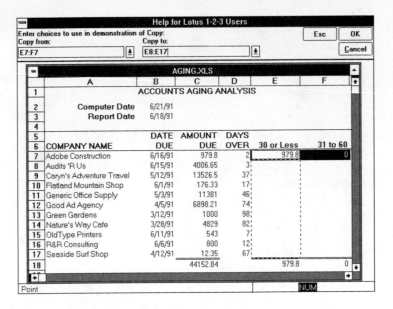

Fig. 5.5. Excel displays a 1-2-3 Help bar when you finish the command.

To select a range using Excel techniques, drag across the range with a mouse or move to one corner of the range; then hold down the Shift key as you move by keyboard to the opposite corner.

Press the Esc key to back up from a mistake.

6. When the 1-2-3 Help bar is filled out, press Enter or click on the OK button to see the demonstration using the commands and worksheet range you selected.

Moving and Selecting

 While you are learning Excel, you may want to use 1-2-3 keystrokes to move and select cells. Excel has many more shortcut keys, function keys, and movement and selection keys than are available in 1-2-3. You will find yourself more productive if you learn the Excel keys listed in the following chapters. While you learn Excel, you may want to use these alternate navigation keys. To use alternate navigation keys in Excel, follow these steps:

1. Choose the Options Workspace command by pressing Alt, O, and then W.

2. Select the Alternate Navigation Keys check box by holding down the Alt key as you press K (Alt+K).

Return to the normal Excel navigation keys by following the same procedure and deselecting the Alternate Keystrokes check box. (A check box is selected when an X appears in it.)

The alternate navigation keys are listed in table 5.1.

Table 5.1
Alternate Navigation Keys

Alternate Key	Alternate Action	Excel Action
Arrow keys	Move active cell	Move active cell
Ctrl+left/ right arrow	Move one screen	Move to the edge of a block of data as in a 1-2-3 End, arrow move
Page Up/Down	Move one screen	Move one screen
Home	Move to A1	Move to first cell in row
End	Press End, then arrow to move to edge of a block of data	Move to rightmost column of data

To select cells as you move across them, hold down the Shift key and press a movement key. To select a range of cells from the active cell to the edge of a data block, move to the first cell, press End, and then hold down the Shift key as you press the arrow in the direction you want to select. To select a range of cells with the Goto key, press F5, enter the range you want using a colon (:) to separate cell references (as in B5:C12), and then press Shift+Enter.

While the Alternate Navigation Keys option is selected, you also can enter text, functions, and formulas. You can use methods that are similar to those in Lotus 1-2-3. See table 5.2.

Table 5.2
Alternate Data-Entry Keys

Keystroke	Result
'	Left align following text in cell
"	Right align following text in cell
^	Center following text in cell
\	Fill cell with following characters
@	Precede a function or formula (optional)
+ – (1 to 9	Start a formula (or use Excel's =)

Using Function Keys

Many of the Excel function keys are the same as those in 1-2-3. Excel has many additional function and shortcut keys available. You hold down Shift, Ctrl, or Alt as you press the function key. Additional Excel function keys are listed in the Quick Reference Card at the back of the book. Table 5.3 lists compatible Excel and 1-2-3 function keys.

Table 5.3
A List of Compatible Excel and 1-2-3 Function Keys

Function Key	1-2-3	Excel
F1	Help	Help
F2	Edit	Edit
F4	Absolute Reference	Absolute Reference
F5	Goto	Goto
F6	Window	Next Pane
F9	Calc	Calculate Now (all worksheets)
Shift+F9	N/A	Calculate Document (active document only)

Excel recalculates data tables automatically, so there is no need for the F8 key to calculate tables. (You can toggle automatic table calculation on or off through the menu.) The Graph key, F10, is unnecessary in Excel because you can display graphs simultaneously with their supporting worksheets.

Making the Transition Smoothly

When you change from Lotus 1-2-3 to Excel, remember the following important concepts:

- Sometimes learning a new skill that is similar to an old skill can be difficult. An old skill can interfere with a new, but similar skill. If you understand that this happens and you use Excel's Lotus 1-2-3 Help features, you will find that Excel and its related Windows programs are well worth the transition.

- Make changes to an Excel sheet or chart by first selecting the cells or graphics you want to change, and then choosing the command to affect the cells or graphics. (See "Following Excel Procedures.")

  Lotus works the opposite way. In 1-2-3, you choose a command and then select the cells to be affected. The advantage of Excel's method is that after an Excel command is completed, the range remains selected so you can make additional changes to the same selected cells or graphical item.

- Although you can choose to activate Excel menus by pressing the / (slash) key, it is not a good idea. Use the Alt key.

  Pressing the / key prepares your mind for a string of 1-2-3 commands. When you try to type Excel commands, you slow down and create errors. Instead, use the Alt key to activate Excel menus. The Alt key is the standard menu key used by all Windows and OS/2 Presentation Manager programs. Use the **O**ptions **W**orkspace command with the **L**otus 1-2-3 Help option selected. When you press the / key, Excel will give you Lotus Help.

- Use Excel's **H**elp **L**otus 1-2-3 commands to learn Excel while you continue working with Lotus keystrokes or commands. (See the next section.)

The Help Lotus 1-2-3 feature will accept your Lotus keystrokes and demonstrate how to accomplish the same command using Excel. This feature actually demonstrates the Excel command on your worksheet, using the range of cells you select. The result is that you can continue to work and learn at the same time.

- Press F1 whenever Excel displays a dialog box that you aren't familiar with.

When a dialog box or error box is displayed, press F1 to see an explanation of what each option does. Press Alt+F4 to close the Help window. If you do not want to complete the dialog box, press Esc.

- Operate Excel with the mouse, touch-typing, arrow keys, function keys, or shortcut keys.

Excel and many Windows programs are designed to be very flexible. You aren't limited to one mode of operation. Use a combination of whichever methods make you most productive. Once they are proficient, most people find that a combination of mouse and shortcut keys gives them the greatest speed. The easiest way to learn and remember is with the mouse.

Excel contains many features and extensive Help files to help you learn Excel and easily convert your worksheets and charts.

Getting Help with 1-2-3

To see Help information on how to switch from Lotus 1-2-3 to Excel, choose the **Help Index** command by pressing Alt+H, then I. Press the Tab key to select Switching from Lotus 1-2-3; then press Enter. Press Tab to select the topic you want; then press Enter. You can jump between locations in Help files, search for topics, and print the Help information you see. Close the Help window by holding down Alt and pressing F4 (Alt+F4). The Help feature is described in more detail in Chapter 2, "Operating Windows."

Following Excel Procedures

Excel follows a standard procedure for changing a worksheet, chart, or macro. Use these same steps for nearly all commands:

1. Select the cell, range, or graphical object to be affected.

2. Choose a command.

3. Select options from a dialog box, if necessary; then choose OK or press Enter.

Moving and Selecting Cells and Ranges

The *active* cell is the cell surrounded by a darker border. Your data entry or pasted data goes into the selected cell. Commands affect the selected cell.

A *range* of cells is a rectangular group of selected cells. In Excel you can select a discontinuous range so that a single command affects multiple areas at one time. You also can select multiple discontinuous rows and columns and with one command change their contents. Within a range, the active cell is white.

To move the active cell, use the arrow keys, page keys, or Ctrl+arrow. An alternate method is to press the Goto key, F5, enter a location, and press Enter. A previous section in this chapter (see "Moving and Selecting") describes how to switch Excel's keyboard to use alternate keystrokes for moving and selecting. These alternate keystrokes are similar to those used in Lotus 1-2-3.

For commands such as formatting, editing, and entering data, you must *select* the cell or range of cells to be affected. Selected cells appear in reverse video. Selected graphical items appear enclosed by small white or black squares. To select a cell range by keyboard, follow these steps:

1. Move to one corner of the rectangular range you want selected.

2. Hold down the Shift key, and move to the opposite corner of the range by pressing the movement keys.

3. Make your menu selection.

If you are using a mouse, follow these steps:

1. Click on a cell at one corner of the range.

2. Hold down the mouse button, and drag the mouse pointer to the opposite corner.

3. Release the mouse pointer.

Chapter 6, "Creating Worksheets," lists numerous shortcuts for selecting ranges and for accelerating movements by key or by mouse.

Selecting Commands from Menus

Excel commands appear on menus pulled down from a menu bar at the top of the screen. The Status bar at the lower left corner of the screen explains each menu or command as you select it.

To choose a command with the keyboard, follow these steps:

1. Press Alt to activate the menu bar.

2. Press the underlined letter in a menu's name to select the menu.

3. Press the underlined letter in the command.

Throughout this book, the *letter* that activates a menu, command, or dialog box option appears in bold within a word. For example, the menu for file commands is **F**ile; you choose the **F**ile command by pressing Alt, then F.

To operate the mouse, move the mouse so that the on-screen pointer moves. The pointer changes shape depending upon what it does at a specific location on the screen. To execute commands, put the tip of the pointer on a word or item and press the left mouse button. This is a *click*. Perform a *double-click* by rapidly clicking twice without moving the mouse. Accomplish a *drag* by putting the pointer on an item, then holding down the mouse button as you move the mouse pointer to another location.

To choose a command with a mouse, click on the menu name; then click on the command in the menu.

Commands that are grey are not available. They may be inappropriate to the current situation or may require a previous action.

Commands followed by ellipses (...) display a dialog box. A *dialog box* is a pop-up window in which you can select options and enter data. Dialog boxes give you a chance to refine your command.

Selecting from Dialog Boxes

Some Excel commands need additional information. Rather than use multiple layers of menus, Excel commands display a dialog box like the one shown in figure 5.6. A dialog box lets you immediately see all the default settings and available options. You can change just what you need to change.

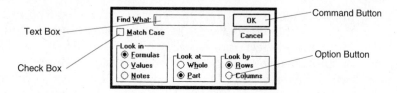

Fig. 5.6. *A dialog box gives you access to all of a command's options.*

To select an option from a dialog box, hold down Alt as you press the underlined letter in the name of the option you want. If you are using a mouse, click on an option or text box.

Check boxes are square and contain an X when selected. Each check box is independent of others, so you can select them in any combination.

Round option buttons come in groups. You can select only one at a time. To select an option button, hold down Alt and press the underlined letter in the name of the group of buttons. Then use the arrow keys to select the option you want. With a mouse, click on the option button.

List boxes contain lists of alternatives. To select a list box, hold down Alt as you press the underlined letter in the list name. Press up- or down-arrow keys to select an alternative from the list. With a mouse, click on the up or down arrow in the scroll bar alongside the list to scroll through the list; then click on your selection.

Some lists look like text boxes with a down arrow on the right side. To display the list, select the list with Alt+letter; then press Alt+down arrow to pull down the list. Use up or down arrows to move between alternatives. With a mouse, click on the down arrow to display the list; then click on your selection.

Complete a dialog box by clicking on the OK button or pressing Enter. To back out of the dialog box, click on the Cancel button or press Esc.

Entering Formulas

Enter formulas by selecting a cell, then beginning the formula with a plus sign (+) or an equal sign (=). (Turn on the Alternate Navigation **Keys** option described previously if you want to precede formulas with Lotus 1-2-3 formula symbols.) Once you have started a formula, you can enter cell references by typing, by moving to a cell using keys, or by clicking on the cell. You can use the Goto key, F5, during formula entry. Press the Enter key to enter a formula or press Esc to back out.

When the alternate keystrokes option is selected, functions can be preceded by an @ sign, but they do not have to be. You can paste functions and their arguments into worksheet or macro sheet cells by choosing Formula Paste Function and selecting the Paste Arguments check box. This technique is helpful when you forget what the arguments are or the order in which they should be typed. (An argument is the information enclosed by the parentheses that follow a function.)

Press the Edit key, F2, to edit the formula in the active cell. Press the Absolute Reference key, F4, to cycle between absolute and relative references while entering or editing a cell reference.

If an error box is displayed when you attempt to enter a formula, press F1 for Help. After reading the Help messages, press Alt+F4 to close the Help program.

Creating Macros

Whether or not you learned how to create and use 1-2-3 macros, you can quickly record your own macros in Excel. Excel records your keystrokes on a separate macro sheet. You can play this "macro recording" back exactly as created, or you can edit it so that dialog boxes pause for operator entry, or input boxes appear asking for data.

One of the most productive things you can learn is how to record macros and make them display dialog boxes, data-entry boxes, and alert boxes. The Macro Quick Start in Chapter 28 will take you step-by-step through creating your first macros.

Of course, you also can write macros using Excel's extensive macro language. The language has 277 macro functions in addition to the 146 worksheet functions. With the macro language, you can create custom menus and dialog boxes. Instead of memorizing commands and arguments, you can paste macro functions and their arguments from a scrolling list.

In Excel, you also can write function macros that work the same as built-in worksheet functions. You can use these function macros just as though they came with Excel.

Excel macros occupy their own sheets, so you can use them with any worksheet, chart, or database.

Retrieving and Saving 1-2-3 Files

Loading and saving 1-2-3 files in Excel is easy. Because of program differences, however, an alert box will display discrepancies.

Opening 1-2-3 Worksheets and Charts

To load a 1-2-3 worksheet file, follow these steps:

1. Choose the **File Open** command.

2. Select the File **N**ame text box, and type a new file pattern of *.WK? that will display Lotus 1-2-3 files.

   Figure 5.7 shows the File Open dialog box with the File **N**ame box edited to display Lotus files.

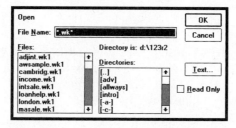

Fig. 5.7. *Change the File Name box to see a list of Lotus 1-2-3 files.*

3. Choose the OK button, or press Enter to list the files.

4. Select the **F**iles list box by pressing Alt+F or clicking in it. Click on the file name you want, or press the up- or down-arrow key to highlight the name of the file you want to open.

5. Choose the OK button or press Enter.

6. If charts are part of the Lotus 1-2-3 worksheet, you will be asked if you want to convert charts. If you respond **Y**es, Excel will convert each chart attached to the worksheet to a chart in its own window.

7. If Excel encounters a formula it cannot translate, Excel displays an alert box containing the reference for that formula. The value of the 1-2-3 formula is put in the corresponding cell of the Excel worksheet.

The Lotus file you selected is opened and automatically converted. Notice that the document's title bar still shows that the file has a Lotus extension. If you save the file with the Lotus extension, it will save back as a Lotus file and lose any Excel enhancement or charts you add.

While Lotus 1-2-3 files are on-screen, you can treat them as any Excel file. You can link with them, and you can enhance them with Excel formulas and features. Saving the file back to its Lotus format loses all the Excel enhancements.

Excel preserves individual cell links between Lotus 1-2-3 worksheets. The equivalent link exists when the 1-2-3 worksheet is converted into Excel.

Excel opens and converts 3-D files from Lotus 1-2-3 Release 3. Excel converts and maintains the links in the worksheets within the file. The maximum number of worksheets that you can convert from within one 1-2-3 Release 3 file depends on your Excel configuration and memory.

◈ Saving 1-2-3 Worksheets with Excel Format

If you open a Lotus 1-2-3 file into Excel and save it, using the File Save or File Save As command, you will save the file back to its original Lotus 1-2-3 format, thereby losing any Excel enhancements you have added. To preserve the enhancements, you must save the 1-2-3 file with an Excel format.

To save a Lotus 1-2-3 file with an Excel file format, follow these steps:

1. Choose the File Save As command.

2. Type the file name in the Save Worksheet as text box.

3. Choose the Options button to display the File Format dialog box shown in figure 5.8.

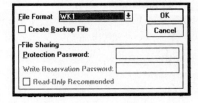

Fig. 5.8. *Use the File Format list to save a file in either Excel or Lotus formats.*

4. Select the File Format list by pressing Alt+F or clicking on the list.

5. Pull down the list by pressing Alt+down arrow or clicking on the down arrow. Select the Excel format, Normal.

6. Choose OK or press Enter to return to the Save dialog box.

7. Choose OK or press Enter to save the file.

✵ Saving Excel Worksheets As 1-2-3 Files

To save Excel worksheets as Lotus 1-2-3 files, follow these steps:

1. Choose the File Save As command, and then type a file name in the text box.

2. Choose the Options button.

   If you opened the worksheet from a Lotus file, a Lotus 1-2-3 format will be selected in the File Format list. Excel automatically saves files back to their original format.

3. Select the File Format list by pressing Alt+F or clicking on the list.

4. Pull down the list by pressing Alt+down arrow or clicking on the down arrow. Then select the Lotus format in which the worksheet should be saved. Use WKS for Lotus 1-2-3 Releases 1 and 1A; use WK1 for Releases 2, 2.01, and 2.2; use WK3 for Releases 3 and 3.1.

5. Choose OK or press Enter to return to the Save dialog box.

6. Choose OK or press Enter to save the file.

If your worksheet used Excel functions that cannot be converted into 1-2-3 functions, Excel displays an alert box asking if you want cells reported that cannot be converted. Tell Excel that you want these cells reported, so that you can write a list of which cells to check later. Formulas that cannot be converted are placed in the Lotus 1-2-3 worksheet with the value found in the Excel sheet. Figure 5.9 shows the alert box referencing a cell that could not be converted.

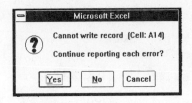

Fig. 5.9. *Excel references cells that cannot be converted to Lotus.*

Noting Translation Differences

Excel automatically converts 1-2-3 worksheets into Excel and saves them back in 1-2-3 format. A few 1-2-3 worksheet characteristics do not convert. When converting from an original Excel worksheet into 1-2-3, remember that Excel has more capabilities than 1-2-3. These extra features and functions cannot be converted to 1-2-3.

Excel does a good job of converting formats, cell protection, formulas, names, and 1-2-3 graphs. However, some characteristics, such as windowing, cannot be converted because of their major differences.

If any 1-2-3 function or formula does not translate into Excel, a dialog box appears showing the cell location of the errant formula. Choose the Yes button if you want to continue seeing these messages in an alert box. Choose the No button if you want to convert the 1-2-3 worksheet without the messages. Cells containing formulas that do not convert will contain the value of the original formula.

Data tables do not translate between either application. Formulas and values in the left column and top row of the tables remain in their original cells; however, you must reapply the Data Table commands for both applications. Excel data tables constantly recalculate and are actually formulas, whereas 1-2-3 tables are generated with the /Data Table command and must be recalculated by pressing a key.

Hidden cells in Excel will be shown when converted to 1-2-3. Excel's seven error values translate into ERR and NA values in 1-2-3 as appropriate.

You can create larger worksheets with Excel than you can with 1-2-3. When Excel rows exceed the limit of a 1-2-3 worksheet, the extra rows wrap around from the top. Some versions of Lotus 1-2-3 can contain only 8,192 rows. If you save an Excel worksheet that contains 8,193 rows to Lotus 1-2-3 Release 2.X, Excel's bottom row will become row 1. If you think this might happen, rearrange your Excel worksheets or make them into multiple linked worksheets.

1-2-3 cannot handle multiple simultaneous ranges, range operators (intersect, range, and union), or array formulas, so these features are not converted from Excel.

Excel loads 1-2-3 graphs that are active in the worksheet or are named with the /Graph Name command. Each named graph appears in its own window. Excel does not save Excel charts as Lotus 1-2-3 graphs because Excel's charts have more features and formats. Excel cannot read or translate Lotus print graph files, PIC files that have been saved for printing with PGRAPH.

Translating 1-2-3 Macros

Excel's Macro Translation Assistant converts simple 1-2-3 macros into Excel macros. To get help translating a 1-2-3 macro, choose the **Help Index** command. When the index of topics appears, press Tab to select Switching from 1-2-3; then press Enter. Next press Tab to select Macro Translation Assistant; then press Enter to see Help information on translating macros. Press Alt+F4 to close the Help window.

> **Tip: *Using Excel's Macro Recorder To Create New Macros***
> Excel's extensive macro language, custom dialog boxes, custom Help program, and ability to link with other Windows programs make the conversion of advanced 1-2-3 macros less than optimal. In nearly all cases, you should record and modify Excel macros rather than translate 1-2-3 macros. Excel's macro recorder is easy to use. With simple modifications to recorded macros like those described in the Macro Quick Start chapter, you can exceed the capability of Lotus 1-2-3 macros.

From Here...

If you are an experienced Lotus 1-2-3 user you may find some initial difficulty in using Excel. A learning dysfunction phase occurs whenever you learn new skills that are similar to old skills. You probably remember the steep learning curve involved in initially learning 1-2-3. It is tough for many people. Learning Excel is much easier, and Excel's more powerful features are accessible. Using Excel is clearly worth the transition.

If you are a power user of Lotus 1-2-3, your skills are not lost; instead, these skills are enhanced. Excel shifts everyone up the productivity curve. Excel beginners perform the equivalent of intermediate 1-2-3 work, and Excel intermediates perform the equivalent of advanced 1-2-3 work. For 1-2-3 power users, Excel opens new horizons. The extensive macro language, array math, the Solver, Q+E, and Dynamic Data Exchange give you access to more power using the same problem-solving knowledge you already have.

If you have read this chapter before other chapters in the book, go through the Quick Start tutorials to develop a solid foundation in Excel. This book includes a Quick Start for building a worksheet, creating a chart, building a database, and creating a command and function macro. After you go through the Quick Starts, try the **Help** Lotus 1-2-3 command. To use your 1-2-3 command knowledge while you are learning Excel and building worksheets, choose the **Options Workspace** command and set the **A**lternate Menu or Help Key to /. Select the **L**otus 1-2-3 Help option. The next time you press the / key, select the **D**emo option, and you will be able to use 1-2-3 commands as you learn Excel.

6

Creating Worksheets

This chapter teaches the basics of using Excel. In this chapter, you learn how to move and scroll across a worksheet, how to select areas in a worksheet to change them, and how to save and open the worksheet, chart, and macro files that you create.

If you need to learn about the parts of an Excel screen and how to operate the menus and dialog boxes, how to move and size windows, and how to use Help, read Chapter 2, "Operating Windows."

Before you continue with this chapter, take a moment to review the concepts that apply to all Windows programs.

To affect any portion of a worksheet, follow these steps:

1. Select the cells, text, or graphic element you want to change.

2. Choose the command or press the shortcut key that makes the change.

3. Select options from the dialog box if one appears.

4. Choose OK or press Enter.

5. Choose another command if necessary to further affect the item that you selected in step 1.

All these steps condense into the most important concept you will use for all Windows programs:

Select, then do!

Learning the Parts of the Excel Screen

When Excel appears, you may see a screen like the one shown in figure 6.1. In this figure, the Excel *program window* fills the entire screen, and a smaller *document window* displays a blank worksheet. Depending on how Excel is configured or was last used, the program window may not fill the entire screen. Chapter 2 describes how to maximize the program so that it fills the screen.

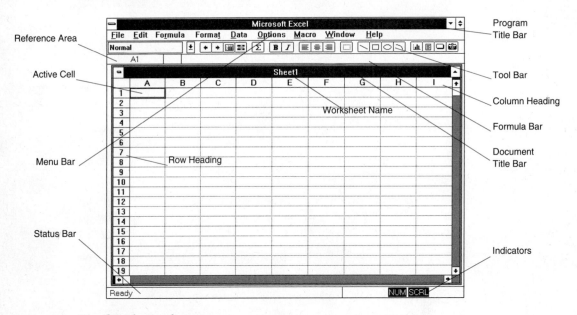

Fig. 6.1. *The Excel screen.*

The document window, Sheet1, has a solid *title bar,* indicating that it is the active document window (see fig. 6.1). You can have multiple worksheets, charts, or macro sheets open at the same time, but you enter data and commands only into the active document window. Inactive windows are normally behind the active window and have a lighter colored or cross-hatched title bar. Figure 6.2 shows the Excel program window with a worksheet, macro sheet, and a chart document. Notice the differences in the title bars.

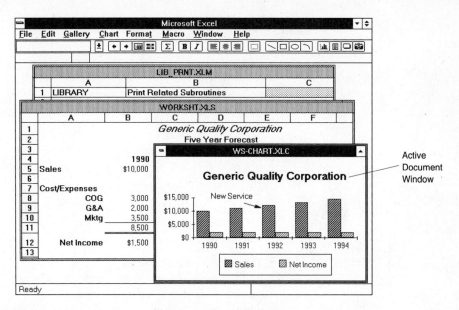

Fig. 6.2. *Excel screen with a worksheet, macro sheet, and chart document displayed.*

The components that make up an Excel screen are described in table 6.1.

Table 6.1
Parts of the Excel Screen

Part	Description
Program window	The window in which Excel runs. Each Windows program can run in its own window. When running Windows in 386 Enhanced Mode, DOS programs also can run in a window.
Document window	The window within the program window, where worksheets, macro sheets, and charts are displayed.
Active window	The window that accepts entries and commands; this window has a solid title bar and is normally the top window.
Title bar	The bar at the top of the window.

continues

Table 6.1 *(continued)*

Part	Description
Tool bar	A bar below the menu bar that gives quick access to commands and tools, such as bold, italic, show outline, styles, and drawing tools.
Formula bar	The area of the screen where you enter text, numbers, or formulas. The formula bar is below the menu bar or tool bar.
Status line	A bar at the bottom of the screen that shows what Excel is prepared to do next; watch it for prompts, explanations of the current command, or guidance.
Indicators	These display modes of operation, such as NUM when the numeric pad is on, SCRL when the Scroll Lock has been pressed, or EXT when the Extend mode is on.

Setting Preferences

Excel contains a number of features that enable you to customize Excel for your own work preferences. The choices that you will make immediately are described here. These preferences enable you to change such things as displaying full or shortened menus, enabling Lotus 1-2-3 movement keys, or changing the mouse buttons and speed. Other preferences, such as setting the numeric keypad for automatic decimal placement (as in a ten-key) or changing worksheet grid colors, are described in later chapters.

Switching between Full and Short Menus

Excel can use either a full or partial set of menus. If you use Excel infrequently or if you are a beginner, the short menus, which show only the most important commands, will make learning easier. If you are more experienced and knowledgeable, you will want the full menus.

The **O**ptions menu displays either a **F**ull **M**enus or **S**hort **M**enus command so that you can switch between these menus. For example, if you are currently using short menus, some commands do not show on the menu and the **O**ptions menu displays the command **F**ull **M**enus. Choose this command to switch to full menus.

Displaying the Tool Bar

The tool bar appears below the menu bar in Excel and gives you quick access to buttons for frequently used commands, drawing and charting tools, and styles. You can decide whether the tool bar is displayed.

To display the tool bar, choose the **O**ptions **W**orkspace command and select the **T**ool **B**ar option. To remove the tool bar from the screen, deselect the **T**ool **B**ar option.

Operating with Lotus Keys

If you are familiar with Lotus 1-2-3, you can use that knowledge to learn Excel. In fact, you can modify Excel so that it helps you switch from Lotus 1-2-3. Chapter 5 describes how to make the transition from Lotus 1-2-3 to Excel.

If you want to use operating methods similar to Lotus 1-2-3 as you learn Excel, choose the **O**ptions **W**orkspace command and type a slash (/) character into the **A**lternate Menu or Help Key text box. Next, select the **L**otus 1-2-3 Help option. These choices will display Excel's help for Lotus users whenever you press the slash key. While in a worksheet, you can press the keys that you would use for a Lotus process, and Excel will demonstrate the equivalent Excel keystrokes. This method, described in Chapter 5, enables you to learn while you continue to work productively.

If you select the Alternate Navigation **K**eys check box after choosing the **O**ptions **W**orkspace command, you can use many of the Lotus cell movement methods, such as End, arrow.

Moving after Entering Data

When you type data, Excel will move the active cell to the next lower cell each time you press the Enter key. If you want the active cell to stay in place, choose the Options Workspace command and deselect the Move Selection After Enter check box.

Customizing the Mouse

You can customize the mouse to operate more slowly, and you can switch the active button to the right side. To customize the mouse, follow these steps:

1. Choose the Excel Control Menu by clicking on it or by pressing Alt, space bar.

2. Choose the Run command.

3. From the dialog box that appears, select the Control Panel option.

4. Choose OK or press Enter.

The Control Panel will appear. This is the same Control Panel that you can open from the Main group window within the Program Manager.

Open the Mouse program and change the settings:

1. To open the Mouse program, double-click on its icon; or press the arrow keys until the icon is selected, and then press Enter (see fig. 6.3).

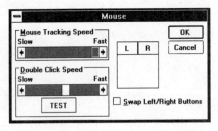

Fig. 6.3. The Mouse dialog box.

2. Change any of the following options:

Mouse Tracking Speed: The speed the on-screen pointer moves with respect to your movement of the hand-held mouse. Use slow while learning.

Double Click Speed: The speed at which you must double-click for a double-click to be accepted. Use slow while learning.

Swap Left/Right Buttons: Swaps the active mouse button to the opposite side. Use for operating the mouse from the opposite hand.

3. Choose OK or press Enter.

4. To close the Control Panel, double-click on its program Control menu; or press the program close shortcut key, Alt+F4.

Addressing Cells

An Excel worksheet is composed of rows and columns—256 columns and 16,384 rows. The intersection of each row and column creates a cell. Within a cell, you can place text, a number, or a formula.

You can refer to a specific cell in the current worksheet in one of two ways: A1 or R1C1. The A1 style of reference indicates a cell by its column letter and row number—B4, for instance. This style is used in Lotus 1-2-3 and is familiar to many people. The worksheet's 256 columns are designated A through IV. You can locate or refer to any cell's contents by the address of the cell's column and row. Figure 6.4 shows a single cell, selected at B4 (column B, row 4).

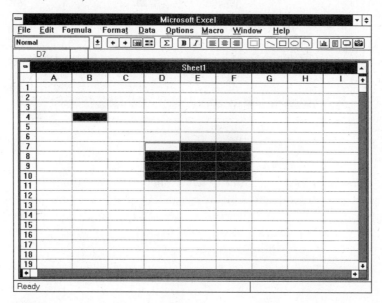

Fig. 6.4. *Selected cell B4 and range D7:F10.*

You can refer to ranges, or rectangular groups of cells, such as the one shown in figure 6.4, with the notation D7:F10. The opposite corners of the range (D7 and F10) are separated by a colon (:). In Excel, you can select multiple ranges at one time. You use ranges when you want a command to affect multiple cells or when you use a formula involving the contents of multiple cells.

The R1C1 style indicates a cell by its row number, R1, and its column number, C1. For example, the single upper left selected cell in figure 6.5 is R4C2 (row 4, column 2). You also can designate a range in R1C1 style. For example, in figure 6.5, the first corner of the range is R7C4, and the opposite corner is R10C6. Using a colon to separate the corners, the complete range is designated as R7C4:R10C6. This style is familiar to users of Multiplan and is easier to use in complex formulas involving relative positions and in macro programming.

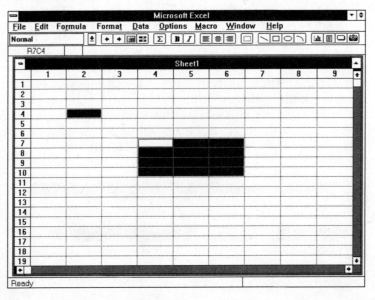

Fig. 6.5. The R1C1 style.

You can switch formulas and the worksheet's row and column headings between the A1 and R1C1 styles by choosing the **Options Workspace** command and selecting or deselecting the R1C1 option. This book uses the A1 style of references, except where indicated in complex formulas or in macros.

Moving around the Worksheet

The Excel worksheet can be very large. If the worksheet were a piece of paper, the entire sheet would measure as wide as two cars and stand as tall as a 30-story building. If you are going to find things on a worksheet, you will need to know how to get around efficiently.

Scrolling with the Mouse

When you scroll a window, it helps to imagine that the worksheet is staying still and you are moving the window over the top of the worksheet. To scroll the window with the mouse, use the scroll bars located at the right side and bottom of each worksheet (see fig. 6.6). The arrows in the scroll bars show the direction the window moves over the worksheet. (Remember: Imagine the window moving over a stationary worksheet.)

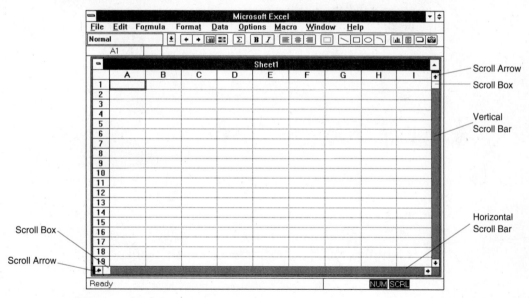

Fig. 6.6. The worksheet with the scroll bars and scroll box labeled.

To scroll the worksheet in single-row or column increments, click on the arrowhead in either the horizontal or vertical scroll bar. The arrowheads point in the direction the window moves over the worksheet. To scroll continuously, put the pointer's tip on a scroll arrow and hold down the mouse button.

The position of the scroll box in the scroll bar shows the relative position of the window on the worksheet. Note the vertical and horizontal scroll boxes to see where you are on the worksheet.

To scroll through the worksheet in increments of a full window, click the mouse pointer in the gray area on either side of the scroll box. For example, clicking in the gray scroll bar below the scroll box moves the window down by the span of one window.

To scroll large expanses, click on the scroll box and drag the box to a new position on the scroll bar. As you drag the box, notice that the row or column position for the new location is shown in the Reference Area at the top of the screen to the left of the formula bar. When you see the row or column that you want to be on, release the mouse button. The window will show the new location.

> **Tip: *Quickly Returning to Your Original Location***
> If your work suddenly disappears from the screen, do not panic. You may have accidentally scrolled to a new location. Check the row and column headings to move back to your original work area. If you cannot see the active cell where you were working last, press Ctrl+Backspace to scroll back so that the active cell is displayed.

Scrolling from the Keyboard

From the keyboard, you can scroll the window over the worksheet using normal movement keys, but you must press the Scroll Lock key first. When Scroll Lock is on, you see SCRL indicated at the bottom of the screen. This indicator means that if you press the arrow or movement keys, the screen will scroll without moving the cells you have selected.

On many keyboards, a light appears on the key or keyboard when Scroll Lock is enabled. Do not forget to press the Scroll Lock key a second time after you are finished scrolling to return the movement keys to their normal function.

The keys that scroll the window are listed in table 6.2.

Table 6.2
Keys That Scroll the Window
Press Scroll Lock and then one of the following keys:

Key	Movement
Up arrow	Scroll up one row
Down arrow	Scroll down one row
Right arrow	Scroll right one column
Left arrow	Scroll left one column
PgUp	Scroll up one window
PgDn	Scroll down one window
Ctrl+PgUp	Scroll right one window
Ctrl+PgDn	Scroll left one window
Home	Move to the top left cell in the window
Ctrl+Home	Move to cell A1

Selecting Cells

Before you can enter, edit, or modify the contents of a cell, you must select the cell or cells you want to change. A selection of multiple cells is referred to as a *range.* The single cell that receives the data or formula you enter is the *active cell*.

The cell defined by a bold border and white background is the active cell. Commands affect all selected cells; data and formulas are entered in the active cell.

Selected cells are highlighted or reversed from the rest of the worksheet. If you select a range of cells, such as those shown in figures 6.4 and 6.5, all the cells will be highlighted, but one cell will have a bold border and white background.

If you want to see the active cell, but it is not visible in the window, press Ctrl+Backspace. The window will scroll to show the active cell. Selected ranges will remain selected.

Selecting a Single Cell

Use either the mouse or the arrow keys to select cells. Selecting a cell with the mouse is easy; just move the mouse pointer over the cell and click the mouse button.

To select a single cell from the keyboard, press the appropriate movement key to move the active cell. Table 6.3 shows the keys that move the active cell. To issue key combinations, such as Ctrl+PgUp, hold down the first key (Ctrl) as you press the second key (PgUp).

Table 6.3
Keys That Move the Active Cell

Key	Movement
Up arrow	Move the active cell up one cell
Down arrow	Move the active cell down one cell
Right arrow	Move the active cell right one cell
Left arrow	Move the active cell left one cell
Tab	Enter data and move the active cell right
Shift+Tab	Enter data and move the active cell left
Enter	Enter data and move the active cell down (when a range is selected or when the **Move Selection After Enter** option is selected from the **Options Workspace** command)
Shift+Enter	Enter data and move the active cell up in the selected range
Ctrl+arrow	Move the active cell in the direction indicated until the edge of a block of data is reached
Home	Move the active cell to column A of the current row
Ctrl+Home	Move the active cell to the first cell in the worksheet (A1)
End	Move the active cell to the end of the row as far as the rightmost column
Ctrl+End	Move the active cell to the last cell in the used portion of the worksheet

Key	Movement
PgUp	Move the active cell up one full window
PgDn	Move the active cell down one full window
Ctrl+PgUp	Move the active cell one screen-width left
Ctrl+PgDn	Move the active cell one screen-width right

The Ctrl key can save you time when you need to move across a worksheet or when you need to move up or down a column. The Ctrl+arrow key combination acts as an express key that moves the active cell as if the cell were on an expressway or an elevator. The Ctrl+arrow combinations move the selected cell in the direction of the arrow until the cell contents change in one of the following ways:

- If the active cell is blank, it moves in the direction of the arrow until it reaches a filled cell.

- If the active cell is filled, it moves in the direction of the arrow until it reaches a blank cell.

Using Goto

The Formula Goto command moves the active cell to any address you request. To use the Goto command, follow these steps:

1. Choose the Formula Goto command or press F5 to display the Goto dialog box.

2. Type the cell address or range you want to go to, or select from the list box the named location you want to go to. The Goto box will appear similar to figure 6.7.

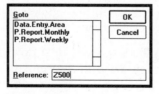

Fig. 6.7. The Formula Goto dialog box.

3. Choose OK or press Enter.

If you choose a named cell or range with the Goto command, the entire range is selected. (Named ranges are cells or ranges that are given a text name, such as Revenue; ranges are discussed in detail in Chapter 7, "Entering and Editing Worksheet Data.")

> **Tip: *Selecting Frequently Used Ranges***
> Use the Goto command to select frequently used ranges quickly. Name the cells or ranges you use frequently with the Formula Define Names command. Once you have named the cells, you can go to and select those cells by pressing F5, selecting the name, and choosing OK. For a shortcut, press F5 and double-click on the name.

When you know the text, number, or formula you are looking for, but you don't know the location, use the Formula Find command. Formula Find locates numeric or text values, partial or whole formulas, or the contents of a note attached to a cell. Chapter 7, "Entering and Editing Worksheet Data," contains more information about the Find command.

Selecting a Range of Cells

Select a range of cells when you want to apply a command to all the selected cells or enter data into the cells.

To select a range of cells with the mouse, click on the cell at one corner of the range, as shown in figure 6.8, and drag to the opposite corner of the range. Release the mouse button. A rectangular range of cells is selected, as in figure 6.9. It does not matter if the pointer wanders on the screen as it moves to the opposite corner—just make sure that the pointer is on the correct cell when you release the mouse button.

If a corner of the range is off the screen, drag the mouse pointer against the document window's edge in the direction you want to move. The window will scroll over the worksheet.

To select cells using the keyboard, hold down the Shift key as you press movement keys. Or press F8, press movement keys, then press F8 again to turn off Extend mode.

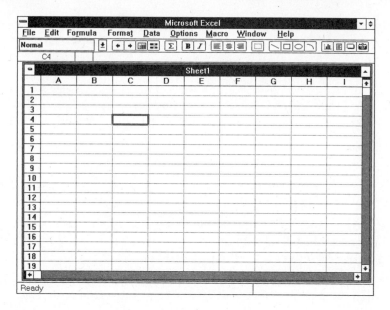

Fig. 6.8. *A selected cell begins a range.*

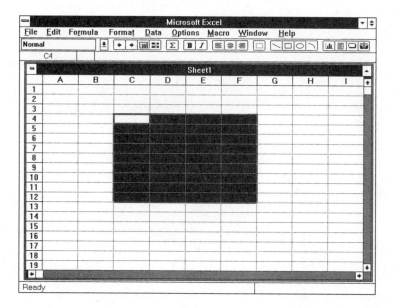

Fig. 6.9. *A selected range of cells.*

In some cases, a range is so large that dragging or pressing keys from one corner to another takes a long time. You can use quicker methods for selecting large areas. To select a large area, follow these steps:

1. Select one corner of the range.

2. Scroll the window so that the opposite corner is displayed. (Do not click in the worksheet. The original corner must remain active.)

3. Hold down the Shift key as you click on the opposite corner. All cells between the two corners will be selected.

1. Move the active cell to a corner of the range you want to select, as shown in figure 6.8.

2. Hold down the Shift key and press the movement keys to move across to the opposite corner. The active cell remains at the original corner, as shown in figure 6.9.

   If the opposite corner is outside the edge of the window, continue to hold down the Shift key and press the movement keys. The window will scroll to let you see the direction you are selecting.

If you have a large range to select using the keyboard, follow these steps:

1. Select one corner of the range.

2. Choose the Formula Goto command or press F5.

3. Type the cell reference of the opposite corner in the Reference text box.

4. Hold down the Shift key as you choose the OK button, or press Enter.

To select a range different from where you are located, choose the Formula Goto command, or press F5 and type a range address in the Reference box, such as A5:F12. Choose OK or press Enter. In this case, the active cell will be A5 and the range selected will be from A5 to F12.

You also can select ranges using the F8 function key to turn on Extend mode. Extend mode produces the same result as continuously holding down the Shift key.

To select a range, follow these steps:

1. Select a corner of the range by mouse or keyboard.

2. Press F8 to enter the Extend mode. Extend mode acts the same as holding down the Shift key as you move. Notice the EXT indicator at the bottom of the window.

3. Select the opposite corner of the range by clicking on it or moving to it with the movement keys.

4. Press F8 again to turn off Extend mode.

As long as EXT is displayed in the status line, the first corner selected remains anchored.

Keep in mind that you can use all the movement keys combined with the Shift or F8 key to select a range with the keyboard. Table 6.4 lists shortcut keys for selecting ranges.

Table 6.4
Shortcut Keys for Selecting Ranges

Key	Extend selection from active cell to
F8	Last cell selected
Shift+arrow	Last cell selected
Shift+Home	Beginning of row
Shift+Ctrl+Home	Beginning of worksheet (A1)
Shift+End	Last cell used in worksheet
Shift+space bar	Entire row of active cell
Ctrl+space bar	Entire column of active cell
Shift+Ctrl+space bar	Entire worksheet
Shift+PgUp	Cell in same column one window up
Shift+PgDn	Cell in same column one window down
Shift+Ctrl+arrow	Edge of the next block of data in the direction of the arrow key

Tip: *Adjusting a Selected Range*
To keep a range selected and move the selected area of any corner in the range, follow these steps:

1. Press Ctrl+. until the active cell is in the corner opposite from the one you want moved. Each press of Ctrl+. moves the active cell to the next corner.

2. Hold down the Shift key and press a movement key. The window will change to show you the corner being moved.

Selecting Multiple Ranges of Cells

Excel has the capability to select multiple nonadjacent ranges simultaneously. This capability enables you to format multiple ranges with a single command, print different parts of the worksheet with a single command, or erase multiple data-entry cells with a keystroke. To select multiple ranges, follow these steps:

1. Select the first range.

2. Hold down the Ctrl key as you select each additional range.

3. Release the Ctrl key.

1. Select the first cell.

2. Press F8 to enter Extend mode (EXT) and select a range.

3. Press Shift+F8 to enter Add mode (ADD) so that you can move while keeping the current selection.

4. Move to a corner of the next range.

5. Repeat steps 2, 3, and 4 until you have selected all the ranges you need.

Remember that pressing F8 lets you select multiple adjacent cells. Pressing Shift+F8 lets you keep the current selections while you move to a nonadjacent cell to start a new range.

Selecting Rows and Columns

Some operations are quicker if you select an entire row or column at one time. Formatting is also more memory efficient if you select and format an entire row or column instead of formatting each cell in the row or column.

To select an entire row or entire column with the mouse, click on the row or column heading. For example, click on the number 5 at the left edge of the document to select row 5. You can select adjacent rows or columns by dragging across the headings or by clicking on the first and Shift+clicking on the last. Select multiple nonadjacent rows or columns by holding down the Ctrl key as you click on each heading.

To select the row containing the active cell with the keyboard, press Shift+Spacebar. Press Ctrl+Spacebar to select the column containing the active cell. Once you have a row or column selected, you can select additional adjacent rows or columns by holding down the Shift key as you press the arrow movement keys.

Figure 6.10 shows how you can select multiple rows and columns before you give a single bold command or click on the bold button in the tool bar. These rows and columns were selected by holding down the Ctrl key and clicking on each row or column heading.

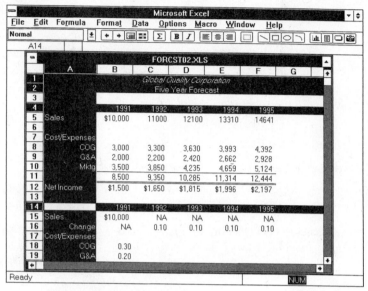

Fig. 6.10. *Selected rows and formatting.*

Selecting Cells by Their Content

Excel contains a valuable command that enables you to select cells by their content or by their relationship to formulas. You will find this command useful when you check a worksheet for the location of notes. (Cells can contain hidden notes.) You also will find this command valuable when you want to locate errors in a worksheet.

To select cells according to their content, first make sure that you are using full menus; then follow this procedure:

1. Select a single cell if you want to check the entire worksheet for a specific cell content, or select a range of cells if you want to check cells within a range.

2. Choose the Formula Select Special command (see fig. 6.11).

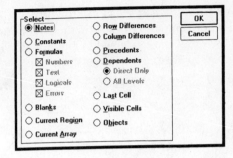

Fig. 6.11. *The Formula Select Special dialog box.*

3. Select one of the following options:

Notes: Selects cells containing notes (Shortcut: Ctrl+?)

Constants: Selects cells containing constants of the type specified in the check box below

Formulas: Selects cells containing formulas that produce a result of the type specified in this check box:

Constant/Formula type:

Numbers: Selects cells containing numbers
Text: Selects cells containing text
Logicals: Selects cells containing logical values
Errors: Selects cells containing errors

Blanks: Selects blank cells

Current Region: Selects a block of rectangular cells surrounded by blank rows, columns, or the worksheet border (Shortcut: Ctrl+*)

Current Array: Selects the array containing the active cell (Shortcut: Ctrl+/)

Last Cell: Selects the lowest, rightmost cell used by the active worksheet

Visible Cells Only: Selects the visible cells; prevents changes to collapsed outline data or hidden rows or columns

Objects: Selects all graphical objects

4. Choose OK or press Enter.

After you select cells with the Formula Select Special command, you can maintain the selections and move between the cells by pressing Tab, Shift+Tab, Enter, or Shift+Enter. This technique enables you to move the active cell between selected cells and see the contents, such as formulas, in the formula bar.

Managing Files

In the text that follows, you learn how to save, open, clear, and delete Excel documents. You find out how to save your work in progress so that you can restore it.

Opening a New Document or Template

When you start Excel, the program opens with a blank worksheet titled Sheet1, but you can open new worksheets, templates, charts, or macro sheets at any time. If you open a template, you open a worksheet that has been already constructed and is ready for operations. Templates make it easy for you to find and open master documents used to create other documents. Templates are covered in Chapter 11, "Building Systems and Managing Multiple Windows."

To open new documents, follow these steps:

1. Choose the File New command.

2. Select the worksheet, chart, macro, or template from the New list box (see fig. 6.12). Your dialog box may show available templates that are different from those in the figure.

3. Choose OK or press Enter.

Each additional open document reduces the memory available to your computer. Depending on your computer and its memory, the reduced memory can limit the size of files you can later open; the reduced memory also may lower performance. When you close nonessential document windows, you free memory and improve performance.

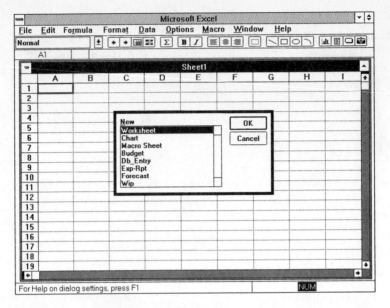

Fig. 6.12. The File New dialog box.

Opening an Existing Document

To open an existing document, follow these steps:

   1. Choose the **File O**pen command (see fig. 6.13).

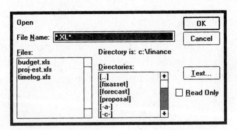

Fig. 6.13. The File Open dialog box.

   2. Open, if necessary, the disk and directory that contain the file you
      want.

Open the drive that contains the file by scrolling through the Directories list box, clicking on the drive letter, and then clicking on OK. Drive letters are in square brackets, [A], [B], etc. Now, scroll through the Directories list box, click on the directory name you want, and then click OK. Go to higher (parent) directories by clicking on [..], and then on OK.

Select the Directories list box by pressing Alt, D. Move to the drive letter by pressing the up- or down-arrow keys, and then press Enter. Press Alt, D to reselect the Directories list box, press the up- or down-arrow keys to select a directory, and then press Enter. Go to higher (parent) directories by selecting [..] and pressing Enter.

3. If the file is an Excel file, skip to step 3. If the file name that you want does not use an extension with XL, you must change the file pattern in the File Name text box.

Drag across the text in the File Name text box, type *.*, and then click on OK to see all files.

Press Alt+N to select all the text in the File Name text box, type *.*, and then press Enter to see all files.

4. Select the file that you want from the Files list box.

Click on the file name.

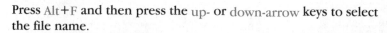

Press Alt+F and then press the up- or down-arrow keys to select the file name.

5. Choose OK or press Enter.

Worksheets can have two types of password protection. The password can protect the worksheet against unauthorized opening, and the password can protect against changes saved back to the original name. If the file that you want to open is protected, you will be prompted for the password. Type the password, using the exact upper- and lowercase letters as the original password, and then choose OK or press Enter.

If the worksheet has been saved with the read-only option recommended, you will be asked whether you want to open the file as a read-only file, open it so that you can make changes, or cancel the file opening.

Tip: *Opening Files Quickly with a Double-Click*
To quickly change directories and open files, press Ctrl+F12. This command displays the File Open dialog box. Once the dialog box is open, double-click on the directory you want to change to, and then double-click on the file you want to open. Double-clicking simultaneously selects the name and chooses OK.

The file extension can help you find the file you want. Excel files use different file extensions for each type of file. Changing the file extension in the File **Name** text box and choosing OK will display files that match the extension you typed. For example, to see chart files, type *.**XLC**; to see Lotus 1-2-3 files, type *.**WK***; to see all files, type *.*. Excel extensions are described in table 6.5.

Table 6.5
Excel File Extensions

Extension	File Type
.XLS	Worksheet
.XLC	Chart
.XLM	Macro sheet
.XLT	Template sheet
.XLW	Workspace (a group of documents that will all open together)
.XLA	Add-in programs

Changing Disks and Directories

Excel displays files, directories, and disks in the File **O**pen and File **S**ave dialog boxes. With these dialog boxes, you can change the directory and disk that Excel uses for saving and retrieving. The current drive and directory appear as text in the middle of these boxes.

Use the **Directory** list box to select a new disk or to change the directory (see the preceding section). You do not have to select a file to change directories or disk drives. When you reach the step to select a file, you can choose Cancel or press Esc and remain in the disk or directory that you selected.

Some sample listings in the **Directory** box are described in table 6.6. The directories in the table reflect the directories shown in figure 6.13.

Table 6.6
Directory List Box Options

Directory Box	Path Name
[-A-]	A:, the diskette drive
[-C-]	C:, the current directory
[..]	The current directory is C:\FINANCE; [..] changes directories to C:\
[FIXASSET]	C:\FINANCE\FIXASSET
[FORECAST]	C:\FINANCE\FORECAST

Saving Documents and Templates

You should save your documents every 15 to 20 minutes. You may also want to use version numbers in file names, such as FORCST03.XLS and FORCST04.XLS, each time you save. In this way, you always can return to previous versions of your work. If you save to the same file name each time, the previous work is replaced. (Delete old versions of work with the **File Delete** command or with the File Manager from Windows.)

The File Save **As** command (see fig. 6.14) also is the easiest method of saving your worksheet data into formats readable by other Windows and DOS programs. Chapters 33 and 34 explain how to save Excel files in formats that you can use with other programs, such as Lotus 1-2-3, dBASE, or many forms of text files. To learn how to save a worksheet as a template, see Chapter 11, "Building Systems and Managing Multiple Windows."

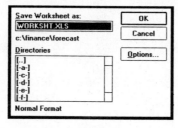

Fig. 6.14. The Save As dialog box.

To save the active worksheet, chart, or macro sheet, follow these steps:

1. Activate the document that you want to save. (The document window on top is the file that will be saved.)

2. Choose the File Save As command, or press F12 or Alt+F2.

3. If you want to save to a different drive or directory, select the drive or directory from the Directories list box and choose OK.

4. Enter a new name or edit the existing name in the name box. Do not type a file extension.

5. If you want to make a backup copy of the file, select Options and then select the Create Backup File option. The backup file has the same name with a BAK extension.

6. Choose OK or press Enter.

Use DOS file names with one to eight characters. File names can include letters, numbers, and some symbols. Because only some symbols can be used, the best practice is to use only the underline (_) and the hyphen (-). Excel automatically enters the correct file extension.

> **Tip:** *Never Use Spaces in File Names!*
> File names never can include spaces. Spaces confuse DOS's capability to store the file with the name you want. Also, don't use periods in file names, other than the period before the extension.

For safety, you may want to use the Save As command instead of the Save command. The Save As command shows you the directory and gives you a chance to change the file name for each save. The File Save command saves the document under the name last used.

Password Protecting Your File

You can protect your documents against unauthorized opening or unauthorized changes by saving them with different types of passwords. To add protection to a file, choose the Options button from the Save As dialog box. The dialog box shown in figure 6.15 appears.

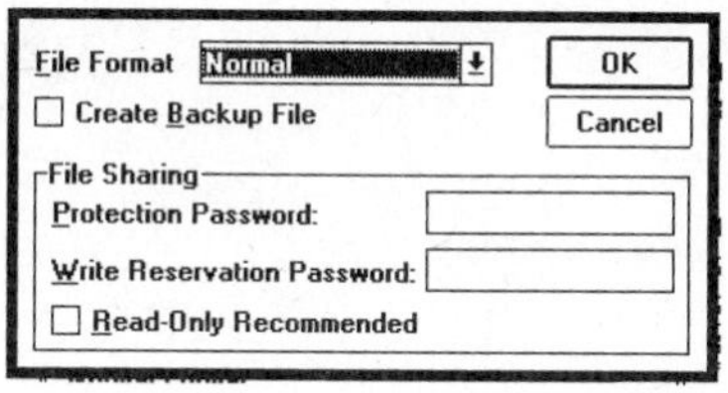

Fig. 6.15. The Save As Options dialog box.

To protect a file so that a password is requested before the file can be opened, type a password of up to 15 characters into the **P**rotection Password text box. The password can contain text, numbers, spaces, and symbols. Remember to note upper- and lowercase letters. You will be asked for the exact upper- and lowercase letters that you used originally. Because asterisks show on-screen in place of the password, you will be asked to reenter the Protection password to ensure that you typed it correctly. You can use passwords to protect templates and add-in documents.

If you want to ensure that only authorized users can change a file, type a password in the **W**rite Reservation Password text box. When the file is opened, operators will be prompted for the Write Reservation password. Without the password, operators can only open the file as a Read-Only file. This restriction forces operators to save the file with a new file name and preserves the original file. If operators know the Write Reservation password, they can make changes to the file and save the file over the original file.

If you want to recommend that operators open a file as Read-Only, but not force them to, select the **R**ead-Only Recommended check box. This selection enables operators to make changes to the original without a password, but reminds them to check the **R**ead-Only check box for normal work. This option is best when you want to protect files against accidental changes, but you want all operators to have open access to the files. Files saved from a document with this option on will also have their **R**ead-Only Recommended option selected.

Tip: *Protecting Your Work*
The protection options of Excel do ***not*** prevent you from deleting or erasing a file. Make backup copies of your important work.

If your work is important, keep the original and backup copies in two different physical locations. When you keep copies apart, a fire or vandal can't destroy both your original and your backup.

Saving All Your Work at Once

Excel can save all your windows exactly as they appear on-screen. This is useful for leaving a work session that you want to return to later. This capability also enables you to "package" Excel worksheets, charts, and macros so that others can start all the documents at once with windows arranged in a layout that you design.

When you need to save all the work in progress, choose the **File Save Workspace** command. Type the name you want the work saved under, and choose OK or press Enter. When you are ready to resume work, choose the **File Open** command, look for the file name with the extension XLW, and select the file.

The **File Save Workspace** command saves a list of file names, window positions, and menu settings, rather than saving the actual documents on-screen. Should you later open and modify one of the documents and resave it, the next time the workspace is opened, the modified document will appear with its changes. If you change the file names or if you move files to directories different from the ones under which the workspace was created, the workspace will not be able to open the renamed or moved files. If this happens, re-create the workspace.

> **Tip: *Keeping Workspace Documents in the Same Directory***
> Although a workspace can contain documents saved in different drives and directories, a management problem can arise if files are moved. Keeping all files and the workspace file in the same directory enables you to move all related workspace files together and continue to use the original XLW file that opens the workspace.

Deleting Files

You can delete individual files from within Excel with the **File Delete** command. Choose the **File Delete** command, select the file you want to delete from the list box, and choose OK or press Enter. An alert box appears asking you to confirm the deletion; choose **Yes** to delete.

To delete multiple files at one time, use the File Manager in the Main group of the Program Manager. The book, *Using Microsoft Windows 3,* 2nd Ed., published by Que Corporation, explains how to use the File Manager and lists numerous shortcuts.

After you delete files, you cannot use the **Edit Undo** or Esc commands to restore them.

Closing Documents and Exiting Excel

You can close the active window by choosing the **File Close** command. The mouse shortcut for closing a window is to double-click on the document Control menu to the left of the document's title bar. (Make sure that you double-click on the Control menu to the left of the document's title, not to the left of the Excel title.) By keyboard, you can press Ctrl+F4.

If you made changes since the last time you saved the document, an alert box appears (see fig. 6.16). If you want to save the document before closing, choose **Yes**.

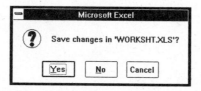

Fig. 6.16. The Close and Save alert box.

> **Tip:** *Closing All Document Windows While Keeping Excel Running*
> To close all the document windows with a single command, hold down the Shift key as you select the File menu. A new command, Close All, appears. Choosing Close All closes all worksheets; you can confirm whether you want to save worksheets that you have changed.

To exit Excel, choose the **File Exit** command or press Alt+F4. With a mouse, double-click on the program Control menu to the left of the Excel title bar. If you made changes to documents since they were last saved, you will be asked whether you want to save the changes.

From Here...

You can operate Excel in any way that fits your style and the task at hand. You can use the mouse, Alt+*letter* menu selections, Alt+arrow key menu selections, or the ever popular shortcut keys. You should, however, avoid using the same commands over and over, year after year, without considering Excel's additional capabilities. Occasionally, you should take the time to scroll through the commands in menus to learn what features are available.

Remember that the **Help** menu contains a great deal of information. You also can get help by pressing F1 when a dialog box is open, or by pressing Shift+F1 and then clicking on a menu and command.

The next chapter deals with data entry and editing. If you are familiar with Lotus 1-2-3, you are familiar with Excel's basic data-entry and editing concepts. Nonetheless, skim these chapters; Excel has many timesaving techniques and powerful features.

7

Entering and Editing Worksheet Data

Excel's value lies in storing, manipulating, and displaying data. But before you can use data in Excel, you must enter it. This chapter discusses the types of data a cell can contain and explains how to enter text, numbers, and dates. You also learn how to create formulas that manipulate data and how to create and use English names, such as Revenue, for cell references instead of using inscrutable references like B37.

In addition to telling you how to enter data, this chapter describes how to edit the contents of a cell and how to move and rearrange the layout of the worksheet. You can save considerable time building worksheets after you learn how to move or copy text or formulas.

Entering Data

Excel worksheet cells can contain values or formulas. The constant values cells can contain are numbers, text, dates, times, logical values, and errors. A logical value, such as TRUE or FALSE, is the result displayed after a condition is tested. Error values, such as #NUM!, occur when Excel cannot properly evaluate a formula in a cell.

When you type a value or formula in the active cell, your entry appears at the insertion point, or cursor, in the formula bar near the top of the screen (see fig. 7.1). The entry appears in the long text box on the right side of the formula bar. The insertion point, a flashing vertical line in the formula bar, indicates where characters you type will appear. As soon as you type or edit in the formula bar, two boxes appear to the left of the formula bar. If you are using a mouse, clicking on the Cancel box cancels an entry; clicking on the Enter box enters the formula bar contents into the active cell.

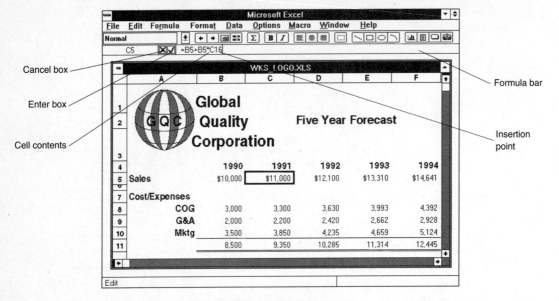

Fig. 7.1. Data and formulas are entered in the formula bar.

To enter data in a worksheet, follow these steps:

1. Select the cell in which you want to enter data.

2. Type the entry.

   The entry appears in the formula bar as you type. If you decide that you want to cancel the entry in the formula bar, click on the Cancel box in the formula bar or press Esc.

3. Enter what you have typed.

 Click on the Enter box in the formula bar.

 Press Enter.

If you want to back out before the value or formula is entered in a cell, press Esc or click on the Cancel box in the formula bar. If the value or formula has just been entered, choose the **Edit Undo** command.

Undoing Edits and Commands

Although Excel cannot correct every wrong command, entry, or edit, the Undo command can undo many mistakes. When you want to undo your last change, choose the Edit Undo command. The Undo command changes to show you the last command it can undo.

Entering Text

Text can include alphabetical characters, numbers, and symbols. To enter text in a cell, select the cell, type the text entry, and then enter the text by clicking on the Enter box or pressing Enter.

You can type as many as 255 characters in a cell. (Note that all the characters may not show in the worksheet if the cell is not wide enough and if the adjacent cell contains data.) When you enter text in a cell that still has the original General format, the text automatically aligns on the left side of the cell.

You can make Excel accept numbers as text by placing an equal sign in front of the numbers and enclosing the numbers in quotation marks. For example, suppose that you enter what Excel would normally consider a number, as follows:

="45,000"

Entering this number as text enables the number to exceed the cell's width. If you enter a number in the normal way and the cell is not wide enough to display it, the cell fills with # signs. Entering a number as text also is useful if you need to create a text heading, for example ($000), that Excel would normally treat as a number. If you use this method, Excel can convert the text number into a number if it is needed within a numeric formula.

If you need to display quotation marks on-screen, you must enclose the quotation marks you want within quotation marks. Enclosing the quotation marks rather than the text results in three quotation marks on either side of the text, as in the following example:

=" " "The Absolute Best" " "

Unlike Lotus 1-2-3, Excel enables you to type phrases that begin with a number directly into the worksheet. For example, the following address is accepted by Excel as text because it contains letters:

45 Oak Ridge Trail

Entering Numbers

Numbers are constant values containing only the following characters:

1 2 3 4 5 6 7 8 9 0 – + / . E e

To enter a number, you select the cell, type the number, and then press Enter or click on the Enter box. You can enter integers, such as 135 or 327; decimal fractions, such as 135.437 or 327.65; integer fractions, such as 1 1/2 or 2/3; or scientific notation, such as 1.35437e2.

As you create worksheets, Excel may display newly entered numbers or formulas as ######## (see fig. 7.2). A cell filled with # signs indicates that the column is not wide enough to display the number in its current format. In this case, you need to change the numeric format or widen the column. Formatting worksheets is described in Chapter 8.

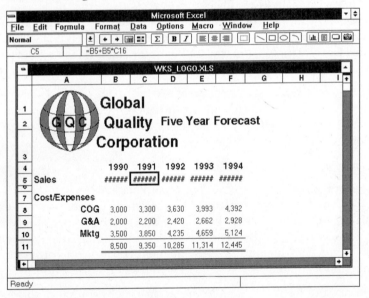

Fig. 7.2. The signs ##### appear when a column is not wide enough to display a number or date.

Electronic spreadsheets like Excel store both the raw number typed into a cell and the format or appearance in which the number should be displayed. When you enter a number in a cell, Excel tries to establish how the number should be formatted. For example, Excel accepts and displays the entries listed in table 7.1 with the formats indicated.

Table 7.1
Excel Formats

Typed Entry	Excel's Automatically Chosen Format	Displayed Result
897	Number, General	897
7999 Knue Rd.	Text, left aligned	7999 Knue Rd.
$450.09	Number, dollar format	$450.09
54.6%	Number, percent format	54.6%
$NF2 3/4	Number, fraction	2 3/4
0 3/4	Number, fraction	3/4
45,600	Number, comma format	45600
678	Number, negative	−678
(678)	Number, negative	−678
4/5/92	Date, m/d/yy	4/5/92
4/5	Date, m/d/yy (current year assumed)	5-Apr

The second example—7999 Knue Rd.—illustrates that if an entry is not a number or date, then Excel stores it as text. This feature is convenient when you are entering database information such as inventory codes or street addresses.

To enter a fraction you must type an integer, a space, and then the fraction. If you are entering only the fractional part, type a zero, a space, and then the fraction. The result is a number that can be used in calculations.

Tip: *Matching the Number Displayed to the Number Used in Calculation*

Excel stores numbers with 15-decimal precision. You can change the format to display fewer digits, but the full number is still used in calculations. Formatted numbers can cause problems if you are not aware of the difference between the formatted display and the number used in calculation. Because the number used in calculations may be slightly different than the number displayed, an equation's result may appear to be incorrect. To solve this problem, review the **Options Calculation** command with the **Precision as Displayed** option selected and the ROUND function, both discussed in Chapter 8, "Formatting Worksheets."

Entering Dates and Times

Excel recognizes dates and times typed in most of the common ways. When you type a date or time, Excel takes your entry and converts it to a *serial* number. The serial number represents the number of days from the beginning of the century until the date you type. Time is recorded as a decimal fraction of a twenty-four hour day.

If Excel recognizes your entry as a valid date or time format, you will see the date or time on-screen. Correctly entered dates appear in the formula bar with the format m/d/yy regardless of how the cell is formatted.

A valid date entry typed into an unformatted cell is aligned as a number, to the right. A valid date entry typed into a cell formatted with a nondate numeric format appears converted to its serial number with that numeric format. For example, if you type **Sep 5, 91** in a cell formatted to show numbers with a comma and two decimal places (#,##0.00), you will see that date appear as 33,121.00.

If Excel does not recognize your entry as a valid date or time format, and you type a text date (such as **Sept 5 91**), Excel treats the entry as text and, in an unformatted cell, aligns it to the left.

To enter a date, type the date into the cell with any of these formats:

    7/8/92
    Jul 8, 92
    8-Jul-92
    8-Jul   (The year from the system date is used.)
    Jul-92   (Only the month and year show.)

In any of these date formats, you can use either a / or - to separate elements.

Enter times in any of these formats:

    13:32
    13:32:05
    1:32:05 PM
    1:32 pm
    1:32 p

The first two examples are from a 24-hour clock. If you use a 12-hour clock, follow the time with a space and A, AM, P, or PM (in either upper- or lowercase). Be sure that you leave a space before the AM or PM. Do not mix a 24-hour clock time with an AM or PM.

You can combine the date and time during entry by using the 5/28/91 12:45 format.

For information about formatting or changing the formats of dates and times, refer to Chapter 8, "Formatting Worksheets."

Tip: *When the Date or Time Does Not Format Automatically*
In some cases when you enter a correctly formatted date or time, the displayed result is not in a date or time format. This occurs when the cell's format has been previously changed from the default, General. To reformat for the correct display, select the cell, choose Format Number, select the date or time format from the list box, and choose OK or press Enter.

Entering Formulas

Formulas perform calculations—the reason for Excel's existence. Formulas automatically recalculate and produce current results when you update data used by the formulas. Formulas refer to the contents of a cell by its address, such as B12. In formulas, you can use math operators, such as + or −, as well as prebuilt formulas, called functions, like SUM or PMT (payment).

A simple formula might appear in the formula bar as follows:

=B12*D15

This formula takes the contents of cell B12 and multiplies it times the contents of cell D15.

In this section, you learn how to build formulas, how to use different types of cell references, and other concepts important to more complex formulas.

Normally, the worksheet displays the results of formulas rather than the formulas themselves. The formula in the active cell is displayed in the formula bar. Figure 7.3 shows the active cell as C11 and its formula displayed in the formula bar.

Figure 7.4 shows the formulas in the worksheet. The formulas are displayed in the worksheet when you choose the **Options Display** command and select the Formulas command.

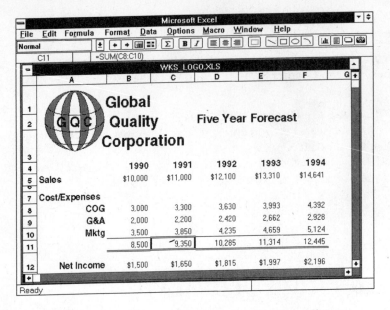

Fig. 7.3. *The formula bar displays the formula in the active cell.*

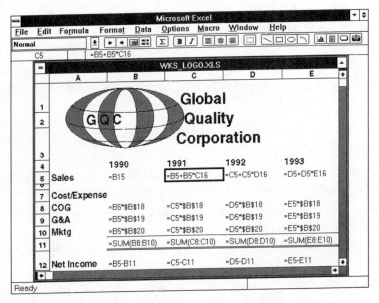

Fig. 7.4. *Formulas also can be displayed in the worksheet.*

To enter a formula, follow these steps:

1. Select the cell that will contain the formula.

2. Type an equal sign (=).

3. Type a value, cell reference, function, or name.

4. If the formula is complete, press Enter or click on the Enter box in the formula bar. If the formula is not complete, continue to step 5.

5. Type a math operator.

6. Return to step 3.

Always separate terms in a formula with operators. Do not leave any spaces in the formula.

Before a formula has been entered, you can clear it from the formula bar by clicking on the Cancel box, an X, which is found to the left of the formula bar. From the keyboard, press Esc.

> **Tip: *Filling a Range of Cells with a Value or Formula on Entry***
> In the Worksheet Quick Start, it would have been convenient to enter the formulas for cells B8, B9, B10, or B11 and have them fill or copy to the right. This is easy to do.
>
> If you know you need to fill a range of cells with the same value or formula, follow these steps:
>
> 1. Select the range of cells to contain the entries.
>
> 2. Enter the value or formula that is appropriate for the active cell.
>
> 3. Press Ctrl+Enter or hold Ctrl and click on the Enter box.
>
> The Ctrl+Enter combination both enters your value or formula in the active cell and copies it into other cells in the selection. Any formulas you enter with Ctrl+Enter adjust their relative cell references to their new locations just as though you had copied them or filled them into the selected cells. (Relative cell references are described in the section "Using Cell References in Formulas.")

Entering Cell References by Pointing

The most accurate method of entering cell references in a formula is by pointing. Although you can type an entire formula, it is often easy to make a typing error or misread the screen and end up with D52 in a formula when it should be D53. When you point to a cell to include in a formula, you actually move the active cell to the cell you want in the formula. It is obvious when you have selected the correct cells.

To enter a cell reference into a formula by pointing, follow these steps:

1. Select the cell for the formula.

2. Type an equal sign (=).

3. Point to the cell you want in the formula.

Click on the cell you want to include in the formula.

Press the movement keys to move the dashed "marquee" around the cell you want to include in the formula.

The address of the cell you point to appears at the cursor location in the formula bar. The cell pointed to is enclosed by a dashed line.

4. Enter a math operator.

5. Point to the next cell.

6. Repeat from step 4 to continue the formula, or enter the formula by clicking on the Enter box or pressing Enter.

Using Cell References in Formulas

You can refer to a cell's location in Excel with either a *relative reference* or an *absolute reference*. Be careful to use the correct type of cell reference in each formula you create. If you understand the difference between the two types of cell references used in Excel, you can avoid creating formulas that change incorrectly when copied to new locations.

All of us use both relative references and absolute references. Suppose, for example, that you are in your office and you want someone to take a letter to the mailbox. Using a relative reference, you would tell the person: "Go out the front door; turn left and go two blocks; turn right and go one block." These directions are *relative to* your office location at the time you give the instructions. If you move to a different location, these directions do not work anymore.

To make sure that your letter gets to the mailbox no matter where you are when you give the directions, you must say something like this: "Take this letter to the mailbox at 2700 Mendocino." No matter where you are speaking, the mailbox will be at one absolute location: 2700 Mendocino. The address *absolutely* will not change.

Relative References

Unless you specify otherwise, Excel uses relative referencing for cell addresses when you enter a formula. This means that cell references in a formula change when you copy the formula to a new location or when you fill a range with a formula. You most often will want formulas to use relative cell references.

In figure 7.5, the formula in cell C5 is =B5+B5*C16. These are all relative references. The formula, translated into English, would read as follows:

Into cell C5, put the number in the cell one column to the left, same row (B5). To that number, add the result of multiplying the number in the cell one column to the left, same row (B5 again) and the number in the cell eleven rows down, same column (C16). Put that result back into cell C5.

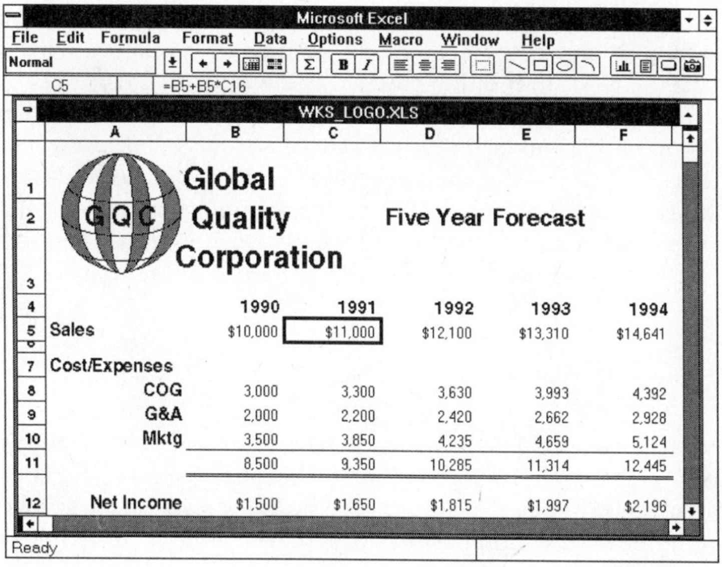

Fig. 7.5. *The relative reference formula in C5 shown in the formula bar.*

You can see the equivalent formula in R1C1, row-column format, by choosing the **O**ptions **W**orkspace command and selecting the **R1C1** option. If you change the formula display to R1C1 format, the formula in the same cell, R5C3, is =RC[−1]+RC[−1]*R[11]C. The R1C1 format makes relative references more obvious because the cell references are presented as the relative change from the current cell. For example, C[−1] means one column left, and R[11] means eleven rows down from the active cell.

When you copy either formula across row 5, the formulas automatically adjust their cell references to their new positions. The copied formulas therefore look like this:

Cell Containing Formula	A1 Format	R1C1 Format
D5 or R5C4	=C5+C5*D16	=RC[−1]+RC[−1]*R[11]C
E5 or R5C5	=D5+D5*E16	=RC[−1]+RC[−1]*R[11]C
F5 or R5C6	=E5+E5*F16	=RC[−1]+RC[−1]*R[11]C

Notice how the formula using A1 format changed to give its cell references the same relative position from the cell containing the formula. Formulas using R1C1 format do not change when copied because the formula always shows the relative position of the cell being used.

Most of the time, you will want cell references to change when they are copied. But in some cases these changes can cause problems. What would happen if the worksheet didn't have a row of values all the way across row 16? What if row 16 had a single value that each copied formula had to use? What if your worksheet had only a single Change number in row 20 to be used for each year's revenue increase? Each of the copied formulas in these cases would have been wrong. When you must copy a formula and you must make sure that some terms in the formula do not adjust to their new locations, you must designate those terms as absolute references.

Absolute References

To keep cell references from changing when you copy or fill a formula to new locations, use absolute references. If you use the A1 formula format, indicate absolute references by putting a dollar sign ($) in front of the column letter or row number that you want to freeze. In R1C1 format, indicate an absolute cell reference by typing a specific row or column number; do not enclose the number in square brackets.

In figure 7.6, the COG factor is referred to using an absolute reference address of $B$18 in A1 format or R18C2 in R1C1 format. In A1 format, the dollar sign in front of each part of the address, B and 18, prevents the cell reference from changing during a copy or fill; in R1C1 format, the specific row and column numbers without brackets prevent the cell reference from changing during a copy or fill operation.

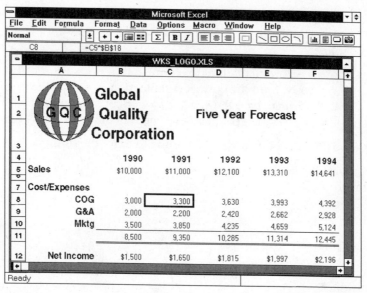

Fig. 7.6. *Absolute reference formulas use a $ to "freeze" a row or column reference.*

The formula in B8, for example, was copied into cells C8, D8, E8, and F8. Cell B8's formula is =B5*$B$18 in A1 format or =R[-3]C *R18C2 in R1C1 format. When copied, only the first term changes in each new cell that the formula is copied into. The second term remains *absolutely* the same. This was necessary because there was a value in B18, but no corresponding values in C18, D18, E18, and F18. Had the formula used B18 instead of $B$18, all the copied formulas would have referenced the blank cells C18, D18, E18, and F18.

You can enter an absolute reference in any of three ways:

- As you enter the formula, type the dollar sign in front of the row or column that you want to remain the same. In R1C1 format, delete the square brackets.

- Choose the Formula Reference command after typing a cell address.

- Move the flashing insertion point in the formula bar to the cell address and press F4, the absolute reference key. (If the formula already has been entered, select its cell and press F2 to edit it.)

To enter an absolute reference using the Formula Reference command or F4 key, follow these steps:

1. Type an equal sign (=) and the cell reference you want to be absolute.

2. Choose the Formula Reference command or press F4, the absolute reference key, until the correct combination of dollar signs appears. For R1C1 format, type the specific row or column number without brackets, or use the Formula Reference command or press F4.

3. Type the next operator and continue to enter the formula.

You can use the Formula Reference command or F4 key when editing an existing formula.

Mixed References

On some occasions, you will want only the row to stay fixed when copied or only the column to stay fixed. In these cases, you need to use a mixed reference, one that contains both absolute and relative references. For example, $B5 prevents the column from changing, but the row changes relative to a new copied location. In B$5 just the opposite occurs. The column adjusts to a new location but the row always stays fixed at 5. A mixed reference in R1C1 format might look like RC2 where the R means the current relative row and C2 means the absolute second column. R2C[–1] means the absolute second row and the relative column one left.

You can create mixed references in the same ways you can create absolute references. Type the dollar signs or specific row and column numbers without brackets, choose the Formula Reference command, or press F4. Each choice of Formula Reference or each press of F4 cycles the cell reference to a new combination.

Each time you select the Formula Reference command or F4, Excel cycles through all combinations of relative and absolute references. Press F4 four times, for example, and you cycle through B22, $B$22, B$22, $B22, and B22.

Changing Between A1 and R1C1 Cell Reference Style

You can switch from the A1 to R1C1 style of displaying cell references by choosing the Options Workspace command, selecting the R1C1 button, and then choosing OK. Figure 7.7 shows a formula in the bar in R1C1 style. To switch from R1C1 style back to A1 style, deselect the R1C1 option and choose OK.

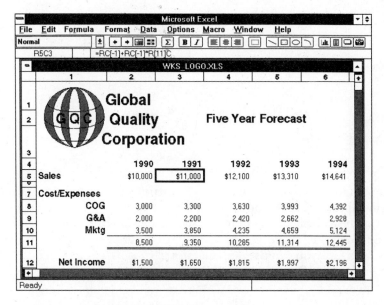

Fig. *7.7. The R1C1 reference style is easier to use for complex formulas and macros.*

Using Operators in Formulas

Operators tell formulas what operations to perform. Excel uses four types of operators:

Operators	*Signs*
Arithmetic	+, −, *, /, %, ^
Text	&
Comparative	=, <, <=, >, >=, <>
Reference	colon (:), comma (,), space ( )

Table 7.2 illustrates with examples how you can use each of the arithmetic operators in formulas.

Table 7.2
Arithmetic Operators

Operator	Formula	Result	Type of Operation
+	=5+2	7	Addition
–	=5–2	3	Subtraction
–	–5	–5	Negation (takes the negative of the number)
*	=5*2	10	Multiplication
/	=5/2	2.5	Division
%	5%	.05	Percentage
^	=5^2	25	Exponentiation (raised to the power of)

Excel can work with more than just arithmetic formulas. The program also can manipulate text, perform comparisons, and relate different ranges and cells on the worksheet. For example, the ampersand (&) operator joins text within quotation marks or text contained in referenced cells. Table 7.3 illustrates how you can use text operators.

Table 7.3
Text Operators

Operator	Formula	Result	Type of Operation
&	="Ms. "&"Gibbs"	Ms. Gibbs	Text is joined.
&	=A12&" "&B36	Ms. Gibbs	Text is joined when A12 contains Ms. and B36 contains Gibbs.

When you need to compare results, you can create formulas using comparative operators. These operators return a TRUE or FALSE result, depending on how the formula evaluates the condition. Table 7.4 lists the comparative operators.

Table 7.4
Comparative Operators

Operator	Type
=	Equal to
<	Less than
<=	Less than or equal to
>	Greater than
>=	Greater than or equal to
<>	Not equal to

Here are some examples of comparative operators in formulas:

Formula	Result
=A12<15	TRUE if the content of A12 is less than 15; FALSE if the content of A12 is 15 or more.
=B36>=15	TRUE if the content of B36 is 15 or more; FALSE if the content of B36 is less than 15.

If a cell contains the text TRUE or true, Excel evaluates the cell as TRUE; if a cell contains the text FALSE or false, the cell is evaluated as FALSE. The number 0 is always evaluated as FALSE, while any nonzero number is TRUE.

Another type of operator is the reference operator (see table 7.5). Reference operators do not make changes to constants or cell contents. Instead, they control how a formula groups together cells and ranges of cells when the formula calculates. Reference operators let you combine absolute and relative references and named ranges. Reference operators are valuable for joining cells together (union) or referring to a common area shared between different ranges (intersect).

Tip: *Referencing an Entire Row or Column*
Use the range operator (:) to reduce your work in formulas. For example, if you want a formula to refer to all cells in column B, type **B:B**. Similarly, the range that includes all cells in rows 5 through 12 is entered as 5:12.

Table 7.5
Reference Operators

Operator	Example	Type	Result
:	SUM(A12:A24)	Range	Evaluates as a single reference the cells in the rectangular area between the two "corners."
,	SUM(A12:A24,B36)	Union	Evaluates two references as a single reference.
space	SUM(A12:A24 A16:B20)	Intersect	Evaluates the cells common to both references (if no cells are common to both, then #NULL results).
space	=Yr92 Sales	Intersect	Cell contents at the intersect of the column named Yr92 and the row named Sales.

Tip: *For 1-2-3 Users*
Excel uses a colon (B12:C36) to designate a range in the same way that 1-2-3 uses two periods (B12..C36). You can use a comma to select multiple ranges (B12:C36,F14:H26) for many functions.

Excel follows a consistent set of rules when applying operators in a formula. Working from the first calculation to the last, Excel evaluates operators in the order shown in table 7.6.

Table 7.6
The Order in which Excel Evaluates Operators

Operator	Definition
:	Range
space	Intersect
,	Union
—	Negation

Operator	Definition
%	Percentage
^	Exponentiation
* and /	Multiplication and division
+ and –	Addition and subtraction
&	Text joining
=, <, <=	Comparisons
>, >=, <>	

You can change the order in which calculations are performed by enclosing in parentheses the terms you want Excel to calculate first. Notice, for instance, the difference between these results:

Formula	Result
=6+21/3	13
=(6+21)/3	9

Changing Formulas to Values

In some situations, such as calculating a number as you enter it in a worksheet, you may want to type a formula and change it to a value on entry. To "freeze" a formula into its resulting value, follow these steps:

1. Select the cell of an existing formula and press F2 (the Edit key), or type the formula in the formula bar.

2. Choose the Options Calculate Now command, or press F9.

   The formula in the formula bar is replaced by its calculated value.

3. Choose OK or press Enter.

> **Tip: *Checking Partial Results in a Formula***
> To find errors in formulas, check the results of terms within the formulas. One of the terms (partial formulas) may be wrong. You can change part of a formula into a value. Select from the formula bar the part of the formula you want to see the result of, and then press F9. For example, if you type the formula =B12*C36+(D12/D35), select the cell references of B12*C36, and press F9, you will see what the result is for that part of the formula. The portion you select must be a valid formula in its own right. (This method also works to evaluate part of a long or nested macro function.)

Naming Cells

If you get tired of trying to decipher the meaning of B36 or F13:W54 in a formula, you can use names to refer to cells, ranges, and multiple ranges. For example, you can give the range F19:L65 an easily recognizable name, such as SALES__REPORT or DATA.ENTRY. Named cells and ranges in Excel are similar to range names in Lotus 1-2-3, but in Excel you can paste names into formulas, create compound names, and even assign frequently used formulas and constants to names.

Using names in worksheets has many advantages:

- Names reduce the chance for errors in formulas and commands. You are likely to notice that you mistyped SAELS_REPORT when you meant to type SALES_REPORT, but you might not notice an error when you type F19:L65. When you enter an unrecognizable name, Excel displays a #NAME? error.

- You can name any frequently used constant or formula and use the name in formulas. (The named constant or formula does not have to reside in a cell.) For example, you can enter a name such as RATE in a formula and then at any later time use the Formula Define Name command to assign a new value to the name RATE. The new assignment changes the value of RATE throughout the worksheet. Nowhere in the worksheet does the value of RATE have to be typed. This technique enables you to create predefined constants and formulas that others use by name.

- Named ranges expand and contract automatically to adjust to inserted or deleted rows and columns. This feature is important for creating charts, databases, macros, and linked worksheets that continue to work no matter how a named range is expanded or contracted.

- Names make finding your way around the worksheet easy. You can choose the Formula Goto command, or press F5 and enter the name of the location you want to go to. Choosing the Formula Goto command and then selecting DATA.ENTRY or MONTHLY.REPORT is a time saver.

- Using names in macros when referring to specific locations on worksheets helps make your macros more versatile. The macros continue to work on rearranged worksheets.

- Names make formulas easy to recognize and maintain. For example, the formula

=Revenue-Cost

is much easier to understand than the formula

=A12-C13.

- Names make typing references to other worksheets easy. You do not need to know the cell reference in the other worksheet. If the other worksheet has a named cell reference, then you can type a formula such as

=YTDCONS.XLS!Sales.

This formula brings the information from the Sales cell in the worksheet with the file name YTDCONS.XLS into the cell in your active worksheet.

- Names are easier to remember than cell references. After you name cells or ranges, you can look at a list of names and paste the names you want into formulas with the Formula Paste Name command (see this chapter's "Pasting Names and Functions into Formulas" section).

Creating Names

When the time comes to create names, you must remember a few rules. Names must start with a letter, but you can use any character after the initial letter *except a space*. Do not use a space in a name; instead, use an underline (_), hyphen (-), or period (.). Be careful when using a hyphen; it may be mistaken for a minus sign, as in SALES-EXPENSES.

Incorrect Names	Correct Names
SALES EXPENSES	SALES_EXPENSES
Region West	Region.West
1989	YR1989
%	RATE

Although names can be as long as 255 characters, you will want to make them shorter. Because formulas also are limited to 255 characters, long names in a formula leave you less room for the rest of the formula, and the full name will not show in a dialog box.

Names can be typed in either upper- or lowercase letters. Excel recognizes and continues to use the capitalization used to create the name.

Do not use names that look like cell references, such as B13 or R13C2.

To name a cell, range of cells, or multiple range, follow these steps:

1. Select the cell, range, or multiple ranges you want to name.

2. Choose the Formula Define Name command.

3. Leave the name Excel proposes, if it is acceptable, or type the name you want in the Name box.

4. Leave the cell reference in the Refers to box, if it is acceptable, or type an equal sign (=) followed by the correct reference. (This procedure is described later.)

5. Choose OK or press Enter.

You can see in figure 7.8 that Excel will often propose a name for the cells you select. Excel looks at the left edge for a text name of a row or looks above for a text name of a column. If you select a range, Excel checks for a name in the upper left corner of the range. If the text contains a blank space, as in the figure, Excel automatically replaces the blank with an underscore to make the name legal. Excel has done this in the figure.

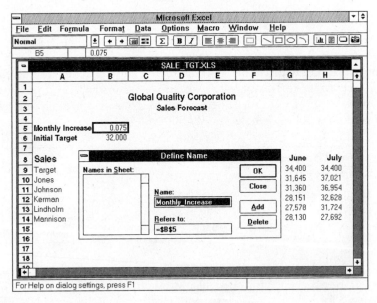

Fig. 7.8. Formula Define Name will attempt to propose names for the cell or range you select.

Tip: *Why Range Names Don't Show in Formulas*
Excel does not immediately replace existing cell references in formulas with range names. You have the advantage of specifying the areas of the worksheet where formulas show the range names. This procedure is described in the "Applying Names" section later in this chapter.

Creating Names from Existing Text

If you have built a text skeleton for your worksheet (as described in Chapter 4, "Designing Worksheets"), you can use the text on the worksheet to assign names to adjacent cells. Moreover, by selecting a range of cells, you can assign a number of names at the same time.

To assign a number of names at the same time, use the Formula Create Names command. You then can choose whether Excel uses as names the existing text along one or more edges of the selected area.

To create names using text in the worksheet, follow these steps:

1. Select the range of cells you want to name. Be sure to include the row or column of text cells that compose the names (see fig. 7.9).

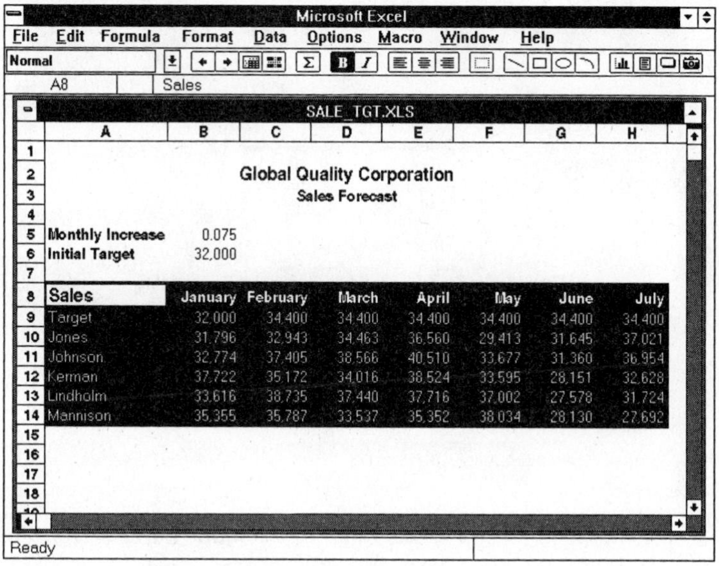

Fig. 7.9. Include text you want as names in the range you select.

2. Choose the Formula Create Names command. The dialog box
   shown in figure 7.10 appears.

Fig. 7.10. *The Create Names dialog box enables you to choose the location of
text that will be used as names.*

3. Select the Top Row option to use text in the top row of the selection as names for the columns. Similarly, the Bottom Row option
   uses the bottom row of text as names for the columns. The Left
   Column option uses text in the left column to name the rows to the
   right of the text; and the Right Column option uses the text in the
   right column to name the rows to the left of the text.

4. Choose OK or press Enter.

In figure 7.11, the cells in the columns are named with the names at the top
of each column. In figure 7.12, each of the selected rows is named with the
names down the left column of the selected area.

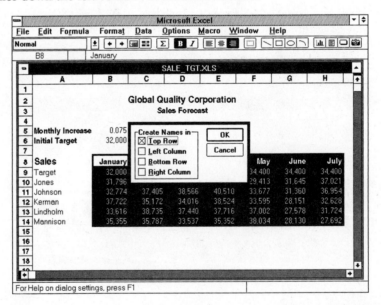

Fig. 7.11. *Use names at the top of these columns to name the cells going down.*

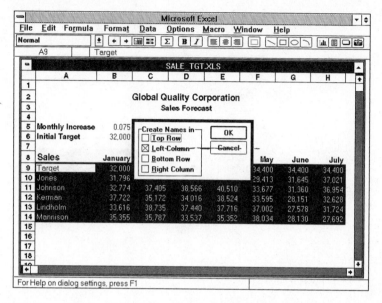

Fig. 7.12. *Use names at the left of rows to name the cells going across.*

If you attempt to assign a duplicate name, a dialog box appears, warning you that the name is already in use. Choose the Yes button to update the name to the new references; choose the No button to retain the old name and references; or choose the Cancel button to retain the old name and back out of creating new names.

If you use Formula Create Names to name cells, make sure that the text in the cells does not violate the rules for names. Remember that names cannot begin with numbers. An alert box appears to tell you when text cannot be accepted as a name. The mistake most often made is using characters such as %.

Text in cells used as names can include spaces. Excel automatically replaces the space with an underscore mark in the created name. For example, SALES RATE in a cell becomes the name SALES_RATE.

You can select more than one box from the Create Names dialog box. As a result, you can name cells in different orientations with different names. If you select two options that overlap, then any text in the cell at the overlap is used as the name for the entire range. For example, if you select both the Top Row and Left Column options, then the text in the cell at the top left of the selected range is the name for the entire range. In figure 7.13, the name SALES applies to the range B9:H14, the names on the left apply to the rows, and the names at the top apply to the columns.

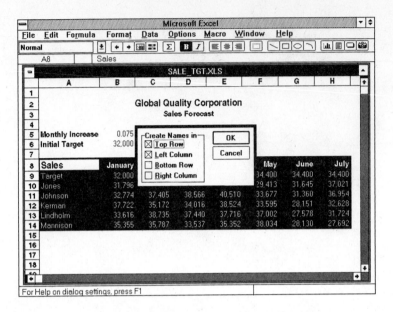

Fig. 7.13. *Text at the top left of a range is proposed as the name for the range.*

As part of your worksheet documentation, you should include a list of the names used. Excel can paste into your worksheet a complete list of names and the cells they name. Move the active cell to a clear area and choose the Formula Paste Name command followed by the Paste List button. A list of all the names and corresponding cell addresses appears in your worksheet.

Changing or Deleting Names

Sometimes you will want to change a name or the cells that the name refers to. Also, from time to time, you may want to delete names that are no longer needed. Deleting unneeded names keeps your list of names free of clutter.

To change a name or the cells that the name references, follow these steps:

1. Choose the Formula Define Name command. (This is the same command you use to name a cell or range of cells manually.)

2. Select from the list box the name you want to change.

3. Select the Name box or the Refers to box.

4. Edit the name or cell reference in the appropriate text box. Use the arrow keys, Backspace, and Delete keys to edit in the text box.

5. Choose OK or press Enter.

To delete a name, select the name you want to delete. Then choose the Delete button.

Caution: After you have deleted a name, selecting Cancel does not undelete it.

Applying Names

When you create or define names, they do not automatically appear in existing formulas in the worksheet. If you create formulas before names, you need to apply the names to the formulas. With the Formula Apply Names command, Excel gives you the capability to select where you want names applied (see fig. 7.14).

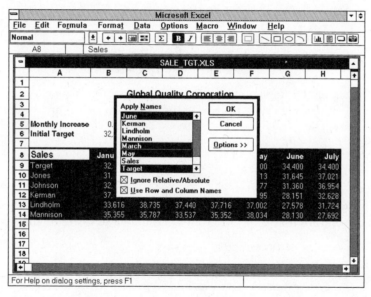

Fig. 7.14. *To apply names to existing formulas, use the Formula Apply Names command.*

To apply existing names to formulas containing named cell references, follow these steps:

1. Select a single cell if you want to apply names to the entire worksheet, or select a range to apply names to formulas within the range.

2. Choose the Formula Apply Names command.

3. Select names to apply from the Apply Names dialog box.

Click on each name you want to apply. Holding Shift enables you to select multiple names.

Press the up- or down-arrow key to move through the list. Hold down Ctrl to move without selecting, and press space bar to select additional names. Shift+arrow selects adjacent names.

4. Select the Ignore Relative/Absolute check box if you want names to replace absolute and relative references. Deselecting this box applies absolute names to absolute references and relative names to relative references.

5. Select the Use Row and Column Names check box if you want Excel to rename cell references that can be described as the intersect of a named row and a named column. In figure 7.13, for example, cell G10 can be referenced as Jones June. Deselect this box if you want only individual cell names to apply to cell references.

6. Select the Options button to omit row or column names when the cell containing the formula is in the same row or column as the name. The following options are available:

Omit Column Name if Same Column
Omit Row Name if Same Row

After selecting Options, you can also select the order in which you want row and column names to appear. Simply select or deselect the options for Name Order: Row Column and Column Row.

7. Choose OK or press Enter.

Tip: *The Conservative Approach to Applying Names*
If you want to be conservative when you apply names to cell references, then deselect both the Ignore Relative/Absolute and the Use Row and Column Names check boxes. With these two boxes deselected, names replace only exact matches.

Naming Formulas and Values

Your worksheets are much more readable and understandable if you create names for commonly used constants or frequently used formulas. You can name any number or formula, and then use that name in a cell or formula. The number or formula does not have to be in a cell.

To name a value or formula you enter, follow these steps:

1. Choose the Formula Define Name command.

2. Select the Name text box and enter the name.

3. Select the Refers to box.

4. Type the constant number or the formula. Enter the formula or constant as you would in the formula bar. You can edit in the Refers to box as you edit in the formula bar.

5. Choose OK or press Enter.

Figure 7.15 illustrates how a formula is assigned a name. Because the formula or constant stored in the name does not have to be stored in a cell, your worksheets stay neater and are easier for inexperienced users to work with.

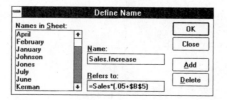

Fig. 7.15. *Assign frequently used formulas or constant values to a name.*

If you build formulas in the Refers to box by pointing to cell references (clicking on them or moving to them), Excel supplies only absolute references (such as $D$15). These references are absolute because a name usually applies to one specific location on a worksheet. You can type relative references or edit out the dollar signs to create names that act like relative references. (Named relative reference formulas can be confusing to use, so be careful.) For example, if the active cell is C6, you might type the formula =C12 in the Refers to box. You could give the formula the name RIGHT6. You then can use the name RIGHT6 in a formula or cell in order to pick up the contents of the cell six cells to the right of the cell containing =RIGHT6. Move the Define Name dialog box if it is in the way of the cell you need in a formula.

Increasing Data-Entry Efficiency

Data entry is usually tedious, but it must be done correctly. The following sections show you how to speed up the data-entry process.

Entering Data for Accounting

If you are accustomed to using a 10-key keypad that enters decimal points automatically, you will appreciate the fixed decimal feature of Excel. You can make Excel automatically enter the decimal by choosing the **Options Workspace** command. When the Workspace dialog box appears, select the Fixed Decimal check box. In the **P**laces text box, enter the number of decimal places you want (2 is normal). Choose OK or press Enter.

Now, for example, to enter the number 345.67, you can type **34567**. When you press Enter, Excel enters the number and inserts the decimal point. You can override the automatic decimal placement by typing the decimal in the number you enter.

The feature continues to work until you turn it off by deselecting the **F**ixed Decimal check box.

Entering Data in a Range

To quicken the data-entry process, select the range in which you want to enter data; the active cell will move automatically after pressing a data-entry key. This feature is especially convenient for data-entry forms and databases. Figure 7.16 shows a selected data-entry area.

To enter data in a selected area, press the appropriate key:

Key	*Action*
Tab	Enters data and moves right in the selected area; at the right edge of the selected area, wraps to the left.
Shift+Tab	Enters data and moves left in the selected area; at the left edge of the selected area, wraps to the right.

Key	Action
Enter	Enters data and moves down in the selected area; at the bottom of the selected area, wraps to the top.
Shift+Enter	Enters data and moves up in the selected area; at the top of the selected area, wraps to the bottom.

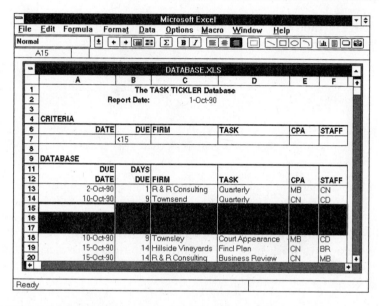

Fig. 7.16. *Selecting data-entry cells before typing automatically moves the active cell to the correct location.*

When the active cell reaches the edge of the selected area, it automatically wraps around to the next appropriate cell. For example, if you are pressing Tab repeatedly, the active cell reaches the right edge and then jumps to the first cell in the next row of the left edge.

Using Data-Entry Shortcuts

As you enter data in a database, you may want to copy information from the cell above the active cell or insert the current date and time. Excel has shortcut keys that make these tasks easy and convenient to do.

Key	Action
Ctrl+' (apostrophe)	Copies the formula from the cell above (cell references are not adjusted to the new location).
Ctrl+" (quotation mark)	Copies the value from the cell above.
Ctrl+; (semicolon)	Inserts the date.
Ctrl+: (colon)	Inserts the time.

Working While Excel Recalculates

When Excel recalculates, it only calculates those formulas involved with the data that has changed. This means it recalculates faster, and you spend less time waiting.

When it recalculates, Excel incorporates two additional features that can increase your productivity. First, you can continue entering data, changing formulas, or giving commands as the worksheet recalculates. Excel incorporates the changes you make as it recalculates. Secondly, you can start a recalculation on a worksheet, activate other Windows programs, and work in them as Excel continues recalculating the worksheet.

Choosing When To Recalculate

Excel normally recalculates each time data changes. This can slow down data entry if a worksheet is large and requires a long calculation time. In that case, you may want to disable automatic recalculation.

To disable automatic recalculation, follow these steps:

1. Choose the Options Calculation command to display the dialog box shown in figure 7.17.

2. Select the Manual option for manual recalculation, or select Automatic Except Tables to recalculate the worksheet without recalculating data tables.

3. Choose OK or press Enter.

Fig. *7.17. Control when and how Excel recalculates with the Calculation dialog box.*

When manual calculation is selected, a Calculate message appears in the status bar whenever you make a change to the sheet. This message indicates the worksheet must be recalculated before the results will be correct.

When manual recalculation is turned on, the worksheet does not automatically recalculate. What you see on the screen or print could be wrong. If the Calculate message appears at the bottom of the screen, make sure that you choose the **O**ptions Calculate **N**ow command or press F9 to recalculate documents before printing or using the results. If you want to calculate only the active document, hold down the Shift key as you choose **O**ptions and choose the Calculate Document command, or press Shift+F9. Reselecting the **A**utomatic calculation option will also calculate the document.

Some large worksheets, tables, or databases can take a long time to recalculate. Because Excel normally recalculates before saving a file, the recalculation time can be bothersome. To turn off recalculation before saving, choose the **O**ptions Calculation command, select the **M**anual option, and deselect the Recalculate Before **S**ave check box.

Editing Cell Contents

Whether you are editing a text box in a dialog box or a formula in the formula bar, you use the same editing principles used in all Windows programs. Before you can edit text, you must display the dialog box containing the text or put the cell's contents in the formula bar. To do this, follow these steps:

1. Select the cell or choose the command that displays the dialog box.

2. Move the insertion point into the text.

Move the pointer over the text until it changes into an I-beam. Position the pointer in the text you want to edit, then click. A flashing insertion point indicates where typing and editing take place.

If you have selected a cell, press the Edit key, F2. If you need to edit a text box in a dialog box, press Alt+letter to activate the text box, then type or arrow to the text you want to edit.

Table 7.7
Shortcut Keys and Mouse Actions for Editing Formulas

Key	Mouse	Action
F2	Click in bar	Moves the cursor into the formula bar for editing.
F4	Formula Reference	Cycles the cell reference touching the insertion point of all combinations of absolute and relative references.
Ins	N/A	Toggles between Insert and Typeover modes.
Del	N/A	Clears the selected characters or character to the right of the insertion point.
Backspace	N/A	Clears the selected characters or character to the left of the insertion point.
Ctrl+Del	N/A	Clears all characters from the insertion point to the end of the line.
Shift+Del	N/A	Cuts the character or selection to the right of the insertion point.
Ctrl+Ins	Edit Copy	Copies the selection to the clipboard.

Key	Mouse	Action
Shift+Ins	Edit Paste	Pastes the text at the insertion point, or replaces the selected characters.
Home	N/A	Moves the insertion point to the front of the formula bar.
End	N/A	Moves the insertion point to the end of the formula bar's contents.
Shift+Home	Drag up and left	Selects all characters from the insertion point to the front of the formula bar.
Shift+End	Drag down and right	Selects all characters from the insertion point to the end of the formula bar.
Shift+arrow	Drag across	Selects characters during a move.
Ctrl+left/ right arrow	Double click	Move a word or formula term at a time.
Shift+Ctrl+ left/right arrow	Double click, Shift+Drag	Select a word or formula a term at a time.

Inserting Text

To insert information in a dialog text box or formula bar, move the insertion point into the text by clicking the I-beam pointer at the spot where you want to insert text, or press F2 and move the insertion point with arrow keys. Once the insertion point is at the correct spot, begin typing.

When you need to insert the same text in several places, select the text and copy it with the Edit Copy command. Then move the insertion point to the spot where you want to place the text and choose Edit Paste.

Excel normally is in Insert mode, so what you type inserts itself at the insertion point. If you want to type over existing text, press Ins (Insert), and then type. Pressing Ins a second time toggles you back to Insert mode.

You can delete single characters to the left of the cursor by pressing Backspace. Delete single characters to the right of the cursor by pressing Del.

> **Note: *Protected Cells Cannot Be Changed***
> When Excel beeps and prohibits you from editing a cell's contents, the cell may be protected against changes. Protection is described in Chapter 8, "Formatting Worksheets."

Editing in the Formula Bar

You can edit Excel formulas with the same techniques you used to build them. For example, you can paste named ranges and functions into formulas or refer to cells and ranges by pointing to them. Excel even has a find-and-replace function that can help you repeat changes throughout the worksheet.

> **Tip: *Putting Problem Formulas "On Hold"***
> The time may come when you know that a formula contains an error, but you cannot seem to find it. Because of the error, you cannot enter the formula. If you press Esc, the formula bar will clear and you will lose the formula. To preserve your formula so that you can return to it later, delete the equal sign at the front and press Enter. The formula becomes text in the cell. When you have the time or the insight to fix the formula, reselect that cell, type the equal sign back in, and fix the formula.

Finding Formulas

The Formula Find command finds whatever you want in the worksheet (or database), including text or formulas. You can use the Formula Find command to locate formulas that contain a unique term, a specific text label, a cell note containing a specific word, or error values. The Formula Find command is especially helpful when you are correcting a worksheet you may not be familiar with.

To find text or a value with Formula Find, follow these steps:

1. Select the cells you want to search. Select a single cell to search the entire worksheet.

2. Choose the Formula Find command or press Shift+F5 to display the Find dialog box (see fig. 7.18).

3. Type what you are searching for in the Find What box.

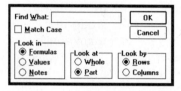

Fig. 7.18. *Use Formula Find to look for values, text in notes, or terms in a formula.*

4. From among the Look In options, select the option that describes the items you want to search through:

   Formulas   Search through formulas in the cells indicated.

   Values   Search through values in the cells indicated.

   Notes   Search through notes attached to the cells indicated. (Notes are hidden descriptive text that can be attached to cells.)

5. Select one Look At option to define how much of the cell contents must match:

   Whole   The entire cell contents must match.

   Part   A part of the cell contents must match.

6. Select the Look By option that describes the direction in which you want the search to proceed:

   Rows   Search across rows starting at the current cell.

   Columns   Search down columns starting at the current cell.

7. Choose OK to find the next match, or press Shift and choose OK to find the previous match. Choose Cancel to stop finding items.

After you have completed step 7 and find the item, edit the formula with normal editing procedures.

To quickly find the next cell that satisfies the same conditions, press F7 to find the next occurrence, or press Shift+F7 to find a previous occurrence.

Formula Find cannot be used with comparative operators such as =, <, and >=. For example, entering <12 in Cell Find creates a search for the text <12 rather than for numbers less than 12. If your data is properly laid out, you can search on many different criteria using the techniques described in the database chapters.

You can search for "near misses" by using wildcards. You can use an * in the Find What box to search for any group of characters, numbers, or cell references, and use a ? to search for any single character or part of a cell reference. For example, if you type =B12*(C3+*) in the Find What box, Excel will look for formulas that have anything as the last term in the parentheses. If you type =B?, Excel will find formulas with first terms that are relative references in the B column.

> **Tip: *Finding External Reference Formulas***
> Find cells linked to other cells, worksheets, or Windows programs by searching for occurrences of an exclamation mark. Use the Look in Formulas and the Look at Part options.
>
> To find cells that feed into the current formula or cells that depend upon the current formula, use the Formula Select Special command and select the Precedents or Dependents options. The Direct Only and All Levels options indicate how many levels of precedents or dependents should be selected.

Making Multiple Changes with Formula Replace

The Formula Replace command is a big help when you overhaul a worksheet. The command works the same way as a search-and-replace command does in a word processing program. You tell Excel what the new text will be and what text it will replace. You can replace selectively or replace throughout the entire worksheet.

Formula Replace can save you from financial mistakes. If you must make major changes to a term or formula used throughout a worksheet, missing a single formula can have dire consequences. With Formula Replace, you can be sure that you have found and replaced all the incorrect formulas or terms.

To search and replace, follow these steps:

1. Select the cells you want to search. Select a single cell to search the entire worksheet.

2. Choose the Formula Replace command to display the Replace dialog box (see fig. 7.19).

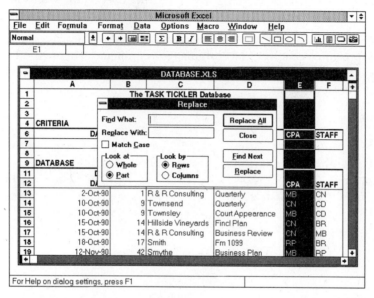

Fig. 7.19. *The Formula Replace command is valuable for making changes quickly throughout your worksheet or database.*

3. Select the Find What box and type the text, cell reference, or formula term to be replaced.

4. Select the Replace With box and type the replacement text.

5. Select the Look At option:

Whole	The text in the Find What box must match the entire cell contents.
Part	The text in the Find What box can match any part of the cell contents.

6. Select the Look By option:

Rows	Search across each row.
Columns	Search down each column.

7. Choose the Replace **A**ll button to find and replace all matches, **F**ind Next to find the next match, or **R**eplace to replace the current found item. Choose Close to stop the **R**eplace command and put away the dialog box. Choosing Close does not undo replacements that already have occurred.

If you need to undo changes you have made, choose the Undo Replace command.

To search for items to replace, you can use the * and ? wildcards as described in the previous section on the Formula Find command. This method can be a very efficient way to change formulas or database contents in a portion or in the entire worksheet.

> **Tip:** *Recalculating Selected Portions of a Worksheet*
> To recalculate only selected cells on a worksheet, select all the cells you want to recalculate, then use the Formula Replace command to replace the equal signs (=) with equal signs (=). This causes each formula to recalculate as though it were reentered. However, the results of this method may be inaccurate if you do not include all cells involved in the calculations.

Editing Absolute and Relative References

To change an absolute or relative cell reference that is already entered in a formula, follow these steps:

1. Select the formula.

2. Move the insertion point to the cell reference you want to change.

3. Press F4 to cycle through combinations of absolute and relative cell references.

4. When the formula is displayed correctly, press Enter.

Figure 7.20 shows a formula bar with the insertion point in a cell reference before F4 was pressed. Figure 7.21 shows the effect of pressing F4 one time.

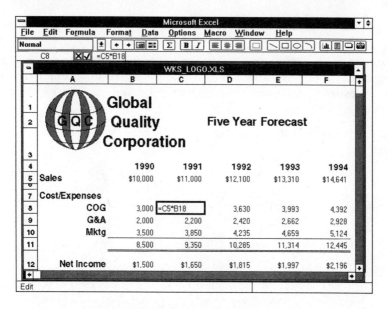

Fig. 7.20. *Move the insertion point next to the cell reference you want to change.*

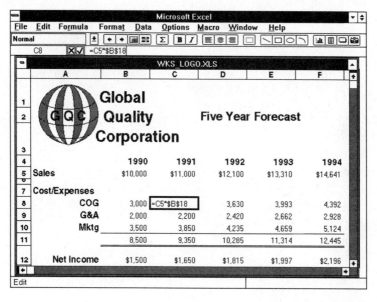

Fig. 7.21. *Each press of the F4 key changes the mix of absolute and relative references.*

Entering New Cell References

Using the same techniques you used to create formulas, you can edit formulas to change or add new cell references. You can enter new cell references by typing them, pointing to them and clicking on them, or moving to them with the movement keys.

To insert a new cell reference or range into an existing formula, follow these steps:

1. Position the insertion point in the formula bar where you want the new cell reference or range. Select a cell reference or range you want to completely replace. (Drag across it with the pointer or use Shift+arrow keys.)

2. Type or point to the new cell reference.

Type or click on the new cell reference. If your new reference is a range, click on one corner and drag to the opposite corner.

Type the new cell reference or press the movement keys to move to the cell you want as the new reference. To include a range in the formula, press the movement keys to move to one corner of the range, hold down Shift, and move to the opposite corner of the range.

Watch the formula bar as you perform step 2. The new cell reference replaces the old.

3. Add cell references, or choose OK or press Enter. Press Esc to back out of your changes.

> **Tip: *Adding Names or Distant Cell References to Formulas***
> If you are adding cell references to a formula by pointing to them, you can go to the distant location by pressing the F5 key. Once there, you can select that cell or another close by. If the cell or range you want to add is in the Goto box that appears after pressing F5, choose the name from the Goto box. The name will appear in the formula, and the selected named cells will display.

Pasting Names and Functions into Formulas

If you have named cell ranges or are using Excel's prebuilt functions, you can paste existing names or functions into formulas. Excel lets you choose the name or function you want from a list, and then paste it into a formula. This is easier and more accurate than typing.

To paste a name or function into an existing formula, follow these steps:

1. Move the insertion point in the formula bar to where you want the name or function.

2. Choose Formula Paste Name to display the dialog box shown in figure 7.22, or choose Formula Paste Function to display the dialog box shown in figure 7.23.

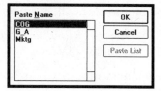

Fig. 7.22. The Paste Name dialog box.

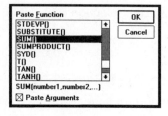

Fig. 7.23. The Paste Function dialog box.

3. From the list box, select the name or function you want to paste.

4. Choose OK or press Enter.

Tip: *Double-Clicking To Save Time*
You can select from most list boxes and choose the OK button simultaneously by double-clicking on your selection in the list.

Changing Worksheet Layout

After you have drafted and tested your worksheet, you may find that you need to reorganize or restructure the layout of the worksheet. This is especially true if you inherit old worksheets or need to convert old Lotus 1-2-3 spreadsheets. When you restructure, you may need to delete or insert cells, rows, and columns.

Shortcut keys that are very helpful to reorganizing the worksheet layout are shown in table 7.8.

Table 7.8
Shortcut Keys for Changing the Worksheet Layout

Key	Action
Del	Clears selected cells; same as **Edit Clear**. Select whether to clear **All**, **Formats**, or **Formulas**.
Ctrl+Del	Clears selected formulas; same as **Edit Clear** with **Formulas** selected.
Backspace	Clears the formula bar; activates and clears formula bar.
Ctrl+Ins	Copies the selection so it can be pasted; same as **Edit Copy**.
Shift+Del	Cuts the selection so it can be pasted; same as **Edit Cut**.
Shift+Ins	Pastes at the selected cell; same as **Edit Paste**.
Alt+backspace	Undoes last command from **Edit** menu.
Ctrl+backspace	Repositions the worksheet so that the active cell is in view.

Clearing Cell Contents

Excel gives you alternatives when clearing or erasing cells. You can clear or erase everything in a cell or range, erase the format only, erase the formulas only, or erase the notes only.

Note: *Clear and Delete Do Different Jobs*
When many people first use Excel, they make the mistake of choosing the **Edit Delete** command to remove the contents of a cell. They should use the **Edit Clear** command. The **Edit Delete** command removes the actual cell from the worksheet, like pulling a brick out of a wall. The **Edit Clear** command leaves the cell in place, but erases the cell's contents.

Note: *Never Use the Space Bar To Clear or Erase*
Novice worksheet users commonly think they can type a blank space and then press Enter to erase a cell's contents. Beware! Blank spaces create problems. For example, in some worksheet functions and database commands, Excel does not see that cell as blank, but as a cell containing a blank character. Uncovering this problem can be difficult.

To clear the contents of a cell, follow these steps:

1. Select the cell or range of cells you want to clear.

2. Choose **Edit Clear** or press the Del key to display the Clear dialog box (see fig. 7.24).

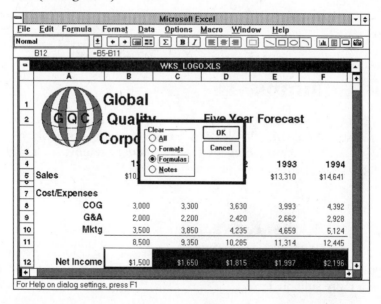

Fig. 7.24. *Pressing the Delete (Del) key enables you to clear different characteristics of a cell.*

3. Select the button that describes what you want cleared:

All	Clears cell contents and notes; returns the format to General format.
Formats	Returns the format to General format.
Formulas	Clears formulas but does not change formats or notes.
Notes	Clears notes but does not change formulas or formats.

4. Choose OK or press Enter.

If you want to clear other cells immediately after this, you can save steps by choosing **Edit Repeat Clear**.

If you accidentally clear a cell's contents, *immediately* choose the **Edit Undo** command. This command undoes your most recent edit.

Cells that have been cleared appear as zeros to formulas. Clearing cells may cause formulas that depend on those cells to produce errors. To find formulas with errors, choose the **Formula Select Special** command and select the **Formula** option. Turn off all the check boxes, but leave the **Errors** check box selected; then choose OK or press Enter. All cells containing error values (such as #NAME?) are selected. Press Tab to move between the selected cells.

Deleting and Inserting Cells, Rows, and Columns

With Excel, you can delete or insert entire rows or columns. You also can easily delete or insert cells, leaving the surrounding rows or columns unaffected. This technique enables you to add or remove cells without having to change entire rows or columns.

Deleting Cells, Rows, and Columns

The **Edit Delete** command removes cells, rows, or columns from the worksheet. This command is useful when rearranging your worksheet to give it a more suitable layout.

Edit Delete is different than the **Edit Clear** command. The **Edit Clear** command clears a cell's contents or format, but it leaves the cell intact. **Edit Delete** completely removes cells, rows, or columns; it doesn't just remove their contents.

When **Edit Delete** deletes cells, it completely removes the selected cells and "slides in" other cells to fill the gap. You can choose the direction in which remaining cells will move. Figures 7.25 and 7.26 show a worksheet before and after cells were deleted. The lower cells were moved up to fill the gap. Notice that the worksheet area to the right of the deleted cells was not affected. **Edit Delete** is an excellent command for sliding rows or columns into a new location without affecting adjacent cells.

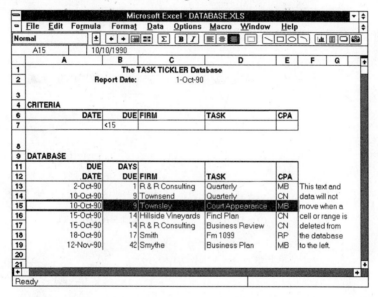

Fig. 7.25. *A worksheet before cells are deleted.*

When you need to *remove* cells, rows, or columns from the worksheet, follow these steps:

1. Select the cells or range to be deleted, or select cells in the rows or columns to be deleted.

2. Choose the **Edit Delete** command, or press Ctrl + – (minus). The Delete dialog box appears (see fig. 7.27).

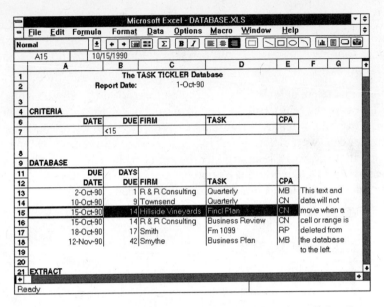

Fig. 7.26. Surrounding cells fill in the gap after cells have been deleted.

3. If you want to delete cells, select the direction in which you want remaining cells to move:

Shift Cells Left   Cells to the right of the deleted cells move left.

Shift Cells Up   Cells below the deleted cells move up.

 If you want to delete the row(s) or column(s) containing the selected cells, select one of the options:

Entire Row   Deletes each row containing a selected cell.

Entire Column Deletes each column containing a selected cell.

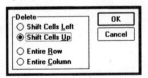

Fig. 7.27. Delete dialog box.

4. Choose OK or press Enter.

To undo an incorrect deletion after making it, choose Edit Undo Delete immediately.

You can delete rows or columns quickly by selecting the entire row or column and then using the Edit Delete command or pressing Ctrl+ – (minus). (Click on row or column headings to select the entire row or column, or press Shift+space bar to select a row and Ctrl+space bar to select a column.)

Depending on the design and layout of the worksheet, deleting cells, rows, or columns that contain information used by formulas can cause errors. Because the cell and its contents no longer exist (the deleted cell is not just blank; it's gone), formulas that used that cell cannot find a cell to reference. They will produce a #REF! error. To make sure you do not delete rows or columns containing formulas or values, first select the rows or columns and then use the Formula Select Special command to see if they contain formulas or values.

> **Tip: *Excel Preserves Ranges If You Delete a Range Boundary***
> In Lotus 1-2-3, if you delete a row or column that contains a range boundary, formulas and functions that depend on that range "blow up"; you also will lose the ranges stored in menus. If you delete a row or column on a range boundary in Excel, Excel reduces the range to compensate. In other words, with Excel you can delete the last row of a database or SUM column without producing errors and destroying your worksheet.

Inserting Cells, Rows, and Columns

Sometimes you must insert cells, rows, or columns to make room for new formulas or data. You can insert cells, rows, or columns as easily as you can delete them.

To insert cells, rows, or columns, follow these steps:

1. Select a cell or range of cells where you need new cells inserted. Or select cells in the rows or columns where you want to insert rows or columns.

2. Choose the Edit Insert command, or press Ctrl+ + (plus). The Insert dialog box appears (see fig. 7.28).

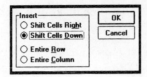

Fig. 7.28. Insert dialog box.

3. If you want to insert cells, select the direction you want selected cells to move when blank cells are inserted:

Shift Cells **R**ight   Selected cells move right.

Shift Cells **D**own   Selected cells move down.

If you want to insert rows or columns, select the option button:

Entire **R**ow   Insert a row at each selected cell.

Entire **C**olumn   Insert a column at each selected cell.

4. Choose OK or press Enter.

In figure 7.29, a range of cells has been selected where blank cells will be inserted. Figure 7.30 shows the results after insertion. Notice that the data in the cells to the right of the inserted area, F15:F16, has not moved. Only the cells below the insertion move down to make room for the inserted cells.

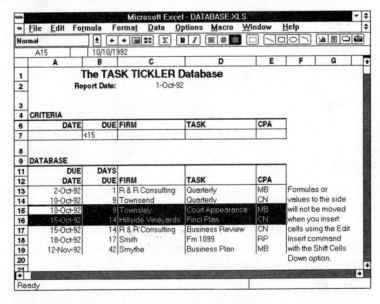

Fig. 7.29. Cells will be inserted in the selected range.

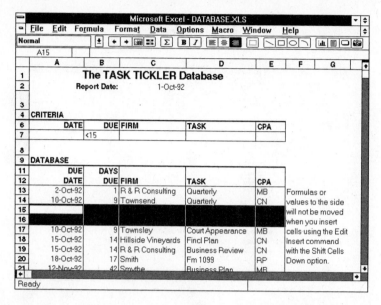

Fig. 7.30. *Existing cells move to make room for inserted cells.*

Excel takes some of the work out of inserting. In most cases, when you insert a row or group of cells, you want each inserted cell to have the same format as the cell above. Excel automatically formats the inserted row or cells with the format above. If you don't want this format, use the method described in Chapter 8 to format the new cells.

Moving Cell Contents

Cutting and pasting is a valuable function for reorganizing your worksheet. You "cut out" a range of cells and "paste" them elsewhere. This operation moves cell contents, the format, and any note attached to the moved cells.

Formulas remain the same when you move them by cutting and pasting. You do not need to worry about relative and absolute cell references. To move a cell or a range to a new location, follow these steps:

1. Select the cell or range you want to move.

2. Choose **Edit Cut**, or press Shift+Del. The cells you have selected appear surrounded by a *marquee*—a moving dashed line like the one shown in figure 7.31.

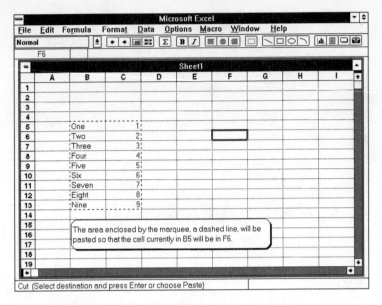

Fig. 7.31. The marquee—a dashed line—shows the cut range.

3. Select the cell at the upper left corner of where you want the pasted cells.

4. Choose **Edit Paste**, or press **Enter**.

The cells you selected in the first step are cut out and moved to the location you indicated. The area from which they were cut is blank and has a General format. If you accidentally paste over existing data or formulas, choose the **Edit Undo** command. (Pasting over existing cells replaces the cell's previous content and format with the pasted content and format.)

You need to select only the upper left corner of the new location. The move procedure is similar to moving a picture from one place on a wall to another. You do not need to describe where all four corners of the picture go; you need to specify only the upper left corner.

As you select the range to cut, notice the Reference Area at the left of the formula bar; it shows you the size of the range you are cutting out (for example, 8R X 4C). This will help you determine whether you can move the data without pasting over existing cells and replacing their contents.

 In some cases you can move cells into a new location and move existing cells aside. This technique uses the **Insert Paste** command. To insert pasted cells, follow these steps:

1. Select the cells you want to move.

2. Choose the **Edit Cut** command, or press Shift+Del.

Figure 7.32 shows a cut range marked by the marquee.

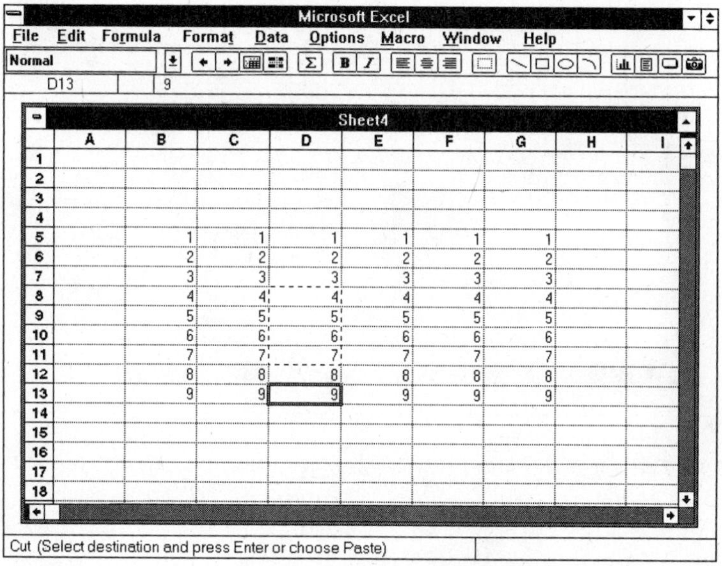

Fig. 7.32. The marquee encloses cells to be cut out.

3. Select a cell in the same row or column as the top left corner of the original range you selected. In the figure, cell D13 is the cell where the pasting occurs.

4. Choose the **Insert Paste** command. Figure 7.33 shows where the inserted cells are and where the previous cells have moved.

The cells you cut will insert themselves. The contents of the existing cells will move to fill the vacuum left by the cut cells. The Insert Paste command is only available when the cell selected to paste into is in the same row or column as the top left cell of the cut cells.

Copying Cell Contents

You can save yourself a lot of data-entry time with Excel's Copy and Fill commands. Instead of typing each formula in a worksheet, you can type a few formulas and copy or fill them into other cells. You even can copy the formula and format at the same time.

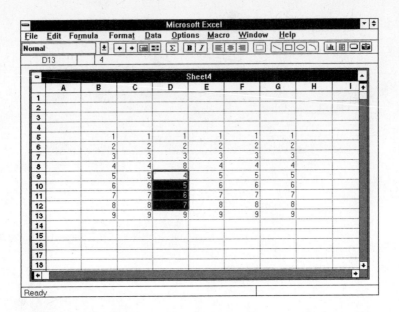

Fig. 7.33. Existing cells move to make room for cells entered with Insert Paste.

> **Note: *Copying Formulas May Produce Errors from Relative References***
> Some formulas will not produce the correct results when copied because cell references within the formulas change relative to their new cell locations. Always cross-check copied or filled formulas to ensure that they produce reasonable results. If you suspect an error, review the descriptions of relative and absolute cell references.

Filling Any Direction

Worksheets would take a long time to build if you had to type every formula. In many cases, you can use the same or similar formula across a row or down a column. The Edit Fill commands let you fill an existing formula into adjacent cells. In many cases, this is easier than using a Copy command.

You can fill cells left or right across a row and up or down a column. To fill cells to the right or down, follow these steps:

1. Select the row or column you want to fill. The cell containing the formula or value used to fill other cells must be on the outside edge. Figure 7.34 shows cells in the worksheet selected prior to filling.

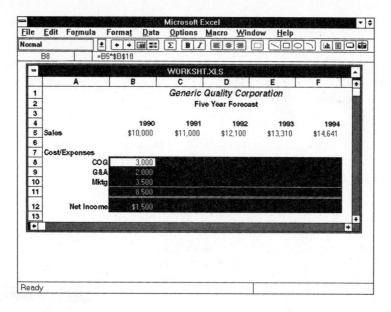

Fig. 7.34. *Select the original cells and the cells you want filled.*

2. Choose **E**dit Fill Rig**h**t to fill right, or choose **E**dit Fill Do**w**n to fill
down from the dialog box. To fill up or left, hold down the Shift
key as you choose the **E**dit command and select **E**dit Fill Left (**h**) or
Edit Fill Up (**w**). Figure 7.35 shows the resulting filled cells.

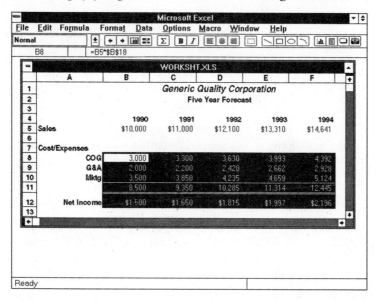

Fig. 7.35. *The Fill commands fill the original formula or value into the rest of*
the range.

3. Check to see that the filled formulas have produced reasonable answers.

The result of an Edit Fill command is the same as copying. Relative references adjust to their new locations. Duplicated formulas or values replace any cell contents they cover.

Shortcut keys for filling are Ctrl+> to fill right and Ctrl+< to fill down.

If you are filling an area involving hidden rows or columns or outlines, you may want to fill visible areas only. To avoid filling these hidden areas, choose the Formula Select Special command with the Visible Cells option, or click the Select Visible button in the tool bar after you select the cells in the first step.

> **Note:** *Filling Cells as You Enter Data or Formulas*
> You can fill cells as you enter data or formulas if you first select the cells or ranges to be filled. (You can fill nonadjacent ranges.) Next, type the formula or value in the active cell. Instead of pressing Enter, press Ctrl+Enter. Formulas and values are copied into all selected cells just as though you used a Fill or Copy command.

Copying Cell Contents to New Locations

Copying works well for duplicating values or formulas to cells that are not adjacent to the original. Copying adjusts formulas to their new locations. Other chapters in the book describe how copying is also used to transfer information to other Windows applications, link worksheets together, and link worksheets and charts.

To copy a cell or range to a new location, follow these steps:

1. Select the cell or range of cells you want to copy. As you copy, check the size of the range you are copying by watching the Reference Area to the left of the formula bar.

2. Choose the Edit Copy command, or press Ctrl+Ins. The cells to be copied appear surrounded by a marquee (a moving dashed line).

3. Select the cell at the top left corner of where you want the duplicate to appear. Check to see if other cell contents will be written over. If needed cells will be overwritten, press Esc and use the Edit Insert commands described previously to make room for the duplicate cells.

4. Choose the Edit Paste command or press Shift+Ins to paste and retain the copy in memory. Press Enter to paste one time.

Because the size and shape of the copied area is already established, you need to indicate only the upper left corner of the paste location. Selecting the wrong size area to paste into prevents Excel from pasting and causes an alert box warning to appear.

You can make multiple copies of a range with a single command. Remember to select only the top left corners of where you want each of the duplicate ranges to go. Figure 7.36 shows the marquee around a copied column of formulas and the top of each column where the original column will be pasted. Notice that pasting in multiple columns is like hanging wallpaper: you need to indicate only where the tops of each roll of wallpaper will go; the wallpaper hangs down correctly by itself. Figure 7.37 shows the pasted columns.

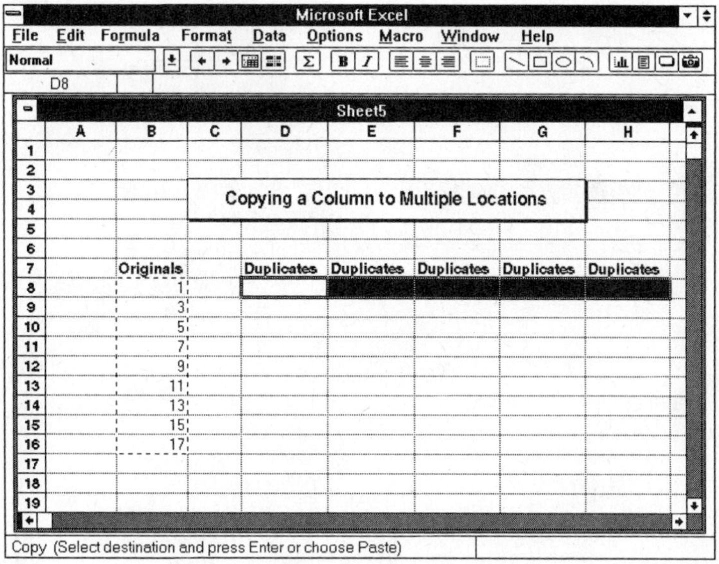

Fig. 7.36. Select the top cell where you want duplicated columns to appear.

Figures 7.38 and 7.39 show how to copy an original row into multiple rows. Notice that only the left cell is selected where each duplicated row will be pasted.

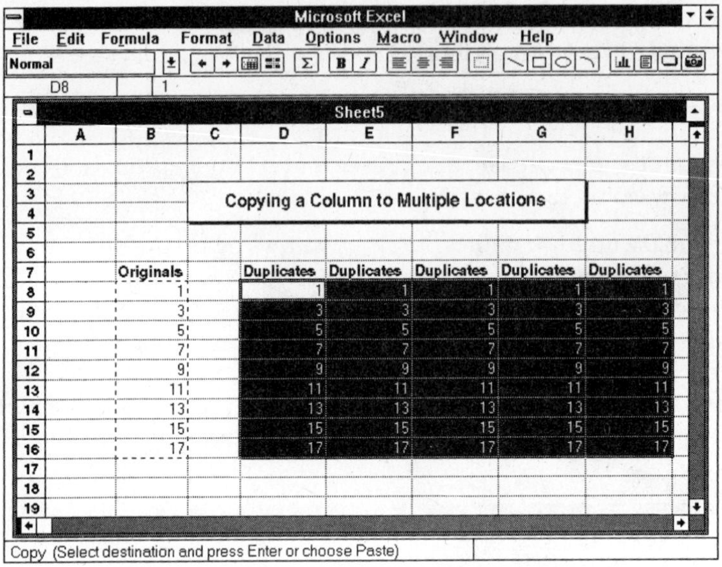

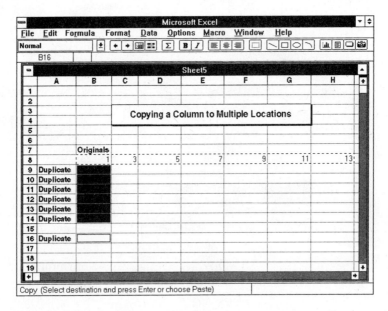

Fig. 7.37. Columns after pasting.

Fig. 7.38. Select the left cell where you want duplicated rows to appear.

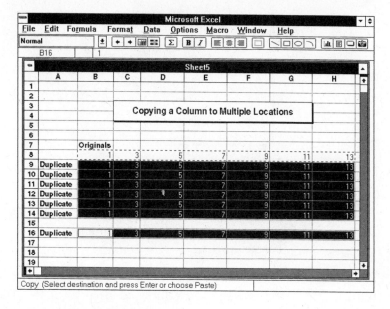

Fig. 7.39. *Rows after pasting.*

Pasting Cell Contents with Special Effects

The Edit Paste Special command is handy when you want to copy and paste part of a cell's contents, such as its format or value, but not both. You can reorient database layouts into worksheet layouts and vice versa. The command also enables you to combine the contents of cells by pasting them together. This feature is very useful when you need to combine or consolidate different parts of a worksheet. (Consolidation is covered extensively in Chapter 12, "Linking and Consolidating Worksheets.")

To use the Edit Paste Special command for any of its many operations, follow these steps:

1. Select the cell or range of cells.

2. Choose the Edit Copy command.

3. Select the upper left corner of where you want to paste.

   If you are transposing (flipping) rows and columns, be sure to consider which cells will be covered when the pasted area is rotated 90 degrees.

4. Choose **Edit Paste Special** to display the dialog box shown in figure 7.40.

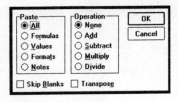

Fig. 7.40. The Edit Paste Special dialog box.

5. Select the characteristics you want transferred:

All   Transfer all of the original's contents and characteristics.

Formulas   Transfer only the formulas.

Values   Transfer only the values and formula results. (This option converts formulas to values.)

Formats   Transfer only the cell format.

Notes   Transfer only note contents.

6. Select from the dialog box how you want the transferred characteristics or information combined with the cells being pasted into:

None   Replace the receiving cell.

Add   Add to the receiving cell.

Subtract   Subtract from the receiving cell.

Multiply   Multiply by the receiving cell.

Divide   Divide into the receiving cell.

7. Select the **Skip Blank** check box if you do not want to paste blank cells on top of existing cell contents.

8. Select the Transpose check box if you want rows changed to columns or columns changed to rows.

9. Choose OK or press Enter.

> **Tip:** *Freezing Formulas into Results*
>
> By copying the range of formulas you want to freeze, you can convert formulas into their results so that they do not change. Then, without moving the active cell, use **Paste Special** with the **Values** and **None** check boxes checked to paste the values over the original formulas.

The Transpose option in the **Paste Special** dialog box can save you time and work if you use database information in your worksheets or worksheet data in your database. The Transpose option rotates a range of cells between row orientation and column orientation. This option is useful for switching between a database's row layout and a worksheet's column layout. You cannot transpose over the range containing the original data. Figure 7.41 shows an original range on the left and its transpose on the right.

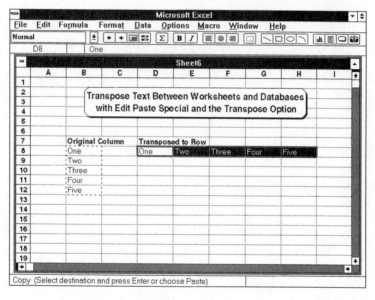

Fig. 7.41. *Transposed ranges, original on left.*

Tacking Notes onto Cells

Notes are messages attached to worksheet or database cells. They appear in special dialog boxes or are printed when you request. You attach notes to cells for two reasons: to preserve your sanity and to preserve your business.

Include in notes any information that is helpful to the next person using the worksheet. That next person might even be you in two months—after you have forgotten how and why the worksheet operates.

You can put many things in a note. For example, in cell A1 put:

- the author's name
- the auditors' names
- the date of the last review for accuracy

In data-entry cells, put the following:

- worksheet's assumptions
- data-entry limits
- the historical significance of a value (such as the high sale of the year)

In formula cells, put the following:

- the origin or verification of a formula
- analytical comments about a result ("Pete, this profit margin is too low!")

Adding, Editing, and Deleting Notes

To add a note to a selected cell, follow these steps:

1. Choose the cell you want the note attached to.

2. Choose the Formula Note command or press Shift+F2 to display the Cell Note dialog box (see fig. 7.42).

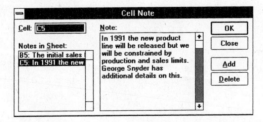

Fig. 7.42. Cell Note dialog box.

3. Enter text in the Note area.

4. Press Enter or choose OK when the note is completed.

A small red dot at the upper right corner of a cell indicates the cell contains a note. To turn these indicator dots on or off in the display, choose the **Options Workspace** command and select or deselect the Note Indicator option. The default setting for the note indicator is on. If you prefer for it to always be off, save a workspace with the Note Indicator deselected and open the workspace when you start Excel. Workspaces are described in Chapter 11, "Building Systems and Managing Multiple Windows."

The Notes in Sheet box lists all the notes in the worksheet preceded by their cell references. When you select a note from the list, the text appears in the Note box, and the cell reference appears in the Cell box. You can view another note by selecting it from the Notes in Sheet list.

The **Add** button adds information from the Note box to the cell shown in the Cell box. This method lets you add new notes to cells without having to return to the worksheet. You can enter cell references in the Cell box by typing them or by clicking in the Cell box and then clicking on the cell in the worksheet.

To edit a note, select the cell and choose the Formula **Note** command. Then edit the note as you normally edit text in Excel. To delete a note, select it from the Notes in Sheet box, and then choose the **Delete** button.

Displaying and Finding Notes

If the Note Indicator option is selected, a red dot appears in the top right of cells containing notes. To display the note behind a cell, double-click on the cell, or select the cell and press Shift+F2. Select all the cells containing notes by choosing the Formula Select Special command and selecting the **Notes** option or by pressing Ctrl+?. Move between the cells containing notes with Tab or Shift+Tab, and press Shift+F2 to read the note behind the cell.

Use the Formula **Find** command to search quickly through cells and find a note that contains a pertinent word. Select the Look in Notes option in the Find dialog box, and choose the Look at **Part** option to find any occurrence of the word in context.

From Here...

You can use the worksheet you created in Chapter 3, "Worksheet Quick Start," to experiment further with different methods of entering formulas and data. If you already have worked through the Quick Start, reopen the worksheet and try some of the data-entry and editing techniques described in this chapter. Chapter 23, "Entering and Sorting Data," describes additional data-entry methods useful with databases.

When you begin editing, you probably will use the Edit menu primarily, but do not stop with the menus. As you gain confidence, try the shortcut keys listed in table 7.8. You will find that you quickly can cut, copy, or paste with just a few keystrokes.

At this point, you will want to work through the next chapter, Chapter 8, "Formatting Worksheets." Chapter 8 shows you how to "dress up" your worksheets. After you have experimented with some of the ideas the chapter contains, you should be ready to build and format your own worksheets.

8

Formatting Worksheets

A ppearance isn't everything, but it counts for a great deal when you need to communicate with confidence. In the eyes of others, your worksheet may have little merit if important information is obscured.

Excel has formatting features that make worksheets and databases easier to read and understand. In addition to changing column widths or selecting predefined numeric and date formats, you can create your own numeric and date formats; change the height of rows; change the font, size, color, and style of characters; hide the grid; and shade or color ranges. With Excel, your printed worksheet or database can look as though it just came from the typesetter. You can drive your point across with emphasis and elegance.

Changing Character Fonts, Sizes, Styles, and Colors

You see different character fonts and styles everyday. *Fonts* are the various typefaces used in printed materials. Font heights are measured in *points;* there are 72 points per inch. Fonts also appear in different styles: plain, bold, italic, underline, and strikeout. Figure 8.1 shows examples of different fonts with various point sizes and styles.

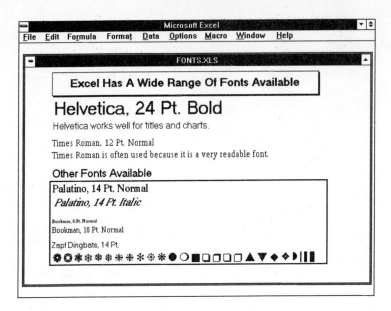

Fig. 8.1. *Excel enables you to use easily the fonts available to your printer.*

Excel can use up to 256 different fonts on a worksheet. If you use more than a few fonts per worksheet, however, your worksheet may look like a ransom note made from assorted magazine clippings.

> **Tip:** *Ensuring Consistency by Formatting with Styles*
> You can save time when formatting by first creating a *style.* A style *associates,* or ties, a group of format preferences to an assigned name. The style name applies the formats collectively. Applying the style name to a cell or range applies all the formats associated with that style name. Changing the definition of a style name changes the format in all cells that have that style. Styles are described near the end of this chapter in the section "Creating Styles."

You can use one of three methods to change the appearance of your data: the menu, the tool bar, or the shortcut keys.

To change the font, size, or style of characters through the menu, follow these steps:

1. Select the cell, range, or multiple ranges.

2. Choose the Format Font command (see fig. 8.2).

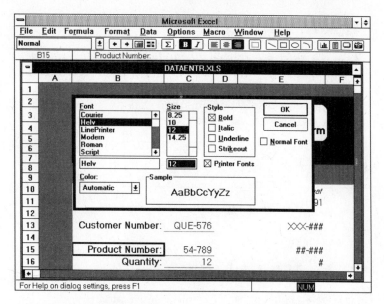

Fig. 8.2. *The Format Font dialog box.*

3. Select the Printer Fonts check box before selecting fonts. When this check box is selected, the Font list shows the fonts that your printer can print. When the check box is deselected, the Font list shows fonts that you can display on-screen.

4. Select the font from the Font list. Check the Sample box to see how that font appears.

5. Select the point size from the Size list. (Recall that there are approximately 72 points per inch of height.)

6. Set the style selection for the font. Select from Bold, Italic, Underline, and Strikeout. Leave all of these check boxes unselected for a font without styling.

7. Select a color from the Color list. Click on the down arrow; or press Alt, C, and then Alt+down arrow.

8. Choose OK or press Enter.

If you want to return the selected cells to the default font style, use the same procedure and select the Normal Font check box.

Using the Tool Bar

The tool bar is a quick way of changing to bold and italic font styles if you are using a mouse. Display the tool bar with the **Options Workspace** command and select **Tool Bar**. To bold or italicize a cell, range, or text selected in a text box, make your selection and then click on the bold or italic icon in the tool bar, as shown in figure 8.3.

Bold icon —— 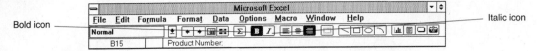 —— Italic icon

Fig. 8.3. Use the tool bar to change fonts to bold and italic.

Using Shortcut Keys

To format selected cells quickly, use these shortcut keys:

Format	*Shortcut key*
Normal style	Ctrl+1
Bold (toggle on/off)	Ctrl+2
Italic (toggle on/off)	Ctrl+3
Underline (toggle on/off)	Ctrl+4
Strikeout (toggle on/off)	Ctrl+5

Aligning Numbers and Text

In an unformatted cell, text aligns against the left edge of the column, and numbers align against the right edge. To enhance your worksheet, you can align values or formula results so that they are left, right, or centered in a cell. You also can easily fill cells with a character that you specify (such as a dash or equal sign) to create lines across your worksheet. Excel also word wraps text within a cell. If the text exceeds the width of the cell, the cell height increases to contain multiple lines.

By using the three Alignment icons on the tool bar, you can quickly align text. To align cell contents with the tool bar, follow these steps:

1. Select the cell or range containing the contents you want to align.

2. Click on the Left, Center, or Right icon in the tool bar (see fig. 8.4).

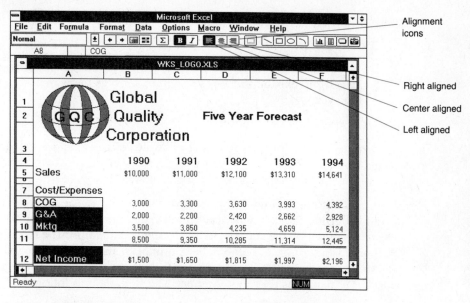

Fig. 8.4. The Alignment icons in the tool bar help you align cell contents.

To use the menu to change the alignment of cell contents, follow these steps:

1. Select the cell or range of cells that you want to format.

2. Choose the Format Alignment command to display the Alignment dialog box (see fig. 8.5).

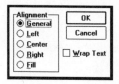

Fig. 8.5. The Alignment dialog box.

3. Select one of the following alignment buttons:

   General aligns text to the left and numbers to the right (the default).

   Left aligns cell contents against the left edge.

   Center aligns cell contents around the cell's center. Characters may extend outside the cell.

Right aligns cell contents against the right edge.

Fill repeats the text to fill the cell.

4. Select the **Wrap Text** check box if you want text to wrap within the cell and expand the row's height to show as many lines as necessary.

5. Choose **OK** or press **Enter**.

To save time when formatting, select multiple cells and ranges and give a single command. Use Ctrl+Drag to select nonadjacent areas with the mouse; or use Shift+F8 to add nonadjacent areas by keyboard.

Figure 8.6 illustrates how the **Wrap Text** option works. The text in cell B4 extends outside the cell, whereas the text with the **Wrap Text** option selected wraps within the cell, B7, to form a single paragraph. The formula in the bar illustrates how to combine text, numbers, and dates within a single cell, as you see in cell B10. The formula bar show the concatenation formula in cell B10 that joins text and numbers. The formula is as follows:

=B12&TEXT(C12,"mmmm")&D12&Text(E12,"$#,##0")&"."

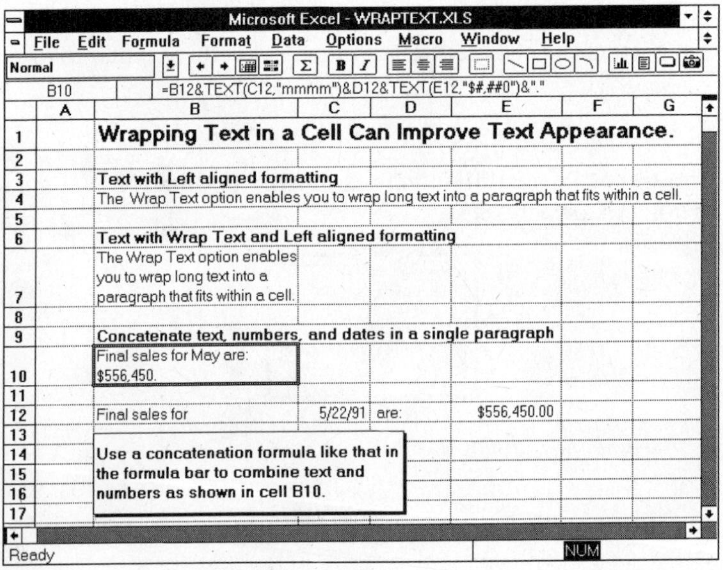

Fig. 8.6. Use Wrap Text to fit paragraphs into a cell.

Justifying Paragraphs

Excel has a primitive word processing function in its Format Justify command. If you want to create a box of text that uses more formatting options, examine the text boxes described in Chapter 9, "Drawing and Placing Graphics in Worksheets."

The Format Justify command takes long strings of text, divides them into lengths that you specify, and reenters each length in its own cell. The result appears as a paragraph with each line starting in the next lower cell. You can use Format Justify to join and wrap strings of text that are not in the same cell. Cell heights do not change as they do with the Wrap Text option of the Format Alignment command.

The worksheet shown in figure 8.7 contains strings of text that would look better if they were of similar length. Cells A2, A3, A4, A6, and A7 contain the text. The selected range, A2 through D12, defines how much space the text can occupy after justification. Choose the Format Justify command, and the text will appear as shown in figure 8.8.

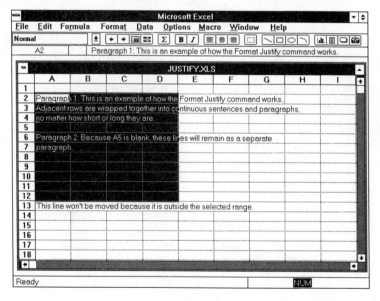

Fig. 8.7. *The selected text will be justified to fit within the selected range.*

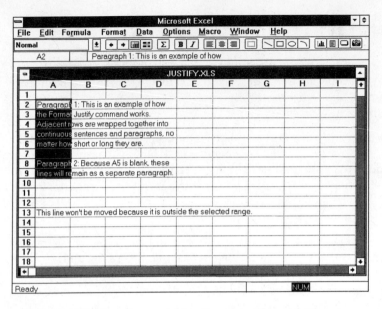

Fig. 8.8. *After justification, the text wraps for a smoother appearance.*

Blank lines occurring in text remain blank after justification. This feature keeps paragraphs separated before and after justifying. Text in adjacent rows, no matter how short a line, merge to form continuous sentences and paragraphs. Data outside the range that you specify does not move when you choose the Justify command.

If the text cannot justify and fit within the range you specify, Excel displays an alert box. If you choose OK rather than Cancel, the text justifies even though it won't fit into the area you specified. The Justify command will not move numbers or formulas down to make way for text; therefore, text may overwrite numbers or formulas.

If you accidentally cover information with justified text, immediately choose the Edit Undo Justify command. When there is insufficient space to justify text, either select a larger area in which to justify the text or move the obstructing information.

Formatting Numbers

Excel has 23 numeric and date/time formats that are already defined. In addition, you can design your own custom formats. These custom formats can contain characters and symbols that you specify, designate the precision you want, and use 16 different colors. The format can even change according to the range of values in the cell.

Cells that have not been used or that have been cut or cleared have the General numeric format. This means that Excel displays a number to the greatest precision possible. If the number is too large or small, the display will appear in scientific format, as for example, 5.367 E+05.

Applying Predefined Numeric Formats

Excel guesses the format you want for a number, depending on the format used when the number is entered. For example, if you enter the number $12.95 into a General format cell, Excel automatically formats the cell for currency ($X,XX0.00). Enter a percentage, such as 15%, and you will see it in the worksheet as 15% (even though it appears in the formula bar as .15).

> **Tip: *When the Column Is Too Narrow for the Display***
> If a cell fills with the characters ####, the column is not wide enough for the number in its current format. To correct this problem, widen the columns. If widening the columns causes formatting problems elsewhere in the worksheet, use the TEXT function to change the number to text. The number or date can then exceed cell width and can have any format, including custom formats. The formula bar in figure 8.6 shows examples of uses of the TEXT function. The custom numeric and date functions are described in a following section.

To format cells for a specific numeric appearance, follow these steps:

1. Select the cells that you want to format.

2. Choose the Format Number command to display the Format Number dialog box (see fig. 8.9).

3. Select the format you want from the Format Number list. Custom formats that you have created appear at the bottom of the list.

4. Choose OK or press Enter.

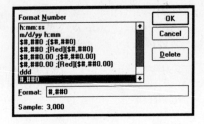

Fig. 8.9. *The Format Number dialog box.*

The Style list on the tool bar includes predefined styles for some numeric formats. Choose Comma for comma format with two decimals, Currency for dollar format with two decimals, and Percentage for the percent format with a percent sign.

Shortcut keys that bypass the Format Number command and immediately format the selected cell include these:

Format	Shortcut Key
General	Ctrl+~
#,##0.00	Ctrl+!
$#,##0.00_);($#,##0.00)	Ctrl+$
0%	Ctrl+%
0.00E+00	Ctrl+^
d-mmm-yy	Ctrl+#
h:mm AM/PM	Ctrl+@

Formats in the Format Number list and custom formats have four parts. These four parts are as follows:

Positive format;Negative format;Zero format;Text format

Notice that each of the formats is separated from the next by a semicolon. The first position specifies the format for positive numbers in the cell, the second for negative numbers, and so on. Although not all these format positions are used in the predefined formats, they are useful with custom formats.

The symbols used in the predefined numeric formats act as placeholders or format specifiers. Notice that the 0 acts as a placeholder and displays a 0 in the number when no number is in that position.

The symbols "_)" following a positive format ensure that positive numbers leave a space on the right the same width as the right parenthesis) on negative numbers. This ensures that positive and negative numbers align evenly down the right edge of the columns. Formatting characters are described in more detail in the next section.

Predefined numeric formats in the Format Number list are as follows:

Format	Number Entered		Formatted Display
	2500	–2500	.5
General	2500	–2500	0.5
0	2500	–2500	1
0.00	2500.00	–2500.00	0.50
#,##0	2,500	–2500	1
#,##0.00	2,500.00	–2500.00	0.50
$#,##0_);($#,##0)	$2,500	($2,500)	$1
$#,##0_);[RED]($#,##0)	$2,500	($2,500)*	$1
$#,##0.00_);($#,##0.00)	$2,500.00	($2,500.00)	$0.50
$#,##0.00_);[RED]($#,##0.00)	$2,500.00	($2,500.00)*	$0.50
0%	250000%	–250000%	50%
0.00%	250000.00%	–250000.00%	50.00%
0.00E+00	2.50E+03	–2.50E+03	5.00E-01
# ?/?	2500	–2500	1/2
# ?/?	2500	–2500	1/2

*This negative number displays in red.

Designing Custom Numeric Formats

You can design your own numeric formats for financial or scientific tasks and create formats for catalog numbers, telephone numbers, international currency, and so forth. Any time you need to display a number in a special way, consider using a custom numeric format.

To create custom formats you can use anywhere on the worksheet, follow these steps:

1. Select the cells that you want to have the custom format.

2. Choose the Format Number command.

3. If an existing format is close to your desired custom format, select that format from the Format Number list.

4. Edit the custom format's pattern in the Format text box, as shown in figure 8.10.

Fig. 8.10. Type custom formats in the Format text box.

5. Choose OK or press Enter.

To test the custom format in the selected cell, type in positive, negative, and zero values and watch the displayed result.

You can reuse this custom format on any cell in the worksheet by scrolling to the bottom of the Format Number list and selecting it as you would a predefined format.

Excel uses a semicolon (;) to separate the formats for positive, negative, and zero formats:

positive format;negative format;zero format

Consider the custom format $#,##0_);($#,##0); "Zero" displays a positive number in the $#,##0 format, a negative number in the ($#,##0) format, and the text Zero for a zero.

Symbols that you can use when creating custom formats are shown in table 8.1.

Table 8.1
Formatting Symbols for Custom Formats

Formatting Symbol	Result
General	Uses the default format for unformatted cells. Displays numbers as precisely as possible for column width. Displays in scientific format for very large or small numbers.
#	Acts as a placeholder for digits. Zero is not displayed if a number is absent. Decimal fractions round up to the number of #'s to the right of the decimal. For example, the value 3.5 with format $#,###.## is displayed as $3.5, and the number .245 as $.25.

Formatting Symbol	Result
0	Acts as a placeholder for digits. Used to display a zero if no number is entered. Decimal fractions round up to the number of 0's to the right of the decimal. For example, the value 3.5 with a format $#,##0.00 is displayed as $3.50, and the number .245 appears as $0.25.
?	Acts as a placeholder for digits in the same way as the 0 does. Insignificant zeros are removed and spaces inserted so that numbers will still align correctly.
_(underscore)	Skips the width of the *character* following the underscore; for example, typing _) at the end of a positive format inserts a blank that is the width of the). This enables a positive number to align correctly with a negative number enclosed in ( ). Without the _), the character at the far right on the positive number would align with the closing) of a negative number.
. (decimal)	Marks the location of the decimal point. Use a 0 to the left of the . (decimal) to indicate a leading zero.
, (comma)	Marks the position of thousands. You need to mark only the location of the first thousand.
%	Multiplies the entry by 100 and displays the number as a percentage with a % sign. A decimal number is actually in the formula bar.
E–E+e–e+	Displays the number in scientific notation. One or more 0's or #'s to the right of the E or e indicate the power of the exponent.
: $ – + ( )	Displays this character in the same position in the formatted number.

continues

Table 8.1 *(continued)*

Formatting Symbol	Result
/ (slash)	Serves as a separator in fractions. Type a decimal fraction, such as 1.667, into the cell; or type a leading integer followed by a fraction, as in 1 2/3, to produce a fractional display of 1 2/3.
\ (backslash)	Indicates a single text character or symbol when it precedes an entry.
"text"	Displays the specified text within quotation marks.
* *character*	Fills the remaining column width with the character following the asterisk (one asterisk per format).
@	Acts as a format code to indicate where text will appear in the format.
[*color*]	Formats cell content with the color specified (described in a later section of this chapter).
[*condition value*]	Uses conditional statements within the number format to specify when a format will be used. Conditions can be <, >, =, >=, <=, and <>. Values can be any number.

Figure 8.11 shows examples of custom formats and how they can be used. The format shown in column C was entered in the Format Number dialog box as a custom format. This format was then used to format the number in column D so that the number is displayed as you see in column E.

Figure 8.12 shows uses for custom numeric formats beyond just formatting numbers.

Display text by enclosing the text in quotation marks and inserting the text elements at appropriate locations between semicolons. If you want a part number always to be preceded by P/N and to show a hyphen before the last three numbers, create a custom format such as the following:

"P/N "####-###;"Use Positive";"Enter Number"

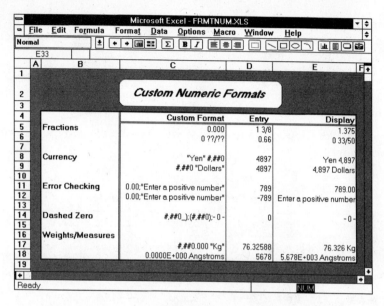

Fig. 8.11. *Use custom formats to design your own numeric formats.*

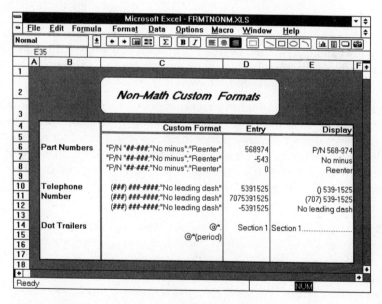

Fig. 8.12. *Custom formats can be used for more than just numbers.*

With this format, the number 5768953 is displayed as P/N 5768-953. Entering a negative number displays the text Use Positive, and entering a zero produces the text Enter Number.

To hide numbers, don't put a format code between semicolons where Excel expects one. For example, in table 8.2, the second example hides negative numbers and zeros.

Table 8.2 gives some examples of ways you can use text and the semicolon to your advantage.

Table 8.2
Custom Formats That Hide Values

Custom Format	Positive	Negative	Zero
$#,###_);($#,###);	$2,500	($2,500)	
$#,###_);;	$2,500		
$#,### ;($#,###);"Zero"	$2,500	($2,500)	Zero
;;	All values hidden, but used in calculation		

A double semicolon hides all numbers. Hidden numbers are still in the worksheet and can be used by other formulas. You will see these numbers in the formula bar if you select a cell containing one of them. Select and reformat cells to redisplay hidden numbers.

Negative numbers enclosed in parentheses will be out of alignment with positive numbers in the same column because of the parentheses around the negative number. Typing _) after the positive format puts a space on the right side of positive numbers to compensate for the) used on the right side of negative numbers. This ensures that positive and negative numbers will align evenly when right aligned.

Tip: *Setting Windows 3 Formats for Your Country*
Set the numeric, date, and time formats throughout your worksheet from the Control Panel. Choose the program Control menu (Alt, space bar) and then the Run command. Select the Control Panel option from the displayed box, and then choose OK. When the Control Panel appears, open the International program. Set the Country, Language, Keyboard Layout, and Measurement you will be using. You may need your installation disks the first time you select another country's formats. After changing countries, you will have that country's formats available within Excel and other Windows programs.

Formatting Cell Contents with Color

Color formats can help you pick up discrepancies in data entry or flag numbers that are out of tolerance. The color format works on a cell along with the numeric or date formats.

You must type the color symbol in the custom format within the portion of the format where you want the color. Color formats in the text position change the color of text. For example, if you want the positive format to be blue and the negative format to be red, use a format such as the following:

[BLUE]$#,##0.00_0;[RED]($#,##0.00)

Colors that you can use include the 8 named colors and any of the custom colors. Mix custom colors with the **O**ptions Color Palette command. Colors on the palette are numbered from top to bottom and from left to right. (The top left is 1; the lower right is 16.) The colors specified by name are as follows:

[BLACK]
[WHITE]
[RED]
[GREEN]
[BLUE]
[YELLOW]
[MAGENTA]
[CYAN]
[COLOR#] (where # is a color numbered from 1 to 16 on the color palette)

Using Formats for Different Values

When you use the [*condition value*] formatting symbol, you can format a cell so that numbers appear in different formats or colors, depending on the value of the number. This technique is especially valuable for error-checking on data entry, for exception reporting from analysis, and for Executive Information Systems.

For example, the following format makes all numbers in the cell use the 0.00 numeric format, but the numbers appear black when greater than or equal to 1,000, red when less than or equal to 500, and blue for any number in between these values:

[BLACK][>=1000]0.00;[RED][<=500]0.00;[BLUE]0.00

Deleting Custom Formats

To remove custom formats, choose the Format Number command, select the custom format from the Format Number list, and choose the Delete button. You cannot delete predefined formats.

Hiding Zeros

Hiding zeros often makes worksheets easier to read. In Excel, you have three options for hiding zeros: hiding them throughout the worksheet, creating a custom format, or using an IF function.

To hide zeros throughout the entire worksheet, choose the Options Display command and deselect the Zero Values box. Select the Zero Values box when you want to see the zeros.

Use a custom format to hide zeros by using the semicolon to indicate a zero format, but do not enter any format for zero numbers. For example:

```
$#,###_);($#,###);
```

In formulas, use an IF function to hide a zero with a formula, such as in the following:

```
=IF(A12+B12=0,"",A12+B12)
```

This formula says that if A12+B12 equals zero, Excel displays what is between the quotation marks, which is nothing. (Beware of using a space to indicate zeros; this causes problems in some databases or numeric and text functions.) If A12+B12 does not equal zero, Excel displays the result of the formula.

Understanding the Danger in Formatted Numbers

The formatted values that appear on-screen may not be the same values used in calculations. This discrepancy can cause the displayed or printed result to be different from manually calculated answers.

Figure 8.13 illustrates this problem. Worksheet columns C and D contain the numeric values. Columns E and G contain the same formula that multiplies the adjacent cells in C and D. Cells E15 and G15 contain SUM( )

functions that sum their respective columns. Notice that the total for columns E and G do not agree with the total of the displayed numbers. Column G has been formatted to appear with two decimal places, but the actual numbers used in calculation have three decimal places. That third decimal place causes the displayed and actual results to appear different.

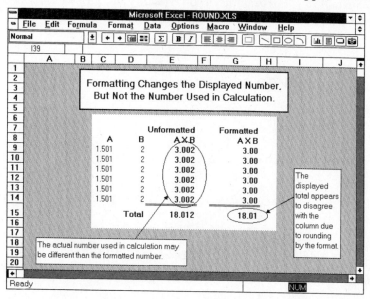

Fig. 8.13. *Formatting rounds the displayed number, but not the calculated number.*

You can resolve the problem either for the entire worksheet or for individual cells. To resolve the problem for the entire worksheet so that the numbers displayed match those used in calculation, choose the **Options Calculation** command and select the **Precision** as Displayed check box. When you choose OK or press Enter, you are warned that constant numbers throughout the worksheet will be permanently rounded to match cell formatting.

A second method enables you to round individual cells. This method uses the ROUND( ) function. For the example in the figure, you would use the formula =ROUND(C9*D9,2) in cell E9. This formula rounds the multiplied value before it is summed. Always round before doing further calculations. Rounding the SUM( ) results in E15 will not solve the problem. Numbers must be rounded before they are totaled.

Formatting Dates and Times

Type dates and times in cells the way you are accustomed to reading or writing them. Excel recognizes dates and times entered in any of the formats shown in table 8.3. For example, if you type the date 1/12/92 into a cell with the General (default) format and then press Enter, the cell is automatically formatted in the m/d/yy format.

Table 8.3
Predefined Excel Date and Time Formats

Format	Example
m/d/yy	12/24/91
d-mmm-yy	24-Dec-91
d-mmm	24-Dec
mmm-yy	Dec-91
h:mm AM/PM	9:45 PM (12-hour clock)
h:mm:ss AM/PM	9:45:15 PM (12-hour clock)
h:mm	21:45 (24-hour clock)
h:mm:ss	21:45:15 (24-hour clock)
m/d/yy h:mm	12/24/88 21:45 (24-hour clock)

If the cell is in the default General format, you do not need to format the cell. Excel changes the General format automatically to agree with the date and time format that you first enter. You can change this format or create a custom format at any time.

If you enter a date or time and see it appear on the left side of the cell, Excel did not interpret your entry as a date or time, but accepted it as text. Check to see if the formula bar shows the date in the pattern m/d/yy. If so, the entry was accepted as a date.

When Excel accepts a date or time, the program automatically calculates the serial number—the number of days from the beginning of this century to the date you enter. (This serial number can be used to perform date arithmetic, such as calculating the days between dates.)

Time is calculated as the decimal portion of 24 hours. To see the serial number in a date/time cell, reformat the cell to General format.

The following shortcut keys can save you time when entering and formatting dates and times:

Shortcut Key	Format Result
Ctrl+;	Insert current date
Ctrl+: (Shift+;)	Insert current time
Ctrl+@	Format h:mm AM/PM
Ctrl+#	Format d-mmm-yy

Using Predefined Date and Time Formats

Regardless of how you enter or calculate the date and time, you can display the date and time in a predefined or custom format. You also can select a different color for the cell's contents or set a format for dates and times within a range.

To change the date and time format of a cell, use the same process as with formatting a number. Select the cells or range of cells that you want to format. Choose the Format Number command, select a date/time format from the list box, and choose OK or press Enter.

Creating Custom Date and Time Formats

If you can't find the date or time format you want, you can create it with the same process used to create custom numeric formats. The only difference is that different formatting symbols are used for date and time formatting. The custom formatting characters you can use for date and time are shown in table 8.4.

Table 8.4
Date and Time Characters for Custom Formats

Type	Display Result
General	Serial date number of days from the beginning of the century. For example, Dec 24, 1991 is 33596. Times appear as decimal portions of 24 hours.
Days	
d	1 to 31, day number; no leading zero.
dd	01 to 31, day number; leading zero.
*Months**	
m	1 to 12, month number; no leading zero.
mm	01 to 12, month number; leading zero.
mmm	Jan to Dec, three-letter abbreviation.
mmmm	January to December, full name of month.
Year	
yy	00 to 99, two-digit year number.
yyyy	1900 to 2078, full-year number.
Hours	
h	0 to 24, hour number; no leading zeros.
hh	00 to 24, hour number; leading zeros.
*Minutes**	
m	0 to 59, minutes; no leading zeros.
mm	00 to 59, minutes; leading zeros.
Seconds	
s	0 to 59, seconds; no leading zeros.
ss	00 to 59, seconds; leading zeros.
AM/PM	am/pm
A/P	Displays the hour using the 12-hour clock.
Separators	
–	Places dash divider between parts.
/	Places slash divider between parts.
:	Places colon divider between parts.

* Excel interprets m characters that follow an h as minutes.

Some examples of custom date formats are shown in table 8.5.

Table 8.5
Custom Date and Time Formats

Format	Display
mmmm d, yyyy	April 1, 1991
d mmm, yy	1 Apr, 92
yy/mm/dd	92/04/01
[BLUE] d mmm, yy	1 Apr, 91 (in blue)
[RED][>=33596] d mmm, yy;d mmm, yy	24 Dec, 91 (in red) 23 Dec, 91 (in black) (The number 33596 is the serial date number of 24 Dec, 91.)

To find the serial date number for a date to use in a conditional format, enter the date in a cell so that it appears in date format and then change the format to General. The serial date number will appear.

Formatting Rows and Columns

You can improve the appearance of your worksheet or database by adjusting column widths and row heights. Appropriate adjustments also help you fit more data on a page. You even can hide confidential data in a row or column. This section describes these tasks.

Adjusting Column Width

You can adjust one or more columns in Excel to get the best appearance in your worksheet or to fit the maximum data on-screen or in a printout. If a column is not wide enough to display a number, date, or time, Excel lets you know by displaying ###### in the cell.

> **Tip:** *Adjusting Columns to the Best Fit*
> Double-clicking on the *column heading* separator on the right side
> will adjust a column to fit its widest contents.

To change one or more column widths, follow these steps:

1. Select the column(s) by dragging the pointer across the column
   headers (see fig. 8.14). You do not need to select the column to
   change a single column. (Select nonadjacent columns with
   Ctrl+Click.)

Column heading

	A	B	C	D	E	F	G	H	I	J	K
1											
2					Five Year Forecast						
3											
4			1990		1991		1992		1993		1994
5	Sales		$10,000		$11,000		$12,100		$13,310		$14,641
6											
7	Cost/Expenses										
8	COG		3,000		3,300		3,630		3,993		4,392
9	G&A		2,000		2,200		2,420		2,662		2,928
10	Mktg		3,500		3,850		4,235		4,659		5,124
11			8,500		9,350		10,285		11,314		12,445
12	Net Income		$1,500		$1,650		$1,815		$1,997		$2,196
13											
14			1990		1991		1992		1993		1994
15	Sales		10,000		NA		NA		NA		NA
16	*Change*		NA		0.10		0.10		0.10		0.10

Fig. 8.14. *Select nonadjacent columns with a Ctrl+Click on each column heading.*

2. Move the pointer onto the vertical line to the right of the column
   heading that you want to widen. For example, to widen column B,
   move onto the line between the B and C headers. The pointer
   changes to a two-headed horizontal arrow.

3. Drag the column left or right until the shadow is where you want it,
   and then release the mouse button.

1. Select cells in the columns that you want to change. Change
   multiple columns by selecting a cell in each column that you want
   changed. Chapter 6 describes how to select adjacent or
   nonadjacent cells.

2. Choose the Format Column Width command (see fig. 8.15).

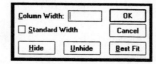

Fig. 8.15. The Column Width dialog box.

3. Enter the column width as the number of Normal style characters.

4. If you want Excel to adjust the column width to fit the longest string of characters in the column, select the Best Fit button.

5. Choose OK or press Enter.

To return column widths to the default setting, select the Standard Width check box.

Hiding Columns

When you generate a database or worksheet for multiple users, you may not want to print all the information that you enter. You can temporarily hide columns so that they do not appear on-screen or print.

To hide selected columns, choose Format Column Width and select the Hide button. Unhide columns by selecting cells that span the hidden column; then choose the Format Column Width command and select the Unhide check box.

Adjusting Row Height

You may want to change row heights to create more space for titles or more space between subtotals and grand totals. The procedure for changing the height of rows is similar to that for changing column widths. Row heights change automatically to accommodate the tallest font in the row. Before making a row height smaller, you may want to make sure that you won't be cutting off the tops of large characters.

To change the height of one or more rows, follow these steps:

1. Select one or more rows. Drag across row headings, or use Ctrl+Click to select nonadjacent rows (see fig. 8.16).

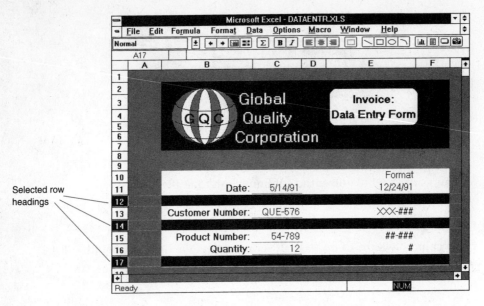

Selected row
headings

Fig. 8.16. Select nonadjacent rows with a Ctrl+Click on each row heading.

2. Move the mouse pointer onto the line below the heading of the row that you want to change. When correctly positioned, the mouse pointer changes to a two-headed vertical arrow.

3. Drag the two-headed arrow up or down until the shadow of the row bottom is where you want it. Then release the mouse button.

1. Select a cell in each row that you want to change.

2. Choose the Format Row Height command (see fig. 8.17).

Fig. 8.17. The Row Height dialog box.

3. Enter the height in the Row Height text box.

4. Choose OK or press Enter.

If you want to return the row to normal height, select the **S**tandard Height check box.

✦ Hiding Rows

To hide rows of information, use the same steps that you use to change the row height. When the Row Height dialog box appears, select the **H**ide button.

Hide selected rows by choosing the Forma**t R**ow Height command and selecting the **H**ide button. Unhide rows by selecting cells that span the hidden row; then choose the Forma**t R**ow Height command and select the **U**nhide check box.

Coloring, Shading, and Bordering Cells

Shading, borders, and even colors can dress up your worksheet or reports to make important information stand out. These features create an impression of high-quality, polished work. This section explains the special formatting changes that you can make.

Shading and Coloring Cells

You can add emphasis and polish to your worksheets by using different shadings and patterns as backgrounds for tables of numbers, as shown in the examples throughout this book. Figure 8.18 shows the 18 black-and-white patterns available. The number shown in each shaded cell is used by the PATTERNS macro function to specify a shade.

You also can create these shadings by using foreground and background colors. Colors can emphasize screen display, output printed to any color-capable Windows-compatible printer, and output projected on-screen with a color screen projector.

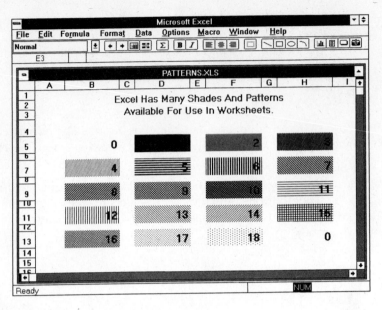

Fig. 8.18. You can choose from 18 patterns.

To add a pattern in black and white or color to your worksheet, follow these steps:

1. Choose the Format Patterns command. The Cell Shading dialog box is displayed, as shown in figure 8.19.

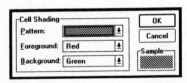

Fig. 8.19. You can use 16 foreground and background patterns.

2. Select a pattern from the Pattern pull-down list.

3. If you want a colored pattern, select a foreground and a background color from the Foreground and Background pull-down list. Check the Sample area in the lower right corner of the dialog box to see the color and shade.

4. Choose OK or press Enter.

You can use as many as 16 colors for the foreground or background. The 16 colors available are specified on the color palette. Use the **O**ptions Color Palette command to change the available colors. This command is described in Chapter 35, "Customizing Excel."

If you use a particular color or shade frequently, assign a color numeric format to a style name. Styles are described later in this chapter.

> **Tip: *Changing the Color of Cell Contents and Gridlines***
> Change the color of cell contents by specifying a color for content using a custom numeric format. These formats are described in a previous section of this chapter.

To change the color of the gridlines and the row and column headings in a worksheet, choose the **O**ptions **D**isplay command and select a color from the Gridline & Heading Color pull-down list.

Adding Borders and Lines

You can place borders around cells or use borders as lines and double-underlines under cells to add emphasis, to define data-entry areas, or to mark totals and subtotals. When combined with shading, borders make your documents easier to read and give them flair.

Borders are displayed better if you turn off the gridlines in a worksheet. Use the **O**ptions **D**isplay command with the **G**ridlines check box deselected to turn off gridlines.

Figure 8.20 shows examples of vertical and horizontal lines created with the Border command.

> **Tip: *Using the Borders Command for Lines***
> Many Lotus 1-2-3 users are accustomed to creating lines or double-underlines by filling cells with dashes or equal signs. Although you can continue to do this in Excel, a more effective method is to use Excel's Forma**t B**order command and select one of the many under-line alternatives.

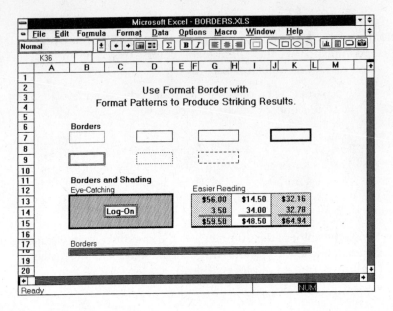

Fig. 8.20. The Format Border commands draw many types and weights of lines.

To add borders (or borders used as lines) on selected cells, follow these steps:

1. Select the cell, range, or multiple ranges.

2. Choose the Format **B**order command (see fig. 8.21).

Fig. 8.21. The Format Border dialog box.

3. Select the part of the cell or range that you want bordered.

4. Select the style of line you want for the border. Use the double-underline style for totals. Press Alt, E, and then use the arrow keys to move between different styles.

5. Select the color you want for the border from the Color drop-down list box. Click on the down arrow or press Alt, C, and then Alt+down arrow. Use the arrow keys to move to the desired color.

6. Choose OK or press Enter.

Outline puts a border around the outside of the selected cells. To put lines inside a range, select one or more of the other options.

Although the Border dialog box includes a Shade check box, use the Format Patterns command to shade. This command offers colors and more levels of shading.

❖ Creating Styles

Styles are a powerful formatting feature in Excel that can save you time and produce more consistent formats. Styles enable you to apply consistently a group of formats. By giving the combined formats a style name, you can apply that combination to cells by choosing the style name, rather than by choosing all the individual formats. If you later change the definition of formats associated with that style, all cells having that style will immediately change to the new definition.

Styles are helpful because they eliminate the need to choose multiple commands for repetitive formats, and they reduce the need to reformat worksheets. If you work in a company where a standard appearance for proposals and presentations is important, styles can ensure that everyone uses consistent formatting. The company can create preferred styles for titles, headings, bodies of financial reports, and totals. Everyone can then use these styles to reduce the workload and produce a consistent corporate image.

A style can contain all the formatting you use for Number, Font, Alignment, Border, Pattern, and Protection. You can even specify which of these format types should not be used in a style so that an existing format in a cell remains after the style is applied. For example, a style can specify a numeric format and font but leave the existing color unchanged.

You can use styles in worksheets, templates, and macro sheets. The default Excel worksheet comes with a few predefined styles: comma, currency, normal, and percent. Normal is the default format for the entire worksheet. Redefining the formats associated with the Normal style changes the format used throughout a worksheet in those cells not affected by special formatting.

Applying a Style

You can apply a style in two ways. Both ways require that you first select the cell or range to which you want the style's formats applied. Then you choose the style from the Style list on the tool bar or from the Format Style dialog box.

If you are using a mouse and the tool bar is displayed, you can quickly choose a style from the tool bar. To apply a style, follow these steps:

1. Select the cell or range that you want to format.

2. Select the Style list in the tool bar by clicking on the down arrow (see fig. 8.22).

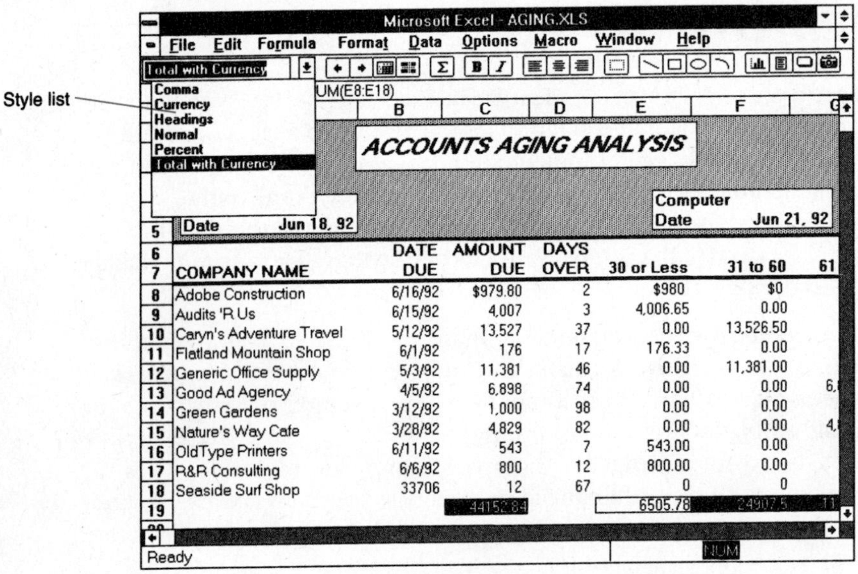

Fig. 8.22. The Style list is displayed on the left side of the tool bar.

3. Click on the name of the style that defines the formats you want to apply.

If you have a large number of style names in the worksheet, you may find it quicker to select the Style box in the tool bar, type in a name, and press Enter.

To apply a style using the dialog box, follow these steps:

1. Select the cell or range you want the style applied to.

2. Choose the Format Style command (see fig. 8.23).

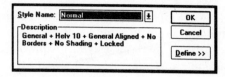

Fig. 8.23. The Format Style dialog box.

3. Select the style name from the Style Name list box, or type the name in the box (see fig. 8.24). When you select or type the name, the Description box shows the formats that are contained in that style.

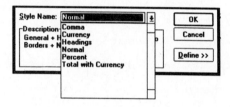

Fig. 8.24. The Format Style dialog box with the list displayed.

4. Choose OK or press Enter.

Whether a style's formats overwrite existing formats in a cell depends on whether the Style Includes box was selected to override conflicting styles (the Style Includes box drops down when you select **Define**). For example, if **P**attern in the Style Includes box was deselected when the style was created, you can use the style on any cell without changing the existing pattern in the cell.

Creating or Copying Styles

You can create styles in three different ways. You can create them by using the format in a cell as an example; you can create them by choosing formats from dialog boxes; or you can use *merge* to use styles that exist on another worksheet.

Creating a Style by Example

If there is a cell on the worksheet or macro sheet that already has the formats you want associated with a style, you can use the formats in the cell to define a new style. You can use this method of *style by example* to create styles with either the tool bar and mouse or with the Format Style command.

To create a style with the tool bar, follow these steps:

1. Select the cell that contains the formats you want in a style.

2. Type the new style name in the Style box on the tool bar.

3. Press Enter to create the new style, or press Esc to back out.

To create a style by example by using commands, follow these steps:

1. Select a cell containing the formats you want in a style.

2. Select the Format Style command.

3. Type the new style name in the Style Name text box.

4. Choose OK or press Enter.

Notice that you can read a description of what the current cell's formatting contains—what the new style will contain—in the Description box within the dialog box.

Creating a Style through Commands

If you do not have a mouse or if an example does not exist in the document, you can define a style by selecting formats just as you would select formats from the Format commands dialog boxes.

To define a style using the Format Style command, follow these steps:

1. Choose the Format Style command.

2. Select the Style Name list box, and type a new name. You will not be warned if you are about to change an existing style. To make sure that you are not using an existing name, click on the down arrow and scroll through the list; or press Alt, S, then Alt+down arrow and scroll down.

3. Choose the Define >> button to expand the dialog box (see fig. 8.25).

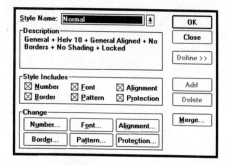

Fig. 8.25. *The expanded Styles dialog box enables you to define styles.*

4. Select the formats you want to associate with this style by selecting the appropriate check boxes in the Styles Includes box. Any formats with the check box deselected will not be used in the style.

5. Select an available formatting button from the Change box.

6. In the Format dialog box that appears, select the formatting options you want to associate with the style. Choose OK or press Enter.

When you select a Change button, such as Number, the dialog box that corresponds to its Format command will appear. For example, if you choose the Number button, the Format Number dialog box will be displayed (see fig. 8.26).

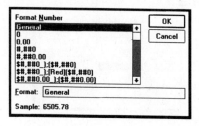

Fig. 8.26. *Change buttons display the same formatting dialog boxes as do the Format commands.*

7. Repeat steps 5 and 6 until the style contains the formatting you want, as defined in the Description box.

8. If you want to keep this style and define more, choose the Add button. If you want to keep this style and apply it to the selected cells, choose OK or press Enter. If you want to keep this style, but not apply it to the selected cells, choose Close.

Deselecting a format check box under Styles Includes does two things. While the Styles dialog box is open, it grays the corresponding button under Change so that this format cannot be changed. Once the style is defined and you apply it to a cell already containing formats, the cell will keep its original formatting for those formats that were deselected in the Styles Includes box.

Copying Styles between Documents

You may have worksheets or macro sheets that contain the styles you want on other worksheets and macro sheets. You can copy styles between documents through a process called *merging*. But you must take into consideration that all styles from the source document are merged in; unless you specify otherwise, these will replace styles in the target document having the same name.

To copy styles from a source document to a target document, follow these steps:

1. Open both documents and activate the document that will receive the styles.

2. Choose the Format Styles button.

3. Choose the Define >> button.

4. Choose the Merge button (see fig. 8.27).

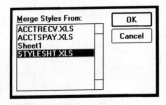

Fig. 8.27. The Merge Styles From dialog box.

5. Select from the Merge Styles From list the source document that contains the styles you want to copy.

6. Choose OK (see fig. 8.28).

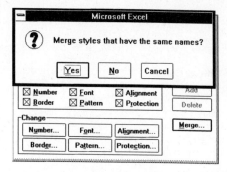

Fig. 8.28. *Excel asks if you want to replace existing style names with merging styles that have the same name.*

7. If the source document contains styles with the same name as the target document, select one of these alternatives:

Yes, if you want the source styles to replace styles with the same name in the target document.

No, if you want to merge all styles except those with the same name.

Cancel, if you don't want to merge styles.

8. Choose the Close button to close the dialog box without applying a style.

Redefining a Style

In addition to saving time used in applying multiple formats, styles also save you time when you need to reformat a document. If your document uses styles, you need only to redefine the style, and all cells using that style will immediately reformat to match the style's new definition.

If you decide that you need a format different from the one used in an existing style, you have two choices: either create a new style for use with new formatting or redefine an existing style. The advantage to redefining an existing style is that all cells that currently have that style will update to use the new formats in the redefined style. This makes it easy for you to reformat all the headings, titles, dates, or totals in a document. For example, if you redefine the formats associated with a style named Headings, all cells that use the Headings style will take on the new format definition.

Redefining a Style by Example

To redefine a style using an example, follow these steps:

1. Select a cell that is formatted with the style you want to redefine.

2. Format that cell so that it has the new formats you want for the style's definition.

3. Apply the style name to the cell as you did when you first applied the style. Use either the tool bar or the Format Style command.

4. When the dialog box appears (see fig. 8.29), choose one of these alternatives:

   Yes, to redefine the existing style.

   No, to keep the existing style and apply it again to the cell.

   Cancel, to make no changes to the style or cell.

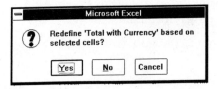

Fig. 8.29. This dialog box appears when you redefine a style by example.

Redefining a Style through Dialog Boxes

If a style is complicated or if you know exactly how you want to redefine the style, you will want to redefine the style through dialog boxes. To redefine a style through dialog boxes, follow these steps:

1. Choose the Format Style command.

2. Choose the Define button to expand the dialog box.

3. If you want to see the existing style description in the Description box, select the style name from the Style Name box. If you want to see a description of the formats in the selected cell, type the name of the style in the Style Name box.

4. Deselect check boxes in the Styles Includes box that you do not want the style to have.

5. Select the Change buttons and make the changes you desire to the formats defined for the style.

6. Choose OK to redefine the style and apply it to the current cell; or choose Add to redefine the style and keep the dialog box open for more definitions; or choose Close to close the dialog box without applying the style to the selected cell.

Redefining the Default (Normal) Style

The default, or global, format is stored in Excel's Normal style format. If you type an unformatted cell, the Normal style is used. If you redefine the Normal style, all the cells that you did not format separately will change to match the new Normal definition.

To redefine the Normal style, redefine the formats associated with the Normal style. Use either the style by example or the dialog box method to redefine the Normal style.

Deleting a Style Name

If you no longer use a style, delete it to prevent clutter and make other styles more accessible. To delete a style, follow these steps:

1. Choose the Format Style command.

2. Select the style that you want to delete. Predefined styles cannot be deleted.

3. Choose the Define button.

4. Choose the Delete button.

5. If you want the cell to return to Normal style, choose OK or Close. If you want to apply a new style, select the style and choose OK.

Controlling the Worksheet Display

You can change many characteristics of Excel's worksheet display so that worksheets and databases are displayed with custom appearance. By removing gridlines, row and column headings, and scroll bars, you can create windows that appear to be custom programmed.

Formatting the Entire Worksheet

Set formats when you begin your worksheet. After planning your worksheet and drawing thumbnail sketches, set the entire worksheet to the most common formats that you plan to use. To set formats for the entire worksheet *before* you make any other entries, follow these steps:

1. Select the entire worksheet by clicking to the left of the column A header or by pressing Shift+Ctrl+space bar.

2. Choose the format commands.

3. Use the worksheet—or save the worksheet as a template or workspace if you want to preserve these formats and workspace settings for future use.

Hiding Row and Column Headings

You can create special displays in Excel for data-entry forms, on-screen information, and help screens. These displays appear as they would in an uncluttered paper printout when you remove row and column headings. Choose the **Options Display** command and deselect the **Row & Column Headings** check box. This action does not affect the row and column headings for printing.

Displaying Formulas

You will want to display formulas on-screen or in your printout at particular times: when debugging your worksheet (finding and correcting problems), when reviewing an unfamiliar worksheet, or when printing a documentation copy of the worksheet for future reference. To show the formulas in a worksheet, choose the **Options Display** command and select the **Formulas** check box.

When printing a worksheet to show formulas, make sure that the **Row & Column Headings** check box is selected from the **File Page Setup** command.

Turning Off Gridlines and Changing Grid Color

Turning off the gridlines displayed on-screen gives a better appearance to final results. You may want the gridlines on while you build formulas. To turn the screen gridlines on or off, choose the **Options Display** command, and select or deselect the **Gridlines** check box.

Figure 8.30 illustrates how a data-entry form without gridlines appears more like a paper form. This kind of display can make data entry easier and reduce mistakes.

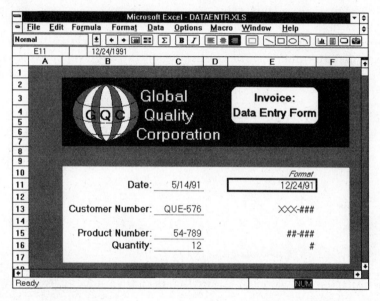

Fig. 8.30. The screen appears more like a paper presentation with the gridlines off.

To change the color of the gridlines and headings, follow these steps:

1. Choose the O ptions D isplay command.

2. Select Gridline & Heading C olor by clicking on the down arrow or by pressing Alt , C , and then Alt +down arrow .

3. Select the color that you want.

4. Choose OK or press Enter .

If you want to color individual cell or range contents, use the Format **Patterns** command described earlier in this chapter.

Protecting Worksheets from Change

If you develop Excel worksheets for use by inexperienced operators, if you create worksheets for sale, or if you work in the mistake-filled hours after midnight, you will find this section helpful. With Excel, you can protect cells, graphical objects, and windows. If you need to protect confidential or proprietary information, you can also hide formulas so that they do not appear in the formula bar. You can use a password to prevent unauthorized people from changing the protection status or the display of hidden information.

The procedure for protecting a worksheet and its contents uses two commands. The first command formats the cells or objects that you want to be unprotected. The second command turns on protection for all the cells or objects that have not been unprotected.

Marking Cells for Protection and Hiding Formulas

Cell protection is a valuable feature that prevents someone from accidentally entering data over the top of a formula and prevents unauthorized users from changing your formulas. You also can specify whether a cell's contents are visible in the formula bar. Although the cell contents are hidden from the formula bar, the cell's value or formula results still appear in the worksheet.

The default format for all cells is protected and visible. Using the following steps, you can change cell formats to be unprotected or hidden. Protection and hiding do not take place until you give the **Options Protect Document** command.

To unprotect or hide a cell's contents, follow these steps:

1. Select the cell or range that you want to be unprotected or whose contents you want to hide from the formula bar.

2. Choose the Format Cell Protection command (see fig. 8.31).

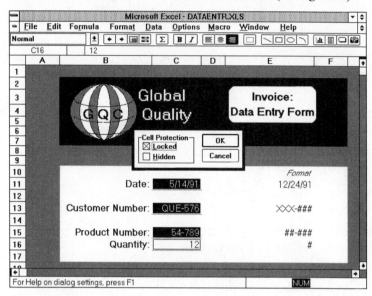

Fig. 8.31. The Cell Protection dialog box.

3. Deselect the Locked check box to mark the cell or range as one that can be changed.

4. Select the Hidden check box to mark the cell or range as one whose contents will not show in the formula bar. You can continue to change all cells on the worksheet and see any cell contents until you turn on protection for the worksheet.

5. Choose OK or press Enter.

To turn on protection, choose the Options Protect Document command (see fig. 8.32). Select what you want to protect: Cells, Windows, or Objects. Enter a password if desired in the Password text box. Choose OK or press Enter.

Protected windows and objects cannot be moved, sized, or formatted. Protect objects that you want to lock into place on a worksheet, and protect windows that are prepositioned for novice users.

If you don't enter a password, worksheet protection is turned on. To turn it off, choose the Options Unprotect Document command. No password will be asked for.

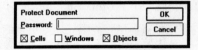

Fig. 8.32. *Use the Protect Document command to protect cell contents, window position, and graphical objects.*

After you protect the worksheet, look through some of the menus. Notice that most of the commands are grayed and unusable.

Don't forget your password! If you do, you won't be able to get back in and change the worksheet. Here are a few helpful hints for choosing passwords:

- Remember the characters that you capitalize in a password. Passwords differentiate between upper- and lowercase letters.

- Avoid using passwords that are easy to figure out, such as the following commonly used choices:

> Mother's maiden name
> Spouse's maiden or middle name
> Birthdate
> Employee number

- Don't stick your password to the computer with a piece of tape. (Don't laugh; people do it!)

- Use symbols or uncommon capitalization in a name that you won't forget.

- Have a senior officer in the company keep a confidential list of passwords to make sure that a password is accessible if the original guardian isn't.

- Change passwords whenever you doubt security.

From Here...

Many people who use spreadsheets learn only the basic procedures for entering, editing, formatting, and printing. After you cover Chapter 16, "Printing Worksheets," you will know enough to start creating and using Excel worksheets. However, by exploring Excel's numerous other worksheet capabilities, you will be able to use your knowledge to improve your work.

If you feel that you don't have enough time to explore further, at least look over these topics: "Printing Worksheets," in Chapter 16, and the discussion of the SUM( ) and ROUND( ) functions in Chapter 10.

If you plan to learn more about Excel at this time, congratulations. From here, you probably should scan the chapter "Using Functions," and then read "Building Systems and Managing Multiple Windows" and "Linking and Consolidating Worksheets." These chapters are useful in nearly all business and engineering situations.

Before you stop and decide you have learned enough to get by, make a commitment to go through the Chart, Database, and Macro Quick Starts. They take less than two hours total, and you can spread them out over the next month. You will find that the worksheet is only one way that Excel can help you be more productive.

9

Drawing and Placing Graphics in Worksheets

E xcel gives you the power to communicate with emphasis and polish. Your Excel worksheets can contain more than just numbers—the layouts can include any of these elements that add information and value to your reports:

- Drawings composed of lines, arrows, ovals, circles, rectangles, and squares

- Text boxes containing titles or paragraphs of word-wrapped text

- Pictures of charts or worksheet ranges that are automatically updated when you update the charts or ranges

- Professional graphics, illustrations, or logos from Windows drawing programs or scanned artwork

- Macros linked to graphic objects—selecting an object runs a macro

All of these features (and more) are discussed in this chapter. All of the features in this chapter are new with Excel 3 for Windows.

Excel's information and analysis systems now can carry out more functions—in less time and at a fraction of the cost—than many high-end executive or management information systems. Excel's analytical and charting power, combined with worksheet graphics and macros, provides the publishing and design capability of systems costing more than $100,000.

Figures 9.1, 9.2, 9.3, and 9.4 show how you can enhance information displays, Excel program controls, and printed worksheets by using the tools described here and in the charting sections.

Figure 9.1 shows an Excel worksheet that is the front-end to a management information system. This system enables users to retrieve business information from global divisions. Users click on an area of the globe and then click on one of the macro buttons at the bottom of the screen. A shaded pattern sets off important screen areas. Two graphics have been imported—the globe and the world map. Text boxes create the title at the top and the instructions at the bottom. Invisible rectangles and ovals (borders and fills set to None) are placed over areas of the globe. These invisible areas, as well as the macro buttons at the bottom of the screen, are assigned to macros, as described in Chapter 30, "Modifying and Programming Macros."

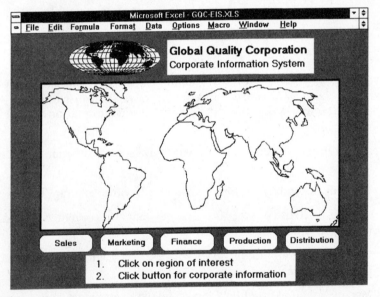

Fig. 9.1. *Link graphics and imported pictures to macros to create an executive information system front-end.*

Figure 9.2 shows the use of charts, linked cell pictures, text boxes, ovals, and arrows. Shading sets off screen areas. The chart titles and analysis box are created with text boxes. The arrow and oval are drawn with tools from the tool bar. The two charts are embedded charts. The small bar chart in the lower right corner was drawn on top of the larger chart. For better positioning, text boxes with invisible (None) borders and fills are used for chart titles. The numeric chart at the top right corner shows stock details for the last three months. This chart was created by taking a picture of cells from the stock data worksheet and embedding and expanding the cell picture on the worksheet. Figure 9.11, later in this chapter, shows how double-clicking on embedded cells displays the worksheet area from which the picture came.

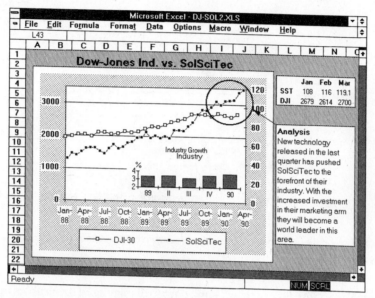

Fig. 9.2. *Combine embedded and overlapped charts and cell pictures for a concise display of a great amount of information.*

Figure 9.3 shows how Excel's graphic capabilities can enhance even simple worksheet information. Shading and thick underlines delineate information. Text boxes aligned with row and column grids create the column titles. You can perform this technique by holding down the Ctrl key as you draw the text boxes. Each text box is text-center aligned and has a shadow border.

Figure 9.4 shows an accounts receivable worksheet. The worksheet is set up so that all the aging analysis is in one screen. A light shading helps differentiate parts of the screen. A database below the screen contains accounts receivable information. By typing into cell D5 the number of days overdue, a list of overdue accounts is generated in the table at the left. Clicking on the macro button at the top left corner extracts simple data from the database to fill out the table of overdue accounts by name. Chapter 25 explains how to extract a list of information from a database; Chapters 28, 29, and 30 explain how to create a macro and assign it to a button to automate the process.

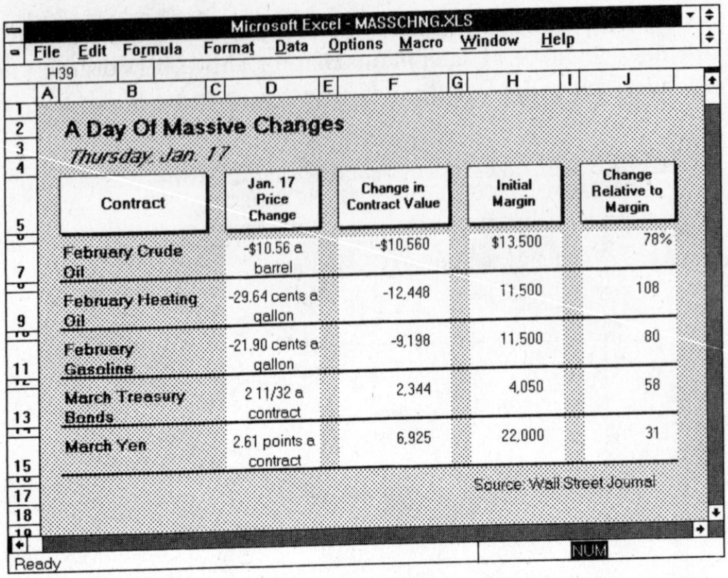

Microsoft Excel - MASSCHNG.XLS									

A Day Of Massive Changes

Thursday, Jan. 17

Contract	Jan. 17 Price Change	Change in Contract Value	Initial Margin	Change Relative to Margin
February Crude Oil	-$10.56 a barrel	-$10,560	$13,500	78%
February Heating Oil	-29.64 cents a gallon	-12,448	11,500	108
February Gasoline	-21.90 cents a gallon	-9,198	11,500	80
March Treasury Bonds	2 11/32 a contract	2,344	4,050	58
March Yen	2.61 points a contract	6,925	22,000	31

Source: Wall Street Journal

Fig. 9.3. *Shading and borders make even simple tables attractive and easier to read.*

The two charts are linked to the same data to display aged receivables in two different ways. Text boxes with invisible borders and fills create chart titles. This technique enables the charts to be larger within their chart area. Figure 9.10 shows one of the embedded charts activated so that it can be reformatted or updated. The information to create the charts comes from a database analysis that uses the **Data Table** command and DSUM function. The **Data Table** command is described in Chapter 13; Chapter 27 describes the **Data Table** command used with DSUM functions to analyze databases.

Creating Graphic Objects

Excel worksheets can contain graphic objects that appear on-screen and print on the worksheet printout. These objects reside in layers that cover the worksheet. Excel offers four fundamental types of objects: objects drawn with Excel tools, pictures taken of worksheets or charts, text boxes containing miniature word processing pages, and graphics from drawing programs or from scanners.

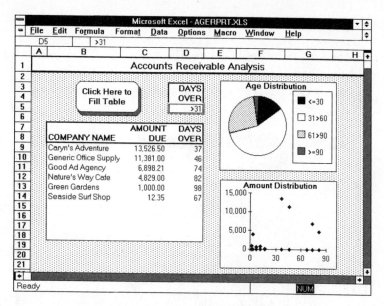

Fig. 9.4. *Get the big picture quickly by combining different views of the same information.*

> **Note: *Most Graphics Require a Mouse***
> Nearly all work with worksheet graphics requires a mouse. Few features are available for graphic objects without the mouse. One of the few things you can do with a keyboard is take a picture of a worksheet or chart and paste it onto the worksheet.

Using Drawing Tools

The Excel tool bar comes with a collection of drawing tools to help you produce an attractive worksheet. You can use the tools to emphasize points and polish the worksheet.

> **Tip: *Placing Graphics on Charts***
> You cannot draw directly on an Excel chart, but you can create floating text that "wraps" in text boxes. You can also paste graphic objects (for example, drawings of cars or trains) into charts, creating a picture chart in which objects replace column, bar, or line markers. This Excel feature is covered in detail in Chapter 19, "Formatting Charts."

The tool bar, used for drawing objects in Excel, is shown in figure 9.5. To display the tool bar above your worksheet, choose the **Options Workspace** command and select the **T**ool bar check box. Press Ctrl+7 to quickly toggle the tool bar on and off.

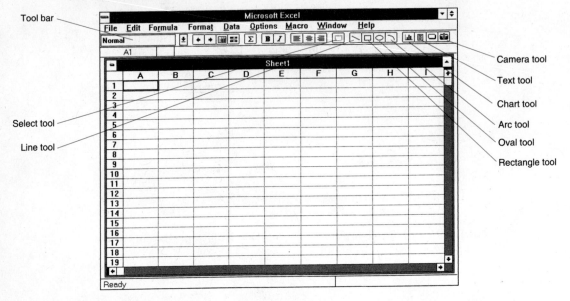

Fig. 9.5. *The right side of the tool bar contains icons used to draw, create, and select graphic objects.*

The right side of the tool bar contains icons used to draw, create, and select graphic objects. Each tool has a specialized function, as described in table 9.1.

Table 9.1
Graphic Tools

Tool	Function
Select tool	Selects groups of objects by dragging a rectangular *marquee* around them.
Line tool	Draws lines or arrows.
Rectangle tool	Draws rectangles or squares.
Oval tool	Draws ovals or circles.
Arc tool	Draws arcs.
Text box tool	Draws boxes for word-wrapped text.

Tool	Function
Camera tool	Captures pictures of worksheet ranges or charts as linked or unlinked graphic objects.
Chart tool	Inserts a chart into the worksheet.

To use most of the drawing tools, you click on the desired tool, then drag the mouse pointer across the worksheet to create the object. After you create the object, you can change border colors and thicknesses, and you can change the pattern that fills the object.

Drawing Lines, Ovals, Rectangles, and Arcs

With the drawing tools available in the tool bar, you can add enhancements to your worksheet. These enhancements include boxes and arrows that pinpoint specific data, shadow box frames, simple logos, and special macro buttons.

You will use the lines, ovals, rectangles, and arcs as basic drawing elements in Excel. After formatting your worksheets with patterns and line widths, you can layer and combine these simple shapes to create more complex drawings. If the Excel drawing tools don't produce the result you need, you can paste in drawings created with Windows applications programs such as Windows Paintbrush, CorelDRAW!, or Micrografx Designer. The process of pasting drawings into Excel is described in Chapter 33, "Using Excel with Windows Programs," and later in this chapter under the heading "Importing Graphics."

To draw a line, oval, rectangle, or arc, follow these steps:

1. Select the drawing tool you want by clicking on it. The mouse pointer symbol is replaced with a cross hair symbol.

2. Move the cross hair to where you want to start the drawing.

3. Follow these procedures if you want to constrain drawing to certain positions:

   Hold down the **Shift** key to keep lines vertical, horizontal, or at 45 degrees; ovals and arcs circular; and rectangles square.

   OR

   Hold down the **Ctrl** key to align the corner of the object with cell gridlines.

4. Drag the cross hair until the object has the size and orientation you want.

5. Release the mouse button to complete the object.

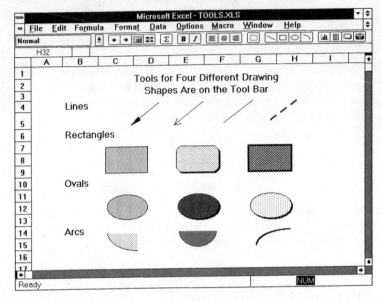

Fig. 9.6. *Drawing tools produce many different shapes.*

The object will appear *selected* when you finish. Selected objects display black *handles* at the edges and corners of an invisible rectangular frame enclosing the object. Objects must be selected before you can format or change them. Functions described later in this chapter change the lines, borders, and patterns used in an object.

To deselect a tool after you have clicked on it, click on it again or press Esc. To remove a graphic object, you must delete it. The procedure for deleting is described later in this chapter.

If you want to draw multiple objects using the same tool, hold down the Ctrl key before you select the tool from the tool bar. You now can draw multiple objects of the same type. The tool stays selected when you finish drawing an object. To return to Normal mode, click on the same tool again or press Esc.

> **Tip: *Using Print Preview To See Where Graphics Will Print***
> The worksheet in a window does not accurately show where objects will appear when printed. Use the Print Preview screen, and choose the Zoom option to see the location of printed objects.

Drawing Text Boxes

Excel enables you to place text boxes of word-wrapped text anywhere on the worksheet. You can edit and format the text in these miniature pages just as you edit and format text in most Windows word processing software. Figures 9.1 through 9.4 show how you can enhance a worksheet or chart with text.

When positioned over worksheet tables, text boxes make excellent titles. Because text boxes "float" in a layer over the worksheet, you can position a title of any size anywhere without affecting worksheet row or column positions.

To draw a text box, follow these steps:

1. Click on the Text box tool. The mouse pointer becomes a cross hair.

2. Hold down the **Shift** key if you want a square text box.

3. Drag from the corner where you want the text box to start until you reach the place where you want the text box to stop.

4. Release the mouse button.

When you release the mouse button, a flashing insertion point appears within the text box, indicating that you can begin typing text. Type continuously (as you would with word processing software); the text will wrap as you reach the margin. If you type more text than will fit in the box, the box contents will scroll so that you can see what you are typing; the full contents will not be visible. If you later decide to change the size or shape of the text box, the text inside will wrap to fit the new shape.

To edit material in the text box, use the arrow keys to move the insertion point in the text. Press Ctrl+left arrow or right arrow to move by whole words. Use Del or Backspace to delete a character or selected characters. To insert new material, begin typing at the insertion point. To replace existing text, select the section to be replaced; then type the new text. To select with the keyboard, hold down Shift as you move with the arrow keys. Select entire words by pressing Shift+Ctrl+left arrow or right arrow.

Text in a text box is different from text in a cell. In a cell, all the words and characters must have the same format. In a text box, formats can vary. To change the format of text in a text box, select the text to be changed, then format it using the Format Text, Font, or Patterns commands. Selecting the Automatic Size check box on the Format Text command menu makes the text box fit tightly around the text. You also can click on the Bold and Italic icons in the tool bar to change characters, or click on the Left, Right, or Center icons to change alignment of all text in the box.

> **Tip:** *Letting Worksheet Contents Show through a Text Box*
> When you want to frame worksheet contents and include text, use a
> text box that has its pattern formatted with a fill of None.

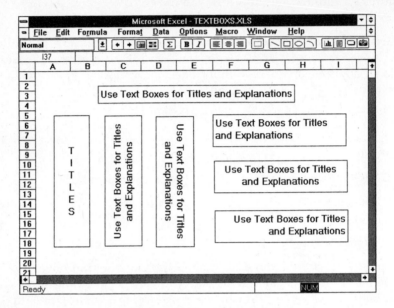

Fig. 9.7. Format, align, and rotate text boxes as needed.

Notice in figure 9.7 that you can rotate text in a text box. Figure 9.8 shows the Format Text dialog box used to rotate text. After text rotates and you select it to edit, the text orients itself vertically.

Creating Pictures of Worksheets and Charts

You can make worksheet information easier to understand by presenting related data and charts on the same page. For example, with your numeric forecasts, you may need to show a table of census data and a chart of those forecasts; these related items can appear on the worksheet.

You can combine worksheets and charts on the same page in two ways. You can create a picture of a worksheet range or chart and paste it onto the appropriate spot on a worksheet, or you can embed the picture in a worksheet. Pasted pictures are not updated when the original changes. Embedded pictures can be reformatted and updated when the original worksheet range or chart changes.

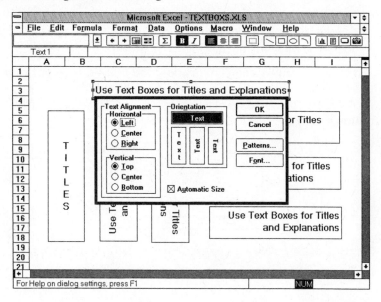

Fig 9.8. *Use the Format Text dialog box to rotate the contents of text boxes.*

Putting Pictures of Charts in a Worksheet

Displaying or printing charts and worksheets together on the same page is an important Excel feature. This feature enables you to create printouts that illustrate your point with a chart, while presenting details in a worksheet. You even can add a text box on the same page to give written explanation. Figure 9.4 illustrates the use of charts on a worksheet.

You can put two types of chart pictures on an Excel worksheet: an unlinked picture of a chart and an *embedded*, linked picture of a chart. Use unlinked pictures when you do not want the chart picture to change, even when the data changes. Because worksheets with unlinked charts load and recalculate faster, it may be better to use an unlinked chart picture if your worksheet needs frequent recalculating, or if the chart will not require updating.

Embedded charts contain external references linking the embedded chart to the data that created it. When the data changes on the worksheet, the embedded picture changes. You can double-click on an embedded chart to open the chart into a window, where you can use normal charting techniques to reformat the chart. Activating and formatting embedded charts is described in more detail in the chapters on charting.

You can copy a picture of an existing embedded chart in a worksheet or copy a picture of a chart document. To create either an embedded or an unlinked picture of a chart, follow these steps:

1. Select the chart by activating the chart document (if it is a chart document in its own window) or by double-clicking on a chart embedded in a worksheet.

2. To create an embedded chart, choose the Edit Copy command and go to step 5. To create an unlinked chart, hold down the Shift key and choose the Edit Copy Picture command. The dialog box (shown in figure 9.9) asks which picture you want.

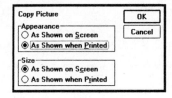

Fig. 9.9. *You can copy a chart picture as it appears on-screen or as it appears when printed.*

3. Select the copy options you want, depending on which picture appears better when pasted.

   Appearance
   As Shown on Screen copies the picture as it appears on-screen. As Shown when Printed copies the picture as it appears when printed.

   Size
   As Shown on Screen copies the size shown on-screen. As Shown when Printed copies the printed size.

4. Choose OK or press Enter.

5. Activate the worksheet in which you want to paste the chart.

6. Select a cell that will be the upper left corner for the picture. Select an object if you want to replace that object with the picture.

7. Choose the Edit Paste command.

The picture will appear on the worksheet, selected and ready for formatting. Figure 9.10 shows two charts pasted into a worksheet.

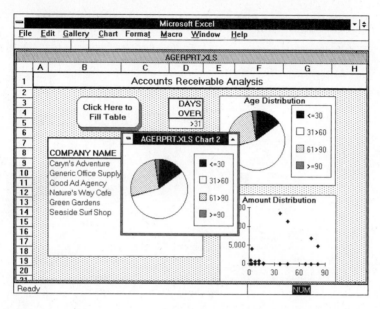

Fig 9.10. *Charts on worksheets can be linked or unlinked to the data.*

Finding the best choice of these copy options—so that text and charts appear accurately positioned—may depend on your printer and the fonts available. The most reliable choice is As Shown on Screen for both options.

Embedded charts remain linked to the worksheet data they use. Even if you create an embedded chart by copying a chart from a document window, the embedded chart links back to the worksheet that supplied the original data. Refer to the chapters on charting to learn how to activate and reformat embedded charts.

Putting Pictures of Cells in a Worksheet

Linked or unlinked pictures of cells can help you get past layout or formatting obstacles you may face when building reports or displays. Pictures of cells are like snapshots of a selected worksheet or macro range. You can put those snapshots anywhere on the same or a different worksheet or macro sheet. Figure 9.11 shows a picture of cells at the top right corner of the background worksheet.

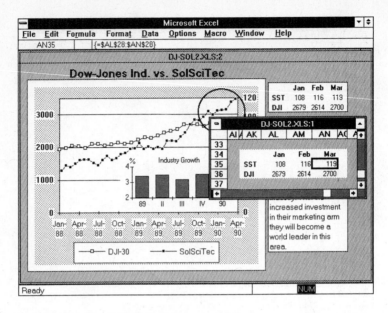

Fig 9.11. Pictures of cells link back to original data.

Each picture appears in its own box and can be formatted, sized, or moved separately. Pictures can be linked or unlinked. Linked cell pictures are updated when their original data is changed.

Cell pictures give you the flexibility to organize your macro sheet or worksheet in the best way for data entry, analysis, or programming. You can copy reporting and print areas as pictures and arrange them on pages alongside text boxes and charts. You can have separate print areas all printed on the same page. If the cell pictures are linked, they will be updated when the source cells are changed.

An advantage of linked cell pictures is that you can use them to create tables or boxes containing information from another area of the worksheet or macro. You can size the linked picture into a small box, double-click on the box, and then scroll through the box to see the source cells. It's like having a telescopic window to other parts of the worksheet.

Embedded (linked) cell pictures are useful for data that changes frequently. However, worksheets with embedded cell pictures take longer to load and to recalculate. If your data does not change frequently, or if speed is critical, you might choose to use unlinked cell pictures.

To copy linked pictures of cells using the Camera tool from the tool bar, follow these steps:

1. Select the cells you want to use for the picture.

2. Click on the Camera tool at the far right on the tool bar. The mouse pointer becomes a cross hair.

3. Activate the worksheet or macro sheet in which you want the picture to appear.

4. Click on the upper left corner of the area where you want the cell picture to appear.

The linked picture of cells will be pasted into place with its upper left corner at the cross hair.

To copy linked pictures of cells by using commands, follow these steps:

1. Select the cells you want to use for the picture.

2. Choose the Edit Copy command.

3. Activate the worksheet or macro sheet, and select the cell where you want the upper left corner of the picture to appear.

4. Hold down the Shift key and choose the Edit Paste Picture Link command.

Pasted cell pictures are updated when data changes or when you change the worksheet display of the source cells. For example, Excel will update pasted picture cells when you change the display of the source cells by turning gridlines on or off.

To update cell pictures or change the formats in source cells, double-click on the embedded cell picture. If the source macro sheet or worksheet for the cell picture is open, it will activate and select the range of the linked cells. If the source sheet is not open, Excel will open the sheet and select the range. When the range is selected, change the data, formulas, or formats as desired. The cell pictures will be updated automatically.

To copy unlinked pictures of cells, follow these steps:

1. Select the cells you want to use for the picture.

2. Hold down the Shift key and choose the Edit Copy Picture command.

3. Select the copy options you want, depending upon which picture appears better when pasted.

Appearance
As Shown on Screen copies the picture as it appears on-screen. As Shown when Printed copies the picture as it appears when printed.

Size
As Shown on Screen copies the size shown on-screen.
As Shown when Printed copies the printed size.

4. Choose OK or press Enter.

5. Activate the worksheet or macro sheet, and select the cell or object where you want the picture to appear.

6. Choose the Edit Paste command.

Tip: *Changing Either Display Setting of Unlinked Pictures*
Unlinked pictures can display gridlines as well as row and column headings. If you do not want row and column headings or gridlines to appear on pictures of a worksheet, use the Options Display command to deselect the Gridlines and Row & Column Headings options.

Importing Graphics

If you aspire to produce worksheets that any graphic artist would be proud of, you needn't be limited to the drawing tools in the Excel tool bar. You can create drawings in almost any Windows graphics program, copy the drawings, and then paste them into your worksheet where you can resize and move them. You can also add pictures, photos, or hand drawings to your worksheet by scanning them with a digital scanner, copying the image, and pasting the image into the worksheet. Excel will accept any graphic that can be copied into the clipboard in the Windows Metafile format.

Putting graphics in your worksheets can do more than just make the worksheets more attractive. Now you can put your company logo on worksheets; add architectural or engineering symbols to specifications, plans, or bids; add schematics or drawings that explain proposals; or create graphic "push-buttons" that run macros when clicked on.

Tip: *Storing Frequently Used Images in a Worksheet*
If you frequently use the same graphics or pictures, you can save time by collecting them in an Excel worksheet. For example, you can draw graphics and pictures with programs such as Windows Paintbrush or CorelDRAW!, then copy the graphics and paste them into a worksheet that acts as a scrapbook. Be sure to give the worksheet/scrapbook a descriptive name, such as TRNSPORT.XLS, BUSINESS.XLS, ENGNEER.XLS, SYMBOLS.XLS, and so on.

Storing your graphics and pictures in a worksheet makes it easy to find the graphic you want, copy it, and paste it into the worksheet you are working on. There's no need to start the Windows graphics program. Figure 9.12 shows part of an Excel worksheet serving as a scrapbook. You can store images like these in reduced size in a worksheet and resize them after you paste them into the worksheet.

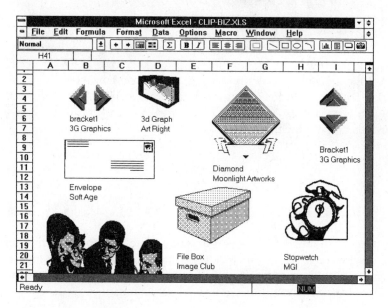

Fig. 9.12. *Use a worksheet as a scrapbook to store frequently used graphics or symbols.*

To copy graphics from another Windows program for use in Excel worksheets or macro sheets, follow these steps:

1. Activate the drawing program and select the graphic you want to copy.

2. Choose the **Edit Copy** command or the appropriate program procedure to copy the selected graphic to the clipboard.

3. Activate Excel and select the cell or object where you want the graphic to appear.

4. Choose the **Edit Paste** command.

After the graphic is on the Excel worksheet or macro sheet, you can treat it like any other graphic object. You can link a macro to it, resize or move it, or change its borders.

> **Tip:** *Using Clip Art for High-Quality Graphics*
> Clip art is artwork that professional artists have drawn and sold for reuse by nonartists. Clip art usually comes in collections by subject matter, such as transportation (trucks, cars, planes, etc.), business (dollar symbols, people, computers, etc.), and so on. Clip art works with most major graphics programs. A few programs, such as CorelDRAW!, include collections of clip art. CorelDRAW! comes with 300 clip-art images. Many of the drawings in this book are the clip-art images that are included with CorelDRAW!.

Working with Graphic Objects

You can format the graphics you draw or paste into Excel with different borders, patterns, and colors. You also can group multiple drawings into a single graphic, fix graphics to a cell location, change the order in which graphics overlap, and protect graphics from change.

Selecting Graphic Objects

In all Windows programs, you must select an item before you can change it. Graphic objects that have been selected are enclosed in an invisible rectangular *frame*. The corners and edges of the frame display black squares, or *handles*, that you use to move the object. Figure 9.13 shows a graphic object with frame and handles.

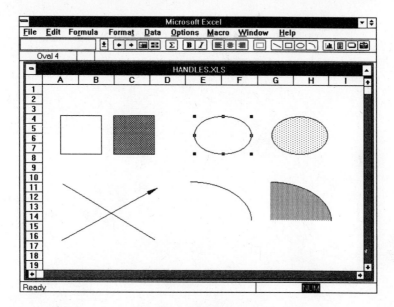

Fig. 9.13. You can move selected objects enclosed by black handles.

Each graphic object is identified by its type and a number that indicates the order in which it was created. The identifier of the selected object is displayed in the Reference Area to the left of the formula bar. Examples of identifiers include Rectangle 1, Arc 2, Oval 5, and Picture 8.

When you move the mouse to select an object, watch the mouse pointer. It must be shaped like an arrow to select the object. The pointer changes to an arrow over the inside of a filled object or picture and on the border of transparent objects, pictures, or text boxes.

To select a single object, move the mouse pointer over the object's border or center; then click. To select multiple objects, click on the first object, then hold down the Shift key as you click on additional objects.

Figure 9.14 shows a group of selected objects. If multiple objects are grouped closely together, you can select them by enclosing them with the Selection tool (see fig. 9.15). To use this method, click on the Selection tool in the tool bar, then drag the cross hair across all the objects. As you drag, a rectangular marquee encloses the objects. You must completely enclose an object to include it in the selection. When you release the mouse button, all enclosed objects will be displayed with black handles, and the marquee will disappear.

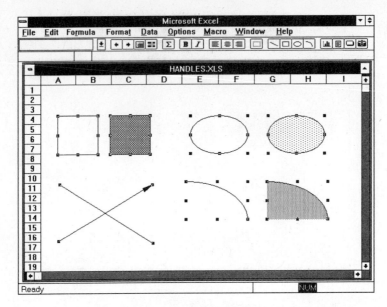

Fig. 9.14. *Select a group of objects with Shift+click or with the Selection tool.*

Selection
tool

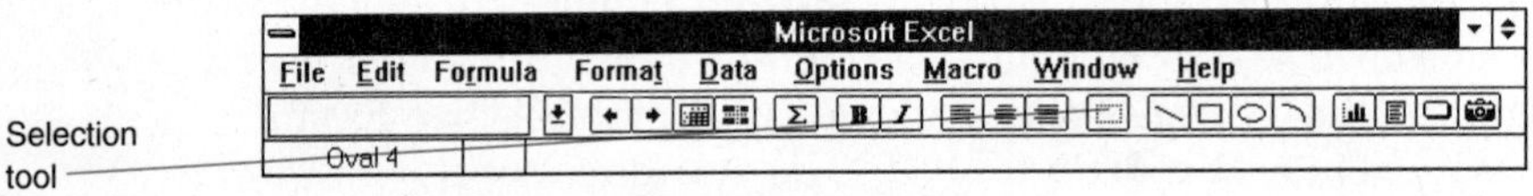

Fig. 9.15. *Click on the Selection tool and drag across multiple objects to select them all.*

To enlarge the area enclosed with the Selection tool, click again on the Selection tool and hold down the Shift key as you drag across additional objects. To select all graphic objects in a worksheet, choose the Formula Select Special command, select the Objects option, and choose OK.

If you want to exclude a few objects from a large group you have already selected, hold down the Shift key and click on the individual objects you want to deselect. You can exclude a group of objects by clicking on the Selection tool, holding down the Shift key, and dragging the mouse pointer across the group. To deselect all objects, press the Esc key or click on a cell in the worksheet.

Graphic objects can have macros assigned to them. Clicking on such an object causes the macro assigned to it to run. To select an object without running its assigned macro, press and hold the Ctrl key when you click on the object.

Deleting Graphic Objects

Deleting graphic objects is straightforward. Click on the object to select it; then press Del or Backspace or choose the **Edit Clear** command. When deleting text boxes, make sure that you have the box selected and not the text. Select a text box by clicking on its edge.

If you accidentally delete an object that you want to keep, immediately choose the **Edit Undo** command.

Formatting Graphic Objects

Excel gives you a wide array of colors, patterns, and line styles to use for formatting objects. You can change lines to arrows with heads of different weight and size. You also can change the thickness, style, and color of borders, and the fill pattern and color used within objects. Some objects even can use rounded corner or shadow box options.

Formatting Lines and Arrows

You can format lines for thickness, line style, and color. You also can put arrowheads on your lines. To format a line, follow these steps:

1. Select the line you want to format.

2. Double-click on the line or choose the **Format Patterns** command. Figure 9.16 shows the Line pattern dialog box.

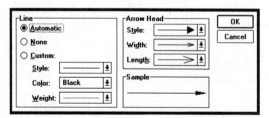

Fig. 9.16. Select lines and arrowhead styles from the line pattern dialog box.

3. Select from the Line options. To use the default line format, select Automatic. Select None for an invisible line. Select Custom to select Style, Color, and Weight of line from the pull-down list.

4. Select from the Arrowhead options if you want an arrow. Select from the Style, Width, and Length pull-down list to choose the type of arrowhead. Figure 9.17 shows the list for different arrowhead lengths.

Arrowhead lengths list

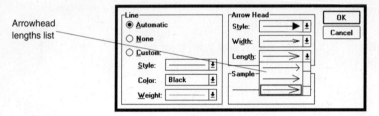

Fig. 9.17. Select the style, width, and length of arrowhead you prefer.

5. Check your selection in the Sample box at the lower right corner of the line patterns dialog box. Change your selections if necessary.

6. Choose **OK** or press **Enter**.

Figure 9.18 shows examples of different lines, weights, and arrowheads.

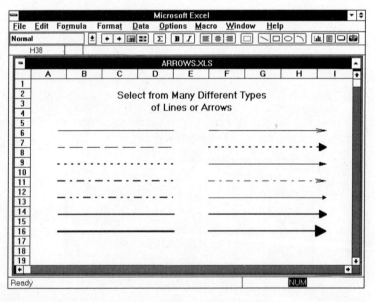

Fig. 9.18. You can create lines with different weights, colors, and arrowhead styles.

Formatting Borders and Patterns

All the graphic objects you draw in Excel can be formatted with different colors, patterns, and line styles or weights.

To change the fill pattern or border of an object, follow these steps:

1. Select the object or objects.

2. Double-click on the object to display the Patterns dialog box, or choose the Format Patterns command if the object is an embedded chart or linked picture. (Hold down the Ctrl key while clicking if the object has an assigned macro.) Figure 9.19 shows the Patterns dialog box for a pattern that has previously been selected.

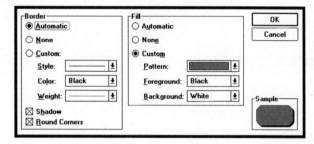

Fig. 9.19. The Patterns dialog box gives you many options for formatting objects.

3. Select from the Border group the style, weight, and color of border. Click on the down arrow to the right of a pull-down box to see the full list of selections.

4. Select the Shadow check box if the object needs a shadow.

5. Select from the Fill group the pattern and colors for the fill. Fill patterns use two colors. Select different colors from the Foreground or Background pull-down list to see how the color patterns appear. Select None if you want an invisible fill that lets the background show through.

6. Review your selection in the Sample box at the lower right corner of the patterns dialog box. Change your selections if necessary.

7. Choose OK or press Enter.

Figure 9.20 shows examples of patterns you can use to fill objects.

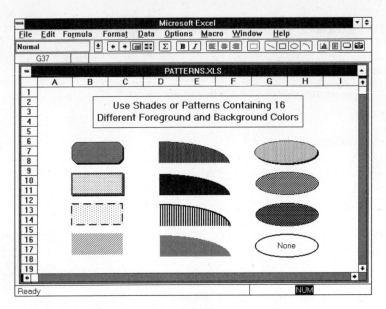

Fig. 9.20. Patterns use foreground and background colors.

If you are unsure of which colors, weights, or patterns to use, or if you want to return to default colors, select the Automatic option for these commands.

To format objects that are pictures linked to other documents, you must reformat the source document for the link. Open the source document by double-clicking on the object. Then reformat the source document as you like.

> **Tip:** *Creating Invisible Fills To Let the Worksheet Show Through*
> To highlight important results, draw rectangles or ovals around cells. Then use the None option to fill the rectangle or oval, letting the worksheet data show through the rectangular or oval border.

Sizing, Moving, and Copying Graphic Objects

You can size and move graphic objects just as you would in other Windows programs.

To resize an object, select it so that you can see the black handles. Move the mouse pointer over a handle until the pointer becomes a cross hair. To change the size in one dimension (height or width), drag a handle in the middle of one side. To resize two sides, drag a corner handle.

To resize an object while keeping its proportions, hold down the Shift key; then drag a corner handle. To see the proportions of an imported graphic or embedded chart that you are resizing, watch the Reference Area to the left of the formula bar. This area shows proportions as a percentage of the original object size.

To move an object, select it; then drag the object to its new location. Be sure to drag objects that have an invisible (None) fill and all text boxes by their edges. If you drag an object by its black handle, you will resize it. If you need to move an object a long distance, cut the object to the clipboard, move to the new location, and paste the object in place.

Move multiple objects by selecting them together, then dragging them to the new location.

To *constrain* movements to vertical or horizontal, hold down the Shift key while dragging. If you want the object to align on underlying cells, hold down the Ctrl key as you drag an object.

To cut or copy objects, select them; then choose the **Edit Cut** or **Copy** command. Select the new location for the object; then choose the **Edit Paste** command.

Grouping Graphic Objects

Grouping objects together fuses them into a single object. When related objects are fused, they are easier to move and size. You can ungroup objects if you later need to separate them.

To group objects together, select the objects you want to group using one of the multiple-selection techniques; then choose the **Format Group** command. To separate a group into its individual elements, select the group; then choose the **Format Ungroup** command.

Reordering Layers of Graphic Objects

Objects in Excel overlap each other in layers. Because objects overlap in the order in which they were created, the most recently drawn or pasted object appears in front. Figure 9.21 shows a text box that was created before the shaded box that partially covers it.

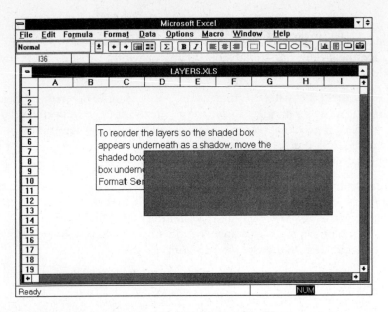

Fig 9.21. The most recently created objects appear in front.

To reorder the layers so that the shaded box appears behind the text box as a shadow, move the shaded box to be slightly offset from the text box; then choose the Format Send to Back command. Figure 9.22 shows the text box in front with a shadow box background. (To bring an object to the front, select it; then choose the Format Bring to Front command.)

You can hide all graphics so that you can see the worksheet underneath the graphic objects. Hide all objects by choosing the Options Display command and selecting the Hide All option. Deselect the Hide All option to redisplay objects. Pressing Ctrl+6 toggles between normal object display, displaying placeholders, and hidden objects.

Fixing Object Positions

You can position objects relative to their underlying cells in three ways. These three ways enable you to specify how an object behaves when you insert, delete, or change the dimensions of underlying rows and columns.

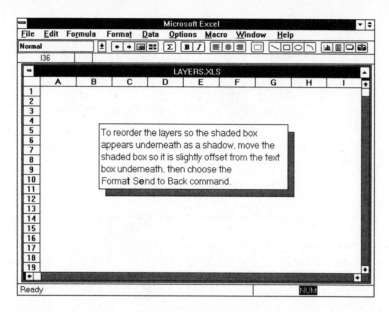

Fig. 9.22. Reorder layers of objects by bringing one to the front or sending one to the back.

Drawn objects, such as text boxes, rectangles, and ovals, are attached to underlying cells; when you affect the underlying cells, the objects move and change shape. The Move and Size with Cells option is automatically selected with drawn objects; this option attaches the object to the cells under the object's top left and lower right corners. This option is useful when you draw rectangles or ovals around specific data on the worksheet, or when you use lines or arrows drawn between two points. As the underlying sheet changes, the end-points of the object remain fixed—still enclosing the data if the object is a rectangle or oval, and still pointing to the correct items if the object is a line or arrow.

When first created, an embedded chart or pasted graphic is attached to the underlying cell at the upper left corner of the object. An object moves with the cell during insertions, deletions, or dimension changes; but the size and proportion of the object remains the same. During cell changes, pictures and charts stay proportional, and they continue to look the way you want them to look.

Use the Move and Size with Cells option if you want an object to change size and shape relative to the worksheet cells it covers.

To change how an object is attached to underlying cells, follow these steps:

1. Select the object.

2. Choose the Format Object Placement command. Figure 9.23 shows the Object Placement dialog box.

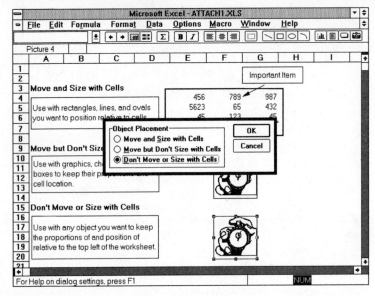

Fig. 9.23. Object Placement controls how worksheet changes affect objects.

3. Select one of the following attachment options.

Move and Size with Cells	Attaches an object to the cells under the object's top left and lower right corners. The object moves or changes size with the underlying cells, rows, or columns. This is the normal attachment when objects are first drawn.
Move but Don't Size with Cells	Attaches the object only to the cell underlying the top left corner of the object. The object moves with the cell during insertions or deletions, but it keeps its original size and proportions. This is the normal attachment when graphics are pasted or charts are embedded.
Don't Move or Size with Cells	Objects are not attached to the underlying worksheet. They must be moved and sized by themselves.

4. Choose **OK** or press **Enter**.

Use the Move but Don't Size with Cells option for charts, pasted graphics, groups of lines, and rectangles and ovals you have created a logo or design with. This option keeps the graphics in position, but prevents them from stretching.

If you don't want objects to change shape or move, use the Don't Move or Size with Cells option. This option preserves an object's shape and keeps it fixed in position relative to the top left corner of the worksheet.

Figure 9.24 shows objects with different attachments. Figure 9.25 shows the same worksheet after a column is inserted.

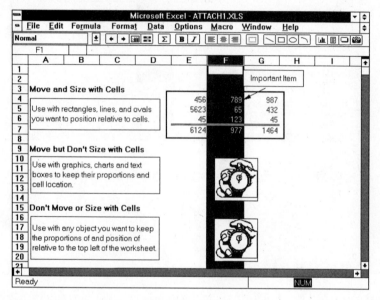

Fig. 9.24. *You can use three methods of attaching objects to the underlying worksheet.*

Protecting Objects

You can protect objects to keep other people from changing them. You protect objects just as you protect cells. Mark the objects you want to remain unprotected by choosing the Forma**t** Object Protection command and de-selecting the **L**ocked check box. To activate protection for the worksheet, choose the **O**ption **P**rotect Document command, select the **O**bjects check box, and enter a password if desired. Choose OK. Those objects that were unlocked prior to document protection can be changed when the document protection is turned on.

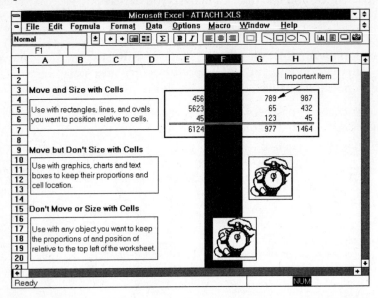

Fig. 9.25. *Attachment methods work differently when the underlying worksheet changes shape.*

Improving Performance

When you scroll windows or recalculate a worksheet that contains graphic objects, Excel redraws the objects. Because redrawing objects requires extra computer power, Excel's performance may slow down. Remember: Excel can show all objects, show placeholders for better performance, or hide all objects so that you can see the underlying worksheet. To speed up Excel's performance, change the display of objects. Choose the **Options Display** command, and select the Hi**d**e All option or **S**how Placeholders. Toggle between these display modes by pressing Ctrl+6. Behind the Display dialog box, you can see the shaded placeholders that take the place of graphic objects. Figure 9.26 illustrates the display options.

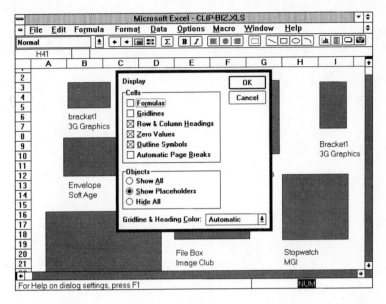

Fig. 9.26. *For increased performance, choose to display object placeholders or hide objects.*

From Here...

Graphic elements, artwork, shading, and embedded charts all make your worksheets and screens more attractive. But they do much more. By using these elements properly, you can add emphasis to important points, lead the eye to critical data, and make information more accessible.

Many business people, engineers, and scientists like to see the overall picture, then focus on the details of specific areas. By combining embedded charts, pictures of tables from the worksheet, and text boxes, you give these readers the opportunity to absorb information in several ways. They can quickly scan a chart for trends, examine the adjacent backup table for specific numbers, and read the text box for explanation.

Now that you are familiar with graphics, you can add a new dimension to your worksheet by assigning macros to graphic objects. When the operator clicks on an object, the macro assigned to that object runs. This feature enables you to put icons on worksheets to perform specific operations. For example, clicking a small picture of a printer could print the selected area, or clicking on a map section could display reports for offices in that area. Before you begin working with macros, you may find it helpful to go through the Macro Quick Start chapter. Chapters 28–32 describe macros.

One form of graphics mentioned in this section is embedded charts. For more information on using charts, see the Chart Quick Start or the charting section, Chapters 18–20, that follow the Quick Start. If you want to learn more about working with graphics that are brought in from programs such as Windows Paintbrush, CorelDRAW!, or Micrografx Designer, read Chapter 33, "Using Excel with Windows Programs."

10

Using Functions

E xcel uses prebuilt worksheet functions to perform math, text, or
logical calculations or to find information about the worksheet.
Whenever possible, you should use functions rather than writing your own
formulas. Functions are fast, take up less space in the formula bar, and
reduce the chance for typographical errors.

Functions act on data in much the same way that equations act on numbers.
Functions accept information, referred to as *arguments*, and return a result.
In most cases, the result is a math calculation, but functions also return
results that are text, references, logical values, arrays, or information about
the worksheet. The functions listed in this chapter can be used in worksheets
and in macro sheets. Your macros can have all the analytical capability of
worksheets.

In the first part of the chapter, you will learn what functions are and how to
use them. The latter part of the chapter is a directory of Excel's 146
worksheet functions with descriptions of the arguments that the functions
use. The directory is segmented by types of functions and includes examples
for many of the functions.

Understanding Functions

Functions accept data through *arguments*. You enter arguments, enclosed
in parentheses, after the function name. Each function takes specific types

of arguments, such as numbers, references, text, or logical values. Functions use these arguments in the same way that equations use variables.

If, for example, you want to write an equation to determine a mortgage or loan payment, you need the following information:

Argument	Description
rate	Interest rate per period
nper	Number of periods
pv	Present value (starting value of loan)
fv	Future value (ending value at loan completion)

Because the equation for an amortized loan payment requires many complex terms, you are more likely to make typographical errors. In addition, Excel solves an equation you enter more slowly than it solves a built-in function for the same operation.

Instead of manually entering a long equation to calculate the loan payment, you can use one of Excel's worksheet functions, PMT. Within parentheses, you enter the values or references for the information needed to do the calculation. The PMT function is entered in this form:

=**PMT(*rate, nper, pv, fv, type*)**

The arguments here give the same information as just described, but with the addition of the argument *type*. Some functions return different answers depending on the value of *type*. In the case of PMT, Excel can calculate payments for different types of loans depending upon the value used for *type*. An actual PMT function might look like this:

=PMT(Mo.Int,A12,B36)

Here, Mo.Int is the name of the cell that contains the monthly interest rate (*rate*), A12 contains the number of months (*nper*), and B36 contains the present value (*pv*). The arguments *fv* and *type* are optional and were not used in this calculation of a simple mortgage payment.

Excel uses various types of arguments for different types of information. As shown in table 10.1, you often can tell the required types of arguments by the names of the arguments. The argument names appear within the parentheses in this chapter's directory, in the Microsoft reference manual, in the on-line Excel Help file, and in the formula bar (when functions are pasted into formulas with the Formula Paste Function command).

Table 10.1

Argument	Type	Sample Function and Argument Names
text	text (in quotation marks or a reference)	**LEFT(*text*,*num_chars*)**
value	value (text in quotation marks, a number, or a reference)	**LOOKUP(*lookup_value*,*array*)**
num	numeric (a number or a reference)	**RIGHT(*text*,*num_chars*)**
reference	cell reference	**COLUMN(*reference*)**
serial_number	date/time number (or a reference)	**DAY(*serial_number*)**
logical	logical (or a reference)	**OR(*logical1*,*logical2*,...)**
array	array (or a reference)	**TRANSPOSE(*array*)**

The area between parentheses never contains a space. Instead, some argument names include an underscore, as in *num_chars*. Each argument is separated by a comma.

Some functions can have as many as fourteen arguments. These functions, such as the OR function, show the additional arguments with ellipses (...).

Some functions have optional arguments, which are shown in the directory in *italic type*. (Mandatory arguments are shown in ***bold italic type***.) If you leave out all the optional arguments, you do not need to enter their preceding commas. If you use some of the optional arguments, you must enter the commas that would have preceded the omitted optional arguments. These commas act as place holders so that Excel understands the position of the optional arguments that you do enter. For example, the following is the format of the PMT function with all its arguments:

PMT(*rate*,*nper*,*pv*,*fv*,*type*)

If you omit the *fv* optional argument, but use the *type* argument, you would enter the function as

PMT(*rate*,*nper*,*pv*,,*type*)

Make sure that you enclose text within quotation marks (""). Text contained in a cell and referenced by the cell address does not have to be in quotation marks. Do not enclose range names in quotation marks. If your text includes a quotation within a quotation, use two quotation marks to begin and end each internal quotation. For example, to find the length of the phrase

　　She said, "So!"

you must use

　　=LEN("She said,""So!""")

Text values, including the quotation marks, can be up to 255 characters long.

Tip: *Producing Blank Cell Displays*
To produce a blank cell display, use two quotation marks with nothing between them, as in this example:

　　=IF(A12>15,"","Entry must be greater than 15!")

When A12 is greater than 15, nothing is displayed in the cell, because the TRUE portion of the IF function returns "". When A12 is 15 or less, this message is displayed:

```
Entry must be larger than 15!
```

Entering Worksheet Functions

You can enter worksheet functions as a single entry in the formula bar, such as this:

　　=PMT(A12,B36,J54)

Or, worksheet functions can be part of a much larger formula, including nested functions that are within other functions, as in this example:

　　=IF(LEFT(A12,4)="VDT",SUM(B36:B54),SUM(C36:C54))

You can enter functions by manually typing the function or by pasting the function into the formula bar. One function, SUM, also can be selected from the tool bar.

Typing Functions

You can type any function into the formula bar just as you would type in a formula. If you remember the function and its arguments, typing may be the fastest method. If you are unsure of the function's spelling or its arguments, paste in the function.

Entering the SUM Function from the Tool Bar

The most frequently used function is SUM. This function totals the numeric value of all cells within the ranges it references. For example, SUM can total all the cells between two endpoints in a column or row. Because SUM is used so frequently, an Auto-SUM icon, which you can use to total adjacent columns or rows automatically, appears on the tool bar. As well as entering the SUM function, the Auto-SUM tool selects the cells in the column above the SUM or in the row to the left of the SUM. SUM is very useful for totalling columns of expenses or rows of sales by region.

Before using the Auto-SUM tool, turn on the tool bar by choosing the **Options Workspace** command and selecting the **T**ool Bar option. Figure 10.1 shows how to enter a SUM function in cell B11 by using a mouse. Select cell B11, below the column you want to total, and then click on the Auto-SUM tool. Excel inserts the SUM function and enters that column's range between parentheses, as shown in the figure. You can continue the formula by adding more terms, or you can enter the SUM function into the cell by clicking on the SUM tool a second time.

Pasting Functions and Arguments

A good way to enter other functions is to paste them into the worksheet by selecting them from a scrolling list. You also can choose to have Excel paste in prompts to remind you of the arguments and their correct order. To paste a function and its arguments into the worksheet, follow these steps:

1. Select the cell where you want to enter the function.

2. Choose the Formula Paste Function command to display the dialog box shown in figure 10.2.

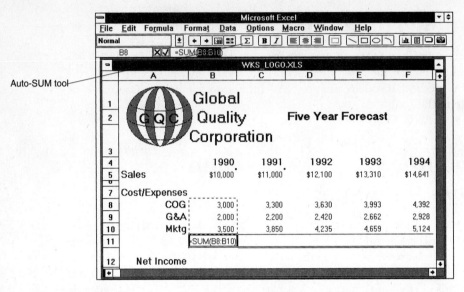

Auto-SUM tool

Fig. 10.1. The Auto-SUM tool enters a SUM function in the selected cell.

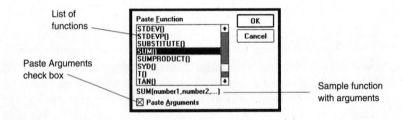

List of functions

Paste Arguments check box

Sample function with arguments

Fig. 10.2. The Paste Function dialog box.

3. Select the function that you want from the list box. (To scroll quickly to a function, select the list and then press the first letter of the function.)

4. Select the Paste Arguments check box box to insert a prompt for each argument.

5. Choose OK or press Enter.

A pasted PMT function and its arguments appear in the formula bar in figure 10.3. Notice that the prompts for arguments are displayed within the parentheses.

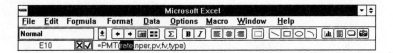

Fig. 10.3. Paste functions and arguments for accuracy and ease.

You must replace the argument prompts with actual values or references in order for the function to work correctly. Functions containing argument prompts that have not been replaced will return #NAME? errors because Excel attempts to use the prompts as range names which do not exist.

Editing Functions

To edit pasted arguments, follow these instructions:

 Double-click on the argument prompt to select the argument text between commas. Now type in a reference or click on the worksheet reference you want.

 Press the Edit key (F2). Move to the beginning of the argument text and press Shift+Ctrl+right-arrow key. This procedure selects the text from the cursor location to the position past the next comma. Type the value to replace the argument text and its trailing comma.

> **Tip: *Creating Your Own Functions with Excel's Function Macros***
> If you need business, financial, science, or engineering functions that are not built into Excel, add them yourself with function macros. Function macros appear in the Formula Paste Function list and act the same as predefined worksheet functions. The "Command and Function Macro Quick Start" (Chapter 28) guides you through creating your first function macro.

Getting Help with Functions

 Excel contains extensive on-line Help for functions. If you forget how to use a function or what an argument represents, use the Help files that are always available. To access Help with functions, choose the **Help Index** command.

Choose the underlined choice, Worksheet Functions, by clicking on it or by pressing Tab until it is selected, and then pressing Enter. A list of specific functions and generic function groups appears.

Choose the function or function group that you need assistance with by clicking on the underlined words or by pressing Tab or the PgUp or PgDn keys to select the function and then pressing Enter. A Help screen similar to the one in figure 10.4 appears. Back up to the previous screen by pressing Alt+B or by clicking on the Backup button. Press Alt+F4 to remove the Help screen.

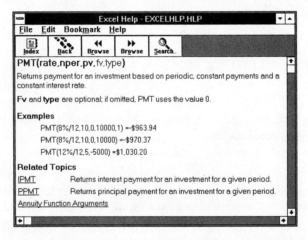

Fig. 10.4. *Extensive function Help is available.*

Excel Function Dictionary

In the function dictionary that follows, each Excel function is listed with its arguments. The directory also includes explanations, limitations, examples, and tips. Function definitions are grouped by type and are listed in alphabetical order within each group. The function groups are as follows:

- Database
- Date and Time
- Financial
- Information
- Logical
- Lookup
- Mathematical

- Matrix
- Statistical
- Text
- Trigonometric

Database Functions

Each of Excel's database functions uses the same arguments: *database*, *field*, and *criteria*. The descriptions of these arguments in the discussion of DAVERAGE apply to all the database functions. Examples of database functions and tips to help you analyze your database contents are provided in Chapter 27, "Building Extensive Databases."

The *criteria*, *field*, and *database* arguments used in D*functions* do not have to be the same as those used in **Data Set Database** or **Data Set Criteria**. You can have several D*functions* working at the same time on different databases, and each function can have its own criteria.

DAVERAGE(*database*, *field*, *criteria*)

This function averages the numbers in the *field* of the *database* for records that match the query in *criteria*.

For the *database* argument, you can specify a range (such as B36:D54), a range name (such as INVENTORY), or the name DATABASE (which you create with the **Data Set Database** command). The *criteria* argument can be a reference (such as B12:D13), a name (such as Crit.Sales), or the name CRITERIA (which you create with the **Data Set Criteria** command). The *field* argument specifies the column to average. You can specify the *field* by its field name in quotation marks ("Sales"), by a reference to a cell containing the field name, or by a number (1 is the first field (column), 2 the second, and so on).

The *database*, *field*, and *criteria* arguments do not have to be the same as those used for the **Data Find** and **Data Extract** commands. This means that you can analyze multiple databases on the same worksheet. If you want to analyze multiple databases with range names, give each database and criteria a unique name, such as Crit.Sales.1 and Crit.Sales.2.

The following examples are valid DAVERAGE functions:

    =DAVERAGE(Database,2,Criteria)

Where Database and Criteria are set with the **Data Set Database** and **Data Set Criteria** commands, and the second field will be averaged.

=DAVERAGE(B12:H534,"Days",Crit.Sales)

Where the *database* being analyzed is in B12:H534, the *field* being averaged has the heading Days, and the *criteria* is in a range with the name Crit.Sales. Notice that when the name of a field heading is used, it is enclosed in quotation marks.

DCOUNT(*database, field, criteria*)

Counts the numeric records in the *database field* that satisfy the *criteria*.

Limits: If the *field* argument is omitted, DCOUNT counts all records in the *database* that satisfy the *criteria*.

DCOUNTA(*database, field, criteria*)

Counts the number of nonblank cells in the *field* of the *database* for those records that satisfy the *criteria*.

Limits: If the *field* argument is omitted, DCOUNTA counts all nonblank records in the *database* that satisfy the *criteria*.

 ### DGET(*database, field, criteria*)

Extracts from the *database* the single record that matches the *criteria*. If no records match the *criteria*, #VALUE! is returned. If more than one record matches the *criteria*, #NUM! is returned.

DMAX(*database, field, criteria*)

Finds the largest number in the *database field* for records that satisfy the *criteria*.

DMIN(*database, field, criteria*)

Finds the smallest number in the *database field* for records that satisfy the *criteria*.

DPRODUCT(*database, field, criteria*)

Multiplies all values in the *field* of the *database* for records that satisfy the *criteria*. This function is similar to DSUM, but the values are multiplied rather than added.

DSTDEV(*database, field, criteria*)

Calculates the standard deviation of a sample population, based on the numbers in the *field* of the *database* for records that satisfy the *criteria*.

DSTDEVP(*database, field, criteria*)

Calculates the standard deviation of the entire population, based on the numbers in the *field* of the *database* for records that satisfy the *criteria*.

DSUM(*database,field,criteria*)

Totals all numbers in the *field* of the *database* for records that satisfy the *criteria*.

DVAR(*database,field,criteria*)

Calculates the estimated variance of a sample population, based on the numbers in the *field* of the *database* for records that satisfy the *criteria*.

DVARP(*database,field,criteria*)

Calculates the variance of an entire population, based on the numbers in the *field* of the *database* for records that satisfy the *criteria*.

Date Functions

Excel records dates and times as serial numbers. A date is the number of days from January 1, 1900, to the date you specify; a time is a decimal fraction of 24 hours. Serial numbers provide the capability to calculate elapsed days, future times, and so on. For example, the serial number for January 1, 1992, 6:30 PM, is 32142.7708333, where 32142 is the number of days from the beginning of the century and .7708333 is the decimal fraction of 24 hours representing 6:30 PM.

Under Windows and OS/2, Excel normally counts dates from the beginning of the year 1900. (On the Macintosh, Excel uses a date system based on 1904.) If, however, the 1904 Date System option is selected in the Options Calculation dialog box, the first day for serial dates is January 1, 1904. You may need to select this option when you are reading Excel worksheets created on the Macintosh. The following definitions and examples assume that the 1904 Date System is not selected.

> **Tip: *Typing Date and Time Entries***
> The same date and time formats that you type into a worksheet, such as 10/12/91 or 9-Sep-92, can be used with worksheet functions. When a function's argument is *serial_number*, you can use the serial date number or a reference to a cell containing a date or time, or you can enter a date as text in the argument, such as "24-Dec-92". Remember to enclose the text date in quotation marks because it is treated as text.

DATE(*year,month,day*)

Produces the serial number for a specific date. Use the DATE function to calculate a serial number from formulas that produce a numeric year, month, or day. Enter numbers for the *year*, *month*, and *day* or reference cells that contain numeric values or formulas.

Limits: Excel returns serial numbers for dates between January 1, 1900, and December 31, 2078. Enter years between 1900 and 2078 (or 00 and 178), months from 1 to 12, and days from 1 to 31.

Example: DATE(1988,7,B11) produces the serial number 32336 if B11 contains the day number 12.

> **Tip: *Finding the First Day of Each Quarter***
> DATE(1992,CHOOSE(*QTR*,1,4,7,10),1) produces serial numbers for the first day of each quarter when *QTR* refers to a cell that contains a number between 1 and 4. Use Format Number to format the cell containing a serial number so that it appears as a date.

> **Tip: *Using Excel's Equivalents to 1-2-3's @DATE and @DATEVALUE***
> Do not use Excel's DATE and DATEVALUE functions to enter dates as you would with the @DATE and @DATEVALUE functions in 1-2-3. Cells in Excel directly accept dates as they normally are typed in American and European formats, such as 12/24/92.

DATEVALUE(*date_text*)

Converts a date written as text into a serial number. The *date_text* can be in any of Excel's predefined date formats. These formats are found in the list box of the Format Number command's dialog box. Excel accepts text dates entered in formulas or directly into cells. The function is most useful with formulas.

Limits: Excel returns serial numbers for dates between January 1, 1900, and December 31, 2078. Enter years between 00 and 178, months from 1 to 12, and days from 1 to 31.

Example: DATEVALUE("24-Dec-92") produces 33962.

DAY(*serial_number*)

Converts a *serial_number* to the number of the day of the month between 1 and 31. Format the cell as a number.

Limits: The serial number must be in the 0 to 65380 range.

Examples: DAY(32501) produces 24.

DAY("24-Dec-91") produces 24.

DAY(B11) produces 24 when B11 contains 24-Dec-91.

 DAYS360(*start_date,end_date*)

Produces the number of days between the *start_date* and the *end_date* in a 360-day year. These calculations are necessary for accounting and finance systems based on twelve 30-day months.

Limits: If the *end_date* occurs before the *start_date*, Excel returns a negative number.

Example: DAYS360("4/1/91",B12) produces 90 when B12 contains the date 7/1/91.

HOUR(*serial_number*)

Hours are the fractional part of a day in a serial number. HOUR returns the number of hours (based on a 24-hour clock) for the fractional day in the *serial_number*. Format the cell as a number.

Examples: HOUR(32501.75) produces 18.

HOUR("24-Dec-92 18:00") produces 18.

MINUTE(*serial_number*)

Returns the number of minutes from a *serial_number*. The fractional part of a day is based on a 24-hour clock. The number of minutes returned is between 0 and 59. Format the cell as a number.

Example: MINUTE(32501.75456) produces 6 minutes.

MONTH(*serial_number*)

Converts the *serial_number* to the number of the month (from 1 to 12). Format the cell as a number.

Examples: MONTH(32501.7546) produces 12.

MONTH(B14) produces 12 if B14 contains "24-Dec-92".

NOW( )

Calculates the serial number of the date and time in the computer's clock. Excel updates the date and time only when the worksheet is opened or recalculated.

Limits: You must include the empty parentheses when entering this function. NOW does not use an argument.

> **Tip: *Stamping Your Worksheets with the Date and Time***
> Use the NOW function to stamp a worksheet with the date and time of printing. Enter NOW in a cell formatted with the **Format Number** command as a date/time format. Each time you retrieve the worksheet or recalculate, the cell contents will be updated. Use **Edit Paste Special** with **Values** selected to freeze a date or time. Do not use NOW in a header or footer; use the codes &D and &T for date and time.

SECOND(*serial_number*)

Returns the number of seconds (between 0 and 59) in the fractional part of the *serial_number*.

Examples: SECOND(32501.753) produces 19.

          SECOND("24-Dec-92 18:04:19") produces 19.

TIME(*hour, minute, second*)

Calculates the serial number when given the *hour*, *minute*, and *second* of time on a 24-hour clock.

Example: TIME(18,4,19) produces .752998.

TIMEVALUE(*time_text*)

Converts a time written as text into a serial number. The *time_text* must be enclosed in quotation marks and must use one of Excel's predefined date or time formats.

Limits: You must enclose the text in quotation marks and use one of Excel's predefined date or time formats. The date is not converted.

Examples: TIMEVALUE("18:04:19") produces .752998.

          TIMEVALUE("12:00 PM") produces .5.

TODAY( )

Calculates the serial number of the computer's current date. This acts the same as the NOW function, but does not return the time portion of the serial number. Excel updates the serial number when the worksheet is opened or recalculated.

WEEKDAY(*serial_number*)

Converts the *serial_number* to the day of the week. The result is a number from 1 (Sunday) to 7 (Saturday).

Examples: WEEKDAY("24-Dec-92") produces 5 (Thursday).

WEEKDAY(B12) produces 5 when cell B12 contains 24-Dec-92.

A similar function is combined with the CHOOSE function in Lotus 1-2-3 to calculate the day of the week. In Excel, it is more efficient to format the cell with the custom date format, *ddd* or *dddd*. This produces Thur or Thursday. You also can create a text string with a formula such as TEXT(B12,"*dddd*"), which produces Thursday. Creating a text string with the TEXT function enables the word "Thursday" to exceed the cell width and to be combined with other text values for use in invoices and calculated titles.

YEAR(*serial_number*)

Converts the *serial_number* into the year.

Example: YEAR(33962) produces 1992.

Financial Functions

Instead of typing financial formulas, you can use Excel's financial functions. Excel functions operate faster and with less chance of error than typed formulas.

Excel provides a family of functions that solve annuity problems. An annuity is a series of even cash flows over a period of time. For example, cash flows may be rent payments coming in according to a regular time period or payments that you make to a retirement fund. A few of the functions that involve annuities are as follows:

> **FV(*rate,nper,pmt,pv,type*)**
> **NPER(*rate,pmt,pv,fv,type*)**
> **PMT(*rate,nper,pv,fv,type*)**
> **RATE(*nper,pmt,pv,fv,type,guess*)**

The *rate* is the periodic interest. The interest period must have the same unit as *nper*—the number of periods (such as months) in the life of the cash flow. For example, the annual interest rate should be divided by 12 if payments or receipts are monthly.

The *pmt* (payment) is the constant amount paid or received in each period on an investment or amortized loan such as a mortgage. Normally, *pmt* contains both principal and interest. Enter cash you pay out, a negative *pmt* (payment), as a negative amount in the function. The worth of something at the end of the last period is the *fv* (future value), and *pv* (present value) is the worth of something at the beginning of the period.

Some functions perform different tasks depending on the number you enter as the *type* argument. When *type* equals zero, cash flow is assumed to be at the end of the period. If *type* equals 1, cash flow is assumed to be at the beginning of the period. If no value is entered for *pv* or *type*, each is assumed to be zero.

guess is your best estimate of the final rate. Usually, a *guess* between 0 and 1 will produce an answer. If *guess* is not entered, a *guess* of 10 percent (.1) is assumed. If your *guess* is too far off, Excel cannot find an answer and #NUM! error is returned.

> **Note: *When* #NUM! *Appears in Financial Functions***
> If #NUM! appears after you enter one of the financial functions, you may have incorrectly entered the positive or negative signs for *pmt*, *pv*, or *fv*. Remember that money you are paying out should appear as a negative number.

Excel also includes functions to analyze uneven cash flows and to calculate depreciation. A few of these functions are as follows:

> **IRR(*values,guess*)**
> **MIRR(*values,finance_rate,reinvest_rate*)**
> **DDB(*cost,salvage,life,period,factor*)**
> **VDB(*cost,salvage,life,start_period,end_period,factor,no_switch*)**
> **DDB(*cost,salvage,life,period,factor*)**

Calculates the depreciation for the *period* you indicate, using the double-declining balance depreciation method. You must indicate the initial *cost*, the *salvage* value at the end of depreciation, and the *life* of the item. *factor* is how quickly the balance declines. If omitted, *factor* is assumed to be 2 for double-declining depreciation.

Limits: The *period* and economic *life* must be in the same units. Check with your CPA or accountant to determine the appropriate economic life.

The function uses the following equation in its calculations:

DDB=((*cost*−prior total depreciation)*factor)/*life*

Example: The lathe in your factory cost $130,000 and will be worth $4,800 at the end of its economic life in 15 years. What is the depreciation amount at different points in the life?

DDB(130000,4800,15,12) results in $3,591.33 for year 12.

DDB(130000,4800,15*12,12) results in $1,277.39 for the month 12 in the first year.

 FV(*rate,nper,pmt,pv,type*)

Calculates the future value of a series of cash flows of equal *pmt* amounts made at even periods for *nper* periods at the constant interest *rate*. A lump sum, *pv*, can be invested at the beginning of the term.

Limits: If no values are entered for *pv* and *type*, they are considered to be zero.

Example: You invest $2,000 as a lump sum, and you add $100 at the beginning of each month for 5 years (60 months) at an interest rate of 8 percent compounded monthly. Use the following function to find the worth of the investment at the end of the term:

FV(.08/12,60,−100,−2000,1)

The result is $10,376.36. Notice that amounts you pay out are negative, and amounts you receive are positive.

IPMT(*rate,per,nper,pv,fv,type*)

Calculates the interest portion of a payment on an annuity. You can use this function to calculate the interest paid on a mortgage at some period, *per*, within the term of the mortgage, *nper*.

Limits: The value of *per* must be in the range 1 to *nper*. If no values are entered for *fv* and *type*, they are considered to be zero.

Example: A flat-rate mortgage of $150,000 is made at 10 percent interest for 30 years. How much was paid toward interest in the 14th month? Use this function to calculate the answer:

IPMT(.10/12,14,360,150000,0,0)

The result is $-1242.44. The result rate is negative because it is the amount you paid out.

IRR(*values,guess*)

Produces the internal rate of return for the series of periodic cash flows found in *values*. The function uses your *guess* as to the rate of return as a starting point for estimation. The result is the rate of return for a single period.

The *values* can be positive and negative cash flows of uneven amounts contained in a range or array of referenced cells. The cash flows must be in the order received. The array or range of values must include at least one sign change (or Excel returns a #NUM! error). If you paid money out at time zero in the investment, the initial value should be a negative number.

guess is your best estimate of the final rate. Usually, a *guess* between 0 and 1 will produce an answer. If *guess* is not entered, a *guess* of 10 percent is assumed. If your *guess* is too far off, Excel cannot find an answer and a #NUM! error is returned.

The IRR function makes continuous estimates of the rate of return until two estimates differ by no more than .00001%. If this resolution cannot be reached after 20 tries, IRR produces the error value #NUM!. If this occurs, change the *guess* and recalculate.

Limits: The IRR method used by all spreadsheets can produce a different solution for each change of sign in the cash flow. You must try different guesses to find the most accurate solution. The IRR method does not allow you to reinvest positive cash flows or save for negative cash flows at realistic rates. The MIRR function produces more realistic results.

Example: Figure 10.5 shows the forecasted cash flows from an apartment complex. Year 0 is the purchase price plus rehabilitation costs. The internal rate of return function in cell G6 is

        IRR(D5:D15,0.1)

        The result of the function is 0.1111655, or 11 percent return. (Cell G6 shows a text version of the function used in cell G5.)

MIRR(*values, finance_rate, reinvest_rate*)

Calculates the modified internal rate of return from a series of positive and negative cash flows in the range *values*. The *finance_rate* specifies the cost of the investment funding. The *reinvest_rate* is the safe rate at which positive cash flows may be reinvested.

Limits: At least one positive and one negative cash flow must be specified.

Example: Consider the same forecasted cash flows from an apartment complex as those used for the IRR function in figure 10.5. For this example, a finance rate of 12 percent and a reinvestment rate of 7 percent are used to make the calculation more realistic. (Finance rate is the rate charged to you on money that you borrow for the investment; reinvestment rate is the rate at which you can reinvest positive cash flows in a safe instrument, such as a CD.) The function in cell G10 is

MIRR(D5:D15,G8,G9)

The result is .104732. This result is a half percent less than it was with the IRR method. On projects with different cash flows or with large amounts, the difference between the IRR method and MIRR method can be substantial. The MIRR method is more realistic.

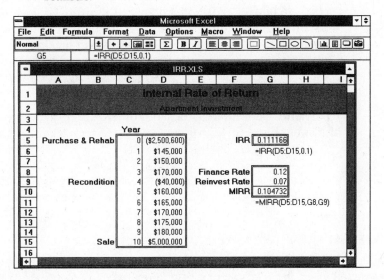

Fig. 10.5. *Although IRR is commonly used to analyze cash flows, MIRR returns a more accurate result.*

NPER(*rate,pmt,pv,fv,type*)

Calculates the number of periods required to create the annuity specified by the given arguments.

Limits: If no values are entered for *fv* and *type*, they are considered to be zero.

Example: NPER(0.10/12,–500,10000) produces 21.969, or **22** payments.

NPV(*rate,value1,value2,...*)

Calculates the net present value of a series of cash flows found in the range or array of *value1*, *value2*, and so on, given a discount rate equal to *rate*. The net present value of a series of cash flows is the value that a future stream of cash represents in terms of cash today, given the fact that future cash can be invested to earn the *rate* percentage.

Limits: The cash flows are considered to be at the end of each period. Cash flows do not have to be equal amounts. The rate must be the rate per period. There can be up to 13 values.

Example: You purchased a piece of equipment for $40,000 cash. You could have invested the cash at 8 percent. At the end of each year for the next five years, the equipment will have saved you $9,000, $6,000, $6,000, $5,000, and $5,000, respectively. At the end of the sixth year, the equipment saves you $5,000, and you sell the equipment for $20,000. Is the purchase worth making?

The net present value of the purchase is

NPV(0.08,9000,6000,6000,5000,5000,25000).

If the values were entered in an array or range of cells the formula also could be

NPV(.08,C15:H15)

The result is $41,072.67. The purchase saved you $1,072.67 over what an equivalent amount invested at 8 percent would earn.

PMT(*rate,nper,pv,fv,type*)

Calculates the periodic payment for different *type*s and future values (*fv*) of investments given the investment's *rate*, term (*nper*), and present value (*pv*).

Limits: If no values are entered for *fv* and *type*, they are considered to be zero.

Example: Suppose that you want to purchase a one-room bungalow in California with a mortgage amount of $190,000 and a flat-rate mortgage of 30 years at 10 percent. If the annual interest is in B12, the annual term in B13, and the mortgage amount in B14, the function would appear in this form:

PMT(B12/12,B13*12,B14)

The result is $-1667.39. Note that the amount is negative because you will be paying out the mortgage. Make sure that the interest rate and term are in the same units as your payment frequency—for example, term in months, interest per month, and one payment per month.

PPMT(*rate,per,nper,pv,fv,type*)

Calculates the principal portion of a payment made on an amortized investment. This portion is the part of the PMT function that reduces a loan balance.

Limits:　If no values are entered for *fv* and *type*, they are considered to be zero.

Example:　Consider the mortgage described in the PMT function example. The payment toward principal in the 12th month will be

PPMT(B12/12,12,B13*12,B14)

The result is $-92.09, which is negative because you are paying out the money.

PV(*rate,nper,pmt,fv,type*)

Calculates the present value of a series of future cash flows of equal *pmt* amounts made at even periods for *nper* periods at the constant interest *rate*. PV is the amount in current dollars that equals an even cash flow in the future. If the amounts of the cash flow are uneven, use the NPV function.

Limits:　If no values are entered for *fv* and *type*, they are considered to be zero.

Example:　You know that you can afford a car payment of $220 per month for the next four years. Current loans are at 9 percent. How large a loan can you afford? The function you need for the calculation is

PV(0.09/12,48,220)

The result is $8,840.65.

RATE(*nper,pmt,pv, fv,type,guess*)

Calculates the interest rate for the annuity that you define with the arguments.

Limits:　If no values are entered for *fv* and *type*, they are considered to be zero. If you do not enter an estimated interest rate for *guess*, Excel uses ten percent (.1). RATE may return more than one solution, depending on the value used for *guess*. If *guess* is too far from the correct value, Excel may not be able to make an estimate and may return #NUM!.

Example:　RATE(12,–800,9000) results in an interest rate of 1.007 percent per month (12.09 percent per year).

SLN(*cost,salvage,life*)

Returns the annual amount of straight-line depreciation when given the initial *cost* of an item, the *salvage* value at the end of the item's economic life, and the economic *life* of the item.

Example:　SLN(40000,12000,5) produces $5,600 per year depreciation.

SYD(*cost,salvage,life,per*)

Calculates the depreciation for the period, *per*, using the sum-of-the-years depreciation method. You must indicate the initial *cost*, the *salvage* value at the end of the economic life, and the *life* of the item.

Examples: SLN(40000,12000,5,1) produces $9,333 depreciation for the first year.

SLN(40000,12000,5,2) produces $7,467 depreciation for the second year.

 VDB(*cost,salvage,life,start_period,end_period*, *factor,no_switch*)

The variable declining-balance depreciation function returns the depreciation on an asset for the period you indicate. The *cost*, *salvage*, and *life* arguments have the same definitions as described in earlier functions.

Start_period is the period at which you want to start calculating depreciation and *end_period* is the ending period for the calculation. Both must be in the same units as the *life*.

Factor is the rate at which the balance declines. If *factor* is omitted, it is assumed to be 2 (for double-declining balance).

No_switch is a logical argument indicating whether VDB should switch to straight-line depreciation when it is greater than the declining-balance depreciation. Using TRUE for *no_switch* prevents the switch to straight-line method. FALSE, or omitting the *no_switch* argument, enables the switch to straight-line method. All arguments must be positive.

Information Functions

Information functions are necessary when cell contents, ranges, or selected areas must be analyzed before performing a function or macro. Additional macro functions for directory management are available through add-ins. Chapter 15, "Using Excel's Add-In Macros," describes these functions.

 ADDRESS(*row_num,column_num,abs_num,a1,sheet_text*)

Produces a cell reference in text form for the cell indicated by the *row_num* and *col_num*. Use one of four values in *abs_num* to specify the type of reference:

1 Absolute reference (default)
2 Absolute row, relative column

3 Relative row, absolute column

4 Relative reference

If the *a1* argument is TRUE, or omitted, Excel returns A1 style references. FALSE returns the R1C1 style reference. *sheet_text* is the name of the worksheet or macro sheet used by the reference.

Other functions related to ADDRESS are CELL, ACTIVE.CELL, OFFSET, INDEX, ROW, COLUMN, and SELECTION.

Examples: ADDRESS(15,4,2,TRUE) = D$15.

ADDRESS(Counter.Row,4,4,FALSE,"ASSETS.XLS") = ASSETS.XLS!R[25]C[4]

where Counter.Row is a name containing the value 25.

AREAS(*reference*)

Returns the number of areas in *reference*. Use the AREAS function to find how many selections are within an area.

Example: AREAS(PRINTOUT) results in 2 when the range named PRINTOUT is defined as the two ranges A1:F55 and G56:O210.

CELL(*info_type*,*reference*)

Returns information about the cell contents of the active cell, or the *reference* cell. The *info_type* determines what the cell contents are checked for. The possible values of *info_type* and the result returned by the function are listed in table 10.2.

Table 10.2
Results Returned by the CELL Function

info_type	Returned value
"width"	The column width in integer numbers, measured in terms of the currently selected font.
"row"	The row number of the reference.
"col"	The column number of the reference.
"protect"	0 if the cell is not locked; 1 if it is locked.
"address"	The first cell in the reference, given in text form; for example, $B$2.
"contents"	The value in the reference.

continues

Table 13.2 *(continued)*

info_type	Returned value
"format"	The text value showing the cell format; examples:

Format	Text Value
General	G
0	F0
#,##0	,0
0.00	F2
#,##0.00	,2
$#,##0_);($#,##0)	C0
$#,##0_);[Red]($#,##0)	C0-
$#,##0.00_);($#,##0.00)	C2
$#,##0.00_);[Red]($#,##0.00)	C2-
0%	P0
0.00%	P2
0.00E+00	S2
#?/? or #??/??	G
m/d/yy or m/d/yy h:mm	D4
d-mmm-yy	D1
d-mmm	D2
mmm-yy	D3
h:mm AM/PM	D7
h:mm:ss AM/PM	D6
h:mm	D9
h:mm:ss	D8

In addition, – is returned for negative formats that use color and ( ) is returned for negative formats that use parentheses.

"prefix"	The label prefix for alignments:

'	Left alignment
"	Right alignment
^	Center alignment
""	All other alignments

"type"	The text value showing the cell format:

b	Blank
l	Text constant (label)
v	Value (all other values)

"color"	1 if cell is formatted for color with negative number; 0 if it is not.

info_type	Returned value
"filename"	The path and file name of the file that contains the reference; nothing is returned if the sheet has not been saved.
"parentheses"	1 is returned if the cell is formatted so that positive numbers display in parentheses; 0 if positive numbers are displayed without parentheses.

Limits: The CELL function is used primarily with macros translated from Lotus 1-2-3. For greater capabilities with Excel macros, use the GET.CELL macro.

Example: CELL("type",B36) results in b if B36 is blank.

Tip: *Using IF with CELL To Display a Message*
IF(CELL("type",B12)="b","Enter a name here","") results in the text
Enter a name here whenever cell B12 is blank. This prompts for data entry.

COLUMN(*reference*)

Produces the column number of the *reference* cell. If *reference* is an array or a range, then the column numbers of each column in the range return as an horizontal array. If the *reference* argument is not specified, COLUMN produces the column number of the cell that contains the function. *Reference* cannot contain multiple areas. (Use the INDEX function to read values from an array.)

Examples: COLUMN(C15) returns 3.

If Print is the range name of the range C5:E20, COLUMN(Print) returns the array {3,4,5}.

COLUMNS(*array*)

Returns the number of columns in *array*.

Example: COLUMNS(E4:G6) produces 3.

INDIRECT(*ref_text,a1*)

Returns the contents of the cell whose reference is in the cell indicated by *ref_text*. The *ref_text* argument must be an A1 or R1C1 reference or a cell name; otherwise, an error is returned. When *a1* is TRUE, 1, or omitted, INDIRECT expects *ref_text* to be A1 style. When *ref_text* is FALSE, or 0, INDIRECT expects R1C1 style.

Example: INDIRECT(A20) results in 5 if A20 contains the cell reference B35 (without quotes) and cell B35 contains 5.

INFO(*type_num*)

Determines information about the operating system and environment. *type_num* indicates what information you want to learn, as in the following list.

type_num	Returned Value
"directory"	current directory
"memavail"	memory available
"numfile"	number of active worksheets
"osversion"	operating system version
"recalc"	recalculation mode: Automatic or Manual
"release"	Microsoft Excel version
"system"	operating system name: Windows = pcdos; OS/2 = pcos2; Macintosh = Mac
"totmem"	memory available, in bytes; includes memory in use
"memused"	memory used for data, in bytes

IS*function*(*value*)

Excel has nine worksheet functions that determine whether a cell meets certain conditions, such as whether it is blank or contains an error value. Depending on the status of the cell, the IS*function* produces either a TRUE or FALSE *value*.

IS*functions* are most useful when used with the IF function to test whether a cell or range is blank or contains numbers, text, or errors. For example, you might want to prevent the division by zero error, #DIV/0!. Consider the following formula entered in a cell next to C13:

=IF(ISERROR(B12/C13),"C13 must not be zero",B12/C13)

This formula determines whether B12/C13 produces an error. If an error is produced, the formula prints the message C13 must not be zero. If an error is not produced, the division result appears.

You also can use IS*functions* to test for the proper type of entry. This example tests to make sure that B36 contains a number:

=IF(ISNUMBER(B36),"Good entry","Entry not a number")

The IS*functions* and their results are listed in table 10.3.

Table 10.3
Excel IS*functions*

Function	Result
ISBLANK(*value*)	TRUE if *value* is a blank reference; FALSE if *value* is nonblank.
ISERR(*value*)	TRUE if *value* is any error other than #N/A; FALSE for any other *value*.
ISERROR(*value*)	TRUE if *value* is any error value; FALSE if *value* is not an error value.
ISLOGICAL(*value*)	TRUE if *value* is a logical value; FALSE if *value* is not a logical value.
ISNA(*value*)	TRUE if *value* is the #N/A error value; FALSE if *value* is not #N/A.
ISNONTEXT(*value*)	TRUE if *value* is not text; FALSE if *value* is text.
ISNUMBER(*value*)	TRUE if *value* is a number; FALSE if *value* is not a number.
ISREF(*value*)	TRUE if *value* is a reference; FALSE if *value* is not a reference.
ISTEXT(*value*)	TRUE if *value* is text; FALSE if *value* is not text.

N(*value*)

Translates *value* into a number. N translates numbers or numbers as text ("9") into numbers, and logical TRUE into 1. Any other value becomes 0. The N function is used primarily to provide compatibility when converting other worksheets. A related function is **VALUE( )**.

Examples: N("9 nine") produces 0.

N(A12) produces 1 if A12 is TRUE.

Tip: *Converting Numbers Entered in 1-2-3 Worksheets*
Numbers entered into 1-2-3 worksheets preceded by a ', ", or ^ are actually text. When the worksheets are opened in Excel, these "numbers" may not be evaluated as numbers. Use the VALUE or N function to convert the text numbers into numbers that Excel can evaluate.

NA( )

Always produces the error value #N/A, which means "No value Available." NA does not take an argument. You can type **#N/A** directly into a cell for the same result. Include the parentheses after NA.

> **Tip:** *Typing #N/A Directly into Blank Cells*
> Enter **#N/A** into blank data-entry cells. If a data-entry cell is not filled, the formulas that depend upon this cell result in #N/A.

OFFSET(*reference,rows,cols,height,width*)

Returns the reference that is offset from the *reference* cell by a specified number of *rows* or *cols*. The height and width of an offset range can be controlled by the *height* and *width* values. If *height* and *width* are omitted, OFFSET uses the height and width of the *reference*.

OFFSET is an excellent way to retrieve data from a historical table of information. The second example shows how this function can be used to retrieve data from a table of sales histories.

Use OFFSET with the SELECTION and FORMULA functions in macros to select ranges or to enter values on worksheets. Using OFFSET to specify the cell to act on is much faster than concatenating text references. For more information on how OFFSET is used in macros, refer to OFFSET examples in Chapters 29, 30, and 31.

Limits: If the offset extends beyond the edge of the worksheet, the function returns the #REF! error.

Examples: OFFSET(C3,1,2) entered in a worksheet results in the value stored in E4.

           OFFSET(Sales.History,Product.Row,Month.Col) entered in a worksheet returns the value stored in the cell that is offset from the cell named Sales.History by the number of rows stored in Product.Row and the number of columns stored in Month.Col.

           OFFSET(C3,1,2,3,4) returns an array of values three rows high and four columns wide. These values are returned from a range of cells of the same size and whose upper left corner is specified as offset from C3 by one row and two columns, or E4.

           To enter this formula, type values to be returned in cells below and to the right of E4. Then select a range in another location that is three rows by four columns, type the OFFSET function, and press Shift+Ctrl+Enter to enter the function as an array. The cells containing the OFFSET array function return the value from the cell in the corresponding position to E4. If you select a cell range larger than the three-by-four range in which to enter the array, unneeded cells return the #N/A error.

ROW(*reference*)

Results in the row number of the *reference* cell. If *reference* is a range, ROW produces a vertical array of the row numbers. If you don't specify the *reference* argument, ROW produces the row number of the cell in which the function is entered. Use the INDEX function to extract a row number as a specific element within ROW.

Examples: ROW(D5) results in 5.

ROW(D5:F7) results in {5;6;7}. When entered into a single cell, the result displays as 5. When entered by selecting three cells in a column and pressing Shift+Ctrl+Enter, the result displays each row number.

The formula =INDEX(ROW(D5:F7),3,1) entered in a single cell finds the row number in the third row of the first column of the array. The array {5;6;7} has only one column and three rows, so the value returned is 7.

ROWS(*array*)

Produces the number of rows in *array*.

Example: ROWS(B12:D35) results in 24.

 ### T(*value*)

Returns the text equivalent of the *value*. This function is included for compatibility when converting other worksheets.

TYPE(*value*)

Determines the type of a cell's contents and produces a corresponding code, as shown in table 10.4.

Table 10.4
Results of the TYPE Function

Value	Result
Number	1
Text	2
Logical value	4
Error value	16
Array	64

Examples: TYPE(B36) results in 1 if B36 contains a number.

TYPE(B36) results in 16 if B36 contains #N/A.

Logical Functions

The logical functions are powerful worksheet functions that enable you to add decision-making and logical preferences to your worksheets results. The IF statement is useful for testing conditions and making decisions. AND and OR functions can test multiple *criteria* or test conditions for use within IF functions.

AND(*logical1*,*logical2*,...)

Joins test conditions: Returns TRUE if all *logical* arguments are TRUE; FALSE if any *logical* argument is FALSE.

Limits: Arguments must be single logical values or arrays that contain logical values. AND cannot contain more than 14 *logical* values. The #VALUE! error results if there are no logical values in the arguments.

Example: AND(B36,C12>20) is TRUE only when B36 is not zero and C12 is greater than 20.

FALSE( )

Always produces a logical FALSE. Type the parentheses without an argument.

IF(*logical_test*,*value_if_true*,*value_if_false*)

Produces the *value_if_true* when the *logical_test* evaluates as TRUE; produces the *value_if_false* when the *logical_test* evaluates as FALSE. If *value_if_false* is omitted, the value FALSE is returned when *logical_test* evaluates as FALSE.

IF is one of the most valuable functions in Excel; this function can test cells and make decisions based on the cell contents.

> **Tip: *Using IF with Other Logical Functions***
> Use the AND, OR, and NOT functions with the IF function to make complex decisions. Examples of AND and OR can be found in Chapter 13, "Building Extensive Worksheets," and in the macro examples in Chapters 29, 30, and 31.

In macros, *value_if_true* and *value_if_ false* can be GOTO functions or action functions, as in this example:

> IF(Counter>10,GOTO(End),GOTO(Loop))

Limits: Up to seven IF functions can be nested.

Example: IF(Invent.Qnty<Invent.Order,"Reorder","") results in the message Reorder whenever the inventory quantity falls below the order quantity.

NOT(*logical*)

Reverses the result of the *logical* argument from TRUE to FALSE or from FALSE to TRUE. Use this function to return the opposite condition of the logical_test in an IF statement.

Example: IF(NOT(OR(B36=12,B36=20)),"Not a 12 or 20","Is a 12 or 20"). This statement determines whether B36 does not contain a 12 or 20 and produces the message Not a 12 or 20 when the cell does not.

OR(*logical1, logical2,...*)

Joins test conditions: Returns TRUE if one or more *logical* argument is TRUE; FALSE only when all *logical* arguments are FALSE.

Limits: OR is limited to 14 or fewer arguments. Arguments cannot be blank cells, error values, or text. Use IS *functions* within OR functions to test for blank cells, error values, or text.

Example: IF(OR(B36=12,B36=20),"Is a 12 or 20","Not a 12 or 20"). This statement checks whether B36 contains either 12 or 20 and produces the message Is a 12 or 20 when it does. If B36 contains anything else, the message Not a 12 or 20 appears.

TRUE( )

Always produces TRUE. Type the parentheses without an argument.

Lookup Functions

The LOOKUP and MATCH functions enable your worksheets to retrieve a value from within a table. Examples of many of these functions are found in Chapter 13, "Building Extensive Worksheets." INDEX functions enable you to extract specific values from within an array. The OFFSET function, listed previously with Information Functions, enables you to retrieve information that is offset a specified distance from a base reference.

CHOOSE(*index_num,value1,value2,...*)

Chooses from the list of *value*s a value that corresponds to the *index_num*. For example, when the *index_num* is 2, the function chooses *value2*. When used in a macro, the CHOOSE function can have values that are GOTO or action functions.

Limits: CHOOSE displays #VALUE when the *index_num* is less than one or greater than the number of items in the list.

Examples: CHOOSE(B12,5,12,32,14) produces 32 when B12 contains 3.

DATE(1992,CHOOSE(*QTR*,1,4,7,10),1) produces the serial number for the first day of each quarter when *QTR* refers to a cell containing a number from 1 to 4.

HLOOKUP(*lookup_value,table_array,row_index_num*)

Looks across the top row of the range defined by *table_array* until the *lookup_value* is met; then looks down that column to the row specified by *row_index_num*.

Limits: Values in the first row of *table_array* must be in ascending order, both alphabetically (A-Z) and numerically (0-9). The *lookup_value* and the values in the first row of the *table_array* can be text, numbers, or logical values.

If the *lookup_value* is not found, HLOOKUP uses the largest value that is less than or equal to the *lookup_value*. This results in the return of a value even though an exact match for the *lookup_value* is not found. If you want to find an exact match in a table, use the MATCH and INDEX functions in combination, as described in Chapter 13, "Building Extensive Worksheets."

row_index_num begins with 1. To return a value from the first row, use 1, and from the second row, use 2, and so on. If *row_index_num* is less than 1, HLOOKUP produces the #VALUE! error. If *row_index_num* is greater than the number of rows in the table, #REF! is displayed.

Examples: Refer to Chapter 13, "Building Extensive Worksheets," for examples using the HLOOKUP function.

INDEX(*reference,row_num,column_num,area_num*)

In the reference form, INDEX produces a cell reference from within the *reference* specified and at the intersection of the *row_num* and *column_num*. Other functions convert the value returned by INDEX to a cell reference or value as needed.

The referenced area is *reference*. If this area contains multiple ranges, enclose the reference in parentheses, as in (B36:D45,G56:H62). If *reference* contains more than one area, *area_num* can choose between areas. In the preceding example, an *area_num* of 2 will choose G56:H62. If you do not include an *area_num*, Excel assumes it is 1.

The arguments *row_num* and *column_num* choose a cell within the area specified. The first row or column is 1. Omitting the *row_num* or *column_num* or using 0 returns a reference for the entire row or column. A second form of the INDEX function is used with arrays, which is shown next.

Limits: If either *row_num* or *column_num* is outside the specified area, INDEX results in the message #REF!.

Example: INDEX((B2:C5,E7:G9),1,2,2) produces the reference or value in F7, the second area, first row, second column.

INDEX(*array*,*row_num*,*column_num*)

In the array form of INDEX, *row_num* and *col_num* return the value of a cell within the array. The definitions of *row_num* and *col_num* are the same as described in the reference version of INDEX.

Examples: INDEX({3,4,5;8,9,10},2,3) produces 10.

INDEX({3,4,5;8,9,10},0,3) produces the single-column matrix {5;10} when the INDEX function is entered as an array formula by using Shift+Ctrl+Enter.

LOOKUP(*lookup_value*,*lookup_vector*,*result_vector*)

LOOKUP can be either a vector or an array function. This description applies to the vector function. A *lookup_vector* contains a single row or column. This function searches through the *lookup_vector* until the *lookup_value* is found. The function then produces the value that is in the same location in the *result_vector*. If the *lookup_value* can't be found, LOOKUP returns a value corresponding to the largest value less than or equal to the *lookup_value*. If the *lookup_value* is smaller than any value in *lookup_vector*, the message #NA is returned.

Limits: Values in *lookup_vector* can be text, numbers, or logical values. They must be sorted in ascending order to give the correct return.

LOOKUP(*lookup_value*,*array*)

The array form of LOOKUP is similar to HLOOKUP and VLOOKUP. LOOKUP searches for a match to *lookup_value* in the first row or the first column of the *array*, depending on the shape of the array. If the array is square, or wider than tall, LOOKUP searches across the first row for the *lookup_value*. If the array is taller than it is wide, the search proceeds down the first column.

If LOOKUP can't find the *lookup_value*, it finds the largest value less than the *lookup_value*. If *lookup_value* is smaller than the smallest value in the row or column being examined, the message #N/A is returned.

The value returned is taken from the last row or column in the *array* that matches the *lookup_value*.

Limits: The row or column being examined for the *lookup_value* must be sorted in ascending order.

MATCH(*lookup_value*,*lookup_array*,*match_type*)

MATCH returns the position of the match for *lookup_value* in the *lookup_array*. The type of match is determined by *match_type*. The *lookup_value* can be a number, text, logical value, or cell reference.

When combined with the INDEX function, as shown in Chapter 13, the MATCH function enables you to find exact matches to a *lookup_value* or return an error. This prevents the possible use of an incorrect value returned by VLOOKUP, HLOOKUP or LOOKUP.

The types of match are given here with a description of what each match type finds:

match_type	Finds
1, or omitted	Largest value less than or equal to *lookup_value*. The *lookup_array* must be in sorted order. The default is 1 if *match_type* is omitted.
0	First value that is an exact match.
−1	Smallest value greater than or equal to *lookup_value*. The *lookup_array* must be in sorted order.

See Chapter 15, "Using Excel's Add-In Macros," to learn how to add the FASTMATCH function to your worksheets. Chapter 13, "Building Extensive Databases," contains examples of how to use MATCH and INDEX to look up exact matches from a list.

Limits: MATCH returns the row or column position within the array of the found item, not its value or cell reference.

VLOOKUP(*lookup_value,table_array,col_index_num*)

Looks down the left column of *table_array* until the *lookup_value* is met, and then looks across that row to the column specified by *col_index_num*. Values in the first column can be text, numbers, or logical values in ascending order. Upper- and lowercase text are considered the same.

Limits: If VLOOKUP can't find the *lookup_value*, the function searches for the next largest value in the first column. Other limits are the same as described in the discussion of the HLOOKUP function.

Examples: Refer to Chapter 13, "Building Extensive Worksheets," for examples using the lookup functions.

Mathematical Functions

Mathematical functions provide the foundation for the majority of worksheet calculations. Most scientific and engineering functions are found under mathematical functions. If you do not find the function you need, you can create your own by referring to Chapter 28, "Command and Function Macro Quick Start," and Chapter 29, "Creating Macros and Add-In Macros."

ABS(*number*)

Returns the absolute (positive) value of the *number*.

Examples: ABS(–5) produces 5.
　　　　　ABS(5) produces 5.

EXP(*number*)

Returns e raised to the power of *number*. EXP is the inverse of the LN function.

Limits: The value of e is 2.71828182845904.

Examples: EXP(0) produces 1.
　　　　　EXP(LN(10)) produces 10.

FACT(*number*)

Returns the factorial of the *number*. A noninteger *number* is truncated.

Example:　FACT(4) produces 24 (4*3*2*1).

INT(*number*)

Rounds the *number* down to the nearest integer.

Examples: INT(7.6) produces 7.
　　　　　INT(–7.6) produces -8.

> **Tip: *Rounding Numbers in Three Ways***
> Use INT( ) to round a number down to the nearest integer. Use
> TRUNC( ) to truncate a number by removing the decimal portion.
> Use ROUND( ) to round a number to a specific number of places to
> the left or right of the decimal.

LN(*number*)

Returns the natural log of the *number* in base e. LN is the inverse of EXP.

Limits: The value of the *number* must be positive.

Example: LN(3) produces `1.098612289`.

LOG(*number, base*)

Returns the logarithm of the *number* in the *base* specified.

Limits: The value of the *number* must be positive. LOG uses base 10 if the *base* argument is omitted.

Examples: LOG(10) produces `1`.
LOG(64,2) produces `6`.

LOG10(*number*)

Returns the logarithm of the *number* in base 10.

Examples: LOG10(10) produces `1`.
LOG10(100) produces `2`.

MOD(*number, divisor*)

Produces the remainder (modulus), of the *number* divided by the *divisor*.

Limits: The `#DIV/0!` error appears if the *divisor* is zero.

Examples: MOD(7,6) produces `1`.
MOD(32,15) produces `2`.

PI( )

Returns the value of π.

Limits: An estimate of π, 3.14159265358979, is used. The parentheses must be included even though the function does not take an argument.

PRODUCT(*number1, number2,...*)

Multiplies *number1* by *number2* by the rest of the arguments.

Limits: You can specify up to 14 arguments. Arguments that are blank cells, logical values, error values, or text are ignored. Text that can be converted into a numeric value is converted.

Example: PRODUCT(B12:C14) produces 24 when cells B12 through C14 contain the numbers 1, 2, 3, and 4.

RAND( )

Produces a random decimal number from 0 to 1. The function does not take an argument between the parentheses. Press F9, choose Options Calculate Now, or hold down Shift and choose Options Calculate Document to produce new random numbers. Freeze random numbers by copying them with Edit Copy and pasting them on top of themselves. For this operation, choose Edit Paste Special and select the Paste Values and Operations None options.

See Chapter 15, "Using Excel's Add-In Macros," to learn how to add the RANDBETWEEN function to your worksheets.

ROUND(*number,num_digits*)

Rounds the *number* to the number of digits, *num_digits*, specified. If *num_digits* is positive, the number rounds to the specified decimal places to the right of the decimal point. If *num_digits* is zero, the number rounds to an integer. If *num_digits* is negative, the number rounds upward to the left of the decimal point.

Examples: ROUND(456.345,2) produces 456.35.
                ROUND(546789,–3) produces 547000.

> **Tip: *Rounding Up and Down***
> The ROUND(*x,n*) function normally rounds the *x* attribute up or down to *n* decimal places, depending on whether the decimal part of the number is equal to or greater than .5. If you want all numbers to be rounded up, add .5 to the numbers you are rounding, as in this example:
>
>   =ROUND(A12+.5,2)
>
> This formula rounds any value in cell A12 to the next higher number.

SIGN(*number*)

Produces 1 when the *number* is positive, 0 when it is 0, and -1 when it is negative.

Example: SIGN(B12) produces 1 when B12 contains 5, and -1 when B12 contains –23.

SQRT(*number*)

Returns the square root of the *number*.

Limits: The value of the *number* must be positive.

Example: SQRT(25) produces 5.

SUM(*number1,number2,...*)

Calculates the sum of the arguments. Arguments that cannot be converted from text to numbers or error values are ignored.

Example: SUM(B36:B40) produces 25 if the range includes the numbers 3, 4, 5, 6, and 7.

 SUMPRODUCT(*array1,array2,...*)

Results in the sum of the product of the arrays. All the arrays must have the same size. You can specify two to fourteen arguments.

Example: SUMPRODUCT(B8:B10,C8:C10) results in 12 where B8:B10 contains 1, 2, and 3 and C8:C10 contains 2,2, and 2.

TRUNC(*number,num_digits*)

Changes the *number* to an integer by "cutting off," or truncating, the decimal fraction portion. If *num_digits* is omitted, it is assumed to be zero.

Example: TRUNC(5.6) produces 5.

Matrix Functions

In all the matrix functions except TRANSPOSE, *array* is a square numeric array stated as a range (such as B36:C37) or as an array constant (such as {3,54;4,65}). The error value #VALUE! is returned if cells contain text or are empty, or if the matrix is not square. Entry and edit methods and examples for matrix functions are discussed in Chapter 13, "Building Extensive Worksheets." Matrix functions can save memory and produce results using fewer cells than other formulas.

MDETERM(*array*)

Produces the determinant of *array*. The array can be a reference, such as B36:C37, or an array constant, such as {1,2,3;5,6,7;8,9,10}.

MINVERSE(*array*)

Produces the inverse of *array*. The array can be a reference, such as B36:C37, or an array constant, such as {1,2,3;5,6,7;8,9,10}.

Because the MINVERSE function produces an array as a result, you must enter this function as an array formula by selecting a square range of cells of equivalent size, typing the formula, and then pressing Shift+Ctrl+Enter.

MMULT(*array1,array2*)

Produces the product of *array1* and *array2*. The number of columns in *array1* must be the same as the number of rows in *array2*. The arrays must contain only numbers.

Because the MMULT function produces an array as a result, you must enter the MMULT function as an array formula, as described under MINVERSE.

TRANSPOSE(*array*)

Transposes the current *array* so that the first row in the current *array* becomes the first column of the new array, the second row of the current *array* becomes the second column of the new array, and so on.

Because the TRANSPOSE function produces an array as a result, you must enter the TRANSPOSE function as an array formula. Entering the TRANSPOSE function is described in Chapter 13, "Building Extensive Worksheets."

Statistical Functions

Statistical functions can help you with simple problems, such as finding an average or counting items. Statistical functions can also do simple statistical analysis, such as biased or nonbiased standard deviation.

AVERAGE(*number1,number2,...*)

Returns the average (mean) of the arguments. The ranges can contain numbers, cell references, or arrays that contain numbers. Text, logical values, errors, and blank cells are ignored.

Limits: AVERAGE can take from 1 to 14 arguments.

Examples: AVERAGE(B12:B15) produces 3.5 when B12:B15 contains the numbers 2, 3, 4, and 5.

AVERAGE(B12:B15,20) produces 6.8 when B12:B15 contains the numbers 2, 3, 4, and 5.

COUNT(*value1,value2,...*)

Produces a count of the numbers in the arguments. The *value* arguments can be numbers, cell references, or arrays that contain numbers. Text, logical values, errors, and blank cells are not counted.

Limits: You can include from 1 to 14 arguments in COUNT.

Example: COUNT(B12:B15) produces 4 when B12 to B15 contains the numbers 2, 3, 4, and 5. The statement produces 3 if B12 is blank instead of containing 2.

COUNTA(*value1, value2,...*)

Produces a count of the values in the arguments. This function counts text values as well as numbers. Empty cells within arrays or references are ignored. COUNTA determines the number of nonblank cells.

Limits: You can include from 1 to 14 arguments in COUNTA.

Example: COUNTA(A12:A20) produces 8 if cell A13 is the only blank cell.

COUNTA(B12:B15) produces 4 when B12:B15 contains the values 2, "Tree", 4, and "Pine".

 GROWTH(*known_y's, known_x's, new_x's, const*)

Calculates the exponential growth curve that best fits the test data contained in the ranges *known_y's* and *known_x's*. GROWTH then uses the *new_x's* values to calculate new *y* values along the calculated curve. If *const* is TRUE or omitted, the constant term is calculated. If *const* is FALSE, 1 is used for the constant term.

Because the GROWTH function produces an array, you must enter the GROWTH function as an array formula. See Chapter 13 for examples on entering similar trend analysis functions.

 LINEST(*known_y's, known_x's, const, stats*)

LINEST calculates the straight line equation that best fits the data and produces an array of values that define the equation of that line. If *known_x's* is omitted, an array equal in size to *known_y's* is used with values of $\{1,2,3,...\}$.

The line has the equation

$$y = b + m_1 * x_1 + m_2 * x_2 + ...$$

Excel uses a least-squares fit to find the best straight-line fit to the data. The array returned is of the form $\{m_1, m_2,..., b\}$. The constants within that array can be used to calculate *y* values on the line for any given set of x_1, x_2, and so on.

If *const* is TRUE or omitted, the constant term is calculated; if FALSE, the constant is zero. If *stats* is FALSE or omitted, the slope and y-intercept are returned. If *stats* is TRUE, the following statistics are returned:

Standard error for each coefficient
Standard error for the constant b
Coefficient of determination (r-squared)
Standard error for the y-estimate
F-statistic
Degrees of freedom
Regression sum of squares
Residual sum of squares

Examples: Examples of the trend analysis functions are included in Chapter 13, "Building Extensive Worksheets."

 LOGEST(*known_y's,known_x's,const,stats*)

Calculates the exponential curve of the form

$$y=b*(m_1{}^{\wedge}x_1)*(M_2{-}^{\wedge}x_2)*....$$

that best fits the data. When given the data *known_y's* and *known_x's*, the values for *b* and *m* are returned in a horizontal array of the form $\{m_1,m_2,...,b\}$.

If *const* is TRUE or omitted, the constant term is calculated. If *const* is FALSE, the constant is 1. If *stats* is FALSE or omitted, only the slope and y-intercept are returned. If *stats* is TRUE, the function returns the following statistics in an array:

Standard error for each coefficient
Standard error for the constant b
Coefficient of determination (r-squared)
Standard error for the y-estimate
F-statistic
Degrees of freedom
Regression sum of squares
Residual sum of squares

MAX(*number1,number2,...*)

Produces the largest value among the arguments.

Limits: MAX can take up to 14 arguments. Arguments that are error values or text that cannot be interpreted as a number are ignored. Within a referenced array or range, any empty cells, logical values, text, or error values are ignored.

Example: MAX(C2:D4) produces 32 if the numbers in these cells are –2, 4, 32, and 30.

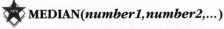 **MEDIAN(*number1,number2,...*)**

Returns the median value of the arguments.

MIN(*number1*,*number2*,...)

Produces the smallest value among the arguments.

Limits: MIN can take up to 14 arguments. Arguments that are not numbers are ignored. If the arguments contain no numbers, MIN produces 0.

Example: MIN(C2:D4) produces -2 if the numbers in these cells are –2, 4, 32, and 30.

STDEV(*number1*,*number2*,...)

Calculates an estimate of the standard deviation of a population from a sample of the population.

Limits: STDEV can take up to 14 arguments. If the arguments include the entire population, use STDEVP.

Example: STDEV(B2:B12) produces 12.12 when the range from B2 to B12 contains 98, 67, 89, 76, 76, 54, 87, 78, 85, 83, and 90.

STDEVP(*number1*,*number2*,...)

Calculates the standard deviation of a population, where the entire population is listed in the arguments.

Limits: STDEV can take up to 14 arguments. If the arguments do not include the entire population, use STDEV.

Example: STDEVP(B2:B12) produces 11.55 when the range from B2 to B12 contains 98, 67, 89, 76, 76, 54, 87, 78, 85, 83, and 90.

 TREND(*known_y's*,*known_x's*,*new_x's*,*const*)

Returns the values along a straight line that best fit the data in the arrays *known_y's*. If a *known_x's* array is omitted, an array of the same size is used that contains the values {1,2,3,...}. For each value in the *new_x's* array, the TREND function produces an array of corresponding *y* values. If *const* is TRUE or omitted, the constant term is calculated. If FALSE, the constant term is zero.

Examples: Examples of the trend analysis functions are included in Chapter 13, "Building Extensive Worksheets."

VAR(*number1*,*number2*,...)

Calculates an estimate of the variance in a population from a sample given in the arguments.

Limits: Use VARP if the arguments contain the entire population.

VARP(*number1*,*number2*,...)

Calculates the variance when given the entire population as arguments.

Limits: Use VAR if the arguments contain only a sample of the population.

Text Functions

Text functions enable you to manipulate text. You can parse text to pull-out portions you need from long strings of text. Or you can change numbers and dates to text so that they can exceed a cell's width without producing a cell filled with #####. Numbers or dates converted to text can be concatenated (joined) to text in titles, sentences, and labels. Text functions are also very important for manipulating text that will be converted to ASCII files to be loaded onto mainframe computers.

CHAR(*number*)

Produces the character corresponding to the ASCII code *number* between 1 and 255.

Example: CHAR(65) is A.

CLEAN(*text*)

Removes from the specified *text* argument any characters that are lower than ASCII 32 or above ASCII 127. These characters are not printed. This function is useful for removing control codes, bells, and non-ASCII characters from imported text.

CODE(*text*)

Produces the ASCII code of the first letter in the specified *text*.

Example: CODE("Excel") produces 69.

DOLLAR(*number*,*decimals*)

Rounds the *number* to the specified number of *decimals* to the right of the decimal point and converts the number to text in a currency format. This text can be concatenated with other text phrases.

Use the DOLLAR function to incorporate numbers in text. For example, consider the following statement:

    ="Your reimbursement is "&DOLLAR(A12,2)&"."

When A12 contains the number 2456.78, this is the result:

```
Your reimbursement is $2,456.78.
```

If you specify a negative number for the *decimal* argument, the function rounds the *number* to the left of the decimal point. If you omit the *decimal* argument, the function assumes two decimal places.

Examples: DOLLAR(32.45,2) results in $32.45.
DOLLAR(5432.45,–3) results in $5,000.

EXACT(*text1,text2*)

Compares *text1* and *text2*: if they are exactly the same, returns the logical TRUE; if they are not the same, returns FALSE. Upper- and lowercase text are considered to be different.

Example: EXACT("Glass tumbler",A12) produces TRUE when A12 contains the text "Glass tumbler", but produces FALSE when A12 contains "glass tumbler".

FIND(*find_text,within_text,start_num*)

Beginning at *start_num*, FIND searches the text specified by *within_text* to locate *find_text*. If *find_text* is found, the FIND function produces the character location where *find_text* starts. If *start_num* is out of limits or a match is not found, the #VALUE! error value is displayed. If *start_num* is not specified, it is assumed to be 1.

Example: FIND(B12,"ABCDEFGHIJKLMNOPQRSTUVWXYZ") produces 3 if B12 contains "C".

FIXED(*number,decimals*)

Rounds the *number* to the specified *decimals* and displays it as text in fixed decimal format with commas. If you omit *decimals*, the *number* is rounded to two decimal places. If you specify a negative number of *decimals*, the function rounds the *number* to the left of the decimal point.

Examples: FIXED(9876.543) produces 9,876.54.
FIXED(9876.543,–3) produces 10,000.

LEFT(*text,num_chars*)

Produces the leftmost number of characters from *text*.

Limits: The value of *num_chars* must be greater than zero. If the value is omitted, it is assumed to be 1.

Example: LEFT(A17,3) produces Que if A17 contains "Que Corporation".

LEN(*text*)

Produces the number of characters in *text*. The LEN function is particularly useful when paired with the LEFT, MID, and RIGHT functions so that portions of long text can be separated.

LOWER(*text*)

Changes *text* to all lowercase.

Example: LOWER("Look OUT!") produces look out!.

MID(*text,start_num,num_chars*)

Produces characters from the specified *text*, beginning at the character in the *start_num* position and extending the specified *num_chars*.

Example: MID("Excel is the worksheet",10,3) produces the.

PROPER(*text*)

Changes *text* to lowercase with leading capitals.

Example: PROPER("excel, the worksheet") produces
Excel, The Worksheet.

REPLACE(*old_text,start_num,num_chars,new_text*)

Replaces the characters in *old_text* with *new_text*, starting with the character at *start_num* and continuing for the specified *num_chars*. The first character in *old_text* is character 1.

Example: REPLACE(A12,8,11,"one") takes the phrase in cell A12
We are many people on an island in space. **and changes
it to** We are one on an island in space.

REPT(*text,num_times*)

Repeats the *text* for *num_times*.

Limits: The value of *num_times* must be positive and nonzero. The maximum number of resulting characters is 255.

Example: REPT("__..",3) produces __..__..__..

RIGHT(*text,num_chars*)

Results in as many characters as specified by *num_chars* from the right end of *text*. The value of *num_chars* defaults to 1 when omitted.

Examples: RIGHT("San Francisco, CA",2) produces CA.

RIGHT(B12,2) produces 02 when B12 contains the numeric ZIP code 95402.

SEARCH(*find_text*,***within_text***,*start_num*)

Begins at *start_num* in the specified *within_text*, searches through it for the *find_text*, and produces the character number where *find_text* begins. The first character position in *within_text* is 1. If *start_num* is omitted, it is assumed to be 1. SEARCH ignores case differences. If *find_text* is not found or if *start_num* is out of limits, #VALUE! is returned.

The wild card ? can be used within *find_text* to specify any single character at that location within the text being found. The wild card * can be used within *find_text* to specify any group of characters at that location within the text being found.

Examples: SEARCH("an","Marathoners run long distances",14) produces 26.

SEARCH("l*g","Marathoners run long distances") produces 17.

SUBSTITUTE(***text***,***old_text***,***new_text***,*instance_num*)

Substitutes *new_text* for *old_text* within the specified *text*. If *old_text* occurs more than once, *instance_num* specifies which occurrence to replace. If *instance_num* is not specified, every occurrence of *old_text* is replaced.

Example: SUBSTITUTE("The stone age","stone","information") produces The information age.

T(***value***)

Returns text when *value* is text; returns blank when *value* is not text.

Examples: T(B12) produces Top if B12 contains "Top".
T(57) produces blank.

TEXT(***value***, ***format_text***)

Converts the numeric *value* to text and displays it with the format specified by *format_text*. The result appears to be a formatted number, but actually is text. Use one of the predefined or custom numeric or date formats to specify the format for the *value*. These formats and custom formats are described in Chapter 8, "Formatting Worksheets." The format cannot contain an asterisk (*) or be in the General format.

Example: TEXT(4567.89,"$#,##0.00") produces $4,567.89.

Center a title with date or number in a cell narrower than the width that would normally display the date or number by using a formula such as this:

"Today's date is "&TEXT(NOW( ),"mmm d, yyyy")

TRIM(*text*)

Deletes all spaces from *text* so that only one space remains between words. This can be useful for "cleaning" text used in databases or imported to or exported from Excel.

Example: TRIM("this   is   the   breathy   loo   k") produces this is the breathy look.

UPPER(*text*)

Changes *text* to all uppercase.

Example: UPPER(B2) produces ENOUGH! when B2 contains "enough!".

VALUE(*text*)

Converts text numbers or dates in one of Excel's predefined formats into numbers that are usable in formulas. Because Excel normally converts numeric text into numbers when necessary, this function is used primarily to ensure compatibility with other spreadsheets.

Limits: The text number must be in one of the predefined numeric formats available in Excel.

Example: VALUE(B2) produces 52 when B2 contains the text "$52.00".

Trigonometric Functions

Trigonometric functions use angles measured in radians. Convert between radians and degrees with these equations:

Radians = Degrees*π/180

Degrees = Radians*180/π

The add-in functions described in Chapter 15, "Using Excel's Add-In Macros," include a function that converts between degrees and radians.

ACOS(*number*)

Produces the arc cosine of the *number* in radians. ACOS is the inverse of the COS function. The *number* must be in the range –1 to 1. The resulting angle will be in the range 0 to π radians (0 to 180 degrees).

Example: ACOS(.2) produces 1.369438406 radians.

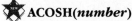 **ACOSH(*number*)**

Produces the inverse hyperbolic cosine of the *number*. The *number* must be greater than or equal to 1.

ASIN(*number*)

Produces the arc sine of the *number* in radians. When given a *number*, the result of a sine function, ASIN produces the original angle measured in radians. The *number* must be in the range –1 to 1. The resulting angle will be in the range –π/2 to π/2 radians (–90 to 90 degrees).

Example: ASIN(.2) produces .201357921 radians.

 ASINH(*number*)

Produces the inverse hyperbolic sine of the *number*.

ATAN(*number*)

Produces the arc tangent of the *number* as a radian angle. ATAN is the inverse of the TAN function. The resulting angle will be in the range –π/2 to π/2 radians (–90 to 90 degrees).

ATAN2(*x_number,y_number*)

Produces the arc tangent for coordinate values of *x_number* and *y_number*. The resulting angle is in the range –π to π radians (–180 to 180 degrees) excluding –π (–180 degrees). If *x_number* and *y_number* are both 0, the function produces the message #DIV/0!.

ATANH(*number*)

Produces the inverse hyperbolic tangent of the *number*. The *number* must be between, but not including, –1 and 1.

COS(*number*)

Produces the cosine of the radian angle *number*.

COSH(*number*)

Produces the hyperbolic cosine of the *number*.

SIN(*number*)

Produces the sine of the radian angle *number*.

Example: SIN(.5) produces .479425539.

SINH(*number*)

Produces the hyperbolic sine of the *number*.

TAN(*number*)

Produces the tangent of the radian angle *number*.

TANH(*number*)

Produces the hyperbolic tangent of the *number*.

From Here...

Use this chapter as a reference guide. Remember that Excel contains a great deal of worksheet help. You can paste functions and prompts for their arguments into formulas by choosing the function from the list provided by the Formula Paste Function command.

To understand what the arguments represent, and for additional information about the limits or use of a function, choose the Help Index command and select the underlined Worksheet Functions. From the list that appears, select the exact function that you need help with, or select the type of function group you are interested in.

Examples of worksheet functions and arrays are in Chapter 13, "Building Extensive Worksheets." Examples of database analysis using D*functions* appear in Chapter 27, "Building Extensive Databases."

11

Building Systems and Managing Multiple Windows

Excel is more than just a worksheet. It is an environment in which you can develop systems for business, science, and engineering. Excel can be a base for developing large computer systems because of its capability to open and link multiple documents. Excel has an extensive set of features and allows you to completely customize its menus and dialog boxes for your own purposes. In this chapter, you will learn the basics of how Excel can open and manage multiple documents.

After reading and experimenting your way through this chapter, you will see worksheets in a new way. You will be able to start Excel and have it automatically load the documents you want to use. You will also be able to open multiple windows onto a single worksheet or divide one window into as many as four panes through which you can see different worksheet areas.

Building a System

Large Excel systems are composed of many documents that work together: worksheets, templates, macros, charts, and add-ins. With Excel's features, you can work on-screen simultaneously with many documents that you frequently use together. Excel even has built-in features that enable you to designate files that will load together or to specify files that will load when you start Excel.

In Excel, building a system of multiple documents consists of a few basic steps. Although every system you build will be different, you may want to follow these steps when building a system that you want to open or run automatically:

1. Create worksheets, charts, macro sheets, add-ins, and templates used in the system. The worksheets should contain formatting styles and custom numeric formats that you want to have available. Macros should add shortcut keys, buttons, or menus to the other documents. Templates should be copied to the XLSTART or alternate startup directory for access through the File New command.

2. Select worksheet settings, such as the following, that you want as defaults when the system opens:

   Hide and protect documents with Window Hide and Options Protect Document

   Worksheet and display settings from Options Workspace and Display

   Chart preferences set in Gallery Preferred

   Custom color palettes set in Options Color Palette and Chart Color Palette

3. Define Auto_Open names in worksheets and templates that will start macros when the worksheet or template opens. Auto_Open macros are described in Chapter 29 and in the following section, "Opening Documents Automatically."

4. Arrange all windows and documents on-screen as you want them to appear when the system starts.

5. Save all documents with their permanent file names to the directories where they will be permanently stored.

6. Save a workspace file using the File Save Workspace command. Use a name that will remind you of the system this workspace contains as, for example, ACCTSREC.XLW or DBANLYS.XLW.

These steps create a system that may involve many documents. You can start the system in different ways:

- If you want the system to start when you start Excel, save the workspace file to the XLSTART directory or your alternate startup directory.

- If you want to start the system from within Excel, use the **File Open** command to open the workspace file.

- If you want to start Excel and the system from an icon in the Program Manager, use the Program Manager's **File New** command to add a program item icon to the open group window. On the **Description** line, type the title of the icon, such as Accounts Receivable. In the **Command Line**, type the path and file name of Excel, EXCEL.EXE, followed by a space, then the path and file name of the workspace that you want this icon to start, such as ACCTSREC.XLW. Such a command line might look like this:

      C:\EXCEL3\EXCEL.EXE D:\ACCT\ACCTSREC.XLW

★ Opening Documents Automatically

If you want a document to open automatically when Excel starts, copy that document into the XLSTART directory, or open the document and save it into the XLSTART directory. This directory is created automatically underneath the directory containing EXCEL.EXE. These are the types of files that Excel will open automatically:

Worksheets	Charts
Macro sheets	Custom applications
Add-ins	Workspace files

Template files, ending with XLT, that are in the XLSTART directory will appear in the list box displayed by the **File New** command, but they will not open automatically.

If you want a macro to run as soon as a worksheet opens, use the **Formula Define Name** command to create the name Auto_Open in the worksheet. In the **Refers to:** text box, enter the name of the macro sheet and the directory where the macro is saved. The **Refers to:** box might contain this entry:

      ='C:\FINANCE\FINMACR.XLM'!SETUP

Here the macro that will run when that worksheet opens is the SETUP macro on the sheet FINMACR.XLM, which is located in the C:\FINANCE directory.

Save the macro sheet into the directory you specified and save the worksheet into the XLSTART directory. When Excel starts, it will open the worksheet in the XLSTART directory. When that worksheet opens, it will start the macro specified by the name Auto_Open.

Using Workspace Files

Excel systems frequently require specific settings and arrangements of multiple documents in many windows. Opening all the files, arranging multiple windows, and setting numerous features can be time-consuming unless you use a workspace file.

Use workspace files whenever you want to open all documents related to a task, open multiple documents on startup, or open documents with nonstandard workspace and display settings.

A workspace file contains a list of the documents, the locations and positions of the windows, and the settings just as they were when the workspace file was created. At any time you can open the workspace file and restore Excel to the way it was when the workspace file was created.

A workspace file does not store the actual documents and the data in the documents, but it does store and retrieve the following:

- Names and directories of all the open documents
- Window position, size, and hidden status
- Options **W**orkspace settings
- Options **D**isplay settings
- Preferred chart type
- Options Calculation settings for Automatic, Manual, or Iteration
- Full or short menu settings
- Info window settings

By creating a workspace that opens specific files, you can open a single workspace file that opens multiple documents and designates settings. The documents that open can be based on templates that contain partially completed worksheets, formatting styles, and macros that automatically change menus and add features.

Saving a Workspace

When you want to save a workspace, open and arrange the documents that you want in the workspace. Set the Options **W**orkspace and Options **D**isplay commands to settings that you want retained in the workspace. When you want to save a workspace file that remembers the workspace, follow these steps:

1. Choose the File Save Workspace command.

2. Type the workspace name in the Save Workspace as: text box. The workspace file ends with the extension XLW, which Excel adds automatically.

3. Choose OK or press Enter

4. If some of the documents have not been saved previously, you are prompted to save the changes.

Save the workspace after you make all document changes, and save each document with a final name. Once the workspace file is saved, it will look for documents with the same names and directories as those that were open when the workspace file was saved. Documents that are updated and changed will still be opened by the workspace file as long as the document's name is the same as the original.

Remember, a workspace file contains only the file names, window positions, and workspace settings. The workspace file does not actually contain the data files. If you save a document to a different name after you saved the workspace, Excel does not know the new name of the document. Deleting, renaming, or moving a document to a different directory will also make it unavailable for opening by the workspace.

Opening a Workspace

When you want to open the files listed in a workspace and revert to all the workspace settings, open the workspace file that contains those files and settings. To open a workspace file, follow these steps:

1. Choose the File Open command.

2. Select a workspace file ending with XLW from the Files list, or type the name and XLW extension into the File Name text box.

3. Choose OK or press Enter.

If files listed in the workspace are not available, an alert box notifies you. The rest of the workspace will open. Some files may not be available because they were moved to other directories, the name was changed, or the file was deleted. If this has occurred, you must re-create the workspace.

Customizing the Workspace

You can customize workspaces to fit your system and the operator's needs. Some of the ways to customize Excel's appearance, along with the commands and dialog box options to make those changes, are in the following list. Choose **Option Display**, and then select the appropriate option.

To Display	*Select*
Formulas and not results	**Formulas**
Gridlines	**Gridlines**
Row & column headings	**Row & Column Headings**
Zero	**Zero Values**
Outline symbols	**Outline Symbols**
Automatic page breaks	**Automatic Page Breaks**
Headings and grids in colors	**Gridline & Headings Color**
Objects	**Show All**
Objects as boxes	**Show Placeholders**
Objects hidden	**Hide All**
Colors for grids	**Gridline & Heading Color**

Choose **Option Workspace**, and then select the appropriate option for these results:

To Do Activity	*Select*
Use R1C1 reference style	**R1C1**
Display the status bar	**Status Bar**
Display the tool bar	**Tool Bar**
Display the scroll bars	**Scroll Bars**
Display the formula bar	**Formula Bar**
Display the note indicators	**Note Indicator**
Use 1-2-3 style movement keys	**Alternate Navigation Keys**
Ignore remote requests for data	**Ignore Remote Requests**
Move the active cell	**Move Selection after Enter**

For example, if you want a window to look like a dialog box, remove the status bar, tool bar, scroll bar, and formula bar by deselecting those options.

For these calculation options, choose **Options Calculation** and select the appropriate option:

To Calculate	Select
After each data or formula change	**Automatic**
After each change but don't recalculate tables	**Automatic Except Tables**
Only after the **Options** **Calculate Now** command or after pressing F9	**Manual**

❖ Building Templates

A *template* is a file used as a form to create other worksheets, macro sheets, or charts. Documents created from a template contain the same layout, text, data, formulas, settings, styles, formats, names, and Auto_Open macros as those in the template.

Templates are useful for any documents that you use frequently and that you want to look consistent. Each of the documents created from a template will be a repeated image of others from the template. Templates can be very useful for forms, such as data entry and expense accounts, or for ensuring consistency in departmental budget presentations.

Opening a Template

Opening a template creates a new document based on the template. The template remains unchanged. The new document will have a temporary name; for example, if the template's file name is DATA.XLT, the documents based on the template will be DATA1, DATA2, and so on.

You can make templates readily accessible by saving them in the XLSTART directory, which is under the directory that contains the EXCEL.EXE program. Templates saved in XLSTART will appear in the list shown in the **File New** command.

You can open a template stored in any directory just as you would open any Excel file. Templates use the XLT file extension.

Creating a Template

Templates can be based on a blank worksheet containing only settings or on an existing document. To build a template, follow these steps:

1. Open or create the document that you want the template to use as a pattern.

2. Choose the File Save As command.

3. Type the template's name in the Save Worksheet as: text box.

4. Choose the Options button.

5. Select the Template format from the File Format list box. This step adds an XLT extension to the file name.

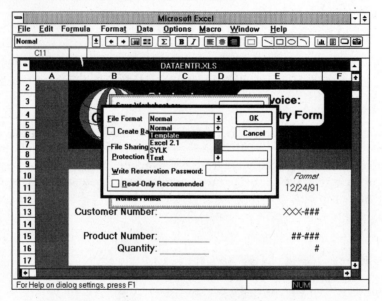

Fig. 11.1. *Selecting the Template file format creates a template from the active document.*

6. Change to the directory where you want the template saved.

7. Choose OK twice or press Enter twice.

Templates can be saved to or opened from any directory. If you save templates to the XLSTART directory, however, you see them listed in the File New dialog box. This makes them easy to open. The list of templates in the File New dialog box is updated only when you start Excel, so templates added during an Excel session will not be shown until you restart Excel.

Templates created from charts do not retain the references to the worksheet data from which the chart was originally created. Chart templates retain only the chart format and use the currently selected worksheet data to create a new chart using the template's format.

To delete a template, use the **File Delete** command in Excel or the File Manager in Windows.

Editing a Template

Editing a template is similar to editing the document on which the template was based. However, there is one extra step. To open the template, choose the **File Open** command and select the template that you want to edit. (Remember, templates use the extension XLT.) Do not press Enter. Press Shift+Enter; or hold down the Shift key and click on OK. This step will open the template and not a document based on the template.

To save the template after editing, choose the **File Save** command. Excel remembers that this is a template, so you do not need to change the file format.

Working with Multiple Documents

Working with multiple documents is a great convenience and time-saver when you want to link worksheets together, view worksheets and graphs simultaneously, or just see multiple documents at the same time.

Opening Additional Documents

When you need to work with additional worksheets, charts, or macro sheets, open the additional documents with **File Open**, just as you opened the first document. When you open documents that are linked to other documents, such as a chart that is linked to an unopened worksheet, you are asked if you want to update the document you are opening using the data from the unopened document.

Activating the Window

If you have multiple worksheets or windows on-screen, you can activate the one you want on top. Using the mouse, move the other windows out of the way by dragging their title bars, then click anywhere on the window you want to activate; the window will appear on top.

With the keyboard, press Ctrl+F6 until the window you want is active; or choose the **W**indow menu, and then choose the window's name from the menu.

Displaying Multiple Windows

You can manually arrange windows by moving and sizing them as described in Chapter 2, "Operating Windows." If you have many windows to reorganize and you have not resized them, you may want to take advantage of some automated assistance. Choose **W**indow **A**rrange All, and the windows will be resized and rearranged so that they are all visible. Figure 11.2 shows three windows after **W**indow **A**rrange All was selected. After you issue the command, the active window appears on the left.

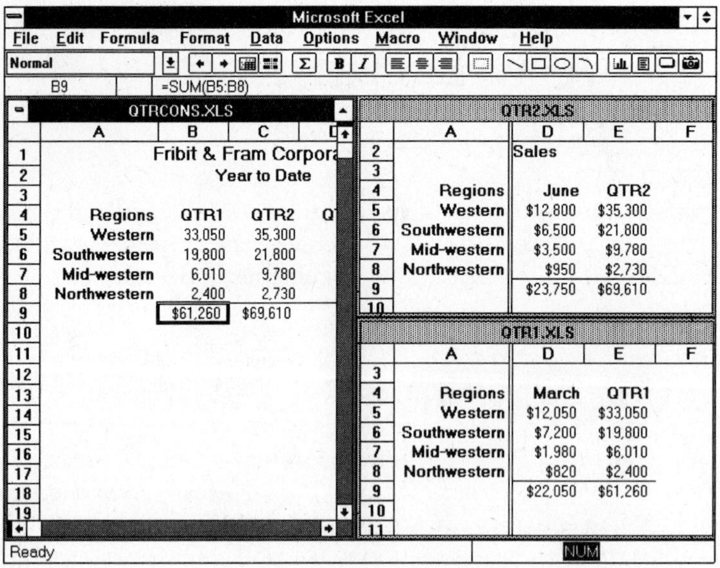

Fig. 11.2. All windows are visible after the command Window Arrange All.

You can add further commands to arrange documents on-screen by opening the file SHEETAID.XLA, which is located in the LIBRARY directory underneath Excel's directory. SHEETAID is described in more detail in Chapter 15, "Using Excel's Add-In Macros."

Hiding and Unhiding Windows

You do not need to keep all your worksheets, charts, and macro sheets on-screen at one time. You can hide documents from view so that the screen appears more organized and less confusing. Hiding documents can also be valuable when you want to hide a macro sheet from beginning operators. A hidden document remains available to other documents with which it is linked.

To hide a window, activate the window so that it is on top, and then select the Window Hide command. The window disappears from the screen, and the Unhide command appears as a choice on the Window menu.

To reveal hidden windows, follow these steps:

1. Choose the Window Unhide command (see fig. 11.3).

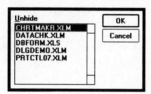

Fig. 11.3. The Window Unhide dialog box.

2. From the list box, select the title of the hidden window you want to reveal.

3. Choose OK or press Enter.

Hidden windows reappear in their former position and size.

If all windows are hidden, the Window menu disappears and the Unhide command appears under the File menu.

Locking Windows in Position

After windows are sized and in the proper positions, you may want to make sure that they stay there. Locking windows in position is a good idea, particularly if the worksheets are used by inexperienced operators or are displayed by macros.

To keep a window from moving or changing size, follow these steps:

1. Position and size the window as you want it.

2. Choose the Options Protect Document command.

3. Select the Windows check box.

4. Enter a password if you do not want others to remove protection.

5. Choose OK or press Enter.

You can scroll through windows that are locked, but you will not be able to resize or move them. You still, however, can enter and edit cells. If cells have been protected with the Format Cell Protection command and if protection for the worksheet is enabled with Options Protect Document, you cannot edit the cells.

To unlock a worksheet, activate its window and choose the Options Unprotect Document command. If a password was used to lock the window's position, you are asked to enter the password.

Viewing a Window through Multiple Panes

Dividing an Excel window into sections enables you to see two or four different views of a worksheet. Multiple panes are particularly useful when you work with databases or large worksheets. Appropriately, each section of the window is referred to as a *pane*. The views are synchronized so that scrolling through one pane also scrolls its counterpart.

You can display both the criteria range and the extract range of a database at the same time. This technique enables you to enter a criterion and see whether the extract matches what you expected. Figure 11.4 shows the criteria and extract ranges of a sample database displayed in two separate panes.

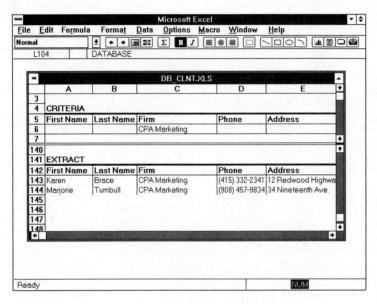

Fig. 11.4. *View different parts of the same worksheet through panes.*

You can place the data-entry area of a large worksheet in one pane and the results in another. If you divide the worksheet into four panes and use **Options** **Freeze** Panes to freeze the panes containing the headings, you can scroll through the worksheet but still see the worksheet's row and column headings.

Breaking a Window into Multiple Panes

Figure 11.5 shows a database window divided into two panes. (Notice how the row numbers jump.) The upper pane shows the database column titles, whereas the lower pane shows the database. With this arrangement, you never lose sight of the column headings as you scroll through a database.

	A	B	C	D	E	F	G	H	
			Microsoft Excel - COMPARE.XLS						
	File	Edit	Formula	Format	Data	Options	Macro	Window	Help
Normal									
	A28		11/1/1990 5:00:00 AM						
	A	B	C	D	E	F	G	H	
1				Well 62, Geysers					
2				Loggings					
3									
4		Analyst: Tom Peterson							
5		Date: Dec 17, 1990							
6		Compare: 11/01/90 to 11/03/90							
7	Log Time	Log Time	C*	GPM	CaCO3	H2S	Se	As	
28	11/1/90 5:00	3D 5Hr	-3.8253822	230.941	0.115551	0.116598	-0.03056	0.091526	
29	11/1/90 5:15	3D 5Hr	1.24052837	-28.2206	0.052581	0.054368	0.011637	0.030376	
30	11/1/90 5:30	3D 5Hr	-1.5624496	136.8894	0.127561	-0.25717	-0.03498	0.159401	
31	11/1/90 5:45	3D 5Hr	-3.9036003	353.9908	-0.05252	-0.01719	-0.01255	-0.01609	
32	11/1/90 6:00	3D 6Hr	1.75934356	285.9913	0.002601	-0.21543	0.044087	-0.16716	
33	11/1/90 6:15	3D 6Hr	-2.0877863	17.40523	0.186699	-0.15361	0.018407	-0.00581	
34	11/1/90 6:30	3D 6Hr	5.27813036	-383.946	0.042713	0.140733	-0.06513	0.008879	
35	11/1/90 6:45	3D 6Hr	10.1674213	-141.396	0.111487	0.091204	0.052956	0.108004	
36	11/1/90 7:00	3D 7Hr	-0.5024012	-174.637	-0.09285	-0.0157	0.002117	0.035986	
37	11/1/90 7:15	3D 7Hr	1.06950479	14.06586	-0.04917	-0.05807	0.011784	0.203535	
38	11/1/90 7:30	3D 7Hr	-7.1852301	-219.912	-0.05531	-0.0368	-0.04744	-0.05621	
39	11/1/90 7:45	3D 7Hr	-4.5923845	-239.669	0.021744	-0.17545	-0.00654	0.208712	
40	11/1/90 8:00	3D 8Hr	4.59071799	151.4242	-0.03858	-0.06699	0.013664	-0.27728	
41	11/1/90 8:15	3D 8Hr	3.44552114	-450.326	0.090031	-0.13439	-0.0413	0.209647	

| Ready | | | | | | | NUM | |

Fig. 11.5. Splitting windows into two panes makes distant areas visible.

To break a worksheet window into panes using the keyboard, follow these steps:

1. Activate the window.

2. Press Alt and then hyphen to display the document Control menu.

3. Press T to select Split from the menu.

   Two gray bars appear that cross the window at its upper left corner. A four-headed arrow appears where the gray bars cross.

4. Use the arrow keys to move the gray bars so that the window divides as you want it.

5. Press Enter to divide the windows as shown.

Figure 11.6 shows two gray bars positioned to divide the window into four sections. If you press the Enter key with the screen as it appears in figure 11.6, the window will split down the right edge of column A and below row 8. Figure 11.7 shows how the vertical and horizontal scroll bars become split after pressing Enter.

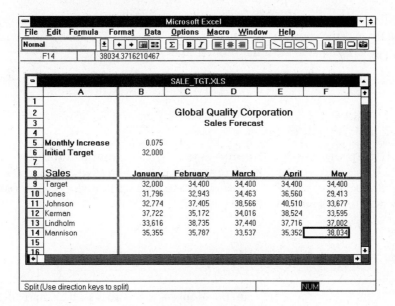

Fig. 11.6. *Split windows so that you can see headings and content no matter where you scroll.*

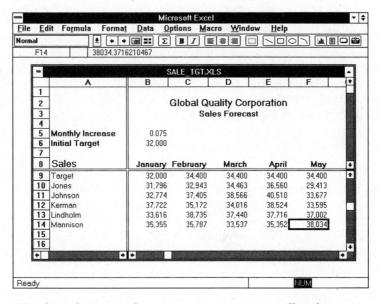

Fig. 11.7. *After splitting windows into panes, you can scroll each pane.*

Before you create panes with the mouse, notice that solid black bars appear at the top of the vertical scroll bar and at the left edge of the horizontal scroll bar. To create panes with the mouse, follow these steps:

1. Drag the solid black bars down or across the scroll bar. As you drag, a gray pane divider shows where the window will be split.

2. Position the gray pane divider where you want the window split, and then release the mouse button.

To resize panes, use the same process you used to create them and move the split bars to a new location. To return a window to a single pane, reselect the Split command; or drag on the black bars and move the gray pane dividers to the extreme edge of a window.

Freezing Headings

You can freeze the panes in position so that you can't change them accidentally. To freeze panes you have already positioned, choose the Options Freeze Panes command.

When panes are frozen, you cannot scroll into the frozen area. You can move the active cell into the frozen area by pressing the arrow keys or clicking on a cell. To "thaw" the frozen panes, choose Options Unfreeze Panes.

You might want to freeze panes in databases that less-experienced operators will be working on. Figure 11.8 shows the worksheet from figure 11.7. The lower right portion of the worksheet can now be scrolled to the right without losing the row headings on the left. Notice that the divider between panes is invisible. The scroll bar scrolls only the area in the lower right portion of the window. In the figure example, the area that can be scrolled is from B9 down and to the right.

> **Tip: *Using Panes To Display Macro Buttons***
> Display macro buttons in the frozen panes so that they are always accessible. Clicking on a macro button runs the macro that the button is assigned to. Macro buttons are described in Chapter 29, "Creating Macros and Add-In Macros."

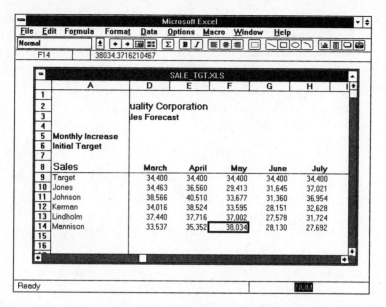

Fig. 11.8. *Freeze panes to prevent scrolling into headings and to prevent panes from moving.*

Activating Different Panes

Using the keyboard, move the active cell clockwise between panes by pressing F6; or press Shift+F6 to move counterclockwise between panes. The active cell moves to the same cell it occupied the last time it was in the pane. With the mouse, you can shift between panes by clicking in the pane you want to activate. Note that jumping between panes often causes windows to reposition.

Removing Panes

When you remove the panes from windows, simply imagine that you want to shrink the top and left panes as much as possible. Then you will be left with a single window pane that fills the screen. If you do not completely move a pane as far as possible to the edge, row or column headings may seem to have disappeared.

Using the keyboard, you can remove panes by pressing Alt, hyphen to display the document Control menu. From the menu, choose Split. When the gray lines and the four-headed arrow appear, move the four-headed arrow to the upper left corner as far as it will go. Press Enter to complete the procedure.

 If you are using a mouse, drag each split bar (solid black bar in the scroll bar) to its farthest point in the scroll bar.

Viewing One Document through Multiple Windows

If you have worked with a large worksheet, you probably wanted to see different parts of the worksheet at the same time. You can do this in Excel by opening new windows of the same worksheet. Although there is still only one worksheet, you can view it through multiple windows. The method discussed previously uses panes that divide a single window. Instead, this method displays additional windows of the same worksheet.

Opening Multiple Windows

In figure 11.9, you can see that windows opened on the same worksheet have the same name in the title bar, but the title of the first window opened ends with :1, the second ends with :2, and so on. The window titles in the figure are DB_CLNT.XLS:1, DB_CLNT.XLS:2, and DB_CLNT.XLS:3. These windows display the same worksheet. Each window can be located and sized separately.

Choose the **Window New** Window command to create a new window onto the current worksheet. You can move, size, and split the new window in the same way as the original. Each window can have different formats, column widths, and display arrangements. In fact, each can appear totally different. However, if you change data or formulas in one window, the change affects all the windows belonging to that worksheet. The number of new windows you can open on a single worksheet is limited only by your computer's memory.

Multiple windows increase your power with Excel. The tips that follow show you a few ways you can tap the power of multiple windows.

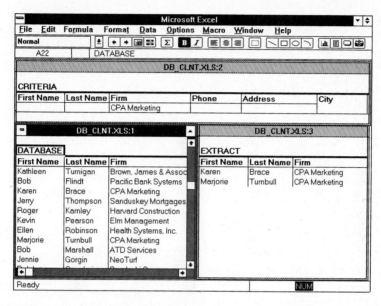

Fig. 11.9. *You can open more than one window on a worksheet.*

Tip: *Data Entry and Help Windows*

Multiple windows can make data entry easier. Arrange windows so that the left window displays the data-entry area. If you need a reminder about account codes, press Ctrl+F6 to activate the window that explains those codes. You can scroll through the account code window to find the code you need.

You also can use multiple windows to create help screens for your programs. Open a window onto the instructional area of the worksheet so that users can scroll to the instructions they need.

Tip: *Debugging and Fixing Problems with a Second Window*

Use Window New Window to create a second or third window onto the active worksheet when you want to debug it. Use Options Display Formulas to format the new window so that it displays formulas. The original window still displays results so that you can see results and formulas at the same time, as shown in figure 11.10. You can see the cell references and the effect of changes more quickly and easily with these two windows.

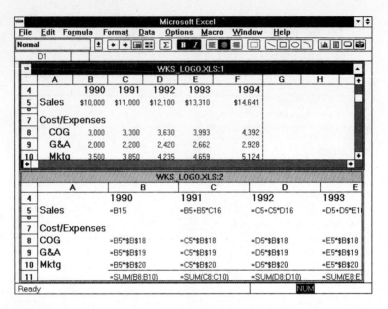

Fig. 11.10. *See results and formulas by opening a second window on the same worksheet.*

> **Tip: *Making Database Queries Easier with a Second Window***
> Jumping between the criteria range, the database range, and the extract range in a database can slow down your work. Instead, set up a window displaying each range. Arrange the windows in a fashion similar to that in figure 11.11. You can even have the windows maximized to full-screen. Whenever you want to use that part of the worksheet shown in another window, press Ctrl+F6 until that window appears on top.

Saving and Closing Multiple Windows

When you save your worksheet to disk, all the windows with their current sizes and shapes are saved. You can set up multiple windows on a worksheet in the arrangement that you use most frequently, and then save the worksheet to disk. When you open the worksheet from disk, all the windows are arranged and sized as you left them.

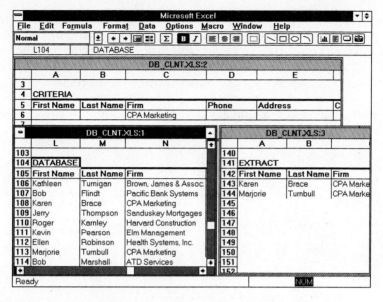

Fig. 11.11. *A second window helps you use your database.*

If you want to save a worksheet with only one window, make sure that you close the extra windows. To close unwanted windows, first activate the window that you want to close. Then select the document Control menu, press Alt, hyphen, and choose the Close command.

From Here...

Excel has all the capabilities necessary to create business, scientific, and engineering applications that work within Windows. By using some of the capabilities shown here, combined with Excel's macro language, you can create powerful solutions.

When you work with multiple worksheets and charts, linking and consolidation are usually required. Chapter 12, "Linking and Consolidating Worksheets," describes in detail how Excel can link cells and ranges between worksheets or consolidate data across multiple worksheets having either the same or different layouts.

Excel's macro language is far more extensive than the simple macro capability found in other worksheets. With it, you can automate processes within Excel, create custom menus and dialog boxes, control other Windows programs, and control data exchange between Excel and other Windows programs. But it's easy to get started with Excel macros. Chapter 28, "Command and Function Macro Quick Start," demonstrates how the macro recorder and three small modifications will quickly help you automate your work.

12

Linking and Consolidating Worksheets

Excel enables you to work with more than one worksheet at a time. You can group worksheets so that formatting and data in one worksheet appear in others; you can link worksheets so that data is shared between worksheets; and you can consolidate worksheets so that data from multiple worksheets is accumulated onto a single worksheet.

Linking makes it possible to divide a large business system into its component worksheets, to test each worksheet separately, and then to link the worksheets together to produce an integrated system. Consolidation enables you to bring together data from multiple worksheets into a single worksheet. Consolidation is often used to accumulate budgets or forecasts from multiple divisions into a unified corporate budget or forecast. Excel enables you either to fix these consolidations so that they don't change, or to link them so that the consolidations update whenever division data changes.

❖ Working with Groups of Worksheets

If you create or work with multiple worksheets that have the same layout, you can save much time by using *workgroups*. Workgroups tie together worksheets or macro sheets so that you can enter data, edit, format, or

369

change display options in multiple sheets at the same time. Workgroups are an excellent way to create documents that are duplicates of each other. (A similar term, *workspace,* denotes a group of files that are opened together; however, once opened, workspace files are independent.)

Creating a Workgroup

Figure 12.1 illustrates three worksheets built with the same layout, worksheet options, and formatting. Creating sheets that are duplicates of each other is easy to do with workgroups. The data is different in each worksheet because each regional office entered its own data.

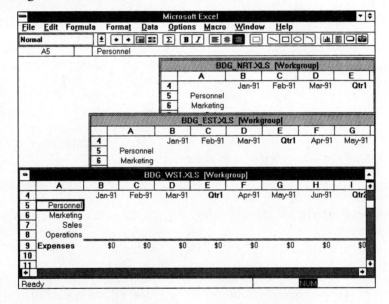

***Fig. 12.1.** Group worksheets together to build duplicates of the same sheet.*

To create a workgroup, follow these steps:

1. Open the worksheets and macro sheets that you want in the same workgroup.

2. Activate the sheet in which you will make changes. Click on the sheet or press Ctrl+ F6 until the sheet is active. This sheet will act as the master for duplication.

3. Choose the Windows Workgroup command to display the Workgroup dialog box shown in figure 12.2. All sheets appear selected.

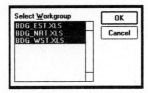

Fig. 12.2. *Select the sheets that you want grouped together from the Workgroup dialog box.*

4. Deselect sheets that you do not want in the same group from the Select Workgroup list box.

 Hold down Shift as you click on sheet names in the list.

 Hold down Ctrl as you press the up- or down-arrow key to move to a sheet name, and then press the space bar to select the sheet.

Shift+ Click or press the space bar on a name to remove it from the list.

5. Choose OK or press Enter.

Notice in figure 12.1 that [Workgroup] appears in the title bars of selected sheets.

If you want to see only the sheets in the workgroup as you work, choose the **Window Arrange Workgroup** command. This command is available only when a workgroup is selected. Sheets that are part of the current workgroup appear in the **Window** menu with a check mark.

> **Tip:** ***Arranging Workgroup Sheets On-Screen***
> Use the SHEETAID.XLA add-in macro to arrange workgroup sheets on-screen. The macro is located in the \LIBRARY directory under the directory in which you installed Excel. Open it to find additional **Window** commands that will help you arrange worksheets. Add-in macros are described in Chapter 15.

If you exit a workgroup and want to return to it, choose the **Window Workgroup** command and notice that the sheets in the last workgroup remain selected. All you need to do is choose OK or press Enter.

If you have an existing workgroup and you want to add or remove other sheets, choose the **Window Workgroup** command. The selected sheets are those of the most current group.

 Hold down the Shift key as you click on the sheet name to add or delete from the list box.

 Hold down the Ctrl key as you move up or down to the sheet name, and then press the space bar.

Exiting Workgroups

As long as you continue to work in the active worksheet, the workgroup will stay intact. As soon as you activate a different document, the workgroup is dissolved. Activate other documents by clicking on them, pressing Ctrl+F6, or choosing them from the **Window** menu.

Entering Formulas and Data in Workgroups

When you want to enter data or formulas across multiple worksheets, follow these steps:

1. Create the workgroup.

2. Enter, edit, fill, or copy data or formulas in the active worksheet just as you would normally.

The entries, edits, or changes you make to the active sheet are duplicated in the same location on other sheets in the workgroup. When you edit a cell's contents in the active sheet and press Enter (or click the Enter box), you place that entry into all the same cells in the workgroup.

Figure 12.3 shows a SUM function entered in the active worksheet. Figure 12.4 shows that the SUM function has been duplicated in other sheets in the group.

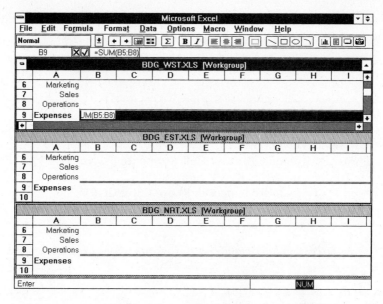

Fig. 12.3. *Enter data, a function, or a formula in the active sheet.*

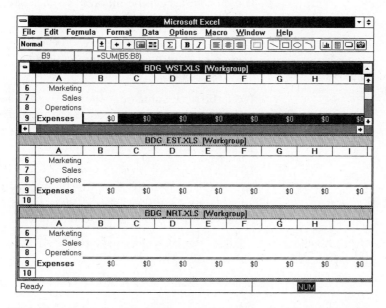

Fig. 12.4. *Changes and entries in the active sheet are duplicated throughout the workgroup.*

If you make a mistake while entering data in a workgroup, choose the Edit Undo command to undo the change in all sheets in the workgroup.

The following commands act across the workgroup in the same way they act on the active sheet:

Menu Commands

File **C**lose, **C**lose All, **P**age Se**t**up, **P**rint

Edit **C**lear, **D**elete, **I**nsert

For**m**at **A**lignment, **B**order, **C**ell Protection, **C**olumn Width, **F**ont, **N**umber, **P**atterns, **R**ow Height, **S**tyle

For**m**ula **G**oto, **P**aste Function, S**h**ow Active Cell

Options **D**isplay, **C**alculate Now, S**h**ort Menus, **W**orkspace

---

The following commands act differently on other workgroup sheets than on the active sheet:

Menu Commands

Data Series	Enters a data series in each sheet of the workgroup. The data series can be different in each sheet if each sheet has a different starting value.
Edit Fill Down/Up or Right/Left	Fills the initial value or formula in each worksheet into the same range as selected in the active sheet.
	To fill the same value or formula across the same range in all worksheets, create the workgroup first; then enter the initial value in the active sheet; then choose the **F**ill command.
	To fill a unique value or formula across the same range in all worksheets, enter the unique value or formula in each worksheet; then create the workgroup; then choose the **F**ill command.
Macro Absolute/ Relative Record	Changes the cell reference type for all sheets in the workgroup.
Macro Record	Records on all macro sheets in the workgroup.
Macro Start Recorder	Works on the single macro sheet in the workgroup in which you selected a cell with the Macro Set Recorder command. Do not include this macro sheet in the workgroup or it may be overwritten.

Copying Cells

You can fill cells or ranges through other sheets in a workgroup, using the **E**dit Fill commands just as you do within a single worksheet. If you have existing data or formulas that you want to copy throughout the same cells or ranges in other sheets, follow these steps:

1. Create a workgroup.

2. Activate the sheet that contains the cells you want to fill through other sheets.

3. Select the cells that you want to fill into other worksheets.

4. Choose the **E**dit Fill Workgroup command to display the Fill Workgroup dialog box (see fig. 12.5).

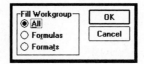

Fig. 12.5. *Use the Fill Workgroup dialog box to fill other worksheets with formulas or formats.*

5. Select the **A**ll option to fill formulas and formats into other sheets. Select Fo**r**mulas to fill formulas only, or select Forma**t**s to fill formats only.

6. Choose OK or press Enter.

Be careful when filling across sheets in a workgroup. You may fill into an area of a worksheet that already contains data or formulas. If you are uncertain about the results of filling, first save the worksheets in the group.

✤ Linking Worksheets into Embedded Boxes

There are two types of worksheet links. One form embeds a picture of a worksheet area into another worksheet. This embedded picture can be updated. The second form links a supporting worksheet's cell or range to another worksheet's cell or range. The following section describes how to link an *embedded picture* of a worksheet area to another worksheet. A later section describes how to link worksheet cells and ranges.

Some Windows programs, such as Excel, enable you to embed objects from one program's documents into another program's documents. An embedded object from Excel can be a cell, a range, a chart, or a complete Excel document. Embedded documents link an image of the original into another document. You can format and update the embedded document whenever you want to.

To create page layouts displaying data from multiple worksheets and charts, you can embed a picture of an Excel worksheet area into another worksheet. This is also an excellent way to create management information displays that bring together data from disparate sources. Embedded cell pictures have these advantages over cell or range links (described later in this chapter):

- Embedded cell pictures (objects) can be quickly opened and updated. When an embedded object is opened, the entire supporting worksheet opens—which makes it easy to change data or to make major corrections to the embedded cell picture.

- Embedded cell pictures can be formatted with most of the same features as text boxes (described in Chapter 9). This formatting makes them attractive and easier to read.

- Embedded worksheet objects can be resized and moved, unfettered by cell locations. This flexibility enables you to create attractive page layouts involving multiple embedded worksheets and charts.

- Embedded cell pictures and charts print together on the page in which they are embedded.

- Embedded cell pictures update on demand rather than automatically. Therefore, you can control the time or frequency of updates.

- Embedded cell pictures can be linked to macros; when such a worksheet is selected, it runs a macro.

Embedded cell pictures have the following disadvantages:

- Embedded cell pictures integrate all the data from the source worksheet into the dependent worksheet, creating very large files.

- Embedded cell pictures are text objects and, as such, cannot be used for calculations. If you need to do calculations with linked data, use the methods in the following sections that describe linking cells and ranges.

❖ Embedding Cell Pictures

Embedding a range from one worksheet into another worksheet involves taking a "picture" of the area from the source worksheet and embedding that picture in the dependent worksheet. To embed a cell picture, follow these steps:

1. Open the worksheet that will supply the picture and the worksheet that will receive the embedded cell picture.

2. Activate the worksheet that will supply the picture

3. Select the range of the worksheet to be pictured.

4. Choose the Edit Copy command.

5. Switch to the dependent worksheet by clicking on it or by choosing it from the Window menu (or pressing Ctrl+F6).

6. Select the cell at the top left corner of the area where you want the cell picture to appear.

7. Hold down the Shift key as you choose the Edit Paste Picture Link command.

To embed a picture of the worksheet using the tool bar and the mouse, follow these steps:

1. Select the range on the worksheet that you want to take a picture of.

2. Click on the Camera icon in the tool bar.

3. Activate the worksheet that will receive the picture.

4. Click on the cell where you want the cell picture embedded.

A picture with black handles around it will appear on the worksheet, as shown in the upper right corner of figure 12.6. Notice that the reference formula linking this formula to the worksheet cells appears in the formula bar while the embedded worksheet is selected. In this figure, the cell picture is from the same worksheet that the picture is embedded on. If the picture is from a different worksheet, the formula bar shows an external cell reference. (External reference formulas are described in the section "Linking Worksheet Cells and Ranges," found later in this chapter.)

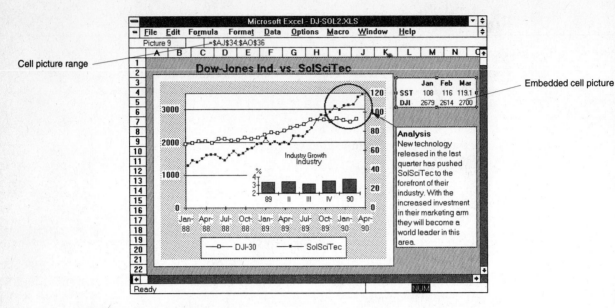

Fig. 12.6. *An embedded cell picture is an object containing the data of the supporting worksheet.*

If you want to paste a picture of a worksheet area onto another worksheet, use the **Edit Paste Picture** command. No link is created. This technique is described further in Chapter 9. To format, resize, position, or protect the embedded worksheet, use the techniques also described in Chapter 9, "Drawing and Placing Graphics in Worksheets."

Updating Embedded Cell Pictures

To update the data or make changes to an embedded cell picture, double-click on the embedded cell picture. Double-clicking on the embedded cell picture opens that supporting worksheet if it is not already open and activates its window. Make changes in this supporting window as you want, save the changes if necessary, and then close the window.

Editing or Changing Links to Embedded Cell Pictures

To delete an embedded cell picture, click on it so that black handles appear on its edges; then press the Del or Backspace key. Choose **Edit Undo** immediately to restore a deleted embedded object.

The external reference formulas used by embedded cell pictures or objects are the same as those used by linked cells and ranges. To change all links involving a supporting worksheet, follow the procedures for File Links in the section that describes changing links between worksheets. When the link is redirected, the embedded cell picture appears blank. Double-click on the embedded cell picture to activate the new supporting document, and then close that supporting document when it appears. The embedded cell picture will now display data from its new supporting worksheet.

If you want to change the link to a single embedded worksheet without changing other links to the same supporting worksheet, click on the embedded worksheet. Edit the external reference formula in the formula bar to refer to the new supporting worksheet's path, file, and cell references. Press Enter. The embedded object will be blank. Double-click on the embedded worksheet to activate the new supporting document, and then close that supporting document when it appears. The embedded worksheet will now display data from its new supporting worksheet.

Linking Worksheet Cells and Ranges

Linked documents share data and the results of formulas. The linked documents update automatically with changes in the document they are linked to.

Linked worksheets let you avoid the problems inherent in large, cumbersome worksheets. You can build small worksheets to do specific tasks, and then link all these *modules* together to form a larger *system*.

Here are some of the advantages of building systems composed of smaller worksheets linked together:

- Systems require less memory because all worksheets may not need to be open simultaneously. Some worksheets can be linked to worksheets that remain on disk.

- Modules can be built separately by different people as long as the data transfer between modules is planned and coordinated. Such cooperation can mean quicker project completion.

- Systems composed of worksheet modules are flexible and can be updated more easily. One module can be redesigned, tested, and implemented without rebuilding the entire system.

- Smaller worksheets recalculate faster than single, large worksheets.

- You can create data-entry modules that operate on separate computers or in separate locations. At a given time, filled-in modules can be linked into the system. This arrangement has a number of advantages: more people can work on the system at once; people can work in separate locations; the work can be completed faster; and the chance that an inexperienced operator will damage the overall system is reduced.

- Systems are easier to maintain and debug when they are built in modules.

- Worksheet modules can be modified for use in different systems.

Understanding Links and Linked Systems

Linking enables one worksheet to share the data in another worksheet. You can link a single cell, a range of cells, and a named formula or constant. The worksheet containing the original data—the source of information—is known as the *supporting worksheet*. The worksheet that receives the linked data is the *dependent worksheet*.

 Supporting worksheets can be either on-screen or on disk; the dependent worksheet can still get the information it needs through the link. When the dependent worksheet opens, it updates linked data that it reads from the supporting worksheet, if the supporting worksheet is on-screen. If the supporting worksheet is on disk, the dependent worksheet reads it from the file. This process occurs whether the link is a simple link between cells or a link within a complex formula.

The cell reference that links the supporting worksheet to the dependent worksheet is known as an *external reference*. When that reference is used in a formula to create a link, the formula is known as an *external reference formula*.

Figure 12.7 shows worksheets linked by an external reference formula. QTR1.XLS supports the dependent ANNUAL.XLS worksheet. The external reference formula in ANNUAL.XLS appears in the formula bar as =QTR1.XLS!$E$5, which indicates that cell B5 on the ANNUAL.XLS worksheet is linked to the contents of cell E5 on the QTR1.XLS worksheet. When the contents of E5 in the QTR1.XLS worksheet changes, the value of B5 of the ANNUAL.XLS worksheet will also change.

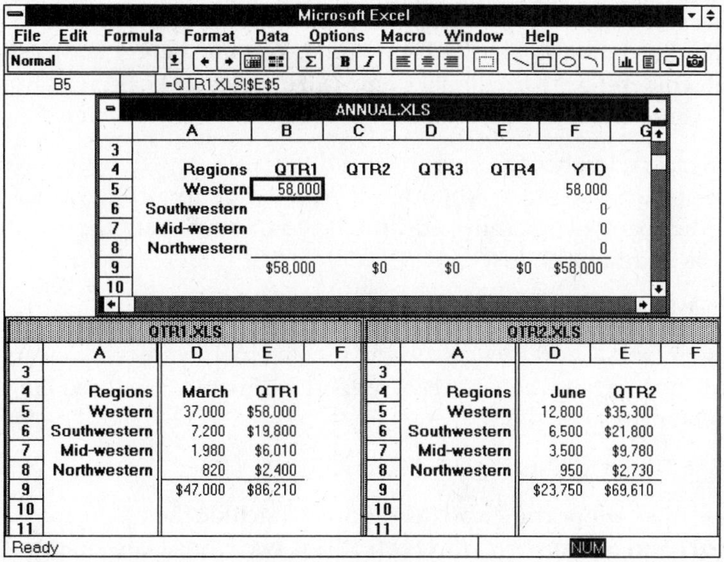

Fig. 12.7. *The QTR1.XLS worksheet supports the ANNUAL.XLS worksheet by feeding data to the dependent worksheet through a link.*

External reference formulas take the following form:

=WorksheetName!CellRef

Here is an actual example:

=QTR1.XLS!$E$5

In this formula, QTR1.XLS is the name of the supporting worksheet that contains the data, and $E$5 is the cell that supplies information to the link. An exclamation mark (!) separates the supporting worksheet name from the cell reference.

An external reference also can span a range of cells. For example, the total in B9 on ANNUAL.XLS could be a single formula that totals the range of cells from the QTR1.XLS worksheet. The formula would appear as this:

=SUM(QTR1.XLS!$E$5:$E$8)

You can link a range of cells to another range of cells of the same size. These links use array formulas and are created with the Edit Paste Link command. An external reference formula on ANNUAL.XLS that links B5:B8 to the supporting cells E5:E8 on QTR1.XLS appears as an array that looks like this:

{=QTR1.XLS!$E$5:$E$8}

The braces, { }, around the formula indicate that it is an array formula. Array formulas act on multiple cells at one time. You must enter and edit array formulas differently than normal single-cell formulas. The braces cannot be typed. These are entered in a special way that is described later.

The external reference formula appears differently, depending on whether the supporting worksheet is open or closed. If the supporting worksheet is open, the external reference formula appears with only the worksheet name, as in this example:

=QTR1.XLS!$E$5

If the supporting worksheet is closed, the external reference appears with the full path name, disk, directory, and file name, enclosed in single quotation marks:

='C:\EXCEL\FINANCE\QTR1.XLS'!$E$9

Because open supporting worksheets do not include their path name in the external reference formula, you cannot have two worksheets open with the same name, even if they are from different directories. You can have links to supporting worksheets with the same names in different directories, but you can have only one of them open at a time.

Linking Cells with Copy and Paste Link Commands

To link a cell or range in a supporting worksheet to a cell or range in the dependent worksheet, use the Edit Paste Link command. In the following steps, the range of E5:E8 on the QTR1.XLS worksheet is linked to cells B5:B8 on the dependent ANNUAL.XLS worksheet:

1. Open the worksheets that you want to link.

2. Activate the supporting worksheet.

3. Select the range of cells that provide the data you want linked (see fig. 12.8).

4. Choose the Edit Copy command.

5. Activate the dependent worksheet. Click on the dependent worksheet, in this case ANNUAL.XLS, and press Ctrl+ F6 until it is active; or choose the worksheet from the Window menu.

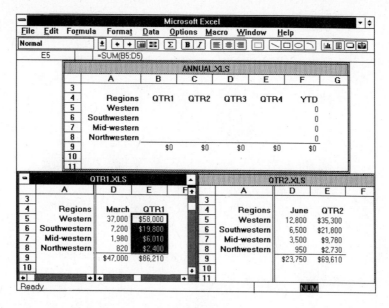

Fig. 12.8. Select the range of cells on the supporting worksheet.

6. Select the top left cell of the range where you want the link to appear.

   In this example, select cell B5 on the ANNUAL.XLS worksheet. Do not select an entire range to paste into; doing so is not only unnecessary, but it increases the chance that you will select the wrong size of range to paste into. You need only select the single cell at the upper left corner of the area that you want to paste.

7. Choose the Edit Paste Link command.

The link appears, as shown in figure 12.9.

Notice in the dependent worksheet's formula bar that cells in the linked range are enclosed in braces, as { }. The braces indicate that the linked range is one array. The entire ranges are linked, not the individual cells. You cannot change individual cells within the array, but you can edit the entire array, as described later in this chapter.

If you use Edit Copy and Edit Paste Link to link a single cell to another single cell, an external reference formula is created that is not an array. You can edit this formula like any other formula.

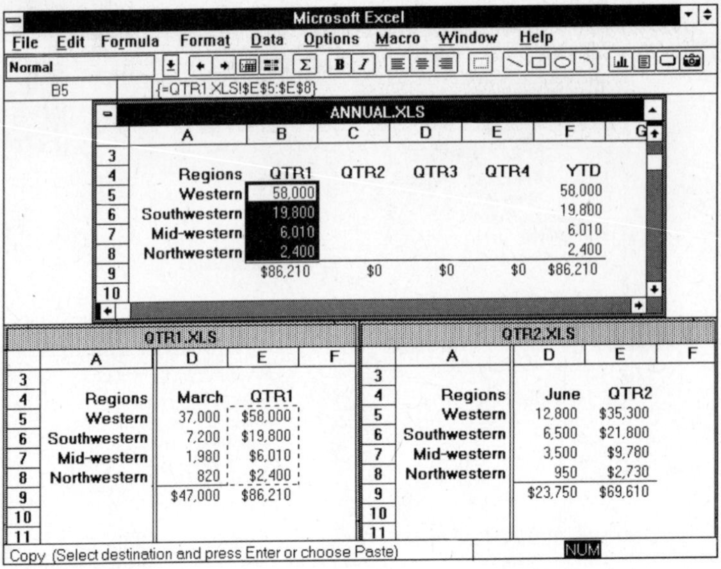

Fig. 12.9. The cells on the worksheet ANNUAL.XLS display data from the supporting worksheet, QTR1.XLS.

Linking Cells by Pointing

If you want to create many links that are individual cells or are links within larger formulas, use the pointing method of creating links. You can enter external references in a formula the same way you build a formula within one worksheet: by pointing to the cell references you want in the formula, even when the cells are on another worksheet. To point to a cell or range so that it is included in a formula, just click on it as you are building the formula; or drag across its range.

To link the dependent cell B5 on ANNUAL.XLS to the supporting cell, E5 on QTR1.XLS, follow these steps:

1. Open the dependent and supporting worksheets.

2. Activate the dependent worksheet.

3. Select the cell that you want to contain the link and start your formula. The formula may be large or as simple as an = sign and the single linked cell.

   In figure 12.10, an equal sign (=) is typed in cell B5 on the ANNUAL.XLS worksheet.

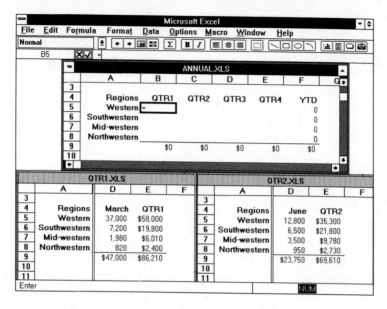

Fig. 12.10. Link cells by pointing to a cell reference in another worksheet.

4. Activate the supporting worksheet, QTR1.XLS, by clicking on it, by choosing it from the Window menu, or by pressing Ctrl+ F6.

5. Select the supporting cell or range on the supporting worksheet. Click on cell E5 or press the arrow keys to enclose E5 in the dashed marquee.

6. Continue building the formula by typing another math operator (math sign); or enter the formula by clicking on the Enter box in the formula bar or pressing Enter.

As soon as you press Enter or type a math operator, the original worksheet reactivates. Figure 12.11 shows the completed external reference formula in B5 as =QTR1.XLS!$E$5.

You can use this pointing method to enter external references within complex formulas such as the following:

=2*SIN(READINGS.XLS!$QE$5)/(B12*56)

You also can point to ranges on other worksheets. For example, consider this formula:

=SUM(SUPPORT.XLS!$F$6:$F$8)

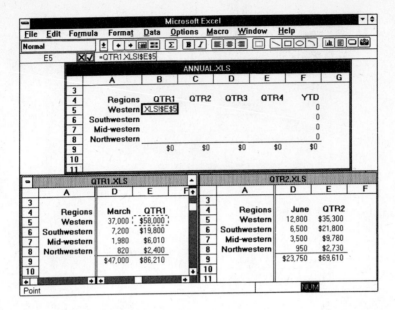

Fig. 12.11. *The resulting link in B5 is created by pointing to a cell on another worksheet.*

This formula was entered by typing **=SUM(** and then switching to the supporting worksheet and dragging across the range F6:F8 with the mouse. To select the range with the keyboard, hold down the Shift key and press the arrow keys until the range is selected. Type the closing **)** and press Enter.

Linking Cells by Typing

If you need to create links to worksheets on disk without ever opening them, you can type in the external reference formula. This technique is helpful if the other file is too large to load with your existing worksheet or if you are so familiar with the supporting worksheet that you can type a reference faster than you can find the cell and click on it.

When you type an external reference to a worksheet that is open, use one of the formats in the preceding examples:

=QTR1.XLS!$E$5

OR

=SUM(QTR1.XLS!$E$5:$E$8)

When you type an external reference to an unopened worksheet that is on disk, enclose the full path name, file name, and cell or range in single quotations. For example:

=ʹC:\EXCEL\FINANCE\QTR1.XLSʹ!$E$9

Typing external reference formulas is easiest when you give cells or ranges a name with the Formula Define Name or the Formula Create Names command. For example, suppose that cell E5 in QTR1.XLS has been named Qtr1.Western. If both the ANNUAL.XLS and QTR1.XLS worksheets are open, you can link them by typing the following formula in the ANNUAL.XLS worksheet:

=QTR1.XLS!Qtr1.Western

When you type formulas containing an external reference as this formula does, the answer appears as soon as you enter the formula. (If you use a range name such as Qtr1.Western, that name must exist on the supporting worksheet. In this example, the Qtr1 in the name Qtr1.Western is not related to the worksheet name QTR1.XLS.)

Creating Links with Names

External reference formulas in a dependent worksheet do not automatically adjust when you rearrange cells in a source worksheet. Rearranging a source worksheet by moving, inserting, or deleting may move the desired data away from the cells to which the dependent worksheet is linked.

For example, in figure 12.11 if the dependent worksheet, ANNUAL.XLS, contains the link =QTR1.XLS!$E$5, then inserting a new row 3 in QTR1.XLS moves the data in cell E5 down to E6. However, the external reference is still linked to the cell E5, which now contains the text heading QTR1.

To make sure that rearranging the supporting worksheet does not ruin links, name the linked cells or ranges and then use the names in the external reference formulas. For example, you could use the Formula Define Name command to name the cell in E5 Qtr1.Western.

To prevent rearrangements in QTR1.XLS from disturbing links, change the link in the dependent worksheet from =QTR1.XLS!$E$5 to =QTR1.XLS!Qtr1.Western. Here Qtr1.Western is the name of the cell $E$5 on the worksheet QTR1.XLS. The section "Editing a Link" in this chapter describes how to edit external reference formulas.

When you link a range of cells using **Edit Paste Link**, an array is created in the dependent worksheet that looks similar to {=QTR1.XLS!$E$5:$E$8}. An external reference array formula links a range of cells in one worksheet to a range of cells in another worksheet. Because an array is involved, you must edit the entire range that makes up the array. To edit the entire range, you must select the entire range and edit the formula. A special entry procedure is required, as described later in this chapter. When you have edited the array formula to include a named range, it will look similar to this:

{=QTR1.XLS!Qtr1.All}

To add a name to the formula in this case, name the range in the supporting worksheet. For example, in figure 12.9, you could give the name Qtrl.All to $E$5:$E$8.

To add that name to the external reference formula in the dependent worksheet, create the link using **Edit Paste Link**. With this command, you can paste the formula into a range such as B5:B8 in the ANNUAL.XLS worksheet, as explained earlier in this chapter. Pasting creates the formula {=QTR1.XLS!$E$5:$E$8} in cells B5:B8. Replace $E$5:$E$8 by selecting all the linked cells involving the range B5:B8. (You *must* have all the cells involved with this formula selected.) Click in the formula bar and notice that the array formula changes to a normal formula. The array brackets disappear. Edit the formula to replace $E$5:$E$8 with Qtr1.All.

To reenter the external reference formula as an array in the selected cells, press Shift+Ctrl+Enter. The formula will now be {=QTR1.XLS!Qtr1.All}. This link will be preserved no matter where you move the range Qtr1.All on the QTR1.XLS worksheet.

Saving Linked Worksheets

When you save linked worksheets, always save the supporting worksheet first. This ensures that the dependent worksheets will store the correct path name and file name of their supporting worksheets.

If you change the name of a supporting worksheet, make sure that worksheets depending on it are also open. Save the supporting worksheet first, and then resave the dependent worksheets. This procedure ensures that the dependent worksheets know the new path name and file name of their supporting worksheet. If a dependent worksheet becomes unlinked from its supporting worksheet, you can relink the worksheets, using the **File Links** command described in the next section.

Opening Linked Worksheets

The linked data in a dependent worksheet updates in different ways when the worksheet is opened. If its supporting worksheets are already open, the dependent worksheet updates immediately on opening. If the supporting worksheets are on disk when the dependent worksheet opens, you then see the alert box shown in figure 12.12.

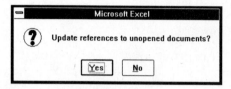

Fig. 12.12. When opening a dependent worksheet, you can choose to keep the old values or update links to files on disk.

If you select **Yes** in the alert box, Excel reads the linked data off the files on disk and updates the dependent worksheet. If you select **No**, Excel retains the values the dependent worksheet had when last saved.

If you already opened a dependent worksheet and want to open the supporting worksheets that feed it, follow these steps:

1. Choose the **File L**inks command to display the Links dialog box, shown in figure 12.13.

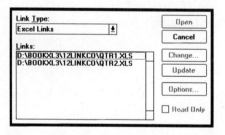

Fig. 12.13. Use the File Links dialog box to change or update links between worksheets.

2. From the Link **T**ype pull-down list box, select Excel Links if it is not already selected.

3. Select the **L**inks scrolling list, and then select those files you want to open. Unopened files appear with their path name.

Select multiple worksheets by holding down Shift and clicking on each name.

 Select multiple worksheets by holding down Ctrl as you press the up- or down-arrow keys to move to different file names. Press the space bar to select each file name.

4. Choose the Open button.

> **Tip: *When the File Links Command Is Grayed***
> Make sure that the dependent worksheet is active. If a worksheet that does not have links is active, the File Links command will appear grayed, indicating that the command is not available.

Changing and Updating Links

To properly maintain a system of linked worksheets, you need to know how to reestablish links that are lost and how to update a large system of links. If supporting worksheets are renamed or moved to other directories, dependent worksheets cannot find the data they need. These links are lost and need to be reestablished.

To reestablish links to a worksheet, or to link a dependent worksheet to a different supporting worksheet, follow these steps:

1. Open the dependent worksheet.

2. Choose the File Links command to display the Links dialog box.

3. From the Link Type pull-down list box, select Excel Links if it is not already selected.

4. Select the Links scrolling list, and then select those files that you want to open (see fig. 12.14). Unopened files appear with their path name.

5. Choose the Change button to display the Change Links dialog box, shown in figure 12.15. The current link is displayed at the top of the dialog box.

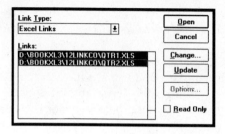

Fig. 12.14. Select the files whose links you want to reestablish or change.

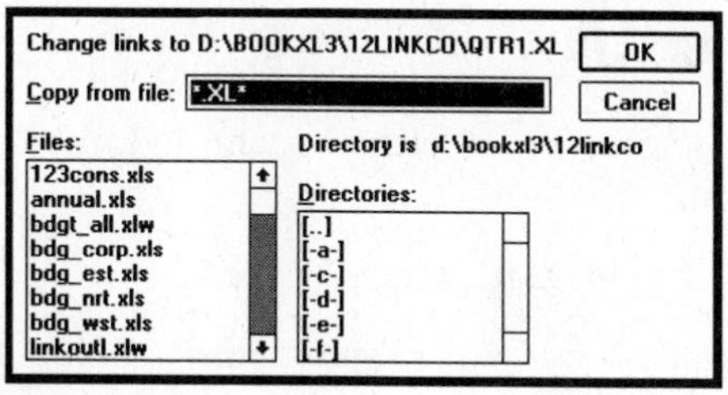

Fig. 12.15. *Change links with this dialog box.*

6. Select a directory and file name to indicate the directory and file of the new supporting worksheet.

7. Choose OK to link to the file name you selected, or choose Cancel to ignore the change.

8. If you selected multiple supporting files, repeat steps 6 and 7, noting at the top of the dialog box which supporting worksheet you are changing.

If you want only to read (not change) information from a supporting worksheet, select the **R**ead Only box from the Links dialog box. This option enables others on a network to read the same worksheet.

If you want to update an active dependent worksheet when its supporting worksheet is on disk, choose the **F**ile Links command, select the supporting worksheet that the active dependent worksheet needs, and then choose the **U**pdate button. The Update button is available only when the supporting worksheet is on disk.

Note: *Passing Changed Data to All Dependent Worksheets*
If worksheet A passes data to B, and B passes data to C, in some cases a change in A will not occur in C. If you change worksheet A, but never open and update B, B will not have the updated data to pass on to C. Consequently, it is important to know the hierarchy of linked worksheets and to update them in order from the lowest supporting worksheet to the highest dependent worksheet.

Editing a Link

You can edit a single external reference formula linked to a cell or range. Consider this example:

=QTR1.XLS!$E$5 or =QTR1.XLS!$E$5:$E$8

Edit the cell the same as you would any formula. Select the cell, and then press F2 or click in the formula bar to edit.

Tip: *Finding External References*
To find cells that contain external references, choose the Formula Find command and select the Look in Formulas option. Next, type an exclamation mark (!) in the Find What text box and choose OK. Press F7 to search forward again or Shift+F7 to search backward. This method is helpful for finding cells containing external links that need to be selectively edited.

Editing an external reference *array formula* requires more steps and a special entry keystroke. When you link a range of cells using Edit Paste Link, you create an array formula in the dependent worksheet that looks similar to {=QTR1.XLS!$E$5:$E$8}. This formula spans multiple cells, linking a range in one worksheet to another. Because an array is involved, you must edit the entire range making up the array; you must select the entire range before you begin editing the formula.

Consider, for example, this formula:

{=QTR1.XLS!$E$5:$E$8}

To edit this formula, select all cells on the dependent worksheet that involve this array formula. Click on one of the cells, and then choose the Formula Select Special command with the Current Array option selected. Or you can press Ctrl+/.

Press F2 or click in the formula bar. Notice that the braces, { }, disappear. Now edit the formula. You may, for example, want to replace the range $E$5:$E$8 with a range name such as Qtr1.All. To reenter the formula as an array, press Shift+Ctrl+Enter; or hold down Shift and Ctrl as you click on the Enter box in the formula bar.

To delete an array formula such as the one just described, you must select and then delete all cells involving the array formula.

Freezing Links

To preserve the values from a link but to remove the external reference, you can freeze the external reference so that it becomes a value. To freeze an external reference, select the cell so that the formula appears in the formula bar. Select the external reference part of the formula by dragging across it or by pressing Shift+left- or right-arrow key. Choose **O**ptions Calculate **N**ow or press F9 to change the selected reference into a value. Press Enter to reenter the formula.

You also can freeze formulas by selecting the cell or range that contains the formulas and choosing the **E**dit **C**opy command. Next, choose **E**dit Paste **S**pecial with the **V**alues option selected and paste directly on top of the original cell or range. This procedure replaces formulas with their values.

Consolidating Worksheets

When you consolidate worksheets, Excel acts on similar data across multiple worksheets and puts the results of calculations in a different worksheet. The data in the multiple worksheets can have identical physical layouts or can have different layouts. If the physical layouts of the supporting worksheets are the same, Excel consolidates data by working with cells from the same relative location on each supporting worksheet. If the physical layouts of the supporting worksheets are different, Excel examines the row and column headings in supporting worksheets to find the data to be consolidated. This method consolidates data by working with cells that have the same row and column headings, regardless of their physical location. Data can be consolidated in more ways than just by totaling similar data. Excel also can create consolidations that calculate such statistical worksheet information as averages, standard deviations, and counts.

A common example of a consolidation is used in corporate budgeting. A corporation accumulates all the division budget forecast worksheets into a single budget forecast worksheet for the entire corporation. Each division updates its own worksheets. Each month the corporation can consolidate the individual division budget worksheets into a single corporate budget worksheet. Figure 12.16 shows 12 months of budget items from 3 sources, BDG_NRT.XLS, BDG_EST.XLS, and BDG_WST.XLS, which are consolidated with the SUM function into the BDG_CORP.XLS worksheet.

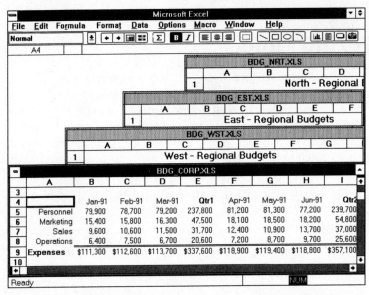

Fig. 12.16. BDG_CORP.XLS contains the consolidation of three divisional budgets.

> **Tip: *Consolidating 1-2-3 Worksheets with Excel***
> If your office uses a mixture of Excel and 1-2-3, remember that Excel can link and consolidate with 1-2-3 worksheets. Follow the same procedures you would use for linking or consolidating with Excel worksheets.

Other examples of business consolidation include sales forecasts and inventory reports. For scientific or engineering uses, consolidation can produce average or standard deviation reports. These reports can include data taken from multiple worksheets produced by various experiments, chromatograph analyzers, well readings, control monitors, and so on.

Understanding Consolidation

When you consolidate, Excel takes data from source areas on different worksheets, calculates the data, and puts that data onto a destination area in the consolidation worksheet. The following general steps provide an overview of consolidating multiple source areas into a destination area:

1. Select the destination area where you want the consolidation to appear.

2. Specify the source ranges that hold the data to be consolidated. A consolidation can have as many as 255 source ranges. The sources do not have to be open during consolidation.

3. Select the way you want the consolidation to act on cells: by their relative locations in each source range or by the row or column headings in the source ranges.

4. Select what you want the destination area to contain: values that do not change or links that update when the sources change.

5. Select one of these types of consolidation:

   AVERAGE
   COUNT
   COUNTA
   MAX
   MIN
   PRODUCT
   STDEV
   STDEVP
   SUM
   VAR
   VARP

Consolidations are handled differently in the destination worksheet, depending on the layout of the destination area that you select, as shown in table 12.1.

Table 12.1
Destinations and Consolidation Results

Destination Selection	Consolidation Result
One cell	Uses as much room on the destination worksheet as needed to consolidate all the categories (items) from the sources.
Row of cells	Fills the consolidation down from the selection. The destination area is only as wide as the selection.
Column of cells	Fills the consolidation to the right of the selection. The destination area is only as tall as the selection.
Range	Consolidates as many categories into the destination as will fit. You are warned if the destination area is not large enough to hold the consolidation.

Consolidating Worksheets by Physical Layout

Consolidate worksheets by their physical layout if the data is in the same position within each source area. The actual location of the source area may be different on each source worksheet. The destination area will have the same layout as the source areas. To consolidate by layout, follow these steps:

1. Select a destination area as described earlier. Select only the data range, because text does not consolidate and because you won't want to consolidate dates used as headings.

2. Choose the Data Consolidate command to display the Consolidate dialog box shown in figure 12.17.

3. Select the Reference text box, and then select or type a source area. Use an external reference of a form similar to =BDG_EST.XLS!$B$5:$E$8. You can select an area in any open worksheet even though the destination worksheet remains the active worksheet. If the source worksheet is on disk, you can type in its full path name and source area enclosed in single quotes.

To activate a source worksheet, click on the source worksheet; or choose the Window menu and select a worksheet. Select the source area on the worksheet by clicking or dragging across it. Move the dialog box if necessary.

 To activate a source worksheet, press Ctrl+F6; or choose the Window menu and select a worksheet. Select the source area by moving to it and then holding the Shift key as you press arrow keys to select, or use the F8 key to extend the selection. Move the dialog box if necessary.

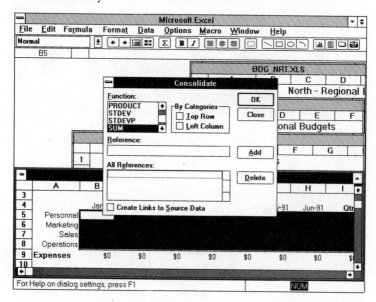

Fig. 12.17. *The Consolidate dialog box enables you to consolidate sheets by location or by data headings.*

4. Choose the Add button to add the source entry to the All References list. The Excel screen will now look similar to figure 12.18, where the BDG_CORP.XLS worksheet is the destination and the source area is one of the BDG.XLS division worksheets.

5. Repeat steps 3 and 4 to add all the source areas to the All References list.

6. Select the type of consolidation you want from the Function list.

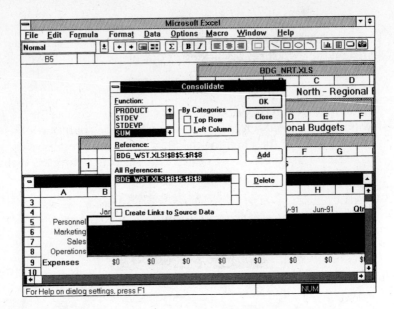

Fig. 12.18. *To prepare for consolidation, you select the source range from each source worksheet.*

7. Deselect the By Categories Top Row and Left Column check boxes. This consolidation uses cell position within the source area, not row or column headings.

8. Select the Create Links to Source Data check box if you want the destination area to be linked to the source areas. This makes the consolidation an outline. Consolidation outlines are described at the end of this chapter.

9. Choose OK or press Enter.

The finished consolidation is shown in figure 12.19.

> **Tip:** *Do Not Include Date Headings in a Consolidation*
> Excel will assume that the serial date number in a cell is a number to be consolidated. The serial date number will throw off the consolidation of numeric data.

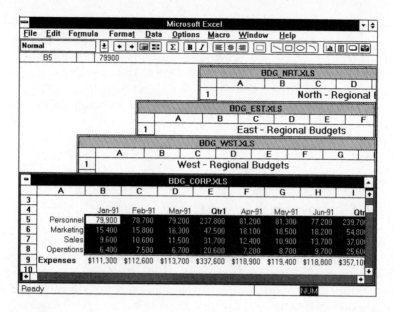

Fig. 12.19. *Consolidating by position requires the same physical layout in all source areas.*

Be aware of how much space the consolidation will take up if you select a single cell as the destination area. A single cell allows an unlimited destination area, which means that as many rows and columns are used for the consolidation as necessary. The consolidation may accidentally cover cells containing information you need.

Text and formulas within the source area are not brought into the destination area. Only values are brought in and formatted. Text in the consolidation sheet already exists because, in most cases, the **W**indows **W**orkgroup command has been used to create matching worksheets. One of these worksheets is used as the consolidation sheet, whereas the others are used as divisional sheets. (Workgroups are described earlier in this chapter.) If you are using a blank worksheet on which to consolidate, copy text from divisional worksheets for use as headings.

You can specify multiple worksheet source areas by using wild cards in the worksheet names. For example, instead of specifying all three sheets, BDG_EST.XLS, BDG_WST.XLS, and BDG_NRT.XLS, and their source areas in the All References list, enter the name in the **R**eference box with a wild card such as BDG_*.XLS. The wild card will refer to WST, EST, and NRT.

You can reduce problems caused in moving or rearranging source areas. Edit the source areas in the **Reference** text box so that you use range names instead of cell references. For example, a consolidation area on all the sheets can be referenced with BDG_*.XLS!BUDGET. The asterisk (*) in the file name is a wild card that refers to EST, WST, and NRT. BUDGET is a range name on each sheet that was named with the **Formula Define** Name command.

Consolidating Worksheets by Row and Column Headings

In most cases, you won't want to consolidate worksheets by position. Doing so means that each division's worksheet must have exactly the same line items and column headings in the same order. For example, the various divisions may have separate budget items or different sales territories selling different products. When you use the following method, source worksheets can contain different items and the headings can be ordered differently, yet the consolidation still works.

When source worksheets have data in different locations or when source worksheets contain different categories to be consolidated, use the names in row or column headings to consolidate. With this method, Excel consolidates data according to the row and column headings of a piece of data and not by the data's cell location. This is the most flexible method of consolidation. The actual location of the source area may be different on each source worksheet.

To consolidate by headings, follow these steps:

1. Select a destination area, as described previously. Include the row or column headings that you want to use as consolidation categories. The headings must be spelled the same as in the source worksheets.

2. Choose the **Data Consolidate** command.

3. Select the **Reference** text box, and then select or type a source area. Include the row and column headings in the source area. You can select an area in any open worksheet. If the source worksheet is on disk, you can type in its full path name and source area enclosed in single quotes. Use a form such as

   =BDGT_EST.XLS!$A$4:$R$8

To activate a source worksheet, click on a source worksheet; or choose the Window menu and select a worksheet. Select the source area on the worksheet by clicking on it or dragging across it. Move the dialog box if necessary.

 To activate a source worksheet, press Ctrl +F6; or choose the Window menu and select a worksheet. Select the source area by moving to it, then holding the Shift key as you press arrow keys to select, or use the F8 key to extend the selection. Move the dialog box if necessary.

4. Choose the Add button to add the source entry to the All References list.

5. Repeat steps 3 and 4 to add all the source areas to the All References list.

6. Select the type of consolidation that you want from the Function list.

7. Select the headings in the source areas by which you want to consolidate. Select one or both: the By Categories Top Row and the Left Column check boxes.

8. Select the Create Links to Source Data check box if you want the destination area to be linked to the source areas. This step makes the consolidation an outline. (Consolidation outlines are described at the end of this chapter.)

9. Choose OK or press Enter.

When you use headings to consolidate, you can specify which categories to consolidate and the order in which you want categories placed in the destination area. To do this, enter the headings in the top row or left column of the destination area. Then include those headings in the selection you make (step 1 in the preceding instructions).

Figure 12.20 shows a destination area with headings down the left column in an order different than the headings in the source areas. Notice that after consolidation (see fig. 12.21) Excel has arranged the consolidated data in the correct rows by headings.

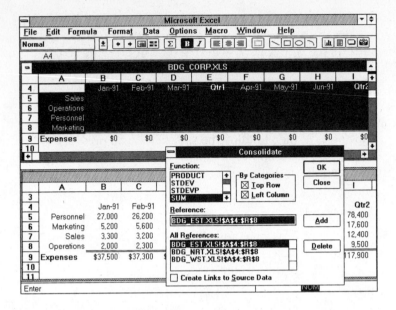

Fig. 12.20. *Enter row or column headings first in the destination area to specify the consolidation order.*

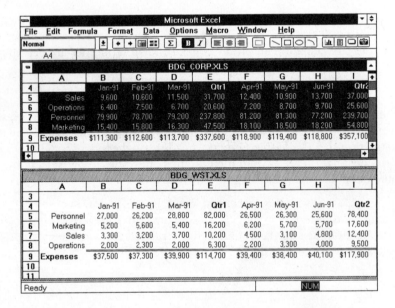

Fig. 12.21. *The consolidation is arranged to match existing headings in the destination area.*

Reduce problems caused by moving or rearranging source areas by editing the source areas in the **R**eference text box to use range names instead of cell references.

Repeating or Editing Links

You can add source areas to the All References list by opening the Consolidate dialog box, selecting the **R**eference text box, and then selecting the source area on a worksheet. Choose the **A**dd button to add the new source area to the All References list.

Delete source areas from future consolidations by selecting the source area in the All References list and then choosing the **D**elete button.

Edit a source area by selecting it from the All References list, editing it in the **R**eference text box, and then choosing the Add button. Delete the original source area from the list if necessary.

Linking and Formatting Consolidated Worksheets

When you select the Create Links to Source Data check box, Excel consolidates by inserting rows and columns into the consolidation area at the appropriate locations. These inserted rows and columns contain external reference formulas that link cells in the consolidation area to cells in each of the source areas. These new rows and columns become part of a worksheet outline. The highest level of the outline shows the consolidation; the lower levels of the outline contain the links to source worksheets. Chapter 13 describes worksheet outlining in fuller detail.

Figure 12.22 shows a destination area in BDG_CORP.XLS created with headings and linking selected. Figure 12.23 shows the same destination area with the outline feature turned on. The highest level of the outline is the consolidation. Lower levels contain links that feed into the consolidation.

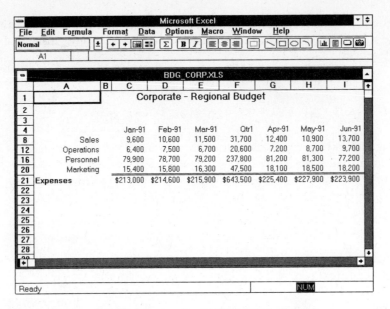

Fig. 12.22. The consolidation area in BDG_CORP.XLS is linked to its sources and uses the headings specified in the dependent worksheet for the consolidation.

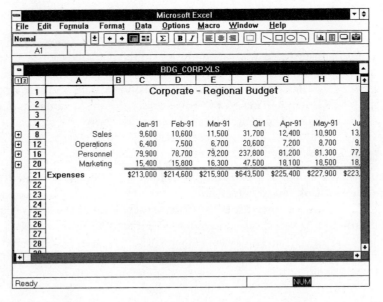

Fig. 12.23. Outlines use row and column buttons that enable you to expand or contract the outline.

There are two important reasons for understanding the relation of linked consolidations and outlines. Each level in an outline (and the linked consolidation) can have a different formatting style. And linked consolidations can be expanded or contracted to show summary or detail views of the consolidated data.

By clicking on the row-level buttons on the left (shown with a +), the outline for rows opens to reveal the links that supply the consolidated cells. Figure 12.24 shows the hidden rows revealed. The consolidation results are actually SUM functions that total the external references in these hidden rows.

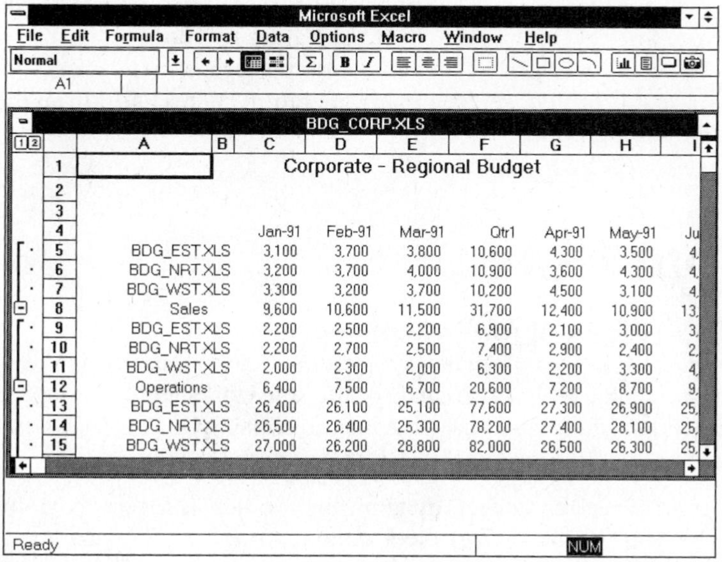

Fig. 12.24. *Expanding the outline's rows reveals the external reference formulas that link to the source areas.*

To apply outline styles to an existing linked consolidation, select the destination area, choose the Fo**r**mula **O**utline command, and choose the Apply **S**tyles button. Refer to Chapter 13, "Building Extensive Worksheets," for information on outlining. Refer to Chapter 8, "Formatting Worksheets," to learn how to change the definitions of outline styles to produce the outline formatting you want.

Manually Consolidating Worksheets

When you need to transfer only values between worksheets and you do not want those values automatically updated, use Edit Paste Special. With Paste Special, you combine the values from one worksheet into another. Paste Special enables you to combine data by pasting values, or by adding, subtracting, multiplying, or dividing values with existing cell contents. Because a link is not established, values are not updated when the supporting worksheet changes.

To consolidate data between worksheets, use Edit Copy to copy cell contents from one worksheet. Activate the other worksheet, and paste with the Edit Paste Special command. Select the Values option to paste the values from the source worksheet. If you want to perform a math operation with the data as it is pasted, select a math operation such as Add from the Operation option group.

From Here...

Excel's capability to display multiple worksheets and to link or consolidate open or disk-based worksheets gives your systems a great deal of flexibility and power. In Excel, you also can link multiple worksheets to a single graph or link worksheets to disk-based database files using Q+E. Q+E is described in Chapter 26, "Linking Excel to Databases with Q+E."

You can link Excel worksheets dynamically to other Windows programs. For example, you can have worksheet data automatically updated by a tele-communication program or have Excel automatically analyze changes to a database inventory. Excel can hold and maintain a mailing list that you link to a mail-merge system in Word for Windows. Linking Excel with other Windows programs is described in Chapter 33, "Using Excel with Windows Programs."

13

Building Extensive Worksheets

Excel contains many commands and features to reduce your workload. This chapter describes commands and techniques that can help you accomplish more in less time.

You will learn how to enter a series of numbers or dates, how to use formulas to manipulate text, and how to write formulas that make decisions based on conditions that you specify. You also will learn how to test input values to make sure that they are in the correct range, how to use lookup tables to find tax or commission rates, and how to use arrays to enter formulas and save memory. If you need to present large sheets of summary and detailed information, you will be interested in the section on creating worksheet outlines. The chapter ends with a section on how to troubleshoot worksheets.

Entering a Series of Numbers or Dates

When building forecasts, budgets, or trend analyses, you often need a series of dates or numbers. You can enter series quickly with the **Data Series** command. A data series can number the items in a database, enter a series of consecutive dates, or create a series of data-entry values for a table of solutions generated with the **Data Table** command.

407

Figure 13.1 shows examples of numeric and date series entered with the **Data Series** command. Note that the displayed dates for the days and months were created with a custom date format. This format is described later in this section.

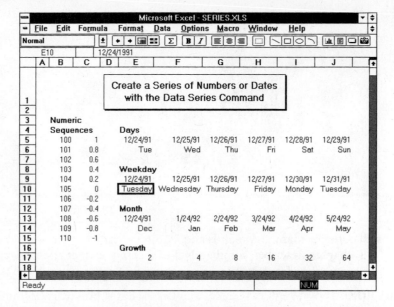

Fig. 13.1. Create numeric or date series with the Data Series command.

To create a series of either numbers or dates, begin with the following steps:

1. Enter the first number or date in the first cell.

2. Select the range of cells that you want filled (see fig. 13.2).

3. Choose **D**ata Se**r**ies to display the Series dialog box (see fig. 13.3).

4. Verify that the **C**olumns or **R**ows option matches the type of range you want filled.

5. Select one of the following Type options:

Linear	Adds the **S**tep Value to the preceding number in the series
Growth	Multiplies the **S**tep Value by the preceding number in the series
Date	Changes to a date sequence

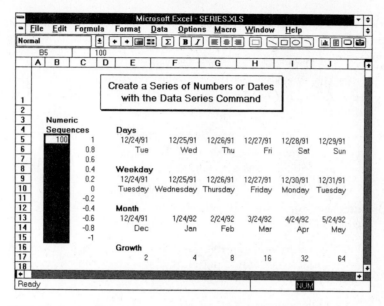

Fig. 13.2. Start your data series with the first number or date.

Fig. 13.3. The Data Series dialog box.

If you are entering a series of numbers and you chose either Linear or Growth in step 5, continue with the following steps:

1. Enter the **S**tep Value. This is the amount by which the series will change from cell to cell. The **S**tep Value can be positive or negative.

   Figure 13.1 shows how a 0.2 **S**tep Value decreases the numbers in column C.

2. Enter the St**o**p Value only if you think you may have highlighted too many cells when you selected the range that you want to fill.

3. Choose OK or press Enter.

Excel stops the series when it reaches either the end of the selected range or the Stop Value. If you use a negative **Step** Value, the Stop Value must be "less" than the starting value. You can type a date or time as the stop value if you type it in a format that Excel recognizes.

If you are entering a series of dates and you chose **Date** in step 5, follow these steps:

1. From the Date Unit area of the Data Series dialog box, select either Day, Weekday, Month, or Year to designate the date increment. (Note that Weekday gives you dates without Saturdays and Sundays.)

2. Enter the Step Value to specify the increment amount. For example, if the starting value is 12/1/91 and you choose Month as the Date Unit and 2 as the Step Value, the second date in the series will be 2/1/92, and the next will be 4/1/92.

3. Enter the Stop Value if you think you may have highlighted too many cells.

   The Stop Value indicates the last date in the series. You can use one of Excel's predefined date formats, such as the one shown in figure 13.4, as the Stop Value.

4. Choose OK or press Enter.

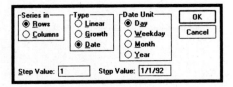

Fig. 13.4. Use a predefined date or time format as the Stop Value.

If you want to display only the name of the month or the day of the week, as shown in rows 6, 10, and 14 of figure 13.1, use custom date formatting. Table 13.1 shows some of these formats. Custom numeric and date formats are described in detail in Chapter 8.

Table 13.1
Date Formats in a Series

Custom Date Format	Display
yy	92
yyyy	1992
mmm	Jan
mmmm	January
ddd	Thu
dddd	Thursday

Using Formulas To Manipulate Text

Excel enables you to manipulate text as well as numbers and dates. Text manipulation comes in handy for combining text and numbers in printed invoices, for creating titles from numeric results, and for using data from a database to create a mailing list.

Use the concatenation operator, the & (ampersand), to join text, numbers, or cell contents to create a text string. Enclose text in quotation marks. Numbers do not need to be enclosed in quotation marks. Do not enclose cell references in quotation marks. You can reference cells containing text or numbers. For example, consider the following formula:

="This "&"and That"

This formula displays the text as follows:

```
This and That
```

You also can join text by referring to the cell address. If A12 contains the text "John" and B12 contains the text "McDougall," you can use the following formula to combine the first and last names:

=A12&" "&B12

The result of the formula is the full name:

John McDougall

Notice that a space between two quotation marks separates the text contained in A12 and B12.

Excel also lets you use a number as text. You can refer to a number as you would a cell filled with text. If A12 contains 99 and B12 contains "Stone St.," use the following formula to create the full street address:

=A12&" "&B12

The result of the formula is the address:

99 Stone St.

When you refer to a number or date in a text formula, the number or date appears in the General format, not as it appears in its formatted display. For example, suppose that cell B23 contains the date 12/24/91 and that you enter the following formula:

="Merry Christmas! Today is "&B23

The result of the formula is this display:

Merry Christmas! Today is 33596

You can change the format with the FIXED, DOLLAR, and TEXT functions. These functions change numbers and dates to text in the format you want. With dates, for example, you can use the TEXT function to produce the following formula:

="Merry Christmas! Today is "&TEXT(B23,"mmm dd, yy")

The result appears as text:

Merry Christmas! Today is Dec 24, 91

You can use any predefined or custom numeric or date format between the quotation marks of the TEXT function.

The TEXT function is a handy way to trick large numbers into exceeding the width of a column without producing the #### signs that indicate a narrow column. The TEXT function also is useful for numeric titles. For example, if you want the number $5,000,000 stored in A36 to fit in a narrow column, use this formula, which displays the formatted number as text so that it can exceed the column width.

=TEXT(A36,"$#,##0")

Using Formulas To Make Decisions

Excel's IF function can make decisions based on whether a test condition is true or false. For example, use IF to test whether it is time to reorder a part, whether data was entered correctly, or which of two results or formulas should be used.

The IF function uses the following format:

IF(*logical_test*,*value_if_true*,*value_if_false*)

If the *logical_test* (condition) is true, the result is *value_if_true*; but if the *logical_test* is false, the result is *value_if_false*. The result values can display text, calculate a formula, or display the contents of a cell. IF functions are valuable in macros for testing different conditions and acting according to the results of the test conditions.

Consider the following formula:

=IF(B34>50,B34*2,"Entry too low!")

In this example, the IF function produces the answer 110 if B34 is 55. If B34 is 12, however, the cell containing the function displays this text:

```
Entry too low!
```

Making Simple Decisions

IF functions are frequently used to make comparisons. Figure 13.5 shows an Accounts Aging Analysis worksheet in which Excel checks how long an amount has been owed. Using IF functions and the age of the account, Excel displays the amount in the correct column.

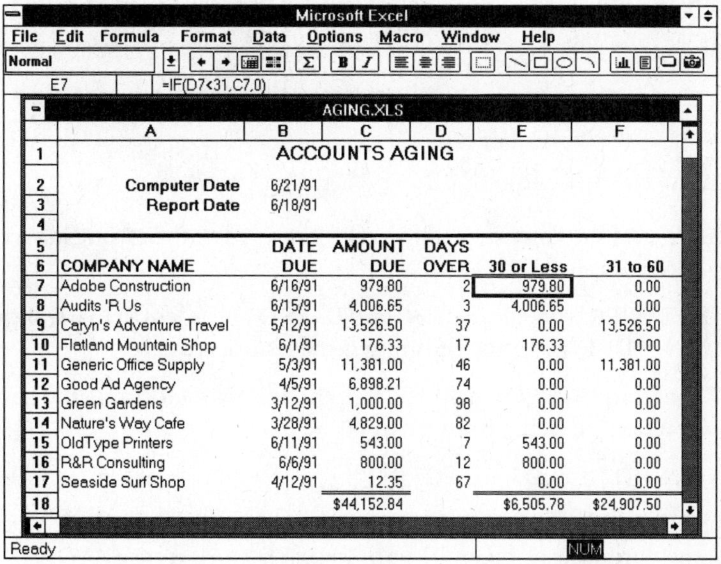

	A	B	C	D	E	F
1	ACCOUNTS AGING					
2	Computer Date	6/21/91				
3	Report Date	6/18/91				
4						
5		DATE	AMOUNT	DAYS		
6	COMPANY NAME	DUE	DUE	OVER	30 or Less	31 to 60
7	Adobe Construction	6/16/91	979.80	2	979.80	0.00
8	Audits 'R Us	6/15/91	4,006.65	3	4,006.65	0.00
9	Caryn's Adventure Travel	5/12/91	13,526.50	37	0.00	13,526.50
10	Flatland Mountain Shop	6/1/91	176.33	17	176.33	0.00
11	Generic Office Supply	5/3/91	11,381.00	46	0.00	11,381.00
12	Good Ad Agency	4/5/91	6,898.21	74	0.00	0.00
13	Green Gardens	3/12/91	1,000.00	98	0.00	0.00
14	Nature's Way Cafe	3/28/91	4,829.00	82	0.00	0.00
15	OldType Printers	6/11/91	543.00	7	543.00	0.00
16	R&R Consulting	6/6/91	800.00	12	800.00	0.00
17	Seaside Surf Shop	4/12/91	12.35	67	0.00	0.00
18			$44,152.84		$6,505.78	$24,907.50

Fig. 13.5. *Use IF functions to test ranges such as the ages of these accounts.*

The first few times you use IF statements, you may want to write an English sentence that states the *logical_test,* or question you want to ask. The question also should state both the results if true and if false. For example, each cell from E7 through E16 uses an IF statement that is the equivalent of this sentence:

IF DAYS OVER is less than 31, show the AMOUNT DUE; but if DAYS OVER is not more than 31, show nothing.

The IF function equivalent of that statement for cell E7 appears in the formula bar as this:

=IF(D7<31,C7,0)

In this example, D7 contains the DAYS OVER for row 7, and C7 contains the AMOUNT DUE for the row. Choose Options Display and deselect Zero Values to prevent the display of zeros in column E.

> **Tip: *Displaying Blank Cells***
>
> If you want to display a blank cell for specific conditions, use a formula such as this:
>
> =IF(D7<31,C7,"")
>
> Nothing is entered between the quotation marks, so this function displays a blank cell for the false condition. Remember that Excel can hide zeros for the entire worksheet if you choose the **Options Display** and deselect the **Zero Values** option.

Making Complex Decisions

In column F of the worksheet shown in figure 13.5, the IF question needs to be more complex:

IF DAYS OVER is greater than 30 and DAYS OVER is less than 61, show the AMOUNT DUE; but show nothing if that is not true.

The IF functions in F7 through F17 use the following formula to check for DAYS OVER in the range from 31 to 60:

=IF(AND(D7>30,D7<61),C7,0)

The AND function produces a TRUE response only when all the elements within the parentheses meet the conditions: D7>30 is true *AND* D7<61 is true. When the AND function produces TRUE, the IF formula produces the value found in C7.

Whenever you want to check for a number within a range of values, use an AND function as shown here; for the AND function to be TRUE, all of the arguments must be true. When you want to check for a specific number, use an OR function. With an OR function, any true argument will produce TRUE. AND and OR functions are described in more detail in Chapter 24, "Finding and Editing Data."

Checking Data Entry

IF functions are also useful for verifying that data falls within allowable limits. You can put an IF function in a cell adjacent to the entry cell to warn the operator when data is out of limits. Consider, for example, the following formula:

=IF(AND(B6>250,B6<500),"","Enter values between 250 and 500")

This formula results in the following warning when the value entered in B6 is not between 250 and 500:

```
Enter values between 250 and 500
```

Looking Up Data in Tables

You can build a table in Excel and look up the contents of various cells within the table. Lookup tables provide an efficient way of producing numbers or text that you cannot calculate with a formula. For example, you may not be able to calculate a tax table or commission table. In those cases, looking up values from a table is much easier. Tables also enable you to cross-check typed data against a list of allowable values.

Excel has two techniques for looking up information from tables. The first method uses three types of LOOKUP functions, similar to those in Lotus 1-2-3. Although easier to use, these functions have the disadvantage of giving you an answer whether the function has found an exact match or not. Also, the list in the table needs to be in sorted order—another disadvantage.

The second method is more precise. It uses a combination of the INDEX and MATCH functions to find an exact match in a table, whether the list in the table is sorted or not. If Excel can't find an exact match, the function returns an error.

Looking up either close or exact matches from tables is valuable for calculating commissions, shipping rates, or checking entered part numbers or descriptions against a known list. Looking up matches from tables can save you time locating information and can cross-check your data entry or actually do the data entry for you.

Using LOOKUP Functions on Tables

Excel has three LOOKUP functions. The function shown in figure 13.6 is VLOOKUP; this function looks down the vertical column on the left side of the table until it finds the appropriate comparison value. The HLOOKUP function looks across the horizontal row at the top of the table until it finds the appropriate comparison value. The third form, LOOKUP, is described in Chapter 10, "Using Functions."

The VLOOKUP and HLOOKUP functions use the following forms:

    VLOOKUP(*lookup_value,table_array,col_index***)**

    HLOOKUP(*lookup_value,table_array,row_index_num***)**

The VLOOKUP function tries to match the value in the left column of the table; the HLOOKUP function tries to match the value in the top row. These values are called the *lookup_values*. The *table_array* describes the range containing the table and lookup values. The *col_index* for the VLOOKUP function or the *row_index_num* for HLOOKUP tells the function which column or row, respectively, contains the result. The first column or row in the table is always numbered 1.

The list you use for comparison in the table must be in ascending order. The cells in C11:C15, in figure 13.6, must be sorted in ascending order for the lookup function to work correctly. The function searches down column one in a VLOOKUP table or across row one in an HLOOKUP table until it meets a value that is larger than the *lookup_value*. If the *lookup_values* are not in ascending order, the function can be misled.

Figure 13.6 shows an example of a VLOOKUP table that locates sales commissions. You will find the VLOOKUP and HLOOKUP commands helpful for looking up data in commission or tax tables because these tables contain data that may be difficult to calculate exactly. For example, the sales that a commission is based on may fall between two numbers in the list. In this example, the formula that finds the sales commission is in cell D5. The VLOOKUP function, as shown in the formula bar of the example, is the following:

    =VLOOKUP(D3,C11:F15,D4+1)

The VLOOKUP formula looks down the left column of the table displayed in the range C11:F15 until it finds a Sales $ amount larger than D3 ($12,425). VLOOKUP then backs up to the previous row and looks across the table to the column specified by D4+1. The formula D4+1 results in 2, the second column of the table. (Sales $ is column 1. The value 1 is added to D4 so that the lookup starts in the Product Class portion of the table.) The VLOOKUP function returns the value .045 from the table. The commission is calculated by multiplying .045 by the amount of sale, which is $12,452.

The lookup functions do not use the headings in row 10. These headings are there for the user.

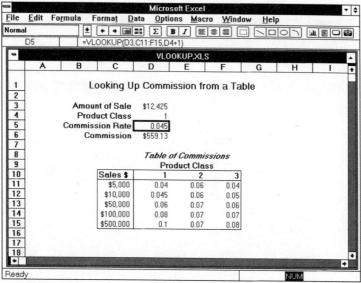

Fig. 13.6. The VLOOKUP function finds information in a vertical table.

Using MATCH and INDEX Functions on Tables

Excel also can look up data from a table and use an exact match to find the information. The list you use for comparison does not have to be in sorted order. If Excel does not find an exact match in the list, an error warns you that the table did not contain a match.

Using exact matches against a list is one way to prevent data-entry errors. For example, imagine a case in which an operator must enter an item number and an item description belonging to that number. Having the operator enter the item description could introduce errors if the description is misspelled or does not match the item number. A better plan is to have the operator enter only the item number and have Excel look up the description. This technique not only reduces typing but cross-checks the item number by displaying either an accurate description or an error message if the number is incorrect.

In figure 13.7, Excel automatically enters the item description when the item number is entered. If the item number is nonexistent, the worksheet displays #N/A in the Description cell (C8).

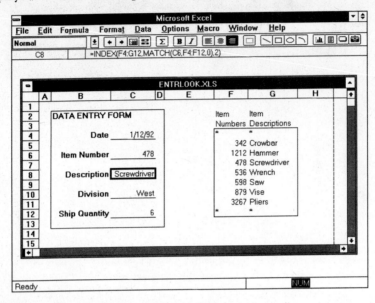

Fig. 13.7. Use an exact match to look up and enter data.

The following formula, found in cell C8, looks up the description and enters it:

=INDEX(F4:G12,MATCH(C6,F4:F12,0),2)

The two functions used in this formula follow this syntax:

=**INDEX(***array,row_num,column_num***)**
=**MATCH(***lookup_value,lookup_array,match_type***)**

In the INDEX function, *array* is the entire range containing data. The *row_num* and *column_num* arguments designate the row and column that specify a value in the *array*. For example, for the range F4:G12, a *row_num* of 5 and a *column_num* of 2 causes INDEX to return Wrench.

In the MATCH function, the *lookup_value* is the value for which you are searching. In the example, this value is the item number found in C6. The *lookup_array* is an array in a row or column that contains the list of values that you are searching. In the example, this array is the column of item numbers F4:F12. The *match_type* specifies what type of match is required. In the example, 0 specifies an exact match.

In the example, then, the MATCH function looks through the range F4:F12 until it finds the exact match for the contents of cell C6. When it finds an exact match, the MATCH function returns the position of the match—in this case, row 4 of the specified range. Notice that the MATCH function finds the first match in the range. For an exact match, the contents of the range F4:F12 do not have to be in ascending order.

You also can omit the *match_type* or specify 1 or –1. If the *match_type* is omitted or is 1, then MATCH finds the largest value in the *lookup_array* that is equal to or less than the *lookup_value*. If *match_type* is omitted or is 1, the *lookup-array* must be in ascending order. If the *match_type* is –1, MATCH finds the smallest value that is greater than or equal to the *lookup_value*. If the *match_type* is –1, the *lookup_array* must be in descending order.

In the formula shown in figure 13.7, the INDEX function looks in the range F4:G12. The function returns the contents of the cell located at the intersection of column 2 and row 4, as specified by the MATCH function. The result is Screwdriver.

The item numbers and descriptions in the table are outlined to identify the table. The asterisks (*) at the top and bottom of the table mark the corners of the ranges. The function continues to work correctly as long as you insert any new data item codes and descriptions between the asterisks.

Calculating Tables of Answers

Because of the "what if" game made possible by electronic worksheets, worksheets are extremely useful in business. Worksheets provide immediate feedback to questions like: "What if we reduce costs by .5 percent?", "What if we sell 11 percent more?", and "What if we don't get that loan?"

When you test how small changes in input affect the result of a worksheet, you are conducting a *sensitivity analysis*. You can use Excel's **Data Table** command to conduct sensitivity analyses across a wide range of inputs.

Excel will create a table showing the inputs that you want to test and displaying the results, so you don't have to enter all the possible inputs manually. Using a combination of a data table and the D*functions*, you can do quick but extensive database analysis of finance, marketing, or research information.

You can have more than one data table in a worksheet so that you can analyze different variables or different database statistics at one time.

You can use **Data Table** in two ways:

- Change one input to see the resulting effect on one or more formulas

- Change two inputs to see the resulting effect on only one formula

Building a Table with One Changing Variable and Many Formulas

One of the best (and most frequently used) examples of sensitivity analysis is a data table that calculates the loan payments for different interest rates. The single-input data table described in this section creates a chart of monthly payments for a series of loan interest rates.

Before creating a data table, you need to build a worksheet that solves the problem you want to test. The worksheet in figure 13.8 calculates a house or car mortgage payment. The formula in cell D7 is this:

    =PMT(D4/12,D5*12,D3)

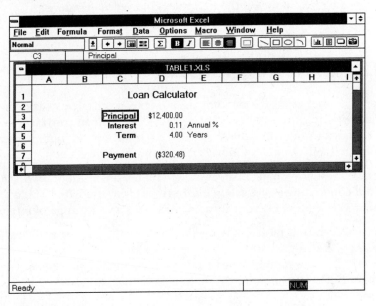

Fig. 13.8. Build a worksheet with a result you want to analyze.

To build a data table, follow these steps:

1. Build the worksheet.

2. Enter the different values that you want tested. (You can enter the values in any sequence.)

   Cells C11:C15 in figure 13.9 show the interest rates to be used as inputs in the sensitivity analysis. When you are testing a single variable, make sure that the upper left corner of the table, cell C10 in the example, remains clear.

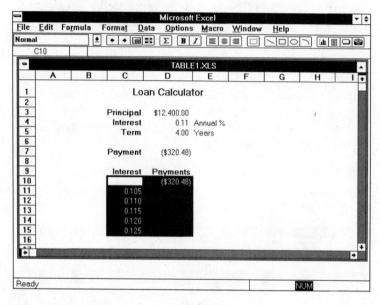

Fig. 13.9. *Enter interest rates to be evaluated.*

3. In the top row of the table, above where the results will appear, enter the address of each formula for which you want answers. You also can enter the actual formula in this cell.

   In figure 13.9, cell D10 contains =D7. Therefore, the results for the payment formula in D7 will be calculated for each interest rate in the table. To see the results of other formulas in the table, enter these formulas in other cells across the top of the table. For example, additional formulas could be entered in E10, F10, and so on.

4. Select the cells enclosing the table. Include the input values in the left column and the row of formulas at the top, as shown in figure 13.9.

5. Choose the **Data Table** command to display the Table dialog box (see fig. 13.10).

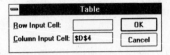

Fig. 13.10. *The Table dialog box.*

6. Enter the **Row** Input Cell or **Column** Input Cell. Click on or point to the cell in which you will type the variable numbers listed in the table.

In this example, the **Column** Input Cell is $D$4. $D$4 is entered in the **Column** Input Cell text box because the variable inputs go down the columns in the table. The reference $D$4 tells Excel to take each value from the column, C11:C15, and substitute the values one at a time into cell D4. After each substitution, the result for that value appears in column D.

7. Choose **OK** or press **Enter**.

The data table will fill with the payment amounts corresponding to each interest rate in the table (see fig. 13.11).

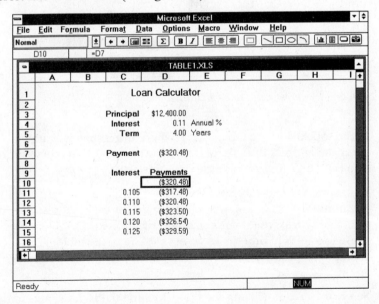

Fig. 13.11. *The Data Table fills with results for each value in the left column.*

If the Table dialog box covers the cells that you want to select as the row or column inputs, move the dialog box. To move the box, drag the title bar; or press Alt and then the space bar and select Move.

> **Tip: *Creating a Sequence of Input Values***
> Use the **D**ata **S**eries command to create a sequence of evenly incremented numbers for use as input values in the data table. The **D**ata **S**eries command is described earlier in this chapter.

Building a Table with Two Changing Variables and One Formula

Figure 13.12 shows how to create a data table that changes two input values, interest and principal (the loan's starting amount). The worksheet calculates the result of a formula for all the combinations of those values. The top row of the table area contains different principal amounts for cell D3, the **R**ow Input Cell. The left column of the table still contains the sequence of interest rates to be used in cell D4.

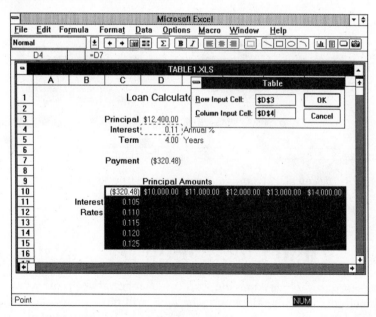

Fig. 13.12. Data tables also can change two input values used by one formula.

Notice that when you use two different input values you can test the results from only one formula. That formula or a reference to the formula must be in the top left corner of the table. In figure 13.12, cell C10 contains the reference =D7 to the payment formula being tested.

The Table dialog box in figure 13.12 shows how the **R**ow Input Cell is entered as $D$3 because the values from the top row of the table will be substituted into cell D3. The **C**olumn Input Cell is entered as $D$4 because the values from the left column of the table will be substituted into cell D4.

Figure 13.13 shows the result of a two-input data table. Each dollar value is the amount you would pay on a loan with that principal amount and annual interest rate. Because each monthly payment represents a cash outflow, the results appear in parentheses to show that the amounts are negative.

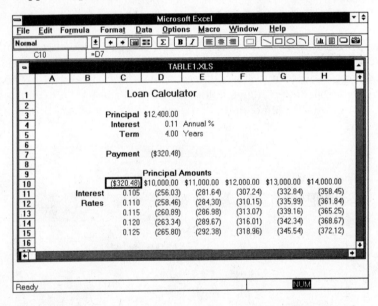

Fig. 13.13. *The completed data table with the results of combinations from two input values, interest and principal.*

Editing and Calculating Data Tables

After your data table is complete, you can change values in the worksheet on which the data table depends. The table will recalculate automatically using the new values. In the example in figure 13.13, typing a new Term in D5 will cause new Payment amounts to appear.

You also can change the numbers or text in the rows and columns of input values and see the resulting change in the data table. In the example in figure 13.13, you can type new numbers or use the **Data Series** command to replace the numbers in C11:C15 or in D10:H10. The data table will update automatically if automatic recalculation is selected.

Large data tables or many data tables may slow down calculation. If you want the worksheet to recalculate, but not the data tables, choose the **Options Calculation** command and select the Automatic except **Tables** option. Recalculate the tables by pressing F9 to calculate all worksheets or press Shift+F9 to calculate the active worksheet. If you are doing a large database analysis, you may not want the worksheet and its tables to recalculate before saving—the normal process. To save without recalculating, choose the **Options Calculation** command, select the **Manual** option, and deselect the Recalculate Before **S**ave check box.

You cannot edit a single formula within the data table. All the formulas in that area are array formulas of the following form:

{=TABLE(*row_input,column_input*)}

To rebuild or expand your data table, select all the cells containing the {=TABLE()} array formula and clear them with **E**dit C**l**ear or by pressing Del and then Enter. Change the data table, select the table area, and choose again the **Data Table** command.

Calculating with Array Math

Arrays are rectangular ranges of formulas or values that Excel treats as a single group. Some array formulas or functions return an array of results that is displayed in many cells. Other formulas or functions affect an entire array of cells, yet return the result in a single cell.

Arrays are a powerful way of doing a lot of calculation in a small space. Arrays also can save memory when used to replace repetitive formulas. Some Excel functions, such as the trend analysis functions discussed in this chapter under "Analyzing Trends," require some knowledge of arrays.

Entering Arrays

Rather than entering or copying a repetitive formula into each cell of a range, you can save memory by entering an array formula. Excel stores an array of formulas in memory as a single formula even if it affects many cells. Also, some Excel functions must be entered as arrays that span a range of cells because the function produces multiple results and each result is displayed in a cell.

Figure 13.14 shows a worksheet for cost estimating with Price in column D and Quantity in column E. To find the sum of the products in column D times column E, you can enter a formula such as =D5*E5 in F5 and copy it down column F. This requires a formula, and space in memory and storage, for each cell containing the formula.

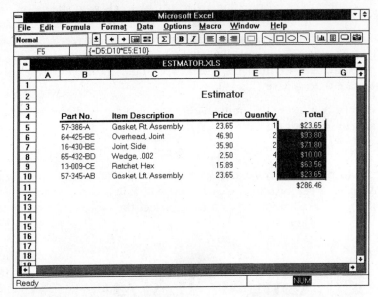

Fig. 13.14. *Entering a repetitive formula as an array formula saves memory and storage space.*

Instead, enter a single array formula in cell F5 that fills the range from F5 through F10 and uses only the memory and storage required for a single formula. To enter a single array formula, follow these steps:

1. Select the range that will contain the array formula—F5:F10 (see fig. 13.15).

2. Enter the formula using ranges by typing it or pointing with the mouse. The formula in cell F5 is =D5:D10*E5:E10.

3. Press Shift+Ctrl+Enter to enter the formula or function as an array.

Instead of multiplying two cells, the formula shown in the formula bar of figure 13.14 multiplies the two arrays D5:D10 and E5:E10. The multiplication is done by taking each corresponding element from the two arrays and multiplying them in pairs—for example, D5*E5, then D6*E6, and so on. The corresponding result is placed in each cell of the range F5:F10, selected before entry.

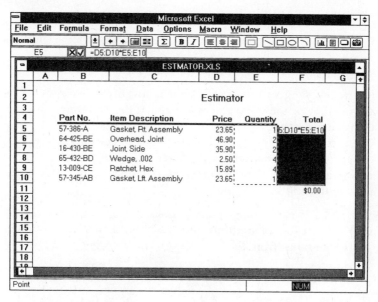

Fig. 13.15. *Select the range, and then enter the array formula.*

Notice that the formula in figure 13.14 appears with braces ({ }) around it. Each cell in the array range F5:F10 contains the same formula in braces. The braces signify that the formula is an array formula and that the array range must be treated as a single entity. You cannot insert cells or rows within the array range, delete part of it, or edit a single cell within it. To change an array, you must select and change the entire array.

You can enter functions that operate on ranges with array math. *Array functions* use an array of values as an input and produce an array of results as an output. Enter array functions the same way as you enter an array formula. Select a range of the correct size to hold the results of the array function, and enter the array formula or function specifying the ranges the formula or function will work on. Then press Shift+Ctrl+Enter.

Suppose, for example, that you want only the total in cell F11 of figure 13.14 and do not need the total price for each part. You can calculate the products and sum them in a single cell with an array formula. To see this result, type the following formula in cell F14:

=SUM(D5:D10*E5:E10)

Enter the formula by pressing Shift+Ctrl+Enter so that Excel treats the formula as an array formula. Excel calculates the sum of the array product. The SUM formula will be displayed in the formula bar with braces around it.

Selecting the Range for an Array

Generally, the range you select in which to enter an array formula or function should be the same size and shape as the arrays used for input. If the array range that you select for the result is too small, you will not see all of the results. If the array range is too large, the unnecessary cells will display #N/A. If an array of a single cell, a single row, or a single column is entered in too large a selection, that element, row, or column is repeated to expand the array to the appropriate size.

In figure 13.14, the array range for each column was 6 by 1 (six rows by one column). The result of multiplying these two arrays is a 6-by-1 array. Therefore, the range from F5 through F10 was selected.

Editing Array Formulas and Functions

Treat arrays as a single entity in which individual cells cannot be edited or deleted. To edit an array formula or function, follow these steps:

1. Move the pointer within the array range.

2. Choose the Formula Select Special command and select the Current Array option, or press Ctrl+/ (Ctrl+slash) to select the array.

3. Click in the formula bar, or press F2 (the Edit key).

4. Edit the array formula or function.

5. Press Shift+Ctrl+Enter to reenter the array.

Analyzing Trends

Excel has four functions that calculate a best-fit line passing through a series of data. You can use these functions to calculate trends and make near-term forecasts.

These functions work by calculating the best-fit equation for either the straight line or exponential growth line that passes through the data. The LINEST and LOGEST functions calculate the parameters for the straight-line and exponential growth-line equations. The TREND or GROWTH functions calculate the values along the straight line or exponential growth line needed to draw a curve or forecast a short-range value.

Before you can use the trend analysis functions, you should be familiar with dependent and independent variables. The value of a *dependent variable* changes when the *independent variable* changes. Frequently, the independent variable is time, but it also can be such things as the price of raw materials, the temperature, or a population size. The independent variable's actual data is entered as the *known-x* argument in the function, and the dependent variable's actual data is entered as the function's *known-y* argument.

Imagine that you own a concrete business that depends on new residential construction. You want to plan for future growth or decline so that you can best manage your assets and people.

After research with the help of the local economic advisory boards, you assemble statistics on housing starts in your service area for the last five years. Figure 13.16 shows the housing starts by year in row 4. After discussion with county planners, you are convinced that your area will continue to grow at the same or a slightly better rate. But what will the number of housing starts be in 1992 and 1993?

In the figure, the independent variables of time (*known_x*) are entered in B3:F3. The dependent variables of housing starts (*known_y*) are entered in B4:F4. If the trend from the past five years continues, you can project the estimated housing starts for the next two years with the following steps:

1. Select the range of cells that you want your straight-line projection to fill, B6:H6, as shown in figure 13.16.

2. Choose the Formula Paste Function command.

3. Select TREND from the list box.

4. Ensure that the Paste Arguments check box is selected so that prompts for arguments are pasted between the function's parentheses.

5. Enter the arguments for the TREND function so that the formula appears as it does in figure 13.16. The syntax for the TREND function is

   TREND(*known_y's,known_x's,new_x's*)

Replace the *known_y's* argument with B4:F4. (Housing Starts are y's because they are dependent on the Year value.)

Replace the *known_x's* argument with B3:F3. (Year is the independent variable.)

Replace *new_x's* with B3:H3. These are the years for which you want to know the values that describe a trend line.

Notice that the selected area in figure 13.16 covers the room for the resulting calculated *y* values.

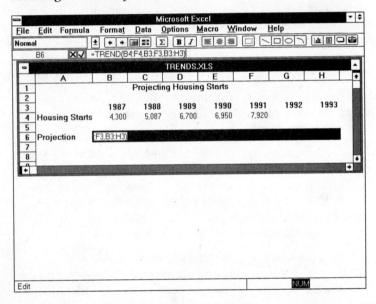

Fig. 13.16. *This worksheet shows the historic data for housing starts.*

6. Press Shift+Ctrl+Enter to enter the TREND function as an array function in the selected range.

The result, shown in figure 13.17, illustrates that years 1992 and 1993 may have housing starts of about 8922 and 9833 if the trend continues.

Notice that the new *y* values in cells B6:F6 don't exactly match the known *y* values in B3:F3. That is because the TREND function calculated the housing starts for those years according to its trend equation (a linear regression). The real number of housing starts in each year will undoubtedly be different. The greater the differences between the real housing starts and projected housing starts, the less likely that the projection will be accurate.

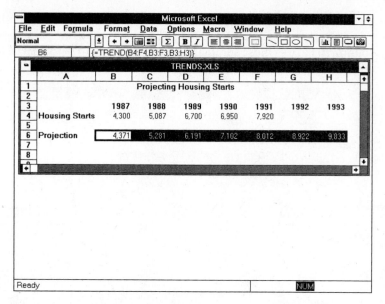

Fig. 13.17. The trend values can help you make short-term projections.

❖ Outlining Worksheets for Summaries and Detail

With Excel you can efficiently display summary and detail information in an outline (see fig. 13.18). When you condense an outline, only the summary information shows. When you expand an outline, the summary and the detailed information show.

Displaying selected levels of information is a real advantage when you need to work with or print worksheets containing different levels of information. The outline enables you to display or print only the amount of information you need. For example, budgets often contain subordinate line items. Operational managers need to see these details, but managers at a different level may need to see the summary level only. Engineers and scientists also find outlines useful. Engineers reviewing large amounts of instrument recordings may want to see only hourly summary statistics of readings taken each minute. When hourly statistics look abnormal, the engineer can expand the outline to show the detail of the recordings taken each minute.

Figure 13.19 shows a history of sales dollars in which time appears horizontally on the worksheet and regions and products appear vertically. The summary and detail information are all shown. Products are summarized by region in rows 9, 13, 17, and 21. Row 22 is a corporate summary. Summaries by quarter are in columns E, I, M, and Q. The Annual summary is in column R. Each of these summaries is a SUM function of the data above or to the left of the function.

	A	B	C	D	E	F	G	H	I
5		Jan	Feb	Mar	Qtr1	Apr	May	Jun	Qtr2
6	Hex Head	4,318	5,955	4,059	14,331	4,412	3,233	3,708	11,353
7	DioFlange	3,223	3,276	3,755	10,255	5,521	5,209	3,287	14,018
8	Crimpex	4,562	4,857	4,464	13,884	6,564	6,946	6,807	20,317
9	East	12,103	14,088	12,279	38,470	16,498	15,387	13,803	45,688
10	Hex Head	4,154	3,565	5,455	13,174	3,299	5,403	5,527	14,230
11	DioFlange	4,014	4,415	5,347	13,776	6,783	4,489	4,192	15,464
12	Crimpex	6,104	6,986	6,002	19,092	4,687	3,801	6,500	14,989
13	West	14,272	14,967	16,804	46,042	14,769	13,694	16,220	44,683
14	Hex Head	6,859	6,000	6,932	19,792	6,859	5,431	5,616	17,906
15	DioFlange	5,194	3,379	4,833	13,406	4,020	5,919	3,582	13,522
16	Crimpex	4,730	3,449	5,115	13,293	3,560	4,089	4,987	12,636
17	North	16,783	12,828	16,880	46,491	14,440	15,440	14,185	44,064
18	Hex Head	5,370	5,210	5,228	15,808	5,519	6,582	4,244	16,346
19	DioFlange	3,281	3,732	3,783	10,796	3,856	3,287	4,697	11,840
20	Crimpex	5,009	6,755	4,056	15,819	3,396	3,441	3,331	10,169
21	South	13,660	15,697	13,067	42,424	12,772	13,311	12,272	38,354
22	Corporate	56,817	57,580	59,030	173,427	58,479	57,831	56,478	172,789

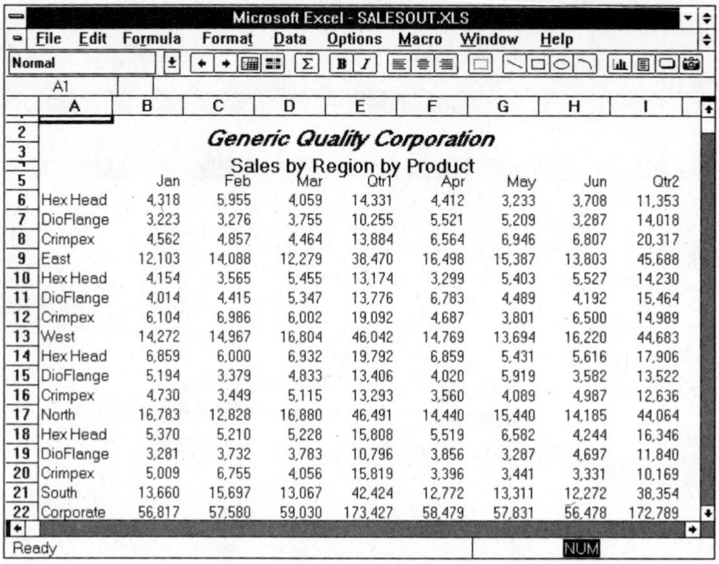

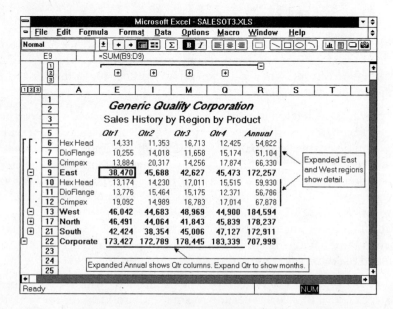

Fig. 13.18. *Normally, worksheets display detailed as well as summary data.*

	A	E	I	M	Q	R
5		*Qtr1*	*Qtr2*	*Qtr3*	*Qtr4*	*Annual*
6	Hex Head	14,331	11,353	16,713	12,425	54,822
7	DioFlange	10,255	14,018	11,658	15,174	51,104
8	Crimpex	13,884	20,317	14,256	17,874	66,330
9	**East**	**38,470**	**45,688**	**42,627**	**45,473**	**172,257**
10	Hex Head	13,174	14,230	17,011	15,515	59,930
11	DioFlange	13,776	15,464	15,175	12,371	56,786
12	Crimpex	19,092	14,989	16,783	17,014	67,878
13	**West**	**46,042**	**44,683**	**48,969**	**44,900**	**184,594**
17	**North**	**46,491**	**44,064**	**41,843**	**45,839**	**178,237**
21	**South**	**42,424**	**38,354**	**45,006**	**47,127**	**172,911**
22	**Corporate**	**173,427**	**172,789**	**178,445**	**183,339**	**707,999**

Fig. 13.19. *Outlines can display data at different summary or detail levels.*

Figure 13.20 shows the history of sales as an outline. In this figure, East, West, North, South, and Corporate rows are summary rows containing the detail of actual product sales. Columns E, I, M, and Q contain, respectively, each quarter's monthly detail.

Notice that some rows and columns have been hidden to show only summary information. North and South rows are collapsed to show only the regional summary. The East and West regions are expanded to show the product detail they contain. Similarly, the quarterly columns could be expanded to show the monthly detail they contain. The Annual column could be collapsed to contain the quarterly as well as monthly columns.

> **Tip: *Using Dates As the Top Row of an Outline***
> When you create an outline automatically, serial date numbers along the top row of the outline may be mistaken for data and disrupt that outline level. If this problem occurs, you can open the old file, type text dates in that row (for example, **May** or **="1/1/92"**), and then re-create the outline. Or, you can manually adjust the levels of rows and columns to correct the outline.

Understanding the Outline Display

Figure 13.20 shows a picture of the the outlining symbols and tools. Outlining tools in the tool bar are used to create, display, change, or select data at a specific outline level. The outlining tools are the following:

Tool	*Description*
Promote	Raises a row or column to a higher level in the outline.
Demote	Lowers a row or column to a lower level in the outline.
Show outline symbols	Displays or hides the outline and its buttons.
Select visible cells	Selects only the cells at the levels displayed in the outline.

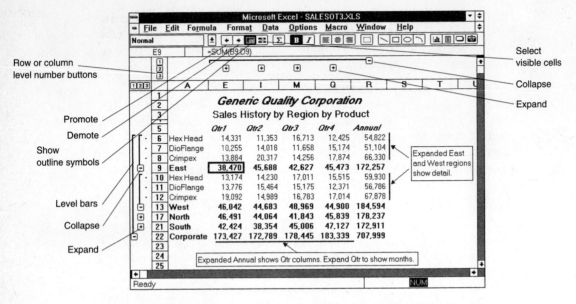

Fig. 13.20. *Outlining uses two tools and special symbols to expand and collapse outlines.*

While an outline is displayed, you will see outlining symbols along the left edge and top of the worksheet that contains the outline. These outlining symbols and buttons expand and collapse levels. You can selectively expand or collapse a selected row or column and its levels, or you can expand or collapse all rows or columns at a specific level. The outlining symbols are the following:

Symbol	Description
Expand(+)	Specifies a level containing lower levels of hidden data. Click to expand and display these levels for the selected row or column.
Collapse (–)	Specifies a summary level within which lower levels may be collapsed. Click to collapse and hide these levels for the selected row or column.
Row or column level number buttons	Specify the number of the row or column level to be displayed throughout the outline.
Level bars	Specifies all rows or columns at a specific level.

Understanding the Worksheet Layout of Outlines

Using Excel, you can create an outline manually, specifying a level for each row or column; or you can let Excel create an outline on the worksheet for you. When you manually create an outline, you use the promote or demote button to specify an outline level for a row or column. You must organize the levels in the outline.

If Excel creates the outline, Excel examines the contents of each cell in the range to be outlined. Depending upon the data and formulas in rows and columns, Excel then creates an outline with appropriate levels. Your outline can have up to seven levels of rows and columns.

Excel examines the range of cells you want to outline, searching for constant data and formulas or functions that have a consistent pattern. For example, Excel checks whether all the SUM functions in a column total the three columns to the left. When Excel finds consistent relationships, it makes these rows or columns summary rows or columns. These rows or columns appear at a higher level in the outline than the rows or columns they summarize.

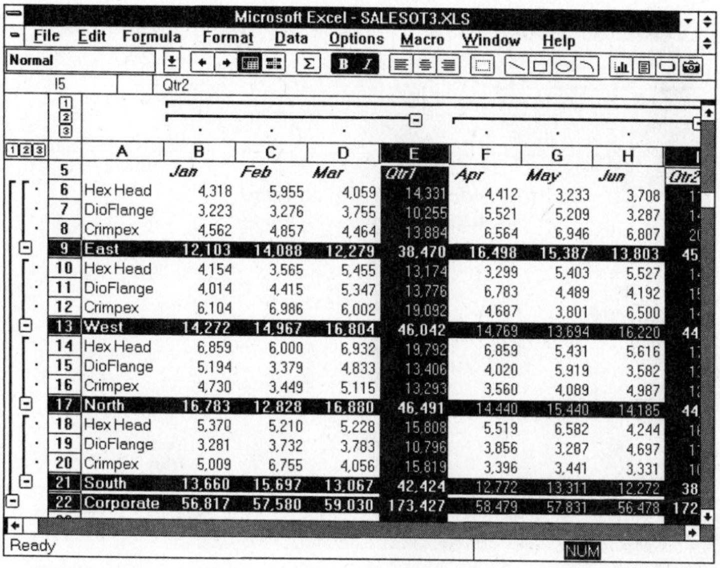

Fig. 13.21. Excel examines the layout of formulas to determine an outline's organization.

In figure 13.21 the shaded cells contain summarizing functions or formulas. The outline symbols show these rows and columns as a higher level in the outline. For example, cells in column E use SUM to total the cells in B, C, and D to the left. Cells in rows 9, 13, 17, and 21 use SUM to total the cells in the three rows above.

The highest levels in the outline are row 21 and column R, shown in figure 13.19 at the beginning of this section. These levels contain simple addition formulas that total lower level SUM functions. Row 21 contains the Corporate total by region; for example, =B9+B13+B17+B21. Column R contains the total of all quarters; for example, =Q6+M6+I6+E6.

All summary directions must be consistent. For automatic outlining to work, all summary columns must have their data on the same side, and all summary rows must have their data either above or below. If your outline mixes the direction in which data is summarized, use the manual method to create an outline.

When you create an outline, Excel assumes that summary rows are below detail rows and summary columns are to the right of detail columns. If you use the Formula Outline command to create the outline, you can specify that summary rows are above detail and summary columns are to the left of detail.

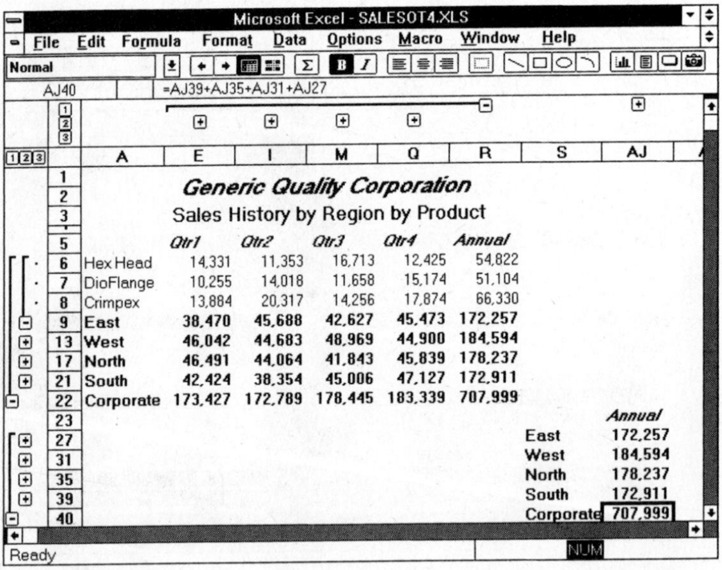

Fig. 13.22. *You can have disjointed outlines, but they are all controlled by the same level numbers.*

A worksheet can contain only one outline, but the outline can be disjointed, spread over different parts of a worksheet. Figure 13.22, for example, shows two outlines that are disjoint. The one at the top left is partially collapsed. The one at the lower right has the same data, but it is collapsed into the cells S23:AJ40. The row or column level number buttons affect both outlines at once, but you can use the Expand (+) or Collapse (–) buttons to manually expand or collapse each outline independently.

> **Tip: *Collapsing and Expanding an Outline***
> Collapsing and expanding an outline can affect other parts of the worksheet. Rows that expand or collapse do so through the entire width of the worksheet. Columns that expand or collapse do so through the entire height of the worksheet. This feature means that you usually will want an outline in rows and columns that are not shared with other cells from the worksheet. If other parts of the worksheet do overlay rows or columns used by the outline, those parts will expand and collapse along with outline changes.

Creating an Outline

You can create an outline using a menu command or using the Show Outline Symbols tool from the tool bar. To create an outline using the menu, follow these steps:

1. Examine the cells you want to outline. Notice whether the summary column is to the left or right of the column data and whether summary rows are above or below the row data.

2. To outline the cells in the range, select a range. To outline the entire worksheet, select a single cell.

3. Choose the Formula Outline command. The dialog box in figure 13.23 appears.

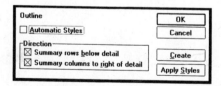

Fig. 13.23. *The Outline dialog box enables you to specify the orientation of your outline.*

4. Select the Automatic Styles check box if you want to apply pre-defined styles to different outline levels.

5. Select the check boxes that define the location of detail data with respect to summary rows and columns:

   Select the Summary rows below detail check box if formulas or functions in rows are below the data they summarize. Deselect if formulas or functions are above the data.

   Select the Summary columns to right of detail check box if formulas or functions in columns are to the right of data. Deselect if formulas or functions are to the left of the data.

6. Choose the Create button.

If you do not apply predefined outline styles, you can apply them later.

If you are using a mouse and have the tool bar displayed, you can quickly create an outline if one does not currently exist. The outline, however, will assume that summary rows are below detail data and that summary columns are to the right of detail data. To use this shortcut, follow these steps:

1. To outline the cells in the range, select a range. To outline the entire worksheet, select a single cell.

2. Click on the Show outline symbols icon. If no outline exists on the worksheet, the dialog box in figure 13.24 appears.

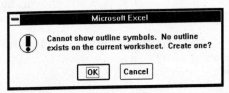

Fig. 13.24. If an outline does not exist, this alert box appears asking whether you want to make an outline.

3. Choose OK or press Enter.

Clearing an Outline from the Worksheet

You can remove all or part of an outline from the worksheet. To remove rows, columns, or the entire outline, raise the level of that part of the outline until it is "above" all outline levels. Removing rows or columns from the outline does not clear them from the worksheet.

To remove all or part of an outline, follow these steps:

1. Select the rows or columns you want removed by selecting the entire row or column. Click on the row or column heading, or press Shift+space bar or Ctrl+space bar.

   To remove the entire outline, select the entire worksheet by clicking in the empty square at the intersection of the column headings and row headings, or press Shift+Ctrl+space bar.

2. If you selected rows or columns, raise the level of the selection by clicking on the Promote symbol (left arrow) in the tool bar or by pressing Alt+Shift+left arrow.

   If you selected the entire worksheet or only a few cells, the dialog box in figure 13.23 appears. Select whether you want to raise rows or columns to a higher level, and then choose OK or press Enter.

3. Continue raising the level of the selection until all the contents of the selection are at the same level.

If you remove an outline or parts of an outline and rows or columns remain hidden, select these rows or columns and choose the Format **R**ow Height or Forma**t** **C**olumn Width commands; then select the **U**nhide button.

Creating or Changing Outlines Manually

You can manually create an outline or change the levels in any outline by selecting rows or columns and then promoting or demoting them. You can create or change outlines this way by using the mouse or by keyboard.

To change or assign a level to a row or column, follow these steps:

1. Select the rows or columns you want to change.

2. Click on the Demote or Promote symbol in the tool bar. With the keyboard, press Alt+Shift+left arrow to promote or Alt+Shift+right arrow to demote.

3. Continue to demote or promote rows or columns as necessary to change your outline.

If you are manually creating an outline, demote rows or columns in the normal worksheet to the level necessary for your outline. When you demote a row or column, the outline symbols appear. Toggle the outline symbols on or off by clicking on the Show outline symbols icon in the tool bar or by pressing Ctrl+8.

If you did not select an entire row or column, a dialog box appears asking whether you want to change a row or column. Select which you want to change, and then choose OK or press Enter.

Expanding and Collapsing the Outline

The real value of an outline is apparent when you expand and collapse the outline to display or work with different levels of data or summary. Although you can most easily use the mouse to expand and collapse, you also can use the keyboard.

> **Tip: *Formatting Text Boxes and Graphics to Prevent Distortion by Outlines***
> Text boxes and graphic objects that overlap an outline may be distorted or disappear when you expand or collapse the outline. To prevent such distortions, format the text boxes or graphic objects with the Format Object Placement command. Although situations vary, you generally can format worksheet or outline titles in a text box with the Don't Move or Size with Cells option. Format arrows with the Move and Size with Cells option. Text boxes explaining data in the outline usually use Move but Don't Size with Cells. This procedure keeps titles over the correct areas, adjusts the length of arrows appropriately, and moves explanatory text boxes without distorting the text inside.

To expand or collapse an outline with the mouse, follow these steps:

1. Display the tool bar by choosing the Options Display command, selecting the Tool Bar check box, and choosing OK. You can toggle the tool bar on or off by pressing Ctrl+7.

2. Display the outline symbols by clicking on the Show outline symbols icon in the tool bar, choosing the Options Display command, and selecting Outline Symbols, or by pressing Ctrl+0.

3. Expand or collapse specific rows and columns or an entire level with one of the following actions:

Expand a specific row or column by clicking on its Expand (+) symbol.

Expand to an entire level by clicking on the appropriate Level number button. Click on the highest numbered button to display all levels.

Collapse a specific row or column by clicking on its Demote (–) symbol.

Collapse to an entire level by clicking on the appropriate Level number button. Click on the lowest numbered button to collapse all levels.

If you are using a keyboard, you can expand areas of an outline by selecting rows or columns, choosing the Format Row Height or Format Column Width commands, and selecting the Unhide check box. This method, however, is not a very elegant way to operate your worksheet. This method also does not enable you to select specific levels you want to display.

A better method of expanding and collapsing an outline is to create the macro shown in figure 13.25. Create this macro following the procedures for a command macro described in Chapters 28 and 29. You cannot record the macro. Either type or paste the functions into the cells as shown. Make sure that you name the title cell at the top using the Formula Define Name command and select the Command option button to make it a command macro. Enter a shortcut key to make the macro easier to use.

To run the macro, select a cell within the outline that is in the row or column you want to display or hide. Run the macro. The first input box that appears asks whether you want to affect the row or column. The second input box asks whether you want to expand or collapse your selection. Enter a 1 or 2 in each of these boxes as directed. The macro does not work if you select a cell outside the outline. A description of each of the macro functions appears in column C.

	A	B	C
1		Outline.Key (a)	
2		=ROW(SELECTION())	Get row number
3		=COLUMN(SELECTION())	Get col number
4		=INPUT("Type 1 for a row or 2 for a column.",1)	Ask: row or column?
5		=INPUT("Type 1 to expand or 2 to collapse",1)	Ask: expand or collapse?
6		=IF(B4=1,B2,IF(B4=2,B3,GOTO(B11)))	Use row or col based on INPUT
7		=IF(B5=1,TRUE,IF(B5=2,FALSE,GOTO(B11)))	Use TRUE (expand) or FALSE (collapse)
8		=ERROR(FALSE)	Disable errors in case outside outline area
9		=SHOW.DETAIL(B4,B6,B7)	Expand or collapse
10		=ERROR(TRUE)	Enable error checking
11		=RETURN()	

Fig. 13.25. *This macro enables you to display or hide selected outline levels using the keyboard.*

Formatting Outlines by Level

Excel will apply predefined formatting styles to each level of the outline. This feature can make report and display formatting easier.

If you want to apply styles when you create the outline, select the Automatic Styles check box from the Outline dialog box.

To apply styles to an outline that already exists, follow these steps:

1. Select the parts of the outline to which you want to apply styles.

2. Choose the Formula Outline command. The Outline dialog box appears.

3. Choose the Apply Styles button.

Chapter 8 describes how to change the definition of a style. By changing the definition of a style, you reformat all cells in the worksheet to which this style applies. This method enables you to efficiently change the appearance of a report.

Copying and Charting from Specific Outline Levels

The worksheet contains all the data at different levels, even though all levels may not be displayed. If you copy or chart from a selection in the outline, the copied area or chart includes data at levels below those that were displayed.

To work with data from the displayed level in the worksheet only, you must specify that you want to work with visible selected cells only. Follow these steps:

1. Select the cells with which you want to work.

2. Click on the Select visible cells icon in the tool bar; or choose the Formula Select Special command, select the Visible Cells option, and then choose OK or press Enter.

   You will see a separation between cells that contain nonvisible data as shown in figure 13.26.

3. Continue working using commands such as these:

   Chart Edit Series
   Edit Copy
   Edit Fill Down/Up

Edit Paste
Edit Paste Link
File New Chart

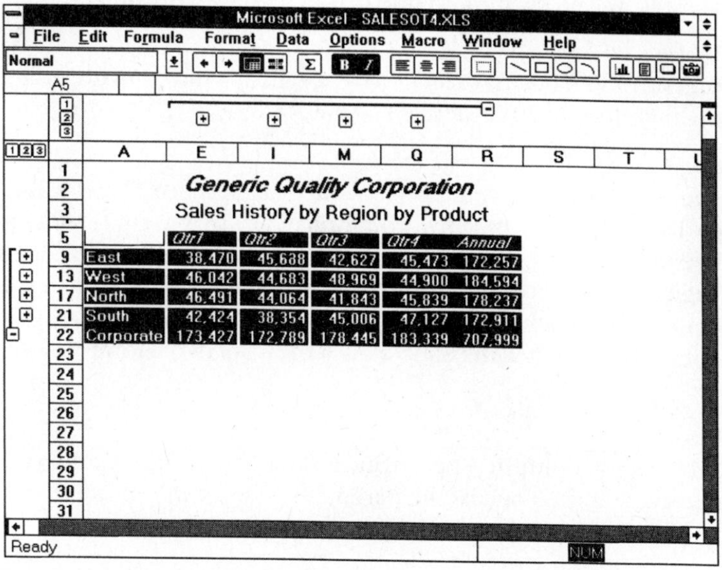

Fig. 13.26. *Select only visible cells to work with displayed data.*

When you paste summary data, the summary formulas are changed to constant values.

Troubleshooting Worksheets, Functions, and Formulas

Surveys show that 30 percent of all electronic worksheets contain errors. This is a terrifying but believable statistic when you consider that most users have been given little or no training, and few are trained in designing or auditing worksheets. Few companies have policies for auditing or documenting worksheets.

Correct worksheets require careful planning and execution. You always should cross-check and review a new worksheet before using it for a critical decision. Excel has built-in commands, macros, and error values to help you discover trouble spots in your worksheets.

Excel includes two features, the Formula Select Special command and the AUDIT.XLA add-in, to make troubleshooting Excel worksheets easier. This section describes these features and includes other tips and techniques to help you resolve problems and find errors in your worksheets.

Problem:
After pressing Enter to enter a formula, Excel beeps and displays an alert box warning that there is an error in the formula.

Solution:
Press the F1 key for Help when you see such an alert box. Excel will display a Help window that lists the most common errors that occur in worksheets. If after reading the Help you cannot find the error in the formula, delete the equal sign (=) at the front of the formula and press Enter. This step enters the formula as text so that you can return later and work on it. To turn it back into a formula, just edit in the equal sign at the front of the formula and press Enter.

Problem:
When typing a complicated formula that includes many pairs of parentheses, you miss one of the parentheses and can't locate it.

Solution:
Excel highlights matching pairs of parentheses as you move the insertion point across one parenthesis of a pair. To see these highlighted, move the insertion point into the formula bar, and then press the right- or left-arrow keys to move the insertion point across a parenthesis. Watch for an opposing parenthesis to highlight. If the highlighted parentheses do not enclose the correct term in the formula, you have found the terms that require another parenthesis.

Problem:
Everything within a function appears correct, but Excel will not accept the entry.

Solution:
A frequent mistake when typing in functions is to miss or delete a comma between arguments. You can reduce the chance of omitting commas and entering arguments incorrectly by entering functions with Formula Paste Function and selecting the Paste Arguments option. To select an argument to be replaced, double-click on the argument prompt that is pasted in, and then type or click on the needed cell. This procedure selects only the argument prompt between commas and replaces it with what you type or the cell that you click on.

Problem:
When auditing a worksheet, you cannot see more than one formula or determine the range names that a cell is part of.

Solution:
You can switch the worksheet to display formulas by choosing the **Options Display** command and selecting the **Formulas** option. The shortcut key is Ctrl+` (grave accent). Open a second window onto the worksheet with the **Window New Window** command; then format one worksheet to show results and the other to show formulas.

If you want to see the range names, formulas, and formats that affect a cell, select the cell and then choose the **Window Show Info** command to display an Information window. Select from the **Info** menu the attributes you want to see about the active cell. While you are troubleshooting a worksheet, leave the Information window open. Whenever you select a new cell, you can switch to the Info window for that cell by pressing Ctrl+F6 to display the Info window updated for the current cell.

Problem:
Large Excel worksheets are difficult to understand without a map showing areas and regions.

Solution:
 Use the AUDIT.XLA add-in that comes free with Excel to add the Audit command to the **Formula** menu. The Audit command enables you to create a miniature map showing all the regions of a worksheet and the types of values or formulas those regions contain. AUDIT.XLA is described in Chapter 14, "Using the Solver."

Problem:
The Circular indicator appears at the bottom of the worksheet. With every recalculation of the worksheet, some of the results grow larger or grow smaller, even though no data has changed.

Solution:
 The worksheet has a circular error—a formula that refers to another cell containing a formula that refers to the first. This error may happen through a chain involving many cells. The formula feeds on itself with progressing recalculations. So, like a snake eating its tail, each recalculation reduces the results; or the results can grow larger, depending on how the formula is built. To find all the cells involved in a circular error, add the Audit command to the **Formula** menu. The AUDIT.XLA add-in that comes with Excel offers this command. Refer to Chapter 14, "Using the Solver," to learn how to use it.

Problem:
In a long formula that contains many parts, one of the smaller terms within the formula is incorrect. You can't find the part of the formula that is producing incorrect results.

Solution:

To see how a term or function within a formula evaluates, follow these steps:

1. Select the cell that produces the incorrect result or an error value.

2. In the formula bar, select the smallest portion of the formula that might be causing this problem. The term you select must be a complete function or portion of a formula that can be calculated by itself. Figure 13.27 shows a portion of an IF function selected. Notice that the complete AND function, including both parentheses and all arguments, is selected.

3. Press the F9 key to calculate the portion you have selected. Figure 13.28 shows how the selected portion in the formula changes to its calculated result, FALSE.

4. Select and calculate other parts of the formula until you find the portion causing the error.

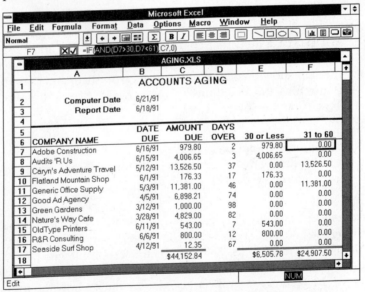

Fig. 13.27. *Select the portion of the formula that you want to check.*

5. Press Esc or click on the Cancel box in the formula bar to return the formula to its original form. If you enter the formula, the result of the formula will replace the equation.

6. Correct the portion of the formula that returned the incorrect answer.

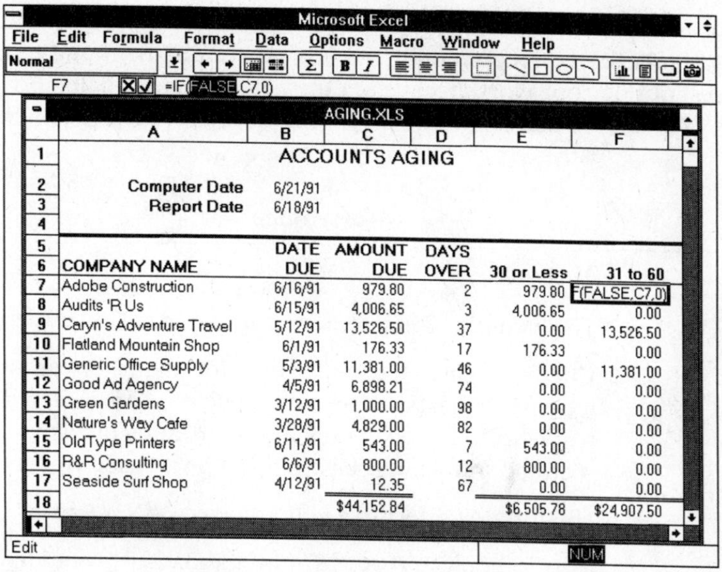

	A	B	C	D	E	F
1	ACCOUNTS AGING					
2	Computer Date	6/21/91				
3	Report Date	6/18/91				
4						
5		DATE	AMOUNT	DAYS		
6	COMPANY NAME	DUE	DUE	OVER	30 or Less	31 to 60
7	Adobe Construction	6/16/91	979.80	2	979.80	F(FALSE,C7,0)
8	Audits 'R Us	6/15/91	4,006.65	3	4,006.65	0.00
9	Caryn's Adventure Travel	5/12/91	13,526.50	37	0.00	13,526.50
10	Flatland Mountain Shop	6/1/91	176.33	17	176.33	0.00
11	Generic Office Supply	5/3/91	11,381.00	46	0.00	11,381.00
12	Good Ad Agency	4/5/91	6,898.21	74	0.00	0.00
13	Green Gardens	3/12/91	1,000.00	98	0.00	0.00
14	Nature's Way Cafe	3/28/91	4,829.00	82	0.00	0.00
15	OldType Printers	6/11/91	543.00	7	543.00	0.00
16	R&R Consulting	6/6/91	800.00	12	800.00	0.00
17	Seaside Surf Shop	4/12/91	12.35	67	0.00	0.00
18			$44,152.84		$6,505.78	$24,907.50

Fig. 13.28. Only the selected portion calculates.

The preceding method of calculating part of a formula displays the contents of arrays. If, in the formula bar, you select a function that returns an array of values and press F9, you will see the values within the array, as in this example:

{2,3,"four";5,6,"seven"}

Commas separate array values into columns. Semicolons separate rows.

Problem:
Warnings appear in cells that do not correctly calculate.

Solution:
When Excel cannot evaluate a formula or function, the program displays an error value in the offending cell. Error values begin with a pound sign (#). Excel has seven types of error values with self-explanatory names (see table 13.2).

Problem:
Searching individual formulas for errors or related formulas takes too long. You would like to select quickly the cells containing errors, cells that feed into the formula in the active cell, or cells that depend upon the result of the active cell.

Solution:

The For**m**ula **S**elect Special command is a powerful ally in auditing and troubleshooting your worksheet. From the Select Special dialog box (see fig. 13.29), you can select specific parts of a worksheet or cell contents.

Table 13.2
Excel Error Values

Value	Meaning
#DIV/0!	The formula or macro is attempting to divide by zero.
	Check: Examine cell references for blanks or zeros. Is it possible that you accidentally deleted an area of the worksheet needed by this formula? An incorrectly written formula may be attempting to divide by zero.
#N/A	The formula refers to a cell that has a #N/A entry.
	Check: You can type **#N/A** in mandatory data-entry cells. Then, if data is not entered to replace the #N/A, formulas that depend on that cell display #N/A. This error value warns you that not all the data has been entered.
	An array argument is the wrong size, and #N/A is returned in some cells.
	HLOOKUP, VLOOKUP, LOOKUP, MATCH, or other functions have incorrect arguments.
	You have omitted an argument from a function. Some functions return #N/A if they cannot correctly evaluate the arguments that you entered. See the function's description in Chapter 10 for more information on the function.
#NAME?	Excel does not recognize a name.
	Check: Use the For**m**ula **D**efine Name command to see whether the name exists. Create it if necessary.
	Check the spelling of the name.
	See whether you used text in a formula without enclosing it in quotation marks. Excel considers the text as a name rather than as text.
	See whether you did not replace one of the Paste Arguments prompts pasted into a function.

Value	Meaning
	Check whether you typed an address or range so that it appears to be a name, such as the cell ABB5 or the range B12C45.
	See whether you referred to an incorrect or nonexistent name in a linked worksheet.
#NULL!	The formula specifies two areas that do not intersect.
	Check: See whether the cell or range reference is entered incorrectly.
#NUM!	The formula has a problem with a number.
	Check: See whether the numeric argument is out of the acceptable range of inputs, or whether the function can find an answer given the arguments you entered.
#REF!	The cell reference is not correct.
	Check: Check whether you have deleted cells, rows, or columns that were referenced by formulas.
	Check whether external worksheet references are still valid. Use the **File Links** command to open source worksheets. If you need to change a link to a worksheet with a different name or directory, use the **File Links** command with the **Change** button on. This is described in Chapter 12 in the section on linking worksheets.
	Check whether a macro has returned a #REF! value from an unopened or incorrect function macro.
	Check to see whether a Dynamic Data Exchange (DDE) topic is incorrectly entered or is not available.
#VALUE!	The value is not the type expected by the argument.
	Check: Verify that values used as arguments are of the type listed in Chapter 10, "Using Functions."

Finding errors such as #REF! or #N/A in your worksheet or in a range is easy. Select the **Formulas** option and select the **Errors** check box. When debugging a worksheet, find what cells feed information into the active cell and what cells depend upon the results in the active cell.

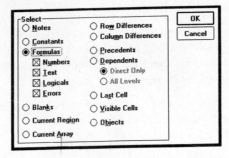

Fig. 13.29. *The Formula Select Special command is a valuable ally in troubleshooting worksheets.*

If you want to see the cells feeding into the active cell, select the **Precedents** option; select the **Dependents** option to see cells that depend upon the active cell. The **Direct Only** option selects cells that immediately feed or depend on the active cell. The **All Levels** option selects cells that feed into or depend on the active cell at any level. The **Direct Only** option is like selecting only your parents or your children. The **All Levels** option is like selecting your entire family tree, backward or forward.

One of the most common errors in worksheets is accidentally typing a number over a formula. To see which cells contain formulas and which cells contain values, select the range you want to troubleshoot, and select the **Constants** or **Formulas** options from the Select Special dialog box. Usually, you will leave all check boxes selected. You may be surprised to find a constant value in the middle of what you thought were formulas!

Press Tab or Shift+Tab to move the active cell between the selected cells, while keeping all other cells selected. Read each cell's contents in the formula bar until you find the cell that contains an error.

Table 13.3
Formula Select Special Options

Option	Action
Constants	Specifies that constants of the following type will be selected.
Formulas	Specifies that formulas with results of the following type will be selected.
Numbers	Selects constants or formulas resulting in numbers.
Text	Selects constants or formulas resulting in text.

Option	Action
Logicals	Selects constants or formulas resulting in logicals (true/false).
Errors	Selects cells with error values.
Precedents	Selects cells that support the active cell.
Dependents	Selects cells that depend on the active cell.
Row Differences	Selects cells in the same row that have a different reference "pattern."
Column Differences	Selects cells in the same column that have a different reference "pattern."

From Here...

The techniques described in this chapter work best when combined with other commands, functions, and techniques. You can find additional techniques, tips, and functions in Chapter 10, "Using Functions," and Chapter 27, "Building Extensive Databases."

14

 **Using the Solver**

E xcel comes with several features that help you find solutions for your worksheets. One feature for use with simple solutions is the Formula Goal Seek command. The other feature is a free add-in program called Solver. Solver is a mathematical tool that can help you find the best solution to certain types of business problems. With the example illustrated in this chapter and the samples that come with Excel, you can learn how to use Solver to find the best answers to your problems.

All of the features discussed in this chapter are new. First, you can read about Excel's Goal Seek feature, which may be sufficient for some of your problem-solving efforts.

Using the Goal Seek Feature

When you know the answer you want, and you just need the input value that makes it so, use the Formula Goal Seek command. With this command, you specify first a solution and then the cell that should be changed to reach that solution. Excel finds the value that results in the specific answer you want.

Understanding When To Use Goal Seek

The Goal Seek command can save you time when you need to "back into" solutions. You may need to use this command to determine the needed growth rate to reach a sales goal or to determine how many units must be sold to break even.

Excel's Goal Seek feature changes one value on a cell until another cell results in the answer you want. To find the answer, the command operates as if it were making repetitive, educated guesses.

When you're using the Formula Goal Seek command, the cell it changes must affect the cell you have specified to reach a specific answer. Because you cannot put restraints on the command, you may end up with solutions that do not make sense, or have problems that get further and further from the answer you specify.

Solving for a Specific Answer

Figure 14.1 shows the worksheet you may have created in the Worksheet Quick Start. While in this worksheet, suppose that you want to use the Goal Seek feature to vary cell B18 until cell F12 reaches the solution of $5,000.

To solve for a specific answer with Goal Seek, follow these steps:

1. Select a cell containing a formula for which you want to produce a specific answer. In the example, this cell is F12.

2. Choose the Formula Goal Seek command. The dialog box shown in the bottom right corner of figure 14.1 appears. Notice that the Set cell field already contains the cell you selected in step 1.

3. In the To value text box, type the solution you want to reach. In the example, the desired solution is $5,000.

4. Select the By changing cell text box, and enter the cell reference of the input cell. This cell must directly or indirectly feed into the formula in step 1. In the example, this cell is $B$18.

    Figure 14.2 shows the completed Goal Seek box.

5. Choose OK or press Enter.

6. If you want to pause or cancel the goal seeking during a long goal seeking process, choose the Pause or Cancel button. Step through the iterative solution process by choosing the Step button. To continue after pausing, choose the Continue button.

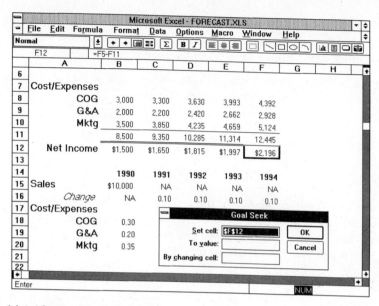

Fig. 14.1. *The Goal Seek dialog box.*

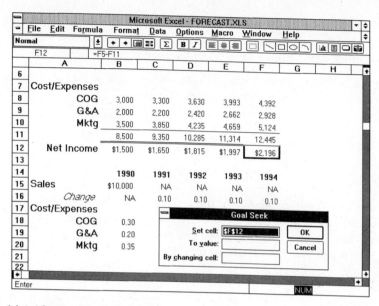

Fig. 14.2. *Enter the solution you want and the cell you want to change to get that solution.*

The input cell selected in step 4 must feed directly or indirectly into the set cell and must not contain a formula. To see which cells are precedents (feed into) the set cell, select the set cell; then choose the Formula Select Special command. Select the **Precedents All Levels** option; then choose OK or press Enter. All cells feeding into the set cell are selected. Press the Tab or Enter key to move among these cells while keeping them selected.

After a solution has been found, you can replace the values in the original worksheet with the new values that show on-screen by choosing OK. Keep the original values by choosing Cancel.

Using Goal Seek with Charts

You can use a chart to search for the goal you want to meet. To do so, you must be in a 2-D column, bar, or line chart. When you drag a marker to a new value position, the Goal Seek dialog box and worksheet appear. Excel then asks which cell you want changed to make the chart value come true.

To find a solution graphically from a chart, follow these steps:

1. Activate the chart and the worksheet on which it depends.

2. Hold down the Ctrl key as you click the data series marker (column, bar, or line symbol) that you want to change to a new value in the chart. A black handle appears on the marker, as shown in the marker at the far right in figure 14.3.

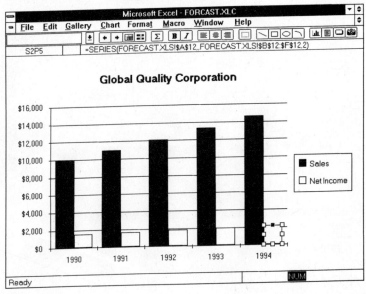

Fig. 14.3. Display the black handle on a chart marker.

3. Drag the black handle so that the marker's end moves to a new value. (In the example, drag the black handle up or down to change the height of the column.) When you release the mouse button, the Goal Seek dialog box appears along with the worksheet to which the chart marker is linked. Figure 14.4 shows the displayed Goal Seek dialog box and worksheet.

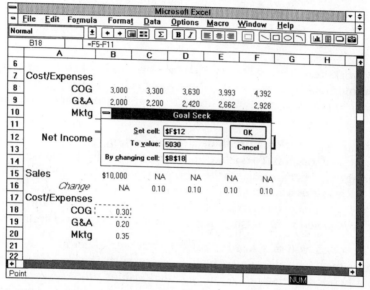

Fig. 14.4. *Use Goal Seek to work backward and find a solution that matches your chart.*

4. In the Goal Seek dialog box, the To value text box is already filled with the value from the chart marker. Change the To value if you need a different value. The Set cell box contains the cell linked to the marker.

5. Select the By changing cell text box, and type or select the cell reference you want to change.

6. Choose OK or press Enter.

Follow the described Goal Seek procedure to find the input value that produces the correct value for the chart marker.

Notice that as you drag the marker, the numeric value of the marker displays in the Reference Area to the left of the File menu. This reference enables you to see the value of the marker as you reposition it.

If the chart marker is linked to a cell containing a number and not a formula, the Goal Seek dialog box does not appear. The number in the worksheet changes to reflect the marker value. This feature helps you to easily enter values into a worksheet when you need a set of values that reflect a certain distribution or pattern.

Using Solver

Many worksheets are too complex for the Formula Goal Seek command to find a solution. A valid solution in these more complex models may require multiple inputs and may have limiting constraints on some of the input values or the output.

Where the Goal Seek feature finds a specific solution, the Solver program finds the *best* solution. To do that, Solver can vary multiple input cells while ensuring that other formulas in the worksheet stay within limits you set. The Solver works the way problems in the real world work—more than one variable must be changed to find an answer, yet other areas of the problem must be watched to make sure that they stay within realistic limits.

In many cases, you may need to rework your worksheet to fit the type of model with which Solver works best. To set up such a worksheet, you must have a better understanding of the relationships among variables and formulas. Solver's payback for your efforts, however, can be extremely high. Solver can save you from wasting resources with mismanaged schedules; help you earn higher rates through better cash management; and show you what mix of manufacturing, inventory, and products produces the best profit.

Understanding When To Use Solver

Use Solver to find the best solution to a problem. Solver is normally helpful for the following types of problems:

- *Product Mix:* Maximizing the return on products given limited resources to build those products.

- *Staff Scheduling:* Meeting staffing levels at minimum cost within specified employee satisfaction levels.

- *Optimal Routing:* Minimizing transportation costs between a manufacturing site and sale sites.

- *Blending:* Blending mixtures of materials to achieve a quality level at minimum cost.

The types of problems with which Solver can work have three important parts. First, problems must have a single objective—for example, to maximize profit or minimize time. Second, problems must have constraints that are typically given as inequalities—for example, the materials used cannot exceed inventory, or the machine hours scheduled cannot exceed 24 hours less maintenance time. Third, the problems must have input values that directly or indirectly affect both the constraints and the values being optimized.

These problems usually fall within two mathematical types: linear and nonlinear. Solver can solve both types of problems. *Linear problems* are those in which the relationship between input and output results in a straight line or flat plane when graphed. If you have a linear problem, Solver has an option for finding solutions faster by using linear programming techniques. Linear formulas are usually simple and have the following form:

$$X=A*Y1+B*Y2+C*Y3...$$

In this syntax, X is the result; A, B, and C are constants; and Y1, Y2, and Y3 are variables.

Solver also solves for the best solution in worksheets involving nonlinear relationships. The following are examples of *nonlinear problems*:

- Sales approach a certain volume and then level off.

- Product quality improves only slightly with increased materials.

- Advertising response increases with ad frequency but then diminishes.

- Product costs vary with different sales volumes.

Some of the forms involving nonlinear relationships include the following:

$$X=Y1/Y2$$
$$X=Y1\char`\^.5$$
$$X=A+Y1*Y2$$

where X is the result, A is a constant, and Y1 and Y2 are input values.

Creating the Sample Worksheet

The worksheet in figure 14.5 illustrates a simple model built to work with Solver. In this worksheet, a city government has started a service named Dirt Cheap, Inc. The service uses many existing resources to produce a positive income stream for the city. In addition, Dirt Cheap reduces and recycles garbage.

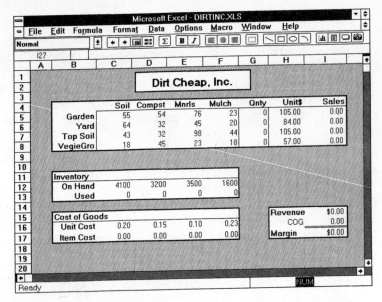

Fig. 14.5. *The Dirt Cheap worksheet solves for the best combination of materials to reach the highest margin.*

Tip: *Keep Names in the Solver Sheet Short*
Names to the top and left of the set cell and constraints are read by Excel and used to generate printed reports. Long or confusing names in these cells may make reports that Solver generates difficult to read.

Dirt Cheap has a collection program for organic garbage, park trimmings, Christmas trees, and so on. The service mulches or composts these items and combines them in different blends with soil and mineral additives to produce high-quality soil and growing mixtures. Some of the labor is volunteer, and materials costs are low except for collection costs.

The worksheet calculates the best combination of raw materials to produce the highest margin, shown in cell I17. No real problem is this simple, but Solver can work within the constraints of the real world to recalculate the best solution given changing conditions.

Much of the Dirt Cheap worksheet is text and constant numbers. To build the worksheet, type the text shown in figure 14.5 to use as a skeleton. Then enter the following numbers and formulas:

Cells	Item	Enter			
C5:F8	Mixture amounts	*C*	*D*	*E*	*F*
	Note: This is an array. Enter the amounts in the indicated cells.	5 55	54	76	23
		6 64	32	45	20
		7 43	32	98	44
		8 18	45	23	18
G5:G8	Product amount	0			
H5:H8	Product price	Numbers 105, 84, 105, 57			
I5	Product $ sold	=G5*H5; then fill down into I6:I8			
C12:F12	Inv. on hand	Numbers 4100, 3200, 3500, 1600			
C13	Inv. used	=$G5*C5+$G6*C6+$G7*C7+$G8*C8; then fill right into D13:F13			
C16	Unit cost	Numbers 0.20, 0.15, 0.10, 0.23			
C17	Item cost	=C16*C13; then fill right into D17:F17			
I15	Revenue	=SUM(I5:I8)			
I16	Cost of goods	=SUM(C17:F17)			
I17	Margin	=I15-I16			

In the model, the values from C5:F5 are the mixture amounts necessary to create a soil product called Garden Blend. The cost for a unit of Garden Blend is $105.00. Solver will find the best quantity, G5, to make of Garden Blend. After the best quantity is found, the sales amount in I5 is calculated by multiplying G5 times H5. This same technique is used for each soil product.

One constraint is that a limited amount of material exists to make the products. The inventory on hand of materials—Soil, Compost, Minerals, and Mulch—is specified in cells C12:F12. Cells C13:F13 calculate the amount of each material used to find the best combination of products. Of course, the amount of materials used cannot exceed the amount of materials on hand.

The cost of each material used is found by multiplying the unit cost for the materials, C16:F16, times the material used, C13:F13. This cost formula is in C17:F17.

The revenue is calculated in cell I15 by totaling the sales, I5:I8. The cost of goods, COG in cell I16, is the total of item costs, C17:F17. The margin is revenue minus cost.

Save this worksheet to disk by using the File Save **As** command.

Installing Solver

Solver involves a program that runs in conjunction with Excel. If you did not install Solver when you installed Excel, rerun the Excel install procedure and select the option to install Solver. You do not have to reinstall all of Excel or Windows.

When you have the Solver files on disk, you can load Solver in one of two ways. If you do not normally use Solver, you do not need to do anything until you begin to use it. The first time you choose the Formula Solver command, the Solver program starts. Watch the Reference Area to the left of the File command to see the percentage of loading completed.

If you use Solver frequently, you can load it automatically on start-up by copying the SOLVER.XLA file into the XLSTART subdirectory. Solver and its XLA files are located in the XLSTART\SOLVER subdirectory.

Solving for the Best Solution

Suppose that for this model, the city council mandates that the goal is to find the best (maximum) margin in cell I17. This objective will help expand the recycling and composting done by Dirt Cheap and may reduce taxes.

The input values that are changed to find the best margin are the quantities of each soil product to be created. At this point, the city sells all the product it makes, so it doesn't have to worry about limits on a product. (Limiting an item's production or availability of resources is described in the sections "Changing Constraints" and "Changing a Limited Resource.") The input values that Solver will find are in G5:G8. For this example, the input values each start with 0. In models that take a long time to calculate, you can reduce calculation time by starting with input values that you believe are nearest to the best solution.

The constraint on the solution is that the inventory used cannot exceed the inventory on hand. In spreadsheet terms, the calculated totals in cells C13:F13 cannot exceed the values in C12:F12. In addition, the values in G5:G8 must be greater than 0 because you cannot produce a negative amount of soil.

To solve for the best solution, follow these steps:

1. Select the cell you want to optimize. In the example, this cell is I17.

2. Choose the Formula Solver command. The Solver loads if it did not when Excel started, and the Solver Parameters dialog box shown in figure 14.6 appears.

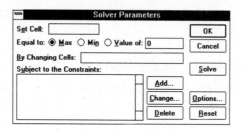

Fig. 14.6. *The Solver Parameters dialog box.*

3. In the Set Cell box, enter the cell you want to optimize.

4. Define the type of relation between the Set Cell and a solution value by selecting one of the following Equal To options:

   Max   Find the maximum result for the set cell.

   Min   Find the minimum result for the set cell.

   Value of Find an exact value for the amount typed in the Value of text box.

   For this example, select the Equal to Max option.

5. Select the By Changing Cells text box; then select the adjustable cells that Solver should change while attempting to find the best answer. For this example, the cells are $G$5:$G$8. You can type the entry, select each cell with the keyboard, or drag across the cells with the mouse. (If the cells you need are not visible, you can move the Solver Parameters dialog box or scroll the worksheet.)

6. Select the Add button to add constraints to the list of constraints. The Add Constraint dialog box displays, as shown in figure 14.7.

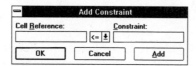

Fig. 14.7. *The Add Constraint dialog box.*

7. Enter the first constraint. In this example, the values in $G$5:$G$8 must be greater than 0. This constraint ensures that Solver will look only for solutions that produce a positive or zero quantity of soil.

Select the Cell **R**eference text box and enter $G$5:$G$8. You can type the cell reference, select it by using the keyboard, or drag across the cells. (If the cells you need are not visible, you can move the Add Constraint dialog box or scroll the worksheet.)

To move to the comparison signs, press Tab or click the down arrow. Then select the >= comparison sign by pressing the down-arrow key or by clicking that sign.

Select the **C**onstraint text box and enter 0.

The completed Add Constraint dialog box for this example appears in figure 14.8.

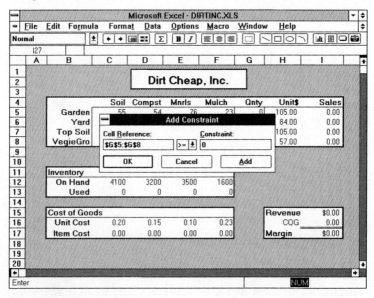

Fig. 14.8. *A completed constraint.*

8. Choose the **A**dd button so that you can add another constraint. When the Add Constraint dialog box reappears, enter the second constraint. For this example, the constraint is $C$12:$F$12>=$C$13:$F$13, which says that the inventory used must always be less than the inventory on hand.

9. Choose the OK button. The completed Solver Parameters dialog box appears (see fig. 14.9).

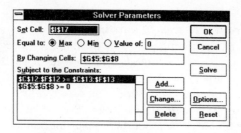

Fig. 14.9. The completed Solver Parameters dialog box.

10. Choose the **S**olve button to run Solver and find the optimal combination of soil products that gives the maximum margin.

11. When Solver finds a solution, another dialog box appears, as shown in figure 14.10. Select **K**eep Solver Solution to keep the solution shown in the worksheet. Select Restore **O**riginal Values to return to the original worksheet values. For this example, select **K**eep Solver Solution and choose **OK** or press Enter. (In this dialog box, you also choose the reports you want to generate, as described later in this chapter in "Printing Solver Reports.")

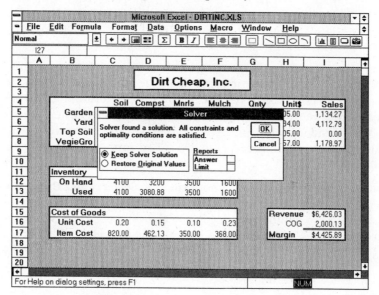

Fig. 14.10. Choose to keep the solution, return to the original answers, or generate reports.

Tip: *Setting Constraints As Inequalities*
In some linear programming programs, you are required to set up constraints as comparison formulas that produce a TRUE or FALSE result. With Solver, you do not have to use this setup. If you have worksheets or mainframe data from programs requiring that method, however, you still can use it with Solver. In the Subject to the Constraints box of Solver, set the constraint equal to a TRUE or FALSE. Do not use 1 or 0 to indicate TRUE or FALSE.

Do not change the values now on the worksheet if you want to try the exercises that follow in this chapter.

Tip: *Working in Other Worksheets While Solver Works*
You don't have to stop your work while Solver does its work. Although you cannot make changes to the worksheet on which Solver is working, you can continue working on other worksheets in Excel.

Solver tells you that you can achieve the best margin if you make 11 units of Garden, 49 units of Yard, no Top Soil, and 21 units of VegieGro. With this combination, the maximized margin is $4,425.89.

Solver stores the dialog box settings within the worksheet containing the problem. (The settings are stored in named formulas.) Because the Solver Parameters dialog box stores previous settings, rerunning Solver with different constraints is easy. You can reset the worksheet by entering zeros into G5:G8 and rerunning Solver. You then see the settings of your most recent solution. This procedure is described in the section "Saving and Loading Solver Data."

If you want to store settings without running Solver, enter the settings as described in the preceding instructions and choose OK. To remove the Solver dialog box without running Solver and without storing settings made with **Options, Add, Change,** or **Delete,** choose Cancel.

Changing a Limited Resource

In real-world situations, limited production resources change. You can see the effect of this change on the solution by changing resources in the worksheet and rerunning Solver. The effect of such changes is known as the *dual value* or *shadow price*. A shadow price tells you what a change in inventory or resources does to the bottom line.

Suppose that the people at Dirt Cheap get a phone call telling them that they can have a hundred pounds of minerals for the cost of the gas required to haul it. For $10, Dirt Cheap can get 100 more pounds of minerals. This exchange throws off the average mineral price slightly, but the big question is, is it worth $10?

To find out the return to margin for 100 more pounds of minerals, change the mineral inventory in cell E12 from 3,500 to 3,600. Enter 0's in G5:G8. Rerun Solver, using the same settings as in the previous problem. Keep this solution so that your worksheet will match the next situation.

Adding 100 pounds of minerals takes the margin from $4,425.89 at 3,500 pounds of minerals to $4,464.24 with 3,600 pounds of minerals. The minerals cost $10 but contributed $38.35 to the margin. They are a good value.

Changing Constraints

The real world doesn't stay steady for long. Things are always changing. But with Solver you can resolve to find an optimal solution quickly even when conditions change.

Suppose, for example, that a major purchaser of Dirt Cheap's soils calls to say that they must have 10 units of Top Soil. On checking the printout, Dirt Cheap's manager finds that no Top Soil was going to be mixed in this run. But she decides to add a constraint that 10 units of Top Soil must be made for this customer. What effect does that change have on the margin?

To see the effect of requiring 10 units of Top Soil, choose the Formula Solver command to open the Solver Parameters dialog box. You need to change the constraints and rerun Solver. To change the constraints, follow these steps:

1. Select the Subject to the Constraints box and select the constraint

   $G$5:$G$8>=0

2. Choose the Change button.

3. Change the constraint to read

   $G$5:$G$6>=0

   Then choose OK.

4. Choose the **A**dd button and enter the constraint

   $G$7>=10

   This statement means that at least 10 units of Top Soil must be made. Choose OK.

5. Choose the **A**dd button and enter the constraint

   $G$8>=0

   Then choose OK.

6. Choose **S**olve to solve for the best margin.

The new solution, with a new limit of 10 units of Top Soil and the additional 100 pounds of minerals from the previous change to the limited resources, yields a result of $4,039.10. This amount is $325.14 less than the margin after adding the 100 pounds of minerals. Satisfying this long-term customer has cost money in the short run, but may have gained invaluable loyalty and word-of-mouth advertising.

You can delete constraints by selecting them and choosing the **D**elete button. Choose **R**eset to reset all settings, cell references, and constraints.

Changing Operational Settings

You can change the technique used by Solver to find answers and change how long it works or how precise an answer it attempts to find. Choosing the **O**ptions button in the Solver Parameters dialog box displays the dialog box shown in figure 14.11. Use these options to control how Solver works. The default settings are appropriate for most problems. Table 14.1 shows the options and their capabilities.

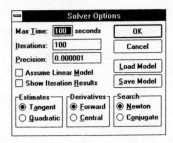

Fig. 14.11. *The Solver Options dialog box enables you to control how Solver works.*

Table 14.1
Solver Option Settings

Option	Control
Max Time	Specify the time in seconds Solver spends finding a solution.
Iterations	Specify the number of times Solver recalculates with attempted solutions.
Precision	Specify how far apart two trial solutions must be before a best solution is declared.
Assume Linear Model	Set Solver to use a linear programming solution method that speeds solutions that are linear. You are warned if the worksheet is not linear.
Show Iteration Results	Show trial solutions when they make significant jumps toward a best solution.
Estimates	Additional solution methods are Tangent and Quadratic. Use Quadratic if the worksheet involves complex formulas that are highly nonlinear.
Derivatives	Specify the method of partial derivatives, using Forward or Central differencing. Central difference can take longer but may result in a closer solution.
Search	Specify a quasi-Newton or Conjugate gradient method of searching.

Printing Solver Reports

Solver generates reports that summarize the results of its solutions. These reports are helpful when you're comparing different constraint conditions or calculating shadow prices that show the effects of changes on final results.

Solver generates two reports: the Answer report and the Limit report. To generate a report after you have solved a model, select Answer or Limit from the **Reports** list when the solution box is displayed (see fig. 14.12). To select both reports from the list, select the first report, hold down the Shift key, and press the up- or down-arrow key, or click.

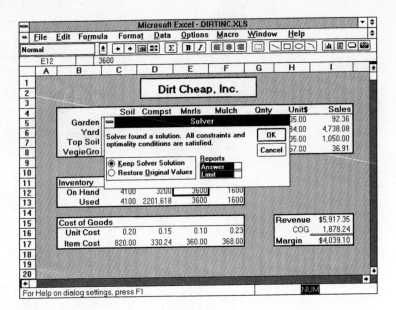

Fig. 14.12. Select the report you want after generating a solution.

The Answer report, shown in figure 14.13, shows the original and final values for the set cell and the adjustable cells. The report also shows the constraints. The constraint analysis tells you whether a constraint was Binding because it equaled the constraint limit, Not Binding because it met the constraint but wasn't bound by it, or Not Satisfied because the constraint could not be met. The Slack values in the report show the differences between the constraints and the final values. In this chapter's example, the Slack is the amount of inventory remaining.

The Limit report shows the set cell value, adjustable cell values, upper and lower limits, and the target result. The upper and lower limits specify how much the adjustable cell can change and still satisfy all constraints. The target result is the set cell value when the adjustable cell value is at its upper or lower limit. This report can show you how much variance is available in adjustable cells. Figure 14.14 shows the Limit report.

Saving and Loading Solver Data

Solver stores in the worksheet the last settings used to solve a problem, or settings that were in the dialog box when you chose OK. (As mentioned previously, the last settings used are stored in named formulas.) The next time you open that worksheet and run Solver, the Solver Parameters dialog box is set as you last used it.

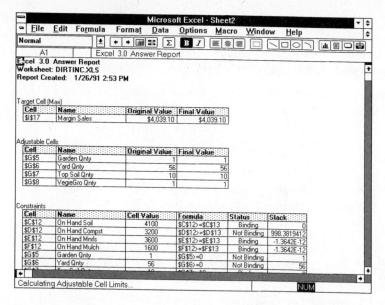

Fig. 14.13. *The Answer report shows original and final results.*

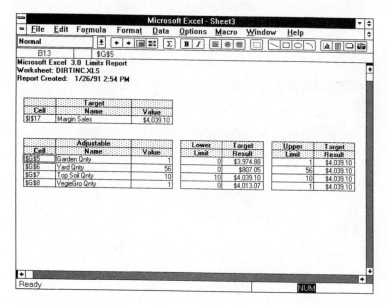

Fig. 14.14. *The Limit report shows how much adjustable cells can change within constraints.*

In some cases, you may want to store predefined settings for the Solver Parameters dialog box. For example, you may have specific sets of constraints that you must consider. You can store each of these sets of constraints in cells on the worksheet and quickly load the settings you need.

You can save and load different Solver models (settings) by using the Options button in the Solver Parameters dialog box. To save Solver settings, follow these steps:

1. Set up the Solver Parameters dialog box with the settings you want to save. Choose OK.

2. On the worksheet, select a range of cells equal to the number of constraints plus two cells for the set cell and adjustable cells.

   If your constraints include a range of cells, be sure to include a cell on the worksheet for each cell in the constraint's range. The range can be any shape. (Making it too large doesn't hurt. Excel advises you if the range is not large enough.)

3. Choose the Formula Solver command. When the dialog box opens, choose the Options button.

4. Choose the Save Model button. Choose Cancel when the Solver Parameters dialog box reappears.

The range fills with the settings from the Solver Parameters dialog box. Figure 14.15 shows an example of saved settings.

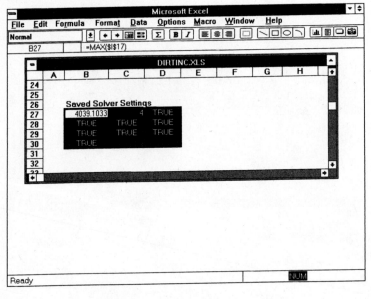

Fig. 14.15. Save Solver settings on the worksheet for later use.

To load settings when you want to rerun a Solver model you have saved on the worksheet, follow these steps:

1. Select the range of cells containing the model.

2. Choose the Formula Solver command.

3. Choose the Options button.

4. Choose the Load Model button.

5. When the Solver reappears with the settings loaded, you can run the Solver or choose OK and run it later.

Understanding the Free Solver Samples

Excel comes with a number of free example worksheets that use Solver to find an optimal or "best" solution. Although simplified, these examples cover many of the classes of problems for which Solver is designed. For these types of problems, Solver saves time over trial-and-error methods.

These example files are located in the SOLVEREX directory. This directory is located under the directory in which Excel is installed. Use the File Open command to open the example file, and then choose the Formula Solver command. You can examine the settings in the Solver Parameters dialog box. You may want to write down the settings and limitations, then return to the worksheet to see how they relate to the problem.

To run Solver on an example, open a worksheet, choose the Formula Solver command, then choose the Solve button. If you choose to keep the solutions that are found, save the worksheet with a different name to preserve the original example.

The example worksheets and their purposes are the following:

File name	Purpose
SOLVER1	Finds the maximum profit by changing the production mix of electronic products where the products share common parts and the sales margin diminishes with increased volume due to sales costs.
SOLVER2	Minimizes the shipping costs from a set of production plants to warehouses while meeting warehouse needs without exceeding plant production.

File name	Purpose
SOLVER3	Finds an employee schedule that meets all shift requirements while minimizing unnecessary staffing.
SOLVER4	Finds the best combination of certificates of deposit and deposit times so that the interest earned is maximized while ensuring that cash-on-hand is available for forecasted needs.
SOLVER5	Finds the combination of stocks in a portfolio that gives the best rate of return for a specific level of risk.
SOLVER6	Finds the value of a resistor that will discharge a circuit to a specific amount within a specific time frame.

From Here...

Worksheets involving Solver can be more difficult to set up but can produce solutions to problems that previously required mainframe computational power. Many of these problems formerly could be solved only by companies with large computers. With Excel and Solver and higher-speed 386 and 486 computers, some of those problems can now be solved on a desktop by large *and* small companies.

15

Using Excel's Add-In Macros

Even with its ease of use, Excel has a more comprehensive set of features than other worksheets offer. But no matter how extensive Excel's features, special industries or special situations are bound to require more. With Excel, anyone who can record or write macros can add features, functions, and commands to Excel so that it works the way it's needed.

Excel comes with 14 add-in programs that serve as examples of the new commands and features you can add. These programs are built with command macros, function macros, and dynamic link libraries. The add-ins are discussed here because they add features to Excel and are helpful to all users—even those who never want to record or write a macro. The first section of this chapter describes different ways you can add these add-in macros and their extra features to Excel without ever having to record or write your own macro. If you want to learn how to record or write your own add-in macros, read Chapter 30, "Modifying and Programming Macros," in the macro section of this book.

Excel comes with the following add-in files located in Excel's LIBRARY directory:

File	Description
ADDINFNS.XLA	Adds six additional worksheet functions.
ADDINMGR.XLA	Enables you to load selected sets of add-ins.
AUDIT.XLA	Adds worksheet troubleshooting features and reports.

File	Description
AUTOSAVE.XLA	Adds a monitor that prompts you to save your work at different time and work intervals.
CHANGER.XLA	Adds a command to quickly change or redefine names in a worksheet.
COMPARE.XLA	Adds a command to compare two worksheets or macro sheets for differences.
DEBUG.XLA	Adds macro troubleshooting features.
FILEFNS.XLA	Adds four macro commands that enable you to manipulate directories or test whether a file exists.
FLATFILE.XLA	Adds additional methods of parsing (separating) text files into worksheet cells.
GLOSSARY.XLA	Adds a glossary feature that stores or inserts frequently used text, numbers, or formulas.
SHEETAID.XLA	Adds additional window arrangment commands.
SLIDES.XLA	Adds a worksheet sequencer that automatically or manually displays documents in order.
SUMMARY.XLA	Adds a summary sheet to a worksheet or macro sheet that stores vital information about authorship, revision date, and so on.
WHATIF.XLA	Adds the ability to test multiple input values and see the results for different combinations of those inputs.

Tip: *Getting Help If You Need It*
If an add-in macro adds a command to a menu or displays a dialog box, you can get on-line help information on its operation. To get help before choosing a command, press Shift+F1 and then choose the add-in command about which you need help—Formula Worksheet Auditor, for example. If a dialog box appears after you choose the command, such as the What If dialog box, press F1 while the dialog box is displayed to access the same helpful window.

Installing and Managing Add-In Programs

Excel's free add-in programs are stored in files ending with the XLA extension. You can find them in the LIBRARY subdirectory under the directory containing Excel. These files are special macros that add features to Excel as though the features were built in. In this section, you learn how to start these add-in macros and how to use the Add-In Manager to manage them. (To learn how you can make your own recorded or written macros into add-ins, read about add-in macros in Chapter 30 in the macro section of this book.)

Starting Add-In Macros

You start an add-in macro when you open the XLA file containing the add-in macro. When that file opens, special commands, shortcuts, functions, or features available through the add-in become accessible. Use the **File Open** command to open XLA files.

If you find some add-ins so useful that you want them available whenever you start Excel, copy those macros' XLA files into the XLSTART directory. If your system uses a different directory as the start-up directory, copy the XLA files into that directory.

You also can start add-in macros along with Excel by copying the Add-In Manager (the ADDINMGR.XLA file) into the start-up directory. With this technique, you can keep a plethora of add-in files elsewhere and put only your Add-In Manager in the start-up directory, making housekeeping easier. For more information on the Add-In Manager, read on.

Managing Add-Ins with the Add-In Manager

The Add-In Manager helps you by opening a collection of add-ins you specify. As mentioned in the preceding section, you can open this collection of files when Excel starts by copying the ADDINMGR.XLA file into the XLSTART directory. (You can use the File Manager to copy the ADDINMGR.XLA file into the XLSTART directory.)

If you have not added the ADDINMGR.XLA file to the XLSTART directory, you still can use it. Start Excel, then use the **File Open** command to open the ADDINMGR.XLA file. This action adds the Add-Ins command to the Options menu. Then choose the **O**ptions **A**dd-Ins command to display the dialog box shown in figure 15.1. In this figure, the Add-In Manager has been configured to open the add-ins shown.

Fig. 15.1. *The Add-In Manager dialog box.*

Add add-in macros to the Add-In Manager by choosing the **A**dd button. A Files dialog box—the same one as the File **O**pen dialog box—appears. Select from this dialog box the XLA file you want to open; then choose OK. When you open the XLA file, the corresponding add-in's name is added to the list in the Add-In Manager dialog box. If worksheets are associated with add-in macros you are opening, you can add the worksheets to this list in the same fashion. Repeat the procedure to add more add-ins or worksheets. Choose the **C**lose button when you are finished.

If you move an add-in macro file to a different directory, you can edit its path and file name by selecting the add-in's name from the list in the Add-In Manager dialog box. Then choose the **E**dit button, select the **P**ath text box, and correct the path. If the add-in macro is in the same directory as the Add-In Manager, choose the **S**ame Directory As the Add-In Manager option. To make an add-in read-only so that network users cannot change it, select the Open as Read Only check box.

Remove add-in macros from the Add-In Manager list by selecting them and then choosing the **R**emove button.

Adding a Sheet Arranger

The multiple sheet aid add-in macro is available when you open SHEETAID.XLA. This macro gives you additional ways of arranging worksheets beyond the normal **W**orksheet **A**rrange All command. In addition, with SHEETAID.XLA you quickly can activate or open the source worksheet that feeds into the linked cell you select.

When you open SHEETAID.XLA, three new **W**indows commands are added: Arrange All Horizontal, Arrange All **P**erspective, and **A**rrange All Vertical. These commands help you arrange open documents on-screen.

SHEETAID.XLA also gives you the ability to display or open quickly a source worksheet that feeds into the current worksheet. To use this feature, select a cell that contains a single external reference to another worksheet. Press Ctrl+D. (When SHEETAID.XLA is not added in, you can duplicate this feature by double-clicking on the linked cell.)

Adding a Worksheet Auditor and Troubleshooter

The worksheet auditor is a tool that goes beyond the troubleshooting prowess of the Formula Select Special options. When you open the AUDIT.XLA macro, the Formula Worksheet Auditor command is added. This command adds four troubleshooting tools: reports of errors, maps of the worksheet layout, interactive tracing of cell dependencies, and a worksheet information report. Choose the Formula Worksheet Auditor command to display the dialog box shown in figure 15.2.

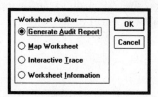

Fig. 15.2. The Worksheet Auditor dialog box.

If you want to see a report of general errors and potential problems on a separate worksheet, select the Generate Audit Report option, click OK or press Enter, and then select check boxes for the following types of reports:

Report	Description
Errors	Prints cells containing error values.
References To Blanks	Prints cell references with formulas that refer to blanks.
References To Text	Prints cell references with formulas that refer to text.
Circular References	Prints cell references and formulas involved in a circular reference. This option can be a lifesaver, but it may take a while to run on large worksheets.
Names	Prints names that are unused or that contain errors.

To see a map that shows your worksheet's layout in miniature, reduce Windows' memory use by closing other programs and unnecessary worksheets, activate the worksheet you want to map, and select the **M**ap Worksheet option from the Worksheet Auditor dialog box. The map is built on its own worksheet, which you can print.

You can trace dependent or precedent cells from a formula with the Formula Select Special command or the Ctrl+[and Ctrl+] shortcut keys. An alternative is to use the Interactive **T**race option of the worksheet auditor. Select the cell you want to trace, choose the Fo**r**mula **W**orksheet Auditor command, and select the Interactive **T**race option. The display splits into two windows. The right is the worksheet; the left is the trace information window. To select dependent or precedent cells to the active cell, choose the Find **D**ependents or Find **P**recedents button. To change the active cell, choose the **R**eset Active Cell button and change the active cell. To retrace through traces you have made, choose the Retrace Move **B**ack or Retrace Move **F**orward button. When you are finished tracing cells, choose the Exit Trace button.

To see audit information regarding your worksheet and an analysis of its contents by type, select the Worksheet **I**nformation option from the Worksheet Auditor dialog box. Another worksheet is opened to contain this information.

Adding the Macro Debugger

You add the macro debugger by opening the DEBUG.XLA file. The debugger gives you additional commands and a new workspace in which to run and debug (troubleshoot) your macros. You also can set *tracepoints* and *breakpoints* in macro cells. When a macro runs and reaches a tracepoint, the macro stops and enters step mode. When a breakpoint is reached, the values and names of cells you previously requested are displayed. From there you can continue, enter single-step mode, or halt.

This debugging utility alters certain formulas in your macro sheet. The formulas that are altered cannot be changed while you are in the debugger. When you leave the debugger, the formulas are returned to normal. For safety reasons, however, saving your macro file before using the debugger— or before making any major changes—is a good idea.

To run the debugger, activate the macro sheet, turn off document protection, and load the DEBUG.XLA add-in. Debug is added to the **Macro** menu. Choosing the **Macro Debug** command displays a new menu from which you debug macro sheets. (You can execute this command only when a macro sheet is open.)

To insert a tracepoint that puts the macro into step mode, select the cell that you want to use as a tracepoint, and then choose the **Debug Set Trace Point** command.

To insert a breakpoint that shows a message or displays variables, select the cell where you want the breakpoint, and then choose **Debug Set Breakpoint**. Type a message that should appear when the breakpoint is reached, and choose OK.

To display variables at a breakpoint, choose the **Debug Breakpoint Output** command. Type the range or variable name or cell reference you want to display, and choose OK. The value of the reference or name appears when the breakpoint is reached during the macro's operation. To remove a variable from the breakpoint, select the variable from the Variables to Output list and choose the **Delete** button.

Remove tracepoints or breakpoints by selecting the cell containing them and choosing the **Debug Erase Debug Point** command.

When you want to run the macro, press Ctrl+F6 repeatedly until the worksheet on which you want to run the macro appears; then choose **Debug Run Macro**. Select the macro from the list, and choose OK. The macro runs as it would normally, but when tracepoints or breakpoints are reached, you enter step mode or see the variables you requested. If your macro switches menu bars away from the Debug menu bar, press Ctrl+R to return to the Debug menu bar.

Other commands on the Debug menu bar are self-explanatory and can help you select or display information useful to debugging macros. For more information on debugging macros, read Chapter 30 in the macro section of this book.

Adding an Auto Save Feature

The AUTOSAVE.XLA add-in saves Excel files for you at the frequency you specify. This macro helps you remember to save. When AUTOSAVE.XLA loads, it adds the Auto Save command to the **Options** menu. Choose the **Options Auto Save** command to display the dialog box in figure 15.3.

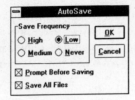

Fig. 15.3. The AutoSave dialog box.

For the Save Frequency setting, you can choose one of the following options:

Option	Frequency
High	Save approximately every 3 minutes.
Medium	Save approximately every 9 minutes.
Low	Save approximately every 30 minutes.
Never	Do not save.

The other options on the AutoSave dialog box are **P**rompt Before Saving and **S**ave All Files. Select **P**rompt Before Saving if you want the program to prompt you before saving. This method is helpful if you prefer to save with a different file name and version number each time. Select **S**ave All Files to save all open Excel documents. Deselect to save only the active document.

Adding a Slide Show

The SLIDES.XLA macro gives you access to the slide show program, which creates a slide show from Excel charts and worksheets. You can have the slide show cycle through open documents either automatically or manually.

Open the SLIDES.XLA macro to add the Slide Show command to the **M**acro menu. Before choosing this command, open all the worksheets you want in the slide show. Scroll documents to display the part of the worksheet you want to show. The slide show displays documents in the same order as if you were pressing Ctrl+F6 to advance to the next slide.

Choose the **M**acro Slide Show command to display the Slide Show dialog box shown in figure 15.4. Select the Advance A**u**tomatically option to advance shows according to the number of seconds you type in the Advance every __ seconds text box. Or select the Advance **M**anually option to advance to the next slide when you press Tab.

Fig. 15.4. The Slide Show dialog box enables you to control how frequently slides appear.

If you want the slide show to operate continuously, select the **K**eep showing the open documents option. If you want the slide show to end after a single pass, select the Show all the open documents **o**nce option.

The **H**ide menus, tool bar & formula bar option does just what it says. When the slide show finishes, the menus, tool bar, and formula bar reappear.

Choose the **R**un button to run the slide show. Quit a show by pressing Q.

Adding Directory Commands

The FILEFNS.XLA add-in gives you four macro functions with which you can create, delete, and find information about directories. These four macro functions are described in the following paragraphs. These functions work only when used within macro sheets.

CREATE.DIRECTORY*(path_text)*
Creates a directory. For instance, CREATE.DIRECTORY("BUDGET") creates the directory named BUDGET as a subdirectory of the current directory. CREATE.DIRECTORY("D:\FINANCE\BUDGET") creates the directory BUDGET as a subdirectory under FINANCE on the D drive. FINANCE must exist.

DELETE.DIRECTORY*(path_text)*
Deletes an empty directory. Returns FALSE if the directory cannot be deleted. This macro uses the same argument syntax as CREATE.DIRECTORY.

FILE.EXISTS*(path_text)*
Returns TRUE if the specified file or directory exists, or FALSE otherwise. The function uses the same argument syntax as CREATE.DIRECTORY. Include the file name in the argument when you're testing for the presence of a file.

DIRECTORIES(*path_text*)
Returns a horizontal array of all subdirectories in the current directory or of all subdirectories in the path you specify. Use the INDEX() function to retrieve a specific name within the returned array. Use the COLUMNS() function to test the returned array for its total number of directories.

As an example of how this function can be used in a macro,

SET.NAME("Dir3",INDEX(DIRECTORIES("C:\FINANCE"),0,3))

stores the name of the third subdirectory under C:\FINANCE in the name Dir3.

> **Tip: *Making Sure To Copy the Dynamic Link Libraries***
> These directory-information macro functions use dynamic link libraries (DLL) stored in the file named FILEFNS.DLL, which is stored in the WINDOWS\SYSTEM directory. If you copy the FILEFNS.XLA add-in macro to other computers, make sure that those computers have the FILEFNS.DLL file in their WINDOWS\SYSTEM directory. If you are using this macro on a network version of Excel, put a copy of the FILEFNS.DLL file in the network's WINDOWS/SYSTEM directory.

Adding Functions

The ADDINFNS.XLA add-in macro adds to Excel six worksheet functions that you can use in your worksheets or macro sheets. After the add-in file is open, you can use these functions just as you would use built-in functions. You can type them without specifying the sheet name, or you can select them from the Formula Paste Functions list.

The added functions are described in the following paragraphs.

BASE(number,*target_base,precision*)
Returns a number as text in the *target_base* system when given a base-10 number. The target base must be between 2 and 36; the default is 16. The *precision* argument refers to the number of decimal places.

DEGREES(*angle_in_radians*)
Returns degrees when given radians.

FASTMATCH(*lookup_value*,*lookup_array,type_of_match*)
Returns the relative position of the *lookup_value* within the *lookup-array*. Different types of matches are made depending upon the *type_of_match*.

Use FASTMATCH rather than the MATCH function when you're searching large arrays. See the discussion of the MATCH function in Chapter 10 for more information.

RADIANS(*angle_in_degrees*)
Returns radians when given degrees.

RANDBETWEEN(*bottom,top*)
Returns a random integer between the top and bottom numbers.

SUMSQUARE(*reference*)
Returns the sum of the squares of all numbers within the *reference* or array. Text and logical values within the reference are ignored.

Adding a Glossary Feature

The glossary add-in is a boon to any operator who frequently enters the same labels, titles, or formulas. The glossary stores frequently used text and formulas and inserts them at your request. It replaces many keystrokes with a few. This add-in is similar to the glossary feature available in Word for Windows or Word.

To add the Glossary command to the Edit menu, open the GLOSSARY.XLA file. To add text or formulas to the glossary, select the cell or range containing the information you want added to the glossary; then choose the **Edit Glossary** command. The Glossary dialog box shown in figure 15.5 will appear. In the **Name** text box, type a short name or abbreviation you want to assign to the contents of the selected cells. Choose the **Define** button.

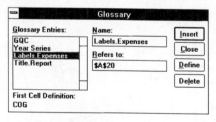

Fig. 15.5. *The Glossary dialog box.*

To insert something from the glossary into a worksheet, select the cell or cells in which you want to insert the information. Choose the **Edit Glossary** command, and select from the **Glossary Entries** list the name you assigned to the glossary contents you need. Choose the **Insert** button.

Delete glossary entries by selecting the glossary name in the dialog box and choosing the **Delete** button. Choose Cancel to exit the dialog box.

Adding a What-If Generator

The what-if macro quickly tests sets of input values on your worksheet by trying all possible combinations. The what-if macro prompts you for a set of values. Then, with your worksheet displayed, these values are plugged into the appropriate cells each time you press Ctrl+T or Shift+Ctrl+T.

To add the **What If** command to the Formula menu, open the WHATIF.XLA file. To set up a data sheet that contains the variables you want tested, choose the Formula **What If** command and select the **New** button. A new sheet appears. When you are prompted, type the name or the cell reference of the input cell you want to receive the values being tested. (You cannot select the cell.) Choose OK. The macro then prompts you for each value you want to test in that input cell. Choose **Done** when you are through entering values.

You are prompted again for the next input cell to be changed. After entering the cell reference, enter the values you want tested in that cell. Choose **Done** after you have entered the last input value for that cell. Continue in this manner until you have entered all input cells and their values. Choose **Done** when the macro prompts you for another input cell reference. All the cell references and input values you have entered have been saved on a worksheet.

To test the input values on your worksheet, activate the worksheet and press Ctrl+Shift+T to cycle through all combinations of input values. To see changes affected by a single input cell, select that cell and press Ctrl+T.

Adding a Document Summary

The SUMMARY.XLA add-in enables you to store summary information easily with the worksheet. This feature is valuable for auditing worksheets or when more than one person updates a worksheet. The summary stores information such as the worksheet title, its size, the date saved and revision number, topics, comments, and the author's name.

To add the Summary Info command to the Edit menu, open the SUMMARY.XLA file. Select this command to display the dialog box shown in figure 15.6. You can edit all information in the Summary Info dialog box except the creation date. Information from the dialog box is stored in hidden names within the worksheet. (Use the NAMES () macro function within a macro to retrieve an array of hidden names. These functions are described briefly in Chapter 32, "Macro Function Directory.")

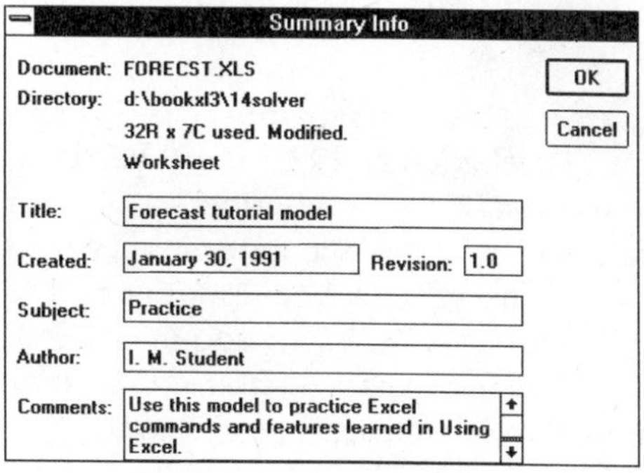

Fig. 15.6. The Summary Info dialog box.

Adding Text File Commands

Opening the FLATFILE.XLA add-in gives you additional methods for working with text files. This add-in macro enables you to save files in *column-delimited* format, in which each field of data aligns in a specific character position. With this add-in, you also can *parse*, or separate, files in which values are separated by nonstandard field delimiters.

Text files are used to transfer information between Excel and personal computer or mainframe programs. For many situations involving text files, you can save or open text files by using the File Save As command and the CSV format for comma-separated values or the text format for tab-separated values. In some exchanges, however, data files are column-delimited—each field aligns within specific columns of characters.

Before you save a worksheet as a flat (column-delimited) file, seeing how characters on the sheet align is often helpful. Because Excel normally uses proportionally spaced characters, columns of characters may appear not to align. To correct this problem, format all involved cells with a nonproportional text such as Courier or Line Printer.

To save a worksheet so that it contains only characters and spaces, open the FLATFILE.XLA file. This adds the Export command to the **Data** menu. Select the cells you want to export to a file, choose the **Data Export** command, and type the file name in the dialog box. Select the **Retain Cell Formats** check box if you want characters to have the alignment and numeric format shown on-screen. One extra space character is inserted between columns if you choose this option. Do not select the Retain Cell Formats check box if you want general alignment and number formatting. Finally, choose the Export button.

To parse or separate a text file into separate cells, use either the **Data Parse** command (a normal Excel command) or the **Data Smart Parse** command (an add-in command). **Data Parse** is described in Chapter 34, "Using Excel with DOS Programs," and is used to separate files in which each field of data is stored in a specific column within a long string of text. The **Data Smart Parse** command is added by the FLATFILE.XLA add-in and enables you to parse (separate) lines of text in which data is separated by a unique character. Each piece of information between those unique characters is put into its own individual cell.

To parse a text file that uses a specific character to separate data, open the text file. Text data opens into a single column. The data being parsed must be in one column for the add-in to work. In that column, select the range of cells that you want parsed. Choose the **Data Smart Parse** command to display the dialog box shown in figure 15.7. Select **Blank Space ( )** if each cell's data is separated from the next cell by a blank space. Select **Slash** (/) if each cell of data is separated from the next cell by a slash. Select the **Other** check box and enter your own single character if it is neither a blank space nor a slash. If you want to include spaces as they are in the file, deselect the **Remove** extra blank spaces check box; otherwise, multiple blanks are replaced by single blank characters.

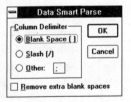

Fig. 15.7. *Select the parsing character from the Data Smart Parse dialog box.*

Adding a Name Changer

The name changer is available when you open the CHANGER.XLA macro. With this feature, you quickly can change the definition of names or replace one name with another. The macro also makes the related change to all uses of the name in formulas throughout the worksheet.

To add the Change Name command to the Formula menu, open the CHANGER.XLA file. Choose this command to display the dialog box shown in figure 15.8 so that you can change names on your worksheet. Select from the From box the name you want to change, type the new name in the To box, and choose the Rename button. You can repeat this procedure until you choose the Close button. You also can delete names from within the Rename a Name dialog box by selecting them and choosing the Delete button.

Fig. 15.8. *Use the Rename a Name dialog box to change cell and range names.*

Adding a Worksheet Comparison Command

If you think that minor changes have been made to a worksheet, the COMPARE.XLA add-in can find them. To use it, open the two worksheets you want to compare. Make one of them active.

Open the COMPARE.XLA add-in and choose the new command that becomes available, Formula Compare. From the Compare to sheet list, select the inactive worksheet you want to compare with the active worksheet. A report of all differences is printed on a new worksheet.

From Here...

Add-ins are useful programs that extend and adapt Excel's capabilities. In addition to the free add-ins provided with Excel and described in this chapter, other add-ins are written to adapt Excel to specific industry problems or to fit specific needs within a business. Other Windows programs that work in synergy with Excel come with add-ins so that the two programs can work together as though they were one. Examples of such programs are Solver from Frontline System, Inc., and Q+E from Pioneer Software. Other programs that work well with Excel are listed in the Appendix.

To learn how to create add-in programs for your own use or for use in your company or industry, begin by learning how to record and modify simple macros. The Macro Quick Start in Chapter 28 takes you through the basics of recording a macro and making modifications that display input and command dialog boxes. The simple procedure for saving a macro as an add-in macro is described in the macro chapters in Part V.

16

Printing
Worksheets

E xcel enables you to use the full capabilities of your printer. Excel reports printed from laser printers can look as though they have been typeset. You will find that you can achieve better quality with your printer than you ever have before.

Figures 16.1 through 16.4 give you some idea of what you can produce. Excel can produce the equivalent of preprinted invoices or "annual report quality" financial statements.

Excel saves you from the trial-and-error process of printing to see the result. You can preview the printed page on-screen before you send it to the printer. You even can adjust margins and column widths in the preview.

The Windows Spooler also increases your work efficiency. The Spooler queues material to be printed, enabling the computer to print while you continue working on other projects.

Reviewing the Printing Process

Usually, your printing process consists of the following steps. These steps, along with the available options, are described in detail later in this chapter.

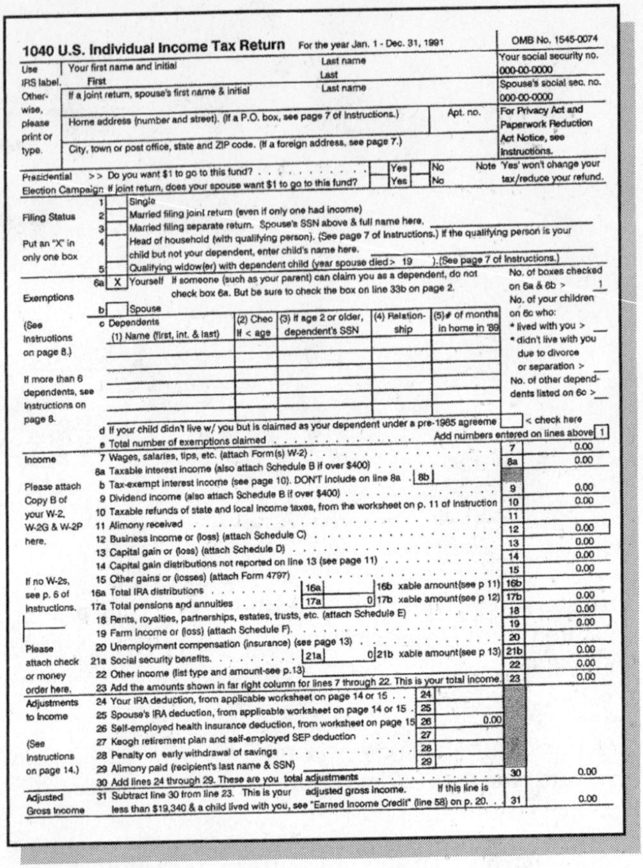

Fig. 16.1. A 1040 U.S. Individual Tax Return form.

1. Choose **F**ile **P**rinter Setup and select your printer. For most printers, you do not need to use the Setup button unless you want to change the printer's default settings.

2. Choose the **F**ile Page Setup command and set borders, page orientation, resolution, and headers and footers.

3. Select the area to be printed and then choose **O**ptions Set Print Area. Do not select the same rows or columns that you selected for Print Titles.

4. Select the rows or columns that you want to print as headings on each page, and then choose the **O**ptions Set Print **T**itles command.

5. Set manual page breaks, if necessary, with **O**ptions Set Page **B**reak.

6. Choose the **File Print** command, or choose the **File Print Preview** command if you want to see how the printed document will appear. While in the preview, choose the **Print** button when you want to print.

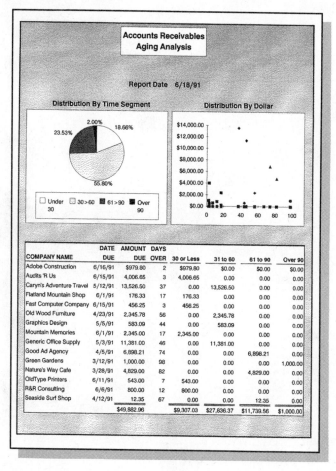

Fig 16.2. *An aging analysis.*

COMPANY NAME	DATE DUE	AMOUNT DUE	DAYS OVER	30 or Less	31 to 60	61 to 90	Over 90
Adobe Construction	6/16/91	$979.80	2	$979.80	$0.00	$0.00	$0.00
Audits 'R Us	6/15/91	4,006.65	3	4,006.65	0.00	0.00	0.00
Caryn's Adventure Travel	5/12/91	13,526.50	37	0.00	13,526.50	0.00	0.00
Flatland Mountain Shop	6/1/91	176.33	17	176.33	0.00	0.00	0.00
Fast Computer Company	6/15/91	456.25	3	456.25	0.00	0.00	0.00
Old Wood Furniture	4/23/91	2,345.78	56	0.00	2,345.78	0.00	0.00
Graphics Design	5/5/91	583.09	44	0.00	583.09	0.00	0.00
Mountain Memories	6/1/91	2,345.00	17	2,345.00	0.00	0.00	0.00
Generic Office Supply	5/3/91	11,381.00	46	0.00	11,381.00	0.00	0.00
Good Ad Agency	4/5/91	6,898.21	74	0.00	0.00	6,898.21	0.00
Green Gardens	3/12/91	1,000.00	98	0.00	0.00	0.00	1,000.00
Nature's Way Cafe	3/28/91	4,829.00	82	0.00	0.00	4,829.00	0.00
OldType Printers	6/11/91	543.00	7	543.00	0.00	0.00	0.00
R&R Consulting	6/6/91	800.00	12	800.00	0.00	0.00	0.00
Seaside Surf Shop	4/12/91	12.35	67	0.00	0.00	12.35	0.00
		$49,882.96		$9,307.03	$27,836.37	$11,739.56	$1,000.00

Installing Your Printer

When you install Windows, you are asked to select the printers you will use. If you want to install or remove printers after Windows is installed, open the Main window in the Program Manager and start the Control Panel program. Press F1 for Help about the Control Panel. Read the information about the

Printers program, and then start the Printers program to install or remove a printer. Windows will need to read your original Windows disks to load the printer driver files.

Global Quality Corporation		Balance Sheet September 30, 1991		

Assets

Current Assets	Current Year	Previous Year	% Change
Current Assets			
Cash	15,007	8,265	181.57%
Accounts Receivable	203,850	448,320	45.47%
Inventory	243,000	241,543	100.60%
Prepaid Expenses	11,400	4,378	260.39%
Investments	95,000	3	0.00%
Total Current Assets	568,257	702,509	80.89%
Fixed Assets			
Buildings	395,577	304,769	129.80%
Leasehold Improvements	3,765	4,356	86.43%
Furniture	27,546	21,587	127.60%
Machinery and Equipment	176,897	87,437	202.31%
	603,785	418,149	144.39%
Less Accumulated Depreciation	156,723	106,734	146.84%
	447,062	311,415	143.56%
Land	69,055	69,055	100.00%
Total Fixed Assets	516,117	380,470	135.65%
	$1,084,374	$1,082,979	100.13%

Liabilities and Shareholder's Equity

Current Liabilities			
Notes Payable	250,000	337,000	74.18%
Trade Accounts Payable	101,900	173,500	58.73%
Accrued Liabilities	35,543	34,200	103.93%
Corporate Income Taxes Payable	21,587	12,423	173.77%
Total Current Liabilties	409,030	557,123	73.42%
Long-Term Debt	213,549	445,638	47.92%
Due to Shareholders	5,690	8,120	70.07%
Deferred Income Tax	4,870	90,230	5.40%
Shareholder's Equity			
Capital Stock	124,000	118,000	105.08%
Opening Retained Earnings	546,789	406,744	134.43%
Dividends Declared	(8,690)	(3,545)	245.13%
Profit/(Loss) for the Period	13,245	4,657	284.41%
Total Shareholder's Equity	675,344	525,856	128.43%
	$1,084,374	$1,082,979	100.13%

Fig. 16.3. A balance sheet.

Selecting the Printer

You may have installed more than one printer when you installed Windows. To select the printer to be used for the next print job, follow these steps:

1. Choose the File Printer Setup command.

Fig. 16.4. Mailing labels.

2. Select the printer and the printer port that you want to use.

3. Select the Setup button if you have not used this printer before. A dialog box similar to the one shown in figure 16.5 will appear.

4. Select the appropriate options for the printer you specified. The Printer Setup dialog box will be different for various printers. Some of the options available are shown in table 16.1.

5. Choose OK or press Enter.

6. Choose OK or press Enter a final time to remove the Printer Setup dialog box.

The printer settings you choose in the Setup dialog box are the default printer settings. For most printers, you use the File Page Setup command to make document printing changes. When you select the Setup button, a dialog box tells you what features should be set with the Page Setup command. Excel continues to print to the printer you select until another printer is selected.

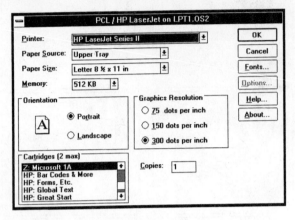

Fig. 16.5. Printer setup dialog boxes vary with each printer.

Table 16.1
Printer Setup Options

Option	Description
Copies	The number of copies printed.
Printer/Memory	The exact model of printer and its memory capacity (to ensure that Windows uses all the features of this model).
Paper Size	The sizes and types of paper available.
Paper Source	Which of the bins your printer may have for different types of paper.
Orientation	The placement of print on the page: *portrait* prints characters on the page as they appear in a normal letter; *landscape* prints sideways on the paper and is useful for making transparencies and charts.
Graphics Resolution	Print quality: printing at high *resolution* slows the printer speed, but produces better graphic images.
Cartridges	Specification of the types of font cartridges available.

If you have questions about the Setup options, choose the **Help** button in the box.

Defining the Page Setup

The **F**ile Page Setup command controls the position of print on the page, reorients the paper if you want to print sideways, specifies custom headers and footers, turns the gridlines on and off, and determines whether the row and column headings are printed.

To change the layout of the printed page, follow these steps:

1. Choose the **F**ile Page Setup command.

2. Change the page options as needed in the Page Setup dialog box (see fig. 16.6). These options are described in more detail in the following sections.

3. Choose the OK button or press Enter.

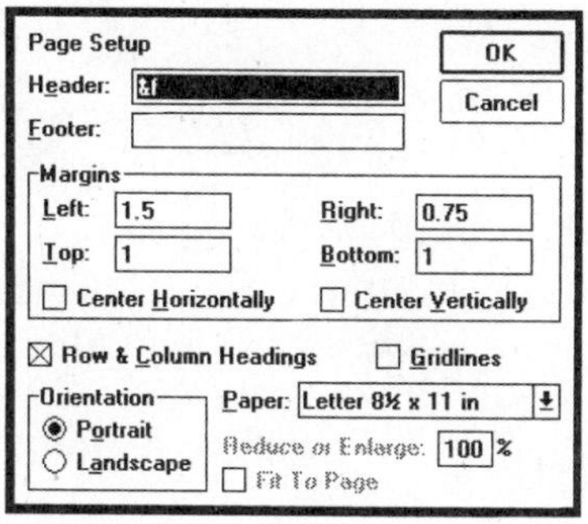

Fig 16.6. *The Page Setup dialog box.*

Setting the Paper Margins

Excel's character width changes with each different font size. Consequently, you need to measure your margins in inches rather than by a count of characters. The default settings for margins are shown in table 16.2.

Measure the margins from the edge of the paper inward. When you set the top and bottom margins, keep in mind that headers and footers automatically print 1/2 inch from the top or bottom of the paper.

Table 16.2
Default Margin Settings

Margin	Default in Inches
Left	0.75
Right	0.75
Top	1
Bottom	1

Many laser printers are unable to print to the edge of the paper in at least one direction. Because of this limitation, you may not be able to set margins of less than 1/4 inch on one or more sides of the paper.

If you want your document to be centered between margins, select the Center Horizontally or the Center Vertically check box.

Turning Gridlines and Row and Column Headings On or Off

For most printed reports, you will not want to print gridlines or the row and column headings. If you turn off these features in the worksheet, they do not show on-screen; however, they can still print. To leave gridlines and row and column headings on-screen and turn them off when printing, deselect the Row & Column Headings or the Gridlines option.

You will probably want to print row and column headings when you print worksheet documentation showing formulas or when you print notes. (If you use Options Display, you can display the formulas on-screen so that they can be printed.)

Creating Headers and Footers

You can create headers and footers that place a title, date, or page number at the top or bottom of each printed page of your worksheet. You even can format them with different fonts, styles, and sizes. Use headers and footers to enter a copyright notice, to document the author, to show the printout date, or to note the source worksheet.

Excel automatically uses the document name as the header and shows the word Page and the page number as the footer. You can either delete these or change them.

Headers and footers use a 3/4-inch side margin and a 1/2-inch margin at the top and bottom. The header and footer cannot be moved within this area. If you specify page setup margins that cross within these boundaries, the document may print over a header or footer.

In the Header or Footer text boxes of the Page Setup dialog box, you can type text and codes to enter and format data automatically. These codes, shown in table 16.3, also are available under the topic "Header and Footer Codes" under the on-line Help (F1).

Table 16.3
Header and Footer Codes

Code	Effect
Position Codes	
&L	Aligns text against left header/footer margin.
&C	Centers text between header/footer margins.
&R	Aligns text against right header/footer margin.
Font and Style Codes	
&"*fontname*"	Prints text that follows in the font specified. Use the same spelling as in the Format Font dialog box and enclose it in quotes.
&*nn*	Prints text that follows in the font size specified by *nn*. Use a two-digit point size: 08, 12, or 14.
&B	Prints text that follows in bold.
&I	Prints text that follows in italic.
&U	Prints text that follows underlined.
&S	Prints text that follows with strikethroughs.
Inserted Data Codes	
&D	Inserts the computer's date.
&T	Inserts the computer's time.
&F	Inserts the name of the document.

continues

Table 16.3 *(continued)*

Code	Effect
Page Codes	
&P	Inserts the page number.
&P+# or &P–#	Inserts the page number plus or minus an adder (#). Use the page code with the plus sign (+) to start printing at a page number greater than the actual page number. Use the page code with the minus sign (–) to start printing at a page number smaller than the actual page number.
&N	Inserts the total number of pages. For example, the header Page &P of &N produces the result Page 6 of 15.
Other	
&&	Prints an ampersand.

> **Note:** *Typing Formatting Codes after the Positioning Code*
> Formatting codes affect the section of the header or footer in which the code resides. Therefore, you must type formatting codes after the positioning codes. For example, to make the center of a header 14-point Times Roman, the font name and size must follow the &C code, as in &C&"Tms Rmn"&14.

As the following examples illustrate, you can combine the codes shown in table 16.3 with your own text to create custom headers and footers. To try these examples, press Alt,E (Header) or Alt,F (Footer) when the Page Setup box is displayed; then type the code line as shown. When you print or preview the document, the result will appear as shown here.

Code: &C&BUsing Excel: IBM Version &RPage &P
Result:

```
                    Using Excel: IBM Version           Page 1
```

Code: &Karen Rose&C&F&R&I&D
Result:

```
Karen Rose                 FORECAST.XCL                 8/15/88
```

Code: &L&D&C&"Tms Rmn"&14ABC Investment Corp.&RMortgage
Banking Div.
Result:

8/15/88　**ABC Investment Corp.**　Mortgage Banking Div.

Headers are printed 1/2 inch from the top of the page, and footers 1/2 inch
from the bottom. If text overlaps the header or footer, use **File Page Setup**
to change the top or bottom margin.

> **Tip: *Print Titles vs. Labels in Headers***
> When you work with databases or large worksheets, you may be
> tempted to put labels in the header so that you can see the labels on
> each page of the printout. Don't! Labels in the header are difficult to
> align with columns and can't be positioned close to the body of the
> report. Instead, use **Options Set Print Titles** to set print titles.

Setting the Print Range

By default, Excel prints the entire worksheet unless you specify otherwise.
When you need to print only a portion of the worksheet, you must define
that area with **Options Set Print Area**. The print area can include more than
one range.

Setting a Single Print Area

The **Options Set Print Area** command controls how much of the document
is printed; the command also controls which cell notes are printed. To
define a single print area, select the range of cells that you want printed and
choose the **Options Set Print Area** command. Cell notes that are within the
selected range will print if you select the **Notes** or the **Both** option from the
File Print command.

After you set the print area, Excel marks the edges of the print area with
dashed lines. For example, figure 16.7 shows the worksheet created in the
Worksheet Quick Start. Excel marked the calculated area, which is selected
in the figure, as the area to be printed when the **Options Set Print Area**
command is chosen. You can see in figure 16.8 the lines that mark the edges
of the print area after **Options Set Print Area** is chosen.

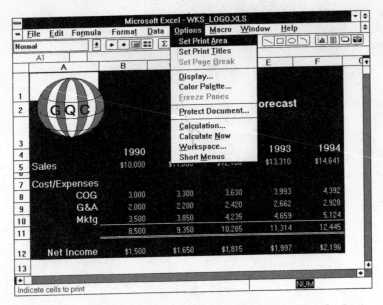

Fig. 16.7. Select the area that you want to print before choosing the Options Set Print Area command.

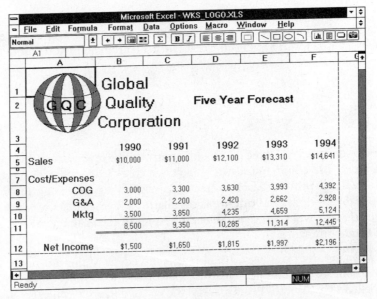

Fig. 16.8. Page breaks mark the page breaks and the edges of a print area.

The Options Set Print Area command creates a named range called Print_Area. You can display this range name and its cell references with the Formula Define Name command.

If you want to return to printing the entire worksheet, select the entire worksheet. (Press Shift+Ctrl+space bar, or click in the blank square above the row heading and to the left of the column heading.) Then choose the Options Remove Print Area command.

Setting Multiple Print Areas

Excel can print multiple ranges with a single print command. Although these ranges print sequentially, each range prints on its own sheet.

Select the multiple ranges that you want to print by using Ctrl+drag or F8 and Shift+F8. Select ranges in the order that you want them to print. Then choose the Options Set Print Area command. This technique works well for creating a single printed report from different areas of a worksheet.

> **Tip:** *Saving Time When Printing*
> If you frequently print the same parts of a document, save time by selecting these areas and giving them a name with the Formula Define Name command. You can even select multiple ranges and give them a single name. Once named, press Goto (F5) and select the range you want to print. Now choose the Option Set Print Area command.

Printing Titles

Repeating printed titles on each page can make large worksheet or database printouts easier to read. For example, when your worksheet is wider than one page, you can repeat row titles along the left margin of each page. You can repeat column titles at the top of each page of a database that spans multiple pages. The Options Set Print Titles command specifies that selected rows or columns will print at the top or left side of each printed page.

To specify titles, follow these steps:

1. Select the entire row(s) or columns(s) of titles that you want on each page. The rows or columns must be adjacent, as shown in figure 16.9.

2. Choose the Options Set Print Titles command.

If an alert box warns that the title area is invalid, make sure that you selected the entire row or column and not just certain cells.

When you select the print range with **Options Set Print Area**, do not reselect the rows or columns that you specified with **Options Set Print Titles**. If you do, the titles will print twice on the page.

To display the currently selected titles, press the Goto key (F5), and then select Print_Titles. To delete Print_Titles, select the entire document and then choose the **Options Remove Print Titles** command.

You don't have to limit yourself to one row or column of titles. As long as the title rows or columns are adjacent, you can include as many as you want.

			Microsoft Excel - COMPARE.XLS					
File	Edit	Formula	Format	Data	Options	Macro	Window	Help

	A	B	C	D	E	F	G	H
1				Steam Well 62				
2				Loggings				
3	Analyst:	Tom Peterson						
4	Date:	Dec 11, 1990						
5	Compare:	11/01/90 to 11/03/90						
6								
7	Log Time	Log Time	C* delta	GPM delta	CaCO3	H2S	Se	Fe
8	11/1/90 0:00	3D 0Hr	-2.5883	-116.6659	-0.0240	0.0524	-0.0278	-0.0193
9	11/1/90 0:15	3D 0Hr	-1.9803	-183.8573	-0.0220	0.0071	-0.0031	0.0331
10	11/1/90 0:30	3D 0Hr	-0.0316	446.0579	0.0558	-0.0454	0.0415	-0.0509
11	11/1/90 0:45	3D 0Hr	2.5050	202.9863	-0.1149	0.0128	0.0098	0.0246
12	11/1/90 1:00	3D 1Hr	-2.3234	209.7980	0.1689	-0.0016	-0.0209	0.0564
13	11/1/90 1:15	3D 1Hr	-5.3186	257.1449	-0.0055	0.0025	0.0162	0.0646
14	11/1/90 1:30	3D 1Hr	-9.7496	-596.2566	-0.1338	0.0736	-0.0033	-0.0767
15	11/1/90 1:45	3D 1Hr	-5.5990	129.8581	-0.1076	0.0261	-0.0640	0.0797
16	11/1/90 2:00	3D 2Hr	0.8763	212.6055	0.0494	0.0613	-0.0377	0.0057
17	11/1/90 2:15	3D 2Hr	-1.4218	145.7752	0.0185	0.0614	-0.0053	0.0250
18	11/1/90 2:30	3D 2Hr	2.1792	-167.0129	-0.0666	0.0459	-0.0528	-0.0445
19	11/1/90 2:45	3D 2Hr	4.9366	-262.4272	0.0646	0.0044	-0.0270	-0.1062
20	11/1/90 3:00	3D 3Hr	2.5623	-183.5901	0.0493	0.0129	-0.0380	-0.0752

Fig. 16.9. The Options Set Print Titles command repeats rows or columns on each page.

Tip: *When Titles Are Printed*
Excel prints titles set with **Options Set Print Titles** only when the selection being printed includes the same rows or columns as the Print_Titles range. Suppose, for example, that you type titles in rows A3:G4 and create Print Titles of rows 3 and 4. If you print data from B36 to H54, you will then have the titles that are in cells B3:G4. If you print the area from H54 to K72, you will have as titles whatever is in H3:K4. Because you did not type titles in this range, you may have blanks or unwanted cell values.

Adjusting the Print Area

After you select a print area, you may need to make adjustments to fit the information on the page. For example, you might want to change the page breaks to keep related data together. You also might want to change the margins or font size so that you can fit the information on the page.

As soon as you set a print area with **Options Set Print Area**, Excel displays dashed lines to mark the page boundaries and automatic page breaks. Automatic page breaks are determined by the cell selection that you make before you choose **Options Set Print Area** and by the margins you specify when you issue the **File Page Setup** command.

Setting Manual Page Breaks

Sometimes you need to insert a manual page break to override an automatic page break. When you insert manual page breaks, the automatic page breaks reposition automatically.

When you choose the **Options Set Page Break** command, the manual page breaks appear above and to the left of the active cell. Figure 16.10 shows page breaks above and to the left of the active cell. Manual page breaks appear on-screen with a longer and bolder dashed line than the automatic page breaks. Page breaks are easier to see on-screen when you remove gridlines with the **Options Display** command.

To insert manual page breaks, move the active cell beneath and to the right of the place you want the break, and then choose **Options Set Page Break**. If you want to set page breaks for only the sides, make sure that the active cell is in row 1 before you invoke **Options Set Page Break**. If you want to set the breaks for only the tops and bottoms of pages, move the active cell to the correct row in column A, and then choose the **Options Set Page Break** command.

A manual page break stays at the location that you set until you remove it. Remove manual page breaks by first moving the active cell directly below or immediately to the right of the manual page break. Then choose **Options Remove Page Break**. (This command appears on the menu only when the active cell is positioned correctly.) Remove all page breaks by selecting the entire document and then choosing the **Options Remove Page Break** command.

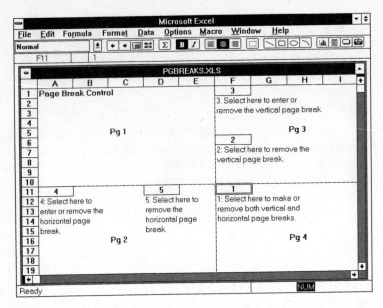

Fig. 16.10. *Manual page breaks appear above and to the left of the active cell.*

> **Note: *When You Can't Remove a Page Break***
> Be sure that you try to remove only *manual* page breaks. You can drive yourself crazy trying to remove an automatic page break that you mistake for a manual one.

Fitting More Data on a Page

You can fit more information on a page by decreasing the margins, decreasing the column widths or row heights, or choosing a smaller font size. On some printers, you can print a proportionally smaller document.

If you used Styles to format your document, you can change fonts throughout the entire worksheet by redefining the style names used in your worksheet. Normal is the style used in cells that have not been formatted. Use a small font size to fit more data on a page. Save your document before you begin changing fonts so that you can easily return to the original document. On PostScript printers, if you need a very small font, you can type in a 6-point font size even when that size is not listed.

Smaller margins produce more room on the paper. Some laser printers can print only within 1/4 inch of the paper's edge.

You also can narrow columns and reduce row height to fit more data on a page. To make sure that all adjustments are the same, select multiple columns before you narrow a column. All the columns will reduce simultaneously.

If your printer is a PostScript printer, you can print a document that is proportionally reduced or enlarged. By making a proportional reduction, you can fit a document to a page without losing or redoing the formatting. You also can use Windows to make a proportional reduction to fit the document to the page.

To reduce a document automatically to fit the page, choose the **File Page Setup** command and select the **Fit to Page** check box. To reduce or enlarge a document, choose the **File Page Setup** command and select the **Reduce or Enlarge** text box. Enter a number smaller than 100 to reduce the page to that percentage of the original. Enter a number larger than 100 to enlarge the page. If your printer is not capable of scaling the print job to fit the page, the **Reduce or Enlarge** and **Fit to Page** boxes will appear gray.

Adjusting Margins and Column Widths While Previewing

You can adjust margins and column widths while in the preview screen. Before adjusting margins with this method, save your document so that you can easily return to the original settings if necessary. To adjust margins or column widths, follow these steps:

1. Choose the **File Print Preview** command.

2. Choose the **Margins** button. Column and margin markers will appear on the preview page in full page view or when zoomed in.

3. Choose the **Zoom** button or click the magnifying glass pointer to zoom in or out of the preview for more accurate viewing.

4. Drag the margin handles (black squares) or the dotted line to a better position.

5. Drag column handles (black T's) or the column gridline to adjust column widths.

6. Choose **Close** to return to the document with these new settings, or choose **Print** to print the document with these settings.

Figures 16.11 and 16.12 show column and margin adjustment from either a magnified or full view.

Previewing the Printout

Instead of printing to check the appearance of your worksheet, you can view a display of the printout with miniature pages such as the page shown in figure 16.13. When you want to examine a preview page up close, you can zoom into the area you want to see.

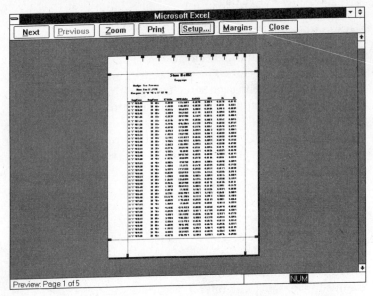

Fig. 16.11. Get the big picture of page fit when you adjust margins and columns.

To preview pages, select the File Print Preview command. The preview screen shows you how the page will print.

To zoom into a portion of the page, choose the **Z**oom button or click the mouse pointer—a magnifying glass—over the portion that you want to magnify. Use the cursor keys or scroll bars to move around in the zoomed-in view. Figures 16.11 and 16.12 show the zoom-in and zoom-out views of the document. To zoom out, choose **Z**oom a second time, or click a second time.

To change pages in the preview mode, use the **N**ext or **P**revious buttons. These buttons appear gray if there is no next or previous page.

After you preview the worksheet, you can print it from the preview screen by choosing the **P**rint button. If you want to change or see the Page Setup settings, choose the **S**etup button. To return to the document, choose the **C**lose button.

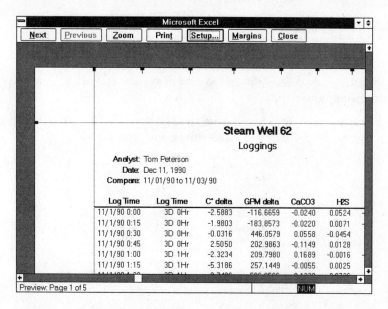

Fig. 16.12. *Zoom in for a precise positioning of margins and column widths.*

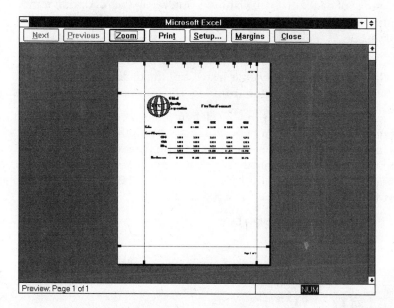

Fig. 16.13. *Previewing enables you to see how the document is positioned on the printed page.*

Printing

With Excel, you can select the range of pages and the number of copies that you want to print. In addition, you can preview the printout on-screen before printing to paper.

Once you are ready to print, choose the **File Print** command to display the print options in the dialog box, as shown in figure 16.14.

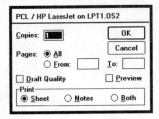

Fig. 16.14. The Print dialog box.

In the **Copies** text box, enter the number of copies you want to print. Specify the range of pages that you want to print; select the **All** option to print the entire print area, or you can enter page numbers in the **From** and **To** text boxes.

When you need a quick print with lower quality characters, select the **Draft** quality check box. The result is faster, but the quality may be lower. If you want to see a preview before printing, choose the **Preview** check box.

Specify what you want to print by selecting the **Sheet**, **Notes**, or **Both** button. **Sheet** prints only the document; **Notes** prints only the notes; and **Both** prints the document, followed by the notes. If you have set a print area, only the document and notes within that area are printed. (To print the cell reference along with each note, make sure that the Row & Column Headings check box is selected from the Page Setup dialog box.)

To print, just choose the OK button. Make sure that your printer is turned on and on-line.

From Here...

Now that you know how to build, format, and print worksheets, you can use Excel to improve the way you work. If you work with data that must be stored, retrieved quickly, and even analyzed for trends and averages, look at Excel's database capability. The Database Quick Start can take you through the basics. If your company uses charts, be sure to work through the Chart Quick Start. Excel's charting capabilities rival those of a program dedicated to charting.

Even if you need Excel only for its worksheet capabilities, examine how you can use macros to speed up repetitive tasks. Excel can record your keystrokes and mouse actions and play them back at your request. By making three simple modifications to a macro recording, you can produce macros that pause dialog boxes for an entry, request information, and display messages. These features are explained in the Macro Quick Start.

Part III

Excel Charts

Includes

Chart Quick Start

Creating Charts

Formatting Charts

Building Complex Charts

We live in a visual world. Almost all our learning comes from what we see. People see and remember trend lines in a chart even when they can't remember the underlying numbers. Variance charts showing the difference between forecast and actual budgets make problem areas immediately visible. The relationships between pricing, volume, and manufacturing become more apparent when presented graphically.

Charts increase understanding and improve communication. Excel's charting capability produces charts with advanced features, yet is quick and easy to use. You can use any of Excel's predefined chart formats to create an initial chart. Then you can enhance and modify that chart to include standard chart items such as arrows, patterns, backgrounds, legends, and movable text. But Excel also gives you advanced capabilities such as using symbols or pictures in place of bars or columns or rotating and zooming 3-D charts.

With Excel, you can create a chart as a document separate from the worksheet or create a chart directly on your worksheet. With a chart on the worksheet, you can see worksheet and chart in the same document on-screen, and they both print on the same page. Charts can even be linked back to the worksheet so that moving a chart's bar or column changes results in the worksheet!

You also should take advantage of Excel's charting with programs such as Word for Windows, Amí Professional, PowerPoint, and CorelDRAW!. Copying Excel charts into these programs extends your ability to communicate.

Excel is one of the first Windows programs to use embedded objects. That means that you can double-click on an Excel chart in a worksheet or embedded in another Windows program and the Excel chart menus will appear so that you can make changes. (The other program must also be capable of handling embedded objects.)

The Chart Quick Start show how easy it is to create charts as separate documents or on your worksheet. You can learn a great deal by experimenting with Excel charts on your own. Charts leave you room for creativity, present information in an easy-to-understand format, and are fun to use as well!

17

Chart Quick Start

T he Quick Start for charts teaches you how to create and customize the chart shown in figure 17.1. To work through the instructions in the Quick Start, you will need to start with a worksheet that contains data. This Quick Start uses the forecast worksheet created in Chapter 3, "Worksheet Quick Start." (The worksheet in the following figures has had a graphic logo added to it, but otherwise it is the same worksheet.) If you did not complete or save that worksheet, then enter the numbers and text as you see them in figure 17.2. You do not need to enter the formulas; entering the numbers and text in rows 4, 5, and 12 will give you enough data to create a chart.

Before beginning this Quick Start, make sure that you have full Excel menus available. Choose the Options command. If the command Full Menus shows, choose that command to make full menus available. If the command Short Menus shows, then you are already in Full Menus.

The Chart Quick Start gives you an overview of Excel's chart capabilities. Remember that you can get help by choosing the Help Index command and selecting Chart. Whenever a dialog box is displayed, you can get help by pressing the F1 key.

Creating a Basic Chart

Excel automatically creates a chart from the worksheet data you select. After you have created a basic chart, you can change the type of chart or enhance the chart.

515

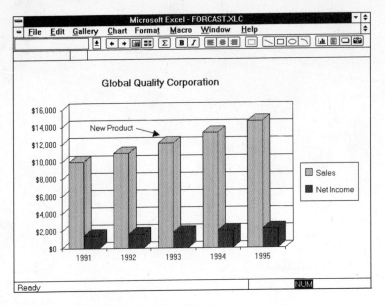

Fig. 17.1. *Create this chart in the Quick Start.*

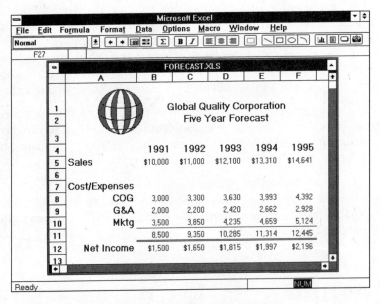

Fig. 17.2. *The forecast worksheet is used to create the chart.*

Excel uses two types of charts. You can create a chart as a separate document in its own window, or you can create a chart that is embedded in a worksheet along with worksheet or database information. Embedded charts display and print with the worksheet. The following steps show you how to create a chart as a separate document and as an embedded document.

> **Tip:** *Placing X-Axis Labels*
> Excel will automatically create a chart from the data selected in the worksheet. Excel positions the X-axis (*category*) labels according to these rules:
>
> - If the selection is wider than tall, the category axis labels are in the row along the top.
>
> - If the selection is taller than wide, the category axis labels are in the column along the left edge of the selection.

The next chapter describes how to create a chart manually and choose which data is used on the category axis. When you include data labels (like the word "Sales" in A5) in the selection, you enable Excel to automatically create titles and legends from text in the worksheet.

Creating a Chart as a Separate Document

If you want to create a chart as a separate document stored in its own file and displayed in its own window, follow these steps:

1. Select the cells to be charted. In this case, select A4:F5. Include the text label in A5.

 Drag from A4 to F5.

 Select A4, hold down Shift, and press the down- and right-arrow keys to select the cells to F5.

2. Choose the File New command.

 Click File, then New.

Press Alt, F, then N; or press F11.

3. Select Chart from the New list(see fig. 17.3).

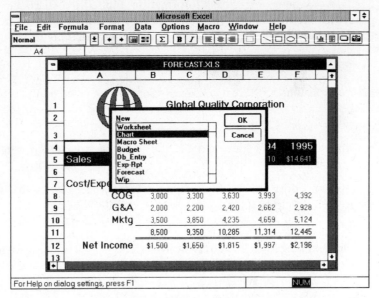

Fig. 17.3. *Select Chart from the dialog box to create a chart.*

4. Choose OK or press Enter.

> **Tip:** *Pressing F11 for an Instant Chart*
> After you select the cells containing the data to be charted, press F11 for an instant chart. (Use Alt+F1 if your keyboard has only ten function keys.)

Excel creates a column chart as shown in figure 17.4. Notice the menu. Because the active document is a chart, the menu now displays chart menu options.

Because you selected a single series of data, the title of the entire chart, *Sales*, comes from cell A5. If there were more data, Excel would use this text as a legend.

Notice that Excel automatically scaled the Y-axis (*value*) axis. Also notice that the value axis uses the same numeric format as the first series of data, row 5, from the selected area.

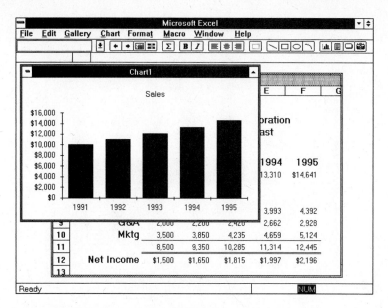

Fig. 17.4. *A simple column chart appears, using the selected data.*

✦ Embedding a Chart in a Worksheet

You can simultaneously create and embed a chart in a worksheet, using a mouse. If you use a keyboard, embed charts in the worksheet by creating them as separate documents and then pasting the charts into the worksheet.

Before you embed a chart in the worksheet, make room for it below the worksheet results. To insert rows in the worksheet, follow these steps:

1. Select the row headings from row 14 to 24. Select the row headings by clicking on the number 14 at the far left of row 14 and dragging down to row 24.

2. Choose the Edit Insert command.

Once you have made room for the chart, embed it by following these steps:

1. Select the cells to be charted. In this case, select A4:F5. Include the text label in A5.

2. Click on the Chart tool in the tool bar. Notice that the mouse pointer changes to a cross hair and the prompt in the status bar tells you, "Click and drag in document to create a chart." The Chart tool is shown in figure 17.5.

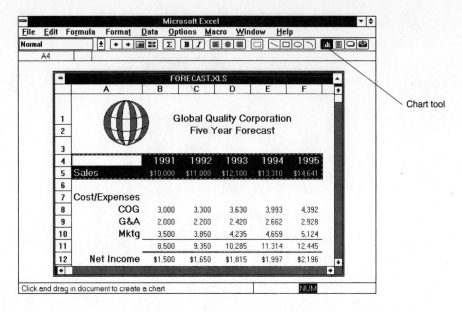

Chart tool

Fig. 17.5. Use the Chart tool on the tool bar to draw the size and location of an embedded chart.

3. Click on the down arrow in the scroll bar until A14 is visible.

4. Drag from the center of A14 to the center of F24. As you touch a screen boundary with the cross hair, the window will scroll to give you more room.

   This step draws a shadow box where the embedded chart will appear. The embedded chart does not have to match cell boundaries.

5. Release the mouse button. The chart will appear on the worksheet within the frame you drew, as shown in figure 17.6.

Changed worksheet data will update an embedded chart the same way changed data updates a chart in a separate document. You can put borders and patterns around the chart outline and add the same features and enhancements you would add to a chart that is a separate document.

Opening an Embedded Chart into a Window

Before you edit, enhance, or format the embedded chart in the following sections, you must open it into a window. To do this, double-click on the embedded chart. The chart will open into a document window. While the embedded document is in a window, you can edit or enhance it the same way you would edit a chart created with the **File New** command.

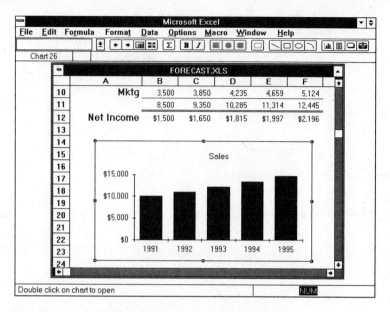

Fig. 17.6. *Embedded charts appear on the worksheet.*

Selecting Chart Types from the Gallery

Excel has six different types of two-dimensional charts, combination charts that combine two of these types, and four different types of three-dimensional charts. You can choose from a total of sixty-eight predefined formats. The predefined formats are variations of the basic chart type. You can customize any of these chart types to fit your needs.

The chart document or embedded chart should now be in its own window and appear as a column chart. (If it does not, see the section "Opening an Embedded Chart into a Window.") A column chart is the default if you have not created a preferred chart setting. To change the column chart to a 3-D pie chart, follow these steps:

1. Choose the Gallery 3-D Pie command.

   Figure 17.7 shows the different types of 3-D pie charts you can select. Pie charts plot only the first *series* of data points. Therefore, if you had selected multiple rows of data, the pie chart would plot only the first row.

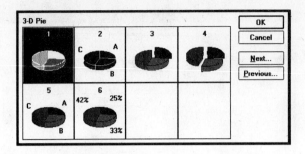

Fig. 17.7. *The 3-D pie chart gallery.*

2. Choose the percentage pie chart, number 6.

 Double-click on the sixth chart type; or click on it, then click OK.

 Type 6, then press Enter.

To make the chart easier to manipulate, maximize the chart's window so that it fills the screen as shown in figure 17.8. To maximize the window, follow these steps:

 Click on the maximize (up-arrow) icon on the right side of the chart's title bar.

 Press Alt, hyphen, and then select Maximize.

Using a mouse, you can "click and drag" wedges in and out of the pie chart, as shown in figure 17.9. Notice that when black handles appear around selected graphical objects, you can move the objects with the mouse. As you withdraw a wedge, the size of the pie decreases. For a presentation, pull the wedge out only a short distance.

The black handles (squares) that appear around some objects when selected indicate that you can drag the object to a new location. White handles around a selected object indicate the object is in a fixed position.

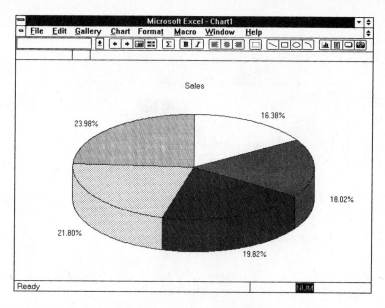

Fig. 17.8. *The maximized pie chart shows percentages.*

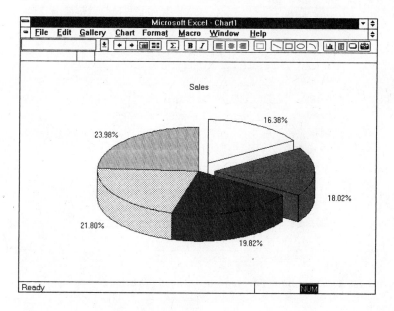

Fig. 17.9. *Drag wedges in or out using the mouse.*

Before adding more data to the chart, change it to a 3-D column chart. To change the chart, follow these steps:

1. Choose the **G**allery 3-D **C**olumn command (see fig. 17.10).

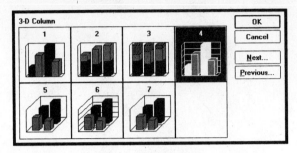

Fig. 17.10. *The 3-D column chart gallery.*

2. Choose the fourth chart type—the one with a horizontal grid. Figure 17.11 shows how the chart changes.

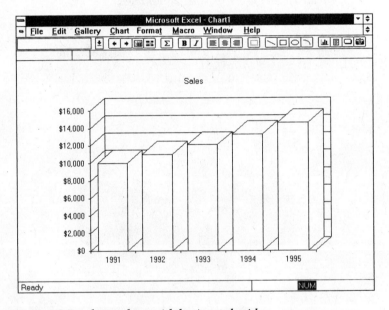

Fig. 17.11. *A 3-D column chart with horizontal grid.*

Double-click on the fourth example.

Type 4; then press ᴇɴᴛᴇʀ.

Customizing a Basic Chart

In this section of the Quick Start, you learn ways to customize the basic chart you have just created. You will add data to the chart. Also, you will add a legend, title, text labels, and an arrow.

Adding Data

Adding a series of data to a chart is as easy as copying data on a worksheet. The current column chart displays the sales for each year. To add the Net Income data to the chart, follow these steps:

1. Activate the worksheet so it is on top by choosing the Window command and selecting the name of the worksheet, FORECAST.XLS, or by pressing Ctrl+F6 until the worksheet is displayed.

2. Select A12:F12, the label and data for Net Income.

3. Choose the Edit Copy command.

4. Activate the chart by choosing the Window command and selecting the name of the chart, Chart1, or by pressing Ctrl+F6 until the chart is displayed.

5. Choose the Edit Paste command to paste the Net Income data into the chart.

The chart should now look like figure 17.12, showing two sets of three-dimensional columns.

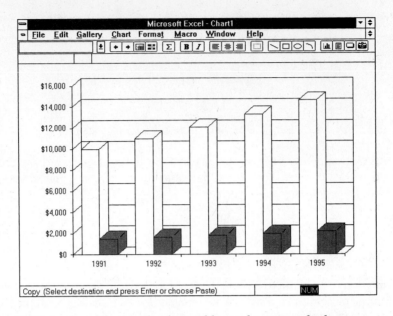

Fig. 17.12. Pasting data into the chart adds another series of columns.

Adding a Legend

Legends help you discriminate between the series of data. To add a legend to the chart, follow these steps:

1. Choose the Chart Add Legend command.

2. Move the legend to a new location.

 Drag the legend to a new location anywhere on the chart, then release.

 Choose the Format Legend command, then select from the options Bottom, Corner, Top, Right, or Left; then press Enter.

3. Move the legend to the right side.

 Drag the legend until it touches the right side and a black, vertical bar appears. Release.

 Choose the Format Legend command, then select the Right option and press Enter.

Notice that the legend has black handles around it, indicating it is selected. While it is selected, you can drag the legend to a new position with the mouse or change its position with the Forma**t** Legend command.

Items on the chart must be selected before you can affect them. They are selected when you first create them. To select an item at a later time, click on it with the mouse or press the up- or down-arrow key to move the selection between groups of items. (The left- or right-arrow keys move the selection between items in the same group.)

Adding a Title

To add a main title to your chart, follow these steps:

1. Choose the Chart Attach Text command.

   The Attach Text To dialog box (see fig. 17.3) gives you the opportunity to attach fixed position titles to the top of the chart, either axis, or a specific column (point of data).

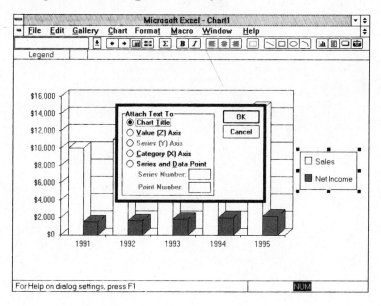

Fig. 17.13. *The Attach Text To dialog box.*

2. Select the Chart Title option and press Enter.

   The word "Title" appears at the top of the chart, enclosed in white squares. White squares indicate a graphical item has been selected but cannot be moved by dragging with the mouse.

3. Press F2, the Edit key, to bring "Title" into the formula bar to be edited.

4. Edit "Title" to become "Global Quality Corporation."

5. Press Enter.

While the title is still selected (showing handles), format its text with a new font and size:

1. Choose the Format Font command.

   The Font dialog box (see fig. 17.14) offers alternatives for text font, size, style, background, and color.

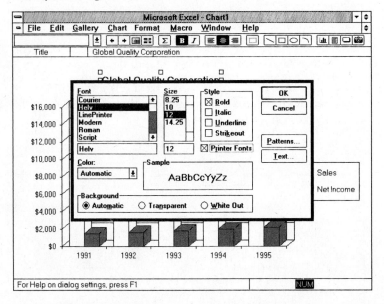

Fig. 17.14. *The Font dialog box is used to change fonts anywhere on the chart.*

2. If you want to print the chart on your printer, select the Printer Fonts check box. If you want to use the Helvetica font, which is shown in the figures but may not print on your printer, deselect the Printer Fonts check box.

3. Choose the Helvetica font with Size 14, Style Bold, Color Automatic, and Background Automatic.

4. Choose OK or press Enter.

The chart will now look like figure 17.15. If you want to remove the handles from a selected object, press Esc.

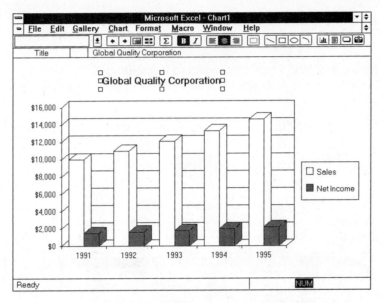

Fig. 17.15. *The attached title stays fixed at the top center of the chart.*

Adding Unattached Text

You can add unattached labels that you can position anywhere. You will find them useful as subtitles and as identifiers for key data. You can also use labels to supplement the chart with information.

1. Before typing unattached text, select a nontext object on the screen so the formula bar is blank. If you select text before you begin to type unattached text, the selected text will be replaced.

 Click on the background or any nontext object.

 Press the up- or down-arrow key to select a nontext chart object.

Pressing the up or down arrow selects different groups of chart objects, such as arrows or columns. Pressing the left or right arrow selects a different object within the same group, such as a specific arrow.

2. Type the words, **New Product**.

3. Press Enter.

   Notice that New Product appears in the middle of the screen, enclosed by black handles. These handles indicate that you can drag the text to a new location.

4. Move the unattached text to the location shown in figure 17.16.

 Click in the middle of the text, drag it, then release.

 Choose the Format Move command. Press the arrow keys to move the text. Use Ctrl+arrow to move in small increments. Press Enter to fix the text's new position.

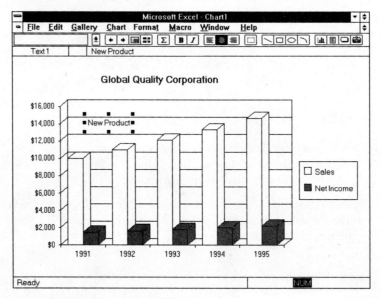

Fig. 17.16. *The unattached text moved into position.*

If grid lines cut the "New Product" text, you can format the background of the box containing the text. Use the Format **P**atterns command, or format the background of the text with the Format **F**ont command.

Adding an Arrow

You can include arrows in a chart to emphasize a specific point on the chart. To add an arrow, follow these steps:

1. Choose the Chart Add Arrow command.

2. Move the arrow to the position shown in figure 17.17, and reduce the arrow's length.

 Drag the middle of the arrow to move the entire arrow. Drag on the black handle at either end of the arrow to resize.

 Choose the Format Move command. Press the arrow keys to move the entire arrow so the tail is on "Product Release." Press Enter. Choose the Format Size command. Press the arrow keys to move the arrowhead into position. Press Enter.

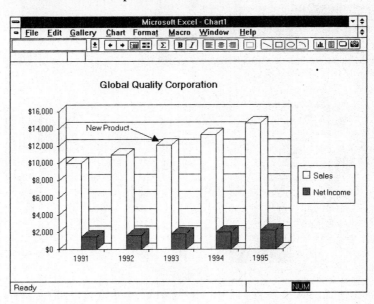

Fig. 17.17. An arrow points from unattached text to a column.

Changing Patterns in a Column

You can change the patterns, colors, or thickness of all lines, arrows, and chart *markers* (bars and columns) in Excel charts. To change the pattern used in the marker for the Sales series of columns, follow these steps:

1. Select the Sales markers (columns). Notice that the first and last markers for Sales will contain white handles when the Sales series is selected.

 Click on any one of the Sales markers.

 Press the up- or down-arrow key until the first and last column for Sales contain a white handle.

2. Choose the Format Patterns command, or double-click on any of the Sales columns. Figure 17.18 displays the border and area shadings and colors.

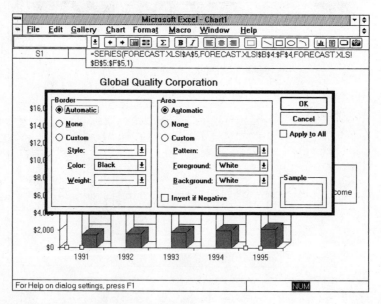

Fig. 17.18. The Format Patterns dialog box.

3. In turn, select the Area Custom Pattern, Foreground, and Back-ground pull-down list boxes and choose a pattern, a foreground color, and a background color. The foreground and background

colors must be different for the pattern to be visible. *Watch the result of your selections in the Sample box.* Figure 17.19 shows the Area Pattern list pulled down.

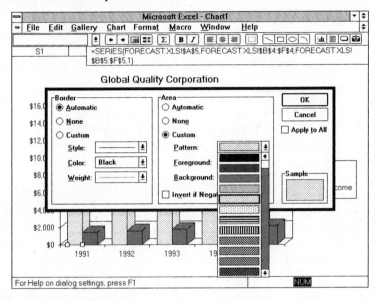

***Fig. 17.19.** Select patterns and colors from the dialog box.*

 Click on the arrow next to a pull-down list; then click on your choice from the list.

 Press Alt and the underlined letter (Alt+*letter*) to display a list, then use the up or down arrow to select from the list. Pull down a list by pressing Alt+down arrow. Press the next Alt+*letter* combination to display the next list.

4. Choose OK or press Enter.

Restoring an Embedded Chart Back to Its Worksheet

If you created an embedded chart, you can restore it back to its position on the worksheet by closing the chart window. With the embedded chart window active, choose the **File Close** command.

Chapter 19 describes how to resize and format embedded charts so that they appear correct on the worksheet. Your embedded chart may require font sizes smaller than the ones used in this Quick Start.

Seeing Worksheet Changes in a Chart

Charts reflect the worksheet data. You can perform different "what if?" calculations in your worksheet and see the results appear immediately in the chart window.

If you are working with a chart embedded in the worksheet, change data in the data-entry cells at the bottom of the worksheet and watch the chart update.

If you created the chart from numbers you typed directly onto a worksheet, change those numbers to see the chart change.

If you are working with a chart that is a separate document, put both the worksheet and chart in windows so you can see them together or switch between them easily.

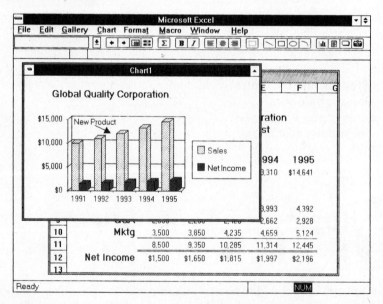

Fig. 17.20. Arrange worksheet and chart windows so you can switch between them easily.

Figure 17.20 shows one way you can position the worksheet and chart windows. You can follow the procedures in Chapter 2, "Operating Windows," to resize and switch between charts and worksheet windows. To position windows, choose the **Windows Arrange All** command.

Saving a Chart

If you created an embedded chart, saving the worksheet saves the chart within it. If you want to save the embedded chart separately, double-click on the chart and save the chart with the **File Save As** command when it is in its own window.

If you created a chart as a separate document, save the worksheet first, then save the chart using the **File Save As** command.

Printing a Chart

To print a chart that is embedded in a worksheet, just print the worksheet. To print a chart that is a separate document, follow these steps:

1. Activate the chart window by pressing Ctrl+F6 or choosing the chart from the Windows menu.

2. Choose the File Print command.

3. Select the Preview check box.

4. Choose OK or press Enter.

5. Change margins in the preview so the chart fills as much of the page as you want.

 Click on the **Margins** button; then drag a margin handle to a new location to reposition the chart.

 Choose the **Setup** button. When the dialog box appears, enter new margins; then choose OK.

6. To print, choose the Print button. To close the preview without printing, choose the Close button.

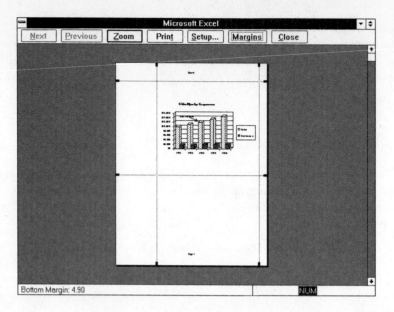

Fig. 17.21. You can adjust margins from within the preview page.

From Here...

If you leave your chart open, you can experiment with it while you skim through the chapters on charting. You might want to explore how you can replace columns and bars with stacked or stretched pictures. For example, you can create a picture chart using pictures, such as stacked cars, to create columns. You also can rotate and zoom 3-D charts. If you are interested in how to draw on a worksheet or include graphical images from other programs or scanners, read Chapter 9, "Drawing and Placing Graphics in Worksheets."

18

Creating Charts

With Excel, you can create charts that are good enough for any boardroom presentation. When you analyze a worksheet or database, you can build any of Excel's 68 preformatted charts with a quick selection of cells and a few keystrokes. Then you can customize the chart with numerous options and overlays. When you print the chart on a laser printer or plotter, the quality rivals that of charts done by graphics art firms.

This chapter explains the details of creating a chart. The next chapter explains the custom formatting features available for Excel charts and how to create picture charts. After finishing these two chapters, you will be able to meet the majority of business charting needs. The final charting chapter explains how to analyze worksheet data by moving chart markers, how to use advanced techniques for manipulating charts, and how to troubleshoot problems in charts.

Figures 18.1 and 18.2 are examples of charts you can create using Excel. When you couple Excel with other Windows software, you can enhance Excel charts even further. Figure 18.2 illustrates how you can paste or embed charts on a worksheet. These charts display and print with the worksheet.

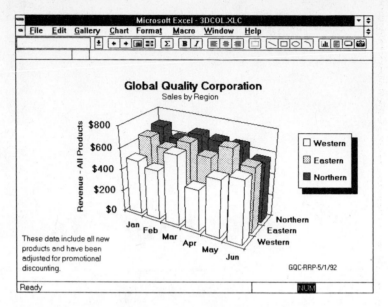

Fig. 18.1. *An example of an Excel chart.*

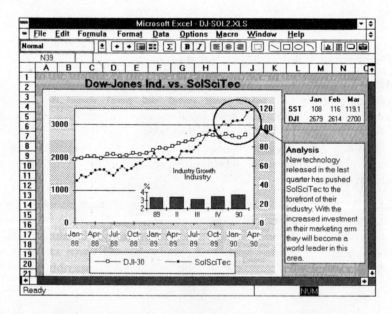

Fig. 18.2. *Embed or paste charts on worksheets for better understanding.*

> **Tip:** *Improving Graphs in 1-2-3 Worksheets with Excel*
> Retrieve the 1-2-3 worksheet and its current and named graphs by
> choosing Excel's **File Open** command, changing the file name wild
> cards from *.XL* to *.WK* so that you can view Lotus files, and
> opening the 1-2-3 worksheet that contains the graphs. When Excel
> automatically translates and loads the 1-2-3 files, the program also
> converts the active 1-2-3 graph and any named graphs into Excel
> charts. Then you can use Excel's charting power to change, enhance,
> or print the chart as you want it. Excel does not translate 1-2-3
> PrintGraph files that end with PIC. Only graphs in the worksheet are
> translated. When you save the translated 1-2-3 worksheet, save it as
> an Excel document with **File Save As** and choose the **Options** button.
> Select the Normal format. 1-2-3 graphs converted to Excel always are
> saved in Excel format; these graphs cannot be saved back as 1-2-3
> charts.

Reviewing the Charting Process

This section gives you an overview of the basic charting process, shows you
a few examples of charts, and explains basic charting terms.

Excel automatically creates charts for you from data you select. The program
uses certain criteria to estimate how you want the data arranged, which data
is used for the *category axis*, and which cells contain labels for chart titles
and legends. In many instances, Excel guesses correctly and automatically
creates a chart. When Excel does not guess correctly, you must create the
chart yourself.

Defining Chart Terms

Excel charts contain many different objects that you can select and modify
individually. Figure 18.3 shows some of these objects, and each object is
described in table 18.1.

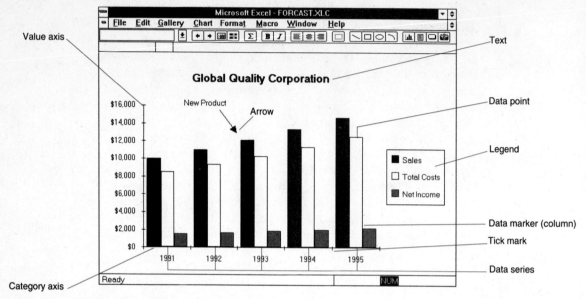

Fig. 18.3. *The parts of a chart.*

Table 18.1
Examining the Parts of an Excel Chart

Object	Description
Arrow	A movable and sizable object that you can format as an arrow or a line. Charts can have multiple arrows.
Axis	The category axis and value axis form the boundaries of a chart and contain the scale against which data plots. The category axis is the horizontal or x-axis and frequently refers to time series. The value axis is the vertical or y-axis against which data points are measured. (Axes for bar charts are reversed. Pie charts have no axes.)
Data point	A single piece of data, such as sales for one year.
Data series	A collection of data points, such as sales for the years from 1988 to 1992. In a line chart, all points in a data series are connected by the same line.

Object	Description
Legend	A guide that explains the symbols, patterns, or colors used to differentiate data series. The name of each data series is used as a legend title.
Marker	An object representing a data point in a chart. Bars, pie wedges, and symbols are examples of markers. All the markers belonging to the same data series appear as the same shape, symbol, and color. In 2-D line, bar, and column charts, Excel can use pictures drawn in Windows graphics programs as markers.
Plot area	The rectangular area bounded by the two axes. This area also exists around a pie chart. A pie chart does not exceed the plot area when wedges are extracted.
Series formula	An external reference formula that tells Excel where to look on a specific worksheet to find the data for a chart. A chart may be linked to multiple worksheets.
Text	Attached text such as titles or axis titles cannot be moved. Unattached text can be moved to any location on the chart and also may be used as text or blank boxes.
Tick mark	A division mark along the category (X) axis.

Tip: *Understanding the Term "Column Chart"*
Excel uses the term "column chart" for charts using vertical columns. Excel's bar charts appear with horizontal bars.

Understanding How To Create a Chart

Usually, creating a chart consists of the basic steps that follow. Each of these steps, along with the specific options you can choose along the way, is described in detail in this or following chapters.

1. Select the worksheet data, including the labels in cells along the short side of the selection that you want to use as legend titles.

2. Choose the File New command, select Chart, and choose OK or press Enter. (Or just press the F11 key.)

3. Choose Gallery, select a chart type, and choose one of the pre-defined styles for that chart type from the gallery.

4. Maximize the chart window so that it is easy to work in and looks more like it will look when printed.

5. Select and then format items on-screen. Make sure that you choose the Printer Fonts check box from the Format Font dialog box so that the chart fonts used match those available in your printer.

6. Add and move custom objects such as titles, floating text, legends, and arrows by choosing them from the Chart menu.

7. Choose the Format Main Chart or Format Overlay command to change the chart type if you need to change the basic type of chart used. (Choosing Gallery after you have customized a chart returns custom features to default settings.)

Creating a Chart Automatically

Excel's design makes creating charts a quick and easy job. Usually you need only to select the data and press F11 to create a chart. (Press Alt+F1 if you don't have an F11 key.) Excel uses three rules to decide how a chart will be created automatically from the selected cells. If the cells you have selected do not meet these rules, you must create your chart manually, as described in "Creating a Chart Manually" in this chapter. Thus, before you take advantage of Excel's automatic chart creation feature, you need to understand the program's three rules.

Understanding Which Charts Can Be Made Automatically

Excel can build a chart for you automatically from selected data and labels in cells if the selected area meets three rules. Excel uses these rules to understand what should be on the horizontal category (X) axis, what should be on the vertical value (Y) axis, and where cell labels used for legend titles are located.

In figures 18.4 and 18.5, the terms *series* and *point* are used. You will see these terms in other examples throughout this chapter. A series is a collection of associated data—the dollar amounts sold of the Rabid Racer bicycle, for example. When charted, a series is a line or bars or columns with the same color. A point is a single instance of data within any of the series. Examples of points in charts are Jan, Feb, Mon, Tue, and so on. A point appears in a chart as a single dot on a line or one column out of a series.

When charted correctly, points appear along the horizontal category (X) axis. The series labels in cells appear as titles in the legend (see figs. 18.4 and 18.5).

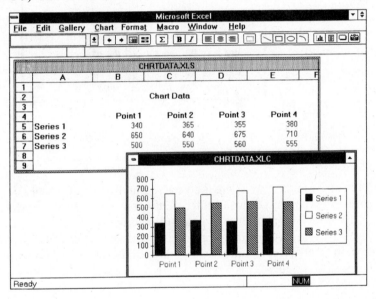

Fig. 18.4. *A selection wider than it is tall, with category labels across the top row.*

First, when Excel examines the data you have selected, the program assumes that the category (X) axis runs along the longest side of the selection. If the selection is wider than it is tall, as in figure 18.4, then Excel assumes that the category labels run across the top row of the selection. If the selection is taller than it is wide, as in figure 18.5, then Excel assumes that the category labels run down the left column of the selection. If the selection is equal in width and length, then Excel assumes that the category (X) axis runs along the longest side.

Second, Excel assumes that labels in cells along the short side of the selection should be used as titles in the legend for each data series. If only one data series exists, Excel uses that label to title the chart. If more than one data series is selected, Excel uses the labels in cells to title the legend.

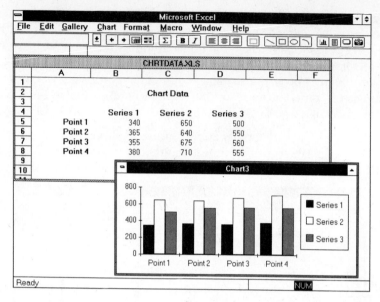

Fig. 18.5. *A selection taller than it is wide, with category labels down the left column.*

Third, if text, a number, or a date is contained in the top left corner of your selection, Excel may get confused as to whether the long side of the selection is category labels or whether it is data and no category labels exist. In this situation, Excel displays the dialog box shown in figure 18.6. This dialog box enables you to tell Excel whether the long side of the data range contains the first data series, category (X) axis labels, or the X values for an XY (scattergram) chart.

Creating the Automatic Chart

To build a chart that has the correct orientation of category data along the longest side, follow these steps:

1. Select the data and labels as shown in figure 18.7.

   Notice that the selected range includes more data points than data series; the range has three series and four data points in each series. Data points are the individual data items, such as revenue for January. A data series in this example is a collection of related data—all the sales for one product, for example.

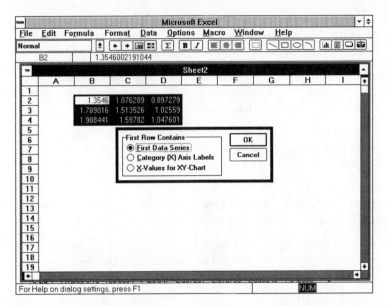

Fig. 18.6. *This dialog box asks you to specify the contents of the long side of the selection.*

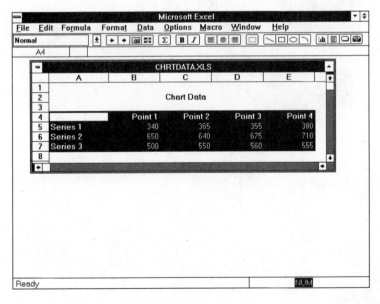

Fig. 18.7. *A worksheet with three data series.*

2. Press F11. (Press Alt +F1 if you don't have an F11 key.) Or choose the File New command, select Chart, and then choose OK or press Enter.

3. If the dialog box shown in figure 18.6 is displayed, select one of the following options to describe the data along the longest side of your selection (your dialog box may be for a column or row).

   Choose First Data Series if the data along the longest side of the selection is a series of data that should be plotted as a line, bar, or column. Because no category labels exist, Excel uses numbers (1, 2, 3,...) for category labels.

   Choose Category (X) Axis Labels if the data along the longest side of the selection should be used as labels for the category (X) axis.

   Choose X-Values for XY-Chart if the data along the longest side of the selection should be used as X data for a scattergram or an XY chart. The chart then is created as an XY or a scattergram type.

   After making your selection in the dialog box, choose OK or press Enter.

Excel plots the data in the default chart type—normally the column chart. Figure 18.8 shows a column chart created with these steps.

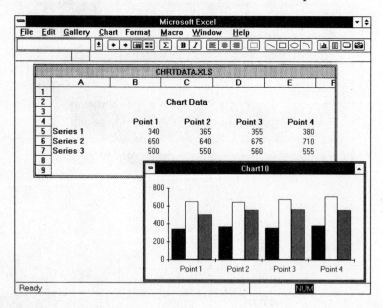

Fig. 18.8. An example of a column chart.

In the chart in figure 18.8, notice that the "Points" (from the top row of the worksheet data) are used as category labels below the category (X) axis. What would happen if a series of data was listed down a column as in figure 18.9? If you select the data shown in figure 18.9 and press F11, the chart in figure 18.10 appears. Notice that the chart still is drawn correctly.

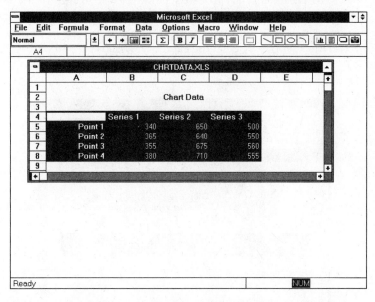

Fig. 18.9. *A worksheet with the data series down a column.*

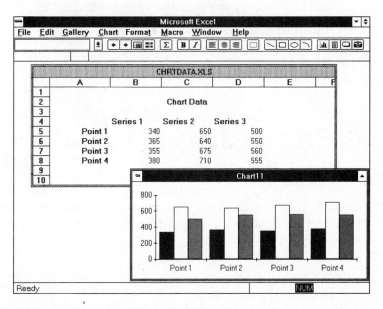

Fig. 18.10. *The chart created from the vertical data series.*

In the preceding two examples, Excel drew the chart as you expected. Excel, however, can "guess" wrong about the vertical or horizontal orientation of data. In this situation, you need to create your chart manually, as described in the next section.

If you want to create a chart from data that is not in adjacent rows or columns, like the selection shown in figure 18.11, then select the rows or columns by using the Ctrl+drag method with the mouse or by pressing Shift+F8 on the keyboard. Select the category (X) axis cells first; then select value (Y) data cells in the same order in which you want the value series to appear on the chart.

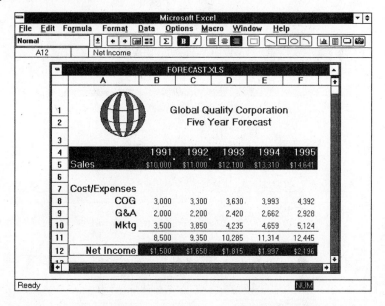

Fig. 18.11. Select nonadjacent cells to chart nonadjacent data.

Creating a Chart Manually

When your chart does not fit the data layout from which Excel can create a chart automatically, you must change the layout of your data or create the chart manually. This section describes how to create charts manually by copying data from the worksheet and pasting the data into a blank chart.

Understanding When To Create Charts Manually

When the data you select for a chart does not meet Excel's three rules for charting, Excel still may create a chart automatically, but it may not be what you expect. A typical symptom indicating that you need to create a chart manually is that your chart's horizontal category (X) axis and vertical value (Y) axis are reversed from what you want (see fig. 18.12). Another symptom occurs when the numbers or dates you want as category (X) axis labels are interpreted as a series of values. This series gets plotted, and the category (X) axis displays a series of integers—1, 2, 3, and so on. Figure 18.13 shows how such a chart looks.

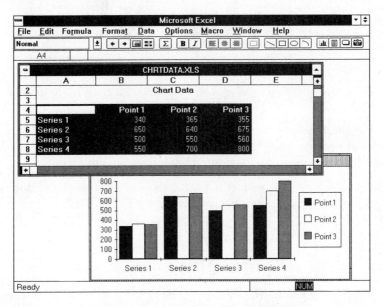

Fig. 18.12. *An automatically created chart with reversed axes.*

First, when the the category (X) axis is along the short side of the selection, create the chart manually. The problem in figure 18.12 occurs because Excel automatically assumes that the category (X) axis always runs along the longest direction of the selection. In this example, the category axis is along the short side of the selection.

Second, when the labels along the long side of the selection should be used in the legend, create the chart manually.

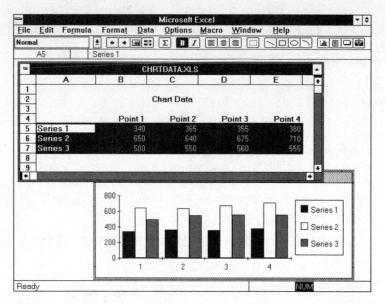

Fig. 18.13. *An example of Excel mistakenly plotting category labels as data.*

Third, if a number or date appears in the top left corner of the selection, Excel may become confused about whether the first row or column is data or labels, so you may have to create the chart manually.

In these situations, or if you try to create an automatic chart and don't get what you want, create your chart manually.

Creating the Manual Chart

To create a chart manually, you copy the selected data from the worksheet and then paste the data into a blank chart document. When you paste into the blank chart, a dialog box asks for the correct orientation of data series and where labels are located.

Suppose, for example, that you have a column chart that has more series than it has data points. In other words, the category (X) axis is along the short side of the selection. Also, suppose that the selection includes series labels that may be needed later for legend titles. If created automatically, the chart appears as shown in figure 18.14. The axes are reversed from what you want.

Do the following steps:

   1. Select the data as shown in figure 18.15.

Notice that the data selected violates rules for automatic charting. The category (X) axis runs along the short side.

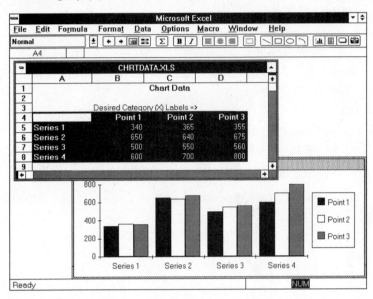

Fig. 18.14. *An automatically created chart with axes reversed.*

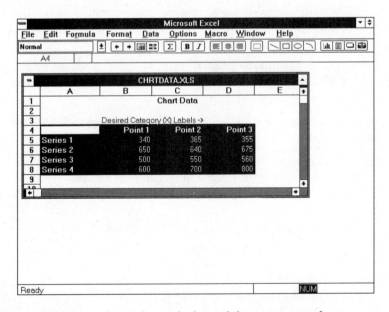

Fig. 18.15. *A layout of data from which Excel does not create the correct chart automatically.*

Later in the procedure, you will need to make selections from a dialog box to orient your chart correctly. Remember the following information about your data:

- Which way are Y values (a plotted line) oriented—across rows or down columns? These are the series.

- If category (X) labels exist, are they across the top row or down the left column?

- If series (legend) labels exist, are they across the top row or down the left column?

3. Choose the Edit Copy command.

4. Press F11. Or choose File New, Chart, and OK.

5. Choose the Edit Paste Special command to display the dialog box shown in figure 18.16.

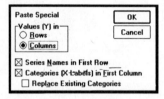

Fig. 18.16. The Paste Special dialog box enables you to change chart orientation and determine which labels are used.

6. Select Values (Y) in Rows if each series of Y data goes across a row or select Values (Y) in Columns if each series of Y data goes down a column.

   (For the example chart in fig. 18.15, you would select Values (Y) in Rows.)

   Excel displays this dialog box with the settings used for automatic charts. If your automatic chart had its category (X) and value (Y) axes reversed, just select the opposite of the displayed Values (Y) in setting. When you select the opposite of the current setting, the check boxes in the lower portion of the dialog box change also.

7. If your selection encloses series names (used in legend titles) for each set of Y values, select Series Names in First Column (Row). (The option text here changes between Column and Row depending on your selection in step 6. For the example, you would select Series Names in First Column.)

8. If your selection encloses category (X) labels, select the Categories (X Labels) in First Row (Column) option. (The option text here changes between Row and Column depending on your selection in step 6. For the example, you would select Categories (X Labels) in First Row.)

9. Choose OK or press Enter.

10. Choose the Gallery menu and select the chart type you want. If you want an XY (scatter) chart, choose the Gallery XY (Scatter) command, select a type of scattergram, and choose OK or press Enter.

Figure 18.17 shows the completed chart and data.

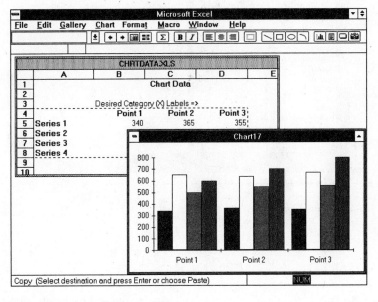

Fig. 18.17. *The manually created chart.*

❖ Creating a Chart on a Worksheet

When you need to present a chart alongside your worksheet or when you need more than one chart per page, create your chart on the worksheet. Charts on a worksheet are displayed with the worksheet and printed with the worksheet.

You can create a chart on a worksheet in two ways. You can embed the chart on the worksheet, as shown in figure 18.18, by using the Chart tool found in the tool bar. Or you can create a chart in its own document window, as the previous sections describe, and then copy and paste the chart onto a worksheet.

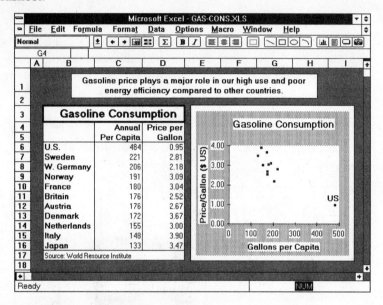

Fig. 18.18. *A chart embedded on a worksheet.*

Using the Chart Tool

To create a chart on a worksheet like the one in figure 18.18, you first must arrange the data in the correct orientation for automatic charting (see "Understanding Which Charts Can Be Made Automatically" in this chapter). Then, if you have a mouse, perform the steps that follow. If you don't have a mouse, you can paste charts on a worksheet by using the technique described in the following section, "Copying a Chart to a Worksheet."

1. Insert rows, columns, or cells to make room for the chart on your worksheet. If your printer does not have small font sizes, you may need a large embedded chart in order for the characters to print correctly.

2. Select the data you want to chart.

3. If necessary, press Ctrl+7 to toggle the tool bar between displayed and hidden. Select the Chart tool from the tool bar.

4. If necessary, scroll the window to where you want the chart.

5. Move the pointer, a cross hair, to where you want a corner of the chart.

6. Drag across the area you want the chart to fill. A dashed line displays the outline of the embedded chart. Release the mouse button to create the chart.

The next chapter describes how to size, move, or expand the embedded chart so that you can format it.

Copying a Chart to a Worksheet

If your data does not meet the requirements for automatic charting or you do not have a mouse, create a chart in its own document window. Then follow these steps to copy the chart into the worksheet:

1. With the chart window active, select the chart by choosing the Chart Select Chart command.

2. Choose the Edit Copy command.

3. Activate the worksheet and select the cell at which you want to place the top left corner of the chart.

4. Choose the Edit Paste command to paste the chart onto the worksheet.

Adding or Deleting Data in Charts

You can add data to your existing charts, regardless of whether they were created automatically or manually. To add data to charts, simply copy the data from the worksheet and paste the data onto the chart. The data you add must include cells for the category (X) axis as well as additional value (Y) data.

If the data you want to add fits the rule that the category (X) axis is along the longest side of the selection, then choose Edit Copy to copy the selection, activate the chart, and choose Edit Paste. The data appears in the chart as a new series.

If the data you want to add does not fit the rules, and its category (X) axis is along the short side of the selection, then choose **Edit Copy** to copy the selection, activate the chart, and choose **Edit Paste Special**. Select from the dialog box in figure 18.16 the options that describe the orientation of the data. Normally, you need to select the opposite option from the one selected in the Values (Y) in group when the box first displays. If the box appears with **R**ows selected, for example, then select **C**olumns. Select the appropriate check boxes and choose OK to paste the data as a new series onto the chart.

Data you paste onto an existing chart does not have to contain the same number of points in its series as the original chart does.

Choosing a Predefined Chart Format

When you build charts, you can use any of the 68 predefined chart formats. The easiest way to create charts is to select the predefined chart closest to the type you want. Then you can customize the predefined chart until it fits your needs. To use a predefined chart, follow these steps:

1. Activate the chart you want to change by clicking the chart window, pressing Ctrl+F6, or choosing the chart's name from the Window menu.

2. Select the Gallery command.

3. From the menu, choose one of these charts:

> Area
> Bar
> Column
> Line
> Pie
> Scatter
> Combination
> 3-D Area
> 3-D Column
> 3-D Line
> 3-D Pie

After you make your choice, you see a dialog box showing the different predefined formats available for that chart. Figure 18.19 shows the gallery of formats available for area charts.

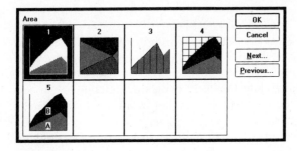

Fig. 18.19. *The gallery of predefined area chart formats.*

4. Select the chart format you want by clicking the square or typing the number.

OR

If the chart you want is not visible, choose the Next or Previous button to go to the next or previous type in the gallery until you reach the chart type you want. Then select a predefined format.

5. Choose OK or press Enter.

Tip: *Selecting the Chart Type*
To select the chart type you want in the Gallery, double-click the box containing the chart. This technique selects the type and chooses OK.

Tip: *Changing Chart Types without Removing Custom Formats*
Choosing a new type from the gallery removes the custom formatting on the chart. Instead of choosing from the gallery to change types on customized charts whose custom formats you want to preserve, use Format Main Chart or Format Overlay.

Reviewing Types of 2-D Charts

Excel's six 2-D chart types plus combination charts give you many options. This section examines how each type of chart generally is used. This information will help you select the correct type of chart to match your data.

✦ 2-D Line Charts

The gallery of line charts is shown in figure 18.20. A *line chart* compares trends over even time or measurement intervals plotted on the category (X) axis. (If your category [X] data points are at uneven intervals, use an XY scatter chart.) Use the line chart in production, sales, or stock market charts to show the trend of revenue or sales over time. In the hi-lo and hi-lo-close charts, numbers 7 and 8 in the gallery, point lines extend from the highest to the lowest value in each category. In the stock market, hi-lo-close charts show the high, low, and closing stock prices on each day.

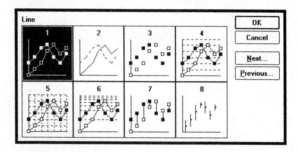

Fig. 18.20. *The gallery of line charts.*

In a 2-D line chart, you can drag a point to a new position, and the worksheet backsolves to meet that result.

2-D Area Charts

The gallery of area charts is shown in figure 18.19. An *area chart* compares the continuous change in volume of series of data. This type of chart adds the data from all the individual series to create the top line that encloses the area, giving the viewer an impression of how different series contribute to the total volume. Use the area chart in sales and production to show how volume changes over time and to emphasize the amount or volume of change. The subjects of area charts may be similar to line charts, such as units shipped per day or the volume of orders over time.

✦ 2-D Bar Charts

The gallery of bar charts is shown in figure 18.21. A *bar chart* is used for comparing distinct (noncontinuous), unrelated items over time. This chart type gives little impression of time but uses horizontal bars to show positive or negative variation from a center point. You can use a bar chart to give a "single point in time" snapshot of budget variance for different items. Bars to the left of center have negative variance, and those to the right have positive variance.

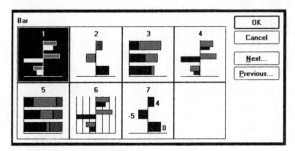

Fig. 18.21. *The gallery of bar charts.*

In 2-D bar charts, you can drag a point to a new position, and the worksheet backsolves to meet that result.

2-D Column Charts

The gallery of column charts is shown in figure 18.22. *Column charts* often compare separate (noncontinuous) items as they vary over time. This chart type uses vertical columns to give the impression of distinct measurements made at different intervals. Column charts frequently are used for comparing different items by placing them side by side. In the Chart Quick Start in Chapter 17, for example, the total sales and total costs are charted in columns by the month.

In a 2-D column chart, you can drag a point to a new position, and the worksheet backsolves to meet that result.

2-D Pie Charts

The gallery of pie charts is shown in figure 18.23. A *pie chart* compares the size of each of the pieces making up a whole unit. Use this type of chart when the parts total 100 percent for a single series of data. Only the first data series in a worksheet selection is plotted. Pie charts work well to show the percentage of mix in products shipped, mix in income sources, or mix in target populations. Wedges in pie charts can be pulled from the pie.

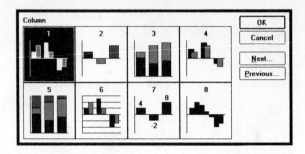

Fig. 18.22. *The gallery of column charts.*

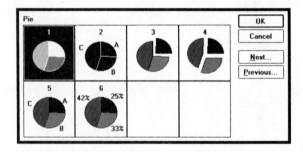

Fig. 18.23. *The gallery of pie charts.*

XY (Scatter) Charts

The gallery of XY (scatter) charts is shown in figure 18.24. A *scattergram* or *XY chart* compares trends over uneven time or measurement intervals plotted on the category (X) axis. (If your category [X] data is at even intervals, use a line chart.) Scatter charts also display patterns from discrete X and Y data measurements. Use scatter charts when you must plot data in which the independent variable is recorded at uneven intervals or the category (X) data points are not specified in even increments. For example, survey data, when plotted with response on the value (Y) axis and age on the category (X) axis, can reveal opinion clusters by age. Much scientific and engineering data is charted with scatter charts.

Combination Charts

The gallery of combination charts is shown in figure 18.25. A *combination chart* lays one chart over another. This type of chart is helpful when you're comparing data of different types or data requiring different axis scales. After a combination chart is created, you can change the type of chart to be used for the main or overlaid chart by using the Format Main Chart or Format Overlay command.

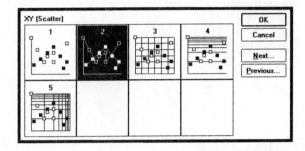

Fig. 18.24. *The gallery of XY (scatter) charts.*

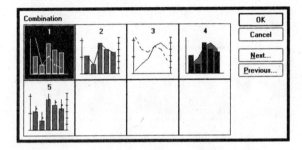

Fig. 18.25. *The gallery of combination charts.*

Reviewing Types of 3-D Charts

Excel's 3-D charts are attractive and work well for presentations or marketing materials. When you are using charts for analytical work, you may find data comparison easier on 2-D charts.

3-D Area Charts

3-D area charts are similar to 2-D area charts, but the 3-D versions enable you to compare series without adding them together. The gallery of 3-D area charts is shown in figure 18.26. Use 3-D area charts for the same types of data as those used in 2-D area charts.

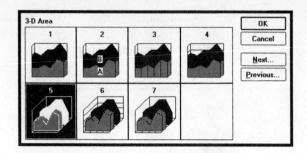

Fig. 18.26. The gallery of 3-D area charts.

3-D Column Charts

You can create 3-D column charts with the columns adjacent to each other or layered into the third dimension. The gallery of 3-D column charts is shown in figure 18.27. Use 3-D column charts for the same types of data as those used in 2-D column charts.

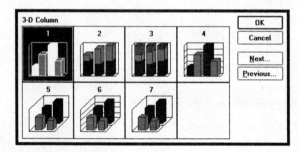

Fig. 18.27. The gallery of 3-D column charts.

3-D Line Charts

3-D line charts also are known as *ribbon charts*. The gallery of 3-D line charts is shown in figure 18.28. Use 3-D line charts for the same types of data as those used in 2-D line charts.

3-D Pie Charts

The gallery of 3-D pie charts is shown in figure 18.29. These types of charts work well for marketing materials or presentations in which an overall impression is required. You can pull the wedges from the pie when you need to discuss the contents of that wedge. Excel can show labels or calculate percentages for wedges. Only the first data series from a selection is charted as a pie.

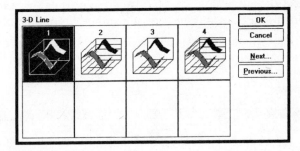

Fig. 18.28. *The gallery of 3-D line charts.*

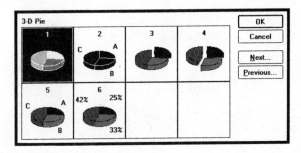

Fig. 18.29. *The gallery of 3-D pie charts.*

Deciding between Line and XY (Scatter) Charts

Line and XY (scatter) charts can be similar in appearance, but they treat data differently when charted. You need to be aware of the differences if you want accurate charts.

You should use a line chart when the category (X) data points are evenly spaced or when the category data points are text and thus spacing does not matter. Category (X) data should be in ascending or descending order. Line charts are most commonly used with business or financial charts in which data is distributed evenly over time or in categories such as Sales, Costs, and so on. Category (X) data, such as time, should be sequential with no data missing.

You should use an XY (scatter) chart when data is intermittent or unevenly spaced. When Excel creates a scatter chart, the program reads the lowest and highest values in the category (X) data and uses these values as the end points for the category (X) axis. The tick marks in between are placed at even intervals between end points. The data then plots along that category (X) axis according to the X data value, not at evenly spaced intervals.

Figure 18.30 shows data plotted in a line chart that should have been plotted in an XY (scatter) chart. The correctly plotted data in an XY (scatter) chart appears in figure 18.31. Notice the difference in the spacing of missed days in the two charts.

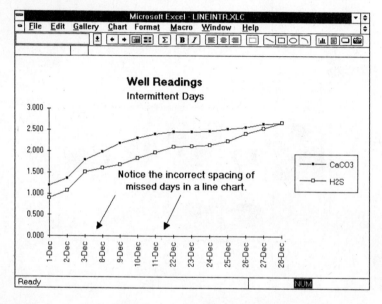

Fig. 18.30. Intermittent data plotted in a line chart, giving an incorrect impression.

Changing the Chart Type

Using the Gallery command to change the chart type in an existing chart removes some of the custom enhancements you may have added and returns the chart to its default colors and patterns. If you need to change the chart type on an existing chart, choose the Format Main Chart command to display the Main Chart dialog box shown in figure 18.32. Select the type of chart you want from the Main Chart Type list. Then select the specific format for that type from the miniature charts shown in the Data View.

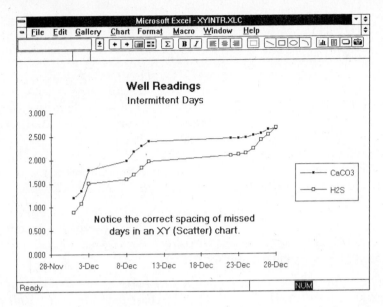

Fig. 18.31. *The same data plotted in an XY (scatter) chart, which shows the correct relationships.*

Remember that combination charts use two different chart types in one chart. To change the type of chart used in either the main or the overlay chart, do not select another type of combination from the **G**allery menu. Doing so removes your custom format. Instead, use the Forma**t** **M**ain Chart or Forma**t** **O**verlay command to change the type of chart used in the main chart or in the overlay chart (see Chapter 19 for more detailed information on using the Forma**t** **M**ain and Forma**t** **O**verlay Chart commands).

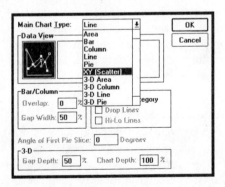

Fig. 18.32. *Use the Main Chart dialog box to change the chart type of existing charts and preserve custom formatting.*

Choosing a Preferred Chart Format

If you deal with the same chart type and format regularly, you may want to designate a specific type and format for Excel to use as the default for new charts you create. Normally, Excel's preferred chart type is column. To change Excel's default chart type and format, activate a chart that has the type and custom formatting you want as the default. Choose the **Gallery Set Preferred** command. Future charts created during this work session will use your preferred format when they first display. If during this work session you want the active chart to revert to the preferred format, choose the **Gallery Preferred** command. When you exit Excel, the preferred format is forgotten.

If you want to use the preferred format at other times, set the preferred chart with the **Gallery Set Preferred** command and then close all files except the preferred chart. Choose the **File Save Workspace** command and give the workspace a memorable name, such as 3DCOLMN.

The next time you want to use the preferred format you saved, open the workspace file (it ends with XLW). The chart that you saved with the workspace file also opens, but you can ignore it. Workspace files remember the chart format settings and **Option Workspace** settings in worksheets.

Saving Charts

Save a chart by activating it and then choosing **File Save As**. If you attempt to close a chart that has not been saved or that has been changed, Excel asks you to confirm whether you want to save the chart.

If you plan to change the name of the worksheets to which a chart is attached, first save the worksheets and then save the chart. Saving in this order stores the correct worksheet name with the saved chart. If you save the chart and then save the worksheet under a new name, the saved chart will not be capable of finding the worksheet.

> **Note:** *Embedded Charts vs. Charts as Separate Documents*
> Embedded charts are saved with worksheets, but charts that are separate documents are not saved with worksheets. Charts in a window are not saved with their associated worksheets. Each chart is separate from the worksheet and must be saved by itself.

Changing Links between Charts and Worksheets

Saving a worksheet with a new name, changing the name of the worksheet file, or deleting the worksheet file causes a problem when the chart looks for the worksheet containing its data.

If one of your charts loses its link to its worksheet, or you need to link a chart to a different worksheet, follow these steps:

1. Open the chart.

2. If you want to establish a link with a different worksheet, open that worksheet.

3. Activate the chart.

4. Choose the File Links command to display the dialog box shown in figure 18.33.

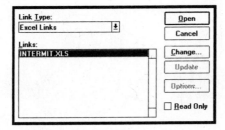

Fig. 18.33. Use the File Links command to open or change source worksheets.

5. Select the worksheet link you want to change in the Links list box.

6. Choose the Change button.

7. Select from the Files list box the name of the worksheet with which you want to establish or reestablish a link. You may need to change directories or disks to find the file. Use the same directory and drive changing techniques you use in the File Open or File Save As dialog box.

8. Choose OK or press Enter.

9. Save the worksheet.

10. Save the chart.

Opening Charts

A chart can be in its own document window or embedded in a worksheet. Either chart can be reformatted.

 To open a chart embedded in a worksheet, double-click the embedded chart. It opens into a chart window. When you are finished formatting the embedded chart, close its document window by choosing **File Close** or by pressing Ctrl+F4. The chart returns to its embedded area.

To open a chart that is its own document, choose the **File Open** command, select the appropriate file name ending with XLC, and choose OK. When you open a chart in its own document window without opening its source worksheet, a dialog box asks whether you want to update the chart (see fig. 18.34). If you choose **Yes**, the chart uses the current values stored in the worksheet file. Choose **No**, however, and the chart uses the values with which it was saved.

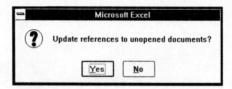

Fig. 18.34. Use this dialog box to choose whether to update a chart that is linked to a worksheet on disk.

To open the worksheets linked to an already open chart, choose the **File Links** command. Select the worksheet file name in the **Links** box and choose the **Open** button.

Printing Charts

Printing charts is similar to printing worksheets. You can print directly from the screen, or you can preview the chart before printing. Previewing a chart gives you a much more accurate view of how the chart will appear when printed. Charts embedded on worksheets print with the worksheets.

 Before you print a chart that is in its own document window, decide how large you want the chart to be on the page. Set the size of the chart on the page by using the **File Page Setup** command to change margins or the **File Print Preview** command with the **Margins** button to change margins. The Page Setup dialog box appears when you choose the **File Page Setup** command, as shown in figure 18.35.

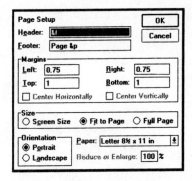

Fig. 18.35. *Use the Page Setup dialog box to set a chart's size.*

> **Tip:** *Making Sure That Your Charts Use Available Fonts*
> If you choose fonts that your printer cannot print, the printed chart
> will not look like it does on-screen. To ensure that your charts use
> fonts available in your printer, choose the Format Font command
> and select the Printer Fonts check box. When the Printer Fonts check
> box is turned on, you can select only fonts that your printer has
> available.

Charts react to print area margins in three ways. If you want the chart to print
in the approximate size shown on-screen, select the Screen Size option in
the Page Setup dialog box. If you want the chart to expand proportionally
until margins are touched, select Fit to Page. The results of a Fit to Page setting
are shown in figure 18.36. If you want the chart to expand in both height and
width until all margins are reached, select Full Page. The same chart in figure
18.36 is shown set at Full Page in figure 18.37.

To print your chart, choose the File Print command and complete the dialog
box. It is the same as the Worksheet Print dialog box described in Chapter
16, "Printing Worksheets."

To preview your chart before printing or to adjust chart size or margins with
the mouse, follow these steps:

1. Choose the File Print Preview command.

2. Examine detail and positioning on the chart by zooming in or out
   on the page. To zoom in, move the pointer (a magnifying glass)
   over an area of interest and click. Click the zoomed page to return
   to expanded view. Choose the Zoom button to zoom and unzoom
   by keyboard.

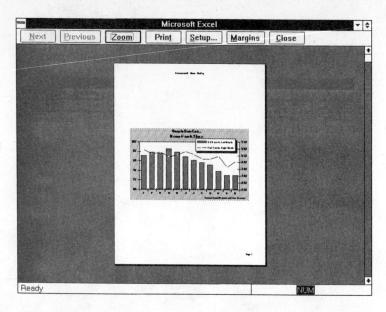

Fig. 18.36. *Use Fit to Page to expand a chart proportionally to the page margins.*

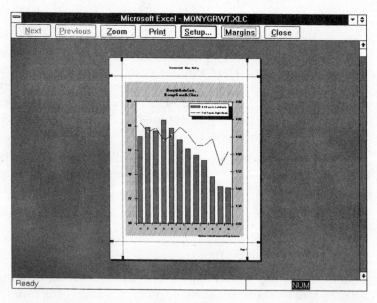

Fig. 18.37. *Use Full Page to expand a chart on all sides to the page margins.*

3. Return to the Page Setup dialog box by selecting the Setup button. If you want the chart to expand in height and width, select the Full Page option from the Page Setup dialog box.

4. Adjust margins and the size of the printing area by clicking the Margins button. Drag the black handles shown in figure 18.37 to change margins and to change the chart size.

5. Choose Print to go to the Print dialog box or Close to return to the chart document.

From Here...

Charts are valuable for communicating information quickly. They enable people to see relationships and detect trends faster than from a table of numbers. If you want to be guided through the building of a chart, go to the preceding chapter, "Chart Quick Start," and work through the short exercise.

In the next chapter, you learn how to add your own custom formatting to charts. If you can select a chart item, then you can change its appearance.

Formatting Charts

I n the previous chapter you learned that you can produce most charts quickly and easily with Excel. In this chapter you will learn how quick and easy it is to apply custom formats to Excel's 68 predefined chart formats.

After you have selected a predefined chart format, you can add lines, arrows, titles, legends, and floating text. You even can create picture charts, in which pictures take the place of columns, bars, or lines.

After you have selected a predefined chart format, you can change the colors, patterns, and borders of chart items; the type and color of the fonts; the position and size of some chart items; and you can add lines, arrows, titles, legends, and floating text. By selecting an axis and then a format command, you can change the scale and the appearance of tick marks and labels. You also can rotate 3-D charts and create picture charts, in which pictures take the place of columns, bars, or lines.

Understanding How To Format Chart Items

After you select one of the predefined chart types, you can customize your chart. You can make it more attractive and easy to understand, while emphasizing the point you want to make.

Customize charts using the same concept you use with worksheets: select, then do! Follow these steps:

1. Select the chart item you want to customize by clicking on it or by pressing an arrow key.

2. Choose the Format command to customize the item, or choose the Chart command to add or delete an item such as a legend, an arrow, or attached text.

3. Select the changes you want to make from the dialog box that appears.

4. Choose OK or press Enter.

All of these steps are explained in detail in the sections that follow.

Selecting Chart Items

Charts are composed of items such as markers, legends, axes, and text. When you customize charts, you add items to the chart, or you format existing items with a new appearance. Before you can format a chart item, you must select it.

To select an item on the chart, click on that item.

To select an item on the chart, first select the class of the item by pressing the up- or down-arrow key. The classes of chart items are as follows:

> Chart background
> Axes
> Legend
> Arrows
> Hi-lo lines
> Markers
> Drop lines
> Plot area
> Gridlines
> Text

Then select the specific item from within its class by pressing the left- or right-arrow key. When you reach the first or last item in a class, the selection skips to items in the adjacent class.

The two largest chart items—the plot area and the chart background—can be selected with the Select Chart or Select Plot Area commands from the Chart menu. You also can click inside the rectangle formed by the axes to select the plot area and outside the rectangle to select the chart.

Selected items have white or black squares, called *handles*, at their corners. Items that are enclosed in white squares cannot be moved or sized (see fig. 19.1). Items that are enclosed in black squares can be moved or sized with the mouse or keyboard (see fig. 19.2).

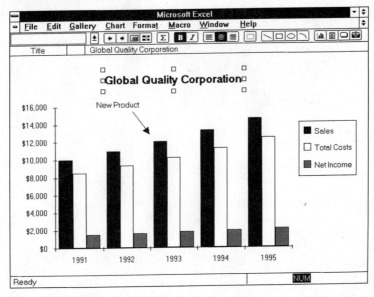

Fig. 19.1. *Items that cannot be moved, such as the title, are enclosed in white handles.*

Moving and Sizing Chart Items

Items that display black handles when selected, such as the legend, arrows, and boxes of text, can be moved anywhere on the screen or resized.

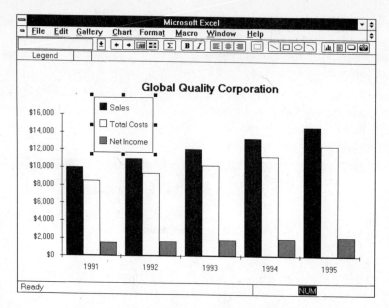

Fig. 19.2. *Items that can be moved, such as the legend, are enclosed in black handles.*

To move an item, follow these steps:

1. Select the item.

2. Move the item.

Drag the item to its new location; then release the mouse button. To move an arrow or text, drag from the center. Do not drag on a black box or you may change the size of the item. A rectangle shows the location of the item as it is moved.

Choose the Format Move command. Press the arrow keys to move the item. Press Enter when the item reaches the correct location. (Note: Before you press Enter, you can return the item to its original location by pressing Esc.)

To resize an item, follow these steps:

1. Select the item.

2. Size the item.

Drag one of the black boxes to expand or contract the item. Drag a handle on the edge of a text box to keep the item's other dimension the same. Drag a handle on the corner of a text box to change two dimensions at once. Words of the text wrap to fit the new box size.

 Choose Format Size, and press the arrow keys to reposition the upper left corner of the box, making it larger or smaller. You may need to move the box after resizing it.

> **Tip: *Moving and Sizing with Precision***
> If the arrow keys provide movements or size changes that are too large, hold down the Ctrl key as you press the arrow keys. Each press of the arrow then makes a significantly smaller change.

Excel automatically resizes pie wedges when you move them. The further you move them from the center, the smaller the wedges and pie become.

Resizing unattached text does not change the size of the text; it changes only the size of the background box surrounding the text.

Adding and Formatting Chart Items

You can add many types of items to Excel charts to make them easier to understand or to pinpoint specific information. This section describes how to add text and text boxes, arrows and lines, legends, and gridlines.

Adding and Formatting Text

Excel charts contain three types of text. First, the chart background includes text along the category (X) and value (Y) or (Z) axes. Excel gets this text from the worksheet data. Excel's second form of text is attached to specific items such as a title, an axis, or a data point. The third form of text is not attached to other items and can be positioned anywhere. Unattached text is useful for more than text labels. It can be used for text comments alongside a chart or to hide portions of the screen.

Attaching Text As Titles or at Data Points

The chart shown in figure 19.3 has text attached to the title position, value (Y) axis position, category (X) axis position, and the third data point marker in the first series.

When you first attach text, temporary text (such as the word "Title") appears at that location surrounded by white selection squares. You can edit this text or type over it to produce the text you want.

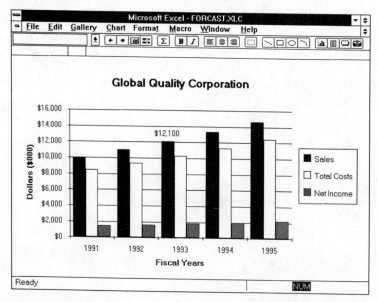

Fig. 19.3. Attached text used for the chart title and axis titles, and as a data point description.

To attach text, follow these steps:

1. If you want to attach text to a data point, select that data point. If you want to attach a text title, begin with step 2.

2. Choose the Chart Attach Text command.

3. Select from the list the location for the attached text:

Item	Location
Chart Title	Centers the temporary text "Title" above the chart.

Item	*Location*
Value Axis	Centers the temporary text "Y" beside the value (Y) axis in 2-D charts or beside the value (Z) axis in 3-D charts.
Category Axis	Centers the temporary text "X" under category (X) axis.
Series (Y) Axis	Centers the temporary text "Y" under the series axis (Y) on 3-D charts.
Series or Data Point	Attaches the value number to the specified data point. On area charts, attaches text to the center of a series.
Overlay Value (Y) Axis	Centers a temporary "Y" beside the overlay's value (Y) axis.
Overlay Category (X) Axis	Centers a temporary "X" under the overlay's category (X) axis.

4. If you chose Series or Data Point, enter the number of the series in Series Number and the number of the data point in Point Number. On area charts, you need only specify the series. If you selected the data point in step 1, these numbers are already entered for you.

   In a column chart, the first series is the column closest to the vertical (Y) axis. In a bar chart, the first series is the bar closest to the horizontal (X) axis.

   A data point is one marker within a series. In a column chart, data points are numbered starting with the one closest to the vertical axis. In a bar chart, data point number one is closest to the horizontal axis.

5. Choose OK or press Enter.

   Temporary text is attached to the point you specified and remains selected. The surrounding white squares indicate that the text is selected, but is not movable.

6. Edit the temporary text as you would a formula: click in the formula bar or press F2, and then edit.

7. Choose OK or press Enter.

You can customize the attached text further by changing its font, size, color, and background using the procedures described in this chapter's "Changing Text Appearance" section.

Deleting Attached Text

To delete attached text, follow these steps:

1. Select the text in the chart. The text will appear in the formula bar.

2. Select the text in the formula bar by dragging across it with the mouse or by pressing F2 and pressing Shift+arrow key.

3. Press the Delete or Backspace key to delete the text from the formula bar.

4. Press Enter or click on the check box.

Add or delete chart axes titles by choosing the Chart Axes command. From the dialog box that appears, select or deselect axes titles that you do or do not want in the chart. Excel reads these chart titles automatically from the chart data on the worksheet.

Adding Unattached Text

In Excel, creating text that can be placed anywhere on a chart is easy and extremely useful. Figure 19.4 illustrates how you can use floating text that is in a comment box to label an arrow.

To add unattached text to a chart follow these steps:

1. Select a nontext item. Make sure that the formula bar is empty.

2. Type the unattached text. Text appears in the formula bar, where you can edit it with normal editing procedures.

3. Press Enter or click on the check box when the text is complete.

The text appears on the chart surrounded by small black squares, which indicate that you can move and size the text background.

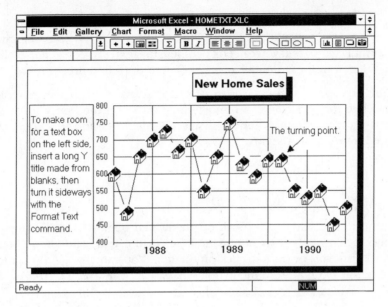

Fig. 19.4. *You can position floating text anywhere.*

 To move unattached text, select the text, then drag the center of the text block to its new location. Size text blocks by selecting the text and dragging one of the black squares to expand or contract the block. Drag a corner to change two dimensions at once. Words within the text box wrap to fit the new block size.

 To move or size unattached text, follow these steps:

1. Select the text by pressing the up- or down-arrow key until any unattached text on-screen is selected.

2. Press the right- or left-arrow key to select the specific unattached text.

3. Choose the Format Move or Format Size command.

4. Move the text or change its size with the arrow keys.

5. Press Enter to fix the text's position or size. (Or, to abandon the process, press Esc.)

As you change the size of the text block, the words wrap to fit the new space.

You also can edit or delete unattached text at any time. Select the text to move it into the formula bar. Press F2 (the Edit key) to move the cursor into the formula bar so that you can edit or delete the text. (To delete unattached text, select it in the formula bar, press Delete, and then press Enter.)

If a text box appears around the unattached text and the box remains when you delete the text, you can remove the box. Select the box, choose the Format Patterns command, and then select Border None and Area None. This procedure removes the box.

Changing Text Appearance

After you have selected a block of unattached text, you can change its appearance with Format commands. Select the text, and then choose Format Patterns; or double-click on the text. You can change the appearance of the text box from the dialog box that appears (see fig. 19.5).

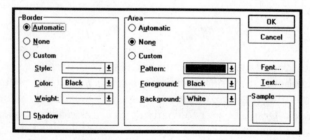

Fig. 19.5. Use the Pattern dialog box to change the appearance of the box surrounding the text.

From within text-formatting dialog boxes, such as that in figure 19.5, you can *tunnel* through to other formatting commands by choosing a tunnel button such as Font or Text.

> **Tip: *Using Fonts That Your Printer Can Print***
> If you choose fonts that are not available in your printer, the printed chart will not look like it does on-screen. When the Printer Fonts check box is on, you can select only fonts that your printer has available.

Selecting Format Font or choosing the Font button displays a dialog box from which you can change the text font, style, and color (see fig. 19.6). You also can change the immediate background behind the text, which is useful for text that overlaps lines or patterns. Select Automatic to use the default background pattern, Transparent to let the area show through, and White Out to remove any pattern behind characters but let the foreground color show.

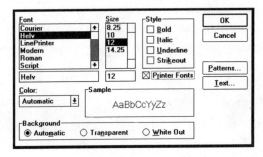

Fig. 19.6. A wide range of fonts and text backgrounds are available.

Tip: *Hiding Selected Parts of a Chart*
The procedure for hiding parts of a chart is similar to the one for creating unattached text. First, create an "empty" unattached text box by making an unattached text box that contains only a single space character. (If the space appears as a blank character in the pattern, select the text and choose Format Font. Next, select Background Transparent so that the character's background is invisible.) While the text block is selected, choose Format Patterns and select a Foreground and Background color that matches the area being covered. Move the box in front of what you want to hide.

 The Format Text command displays a dialog box from which you can change the text alignment and its horizontal or vertical orientation (see fig. 19.7). This feature enables you to rotate value axis titles or text boxes containing explanations.

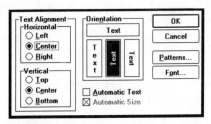

Fig. 19.7. Change text orientation or alignment with the Text dialog box.

Adding and Formatting Legends

Legends explain the markers or symbols used in a chart. Excel creates legends from the labels on the shorter side of the worksheet data series. Figure 19.8 shows an example of a legend. The legend in the figure was customized with border, pattern, and font selections.

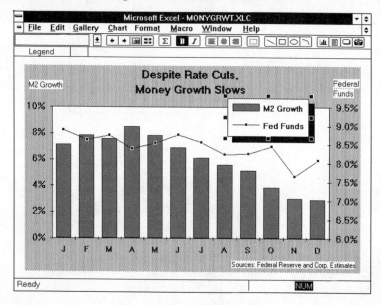

Fig. 19.8. Legends explain which marker represents each data series.

When you want to add a legend, choose Chart Add Legend. The legend appears on the right side of the chart. When a legend exists on a chart, the Add Legend menu item changes to Delete Legend. Use that command to delete a legend.

In the same way that you changed the display characteristics of attached and unattached text, you can change the appearance of a legend. First, select the legend you want to customize (white squares appear at its corners). Then choose Format Font to change the text font, style, size, color, and background. Use Format Patterns to change the border and the foreground and background colors of the area pattern. If you want the legend to blend into the chart so that you do not see the legend's border and background, choose the Invisible option for both Border and Area under Format Patterns.

 You can move the legend to any location on the chart by selecting it, and then dragging it with the mouse. If you move the legend against a chart edge, a black line will appear across the edge to indicate that the chart will move to accommodate the legend. If you move the legend to a central part of the chart, the chart will center in the window. Figure 19.8 shows a legend over a central area of the chart.

From the keyboard, position the legend by selecting it, and then choosing Format Legend. Choose a location from the dialog box shown in figure 19.9.

Fig. 19.9. *Position a legend in a specific location with the Legend dialog box.*

Adding and Formatting Arrows

You really can make your point with an arrow. Use arrows and unattached text to point to spots on a chart that you want to identify or explain. Headless arrows serve as straight lines in charts.

To add an arrow or a straight line to an active chart, follow these steps:

1. Choose the Chart Add Arrow command.

   An arrow that points from the upper left corner to midscreen appears.

2. Move the arrow until its tail is in the correct position.

 Drag the center of the arrow until the arrow is positioned, and then release the mouse button.

 Choose Format Move, and then press the arrow keys to position the arrow. Press Enter.

3. Size the arrow so that it points to the correct spot.

 Drag the black square at the arrow's head so that the head is at the correct spot, and then release the mouse button.

 Choose Format Size, and then press the arrow keys to position the arrow's head. Press Enter.

Move or size arrows in small increments by holding down the Ctrl key as you press an arrow key.

While an arrow is selected, you cannot add another arrow because the Chart Add Arrow command is replaced by Chart Delete Arrow. If you need additional arrows, first select a different item on the chart (then the Add Arrow command appears).

To remove an arrow, select the arrow you want to remove, and then choose the Chart Delete Arrow command.

Move an existing arrow by dragging its middle with the mouse. You can drag on the black square at either end of the arrow to change the arrow's size and position.

Change an arrow's appearance by double-clicking on the arrow, or selecting it and then choosing Format Patterns. The dialog box shown in figure 19.10 enables you to modify the arrow. Notice that the Arrow Head drop-down list boxes enable you to use many different arrowhead shapes and to change an arrow into a line.

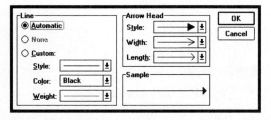

Fig. 19.10. *Use the Arrow Pattern dialog box to make straight lines or to change the line and arrowhead appearance.*

> **Tip: *Making Straight Lines from Arrows without Arrow Heads***
> Change an arrow to a line by selecting the arrow, then choosing Format Patterns. The dialog box shown in figure 19.10 has many alternatives for the color, weight, and style of the arrow's shaft and head. To make a straight line, select the straight line from the Arrow Head Style drop-down list.

Scaling and Customizing an Axis

You can scale and customize the horizontal category (X) axis or the vertical value (Y) and (Z) axes. To change the scale, tick marks, fonts, or colors, follow these steps:

1. Select the category (X) or value (Y) or (Z) axis by clicking on one of the axis lines, or pressing the arrow keys until it is selected. White handles appear at either end of the axis.

2. Select the Format Patterns, Font, or Scale command. A dialog box displays the formatting alternatives.

3. Select the formatting options you want.

4. Choose OK or press Enter.

You can take a shortcut with the mouse. Double-click on the axis you want. When the dialog box for axis patterns appears, select any desired pattern options; then select the Font, Text, or Scale tunnel buttons to make other changes without returning to the Format menu.

Use the dialog box for axis patterns to customize the axis line and the positions of tick marks and labels (see fig. 19.11).

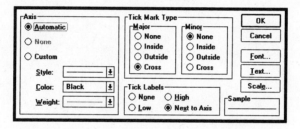

Fig. 19.11. *Use the Axis Pattern dialog box to customize lines, tick marks, and thick labels.*

The dialog box for axis fonts enables you to choose among type styles, sizes, and colors (see fig. 19.12). Be sure to select the Printer Fonts check box to ensure that your chart fonts match those available in your printer.

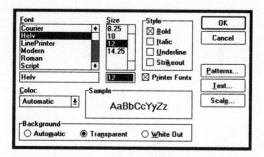

Fig. 19.12. *Use the Font dialog box to change character fonts along an axis.*

The dialog box to change the scale of an axis is different for the category and the value axes. The Category (X) Axis Scale dialog box, shown in figure 19.13, enables you to choose where the vertical axis will cross, how frequently to show category labels, how frequently to display tick marks, and whether to replot categories in reverse (right to left) order.

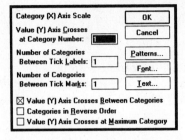

Fig. 19.13. *Use the Category (X) Axis Scale dialog box to control the number of category labels and tick marks.*

> **Tip:** *Making Multiple Changes to Axes Settings*
> When you need to change multiple axes settings, change one setting at a time, see the result, and then change another. Otherwise, the results can become confusing.

In a Scatter (XY) chart, the Category (X) Axis Scale dialog box (see fig. 19.14) enables you to specify the range of the scale and the frequency of major and minor units. Select the Auto check boxes to return the chart to its automatic scaling factors. Change the Minimum and Maximum numbers to change the end points of the category axis. Select the Logarithmic check box to use a log scale on the category axis. If you want to make the value (Y) axis cross at a different point on the category axis, enter the number where you want the value axis to cross in the Crosses At text box.

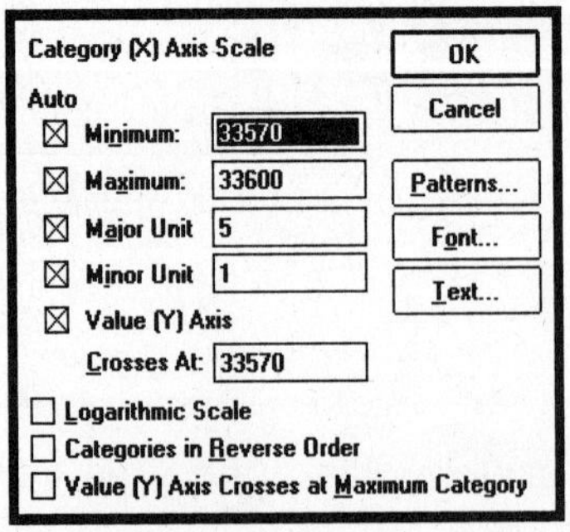

Fig. 19.14. *The Category (X) Axis Scale dialog box on a Scatter (XY) chart.*

In figure 19.14, notice that dates on the category (X) axis appear as numbers in the Minimum and Maximum text boxes. These numbers are the numbers of days from the beginning of the century to the specified starting and ending dates. Because months have an unequal number of days, there is no Major Unit value that produces the same date on the axis for each month. One way to create evenly spaced month/day labels on the category (X) axis is to use a Major Unit value of 29.5. After the axis is scaled, you can correct any month that has a day different from the others by using a floating text label to cover month/day combinations that aren't exact.

The Value (Y) Axis Scale dialog box enables you to choose the units and range of the scale and the point where the category (X) axis crosses (see fig. 19.15). Set the top and bottom limits on the scale by changing the Maximum and Minimum text boxes. Choose the Auto check boxes to return to the default scaling. You also can convert the scale to logarithmic display.

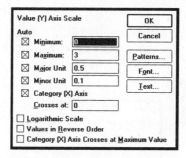

Fig. 19.15. Change scale limits and units on the value (Y) axis.

Tip: *Do not Crowd Tick Marks and Axis Labels*
Some charts, such as charts of stock prices or instrument readings, contain so many data points that the labels and tick marks crowd one another. To reduce this clutter, select the category (X) axis and choose Format Scale. Enter larger numbers into the text boxes for Number of Categories Between Tick Labels and for Number of Categories Between Tick Marks. The larger the numbers you enter, the more distance between labels and between tick marks.

Tip: *Formatting the Appearance of Value (Y) Axis Numbers*
If you want to change the format of the numbers along the value (Y) axis, use the Format Number command to change the format of the first cell in the first value series of data on the worksheet. Use a custom numeric format in that cell if you need a special format in the chart. Scale down values in the chart (for example, showing 1,000,000 as 1,000) by dividing all the worksheet data cells you are charting.

Adding and Formatting Gridlines

Gridlines help viewers compare markers and read values. When you select Chart Gridlines, the Gridlines dialog box (see fig. 19.16) enables you to choose between gridlines that originate from the category (X) axis or from the value (Y) axis. You also can choose whether gridlines originate only from major divisions on the axis or whether they also originate from points between major divisions.

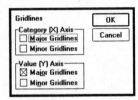

Fig. 19.16. Add gridlines to either axis.

Too many gridlines obscure the chart, making it messy and confusing. In general, do not use gridlines if the chart is for overhead projection. Instead, use gridlines in printed materials where readers need to read charts more precisely.

If you want to display the exact value of a marker, follow these steps:

1. Select the data point on the chart to which you want to attach text.

2. Choose the Chart Attach Text command.

3. Select Series or Data Point, and then choose OK.

In a column chart, for example, this places the numeric value for the column above the column. The value changes and floats as the column changes or moves.

Format the type of line used by gridlines by selecting a vertical or horizontal gridline and choosing the Format Pattern command. Select from the different line styles and weights.

Changing Item Colors, Patterns, and Borders

If an item on a chart can be selected, then you can change its fill color and pattern, border weight and color, and font type and color. You can customize the appearance of anything that shows handles.

Tip: *Creating Custom Colors*
If you want to use colors different from those in the 16 default colors, you can select your own set of 16 colors from a wide range of colors with the Chart Color Palette command. This command and the Options Color Palette for worksheets are described in Chapter 35, "Customizing Excel."

To change the appearance of items, follow these steps:

1. Double-click on the item; or click on it, and then choose the Format Pattern command. A dialog box similar to the one in figure 19.17 will appear.

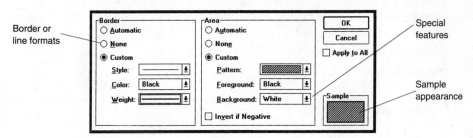

Fig. 19.17. Pattern dialog boxes are similar for all items.

2. Make selections from the dialog box. The lists in pattern boxes are drop-down list boxes, so the list appears only when you select the list box. Click on the down arrow or press Alt+down arrow. Figure 19.18 shows a pattern box with the Area Pattern list dropped down.

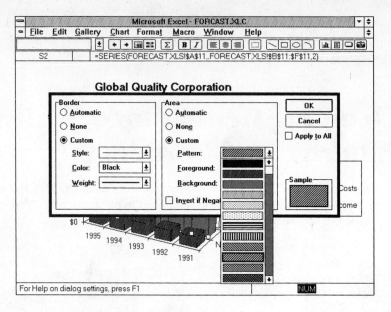

Fig. 19.18. Pattern boxes use pull-down lists.

3. If tunnel buttons such as Font, Text, or Legend appear in the dialog box, choose the button for the format you want to change next.

OR

Choose OK or press Enter.

Pattern dialog boxes are similar for all items. The left group in the dialog box displays formatting alternatives for the border or line in the item. The right group in the box displays formatting alternatives for the fill pattern in the item. A sample of the completed format appears in the lower right corner.

The alternatives in a Pattern dialog box are as follows:

Alternative	Description
Border	
Automatic	Uses default settings.
None	Uses invisible colors.
Custom	
Style	Changes type of line.
Color	Changes color of line. Choose from 16 alternatives.
Weight	Changes the thickness of line.

Alternative	Description
Area	
Automatic	Uses default settings.
None	Uses invisible colors.
Custom	
Pattern	Uses a pattern or shade created from a fore-ground and background pattern.
Foreground	Changes the top color in the pattern. Choose from 16 alternatives.
Background	Changes the bottom color in the pattern. Choose from 16 alternatives.
Tunnel Buttons	Buttons such as Text, Font, or Scale enable you to go to another format command from the pattern box without returning to the Chart menu.
Sample	The Sample box shows you how your selections will appear.

Pattern boxes for items such as arrows include different types of lines and arrowhead shapes.

The largest areas in a chart are the chart background and the plot area. The chart background includes the entire chart; the plot area includes only the area within the axes. You can change the colors, patterns, and boundaries of both areas. Click on the background area, or choose Chart Select Chart or Chart Select Plot Area before choosing the format command. Figure 19.19 shows a chart with patterns for the chart background and plot area, and with the text for the axes in bold.

Transferring Chart Formats

After you create a chart, you can apply formatting from another chart. To transfer a chart format, use the Paste Special command to copy the formatting from one chart and paste it onto another chart. Follow these steps:

1. Activate the chart that has the format you want to copy.

2. Choose the Chart Select Chart command.

3. Choose the **Edit Copy** command.

4. Activate the chart you want to format.

5. Choose **Edit Paste Special**.

6. Select **Formats** from the Paste dialog box.

7. Choose **OK** or press **Enter**.

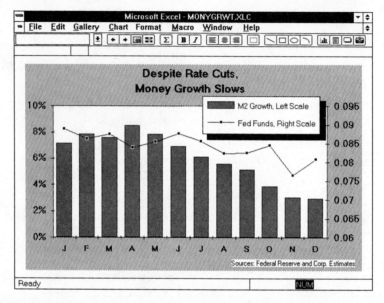

Fig. 19.19. *Format the chart and plot area for a standout appearance.*

Clearing Chart Formats or Contents

You do not have to create a new chart from the worksheet when you want to change all the data or formats. Instead, simply clear the unwanted data or formats from the chart by using these steps:

1. Choose the **Chart Select Chart** command.

2. Choose the **Edit Clear** command, or press **Delete**.

3. Select what you want to clear.

Button	Action
All	Clears the chart.
Formats	Clears the formats, but retains the data series.
Formulas	Clears the data series, but retains the formats.

4. Choose OK or press Enter.

Changing and Modifying Chart Types

If you want to change the type of an existing chart and retain the custom colors and other formatting, choose the Format Main Chart command. Then select the new chart type from the Format Main Chart dialog box (see fig. 19.20). For example, if you have created a customized column chart and you want to switch to a bar chart, select Bar from the Main Chart Type pull-down list. Your custom formatting is preserved if it is appropriate for the new type of chart. Choosing the Gallery Bar command erases all your custom formatting.

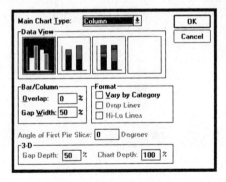

Fig. 19.20. Use the Format Main Chart dialog box to change the type of an existing chart and preserve custom formatting.

You have many options in the Format Main Chart dialog box. When you select the type of chart, different combinations of options become available. Unavailable options are dimmed. Some of these options are shown in table 19.1.

Table 19.1
Main Chart Options

Option	Effect
Bar/Column Overlap	Overlaps bars or columns by a percentage of their width when you enter a positive number. Creates a gap between bars or columns when you enter a negative number.
Bar/Column Gap Width	Creates a gap between groups of bars or columns when you enter a positive number (the percentage of bar or column width).
Format Vary by Category	When the chart includes only one data series, displays each data point in a different color.
Drop Lines	In line or area charts, drops a line from each marker to the category (X) axis.
Hi-Lo Lines	Extends lines from the highest to the lowest value in each category. Use this option with 2-D line charts.
Angle of First Pie Slice	Specifies the angle in degrees clockwise from vertical to the start of the first pie wedge.
3-D Graph Depth	Specifies the distance, measured as a percentage of column width, between series in a 3-D chart.
Chart Depth	Specifies the depth, measured as a percentage of chart width, of a 3-D chart. Use 30 to make a chart 30% as deep as it is wide.

Rotating 3-D Charts

3-D charts may display data in such a way that some series are difficult to see. In figure 19.21, for example, the first series blocks the second series from view. To avoid this problem, you can rotate and adjust 3-D charts using the Format 3-D View command. After rotation, the same 3-D chart appears as shown in figure 19.22.

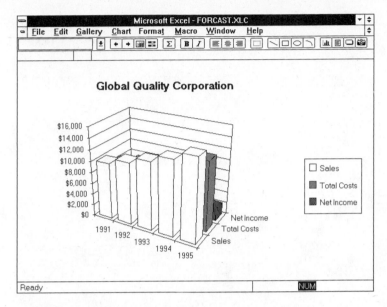

Fig. 19.21. *Some perspectives of a 3-D chart block data series from view.*

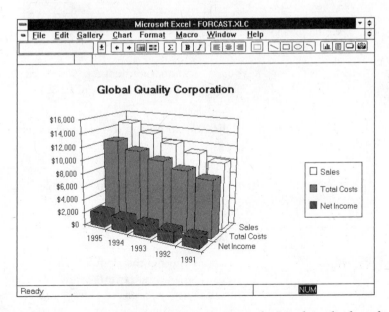

Fig. 19.22. *Rotating and adjusting the perspective of a 3-D chart displays the series from a better angle.*

When you choose the Format 3-D command, the dialog box in figure 19.23 appears. Selections in this dialog box change the angle and perspective from which the 3-D chart is drawn.

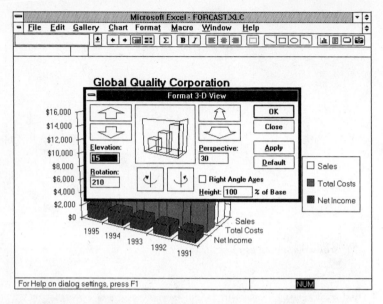

Fig. 19.23. *Rotate the wire-framed chart to rotate your 3-D chart.*

You can use a mouse or a keyboard to rotate or adjust the viewpoint shown in the 3-D View dialog box. Using the mouse is faster and easier.

 Click on the appropriate directional button to rotate or adjust the viewpoint.

 Select the textbox, then type in a number within the range. The options are as follows:

Option	Effect on Chart
Elevation	Changes the height from which you see the chart. Use an angle from –90 to +90 degrees for all charts except pie charts. Use an angle from 10 to 80 degrees for pie charts.
Rotation	Rotates the chart around the vertical (Z) axis. The range is from 0 to 360 degrees.

Option	Effect on Chart
Perspective	Controls the vanishing point or the sense of depth in the chart. Use a number between 0 and 100 to specify the ratio of the front of the chart to its back.
Height _ % of Base	Controls the height of the vertical (Z) axis as a percentage of the chart width (X) axis. Enter a number between 5 and 500.
Right Angle Axes	Freezes axis angles at 90 degrees. Perspective is turned off.

When the wire-frame chart has the orientation you want, choose OK. By choosing the **A**pply button, you can keep the dialog box on-screen and apply the current settings to the chart so that you can see how they look. Choose the **D**efault button to return all dialog box settings to default values.

Creating Picture Charts

Excel charts can use pictures as markers in place of columns, bars, or lines. This feature enables you to make picture charts that grab the eye, and then communicate the information. Figure 19.24 shows how you can use pictures in column charts. Figure 19.25 shows a drawing created in Windows Paintbrush used as a replacement for line markers.

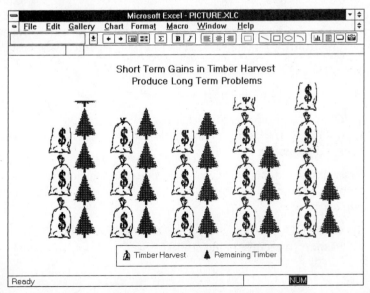

Fig. 19.24. You can use pictures to replace columns or bars.

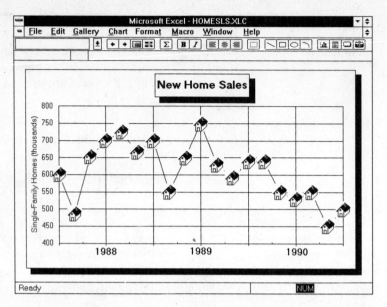

Fig. 19.25. You can use custom pictures to replace the markers on lines.

To replace columns, bars, or lines, you can use pictures from any Windows graphics or drawing program that can copy graphics to the clipboard in the Windows Metafile format. Examples of such programs are Windows Paintbrush (the free program that comes with Windows), CorelDRAW!, and Micrografx Designer. You also can use Excel's worksheet drawing tools to create pictures to copy and paste into charts. Chapter 9, "Drawing and Placing Graphics in Worksheets," describes how to draw on the worksheet.

You can store frequently used pictures in a worksheet that you use as a picture scrapbook. Chapter 9 explains how to paste pictures into worksheets. Copy pictures from the worksheet by selecting them and choosing Edit Copy.

To create a picture chart, follow these steps:

1. Activate your column, bar, or line chart in Excel.

2. Switch to the Windows graphics program in which you want to draw. Press Ctrl+Esc to see the Task List, or press Alt+Tab to cycle between programs.

3. Draw or open the picture you want to use in your chart. (Some graphics programs come with extensive libraries of predrawn art, or *clip art*.)

4. Select the picture, then choose the Edit Copy command. Figure 19.26 shows a picture being copied from Windows Paintbrush.

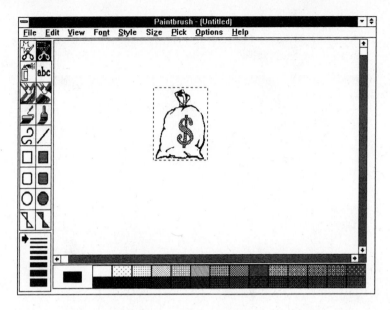

Fig. 19.26. *Copy the picture from a Windows program such as Paintbrush.*

5. Switch back to Excel. Press Ctrl+Esc to see the Task List, or press
   Alt+Tab to cycle between programs.

6. Select the column, bar, or line series (as shown in figure 19.27) that
   you want to contain the picture.

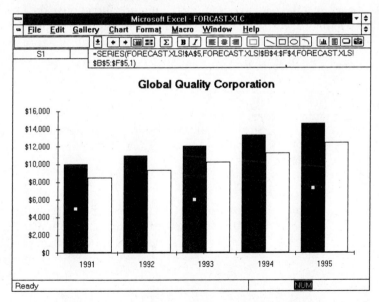

Fig. 19.27. *Select the series that you want to represent with the picture.*

7. Choose the **Edit Paste** command. The picture replaces the series markers, as shown in figure 19.28. The picture may stretch to fit. You can adjust this later.

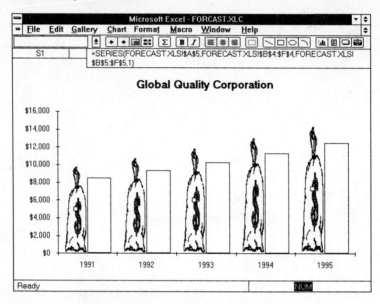

Fig. 19.28. The pasted picture replaces the series markers.

If you want to stretch, stack, or stack and scale the pictures in column or bar charts, then select the series containing the picture and choose the Format Patterns command. From the dialog box shown in figure 19.29, select one of the picture-formatting options. A stacked picture appears in figure 19.30.

The options in the Picture Patterns dialog box are as follows:

Option	Effect
Stretch	Stretches the picture to match the value for each data point.
Stack	Stacks the picture in its original proportions to match the value for each data point.
Stack and Scale	Scales the picture's height to equal the value in the Units/Picture text box, and then stacks the picture to match the value for each data point.

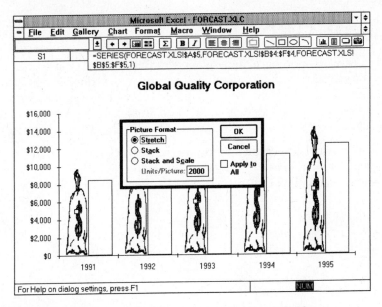

Fig. 19.29. *Select how you want the picture to represent the data.*

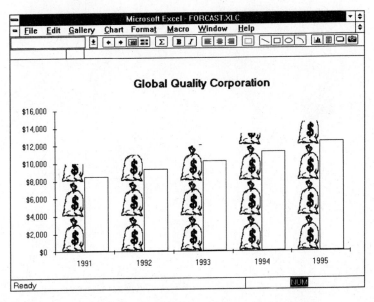

Fig. 19.30. *Stack or scale the picture for a different representation.*

From Here...

You can create impressive, high-quality graphics by using a laser printer or color plotter and the chart formatting techniques described in this chapter. When you reach the point where you need to create overlaid charts, link multiple worksheets to a single chart, or do more complex charting, be sure to read Chapter 20, "Building Complex Charts."

If you have a question or run into trouble as you work with charts, remember that you can get help by choosing topics from the Help menu or by pressing F1 when a dialog box is displayed.

20

Building Complex Charts

W hen you have a situation that requires special charts or you need to go beyond the fundamentals in modifying and formatting charts, the techniques in this chapter will help you. Here, you learn how to solve for worksheet solutions by moving lines, bars, or columns on a chart; link one chart to multiple worksheets; edit the series formulas to control the order of chart markers and the text used in legends; and overlap two charts. This chapter also describes how to prevent a chart from being scrambled when the worksheet is rearranged. Finally, it includes tips for troubleshooting common problems with charts.

Analyzing Worksheets with Charts

In addition to enlivening presentations, charts make excellent analytical tools. Excel charts are linked to one or more worksheets, so playing "what if" games on the worksheets updates the charts that are linked to them. Updating can help to reveal profit-loss crossover points, to forecast inventory quantities, or to quantify trends for different scenarios.

Excel also has the powerful capability to find a worksheet value to match changes in the chart. If you drag a bar, column, or line to a new location in the chart, Excel seeks a new worksheet input that produces the result shown in the chart. This feature provides a quick and easy way to make a visual estimate of a situation and have Excel determine the numbers that correspond to the "visual feel."

Using Charts for "What If"

With Excel, you can make changes to your worksheet and watch the chart immediately reflect those changes. This capability is valuable for performing "what if" types of analysis. Because you can see the effects of your worksheet changes, you can determine emerging trends, crossover points between profit and loss, and mistakes made during data entry.

As figure 20.1 illustrates, you can position worksheet and chart windows so that all windows are visible. As you change a variable in the worksheet created during Chapter 3's Quick Start, the Sales vs. Costs and the Itemized Cost charts reflect the changes immediately. To arrange the windows, use **Window** commands or drag the sides and title bars. (Read Chapter 15, "Using Excel's Add-In Macros," to learn how to add more window-arranging commands to the **Window** menu.)

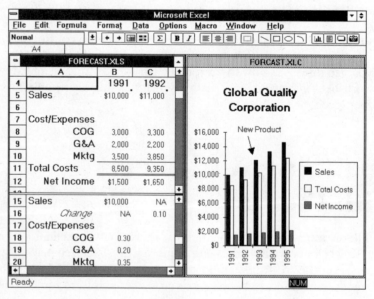

Fig. 20.1. Arrange the windows so that you can watch the changes in the chart as you do "what if" analysis in the worksheet.

Moving Columns, Bars, or Lines To Change Worksheet Values

Excel enables you to move column, bar, or line markers on a chart and cause the corresponding data in the worksheet to change. If the data is not a value, but a formula, then Excel executes the Formula Goal Seek command to find the input value that makes the worksheet correspond to the chart.

To change values on the worksheet from the chart, follow these steps:

1. Open both the worksheet and chart. Activate the chart. The chart must be a two-dimensional column, bar, or line chart.

2. Hold down the Ctrl key and click on the column, bar, or line marker you want to change. A black handle appears on the marker as shown in figure 20.2.

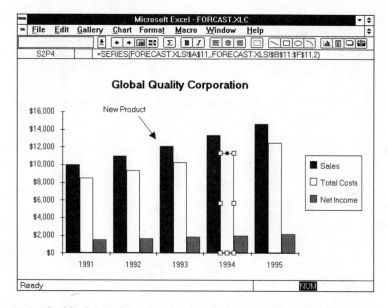

Fig. 20.2. *The black handle indicates that this column can be dragged to a new height.*

3. Drag the black handle to the location you want. Watch the Reference Area to the left of the formula bar to see the changing numeric value for the marker.

4. Release the mouse when the marker is at the location you want.

If the column, line, or bar references a number on the worksheet, that number changes. If the column, line, or bar references the result of a formula, Excel activates the Formula Goal Seek command. This command activates the worksheet for the marker and displays the Goal Seek dialog box, as shown in figure 20.3.

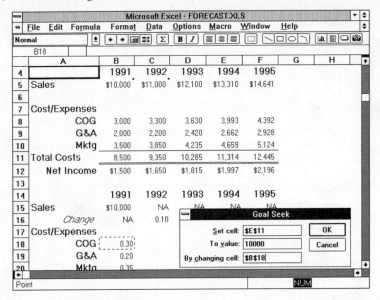

Fig. 20.3. The Goal Seek dialog box asks which worksheet cell should be changed to achieve the result in the chart.

To operate Goal Seek, follow these steps:

1. In the By changing cell text box, select the cell (or type the cell reference of the cell) that you want to change to produce the result in the chart.

2. Choose OK or press Enter.

   Goal Seek iterates through input values to find the value that produces the result in the chart. Then, the Goal Seek dialog box displays the solution.

3. Choose OK or press Enter to enter the new input value in the worksheet, or choose Cancel to return to the original worksheet.

When Goal Seek is complete, Excel reactivates the chart.

The Goal Seek command is described in detail in Chapter 14, "Using the Solver."

Understanding the Series Formula

When you create a chart or add a data series to a chart, Excel links the chart to a data series on a worksheet. Excel creates this link with a series formula.

A series formula tells the chart where the worksheet is located on the disk or network, which worksheet to use, and which cells of that worksheet contain the data to be charted. Each data series has a series formula. As figure 20.4 shows, you can display the series formula in the formula bar by selecting one of the markers in the data series. The formula in figure 20.4 belongs to the first data series (shown with white squares inside the markers). The worksheet corresponding to the chart appears behind the chart.

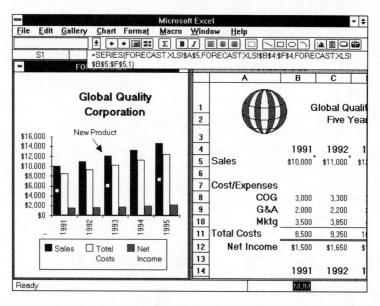

Fig. 20.4. Each set of markers in a chart has a series formula referring to data on a worksheet.

Tip: *Adding, Editing, or Deleting Data Series*
Although you can edit or delete the series formula by hand, it is much easier to use the **Chart Edit Series** command. This command is described under appropriate topics throughout this chapter.

When you examine the worksheet and the related chart, you can see how the series formula works. All series formulas are constructed on this pattern:

=SERIES("*series_name*",*worksheet_name!category_reference*, *worksheet_name!values_reference*,*marker_order_number*)

The *series_name* is either text (in quotation marks) or an external reference to the cell that contains the text label for the data series. An external reference to a text label in a cell is not enclosed in quotation marks. The *series_name* is used in the legend.

The *worksheet_name!category_reference* is an absolute external reference to the worksheet cells that contain the labels for the category (X) axis. The *worksheet_name!values_reference* specifies which worksheet cells contain the (Y) values for the data series.

The *marker_order_number* dictates the order of the data series. In the example in figure 20.4, the *marker_order_number* is 1; therefore, the columns for this data series appear to the left of the other columns. A *marker_order_number* of 2 would make the markers for this data series the second series of markers on the chart.

Editing a Series of Data

 You can add data series to a chart or change existing data series with the **Edit Paste**, **Edit Paste Special**, or **Chart Edit Series** commands. Each has advantages in certain situations. With the Edit Series dialog box you also can link data series from multiple worksheets to a single chart.

Adding a Data Series to a Chart

You can add a data series to an existing chart by copying data from the source worksheet and pasting it into the chart. The selected data must meet the restrictions described in the previous chapters for height and width orientation. For example, you can create a chart made from the Quick Start worksheet by selecting A4:F5 and pressing F11. This chart is shown in figure 20.5.

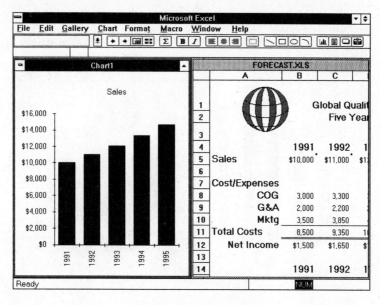

Fig. 20.5. *A simple chart created from one data series.*

To add the nonadjacent data series A12:F12 to the existing chart, follow these steps:

1. Select the data in cells A12:F12 (as indicated on the worksheet in figure 20.6).

2. Choose the **E**dit **C**opy command.

3. Activate the chart and select the **E**dit **P**aste command.

This procedure pastes the data into the chart as shown in figure 20.6.

If the category (X) axis of the data you are pasting into the chart is not the longer axis, then choose the **E**dit Paste **S**pecial command. Select the opposite of the current Row or Column selection, and choose OK.

If you are adding additional data to a Scatter (XY) chart, then select both the new X and Y data. The X and Y data must be in adjacent rows or columns, and the X data must be in the top row or the left column. Paste the X and Y data into the chart with the Edit Paste Special command. Be sure to select the Category (X) Labels in First Row (Column) check box.

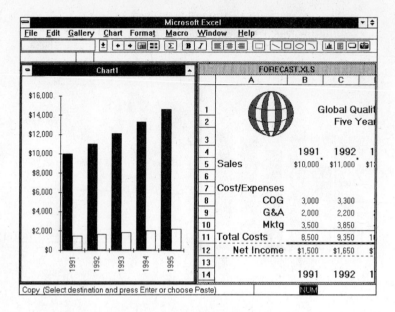

Fig. 20.6. *Additional data series can be pasted into the chart.*

Adding Data from Multiple Worksheets

Once you know how to paste a data series into a chart, you just as easily can create a chart with data from multiple worksheets. For example, you can create a chart that reflects data from four different quarters, even though each quarter is on a different worksheet.

You combine data from multiple worksheets by copying the data from each worksheet and pasting it into the chart. Follow these steps:

1. Create a chart from the worksheet data you want as the first series in the chart.

2. Activate a different worksheet.

3. Select a data series with the same number of data points as contained in the chart. Do not include labels. (If you are adding to a Scatter (XY) chart, the number of data points does not need to be the same, but you must include both X and Y data as described earlier.)

4. Choose the Edit Copy command.

5. Activate the chart.

6. Choose the Edit Paste command. (If you are adding to a Scatter (XY) chart, use the Edit Paste Special command as described previously.)

Deleting a Data Series

When you need to delete a line, area, or series of columns or bars, use the Chart Edit Series command. To delete a series, follow these steps:

1. Select the series you want to delete.

2. Choose the Chart Edit Series command. The Edit Series dialog box appears, as shown in figure 20.7.

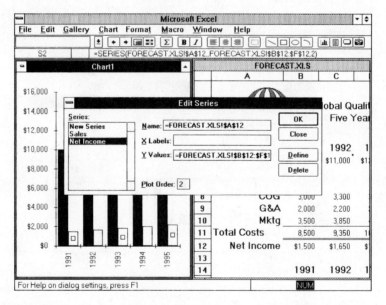

Fig. 20.7. Use the Edit Series dialog box to change or delete chart series.

3. Make sure that the series you want to delete is selected in the Series list, and then choose the Delete button.

4. Make any additional deletions, additions, or edits, and then choose OK. Note that Close does not undo the deletion of a series.

Editing a Data Series

When you extend a series of data on a worksheet, you will probably want to extend the related chart as well. To include the new data on an existing chart, use the **Chart Edit Series** command to extend the range of the data series in the series formula. For example, to add a new year for Sales to the existing chart from the FORCAST.XLS worksheet, follow these steps:

1. Open the worksheet and the chart. Activate the chart.

2. Select the markers (data series) you want to edit. (In this example, select the Sales series.)

3. Choose the **Chart Edit Series** command to display the Edit Series dialog box shown in figure 20.8.

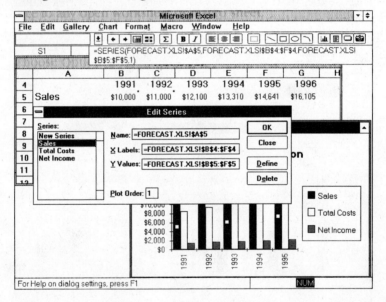

Fig. 20.8. The Edit Series dialog box before the external references are extended to include more cells.

4. Select the **N**ame, **X** Labels, or **Y** Values text boxes.

The **N**ame text box references the cell from which the legend name is taken. You can type in a legend name as a text formula. Consider this example:

="Gross Revenue"

The X Labels text box contains the external reference formula for data used to create the category (X) axis. The Y Values text box contains the external reference formula for the value represented by chart markers.

5. Manually edit the external reference formula in each text box, or select the new data range by dragging across it with the mouse.

Manually edit the reference if it needs only minor changes. For significant changes, such as referencing a distant worksheet range or using a data series from a different worksheet, activate the worksheet and scroll to the data area. The Edit Series dialog box remains on top, but can be moved if necessary. Select the text in the Name, X Label, or Y Label text box you want to change. Select the cells you want to reference by the Name, X Label, or Y Value text box.

Notice that in figure 20.8 the X labels and Y values external references do not extend to column G and do not include the added numbers for 1996. Figure 20.9 shows the updated Edit Series dialog box with the X and Y data ranges extended to include an additional year's data.

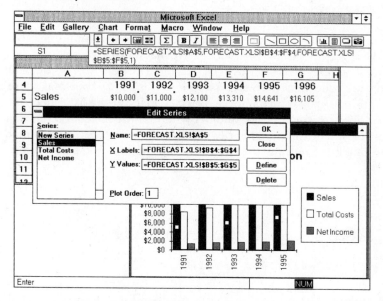

Fig. 20.9. *The updated Edit Series dialog box shows extended external reference formulas that include the additional data locations.*

6. Repeat steps 4 and 5 to edit all text boxes to include the correct locations of other data. Choose the Define button to accept your changes and keep the dialog box open.

7. Choose OK after you have made all changes.

This procedure is necessary because the series formula uses external cell references that are not updated automatically when you change the worksheet. When you move cells, or insert or delete rows and columns, the series formula does not reflect the changes. The chart then may be linked to cells that no longer contain data or that contain the wrong data.

You can avoid this problem completely by naming the cell ranges in worksheets that are linked to charts. Use Formula Define Name or Formula Create Names to name the ranges. Use the Chart Edit Series command to replace the cell references in the series formulas with the range names for those cells. Then the chart will include the named area even if that area moves. If data is added to the end of a data series in the worksheet, redefine the name in the worksheet to include the additional cells.

Reordering Series

The series formula also controls the order of bars or columns in a chart. In their series formulas, the data series have marker order numbers from 1 to the total number of data series in the chart. To reorder the bars or columns, follow the same procedure as you would to edit a data series. Make sure that the data series you want to move is selected in the Series list. Select the Plot Order text box, and type the number you want the selected series to have. Choose OK. The Chart Edit Series command renumbers the other markers accordingly and redraws the chart with the columns and bars in their new order.

Linking Chart Text to Worksheet Cells

The ability to link worksheet text or numbers to attached or unattached (free-floating) chart text is very helpful. This technique can be used to update chart or axis titles when titles on the worksheet change, or to link comments in a worksheet cell to a chart. Figure 20.10 shows a text box that displays the contents of a worksheet cell.

When you edit the worksheet comments, the change appears in the chart text. You even can link a worksheet cell's contents to the data series numbers that are attached to the top of columns or bars. Then the worksheet cell's contents also appear at the top of the column or end of the bar.

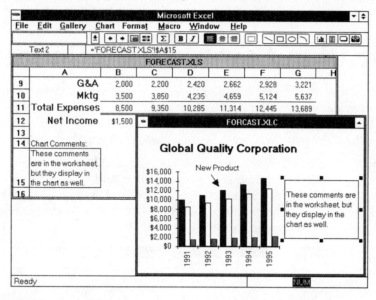

Fig. 20.10. *You can link the contents of a worksheet cell to a text box in the chart.*

To link a worksheet cell's contents to attached or unattached text in a chart, follow these steps:

1. Open the worksheet and the chart. Activate the chart.

2. Create attached text such as titles or data series numbers if you want the cell contents to appear at these points.

3. If you are creating unattached text linked to a worksheet cell, type an equal (=) sign. If you want a cell's contents to appear at an attached text location, select the attached text and replace it with an equal (=) sign.

4. Activate the worksheet by clicking on it (if you can see it), or choose the worksheet from the Window menu.

5. Select the cell containing the text you want to link. You also can select cells containing numbers.

6. Press Enter.

Figure 20.10 shows a worksheet containing information linked to a chart. The unattached text in the chart is selected so that the external reference formula that links the text box in the chart to the worksheet appears in the formula bar.

Creating Combination Charts

Combination charts present two or more series of data on the same chart; they may use two chart types. Combination charts work well to compare trends in two types of data or to look for possible interactions between two sets of data. The two charts are called the *main* chart and the *overlay* chart.

Figure 20.11 shows a combination column chart and line chart created by pasting in a data series, then choosing the Chart Add Overlay command. Marketing expenses were added to the chart created in Chapter 17, "Chart Quick Start," so that the chart now has three data series. In the figure, the third series of data appears as the line.

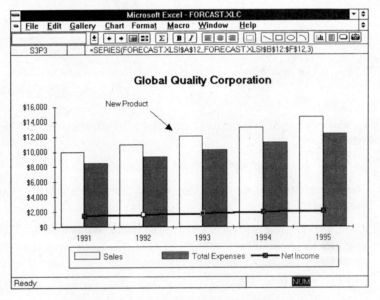

Fig. 20.11. Combination charts combine two types of charts.

Figure 20.12 shows a combination chart where both charts are line charts. This combination enables you to use two value (Y) axes with different scales.

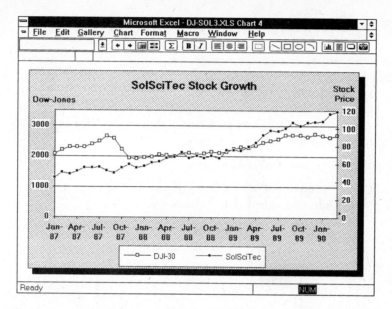

Fig. 20.12. *Use combination charts to plot data series that have different value (Y) axes.*

You can create a combination chart in two ways. The method you choose depends on whether you are creating a new chart or customizing an existing one.

If you are creating a new chart or are working with a chart that has not been customized, you can create a combination chart by choosing the **Gallery Combination** command. You can select from five combination formats.

If your chart has custom features that you do not want to lose, or if you want a combination not included in the gallery combinations, choose **Chart Add Overlay** to create your combination chart. You can alter the type of overlay by choosing Format Overlay as described in this chapter's "Changing the Overlay Chart Format" section. The Format Overlay command is available only when the chart has an overlay.

In combination charts, the chart in the background is the main chart, and the one in the foreground is the overlay. Choosing **Chart Add Overlay** divides the data series evenly, putting the first half of the data series on the main chart and the second half of the data series on the overlay chart. If an odd number of data series exists, then the main chart includes the extra series. For example, if there are five lines being charted, then three will be on the main chart and two will be on the overlay. When an overlay chart already exists on the current chart, the menu command becomes **Chart Delete Overlay**.

Changing the Main Chart Format

You may want to change the type of the main chart during analysis. For example, you might change the main chart from a Line to a Column and then to an Area to see whether different graphic representations reveal something unique. While switching among these chart types with the Format Main Chart command, you can customize the chart with features such as hi-lo lines or overlapping columns.

To change the main chart, follow these steps:

1. Choose the Format Main Chart command. Figure 20.13 shows the Main Chart dialog box that appears.

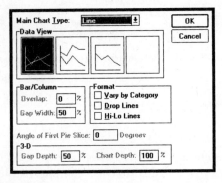

Fig. 20.13. *Use the Main Chart dialog box to change chart types without losing customization.*

2. Select the options you want to use for the main (background) chart in the combination:

Option	Description
Main Chart Type	Changes the chart type to one of the types shown in the Gallery menu, but custom formats are retained. Types available are: Area, Bar, Column, Line, Pie, and Scatter (XY).
Data View	Changes the type of marker or axis presentation within a specific chart type.
Bar/Column Overlap	Specifies how much bars or columns overlap. Enter a positive number as the percentage of overlap. 50 is full overlap. A negative number separates individual bars or columns.

Option	Description
Bar/Column Gap Width	Specifies the space between groups of bars or columns. Measured as a percentage of one bar or column width.
Format Vary by category	Specifies a different color or pattern for each marker in all pie charts or any chart with one data series.
Format Drop Lines	Drops a vertical line from a marker to the category (X) axis. Used on line or area charts.
Format Hi-Lo Lines	Draws a line between the highest and lowest lines at a specific category. Used on 2-D line charts.
Angle of First	Specifies the starting angle in Pie Slice degrees for the first wedge in a pie chart. Vertical is zero degrees.
3-D Gap Depth	Specifies the spacing in depth between markers as a percentage of a marker. 50 changes the space of the depth between markers to 50% of a marker width. Because the chart depth has not changed, this action makes markers thinner. Number must be between 0 and 500.
3-D Chart Depth	Specifies how deep a 3-D chart is relative to its width. Enter a number as a percentage of the chart width. 50 makes the depth 50% of the width. Number must be between 20 and 2000.

Only the options that make sense for the chart type you selected in the Type list are available. Unavailable options are dimmed.

3. Choose OK or press Enter.

Changing the Overlay Chart Format

As you work with your charts, you may find that a different overlay chart type lets you better compare data between the main chart and the overlay chart. To change the type of overlay chart, choose the Format Overlay command and select the options appropriate to the type of overlay chart you select.

The Format Overlay dialog box is shown in figure 20.14. The options in the Format Overlay box are the same as those described for the Format Main Chart dialog box with the exception of the Series Distribution group.

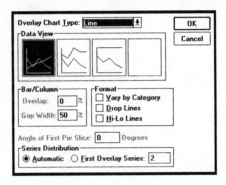

Fig. 20.14. *Use the Format Overlay dialog box to change the type of overlay or the data series used in the overlay.*

The Series Distribution options define where data series are split between the main chart and the overlay chart in a combination chart. If you select the Automatic option, the data series are split evenly between the main and the overlay chart. The first half of the series are assigned to the main chart. If the number of data series is uneven, the main chart receives one extra data series. If there are five data series, for example, the first three data series are used in the main chart and the last two are used in the overlay.

If you want the split between main and overlay charts to begin with a specific data series, select the First Overlay Series and type the number of the first overlay data series in the text box.

> **Tip:** *Changing the Order of Data Series*
> The Series Distribution option specifies where the split between the main and overlay chart occurs; however, it cannot move the fifth data series into a position in the main chart. To change the order in which data series appear, choose the **Chart Edit Series** command, select the series you want to reposition from the **Series** list, and then enter the new position in the **Plot Order** text box.

Whenever a chart with an overlay is active, the Chart menu displays the Delete Overlay command. Choosing Delete Overlay removes the overlay chart and displays all data series on the main chart.

Troubleshooting Charts

You can create enlightening charts from your worksheets. However, even Excel's charts can produce unusual results if you do something outside normal chart operations. The troubleshooting tips that follow reveal some of the ways charts can produce a different result than you expected. These tips also suggest ways you can solve common problems.

Problem:
Excel does not update or redraw the chart after you change data on the worksheet or after you edit one of the chart-related series formulas.

Solution:
Excel may be set for manual recalculation. To update the chart using new worksheet data or a new series formula, choose Chart Calculate Now.

Problem:
You need to update a chart without opening the worksheet.

Solution:
Choose the File Links command, select from the Links list the worksheet from which you want an update, and then choose the Update button.

Problem:
The numbers along the value (Y) axis have too many decimal places and have a format that just doesn't look right with the rest of the chart. What command formats the numbers along the value axis?

Solution:
Excel does not have a command to format numbers along the value axis. Formats along the value axis reflect the formats in the worksheet. To change the format of numbers on the Value axis, use Format Number to format the numbers in the cells of the first data series in the worksheet.

If you need to scale down the numbers on the axis, divide them by 100, 1000, or another appropriate number in the worksheet. Use the numbers resulting from this division to create the chart.

Problem:
When plotting a large amount of data in a line chart, the category (X) labels and tick marks are too close together. How can their appearance be improved?

Solution:
To "thin out" the labels or tick marks along the category axis but still keep all the data, use the Format Scale command:

1. Select the category axis, then choose Format Scale.

2. Select the text boxes for either or both Number of Categories Between Tick Labels and Number of Categories Between Tick Marks.

3. Enter a number larger than the one displayed in the box.

4. Choose OK or press Enter.

If the labels or tick marks are still too close together, repeat the process using a larger number.

Problem:
Some combinations of colors and patterns on charts are aesthetically offensive (ugly!). How are colors and patterns returned to their original selections?

Solution:
You can return to the default colors and patterns by selecting the chart items you want to change, choosing the Format Patterns command, and then selecting the Automatic option.

Problem:
The printed copies of the chart do not look the same as the chart looks in the window. Why does this difference exist, and what can be done about it?

Solution:
Excel may not accurately present fonts or chart item locations in a small window. For a better representation, format charts with the window maximized. To see how your chart will look when printed, choose the File Print Preview command. Click the magnifying glass pointer on areas of the screen that you want to zoom for closer examination. The appearance of print preview is much more accurate than the appearance of the chart in a window.

Problem:
One font appears on-screen, but a different font prints. In addition, not all of the font sizes shown on-screen print on the laser printer.

Solution:
Excel's charts use graphics mode on the laser printer, but characters are created from fonts available to your printer. To reduce the chance of on-screen fonts differing from printed fonts, do the following:

1. Always check the File Printer Setup command to ensure that the correct printer and cartridge are selected.

2. In the Format Font dialog boxes for both the worksheet and the chart, select the Printer Fonts check box. This limits the selection of fonts to ones that you have told Windows (via the File Printer Setup dialog box) that your printer has available. Cells that include unavailable fonts must be reformatted if you select the Printer Fonts check box.

3. If you use soft fonts or a special font cartridge, make sure that you have installed the driver for these fonts so that Windows can work correctly with the fonts.

Problem:
Changing the chart type removes custom formats.

Solution:
When you want to change the chart type of a custom-formatted chart, choose the Format Main Chart command. To change the type of the overlay chart in a combination chart, choose the Format Overlay command. These dialog boxes enable you to change chart types while preserving custom features that are appropriate to the new chart type.

Problem:
After moving a chart or its supporting worksheet to a different directory, the chart loses its link to the worksheet because it cannot locate the worksheet. How can the chart be relinked to its worksheet?

Solution:
Use the File Open command to find the worksheet and open it. Activate the chart so that it is on top. Choose File Links and select the name of the worksheet that was originally linked to the chart. Choose the Change button, and select the replacement worksheet's drive, directory, and file name from the list boxes. Choose OK or press Enter. The old directory and file name of the supporting worksheet is replaced in the chart's series formula by the directory and file name you chose from the list boxes. Save your updated chart.

From Here...

Keep in mind that Excel charts have a wide variety of uses. You can create charts quickly and use them for data analysis, yet they can have the quality of professionally created graphics.

To use your charts inside other Windows programs and some standard DOS applications, refer to Chapter 33, "Using Excel with Windows Programs," and Chapter 34, "Using Excel with DOS Programs." In those chapters, you will learn how to put Excel charts into your word processing documents and how to paste Excel charts into more advanced graphics packages for further enhancement.

Part IV

Excel Databases

Includes

Database Quick Start

Designing Databases

Entering and Sorting Data

Finding and Editing Data

Extracting and Maintaining Data

Linking Excel to Databases with Q+E

Building Extensive Databases

At its simplest, you can think of an Excel database as an automated card file that can store information such as names, phone numbers, and addresses. But Excel databases can serve far broader and more flexible functions. With Excel you can sort, search, extract, and analyze database information. And the database does not even have to reside in the worksheet. It can remain on disk.

You can sort Excel database information in alphabetical and numerical order. And you can sort as many different ways as you want. You can find data that meets conditions you specify, such as finding all accounts that are more than 30 days overdue. You even can use an extract command to withdraw specific information and prepare it for a printed report. Database statistical functions enable you to quickly analyze a database's contents to find information, such as the amount expended in June for project code 1025.

Excel's database is easier to use than other worksheet and database combinations. For example, you can use Excel's database with the same procedures you might use with a Lotus 1-2-3 database. But with Excel, you can use a form that Excel creates automatically. The form makes simple data entry, editing, and searching effortless. And it takes almost no time to learn.

You can link database information to worksheet calculations. Unlike programs that are databases only, the Excel database is an integral part of the worksheet. This feature makes it easy to link database contents to worksheet calculations, or vice versa. You will find this feature particularly important when you want to use database information in worksheet calculations or use worksheet calculations to control database contents.

If you need to use large databases of information that reside on your personal computer's disk or on the mainframe, you can link Excel to those databases with Q+E, a program that comes with Excel. Q+E enables you to link Excel worksheets to data on the disk. You can use Q+E just as part of Excel's **Data** menu, or use it as a separate program to query and edit databases.

To get a quick introduction to Excel's database features, go through Chapter 21, "Database Quick Start." It will show you how easy the Data Form is to use and get you started on more advanced database features.

21

Database
Quick Start

An Excel database helps you store, sort, find, extract, and analyze data. In this Quick Start, you learn how to use the basic database capabilities that are an integral part of Excel.

Microsoft has made the Excel database easy to use by including a data-entry form that Excel creates automatically as soon as you define the range that contains the database. From that form, you can add, delete, edit, and find data in the database. More involved data manipulation, such as finding records that satisfy multiple conditions or extracting data from reports, requires an additional range to hold the questions, or the *criteria,* that you want to ask of the database. If you are familiar with Lotus 1-2-3 database operation, this procedure will be familiar to you.

Before you begin this Database Quick Start, you need to know how to enter and edit data in Excel and how to choose from Excel menus and dialog boxes. If you are not familiar with these techniques, review Chapter 2, "Operating Windows," and Chapter 3, "Worksheet Quick Start."

Setting Up the Database Example

To work through the exercises in the Database Quick Start, you first need to enter the sample database information shown in figure 21.1. Notice that related information is kept in a *record,* which occupies a single row. All the information of the same type is stored in the same *field,* which is contained in a column. A *field name* above each column describes the type of information in that field. Field names must be text or a text formula and can occupy only one row, which appears in row 10 of the example. Although figure 21.1 shows two rows of headings, rows 9 and 10, Excel recognizes only the headings in the row immediately above the database columns. In addition, each field name (in row 10) must be unique.

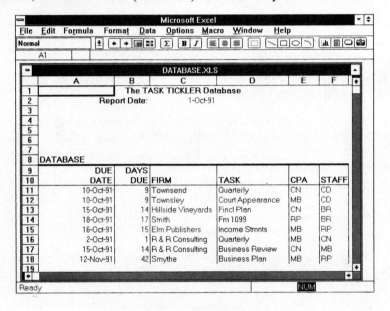

Fig. 21.1. *The sample database for the Database Quick Start.*

To prepare the sample database, follow these steps:

1. Type the data shown in figure 21.1, except for the Days Due information in column B. Be careful to enter the data in the same rows and columns as shown in the figure.

Select the database headings and place thin and thick borders around them by using the Format Border command. Type the date in cell C2 as an Excel date, using a format such as dd-mmm-yy. To ensure that the exercise works correctly, enter the same dates as those shown in column A. Use Format Number to format the dates in a format you want. Widen the columns as necessary.

2. In cell B11, enter this formula:

   =A11-$C$2

   This formula subtracts the Report Date in C2 from the Due Date in A11 to calculate the Days Due.

3. Select the range B11:B18 and choose the Edit Fill Down command to fill the formula down column B of the database. This calculates the Days Due for all the rows in the database.

4. Save your database with the File Save As command.

Sorting Data

Excel has a sort command that enables you to sort information, whether or not it is part of a database. You can use the sort command to reorder work such as lists, forecasting worksheets, or expense account databases. The Data Sort command sorts either by row or by column, allowing you to reorder a worksheet either vertically or horizontally.

To sort the rows of data in the sample database by date and then by firm name, follow these steps:

1. Select the data cells that you want to sort (the range A11:F18, as shown in figure 21.2).

   Always make sure that you have included the full width of the database row to be sorted.

   Do not include database headings in the sort selection. When headings are included, they might be sorted into the data and removed from their column heading position.

2. Choose the Data Sort command. Your screen should look similar to figure 21.3.

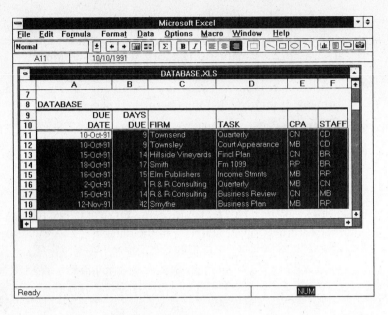

Fig. 21.2. *Data selected for the sort operation.*

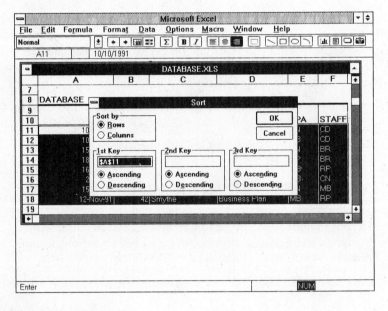

Fig. 21.3. *The Sort dialog box.*

3. Move the Sort dialog box so that you can see the top row of the selected range.

Drag the title bar of the Sort dialog box until the window is positioned.

Press Alt, space bar; then choose **M**ove and press the arrow keys to position the dialog box. Press Enter to fix the new position.

4. Make sure that the **R**ows option is selected to keep each row together during the sort.

5. Enter the **1**st Key as $A$11.

The first key on which you are sorting is Due Date in column A. Choose the top data cell in this column, $A$11. The Due Date will be the first sort item, just as a person's last name is the first sort key in the phone book.

Select the text in the **1**st Key text box, and then click on cell $A$11 in the database. The absolute reference is entered automatically.

Press Alt+1 to select the **1**st Key text box. Type $A$11 or press the arrow keys to move the active cell to A11. The absolute reference is entered automatically.

6. Select the **A**scending order option to sort the dates from the earliest to the latest.

Click on the **A**scending option.

Press Alt+A to select the **A**scending option.

7. Enter the **2**nd Key as $C$11. Where there are rows with the same first key, Due Date, the second key sorts these rows also by the firms' names wherever rows exist that have the same first-key Due Date.

Click in the **2**nd Key box, and then click on cell C11.

Press Alt+2, and then move the active cell to C11.

8. Select Ascending order for the 2nd key. This selection sorts the names from A to Z. The Sort dialog box now should look like the box in figure 21.4.

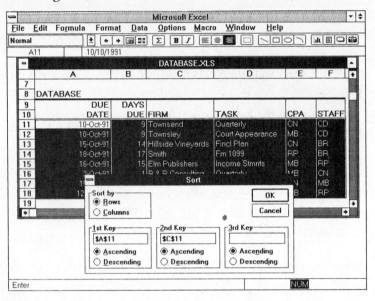

Fig. 21.4. *The sort keys specified in the Sort dialog box.*

9. Choose OK or press Enter.

The data will be sorted by rows, as shown in figure 21.5. Rows containing the same Due Date, such as 10-Oct-91 and 15-Oct-91, are sorted further by firm name.

Setting the Database Range

Before you can use database commands that find or extract information, you must let Excel know where the database is located. To set the database range, follow these steps:

1. Select the database range, A10:F18. Make sure that you include the full width of the rows and the single adjacent row of field names, row 10, above the data.

   Figure 21.6 shows how the single adjacent row of field names is selected along with the data.

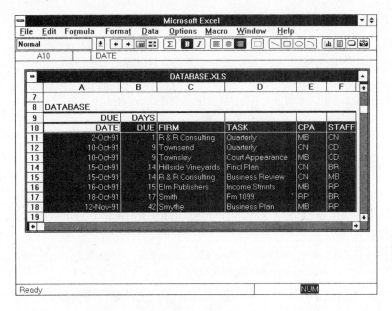

Fig. 21.5. *Database rows sorted by date and then by firm name.*

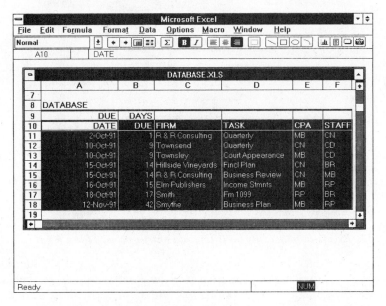

Fig. 21.6. *The data rows and a single field name row are selected before defining the database.*

2. Choose the Data Set Database command.

This command assigns the range name Database to the selected range. Excel looks for field names in the top row of this range.

To check the database range, select a single cell, press the GoTo key (F5), select the name Database from the list, and then choose OK.

Using the Database Form

After you define the location of the database with **Data Set Database**, Excel automatically creates a database form. This form is useful for viewing, adding, deleting, editing, and finding data.

Display the database form by choosing **Data Form**. The form appears in its own window, as shown in figure 21.7.

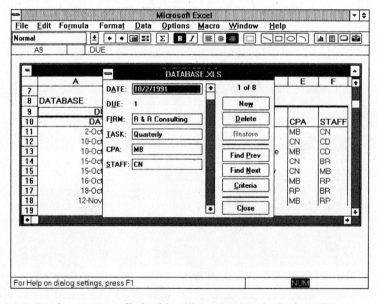

Fig. 21.7. Excel automatically builds a data-entry and edit form for you.

The form uses the names from the top of the database range to label each field. The field names appear on the left side of the form. Most fields have an underlined letter in the field name. The data from one row appears in the text boxes to the right of the field names.

The top right corner of the form shows 1 of 8 to indicate that this is the first of eight records.

The right side of the form contains buttons that are used to add, delete, and find data or to ask a question (Criteria).

Select buttons or data fields to edit by pressing Alt and the underlined letter or by clicking the mouse on the field text or button. The Tab key moves to the next field or button, and Shift+Tab moves backward. Notice that when all letters have been used for underlining, one heading, CPA, may not have an underlined letter. When this happens, use Tab or Shift+Tab to select that field.

Viewing Records

To view the records in the database from the database form, follow these steps:

1. Scroll through the records by using the database form. Watch the top right of the form to see which record you are on.

Click on the arrows in the form's scroll bar or drag the scroll box in the scroll bar.

Press the up- or down-arrow key to move to the same field of the next or previous record. Press Enter to move to the first field of the next record or Shift+Enter to move to the previous record.

2. Choose the Find Prev button repeatedly until the first record is displayed.

Finding Records

You can find specific records (one per row) in the database by specifying a description that records must match. The description of what you want to find is known as the *criteria*.

In the sample database, follow these steps to find those records where the Due Date is 15-Oct-91:

1. From the database form, select the Criteria button.

   The buttons on the form change, and the text box for each field clears so that you can enter the criteria describing the records that you want to match.

2. Select the DATE text box.

Click in the DATE text box.

Press Alt+A or Tab until the text box is selected.

3. Type the following criteria:

10/15/91

The form now should appear as shown in figure 21.8.

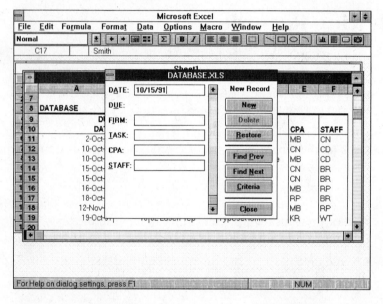

Fig. 21.8. *Use the Criteria form to specify what you want to find.*

4. Choose the Find Next button to search forward through the database from the record you are currently on.

Excel begins searching from the current record and searches forward for the next record containing a Due Date of 10/15/91. Record 4 appears in the form, as shown in figure 21.9.

5. Choose the Find Next button to find the record for R & R Consulting with a Due Date of 15-Oct-91. You will use this record in editing. Choose the Find Prev button to search backward through the database from the current record.

Note that when you conduct this type of search, you can enter criteria in more than one field text box of the database form.

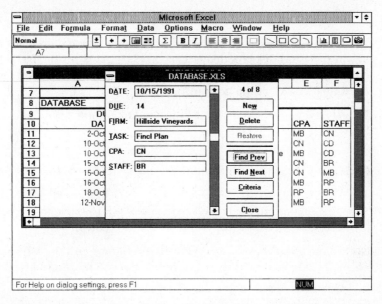

Fig. 21.9. *The database form displays the record that matches the criteria you specified.*

Editing Records

You can edit records from the database form. Because Excel has located the current record, R & R Consulting, you now can change it.

To change the Staff initials from MB to BR, follow these steps:

1. Select the STAFF text box.

 Click in the box.

 Press Alt+S or Tab until the box is selected.

2. Change the initials MB to BR, and then press Enter

Adding Records

Adding new records to the database is as easy as selecting the New button. Follow these steps to add a new record to the sample database:

1. Choose the New button.

   The data form uses blank cells at the bottom of the database for a new record and displays this last record as a blank form. The database range name is automatically extended to include the additional record at the bottom.

2. Type a new record using the data in the fields shown in figure 21.10.

Click in a box, type the information, and then click in the next box.

Type information in a box, and then press Tab to move to the next box. (Pressing Enter moves you to the next record.)

Notice that you cannot enter information into or edit the DUE field. This is a calculated field that cannot be changed or entered within the database form.

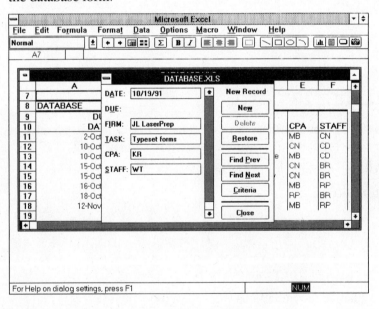

Fig 21.10. New information is typed into a blank form.

3. Choose the Close button to leave the form and retain all the changes and additions to the database.

Figure 21.11 shows the result of your changes in the database. The new record was added in blank cells at the bottom of the database. Excel automatically redefined the database range name to include the new record of information. You can view the new database range by pressing F5, selecting Database from the list box, and then choosing OK.

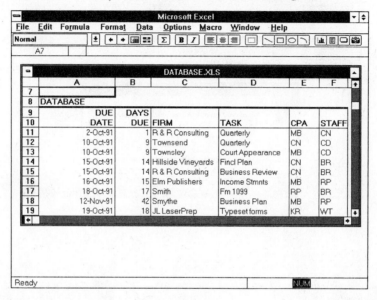

Fig. 21.11. *New records are added to the end of the database, and the database range extends.*

When you add data by using the database form, Excel extends the database range as long as there is room below the database. You are not allowed to add data if room is not available.

Deleting Records

You can use the database form to delete records just as you use it to add records. Follow these steps to delete the record for Elm Publishers from the sample database:

1. Choose Data Form to reopen the database form.

2. Scroll through the records until you reach the added record for Elm Publishers (Record 6).

3. Select the **D**elete button. The alert box shown in figure 21.12 appears, warning that you are about to delete this record permanently.

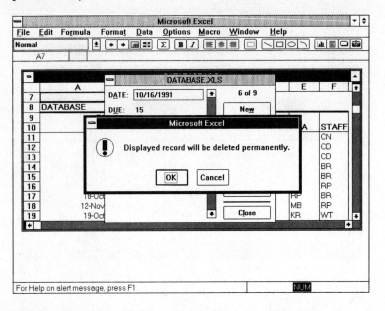

Fig. 21.12. *An alert box warns that you are about to delete a record permanently.*

4. Choose OK or press Enter.

5. Select the Close button to save your changes and to return to the database.

Setting the Criteria Range

To conduct complex searches, extract records, and analyze database contents, you must enter a criteria range on the worksheet. The criteria range contains a minimum of two rows. The top row contains field names that *exactly* match the field names at the top of the database. You do not have to use all the field names, but the ones you do use must be the same as they appear in the database. In the second row of the criteria range (below the field names), enter information describing the records for which you want to search.

Although the criteria range does not need to have borders around it, including borders creates a more attractive appearance and reduces the chance of entering criteria in the wrong cell.

Use the following steps to build a criteria range, as shown in figure 21.13:

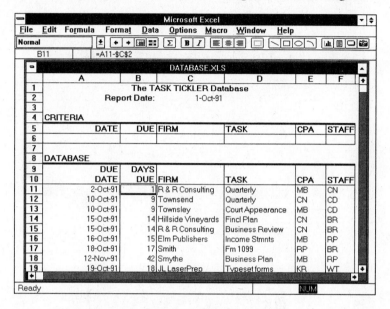

Fig. 21.13. *Adding a criteria range enables you to ask questions of the database.*

1. Enter the word Criteria in cell A4 and make it bold.

2. Copy the field names from row 10 up to row 5 by selecting cells A10:F10 and choosing the Edit Copy command. Select cell A5 and press Enter to paste.

3. Select cells A5:F6, and then use the Format Border command to enclose the criteria range within a border.

You have just entered information for a criteria range. By copying the field names from the database, you ensure that they are exactly the same. You now must tell Excel where that criteria range is located.

1. Select cells A5:F6.

2. Choose the Data Set Criteria command.

The Data Set Criteria command gives the range in figure 21.14 the range name Criteria.

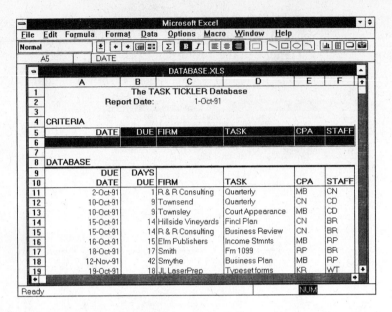

Fig. 21.14. *The criteria range selected.*

Finding Records with the Criteria Range

After a criteria range is selected, you can enter criteria just as you did in the database form. Using a criteria range enables you to enter complex criteria that you cannot enter in the database form. This Quick Start shows you examples of simple criteria that you can enter in the criteria range. More complex criteria are discussed in Chapter 24, "Finding and Editing Data."

One simple type of criteria uses *wild cards* to check for close as well as exact matches in text data. (You also can use wild cards in a data form.) Suppose, for example, that you know a name begins with *Sm* and contains the letters *th*. The asterisk (*) wild card accepts as a match any characters occurring at the same location as the asterisk. In the following example, the asterisk is between *Sm* and *th*. This wild card helps find either the name Smith or Smythe.

In the sample database, use the following steps to enter criteria in row 6 (just as you did in the database form) and to find the records that match that criteria:

1. In cell C6, directly under the FIRM heading, enter

Sm*th

Your screen will look like figure 21.15.

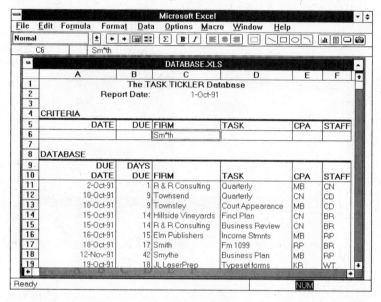

Fig. 21.15. *Criteria using a wild card will find close matches to the data that you specify.*

2. Choose the **Data Find** command. The record containing `Smith` is highlighted.

If the active cell is above the database, the search begins from the top row of the database and goes downward. If the active cell is in the database, the search begins at the row containing the active cell and goes downward.

The screen immediately scrolls to display any record that matches the criteria you entered (see fig. 21.16). The scroll bars change to a new pattern, and a message appears in the status bar to show that the Find command is active.

3. Scroll down to the next matching record:

 Click on the **down arrow** in the scroll bar.

 Press the **down-arrow** key.

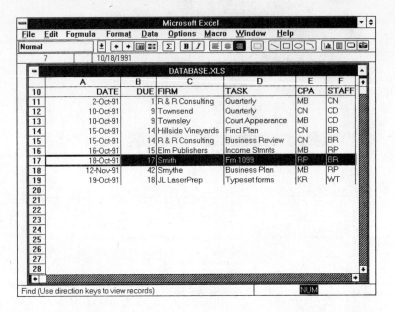

Fig. 21.16. Following the Data Find command, Excel selects the next record that matches the criteria.

The next record in the database contains the FIRM name of Smythe. Smythe also matches the pattern of Sm*th because the asterisk matches the letter *y* and because Excel disregards any characters following the criteria. Notice that the record number appears to the left of the formula bar.

4. Exit the Find mode by clicking outside the database or by pressing Esc.

5. To delete the old criteria from C6, select C6, press Del, and then press Enter. (You are deleting this criteria in preparation for a later example.)

To select the criteria range quickly, press F5, select Criteria from the list, and then press Enter.

Extracting Records for a Report

Using the criteria range you just created, you can command Excel to extract a copy of desired information from the database, copy it to another area, and paste it in. Extracting information is an excellent way to prepare a report or to create a mailing list file to copy into Word for Windows for merging with form letters.

Before you can extract information, you must create an extract range. This range shows Excel the field names of the data you want to extract and where you want the extracted information to be copied.

To prepare your extract range, you must use field headings that *exactly* match the field names in the database. If the headings don't match, Excel cannot match the correct columns.

> **Note:** *How the Extract Range Differs from the Criteria Range*
> The extract range and criteria range are different and separate. The criteria range specifies what you want to find. The extract range indicates where copies of selected information will be pasted.

Use the following steps to prepare an extract range in the sample database:

1. Enter the word **Extract** in cell A20 and make it bold. Bolding the word is not required, but this step makes your extract range easier to find and use.

2. Copy the field names from row 10 down to row 22 by selecting cells A10:F10 and choosing the **E**dit **C**opy command. Select cell A22 and press Enter to paste.

3. Use the **Forma**t **B**order command to outline the extract headings if you want.

Create the extract range by naming it with the **D**ata Set Extract command:

1. Select the extract range headings, A22:F22.

2. Choose the **D**ata Set Extract command.

This procedure names the headings for the extract range with the name Extract.

The extract headings should appear similar to those shown in figure 21.17. Make sure that the names are the same as those in the database headings.

Although the field names in the extract range must match the database field names exactly, the names do not have to be in the same order, nor does the extract range have to include every field name.

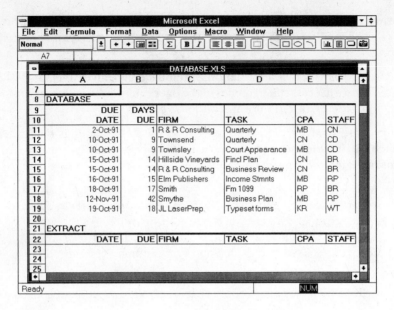

Fig. 21.17. The sample database with extract headings added.

Using the sample database, follow these steps to extract records that contain information due in *less than* 15 days:

1. Delete any previous criteria to ensure that Excel will work only on the new criteria you enter.

2. In cell B6 of the criteria range, directly underneath the DUE heading, enter the following:

   <15

   (Note that < is the symbol for less than. Chapter 24, "Finding and Editing Data," lists other symbols that help you search for **ranges of numbers**.)

3. Choose the **Data Extract** command to display the Extract dialog box (see fig. 21.18).

4. Select the **Unique Records Only** check box to remove duplicate records.

5. Choose **OK** or press **Enter**.

Figure 21.19 shows that the records due in less than 15 days are copied from the database to the rows below the extract headings. The extract range is ready for you to format, print, or copy.

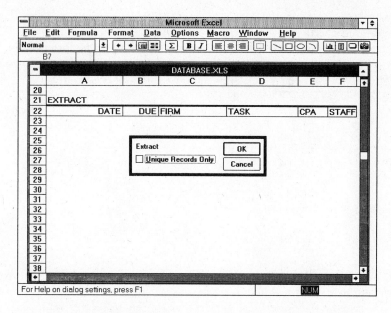

Fig. 21.18. The Extract dialog box gives you the opportunity to remove duplicate records from the copy.

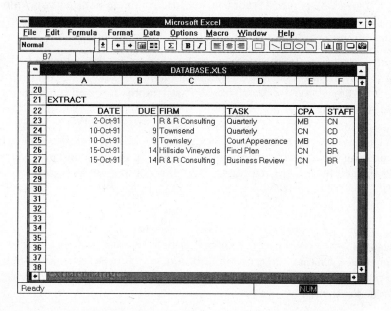

Fig. 21.19. Extracted information appears underneath the appropriate heading.

Note: *Extracting Data into an Unlimited Extract Range*
Excel can extract data into a limited area or an unlimited area. When you highlight only the extract headings, you tell Excel to erase all the cells below the extract headings and use as many cells below as necessary (unlimited area). This technique is convenient when you don't know how many rows of data will be extracted. The practice is hazardous, however, if you have anything below the extract range. Chapter 25, "Extracting and Maintaining Data," describes how to create a limited extract range.

From Here...

The simplest and quickest way to add, delete, edit, and find database information is with the database form. In the chapters that follow, you learn how to use the database form to perform the functions you want.

When you want to perform complex searches, such as finding all records with dates between January 15 and February 15 and with amounts due of more than $500, you will want to use a criteria range to enter your query. Chapters 24 and 25 discuss these criteria and show you how to extract information from the database in order to create reports.

When you understand the fundamentals of Excel's database, make sure that you review the more advanced database techniques described in Chapter 27, "Building Extensive Databases." That chapter has a number of techniques that can save you considerable work and time. For example, the text discusses how to use database statistics functions such as DSUM, a function that can find the total amount due for records with a specific account code. Combining the DSUM function with the **Data Table** command enables you to build a table showing the total by job or account code from data in your database. This one procedure can turn an eight-hour job into a task of just a few minutes.

Because many database operations are repetitive, you may find that using macros in your database operations is helpful. For a quick exercise in macros, see Chapter 28, "Command and Function Macro Quick Start." Chapter 28 demonstrates how easily you can reduce repetitive functions to a single keystroke.

22

Designing Databases

This chapter will help you understand important database terms and concepts. The chapter describes what a database is, explains the parts of a database, advises how to choose the contents for a database, and shows you how to lay out a database on the worksheet. The following chapters, 23–27, explain the details of building and operating databases.

What Is a Database?

The first example of a database that most people encounter is the familiar rolling card file (see fig. 22.1). You can quickly flip through a card file to find information, such as a client's address, phone number, or favorite restaurant. Card files are easy to use as long as the cards are kept in alphabetical order according to a single key word, such as the client's name. Card files can present problems, however, when you want to do anything other than find a client by name. For example, if you wanted to find all the financial analysts in San Francisco, using a card file could take considerable time.

Excel's database handles basic functions, such as finding the kind of information you would write on a card, quickly and easily. Excel also handles complex database jobs, such as analyzing and extracting information in the database.

```
Turnigan, Kathleen      (415) 579-2650

Financial Analyst

Brown, James & Assoc.
213 California St.
San Francisco, CA 94003

Background:        Interned w/Peterman, M.B.A., Stanford

Expertise:         Bond portfolio analysis

Computer experience: Excel expert
```

Fig. 22.1. Cards in a card file are easy to use but time-consuming to search through.

The file card for Kathleen Turnigan contains information related to Kathleen Turnigan. In a computer database, that information is a record. All the information from one file card goes into one database *record*, or a row of related information. Within that row, individual items are stored in *fields* (cells).

Each individual piece of data in the record (row) must be entered in a separate cell. For example, Kathleen's first name goes in one cell (the First Name field), last name in another cell, firm name in a third, and so on. To keep the information organized, each field is assigned to a specific column. For example, first names belong only in column A, last names belong in column B, and so on. Each column is given a *field name*. Figure 22.2 shows how part of Kathleen's card would be entered in row 10 of an Excel database.

An Excel database will have many records. When looking for related information, you will have to tell Excel what field (column) to search. To do this, you must give Excel the exact field name or the field's column number. For example, to find the records in a database for everyone in San Francisco, you might tell Excel to search a field named City. Field names must be text or text formulas. Figure 22.2 shows how the field names and data are arranged within an Excel worksheet.

Figure 22.2 also shows that the information from the card in figure 22.1 now appears in a single record (row) of the database; each cell in the row contains a different field of data. From the field names at the top of each database column, you easily can tell the data each field contains.

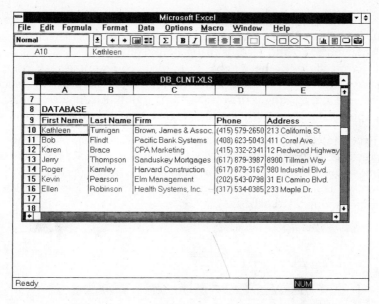

Fig. 22.2. An Excel database with field names as column headings.

What Are the Parts of a Database?

An Excel database can contain as many as three parts:

Range	Description
Database	Where information is kept. An Excel database is kept in a worksheet; related information is entered in rows. Each column of information has a unique field name. With the use of Q+E, you can link Excel to databases on disk.
Criteria	Where you indicate what you want to find or analyze in the database. Contains field names and an area in which you type a specification describing the information you want.
Extract	Where Excel copies desired information from the database. Contains field names and an area in which the copy will be pasted.

Before you can use Excel's database, you must indicate the database range on the worksheet. The range must contain both the data and the field names in the database. To find records using simple queries in the database, you need to specify only the database range. If you want to ask complex questions or extract information for reports, then you also must specify criteria and extract ranges. If you use Q+E to link Excel to a database on disk, you must tell Q+E which file contains the data you want to use.

Tell Excel the location of the database range by selecting the field names and data records, as shown in figure 22.3. Next, choose **Data Set Data**base. This command gives the database and its field names the range name Database. Remember, field names must occupy only a single row. Chapters 21 and 23 describe naming the database.

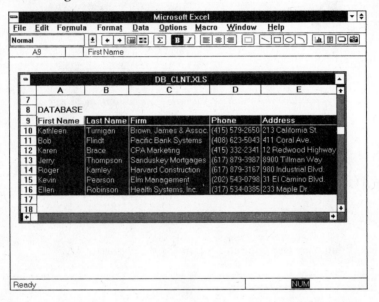

Fig. 22.3. *The database range selected.*

After you name the database range, you can begin to add, delete, edit, and find information. Choosing the **Data Form** command automatically creates a database form with buttons. The form allows you to view one record at a time. Figure 22.4 shows the form created for figure 22.3. Notice that the form shows all fields that were not immediately visible in this part of the worksheet. Chapters 21, 23, and 24 describe the **Data Form** command.

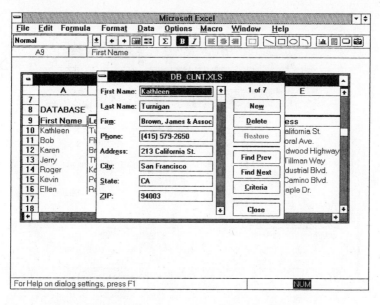

Fig. 22.4. *Excel automatically creates a database form for you.*

If you want to conduct complex searches or extract information from the database, then you also need to specify a criteria range. The criteria range must contain the field names on top and at least one blank row underneath. The field names must be exactly the same as those in the database. In the blank row, you will enter the criteria that specifies what you are searching for. Set the criteria range by selecting the field name headings and at least one row in which to type the criteria. Figure 22.5 shows the criteria range selected. (You do not have to place borders around the criteria range.) Chapter 24 describes complex searches.

The last database area you need to know is the extract range. The extract range is where Excel copies records matching the criteria. For example, you could request an extract of all addresses within a specific ZIP code area. Excel then would copy the addresses into the extract range. Another excellent use of this feature is to create new report formats of subsets of the database.

Figure 22.6 shows a single row of headings selected in preparation for choosing **Data Extract**. Because only a single row of field names has been selected, all cells below the selected extract headings will be cleared before the extracted data is copied down.

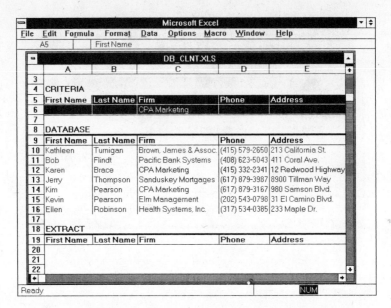

Fig. 22.5. The criteria range is where you indicate what you are looking for.

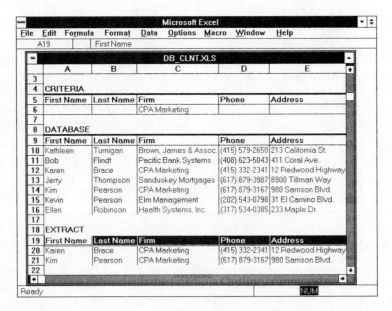

Fig. 22.6. Use the extract range to make duplicate copies of information meeting your criteria.

How Do You Choose the Contents for a Database?

You can save yourself time and trouble by planning your database before building it. As a simple checklist for what data to include in a database and how to name it, consider these points:

- List the groups of data you want in each record—for example, Name.

- Break these groups of data into the smallest elements possible. For example, Name might be divided into separate fields such as First_Name, Last_Name, and Title. This technique makes searching the database easier and enables you to reorder data in new combinations.

- Delete fields you probably will never use. For instance, delete fields that can be calculated in a report. (Why waste memory storing information that can be calculated?)

- Use only text or text formulas in field names. Do not use numeric values.

Choose fields that are small and contain the most usable part of the data. For example, instead of using Name as a single field containing an entire name, use three fields: Title, First_Name, and Last_Name. This technique gives you the option of reordering the data in many different combinations. For example, suppose that your data looks like the following:

Title	First_Name	Last_Name
Ms.	Kathleen	Turnigan

From this data, you can later create any of the following combinations:

Ms. Turnigan
Kathleen
Ms. Kathleen Turnigan
Kathleen Turnigan

You also should keep ZIP codes as a separate field. Never include the ZIP code in the city and state fields. Demographic and market data may be tied to the ZIP code. In addition, you can reduce postage rates by sorting mailings by ZIP code.

Be on the lean side when including data fields. Many business information systems lie unused because some well-meaning person wanted the database to contain too much information. The result is a database that is expensive, time-consuming, and tedious to maintain. When a database isn't maintained, it isn't used. Include only data you can evaluate and keep up-to-date.

How Do You Lay Out a Database?

Before building your database, consider how it fits with the rest of the worksheet and how to coordinate it with other worksheets and databases for your business. Remember: Excel databases and worksheets in different files can be linked together. Here are some additional points to consider:

- Draw diagrams of other databases and worksheets in your business, and notice where the data is stored twice. Can the data be stored in separate files and recombined as needed with the aid of Excel or Q+E?

- Be sure that nothing lies below the extract range. An unlimited extract range clears all cells below it.

- Position the database so that room is available for it to expand downward. If you use **Data Form** to add records (rows) to your database, rows are added without pushing down the information below the database. If not enough room is available to insert cells for the new database, the database form will not let you add a new record.

- If you want to insert rows to add records to the middle of a database, make sure that no worksheet calculations exist on either side of the database. Inserting a row through a database also inserts a row through anything on the sides of the database.

In summary, make a thumbnail sketch or map of how the worksheet is laid out so that you can see whether database expansion will be limited, whether the extract area will erase data below it, and whether rows inserted through the database will insert through other worksheet sections. Comparing the database layout to other parts of the worksheet lets you see where conflicts might exist.

From Here...

The quickest way to learn the basics of Excel databases is to try the Database Quick Start in Chapter 21. The Quick Start requires a little data entry in order to get set up; however, once you have entered that data, the Quick Start goes swiftly. Building the database from the Quick Start will give you a small sample file to experiment on as you read through the other database chapters.

To get started with your database, read Chapter 23, "Entering and Sorting Data," and Chapter 24, "Finding and Editing Data." If you need to perform complex queries or extract information from the database to create a report, refer to Chapter 25, "Extracting and Maintaining Data." If you have large databases or want to link Excel to databases created by other PC programs or from a mainframe, then read Chapter 26, "Linking Excel to Databases with Q+E." Chapter 27, "Building Extensive Databases," shows you how to link databases that are on separate documents and how to analyze database contents, cross-check data entry, and troubleshoot database operations.

23

Entering and Sorting Data

T his and the following chapters describe how to build and use a database that resides on an Excel worksheet. A database is like an automated card-file system that enables you to find information quickly, edit it, sort it, extract and print it, or analyze it. The parts of an Excel database are explained more fully in Chapter 22.

Although Excel is primarily a worksheet, it does have database capability that can help you analyze stock market trends, store expense accounts, and monitor sales figures. The combination of database functions, powerful worksheet analysis capabilities, and charting capabilities makes Excel an excellent tool for business analysis and management systems.

Excel provides two methods for working with a database. The first method uses Excel's automatically generated data form for quick and simple data entry, editing, deleting, and searching. The second method is similar to the method employed in other worksheets. The database is specified in one range of the worksheet, and another range is used for criteria or questions. A third range is specified to hold extracted information. You can use this method for complex searches or when you need to extract information from the database.

Excel's database can hold a single row of data or an entire worksheet full of information. You can put your Excel database on one worksheet and your criteria (questions) on another and have analysis and reports done on yet another worksheet. If the database is too large to fit in a worksheet or the

661

design requires a disk-based database, you can use the free Q+E add-in that comes with Excel to link Excel to external databases. Q+E is explained in Chapter 26, "Linking Excel to Databases with Q+E."

In this chapter, you learn how to build a database and then how to enter information in your database. If you want to keep just a few information records, you will find the discussion on the automatic database form of interest. If you want to enter information in a list (more like the worksheet format), you will find the additional methods valuable.

After creating your database, you may want to keep it sorted for better presentation in reports. Excel's sort command enables you to sort your data in ascending or descending order in as many fields as you want.

Entering the Field Names

The database must have unique field names in a single row across the top of the database. These field names identify each column of data. The database must have at least one row of data directly below the field names.

Figure 23.1 shows the database created in Chapter 21, "Database Quick Start." The formatting shown in the figure is not a requirement; it serves to enhance the database's appearance and to reduce errors. Figure 23.2 shows the mandatory parts of a database: the single row of field headings and the data.

When you enter field names across the top of the database, you must keep the following points in mind:

- Field names must be text or text formulas, such as ="9540."

- Field names cannot be numbers, formulas, logical values, error values, or blanks.

- Field names can include up to 255 characters, but short names are easier to see in a cell.

- Only the names in the row directly above the data are used as field names. You can add a second row above the field names, but that row is for appearance and readability only.

- Names must be different from each other.

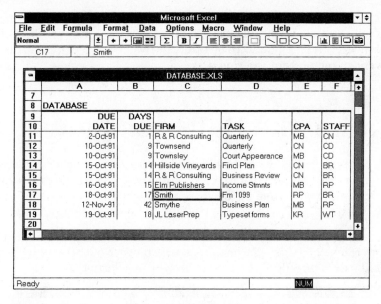

Fig. 23.1. *The database created in the Quick Start.*

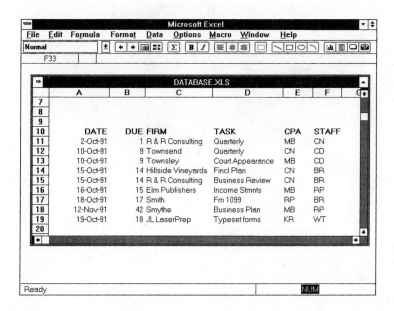

Fig. 23.2. *The essential parts of a database: the field headings and data.*

After you create field names, you will need to add a row or two of data before building the rest of the database. Add one or two rows with normal worksheet entry techniques. After you create the database, you can use more convenient methods of entering data.

Setting the Database Range

After creating field names and adding at least one row of data, you need to set the database range so that Excel will know where the database is located on the worksheet. Setting the database range gives the database the range name Database.

The database range contains the field names in the top row and the data below. Figure 23.3 shows a selected database range. Notice that only the row of field names directly above the data has been selected.

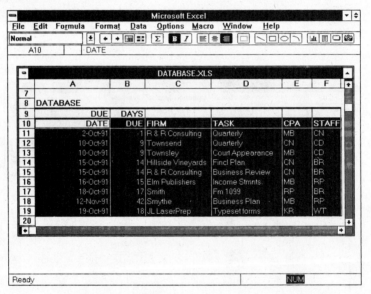

Fig. 23.3. *The database range includes data and a single row of field names above the data.*

To define the location of the database, follow these steps:

1. Select the row of field names and records underneath the field names.

2. Choose the Data Set Database command.

This procedure creates a named range called Database. You can view the currently selected database range at any time by choosing the Formula Goto command (F5) and selecting Database from the list box.

To delete the current database, choose Formula Define Name, select the name Database from the list box, and then select Delete.

You can define only one database at a time with **Data Set Database**. To use a different database, you need to name the new database range by selecting it and again choosing **Data Set Database**. The following tip explains a fast way to do this.

Quickly change between different databases by giving each database a range name with Formula Define Name. Names such as DB_AR, DB_CLIENT, and DB_SALES will make the databases easier to find and remember. After each database range is named, you can switch quickly between databases by following these steps:

1. Choose the Formula Goto command (F5).

2. Select the name of the database you want to use, such as DB_AR, and then press Enter, or double click on the name in the list.

3. Choose the Data Set Database command.

> **Tip: *Using a Macro To Switch between Databases***
> To speed up the above process even more, record a command macro that performs steps 1-3. After the macro is recorded, insert a question mark into the macro. The question mark will pause the Goto dialog box so that you can choose any range name to be set as the database name. To make the Goto box pause, insert a question mark as follows:
>
> =FORMULA.GOTO?("DB_AR")

This formula pauses the Goto dialog box with the name DB_AR selected as the default. The macro enables you to pop up a dialog box with a Ctrl+key combination and select the new database from the Goto list. Chapter 28, "Command and Function Macro Quick Start," and Chapter 29, "Creating Macros and Add-In Macros," explain how to create and modify simple macros.

To move quickly through your databases, from top-to-bottom or side-to-side, use a Ctrl+arrow key combination. You move the active cell across filled cells until the edge of the database is reached. To select cells as you move, also hold down the Shift key (Shift+Ctrl+arrow key).

Entering Data

Now that you have entered the field headings and initial data and have selected the database range, you can use many different methods for entering data. Some methods include the following:

- You can use Excel's automatic database form to enter data. This is the quickest and easiest method of entering data.

- You can enter data into blank rows or cells inserted in the database.

- Use a macro to automate either of these methods or to create a custom dialog box that accepts, verifies, and enters data. Part V of this book explains how to create and use macros.

Entering Data with the Database Form

The easiest method of entering data is with Excel's automatically generated database form. After you have set the database range with Data Set Database, you can use the form to enter data by following these steps:

1. Choose the Data Form command.

   A database form similar to the one shown in figure 23.4 will appear on top of the worksheet.

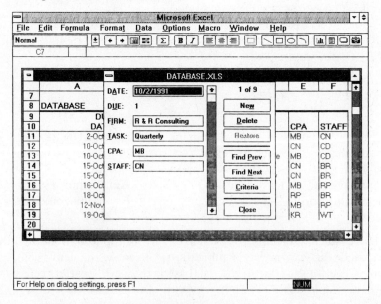

Fig. 23.4. The automatic database form with the first record displayed.

2. Select the New button.

3. After typing data in each field's text box, press Tab or Shift+Tab to travel forward or backward between fields. You can also click in a text box if you use a mouse.

4. To enter additional records, repeat steps 2 and 3.

5. Choose the Close button to quit the form and return to the worksheet.

Selecting the New button or pressing Enter takes the new record you have typed in the form and puts it in the database. Therefore, only use Tab and Shift+Tab until you are ready to save. After selecting Close, save the worksheet to record the additions on disk.

The records added with this procedure are placed below the last row of the database. The database range is extended automatically to include the added records. The data form will not let you add new records if there are not enough blank rows below the current database range. When you create your database, choose a location in the worksheet with enough room to expand.

You can change the data in the new record until you have selected New or Close to add the record to the database. After you add a record to the database, use the editing techniques described in Chapter 24, "Finding and Editing Data," to make changes.

Entering Data Directly into the Worksheet

A second method for entering data is typing directly into rows in the worksheet. Before you use this data-entry method, you must make room in the database range for new records (rows).

To preserve the named range, Database, insert new rows or cells between existing database records (rows). If you insert new rows or cells below the last record of the database, those rows or cells will not be included in the database range. If you insert new rows or cells directly underneath the field headings, the format for the record will not be copied into the blank cells.

If you add new records below the existing database instead of between records, you must select the new database range. Use Data Set Database to rename the database range so that the name Database includes the new records.

Inserting entire rows through the database will move everything in the worksheet below that row. To move down only the cells directly below the database, insert cells in the database. Insert cells in the database when you don't want to disturb areas to the right or left of the database.

In figure 23.5, the cells of the middle two records have been selected so that they can be moved down to allow for the addition of two more records. Cells outside the database are not selected. Notice the markers in column G; these indicate the cell locations outside the selected cells.

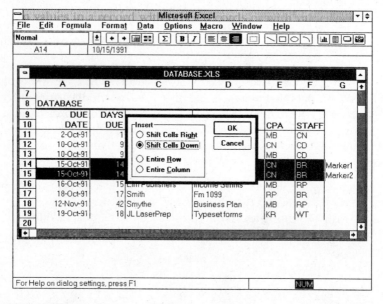

Fig. 23.5. Inserting cells into a database, rather than rows, to preserve the position of information alongside the database.

Choose the **Edit Insert** command to display the dialog box, shown in figure 23.5, for inserting cells. In this box, you specify whether the cells should be moved down or right. Choosing OK moves everything below the selected cells, as shown in figure 23.6. The markers in column G have not moved.

To enter data in the blank cells that you have inserted in the database, follow these steps:

1. Select the cells that will receive data. If you just inserted them, they will still be selected.

2. Type data into the active cell.

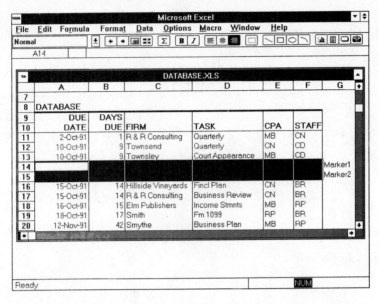

Fig. 23.6. *Blank cells have been inserted into the Database range without moving adjacent cells.*

3. Press one of the keys shown in table 23.1 to enter the data and move the active cell. Be sure to skip over the cells that contain formulas.

4. After the data is entered, press an arrow key to deselect the range.

5. Format the columns of data if necessary.

6. Create and copy formulas down the appropriate columns.

Table 23.1
Data-Entry Keys

Key	Action
Tab	Enter data and move right
Shift+Tab	Enter data and move left
Enter	Enter data and move down
Shift+Enter	Enter data and move up

While you are working within a selected data-entry range, the active cell will remain within the data-entry area. The active cell automatically wraps from one edge of the selected range to the next edge.

Excel has five shortcut key combinations that can speed your data-entry work. The key combinations are shown in table 23.2.

Table 23.2
Shortcut Keys for Data Entry

Key combination	Action
Ctrl+; (semicolon)	Enters computer's current date
Ctrl+: (colon)	Enters computer's current time
Ctrl+' (apostrophe)	Copies formula from cell above without adjusting cell references
Ctrl+" (double quotation marks)	Copies value from cell above
Ctrl+arrow	Moves over filled cells to first blank cell, or moves over blank cells to first filled cell

To create additional data-entry shortcut keys, record a macro (described in Chapter 28, "Command and Function Macro Quick Start"). Load this macro sheet whenever you want the shortcuts available for data entry.

Speeding Up Data Entry

Excel recalculates only the formulas that depend on the changed cells. While Excel is calculating, you can continue to enter data; Excel will stop its calculations momentarily to accept your entry or command. In large databases containing many formulas, constant recalculation can slow data entry.

 To speed up data entry, turn off automatic recalculation by choosing Options Calculation, selecting the Manual option, and pressing Enter. If you want to make sure that the database is recalculated before it is saved, select the Recalculate Before Save check box. Be sure to recalculate if you plan to read the database while it remains on disk through worksheet links or Q+E. Recalculating before the save, when Manual option is on, ensures that the database is up to date when stored on disk.

While Excel is in manual calculation mode, the program will not update the formulas as you enter data. When you make a change that will affect a formula in the worksheet, a Calculate indicator will appear at the bottom of the Excel screen. When you see the Calculate prompt, do not trust formula results displayed on-screen.

To recalculate all open worksheets while staying in manual calculation mode, choose **Options Calculate Now**; or press F9. If you want to recalculate only the active document, choose Shift+**Options Calculate Document**; or press Shift+F9.

After making your database entries, you can return to automatic calculation by choosing the **Options Calculation** command and selecting the **Automatic** option.

Sorting Data

Sorting organizes your data in ascending or descending alphabetical and numeric order. Excel can sort the rows of a database or the columns of a worksheet.

Excel sorts thousands of rows or columns in the time it would take you to manually sort just a few. It sorts on three fields at a time in case duplicates exist in one of the sorted fields. With a simple trick, you can sort on an unlimited number of rows or columns.

When you select **Data Sort**, Excel displays the Sort dialog box shown in figure 23.7. The items that you can select in the box include sort keys and sort order.

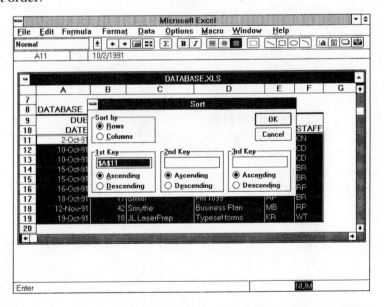

Fig. 23.7. The Sort dialog box enables you to reorganize database rows or worksheet columns.

The keys indicate which fields Excel sorts on. For example, in a telephone book, the first key is Last Name, and the second key is First Name. If there are two people with the name Smith, their first names are used to put all the Smiths in sorted order. In the database shown in figure 23.8, the first sort key is column A (Due Date), the second key is column E (CPA), and the third key is column F (Staff). Notice that the key is an absolute cell reference that can be anywhere in the column you want to sort.

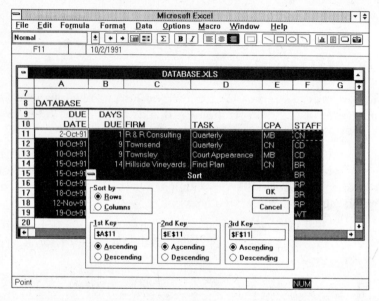

Fig. 23.8. *Excel sorts on three columns or rows at a time.*

The Ascending and Descending options beneath each key tell Excel to sort in A to Z and Z to A order respectively. Excel sorts in ascending order from top to bottom for rows, or left to right for columns. The Descending option reverses this order. In addition, the program uses the following order of priority:

Numbers from largest negative to largest positive

Text

FALSE results

TRUE results

Error values

Blanks

Excel ignores the difference between upper- and lowercase letters, and Excel does not recognize international accent marks. This feature makes finding entries easier.

If you have set international character settings through the Windows Control Panel, Excel will sort in the order used by the country specified.

Be careful when you sort databases that contain formulas. When the rows in the database change order, formulas in the rows adjust to their new locations, which may produce references that provide incorrect results. To avoid this problem, remember that a database row should refer to other cells in the same row. If the formula needs to reference a cell outside the database range, that reference should be an absolute reference so that it doesn't change during sorting.

Performing the Sort Operation

Sorting is easy to use and is helpful for any type of list—not just databases. In fact, you can create quick but useful reports by just sorting database-like information so that the information you need ends up in adjacent rows. (Just print the rows you need.) The result may not look as pretty as a full-fledged database, but it gets the job done quickly.

To sort a database or worksheet, follow these steps:

1. Choose the File Save As command, and save the worksheet to a different file name in case you scramble the data during sorting.

2. Select the data you want to sort.

   Do not select field names at the top of databases. If you include the field names, they will be sorted into the data.

   Select the full width of the database rows if you are sorting by Rows, or the full height of the columns if you are sorting by Columns. Failing to include the full width (rows) or height (columns) can scramble your database or worksheet, leaving part sorted and part unsorted.

3. Choose the Data Sort command.

4. Enter the 1st Key.

   If you are sorting a database by rows (the usual method of sorting), select any cell in the column you want to sort on. If you are sorting by columns (reordering columns), select any cell in the row you want to sort on.

5. Select **A**scending or **D**escending sort order on the **1**st Key.

6. Move to the **2**nd or **3**rd Key, and repeat the procedures in steps 4 and 5.

7. Select **R**ows to keep rows together when sorting databases or **C**olumns to reorder column arrangements.

8. Choose **O**K or press **E**nter.

If you select less than the entire width of your database, the sort function may scramble the database. A database must have its full width selected before sorting, but not necessarily its full height. For example, if you select the First_Name and Last_Name fields in the sort area, but do not include the Phone and Address fields, the First_Name and Last_Name cells will be sorted into a different order than the Phone and Address cells. These results have proved embarrassing for some companies with phone and mailing lists.

This problem occurs most frequently when the database extends past the right of the screen, and you select only the cells visible on-screen. If you sort by columns, the same problem can occur if you do not select the full column height. If you immediately recognize that the sort has created a problem, choose Edit Undo Sort. If you don't immediately recognize the problem, hope that you didn't skip step 1. If you see a problem, retrieve the original copy.

Returning a Sort to Its Original Order

When you want to sort a database and later return it to the original order, you need to add a record index to your database. (This method does not help databases that have been torn asunder by incorrect sorting.) A record index assigns a number to each record according to the record's position, date of entry, or some other ordinal criteria you decide. Figure 23.9 shows an index in column A for the database. You can insert a column or cells to make room for an index.

To index the database records so that you can return them to a previous order, follow these steps:

1. Insert a column on one side of the database.

2. Type a number, such as 1, in the top cell of the column.

3. Select the cell with the number, along with all cells in that column, through the height of the database.

4. Choose the **D**ata Series command, and fill the side column with numbers in increasing order. These numbers are the index numbers.

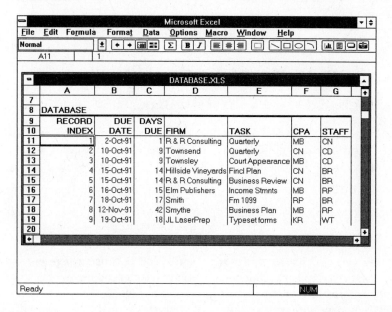

Fig. 23.9. *A record index enables you to return the database to its previous order.*

When you sort, always make sure that you include column A before sorting. When you want to return to the original database order, sort by **R**ows with the first cell in column A as the **1**st key. Make sure that the **A**scending option is selected.

Sorting by Date and Time

Excel sorts date fields by the serial number that lies within any cell containing a date. Sorting works correctly only on dates entered with a date format that Excel recognizes, or on dates created with date functions. (Check Chapters 7 and 8 for information on entering and formatting dates and times.)

In many cases, you can change text dates into serial date numbers by inserting a column, then entering a formula into the column that converts the adjacent date entry. Chapter 10 describes several functions that may be helpful in this process. TRIM removes unwanted blanks; DATE converts month, day, and year to a serial number; TEXTVALUE converts text to serial dates; and LEFT, RIGHT, MIDDLE, and LEN manipulate text into a consistent pattern.

Sorting Account Codes, Service Codes, or Part Numbers

Sorting account codes, service codes, and part numbers can be confusing at first, because these codes may contain a prefix, body, and suffix. For example, your business may use codes such as the following:

AE-576-12

02-88022-09

PRE-56983-LBL

Sorting part and service codes may be difficult because a segment of one code may overlap the character position of a different segment of another code. The result is incorrect sorting. For example, different sections of a code may have different numbers of characters for different items, as in AE-576-12 and AE-2576-12. In this case, AE-576-12 sorts before AE-2576-12, and that's not what you want.

You can solve this problem by making sure that each code segment has exactly the same number of characters. For example, you can enter the examples in the preceding paragraph as AE-0576-12 and AE-2576-12. Because you have added a zero to the first code, both codes have the same number of characters.

You can designate certain fields to contain only numeric entries. For entries that require a specific number of zero placeholders, you can use the custom numeric formats that Chapter 8, "Formatting Worksheets," describes.

For example, the following are two methods of entering the number 0056:

What Is Typed	Numeric Format	Display
="0056"	Any format	0056
56	0000	0056

The first method produces text that follows the numbers in the list. The second method sorts correctly and is much easier to enter. Chapter 8, "Formatting Worksheets," discusses additional methods of formatting numbers for display.

Sorting on More Than Three Fields

With Excel's **D**ata **S**ort command, you can sort on as many fields as you want. You are not limited to just three. You can resort on additional fields as many times as necessary, producing the equivalent of sorting on four, nine, or more fields. The guideline for sorting on more than three keys is to sort the lowest levels first, working your way up to the most important keys.

For example, if you want to sort column A as the **1**st Key, column B as the **2**nd Key, column C as the **3**rd Key, and so on for six keys, you would need a sort like this one:

Key	1	2	3	4	5	6
Column	A	B	C	D	E	F

Even though Excel has only three sort keys, you still can sort by the six columns needed. Your first sort will use the lowest level columns:

Key	1	2	3
Column	D	E	F

A second sort will sort the higher level columns with these keys:

Key	1	2	3
Column	A	B	C

Using Functions To Sort Data

You are not confined to sorting on the contents of a given cell. You have the option of adding to your database a column that contains a function for "pulling out" the sort characteristic you want.

In figure 23.10, column F contains the following function:

=RIGHT(E8,5)

This function extracts the last five characters of cell E8 (the ZIP code). After you have the ZIP codes in column F, you can sort on column F. If you want to permanently convert these calculated ZIP codes into text, copy them and paste them over the originals using the Edit Paste Special command with the Values option selected.

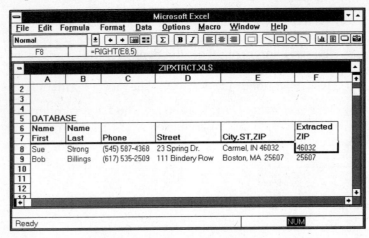

Fig. 23.10. *The RIGHT function pulls ZIP code information out of an address field.*

Rearranging Database Columns

Excel can sort columns as well as rows. This capability enables you to rearrange the columns in your database without extensive cutting and pasting.

Figure 23.11 shows the sample database about to be sorted into a new column order. A blank row inserted at row 11 contains numbers indicating the desired column order. Notice that the Days Due column must remain directly to the right of Due Date in order for the formula in Days Due to calculate correctly after sorting. The Sort dialog box shows that the sort will be by columns and that row 11, the row containing the new column order, will be sorted on.

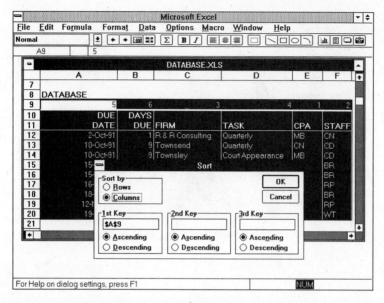

Fig. 23.11. *Columns in the database are rearranged according to assigned numbers.*

Figure 23.12 shows the database after the columns have been sorted in the order specified in row 9. If the Days Due column had not stayed directly to the right of the Due Date column, the formulas would display the error #VALUE!. This error would display because the formulas in Days Due would refer to cells containing text and not dates. Note that you may have to widen columns after you reorder a database in order to get rid of the #### narrow column warning.

Be careful when you perform a column sort on a worksheet such as the one in figure 23.12. Formulas refer to the same relative addresses (for example, two cells left) or refer to an absolute address. When you shift worksheet columns around, the appropriate cell may no longer be where it is expected.

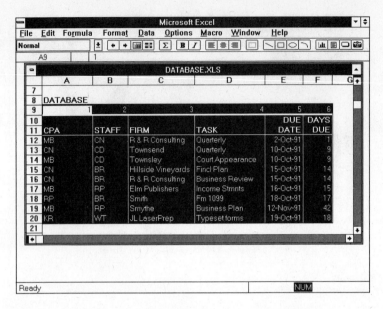

Fig. 23.12. The database after being sorted to rearrange columns.

From Here...

When you have your database set up and data entered, you will probably want to find records that meet a criteria you set. Chapter 24, "Finding and Editing Data," shows you how to search the database for records. You should read Chapter 24 and understand what a criterion is before you go on to Chapter 25, "Extracting and Maintaining Data." Chapter 25 describes how to extract information from the database in order to create a second database or a report.

24

Finding and Editing Data

Databases are used most frequently to find specific information. Excel provides two ways of finding and editing information. Excel's **Data Form** command, which displays the automatic database form, enables you to find data quickly and easily using simple search specifications. If you need to specify a more complex search, you must establish a criteria range and use the **Data Find** command. With the information in this chapter, you will be able to find and edit any type of data in your database. You also can use the methods you learn here to work with external databases on a hard disk or mainframe; these methods are described in Chapter 26, "Linking Excel to Databases with Q+E."

Finding Data

The process of finding data in your database consists of four general steps:

1. Decide what you want to find.

2. Define a pattern that specifies the types of information you want to find. This pattern is known as the *criteria*.

3. Enter that pattern in the database form or criteria range.

4. Choose the Find Next button on the database form, or choose the **Data Find** command when you are working in the worksheet.

681

You will enter criteria in a special range called the *criteria range*. The simplest of criteria are exact matches. For example, if you want to find someone named Smith, you type **Smith** below the Last Name field in the criteria range. Criteria can specify text, dates, numbers, numeric ranges, or logical values (TRUE or FALSE). Criteria can be simple comparisons or complex formulas that involve calculations; criteria can include multiple comparisons or ranges of dates or numbers.

You can use two methods to find information. The easiest method uses the **Data Form** command. The data form accepts only simple comparisons as criteria. The second method of finding information uses a criteria range. After you enter simple or complex criteria in the criteria range, you can use the **Data Find** command to search the database for matching records. This chapter describes both the **Data Form** and **Data Find** methods of finding records.

Finding Data with the Database Form

Excel's database form is excellent for finding records that satisfy simple comparisons. You enter criteria in a blank form and request the next or previous record that matches your criteria. The database form then displays the next or previous record that matches your criteria.

To use the database form to search for records, follow these steps:

1. If you have not done so, prepare the database by selecting the database range and choosing the **Data Set Database** command.

2. Choose the **Data Form** command to display the database form.

3. Select the **Criteria** button.

Selecting **Criteria** changes the buttons on the database form and clears the text box next to each field. Figure 24.1 shows the form ready to accept criteria.

4. Select the text box next to the field you want to search. Click in the box or press Tab for the next box, Shift+Tab for the previous box, or press the Alt+key combination for a particular field.

5. Type the criteria, but do not press the Enter key.

6. Press Tab to move to the next box if you want to type additional criteria.

7. Choose Find Next or Find Prev to move from the current record to the record that meets the entered criteria.

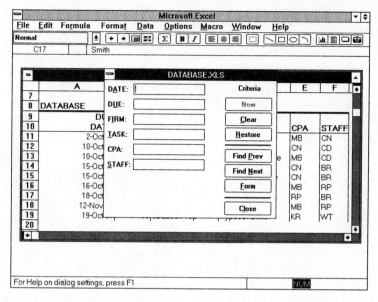

Fig. 24.1. *The database form ready to accept criteria.*

Figure 24.2 shows a database form with criteria entered that will match records where the CPA has the initials MB. In figure 24.3, the criteria in the DUE field indicates that items with less than 15 days will be found. You even can find records that must satisfy criteria in more than one field. For example, the criteria in figure 24.4 specify a search for records with a CPA who has initials CN, the DAYS DUE less than 15 days, and the FIRM name starting with H.

You can use the form to find only simple or multiple comparisons; all comparisons must be true for the record to be found. For example, in figure 24.4, the only records that will be found are those where all three criteria are true. Later in this chapter, table 24.2 shows the different types of comparison operators that you can use in the database form and criteria range.

Because the database form is so easy to use, you will be able to search for data after only a few minutes of practice. If you want to search for complex or calculated criteria, use the Data Find command. The **Data Find** command requires you to type criteria into a criteria range. Criteria in the criteria range do not affect searches done with the data form or criteria entered into the data form.

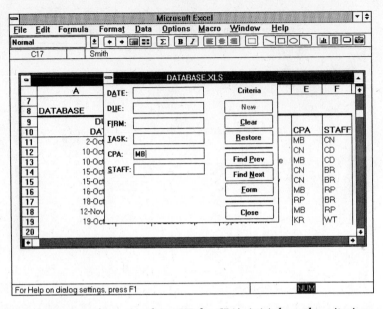

Fig. 24.2. *A database form specifying MB for CPA's initials as the criterion.*

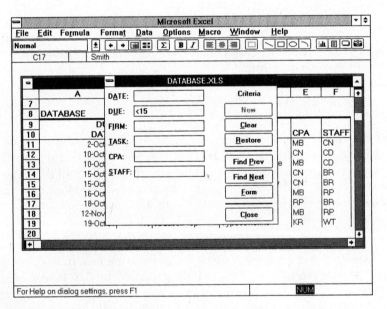

Fig. 24.3. *A database form specifying a due date of less than 15 days as the criterion.*

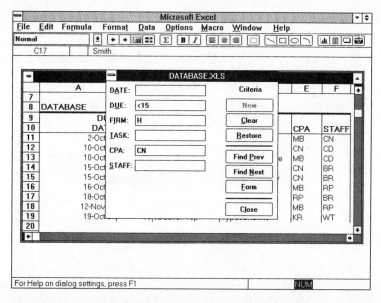

Fig. 24.4. *A form specifying that the DAYS DUE must be less than 15, the FIRM name must start with H, and the CPA's initials must be CN.*

Using the Data Find Command

Although using the **Data Find** command involves more work than using the database form, the command enables you to search for data with complex or calculated criteria. In addition, the command prepares you to use more powerful database features, such as extracting a copy of specific data from a database for use in reports. The command also prepares you for analyzing a database.

Defining the Criteria Range

If you plan to use the **Data Find** command, you need to create and define a criteria range after you have set the database with the **Data Set Database** command. The top row of the criteria range contains field names that must be spelled exactly the same as the field names above the database. The criteria range also includes at least one blank row below the field names. You enter criteria in this row. Excel matches the criteria under a field name in the criteria range against the data under the same field name in the database.

Figure 24.5 shows a selected criteria range. In this example, Format **Border** was used to outline selected cells.

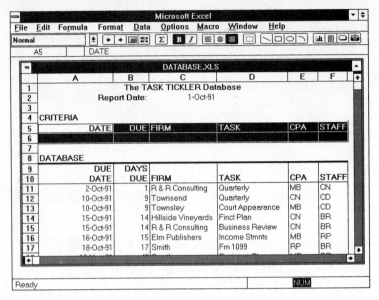

Fig. 24.5. *Borders around a criteria range help identify where to enter questions.*

You define the criteria range in much the same way as you set the database range. Follow these steps to define a criteria range:

1. Copy the field names from the top of the database range to the top row of the criteria range. Copying the field names reduces the chance of mistakes from retyping.

   If the field names in the criteria range do not match those in the database, the **Data Find** command will not work. To make sure that your criteria field names match the database field names exactly, copy them from the database with the **Edit Copy** and **Edit Paste** commands. You need not include every field name in the criteria range. You can include the names in any order you like, as long as they match the field names used in the database. The field names in the criteria range must be either text or formulas that produce text.

2. Select all the field names and one blank row underneath the field names.

   Include only one blank row when you initially create the criteria range. In this blank row, you will type criteria for finding or extracting data. If you create blank rows in addition to the row or rows containing the criteria, the blank rows will tell Excel to find or extract all records in the database. You can see the size of the criteria range by pressing the F5 key and selecting the criteria range from the Goto list. If there are unneeded blank rows in the criteria range, redefine the criteria range without the blank rows.

3. Choose the Data Set Criteria command.

4. While the criteria range is selected, you may want to use the Format Border command to outline the criteria range and make it easier to identify.

Choosing Data Set Criteria names the selected range Criteria. Use Formula Define Name to see the cell address reference or delete the range name Criteria.

Although you can have only one named criteria range at a time, you can quickly switch between criteria ranges. Chapter 23, "Entering and Sorting Data," contains a tip on how to quickly change databases. You can use this same tip to quickly change criteria ranges.

Entering Criteria

After you set the database and criteria ranges, you are ready to search for records in the database. Follow these steps to enter the criteria and invoke the search:

1. Enter criteria in the criteria range.

   The criteria range can contain simple criteria, such as Smith below the FIRM field name in figure 24.6. The criteria range also can contain entries that match ranges of numbers, calculate criteria, and contain TRUE/FALSE comparisons. This chapter's sections "Using Simple Comparisons" and "Using Calculated Criteria" describe simple, complex, and calculated criteria.

2. To begin the search at the first database record, select a cell outside and above the database. To begin the search at a specific record in the database, select a cell in that record.

3. Choose the Data Find command. (If you want to search backward through the database, hold down Shift while choosing Data Find.)

   When Excel encounters a record that meets the criteria you have specified, the window scrolls to display the database record; the status line displays the word Find; and the number of the found record appears in the Reference Area, left of the formula bar. You will also notice that the scroll bars become striped, and the found record appears selected, as shown in figure 24.6. If no records meet the criteria, Excel beeps and displays an alert box.

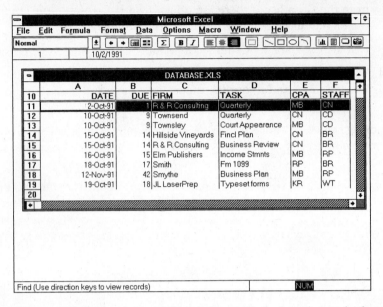

Fig. 24.6. The database appears in the window with the found record selected.

4. Press the up- or down-arrow keys, or click on the scroll arrows, to move to the next or previous matching record. If there are no more matching records, Excel beeps and you are unable to move the cursor.

5. Choose the Data Exit Find command, press Esc, or click on a cell outside the database range to exit Find mode.

While in Find mode, you can scroll through the records that meet the criteria. Use the commands listed in table 24.1 to scroll the database.

Table 24.1
Scrolling a Database

Mouse

Result	Action
Move to next matching record	Click on down scroll arrow
Move to previous matching record	Click on up scroll arrow
Jump to match at least one page (screen height) away	Click in scroll bar

Keyboard

Result	Action
Move to next matching record	Press down arrow
Move to previous matching record	Press up arrow
Move active cell right	Press Tab
Move active cell left	Press Shift+Tab
Scroll right	Press right arrow
Scroll left	Press left arrow
Move to next matching record at least one window away	Press PgDn
Move to previous matching record at least one window away	Press PgUp

While in Find mode, you cannot scroll outside the database either vertically or horizontally. Although you can move outside the database area with arrow keys, doing so cancels the **Data Find** command.

When you are ready to exit from **Data Find**, choose **Data Exit Find** or press Esc.

Tip: *Viewing Criteria and Database Ranges Simultaneously*
As you scroll through your database, you can see two areas of the worksheet at the same time if you split the database window. You can jump back and forth between the split windows by pressing F6 or Shift+F6.

Using the mouse, split the window by dragging the split bar down from the top of the vertical scroll bar. (The split bar appears as a dark bank above the up arrowhead in the bar.) Using the keyboard, press Alt, hyphen key, and then choose Split. Use the down-arrow key to position the split, and then press Enter. To remove the split when it is no longer needed, repeat the procedure and move the split back to its extreme position on the scroll bar.

Using Simple Comparisons

Comparative criteria involve simple equalities or greater- or less-than comparisons. Comparative criteria do not involve mathematical calculations or logical operators, AND or OR. You can use comparative criteria in the database form and in the criteria range. If you need to use complex or calculated criteria, you must use a criteria range in conjunction with the **Data** **F**ind, **E**xtract, or **D**elete commands (see this chapter's section "Using Calculated Criteria").

The simplest and easiest criteria specify text for which you are searching. Figures 24.7 and 24.8 show how a text criteria for the name Smith is entered in the database form (fig. 24.7) and in the criteria row of the criteria range (fig. 24.8) You can see that the criteria is typed exactly as you expect it to be entered in the database. Text criteria is not case-sensitive, so you can match against upper- or lowercase text.

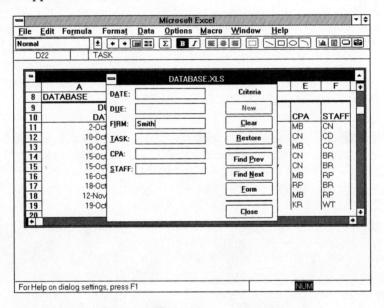

Fig. 24.7. *Text criteria in the database form.*

If you selected **Data** **F**ind or Find Next using Smith as shown in figure 24.7 and 24.8, you would find records containing any of the following:

Smith
Smithely
Smithington

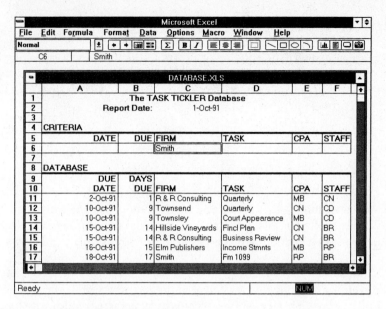

Fig. 24.8. *Text criteria in the criteria range.*

Notice that Excel matches more words than just "Smith." Excel matches the text you enter and accepts any spaces or text after the last character in the criteria. This feature helps you to find records in which a blank space was accidentally typed after the last character.

If you want to find records that contain exactly the word "Smith" and no other variations, then enter the criteria in the criteria range as follows:

="Smith"

Make sure that you enclose the text in quotation marks.

The most frequent database problem is caused by incorrectly clearing the criteria range. If you do not clear criteria from the criteria range, Excel will try to find records that match both the old and new criteria.

To clear the criteria row correctly, select the cells containing the old criteria. Next, choose the Edit Clear command; or press Del, then Enter.

Do not clear cells by pressing the space bar and then pressing Enter. This procedure enters a blank character in the criteria row. Excel then will attempt to find records that contain a blank character in that field.

Finding Near Matches

If you are not sure of the spelling of a word in the database, or you need to find records containing similar but not identical text, you will need a couple of extra cards up your sleeve. In Excel, these are called *wild cards*, and they are part of the game.

The two wild cards used with text criteria are the asterisk (*) and the question mark (?). They represent characters as follows:

? Any single character in the same position
* Any group of characters in the same position

The question mark (?) is useful if you are uncertain how the word you want to match is spelled. For example, if a name in the Last Name field could be either Smith or Smythe, then you would enter your criteria as follows:

sm?th

The ? matches any single letter between the *m* and *t*. Excel accepts the *e* at the end of Smythe because Excel accepts any characters following the end of the criteria word. Because Excel does not distinguish between upper- and lowercase when matching, the program also matches the lowercase *s* in the criteria with the capital *S*.

The asterisk (*) matches groups of characters. You can use it at any location in the text criteria—beginning, middle, or end. To locate data in a field with a name like Gallon_Cans, you might use the criteria `* paint`. This criteria might find the following matches:

blue paint
red paint
yellow paint

If you need to find the actual symbols * or ? in a database, then type a tilde (~) before the * or ?. The tilde indicates that you are not using the * or ? as a wild card.

If you need to use a wild card within an exact match that cuts out the trailing characters, include a wild card like the one shown in figure 24.9:

`="=Sm?th"`

This wild card will find Smith, Smoth, or Smath, but not Smooth.

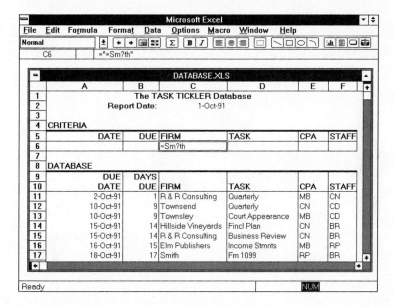

Fig. 24.9. *Use a combination of wild cards and quotes to find an exact match for some characters and a wild card match for others.*

Making Simple Numeric Comparisons

To find an exact match for a number, enter the number in the criteria row directly below the field name. For example, you might enter a number below the Due field in a criteria range or in a database form.

If you want to find numbers greater than or less than a number, enter comparison criteria, such as the criteria in figure 24.3. In this case, the expression <15 tells Excel to search the DUE field (column) for database values that are less than 15. Table 24.2 shows other comparison operators that you can use in the criteria range or database form.

Table 24.2
Comparison Operators

Operator	Meaning	Criteria	Finds
=	Equal	=200	Fields equal to 200
=	Equal	=	Fields equal to blank
>	Greater than	>200	Fields greater than 200

continues

Table 24.2 (*continued*)

Operator	Meaning	Criteria	Finds
>=	Greater than or equal to	>=200	Fields greater than or equal to 200
<	Less than	<200	Fields less than 200
<=	Less than or equal to	<=200	Fields less than or equal to 200
<>	Not equal to	<>200	Fields not equal to 200
<>	Not equal to	<>	Fields that are not blank

Comparing Dates

When you search for dates using comparison criteria, use the comparative operators from table 24.2. Type dates the same way you would type them into a worksheet cell. For example, to search the database shown in figure 24.9 for dates greater than October 14, 1992, you could enter the following criteria under DATE:

>10/14/92

OR

>Oct 14, 92

You can use a date in the criteria that is in any of Excel's predefined date formats.

Using Multiple Comparative Criteria

You can define multiple criteria in the database form by specifying criteria for each field in the form. When you define multiple criteria, all the criteria must be true in a record for Excel to find that record. For example, figure 24.10 finds records that have a DATE DUE greater than 14 *AND* have a CPA's initials of CN.

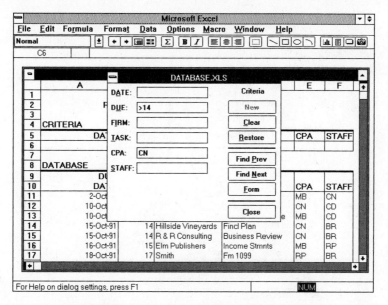

Fig. 24.10. *Multiple criteria in the database form must all be true to find a record.*

When using **Data Find**, you can enter multiple criteria on the same row in the criteria range. When you enter multiple criteria on the same criteria row, then *all* the criteria must be met in order for a record to qualify as a match. Figure 24.11 shows the criteria range where DAYS DUE must be greater than 14 *AND* CPA must be CN. Because both of these criteria are in the same row of the criteria range, a database record must meet both criteria for Excel to find the record.

To find records where one *OR* the other criteria is met, use the criteria range with more than one row and **Data Find**. Insert an additional row in the criteria range for each acceptable criterion. Figure 24.12 shows a criteria range with two rows for criteria. The criteria entries shown below CPA tell Excel to find records where the CPA is MB *OR* the CPA is CN.

Whenever you choose the size of the criteria range, be sure to check the size of the new range with the **Formula Define Name** command. Redefine the range with the **Data Set Criteria** range command, if necessary.

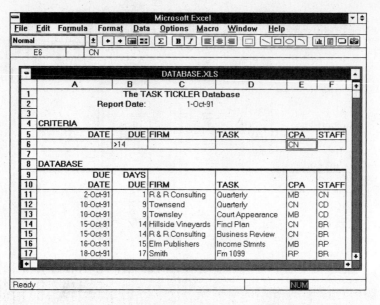

Fig. 24.11. Criteria in the same row of the criteria range must all be true for Excel to find a record.

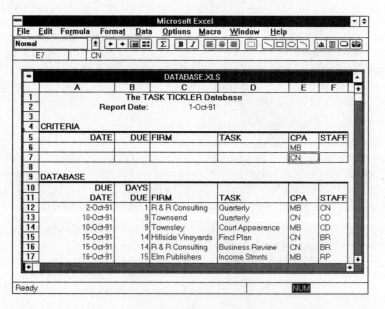

Fig. 24.12. Two rows of criteria that tell Excel to find all records where the CPA initials are either MB or CN.

> **Note:** *Using Two or More Rows in the Criteria Range*
> Be careful when you use two or more rows in the criteria range.
> A blank cell in the criteria range tells Excel to find all values in that
> field. A blank row tells Excel to find all values in every field.
> Therefore, when you leave a row blank in the criteria range, Excel
> finds, extracts, or deletes all data in the database. If you are unsure
> of the size of your criteria range, you can see the range by pressing
> F5 (Goto), selecting the name Criteria, and pressing Enter.

Figure 24.13 shows how you can combine simple criteria to ask complex
questions of your database. The criteria range uses two rows so that you can
find records matching either one value or the other. All the criteria within
either row must be true for Excel to find a record. Here is the English
equivalent of the criteria range in the figure:

The DAYS DUE are less than 15 AND the CPA is CN.

OR

The DUE DATE is 18-Oct-91 AND the FIRM name begins with S.

Excel finds the records that meet these criteria in rows 13, 15, 16, and 18.

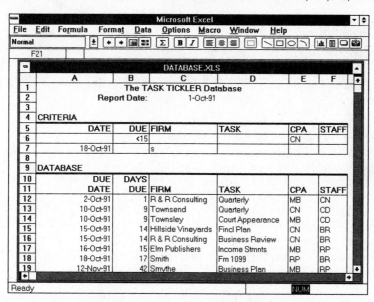

Fig. 24.13. *Multiple criteria specifying AND in the same rows and specifying OR
between rows.*

Using Calculated and Compound Criteria

Using simple comparative criteria is helpful and quick, but in some instances you need to specify more exact data. You may want to find dates between two ranges or even use formulas to calculate what you are searching for. In these cases, you will need to use calculated criteria.

Using Calculated Criteria

You can select records according to any calculation that results in a TRUE or FALSE logical value as a criteria. Calculated criteria are needed, for example, when you want to find records where inventory quantities are less than a specified reorder quantity, where a range of dates are needed but some dates within the range are excluded, or where a mailing list has the ZIP code included with the City and State field.

Figure 24.14 shows an example of calculated criteria that find Parts that were sold for less than 90 percent of Retail price. Notice that the calculated criteria, =E9<0.9*D9, must be entered in the criteria range below a name that does *not* exist in the database. In this example, the name Calc was inserted in the middle of the criteria range. Notice in the figure that Calc is not used as a field name in the database. You can use any text name above the calculated criteria, so long as it has not been used in the database field names.

> **Note: *Entering Calculated Criteria***
> You must enter calculated criteria in the criteria range below names that do not exist as field names in the database.

In your calculated criteria formula, use cell references that refer to cells in the top data row of the database. You nearly always will use relative reference addresses (without $ signs). Use absolute cell references to refer to any cell involved in the criteria that is outside the database.

Calculated criteria can involve multiple fields and equations, but the result must produce a TRUE or FALSE condition. The Excel database commands select those records that produce a TRUE result. Some simple calculated criteria, where the first data row is row 36, are illustrated in table 24.3.

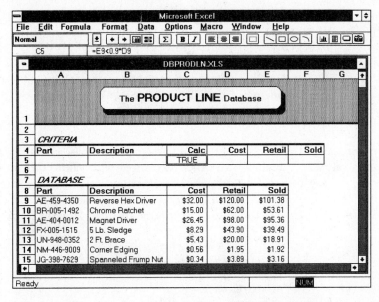

Fig. 24.14. *Calculated criteria must use a new field name in the criteria range.*

Table 24.3
Simple Calculated Criteria

Criteria	Explanation
=B36=G36	Compares the values of fields in the same database row. Selects the record when the value in column B equals the value in column G.
=B36<G36/2	Compares the value in B36 to one half the value in G36. Both cells are in the same record. Selects the record when the value in column B is less than half of the value in column G.
=B36-G36>10	Compares two values in the same database record. Selects the record when a value in column B minus a value in column G is greater than 10.

Tip: *Cross-Checking Comparative or Calculated Criteria*
If you use the correct syntax when you enter a calculated criteria formula, Excel displays TRUE or FALSE in the cell after you enter the formula. TRUE or FALSE applies to the specific cells you used in the formula. Check to see whether TRUE or FALSE corresponds correctly to the evaluation of the cells you used in the criteria formula.

More complex but extremely useful calculated criteria include comparisons between values in a record with other records or with values outside the database. These types of criteria are useful when you want to compare records or use criteria calculated elsewhere in the worksheet. Table 24.4 shows some examples of these types of criteria; the first data row is row 36.

Table 24.4
Complex Calculated Criteria

Criteria	Explanation
=B36–G37>10	Compares values in adjacent database records. Selects the record when the value in column B of one record is more than ten greater than the value in column G of the next record.
=B36=$C$24	Compares a value in a record to a value outside the database. Selects the record when the value in column B equals the value in $C$24, where C24 is a cell outside the database.

As you can see from the table, calculated criteria can involve cell references that are outside the database. However, you must use an absolute reference to refer to any location outside the database range.

Using Compound Criteria

You can use Excel's AND, OR, and NOT functions to create complex compound criteria. This method is useful for specifying complex criteria that cannot be handled by inserting additional rows in the criteria range.

You can use any of the following functions in your compound criteria. In order for a **Data** command to select a record, the compound criteria must return the TRUE or FALSE value as follows:

AND   All conditions must be TRUE.

OR   One condition or the other or both must be TRUE.

NOT   The condition used with NOT is reversed. TRUE changes to FALSE; FALSE changes to TRUE.

Just as you can enter calculated criteria that results in a TRUE or FALSE value, you can enter AND, OR, and NOT functions that evaluate to TRUE or FALSE. For example, consider the database in figure 24.15. For each of the following queries stated in English syntax, the associated compound criteria formula is presented, and the resulting records that Excel finds are listed.

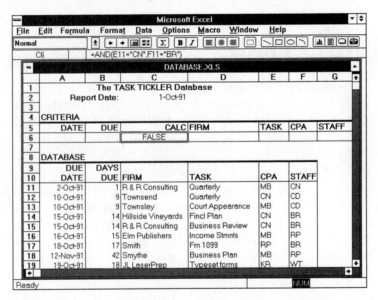

Fig. 24.15. Using AND and OR functions to build complex criteria.

English statement:	The CPA is CN AND the STAFF is BR.
Compound criteria:	=AND(E11="CN",F11="BR")
Result:	Finds the records in row 14 and 15.
English statement:	The FIRM is Townsley OR the FIRM is Smith.
Compound criteria:	=OR(C11="Townsley",C11="Smith")
Result:	Finds the records in rows 13 and 17.

English statement:	The FIRM is NOT Townsley AND the DAYS DUE is 9.
Compound criteria:	=AND(NOT(C11="Townsley"),B11=9)
Result:	Finds the record in row 12.

Note: *AND vs. OR*

AND and OR are easy to confuse. If you are searching a single field for two different text entries (for example, Smith and Jones), use the OR function. An OR function specifies that one name OR the other can be found (TRUE). An AND function specifies that Smith AND Jones must be in the field at the same time—something that will not happen.

Editing Data

Keeping a database current involves two basic functions: ongoing updating of individual records and periodic "scrubbing" to get rid of old records. The balance of this chapter describes how to edit records. The following chapter describes how to manage a database by deleting large numbers of records that meet a specific criteria.

The following descriptions cover two methods of editing the database: editing in the database form and editing directly in the worksheet. In cases where you will be editing one or two records that are easy to find, the database form may be preferable. However, when you have to do a complex search to find the records or when you can copy information from one field into adjacent fields, then you will want to edit directly in the worksheet.

Editing Data with the Database Form

The easiest way to edit individual records is with the database form. If you can find the record using the simple comparative criteria available in the database form, then use the form to do your editing.

Begin by defining the database range with **Data Set Database**. After you have defined the range, follow these steps to find the records you want and edit them:

1. Choose the **Data Form** command.

2. Select the **C**riteria button.

3. To define the records you want to edit, type the criteria. Press Tab or Shift+Tab to move between fields in the criteria form.

4. Select the Find **N**ext button to find the next record matching the criteria.

5. Edit the field contents using normal mouse or keyboard techniques. Press the appropriate Alt+key combination to select a text box, or press the Tab key to move between boxes. Figure 24.16 shows the **T**ask text box selected after pressing Alt+T.

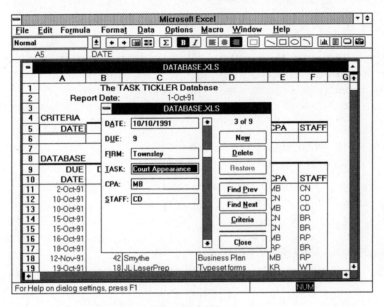

Fig. 24.16. *The Task text box ready for editing.*

6. Press Enter or scroll up or down to save the change and move to the next record. Choose the **R**estore button to restore the changes made during editing. Choosing **R**estore after you leave the record will not restore the data.

7. Select C**l**ose to save the changes and return to the worksheet.

If you need to delete a record you have found with the form, then choose the **D**elete button on the form. The alert message, shown in figure 24.17, will warn that you are about to delete the current record. Choose OK or press Enter to complete the deletion. Keep in mind that deleted records cannot be recovered.

Fig. 24.17. The alert box warns that you are about to delete a record.

Editing Data Directly in the Worksheet

Some of the records you want to edit may require finding calculated or compound criteria. At other times, you may want to edit or format adjacent rows at one time. In these cases, you can enter the criteria in the criteria range, use **Data Find** to find the records, and make your changes directly in the worksheet.

To find the appropriate records with the help of the **Data Find** command and edit data directly in the worksheet, follow these steps:

1. Enter the criteria in the criteria range for the records you want to edit.

2. Choose the **D**ata **F**ind command.

3. Move to the record you want to edit.

4. Select the cell you want to edit by clicking on the cell or pressing Tab or Shift +Tab to move to the cell. If you move outside of the database, the Find mode is turned off.

5. Edit the cell contents by clicking in the formula bar or pressing F2 (the Edit key) and making changes. Going into Edit mode throws Excel out of Find mode. You are now back to editing in a normal worksheet.

6. Press Enter to complete the change.

Usually, you will have to make changes to multiple records that all meet the same search criteria. However, as soon as you begin to edit a found record, Excel takes you out of the Find mode and puts you back into the normal worksheet. To find the next record, you again must choose **Data Find**. If you leave the active cell where it is in the database, Excel will begin looking for the next record after the current one. To save keystrokes, you may want to create a simple command macro that replaces the three keystrokes needed to choose **D**ata **F**ind with a single Ctrl+key combination. The Macro Quick Start in Chapter 28 shows you how to create simple but useful macros such as this one.

If you want to delete a record directly from the worksheet, follow these steps:

1. Use the **D**ata **F**ind command to find the record, then press Esc to return to normal worksheet mode.

2. Select the row or cells you want to delete. If you select cells, be sure to select the full width of the record.

3. Choose the **E**dit **D**elete command.

4. If you are deleting cells, the Delete dialog box asks whether you want to shift the remaining cells up or left. Select the Shift Cells Up option from the dialog box.

5. Choose OK or press Enter.

Be careful if you delete the entire row passing through a database. You may delete information on either side of the database.

If you need to delete a number of records, you may want to sort the database first. Sorting will enable you to find and delete all the records at once. Sorting is described in Chapter 23, "Entering and Sorting Data." You also can use the **D**ata **D**elete command to delete records that meet the criteria you specify.

From Here...

Two important database topics have not yet been discussed in this text: extracting information for reports and maintaining a database. These topics are covered in Chapter 25, "Extracting and Maintaining Data."

If you analyze information kept in databases—such as accounting data, marketing information, or scientific readings from instruments—you should also read Chapter 27, "Building Extensive Databases," to discover how to use database functions and data tables. These features can save you hours of work doing analysis.

25

Extracting and Maintaining Data

This chapter shows you how to create database reports and maintain your database. You will use the **Data Extract** command with what you already learned about criteria to pull information from the database and copy it to a new worksheet location. You also learn how to copy data into a new file and to delete groups of records from your database.

Extracting Data

The **Data Extract** command makes a copy of data that meets the criteria in a criteria range. The copy, which is placed in a section of the worksheet separate from the original database, is useful for creating special reports, for making subsets of the original database, and for preparing data to be transferred to other programs. A special option of the **Extract** command extracts only those records that are unique. The original database remains intact after you extract a copy of the data that matches the criteria.

Like **Data Find**, the **Data Extract** command needs to have the database and criteria ranges specified before it will work. In addition, **Data Extract** needs to know where to put the copied information and how to arrange the columns of data.

A third set of field names—exactly the same as those in the database and criteria ranges—tells Excel which data you want extracted and how you want it arranged. Figure 25.1 shows a small database with the three parts that are important to extracting: the criteria range in A5:F6, the database range in A10:F19, and the field names for the extract range in A22:F22. In figure 25.2, the data meeting the criteria is extracted from the database and copied below the field names in the extract range. Notice that in figure 25.2 the two extracted records each indicate 14 days due, which matches the criteria set in row 6.

			Microsoft Excel - DATABASE.XLS			
File	Edit	Formula	Format	Data	Options	Macro	Window	Help

Normal

B6 = 14

	A	B	C	D	E	F	G
4	CRITERIA						
5		DATE	DUE	FIRM	TASK	CPA	STAFF
6			14				
8	DATABASE						
9		DUE	DAYS				
10		DATE	DUE	FIRM	TASK	CPA	STAFF
11		2-Oct-91	1	R & R Consulting	Quarterly	MB	CN
12		10-Oct-91	9	Townsend	Quarterly	CN	CD
13		10-Oct-91	9	Townsley	Court Appearance	MB	CD
14		15-Oct-91	14	Hillside Vineyards	Fincl Plan	CN	BR
15		15-Oct-91	14	R & R Consulting	Business Review	CN	BR
16		16-Oct-91	15	Elm Publishers	Income Stmnts	MB	RP
17		18-Oct-91	17	Smith	Fm 1099	RP	BR
18		12-Nov-91	42	Smythe	Business Plan	MB	RP
19		19-Oct-91	18	JL LaserPrep	Typeset forms	KR	WT
21	EXTRACT						
22		DATE	DUE	FIRM	TASK	CPA	STAFF
23							
24							

Ready — NUM

Fig. 25.1. The database, criteria, and extract ranges.

The extract range is separate and distinct from the criteria and database ranges. In figures 25.1 and 25.2, notice that three ranges are used. The row of field names selected for **Data Extract** must be separate from the rows of field names that head the database and criteria ranges.

 You can define the extract range in two ways. If you want to use a named extract range, you can select the range and name it with **Data Set Extract**. If you do not name the extract range, Excel uses the currently selected cells as the extract range. These selected cells must have field names in the top row.

Besides having two methods to specify the extract range, you can specify two sizes of extract ranges, limited and unlimited. A *limited extract range* includes the field names at the top of the range and a limited number of cells below the names. The extracted information fills only the cells available in the extract range and then stops. Extracted data that won't fit is left out. You are warned if this happens.

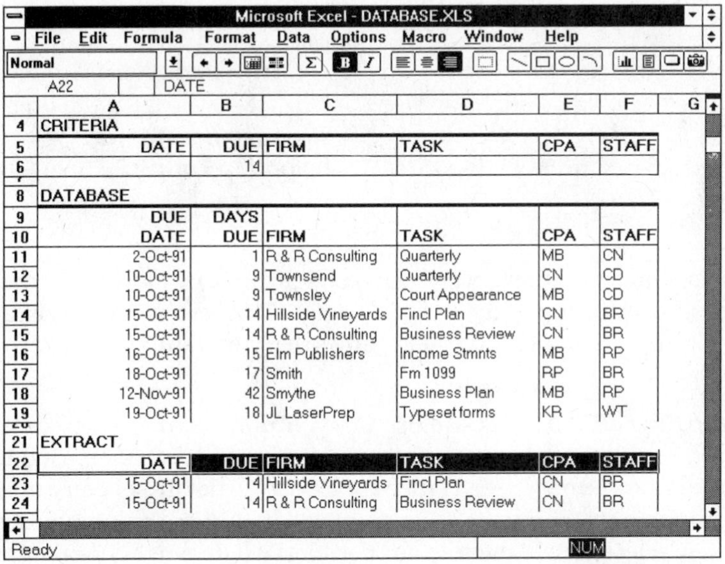

Fig. 25.2. Extracted data is copied from the database and placed below the extract field names.

The other range size is the *unlimited extract range.* In an unlimited extract range, you select only the field names or name only the field names with **Data Set Extract.** The result is an extract range that can be filled with data, beginning with the field names and extending to the bottom of the worksheet. If you are unsure of how much data will be extracted, you should use an unlimited extract range.

> **Note: *Old Data below the Field Names in an Unlimited Extract Range***
>
> Old data or parts of the worksheet below the field names of an unlimited extract range will be cleared. Do not put anything between the field names of an unlimited extract range and the bottom of the worksheet. You will not be warned that all cells below the headings will be cleared. Excel clears this area automatically when you choose the **Data Extract** command to avoid intermingling of the old data with the new.

> **Tip: *Recalculating before You Extract Data***
> If Excel is set to recalculate formulas manually, and the worksheet needs to be recalculated, the word `Calculate` appears at the bottom of the screen. To ensure that all cells contain current values before the extraction, press F9 (Recalculate) before executing the **Extract** command.

The field names at the top of the extract range must be identical to the field names used at the top of the database range. The best way to prepare your extract range is by copying the field names that you want from the top of the database.

But as figures 25.3 and 25.4 illustrate, you don't have to include in the extract range all the field names from the database range, nor must the field names be in the same order as they appear in the database. You can create reports with only the information you need and in the column order you want. Use selected field names and reorder the names as you want them to appear in the extracted data.

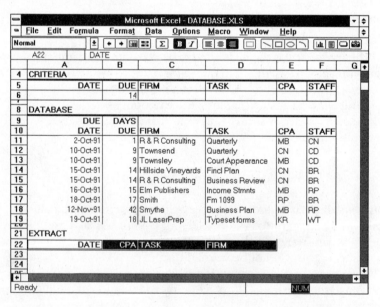

Fig. 25.3. The extract field names do not have to include all the field names; they can appear in a different order from those in the database.

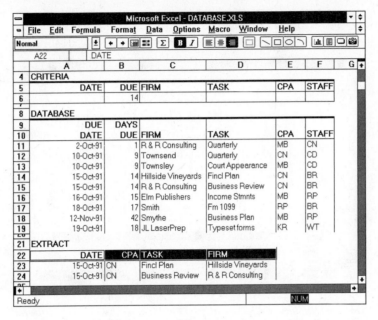

Fig. 25.4. *Reordering field names enables you to structure reports.*

Use the following basic procedure to extract from the database the information you want. Note that each of these steps is described in greater detail in the text that follows.

1. Create field names for an extract range by copying the single row of field names from the top of the database range. Arrange the field names in the order you want the columns of data to appear.

2. Enter the criteria in the criteria range.

 3. If you did not previously name the extract range with **Data Set Extract**, use one of these methods to specify the extract range:

   If you want a temporary extract range, select the extract range. Select only the field names for an unlimited extract range, or select the field names and a limited number of cells below.

   If you want to name an extract range that can be reused by later extract commands, select only the field names for an unlimited extract range; or select the field names and a limited number of cells below, and then choose the **Data Set Extract** command.

Figure 25.5 shows field names selected to create an unlimited range. Figure 25.6 shows a limited range selected.

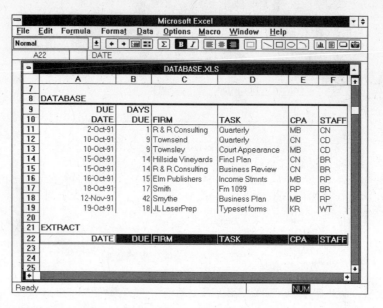

Fig. 25.5. Selecting or specifying only the field names creates an unlimited extract range.

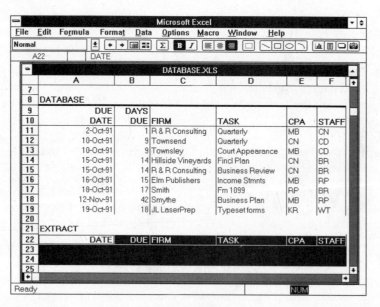

Fig. 25.6. Selecting or specifying the field names and a limited number of cells below creates a limited extract range.

4. Choose the Data Extract command.

5. Select the Unique Records Only option if you do not want duplicate records to appear.

6. Choose OK or press Enter.

Selecting the Extract Range

This section explains in detail the procedures for extracting data in the two sizes of extract range. The benefit of an unlimited extract range is that it allows you to extract an unlimited number of records. This type of extract works well when you don't know how many records will be extracted.

The second, or limited, type of extract range predetermines the area that will hold extracted records. This type of extract works best in a crowded worksheet with limited space.

Extracting a Limited Amount of Data

To extract a limited amount of data, you must select the extract range before you choose the Data Extract command. Select the extract cell that contains the field names, and then select as many cells below as you need to hold the extracted data. Figure 25.6 shows an extract range with the field names selected and a few cells for extracted data.

Excel clears the extract range before copying the extracted data into the range. In this way, the program prevents old and new extract data from mixing.

If Excel attempts to extract more data than will fit into the range you select, the extract continues; however, an alert box like the one in figure 25.7 appears. The alert box tells you that the extract range is full. This message indicates that still more data could be extracted.

When you see the alert box, you have four options: accept the limited amount of data already extracted; create a larger extract range; limit your criteria; or use the technique described in the following section to create an unlimited extract range.

Fig. 25.7. An alert box warns you when the extract range cannot hold all the extracted data.

Extracting Unlimited Rows of Data

You probably will use an unlimited extract range when you are not sure how much data will be extracted. In this case, select only the field names of the extract range, as shown in figure 25.5. Excel extracts all the appropriate data and copies it below the extract field names.

Be careful when designing a worksheet with an unlimited extract range. During the extraction process, Excel clears the cells in all columns below the extract field names to prevent mixing old and new data. During the extraction process, any old data in the extract range is cleared. Never put anything below an unlimited extract range!

Figures 25.8 and 25.9 illustrate the process of extracting data to an unlimited range. In figure 25.8, markers are displayed beneath and to the side of the extract range. Figure 25.9 shows the result of the Data Extract command; the marker underneath the extract range is cleared to make room for the extracted data. Notice that the markers on the side are still intact.

> **Tip:** *Using Extraction To Prepare Data for Other Programs*
> When you extract data from your worksheet, you can select and prepare the data you need to transfer to other programs or to other Excel worksheets. To prepare a database for transfer, first extract the records and fields that you want transferred. Then cut the extracted data out of the extract range and paste it into a new, blank worksheet. Now choose the File Save As command, choose the Options button, and select the file format you want to use when you export (save) the worksheet.

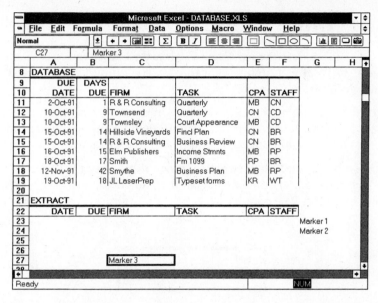

Fig. 25.8. *An unlimited extract range before extraction; markers appear below and to the right of the range.*

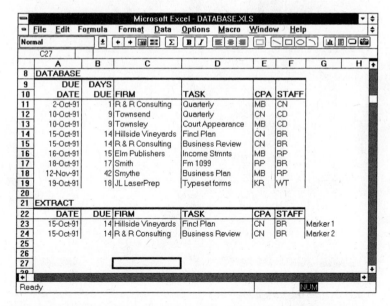

Fig. 25.9. *During extraction, Excel clears the area below the extract field names; here, the marker has disappeared.*

Extracting Unique Records

After you choose **Data Extract**, Excel displays the Extract dialog box, shown in figure 25.10. If you do not want to copy any duplicate data, select the Unique Records Only option.

In figure 25.11, for example, the records in rows 14 and 15 are the same except for one field. If you extract with *all* field headings and the Unique Records Only option, both records appear in the extract range.

If, however, the TASK field is removed from the extract range, only one record is extracted. Without the data in the TASK field, the two records are duplicates. Figure 25.12 shows the result of an extraction where the TASK field name is not part of the extract range.

Fig. 25.10. The Extract dialog box enables you to eliminate duplicate records.

	A	B	C	D	E	F	G	H
8	DATABASE							
9	DUE	DAYS						
10	DATE	DUE	FIRM	TASK	CPA	STAFF		
11	2-Oct-91	1	R & R Consulting	Quarterly	MB	CN		
12	10-Oct-91	9	Townsend	Quarterly	CN	CD		
13	10-Oct-91	9	Townsley	Court Appearance	MB	CD		
14	15-Oct-91	14	Hillside Vineyards	Fincl Plan	CN	BR		
15	15-Oct-91	14	Hillside Vineyards	Business Review	CN	BR		
16	16-Oct-91	15	Elm Publishers	Income Stmnts	MB	RP		
17	18-Oct-91	17	Smith	Fm 1099	RP	BR		
18	12-Nov-91	42	Smythe	Business Plan	MB	RP		
19	19-Oct-91	18	JL LaserPrep	Typeset forms	KR	WT		
20								
21	EXTRACT							
22	DATE	DUE	FIRM	TASK	CPA	STAFF		
23	2-Oct-91	1	R & R Consulting	Quarterly	MB	CN		
24	10-Oct-91	9	Townsend	Quarterly	CN	CD		
25	10-Oct-91	9	Townsley	Court Appearance	MB	CD		
26	15-Oct-91	14	Hillside Vineyards	Fincl Plan	CN	BR		
27	15-Oct-91	14	Hillside Vineyards	Business Review	CN	BR		
28	16-Oct-91	15	Elm Publishers	Income Stmnts	MB	RP		
29	18-Oct-91	17	Smith	Fm 1099	RP	BR		

Fig. 25.11. Extracting unique records with all field names selected; note that both records for Hillside Vineyards are extracted.

	A22		DATE			
	A	B	C	D	E	F	G	H
8	DATABASE						
9	DUE	DAYS					
10	DATE	DUE	FIRM	TASK	CPA	STAFF	
11	2-Oct-91	1	R & R Consulting	Quarterly	MB	CN	
12	10-Oct-91	9	Townsend	Quarterly	CN	CD	
13	10-Oct-91	9	Townsley	Court Appearance	MB	CD	
14	15-Oct-91	14	Hillside Vineyards	Fincl Plan	CN	BR	
15	15-Oct-91	14	Hillside Vineyards	Business Review	CN	BR	
16	16-Oct-91	15	Elm Publishers	Income Stmnts	MB	RP	
17	18-Oct-91	17	Smith	Fm 1099	RP	BR	
18	12-Nov-91	42	Smythe	Business Plan	MB	RP	
19	19-Oct-91	18	JL LaserPrep	Typeset forms	KR	WT	
20							
21	EXTRACT						
22	DATE	DUE	FIRM	CPA		STAFF	
23	2-Oct-91	1	R & R Consulting	MB		CN	
24	10-Oct-91	9	Townsend	CN		CD	
25	10-Oct-91	9	Townsley	MB		CD	
26	15-Oct-91	14	Hillside Vineyards	CN		BR	
27	16-Oct-91	15	Elm Publishers	MB		RP	
28	18-Oct-91	17	Smith	RP		BR	
29	12-Nov-91	42	Smythe	MB		RP	

Fig. 25.12. Unique records extracted without the TASK field; note that only one record appears for Hillside Vineyards.

Tip: *Locating Typos or Cleaning a Mailing List*
Use a unique extract to cross-check databases for typographical errors. Suppose, for example, that you entered a list of part names into a database, with 16 different part names into a total of 320 records. To cross-check for misspelled part names, you can extract unique records using only the field containing the part names. Each of the 16 correctly spelled part names appears once in the extract range. Any misspelled part name appears in the extract range as an additional item. Use **Data F**orm, **Data F**ind, or **Fo**rmula **F**ind to locate the misspelled part name within the database. You can use **Fo**rmula **R**eplace to search for and replace the mistake.

Before you print hundreds of mailing labels from an Excel database, use a unique extract to make sure that you don't print duplicate labels.

Extracting from Another Worksheet

You can extract data to one worksheet from a database on another worksheet. In the following example, all items with a Quantity field greater than 10 will be extracted from the database on the FLIMINV.XLS worksheet and placed in the extract range on the FLIMXTRC.XLS worksheet.

Figure 25.13 shows the two worksheets. The FLIMINV.XLS worksheet contains a database in the range A5:C14 that was named Database with the **Data Set Data**base command.

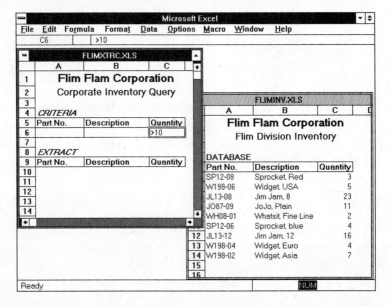

Fig. 25.13. *Criteria and extract ranges are on a worksheet separate from the database.*

The FLIMXTRC.XLS worksheet contains a criteria and an extract range. The criteria range of A5:C6 was set with the **Data Set Criteria** command. The field names that act as headings for the extract in FLIMXTRC.XLS are in cells A9:C9. The extract range is set on this worksheet with the **Data Set Extract** range.

Choosing the **Data Extract** command asks Excel to extract data from the range named Database. In this case, however, the desired Database range is on another worksheet. You must let Excel know where to look for the Database range.

First, activate the FLIMINV.XLS worksheet and use the **Data Set Database** command to name the database. This creates the range name Database for the area A5:C14. Save the FLIMINV.XLS worksheet.

Next, you need to tell the FLIMXTRC.XLS worksheet where the external database is located. To do this, activate FLIMXTRC.XLS and choose the **Formula Define Name** command. In the Define Name dialog box, type a definition of the name Database that tells Excel that the name Database in FLIMXTRC.XLS actually refers to a database on the worksheet FLIMINV.XLS. Type the name Database in the **Name** text box. In the **Refers** to text box, type the external reference for the FLIMINV.XLS database. Enter the external reference this way:

=FLIMINV.XLS!Database

The Define Name dialog box should now look like figure 25.14. This process has defined the Database range on FLIMXTRC.XLS as an external reference to the Database range on the FLIMINV.XLS worksheet.

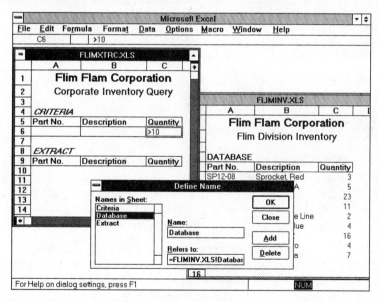

Fig. 25.14. *Use the Formula Define name command to define a database on another worksheet.*

Now use normal extract procedures on the FLIMXTRC.XLS worksheet to extract data. For example, figure 25.13 showed the FLIMXTRC.XLS worksheet set up for an extract where the criteria in cell C6 is >10, so extracted records must have a quantity greater than 10. Figure 25.15 shows the resulting extract from the FLIMINV.XLS database to the FLIMXTRC.XLS extract range.

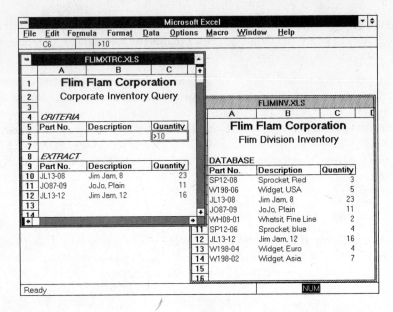

Fig. 25.15. *The completed extract from the FLIMINV.XLS worksheet into the FLIMXTRC.XLS worksheet.*

Creating Database Reports

As figure 25.12 illustrates, you can display extracted columns of data in any order you want. Change the column order of extracted data by changing the order of the field names in the extract range. Keep in mind that you can extract the data you want by using only the field names that you need. Make sure that the field names you use are identical to those used in the database.

 If there's a chance you will reformat or create summary and detail views of your database, consider using Styles and outlining. If you add summary detail to a report, use the Formula Outline command to create an outline from the report. Or manually promote or demote rows or columns using a mouse and the promote or demote icons in the tool bar. Outlines enable you to expand a report to show detail or to contract it to show it in summary. Apply Styles to an outline with the Formula Outline command with the Apply Styles option. Changing the definition of the Styles used in the outline changes the appearance of all rows or columns with that style. Experiment with this process on a simple outline before using it on a large database.

> **Tip: *Hiding Selected Columns To Vary a Report***
> Use one report for different purposes by hiding selected columns or
> rows. Reports for different people may contain data that reflects
> different levels of security or relevance. A report you send to sales
> managers may contain the commissions earned by all salespersons,
> whereas the same report you send to product managers should not
> contain that private information. After you extract data, use the
> **Format C**olumn **W**idth or Forma**t R**ow **H**eight commands with the
> **H**ide button to hide columns or rows.

Maintaining Data

Databases have a tendency to grow and grow. There comes a time when
memory and speed limitations dictate that you clean up. As part of this
process, you need to make backup copies of the old information before
removing it from the working database.

Backing Up Work

An unpleasant surprise awaits you if you continually save your worksheet to
the same file name. When you choose **File Save**, the current Excel file replaces the original file on disk. This practice is fine as long as you never make
a mistake. But what if you accidentally delete the wrong records, make a
number of incorrect edits, or add some incorrect data? If you save garbage
over the good data, you are left with trash.

A conservative policy is to save a printed copy and a disk file of the old data
before deleting it from your working database. Suppose, for example, that
you want to delete all of April's records. Use the **Data Extract** command to
create a printed report of the April records. Then cut out the April extract
report and paste it into a new document. Save this new document as a file
containing only the records that will be deleted.

If you prefer a little more security, save the database you are editing every
15 to 30 minutes, using the **File Save As** command. Each time you save with
File Save As, edit the file name so that it is different from the previous name.
For example, you might want to use a sequence of file names such as the
following:

ACCTS_01.XLS
ACCTS_02.XLS
ACCTS_03.XLS

The last two characters before the extension indicate the file's version number. This numbering technique lets you return to an older file in order to recover previous data. When files get so old that you know you won't need them again, erase them from the disk with **File Delete**; or switch to the File Manager and erase multiple files all at once.

Keep more than one copy of your important database files. In addition, do not keep the backup copy in the same building as the original. Take the backup files to a different building or a bank vault. If your building burns or a thief takes the computers and disks, you still have your data.

Deleting a Group of Records

Your database is of little use unless someone maintains it. Whereas editing, adding, and deleting single records must be done manually, Excel can help you delete groups of records. You delete a group of records in much the same way as you extract a group of specific records. Use the **Data Delete** command to delete from the database all records that meet the criteria you specify. However, because you cannot undo deleted records, adhere to the safety procedures outlined in the following steps:

1. Choose the **File Save As** command and save your worksheet with a unique file name before you delete anything.

2. Enter the criteria for the records you want to delete.

3. Choose the **Data Find** command to make sure that the criteria selects only what you want deleted.

4. Choose the **Data Delete** command to delete records matching the criteria. Excel displays the alert box shown in figure 25.16.

5. Select the OK button or press Enter if you are sure about what will be deleted.

6. Choose the **File Save As** command and save the resulting worksheet with the file name of the original worksheet.

The original file name will now contain the worksheet with the up-to-date database. The file name used in step 1 will contain a backup copy of the database as it was before deleting.

***Fig. 25.16.** This alert box warns that records will be permanently deleted.*

Data Delete shifts records upward to fill gaps left by deleted records. The command also automatically redefines the database range. The rest of the worksheet remains unchanged. Figure 25.17 shows the sample database with a new report date of 16-Oct-91. The criteria range is set to select records where the DAYS DUE has past (where the Days Due field is negative). In figure 25.18, records matching this criterion have been deleted, and the database has closed up to fill the gaps.

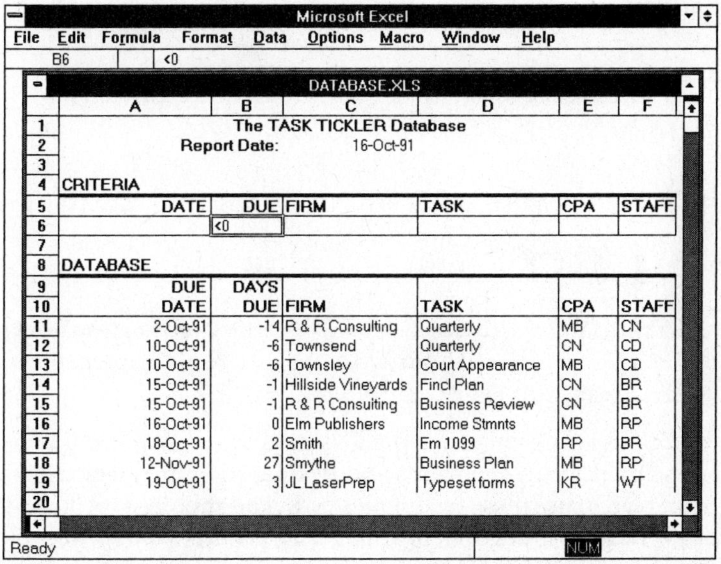

	A	B	C	D	E	F
1		The TASK TICKLER Database				
2	Report Date:		16-Oct-91			
3						
4	CRITERIA					
5	DATE	DUE	FIRM	TASK	CPA	STAFF
6		<0				
7						
8	DATABASE					
9	DUE	DAYS				
10	DATE	DUE	FIRM	TASK	CPA	STAFF
11	2-Oct-91	-14	R & R Consulting	Quarterly	MB	CN
12	10-Oct-91	-6	Townsend	Quarterly	CN	CD
13	10-Oct-91	-6	Townsley	Court Appearance	MB	CD
14	15-Oct-91	-1	Hillside Vineyards	Fincl Plan	CN	BR
15	15-Oct-91	-1	R & R Consulting	Business Review	CN	BR
16	16-Oct-91	0	Elm Publishers	Income Stmnts	MB	RP
17	18-Oct-91	2	Smith	Fm 1099	RP	BR
18	12-Nov-91	27	Smythe	Business Plan	MB	RP
19	19-Oct-91	3	JL LaserPrep	Typeset forms	KR	WT
20						

***Fig. 25.17.** The database before records are deleted with the criterion to delete past records.*

If you have only a few records to delete or records that might be difficult to describe with criteria, you may want to delete them manually. Use **Data Form** to find the records and then select the **D**elete button on the form to delete the current record.

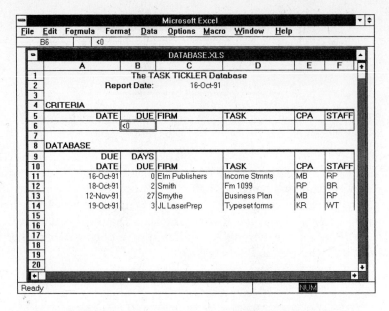

Fig. 25.18. *The database after records specified in the criteria range are deleted.*

From Here...

If you work with large databases and need to extract information from them, or if you need to join material from two databases, read Chapter 26, "Linking Excel to Databases with Q+E."

Chapter 27, "Building Extensive Databases," shows you a number of ways to combine worksheet commands and techniques in the database. Even if you do not plan to use these techniques now, you should skim through that chapter for ideas that might help you in your future work.

26

Linking Excel to Databases with Q+E

O ne of the features that makes Excel powerful is its capability to work with databases that reside on disk or on a mainframe. These databases can be personal computer databases, such as dBASE III Plus or dBASE IV; local area network databases, such as SQL Server; a mainframe database, such as ORACLE; or a text file that contains data from any program. Excel can link worksheets to these databases, copy information from them onto a worksheet, or extract information from a database and put the result on a worksheet.

Excel uses a program called Q+E to work with databases not on an external worksheet (external databases). Q+E is a separate Windows program designed to query and edit databases stored in a personal computer or some mainframes. However, Q+E and Excel work so well together through the use of Dynamic Data Exchange that much of the work involving external databases can be done in Excel. (Dynamic Data Exchange enables Windows programs to pass data and information between themselves.)

This chapter describes only how to use those Q+E features that are available from the Excel **D**ata menu. Q+E is an entire database query and edit program in its own right and would take many chapters and a book of its own to cover fully.

> **Note: *Editing and Appending Database Files***
> You cannot edit or append database files from within Excel by using the add-in macros that come with Excel and Q+E. To edit these files, switch to Q+E and make your changes in Q+E.

Using Q+E

Q+E is a program that enables you to work with different types of database files from within Windows. Because Q+E uses Dynamic Data Exchange, you can closely couple it with some Windows programs, such as Excel and Word for Windows, and give database access capabilities to these programs. Figure 26.1 shows Q+E linked to a dBASE file.

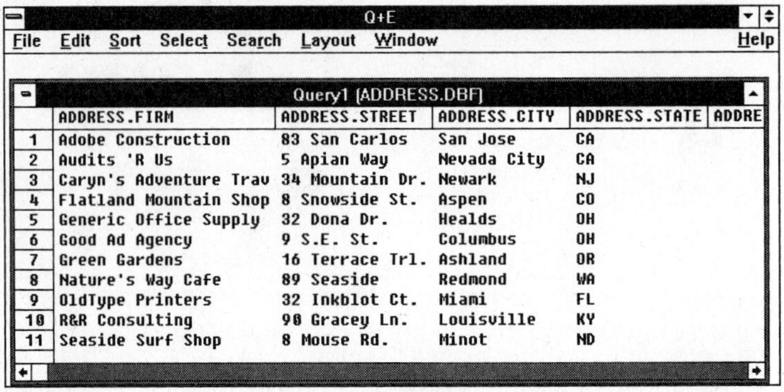

Fig. 26.1. Q+E is a separate program that links database files to many Windows programs.

Q+E works with a variety of database systems. Q+E comes with *drivers* that enable the system to manipulate databases in dBASE II, III, and IV; text files; and Microsoft SQL Server, ORACLE, and OS/2 Extended Edition. With Excel and Q+E, you also can access and manipulate Excel database worksheets on disk, as well as access different types of personal computer text files.

This chapter describes how to use Q+E from within Excel. Even if you are unfamiliar with database concepts, after reading this chapter you will be able to use Q+E to access database, Excel, or text files on disk. The add-in macros, QE.XLA and QESTART.XLA, add new Excel database commands and modify existing Excel commands so that Excel can extract information from files on disk. You will use the knowledge you acquired in previous Excel database chapters.

Q+E is a powerful program. It enables operators to open database files and tables, to query tables based on complex search criteria specified through dialog boxes, or to create and save queries based on SQL SELECT statements. Q+E also can join tables, enabling you to create a single new database by linking together information from two databases containing a common field.

> **Tip:** *Learning More about Q+E's Power by Choosing Help*
> Extensive Help information is available on-line in Q+E. To get help, access the **Help** menu or press F1.

Once Q+E opens a file, you can read and sort data, edit the file and save it, perform calculations such as subtotals, and specify report formats. When files are read into Q+E, you can copy and paste or link them to Excel. When linked data in a file changes, Excel's worksheet is updated.

Installing Q+E

To operate Q+E with Excel, you must install Q+E when you install Excel. When you install Q+E during Excel installation or by itself, Q+E files expand and are copied into special subdirectories. If you did not install Q+E, you still can install it without reinstalling Excel.

One of the first windows during Excel installation enables you to choose extra files and programs to install. To install Q+E, make sure that the Q+E check box is selected. Choose the Drivers button, and select the databases that you want to use Q+E with. You also can select whether you want Q+E to always load simultaneously with Excel.

If you are not sure whether Q+E is installed, use the **File Open** command to look for QE.EXE and QE.HLP in the Excel directory. The subdirectory QE under the Excel directory contains practice files and add-in macros. Other add-in macros for extract commands are located in the XLSTART\QEMACRO subdirectory under the Excel directory.

To install Q+E if it is not installed, rerun the Excel installation program but request to install only Q+E. The Setup program will query which databases you want to access. Most personal computer-based users will want access to Excel, dBASE, and text files. Consult your PC coordinator or Information Systems division to determine whether you should install drivers for Microsoft SQL Server, Oracle, and OS/2 Extended Edition.

Using External Database Commands

The use of Q+E as an integral part of Excel demonstrates how well some Windows programs work together. Q+E comes with three add-in macros that provide commands and features in Excel. The following section demonstrates how to open and use the add-in macro that adds external database extract commands to the **Data** menu.

Adding External Database Commands

You can use three methods to set up Excel so that it adds in the external database commands. These methods are presented here in order of preference, depending on how frequently you plan to use external database commands.

First, if you rarely use an external database, you can add the external database commands and load the Q+E program by choosing the **File Open** command in Excel, changing to the XLSTART\QEMACRO subdirectory under the Excel directory, and opening the add-in macro, QE.XLA. This procedure adds and modifies commands under the **Data** menu and opens the Q+E program.

Second, if you want the external database commands available on the menu, but don't always want Q+E to be running, use the File Manager to copy the file QESTART.XLA from the XLSTART\QEMACRO directory into the XLSTART directory. Then when Excel starts, it opens the QESTART.XLA add-in macro, which adds and modifies commands under the **Data** menu. The first time you use one of the external database commands, the Q+E program opens.

Third, if you always want Q+E to run with Excel and the commands always to be available, copy the QE.XLA file from the XLSTART\QEMACRO directory into the XLSTART directory. When Excel starts, it will add the external commands and immediately run Q+E. Do not leave the QESTART.XLA macro in the XLSTART directory with QE.XLA. If during installation you chose the Drivers button and the option to load Q+E on start-up, then the QE.XLA file was copied into the XLSTART directory for you.

If Q+E starts when Excel starts and you do not want it to, use the File Manager to move the QE.XLA macro out of the XLSTART directory and into the XLSTART\QEMACRO directory.

When you open QESTART.XLA or QE.XLA, the existing database commands are modified to work with external databases. These three additional commands are added to the **Data** menu:

Command	Description
Paste Fieldnames	Reads field names from a file so that you can choose the names you want pasted onto the worksheet at the top of criteria and extract ranges.
SQL Query	Presents a dialog box in which you can write an SQL query that extracts information from an external database.
Activate Q+E	Activates Q+E if it is running, placing Excel in the background. If Q+E is not running, this command starts it.

Understanding How External Commands Work

Most external database commands work similarly to the commands you learned in previous database chapters. A major difference is that you will specify a database that is in a file and not on a worksheet. You will not be able to see the field names at the top of each column because the files are on disk.

Using the new **Data** menu commands, you can paste external database field names onto the worksheet. You will paste these headings into a criteria and extract range; these ranges work the same as the criteria and extract ranges you used with a worksheet database.

After you set the database range and create criteria and extract ranges with appropriate headings, you can extract information from the file on disk.

Specifying Internal and External Databases

You can have a database on the worksheet and multiple databases specified on disk. The **Data Set Database** command keeps track of which database is the active one; the command also enables you to switch between databases.

To set the first external database of a working session, follow these steps:

1. Choose the Data Set Database command. Figure 26.2 shows the database selection dialog box.

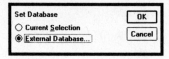

Fig. 26.2. Indicate whether your new database is the current selection on the worksheet or is an external database.

2. If you want to use the selected range on the worksheet as the database, select the Current Selection option. Choose OK or press Enter. (The Current Selection option is the same as the normal Set Database command.) Work with your worksheet database using the procedures described in previous chapters.

   OR

   If you want to use an external database, select the External Database option, and then choose OK or press Enter. Figure 26.3 shows the dialog box that appears.

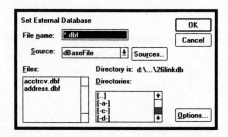

Fig 26.3. Set the source and location of the external database.

3. Select the type of file you are connecting to from the Source pull-down list. Some common file types are Excel, dBASE, and Text. If your database is not on your computer, select the Source button and log on to the database system that contains the information you need. The drivers for these sources must be installed during Q+E installation for the database system to appear in the Sources list. Choose OK

4. Select the location of the file from the Directory list box. (The name of this box may vary for different sources.)

5. Select the file from the Files list.

6. Choose OK or press Enter This step returns you to the Set Database dialog box.

7. Choose the Change or Add button to change existing external databases or to add more databases. Choose OK when you are finished.

> **Tip: *Contacting Pioneer Software for Additional Database Drivers***
>
> Pioneer Software, the makers of Q+E, continually update and develop additional database drivers and Q+E enhancements. For more information, contact Pioneer Software; the address is listed in the Appendix of this book.

Once you set an external database, the Set Database dialog box expands to include the names of external databases that have been set. Figure 26.4 shows the dialog box with multiple external databases set. Choose the Change or Add buttons to change existing database connections or to add more.

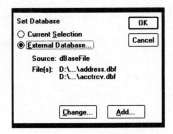

Fig. 26.4. The Set Database dialog box displays all the external databases that are set.

When you are finished with the connection to a remote external database, such as SQL Server or ORACLE, you can free up system resources by choosing the Change button, and then choosing the Source button and logging off.

Setting the Criteria

Although the database is in an external file, you still need field names on the worksheet for use in the criteria and extract ranges. A new command the QE.XLA and QESTART macros add to the **D**ata menu enables you to pull the field names out of a file and paste them into the worksheet.

If you set multiple external databases, you will have field names from multiple databases. To distinguish the names from multiple databases, each field name is preceded by the file name. A period separates the field name and file name to give a syntax of *databasefile.fieldname*.

To paste field names onto the worksheet from a file, follow these steps:

1. Select the left cell of where you want to paste the field names.

2. Choose the **D**ata Paste F**i**eldnames command. The dialog box shown in figure 26.5 will appear.

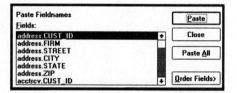

Fig. 26.5. Select the field names you want to use from the Paste Fieldnames dialog box.

3. If you want to paste all field names in a row to the right, choose the Paste **A**ll button. You can reorder or delete names by using Excel editing procedures. Do not follow the rest of these steps.

   OR

   If you want to paste a few names in a special order, choose the **O**rder Fields button. The dialog box shown in figure 26.6 appears.

4. Select a field name from the **A**vailable Fields list, and then choose the Add button.

5. Select additional field names in the order you want and add them to the list. Delete a name by selecting it from the Selected Fields list and choosing the **R**emove button.

6. Choose the **P**aste button to paste the names.

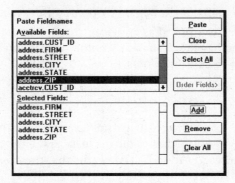

Fig. 26.6. Select the field names and the order in which you want them pasted in this dialog box.

When the field names are pasted onto the worksheet, select the names and one blank row underneath. Next, use the **D**ata Set Criteria command to set the range as the criteria range for the external database. Follow the same procedures as those described in Chapter 21 for setting a criteria range. If you forget to set a criteria range, Excel will extract all the data.

You will not be able to paste field names unless you have set an external database.

If you are using a single current external database and no criteria are calculated, criteria are set in the same way they are set in a worksheet database. When multiple databases are active, computed criteria or extracts must be set differently.

When you have more than one current external database, specify criteria field names with this syntax:

database.fieldname

Suppose, for example, that multiple databases are active and one database has the name ADDRESS.DBF and the field name STREET. The valid field name in the criteria range would be ADDRESS.STREET.

An extract from an external database through Q+E does not evaluate criteria in the same way as an extract from a worksheet. In Q+E, criteria are case-sensitive—uppercase letters match against uppercase letters and lowercase letters match against lowercase letters.

If you need computed criteria, do not create the computed criteria as you would for a worksheet database. For example, with a worksheet database, you would use a criteria where the field name above the calculated criteria is a field name that does not exist. In addition, the calculated criteria in a worksheet database is posed as a logical test. For example, the following criteria tests whether the on-hand inventory in column B is less than the reorder quantity in column C plus 5:

```
Test
=B9<C9+5
```

Here, the name Test does not exist as a field name in the worksheet database. Row nine is the top row of data in the database and is the first row on which the calculated criteria is tested. (This warns that the on-hand inventory is within five units of needing a reorder.)

To build a calculated criteria for an external database, you must use a syntax that is more English-like and is similar to an SQL query. Use the actual field name that you are testing as the field name for the criteria. The test condition is then a comparative, as in this example:

```
ONHAND
<REORDER+5
```

Here, both ONHAND and REORDER are field names that exist in the external database.

Joining Database Extracts

An extremely handy feature of Q+E is its capability to join databases. This feature can save you from the necessity of creating huge database files and from repeating data.

For example, with a normal Excel database that contains the names of business clients and their business addresses, you must keep each person's name and business address in a record (row). This database contains many duplicate entries because many people may work at the same address. This type of database also requires extra data-entry time and increases the possibility of errors as duplicate information is typed. Maintenance and changes to this database can be unwieldy.

A more efficient way of building databases is to have one database contain client names with their company and another database contain companies and addresses. This means that only one address is entered for each company. When you need to create mailing labels, you can join the two databases so that each company address is duplicated where needed. The result is an extract that appears to have come from a single large database.

Using the company address example just described, the criteria to join two databases named CLIENT.DBF and ADDRESS.DBF is as follows:

CLIENT.Company
ADDRESS.Company

Here, the syntax is *database.fieldname*. CLIENT.Company is the field name in the criteria range name. When the extract is performed, this calculated criteria matches records between the databases according to the common field, which is Company. The field name does not need to be Company in both databases, but it must contain matching data. Do *not* use an equal sign before the field name being compared. Both external databases must be set.

Extracting Data from a File

Set an extract range for an external database extract in the same way you set an extract for a database on the worksheet. Copy field name headings down from the criteria range, or paste them in the worksheet with the **Data Paste Fieldnames** command.

To extract from the external database, follow these steps:

1. Set the external database with the **Data Set Database** command.

2. Paste names onto the worksheet with the **Data Paste Fieldnames** command.

3. Arrange and copy those names into criteria and extract range headings. Set the criteria range with **Data Set Criteria**.

4. Enter a criteria. If you do not enter a criteria, Excel and Q+E will attempt to extract all records from the file.

5. Set the extract range by either selecting it or naming it with the **Data Set Extract** command. If you will be using the same extract over and over, use the **Data Set Extract** command. Select or set only the headings if you do not want to limit the number of extracted records. To limit the number of extracted records, select or set the headings and as many cells underneath as you want records. (Do not select the entire row.)

6. Clear the cells in the extract range or below the extract headings. Extracts from external databases do not clear the previous data as do extracts from a worksheet database. If you do not clear previously extracted records, the new records can overlap with the old records and run together.

7. Choose the **D**ata **E**xtract command. Choose OK when asked if you want unique records. The dialog box shown in figure 26.7 appears, showing how many records satisfy the criteria.

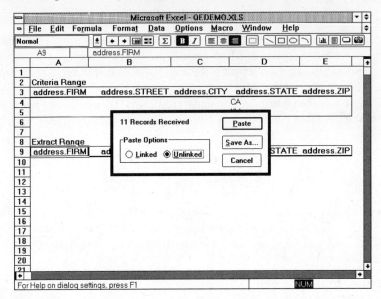

Fig. 26.7. *In this dialog box, you can see how many records satisfy the criteria.*

8. Select the **L**inked or **U**nlinked option to indicate whether you want the data linked to the file via Q+E or whether you want data pasted into cells.

9. Select the **S**ave As button if you want data saved to a file.

10. Choose OK or press Enter. Excel will display the Save As dialog box so that you can enter a file name if you requested the data be saved to a file.

Data that fits your criteria is extracted from the database in a file or from a source; the data then is copied into the extract range as shown in figure 26.8.

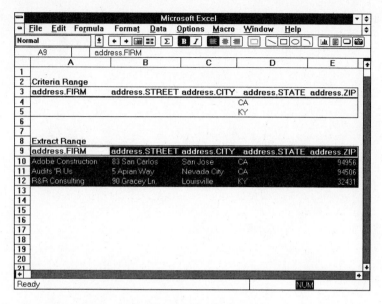

Fig. 26.8. *Extracted data appear on the worksheet.*

From Here...

Q+E enables you to use Excel to analyze and to chart information that is stored in files from other programs. This capability is especially useful for accounting, finance, marketing, or production systems that can save data as dBASE files or are based on SQL Server or ORACLE. Most programs also have the ability to save files or print reports to text files on disk. With the information printed to disk, you can access the information and analyze it in Excel.

Q+E is a program in itself. It has a much wider capability than the Excel-related commands described in this chapter. Q+E includes its own execution command language and Dynamic Data Exchange so that you can create extensive links between databases and Q+E and Windows programs such as Excel, Word for Windows, and DynaComm. To learn more about Q+E commands, refer to the Q+E reference manual that comes with Excel; or activate Q+E from within Excel with the **Data** Activate command, and choose the **Help** Index command. Q+E has extensive Help commands. The QE directory under the Excel directory contains practice and demonstration database and index files.

Building Extensive Databases

Y ou can use Excel's database as just an electronic filing system. However, because it is an integral part of the worksheet, the database has many more uses. You can use database results within worksheet calculations and analyze database contents with worksheet functions.

The collection of techniques and tips repesented in this chapter help you to combine the database with other worksheet functions. The ideas in this chapter also will save you time. Here are some of the techniques you will learn:

- How to reduce errors in worksheets and databases by cross-checking data as it is entered

- How to use database functions, such as DSUM and DCOUNT, to analyze your database and extract summary information that matches the criteria you set

- How to combine the database functions with the **Data Table** command to produce multiple summaries from the database

Cross-Checking Data Entries Automatically

Whether you are entering data in a database form or making entries directly into the cells of a worksheet, you can prevent accidental errors by using formulas that automatically cross-check data as you enter it. Figure 27.1 shows an example of a data-entry form that uses formulas to cross-check entered data. The formula bar shows the formula used to check the data in cell D4.

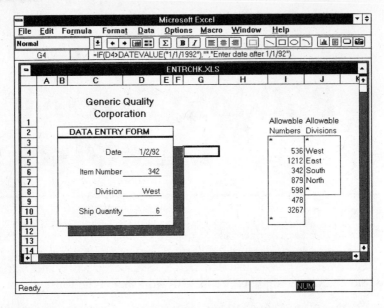

Fig. 27.1. *A data-entry form with tables of allowed inputs.*

Figure 27.2 shows the same form with incorrect data entered. Notice the warnings that appear to the side of the data-entry cells. The formulas used in those cells are given in table 27.1.

Table 27.1
Formulas in Figure 27.1 Cells

Cell	Cross-Check	Formula
G4	Date after 1/1/92	=IF(D4>DATEVALUE("1/1/1992")," ","Enter date after 1/1/92")
G6	Item number in list	=IF(ISNA(MATCH(D6,I3:I11,0)),"Invalid Number"," ")
G8	Division name in list	=IF(ISNA(MATCH(D8,J3:J8,0)),"West, East, South, North"," ")
G10	Range of quantities	=IF(AND(D10>4,D10<21)," ","5 to 20 units")

In each of these formulas, an IF function combined with a conditional test decides whether the entry in column D is correct. The formula in cell G4 checks whether the date serial number from D4 is greater than the date in the IF function. If the serial number is greater, the blank text " " is displayed. If the value in D4 is not greater, the prompting text is displayed.

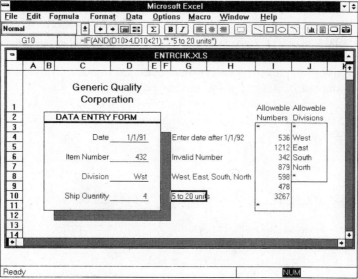

Fig. 27.2. A data-entry form with warnings for incorrect entries.

In cell G6, the MATCH function looks through the values in I3:I11 to find an exact match with the contents of D6. The 0 argument tells MATCH to look for an exact match. When an exact match is not found, the error value #N/A! is returned. The ISNA function detects #N/A! values when a match is not found; it displays the text warning Invalid Number. When a match is found, " " (nothing) is displayed on-screen. Note that when you use MATCH, the items in the list do not have to be sorted as they do with the LOOKUP functions.

Cell G8 uses the same MATCH method to check the division name against acceptable spellings. If you use large lists of possible entries that must be entered accurately, you may want to write custom dialog boxes that contain scrolling lists. Custom dialog boxes are described in Chapter 31.

The value of Ship Quantity must be 5 to 20 units. Therefore, the formula in G10 uses an AND statement to check that the number in D10 is greater than 4 *and* less than 21. When both checks are true, nothing is displayed. If the number is out of the range, the message 5 to 20 Units is displayed.

Analyzing Database Contents

If you ever had to analyze a database by hand, you know it can be a great deal of work. For example, if you have a job-costing database, you have probably had to total amounts by job code. Totaling manually can take hours. The techniques in this section reduce those hours to less than a minute. Excel can search your database for you and calculate totals, make counts, and even perform statistical analysis on data in your database. For example, you can use Excel to count the number of client contacts by sales representative, total the amount for specific account codes by month, or see how repairs are distributed by type.

Using Basic Database Functions

Database functions can perform operations such as counting or totaling the values in a field for only those records that meet your criteria. Three frequently used database functions are DSUM, DCOUNT, and DCOUNTA, which are are similar to SUM, COUNT, and COUNTA. DSUM totals items in a field; DCOUNT counts numeric values in a field; and DCOUNTA counts nonblank cells in a field.

Excel has many other database-analysis functions: DMIN, DMAX, DAVERAGE, DSTD, DSTDP, DVAR, DVARP, DGET, and DPRODUCT. These functions are described in Chapter 10, "Using Functions." Use the same procedure described in the following section for all of these functions.

When you use database functions, you need to specify three arguments: the range where the database is located, the column on which the function will act in the database range, and the range where the criteria is located. The format for database functions is as follows:

> D*function*(*database*, *field*,*criteria*)

The *database* and *criteria ranges* can be the same or totally different from the ranges that you use with **Data Find**, **Form**, or **Extract**. Frequently, operators set up D*functions* to use the same database range as that set with **Data Set Database**, while using a totally different criteria range.

The *field* argument in the function can be either the column number in the database (the first column in the database is 1) or the field name at the top of the database. If you use a field name, such as CODE, make sure that you enclose it in quotation marks (").

> **Tip:** *1-2-3 Numbers Columns Differently*
> When counting the columns in a database for the field argument,
> 1-2-3 starts with zero for the first column or field. Excel starts with
> one for the first column or field.

In figure 27.3, the DSUM formula in cell F18 totals the Amount column for
all records having an Exp Code of 12. Note the formula in F18:

=DSUM(B5:F15,"Amount",B18:B19)

The range B5:F15 is the database, which includes the field names. The range
B18:B19 is the criteria to be used by this function only. The column being
summed is "Amount". This argument also could be specified as 5, or the fifth
column.

In figure 27.4, the criteria range has been reset to B18:C19, and the field
name Date has been added to the criteria range. Now, only those records
with an Exp Code of 12 and a Date of 3/16/92 are totaled.

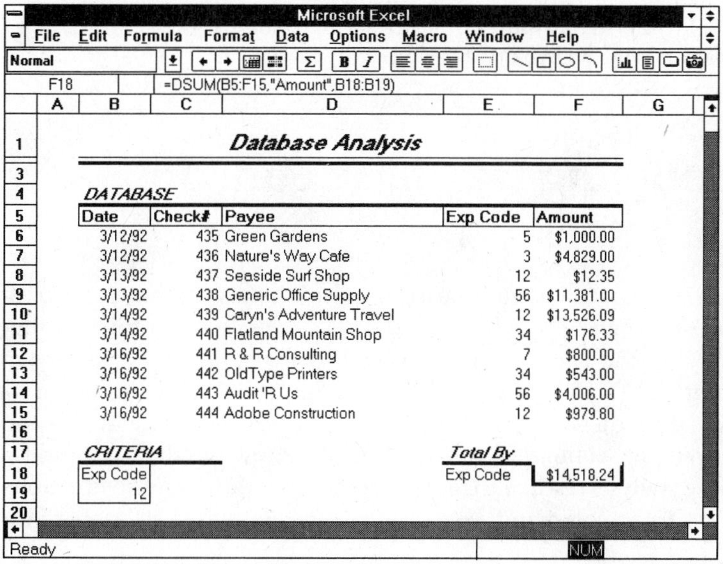

Fig. 27.3. *A DSUM formula in cell F18 totals the Amount column for all records having an Exp Code of 12.*

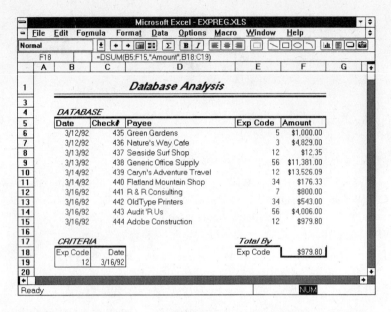

Fig. 27.4. The criteria range is now extended to total the Amount column for records that have an Exp Code of 12 and a date of 3/16/92.

Combining Database Functions with Data Tables

Although database functions are quite useful, they can require a great deal of time if you have many different criteria to type into the criteria range. For example, in the check register shown in figure 27.4, you must type six different Exp Codes into the criteria range and then write down a total. Imagine that you were analyzing 50 or 150 codes. Wouldn't it be easier and faster to let Excel build a table for you that shows all the codes and all the database analysis results? In fact, by combining the database functions with the **Data Table** command, you can have Excel build such a table for you.

It would take a few minutes to manually analyze even the simple database in figure 27.5 for each total by expense code. On a large database, it could take days. When you combine the DSUM function, described in the previous section, with the **Data Table** command described in Chapter 13, "Building Extensive Worksheets," Excel does the work for you.

The **Data Table** command along with the DSUM function in cell F18 takes the expense codes in E19:E24 and produces the total amounts for each expense code, as shown in F19:F24. **Data Table** takes each code from column E and inserts it into the criteria in cell B19. The DSUM result from that criteria is then placed under the DSUM formula in the cell next to the appropriate expense code.

```
┌─────────────────────────────────────────────────────────────────────┐
│ ═                    Microsoft Excel - EXPREG.XLS            ▼ ▲│▼│
│ ═  File  Edit  Formula  Format  Data  Options  Macro  Window  Help   ▲│
│ Normal         ± ◆ ◆ ▦ ▤ Σ B I ▤▤▤ □ ◥□○◗ ▥▤□▥ │
│      F18            =DSUM(B5:F15,"Amount",B18:B19)                    │
│    A   B         C          D                E        F      G       │
│ 4    DATABASE                                                        │
│ 5    Date    Check#  Payee                Exp Code  Amount          │
│ 6     3/12/92  435  Green Gardens              5    $1,000.00       │
│ 7     3/12/92  436  Nature's Way Cafe          3    $4,829.00       │
│ 8     3/13/92  437  Seaside Surf Shop         12       $12.35       │
│ 9     3/13/92  438  Generic Office Supply     56   $11,381.00       │
│ 10    3/14/92  439  Caryn's Adventure Travel  12   $13,526.09       │
│ 11    3/14/92  440  Flatland Mountain Shop    34      $176.33       │
│ 12    3/16/92  441  R & R Consulting           7      $800.00       │
│ 13    3/16/92  442  OldType Printers          34      $543.00       │
│ 14    3/16/92  443  Audit 'R Us               56    $4,006.00       │
│ 15    3/16/92  444  Adobe Construction        12      $979.80       │
│ 17   CRITERIA                             Total By  Exp Code         │
│ 18   Exp Code                                       $37,253.57       │
│ 19                                             3    $4,829.00        │
│ 20                                             5    $1,000.00        │
│ 21                                             7      $800.00        │
│ 22                                            12   $14,518.24        │
│ 23                                            34      $719.33        │
│ 24                                            56   $15,387.00       ▼│
│ ◆│                                                                  ◆│
│ Ready                                              │NUM│            │
└─────────────────────────────────────────────────────────────────────┘
```

Fig. 27.5. *This data table lists expense codes and their totals.*

In figure 27.5, the DSUM function combined with the Data Table command produces a table of expense codes and their totals. The table is in E18:F24, and the DSUM formula is in cell F18. The left column lists each expense code, whereas the right column lists the resulting total amount for the corresponding expense code.

The DSUM formula in cell F18 is this:

=DSUM(B5:F15,"Amount",B18:B19)

This is the same type of formula used in previous examples. The criteria range, B18:B19, again holds the criteria for the Exp Code field. The **Data Table** command takes each value from the left side of the data table and places the values one at a time into the criteria cell B19. It then records the DSUM total for that criteria and puts it in the adjacent cell on the right side of the data table. Chapter 13, "Building Extensive Worksheets," describes how to select the range and use the **Data Table** command to fill in the table.

If figure 27.5 contained 537 different expense codes, the process of entering them in column E down the left side of the data table would be quite time-consuming. Instead, **Data Extract** is used to create a list of all the expense codes used in the database. To create this list of codes, **Data Set Database** and **Data Set Criteria** are used to specify the database and criteria ranges. Because all expense codes should be extracted, no criteria is entered.

The field name Exp Code is copied to cell E18. Then Exp Code in cell E18 is selected, as shown in figure 27.6, and set as the extract with the **Data Set Extract** command. Then the **Extract** command with the Unique Records Only option is used to extract each expense code from the database, just as though creating a report. Expense codes are extracted on the field name Exp Code.

Figure 27.7 shows the result of using the heading Exp Code as an extract range. Because the Unique Records Only option was selected, only one each of the expense codes was extracted. You can use the **Data Sort** command to rearrange the expense codes.

To create a data table, the heading Exp Code must be deleted from cell E18. Chapter 13, "Building Extensive Worksheets," explains how to select and create a table with the **Data Table** command.

Beware! The **Data Extract** command erases all cells below the extract heading. You may want to move the extract heading to a safe area of the worksheet before you extract numbers. Then you can cut and paste the data to the appropriate place on your worksheet after the extraction.

```
 ═                    Microsoft Excel - EXPREG.XLS              ▼ ▲
 ─ File  Edit  Formula  Format  Data  Options  Macro  Window  Help    ▲
Normal          ▲ ← → ▦▦ Σ B I ≡≡≡ □ ◢□○◣ ▥▤□▧
    E18            Exp Code
   A│  B  │  C  │        D        │    E    │    F    │  G  │▲
 4   │DATABASE                                                 │
 5   │Date  │Check#│Payee          │Exp Code │Amount   │      │
 6   │ 3/12/92│  435 │Green Gardens        │       5 │ $1,000.00│
 7   │ 3/12/92│  436 │Nature's Way Cafe    │       3 │ $4,829.00│
 8   │ 3/13/92│  437 │Seaside Surf Shop    │      12 │    $12.35│
 9   │ 3/13/92│  438 │Generic Office Supply│      56 │$11,381.00│
10   │ 3/14/92│  439 │Caryn's Adventure Travel│   12 │$13,526.09│
11   │ 3/14/92│  440 │Flatland Mountain Shop│     34 │   $176.33│
12   │ 3/16/92│  441 │R & R Consulting     │       7 │   $800.00│
13   │ 3/16/92│  442 │OldType Printers     │      34 │   $543.00│
14   │ 3/16/92│  443 │Audit 'R Us          │      56 │ $4,006.00│
15   │ 3/16/92│  444 │Adobe Construction   │      12 │   $979.80│
17   │CRITERIA                        │Total By │Exp Code │
18   │Exp Code│                       │Exp Code │         │
19   │                                                    │
20   │                                                    │
21   │                                                    │
22   │                                                    │
23   │                                                    │
24   │                                                    │▼
 ← │                                                    │ →
Ready                                          │NUM│
```

Fig. 27.6. The Exp Code field heading copied and selected in preparation for extracting expense codes.

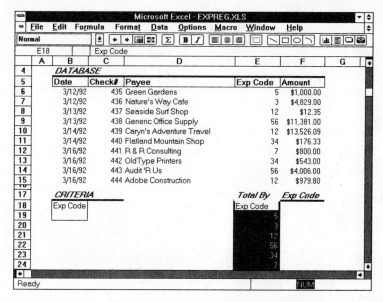

Fig. 27.7. *Extracted expense codes need only to be sorted for use in a data table.*

Troubleshooting Databases

The following section describes some of the more common problems people have when working with an Excel database.

Problem:
The database commands do not work.

Solution:
Use the following checklist to find the problem:

1. Choose the Formula Goto command or press F5, select the database range or the criteria range, and choose OK. Make sure that each range includes a single row of field names at the top of the selected range. The criteria range should contain at least one row in addition to field names. The database range should include one row of field names and all data.

2. Select the rows under the field names in the criteria range, and use Edit Clear to remove any hidden blanks (space characters) in the criteria range.

3. Make sure that field names in the criteria and extract ranges are spelled exactly the same as they are in the database range. Use only text names or formulas that produce text names for headings.

   Field names cannot be numeric. If you must use a numeric field name at the top of a database column, change it into text with a formula such as this:

   ="9540"

4. Make sure that a third set of field names is used for the extract range. The extract range with field names at the top of the range must be set with the **Data Set Extract** command; if it has not been set, it must be selected when you choose the **Data Extract** command.

Problem:
Some of the database commands listed in the book do not appear in the menus.

Solution:
Choose **Options Full Menus**.

Problem:
Calculated criteria does not produce a find or an extract result.

Solution:
Calculated criteria must be entered in the criteria range beneath a heading that is *not* a field name. To use a calculated criteria, create a new field heading that is *different* from any field name in the database. Replace an existing field heading in the criteria range with this new heading or extend the criteria range to make room for the additional heading.

Problem:
Formulas in the database that refer to values outside the database return incorrect results.

Solution:
Make certain that database formulas that refer to cells or names outside the database use absolute references.

Problem:
The **Data Find, Extract,** and **Delete** commands act on the entire database and ignore the criteria.

Solution:
Choose **Formula Goto**, select **Criteria**, and choose the **OK** button. This action selects the criteria range so that you can see it on-screen. Make sure that blank rows do *not* appear in the criteria range.

Problem:

The Data Find, Extract, and Delete commands do not act on records that obviously satisfy the criteria.

Solution:

Complete the following steps:

1. Make sure that the field names at the top of the criteria rows are exactly the same as the field names that head each database column. Use **Edit Copy** and **Edit Paste** to duplicate field names.

2. Use **Formula Goto** to select and verify that the database and criteria ranges are correct.

3. Use **Edit Clear** to erase all "blank" cells in the criteria range. Cells may appear blank, even when they contain blank characters entered with the space bar. Excel tries to find fields that match these blank characters.

Problem:

An exact text search such as ="Smith" finds only a few of the records known to contain Smith.

Solution:

Incorrectly spelled words and blank spaces can prevent what appears to be an exact match. Here are some ways to find near matches:

Type **Smith** (without quotation marks or an equal sign) instead of ="Smith." Smith finds words beginning with Smith, even when the name may be followed by blanks or additional characters.

Use wild cards to find misspelled words. For example, enter **sm?th** to find Smith or Smythe. Enter **?smith** if a leading blank space may have been accidentally entered.

Problem:

A complex criteria using AND and OR does not work as expected.

Solution:

AND statements must satisfy the first condition *and* the second condition simultaneously. OR statements can satisfy either one *or* the other condition or both conditions. Consider this example:

=AND(A15>500,A15<750)

This formula finds records where the data in column A is between 500 and 750. Those are the only values where both conditions are true. Remember, if you are searching for values between two points, use AND. If you are searching for multiple text, such as two names under the same field, use OR.

Problem:
The database does not work correctly with dates.

Solution:
Make sure that dates have been entered with a method that produces a serial date number. Without a serial date number, database functions treat your date entry as text or as a number. For more information, read the sections on entering dates in Chapter 7, "Entering and Editing Worksheet Data."

Problem:
Part of the worksheet disappears whenever **Data Extract** is used.

Solution:
When you select only the field names in the extract range and then use the **Data Extract** command, Excel assumes that you are extracting an unlimited amount of data. Excel then clears the area below the field names in the selected extract range so that extracted data is not mixed with previously extracted data. To review how to extract limited amounts of data, see Chapter 25, "Extracting and Maintaining Data."

Problem:
Data at the bottom of the database is not found or extracted.

Solution:
Use **Formula Goto** to make sure that the bottom rows are included in the database range. Use **Data Form** to add data and preserve the database, or insert new rows through the middle of the database range.

Problem:
Data on the left side of the records does not match data on the right side.

Solution:
The database may have been torn in half and scrambled by a sort operation that did not include all columns. There is no way to repair the problem. Use a previously saved version.

From Here...

After reviewing this and previous chapters, you should be very familiar with Excel's worksheet and database capabilities. To increase your productivity even more, read Chapter 28, "Command and Function Macro Quick Start." You soon will see how easily you can automate database and report creation.

Part V

Excel Macros

Includes

Command and Function Macro Quick Start

Creating Macros and Add-In Macros

Modifying and Programming Macros

Adding Custom Menus and Dialog Boxes

Macro Function Directory

After the first 10 to 20 hours of using Excel, you should be recording macros that will decrease your work load. If you aren't, you should definitely take the time to go through the "Command and Function Macro Quick Start" in Chapter 28. A *macro* is a string of instructions that Excel runs when you request. There are two types of macros: command macros and function macros.

Command macros give you the power to automate frequent tasks that you would do by entering data or choosing commands. Two useful tasks for command macros are printing reports with a single keystroke and creating frequently used charts. Both are macros that beginners can create using the macro recorder. With two or three simple modifications, you can turn recorded macros into macros that display data entry boxes, check data, and pause dialog boxes so that the operator can select options. More advanced command macros produce custom dialog boxes, create new menu bars and commands, control other Windows applications, and even control the exchange of data between Excel and other Windows applications via Dynamic Data Exchange.

The second type of macro is the function macro. With function macros, you can create your own worksheet functions. For example, if you have specific formulas or equations that you want built into Excel, you can create them with function macros. By writing these equations on a macro sheet, you can use your custom worksheet functions with any worksheet. You can even paste them into cells using the Formula Paste Function command.

The chapters in Part V give you the information you need to take advantage of Excel's powerful macro capability.

28

Command and Function Macro Quick Start

Whenever you perform a repetitive action, ask an inexperienced operator to carry out a complex procedure, or customize Excel, you should use a macro.

Excel has two types of macros: *command* macros and *function* macros. Command macros enable you to replace sequences of keystrokes and command choices with a Ctrl+key combination or with a name selected from a list box. Function macros enable you to create customized numeric or text functions for use on worksheets or macro sheets

Excel command macros are easy to create and use. You can create a macro by turning on a recorder, performing the sequence of keystrokes or command choices, and then turning off the recorder. Excel writes the command macro for you. If you decide to edit your recorded macro or write a macro with the Excel macro language, you will find most macro functions easy to understand. A *macro function* is a verb in the macro language. For example, the macro function equivalent to Format Font is FORMAT.FONT.

Excel function macros work just like Excel's built-in worksheet functions. For example, if the built-in PMT function does not do calculations for the types of loans you work with, you can write your own function to do the calculations the way you want.

The Macro Quick Start has two macro examples. The first example demonstrates how to record keystrokes and commands with the recorder and then edit the recording. The second example shows how easy it is to write your own functions to complement Excel's many built-in worksheet functions.

753

Creating Command Macros

Command macros duplicate menu commands and actions on the worksheet. Command macros can be as simple as replacing a few command sequences with a Ctrl+key combination or as sophisticated as any programming language. In fact, the Excel command language enables you to create custom applications with dialog boxes, menus, and links to other Windows programs.

Macros are created on a special macro sheet. A macro sheet looks like a worksheet, but has wider columns. A macro sheet also displays formulas (macro functions). Commands and actions are represented by code words.

There are a number of advantages to creating macros on a sheet. For example, most of the edit and command features you learned for worksheets operate the same way on macro sheets. Also, when macro sheets are separate from worksheets, you can use a macro sheet with different worksheets.

This Quick Start guides you through the creation of a command macro that centers the contents of a worksheet cell, changes the font to Helvetica 12-point, bold, and italic and increases the row height and column width.

The following steps prepare a worksheet for you to work on while recording the macro.

1. Choose **File New**, select Worksheet, and choose OK or press Enter.

2. Move the worksheet to display columns A through E on the right side of the screen as shown in figure 28.1. Note that to do this, your worksheet cannot be maximized.

Drag the title bar to the right.

Press Alt +hyphen. Choose **M**ove and press the right-arrow key. Press Enter when the worksheet is positioned as shown.

3. Type **Global Quality Corporation** in cell C2. Keep cell C2 selected; this is where you will want to use your new macro. The worksheet should now look like figure 28.1.

Make sure that all menu commands are visible before continuing this Quick Start. If you see only two commands under **Macro**, then choose **Options Full Menus** so that all commands are visible.

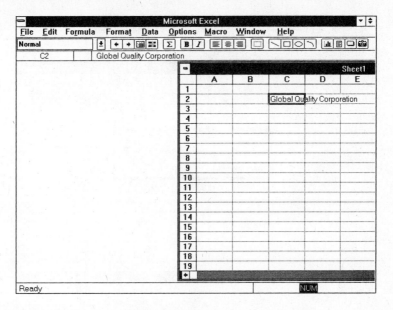

Fig. 28.1. Position the worksheet to make room on-screen so that you can see the macro sheet when it appears.

Now you are ready to record the commands that you want to use when formatting a title. Follow these steps:

1. Choose the Macro Record command. This displays the Macro dialog box shown in figure 28.2.

2. Type **Title**, the name you will use to recognize this macro, in the Name text box. Press Tab to select the Key box and press **T**, the key to be used with Ctrl as the shortcut key for this macro.

3. Choose OK or press Enter.

The recorder is now turned on, and a macro sheet opens behind the worksheet. Because you moved the worksheet to the right, you see the macro sheet at the left of the screen (as shown in figure 28.3). Revealing the macro sheet enables you to see the macro code as it is recorded. Cell A1 at the top of the first column holds the name of the first macro—Title. Its shortcut key appears in parentheses.

Because everything you do is recorded as a code on the macro sheet, follow the rest of the procedures exactly. If you make a mistake, do not worry. You can later edit or delete mistakes on the macro sheet just as you edit or delete formulas on the worksheet. Do not do any editing, however, until you complete the recording and turn off the macro editor!

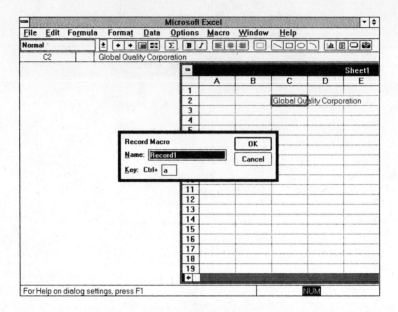

Fig. 28.2. Enter the name and shortcut key for the macro in this dialog box.

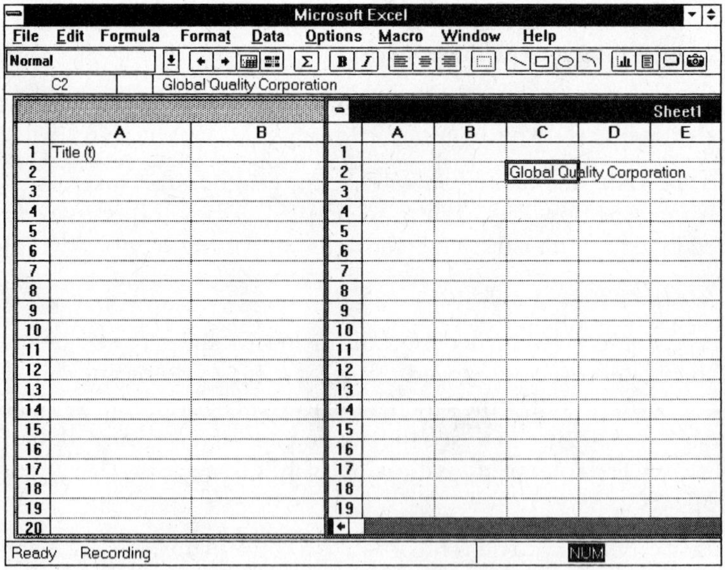

Fig. 28.3. The name of the macro appears at the top of the column.

Follow these steps to give the commands the macro will record:

1. Choose the Macro Relative Record command.

   If Macro Absolute Record appears on the menu instead of Relative Record, then Macro Relative Record has already been chosen. The Relative Record command records all movements of the active cell relative to its last position. Macro Absolute Record records the exact location of the cells selected during the recording. This concept is similar to relative and absolute cell references in worksheet formulas.

2. Choose the Format Font command; select Helvetica 12-point, Bold, and Italic; then choose OK or press Enter.

   Figure 28.4 shows the macro function in cell A2 of the macro sheet. In most cases the function, such as FORMAT.FONT, is very similar to the command chosen from the menu.

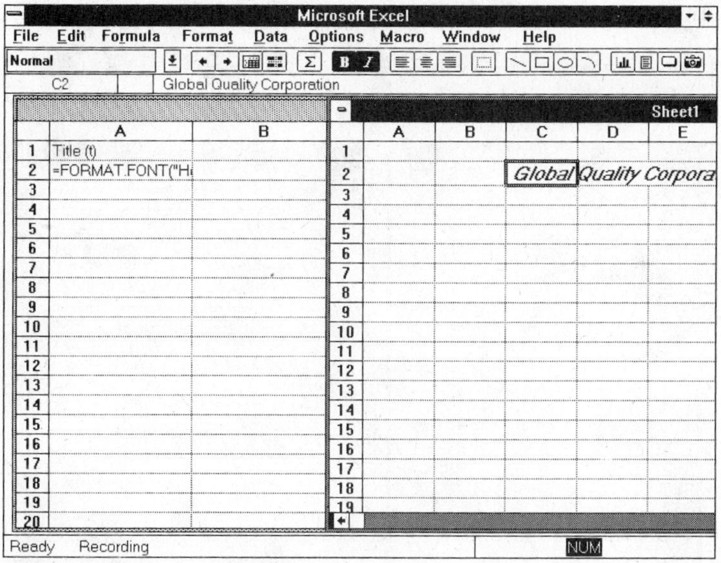

Fig. 28.4. A macro function appears in the next blank cell each time you give a new command.

3. Choose the Format Alignment command, select Center, and choose OK or press Enter.

   The code ALIGNMENT appears in A3, the next cell of the macro sheet.

4. Choose the Format Column Width command, type **20** in the Column Width box, then choose OK or press Enter. You also can record a column-width change that you make by dragging the mouse.

The code COLUMN.WIDTH appears in A4 of the macro sheet.

5. Choose Format Row Height, type **26** in the Row Height box, and then choose OK or press Enter. You also can record a row height change that you made by dragging the mouse.

The function ROW.HEIGHT appears in A5 of the macro sheet.

6. Choose the Macro Stop Recorder command.

The Stop Recorder command inserts a RETURN( ) macro function at the end of the macro recording, marking the end of the macro. The macro sheet now should look like the one in figure 28.5. The column lists the commands and actions in sequence, one macro function per cell.

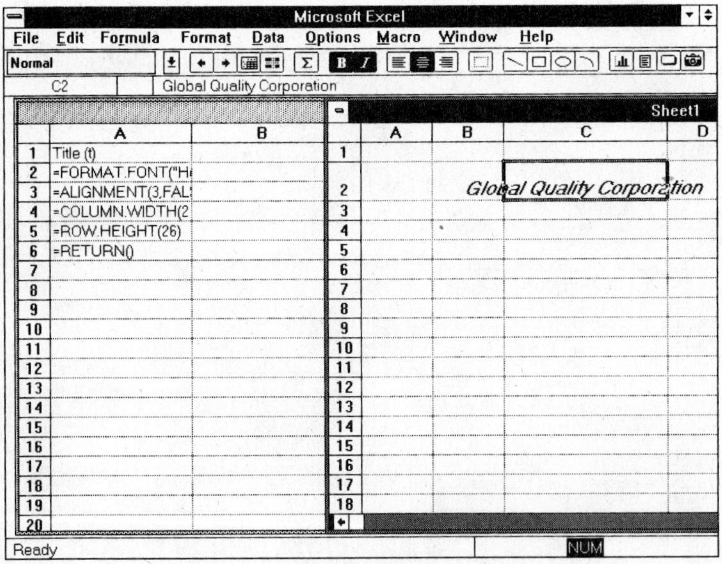

Fig. 28.5. The complete macro after recording is stopped.

Testing the Command Macro

To test your macro, follow these steps:

1. Select cell A5 of the worksheet and type **North Division**

2. Choose the **Macro Run** command.

As shown in figure 28.6, a dialog box displays a list of all macros on all open macro sheets. Notice that the title of the macro sheet precedes the name of the macro. You can have multiple macro sheets open. The left side of the list shows the letter used with the Ctrl key as a shortcut.

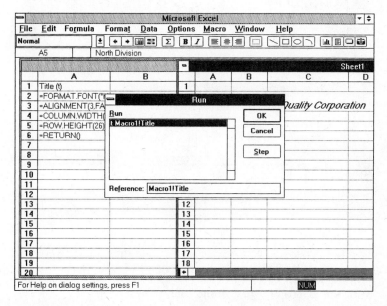

Fig. 28.6. *The **Macro Run** command displays a list from which you can select the macro you want to run.*

3. Select the Title macro from the list box; then choose OK or press Enter.

The macro immediately repeats all the keystrokes you recorded and changes cell A5 to appear as shown in figure 28.7.

Editing the Command Macro

When you see the results of your macro, you may decide that the macro could be more versatile. For example, you may want to leave the columns at the original width, ask the operator to enter the text title, or give the operator the chance to select the font.

Microsoft Excel											

File Edit Formula Format Data Options Macro Window Help

Normal

A5   North Division

Sheet1

	A	B		A	B	C
1	Title (t)		1			
2	=FORMAT.FONT("H					
3	=ALIGNMENT(3,FAL		2			Global Quality Co
4	=COLUMN.WIDTH(2!		3			
5	=ROW.HEIGHT(26)		4			
6	=RETURN()					
7			5	North Division		
8			6			
9			7			
10			8			
11			9			
12			10			
13			11			
14			12			
15			13			
16			14			
17			15			
18			16			
19			17			
20						

Ready   NUM

Fig. 28.7. The macro repeats the same commands to format a new worksheet cell.

To make these changes, you need not re-create the macro; merely edit the contents of the macro just as you would edit the contents of a worksheet.

To review the macro before editing, follow these steps:

1. Select the macro document.

 Click on the macro window so that it appears on top.

 Press Ctrl+F6 or choose **Window** and select the macro sheet by name.

2. Widen column A so that you can read the macro code. The macro sheet should look like the one in figure 28.8.

Before you make any changes, read the macro functions. Macro functions closely mimic the menu commands or actions, so they are easy to read. The information inside the parentheses shows what options were selected from a dialog box or what text was entered. Table 28.1 shows the functions used in your Title macro.

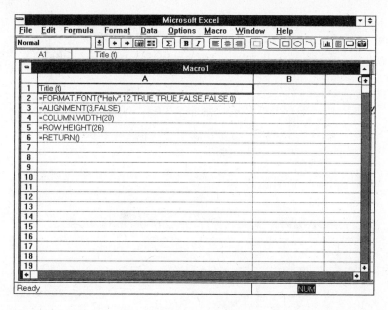

Fig. 28.8. *The macro functions show which options were selected in each dialog box.*

Table 28.1
Codes for Title Macro

Code	Result
FORMAT.FONT("Helv",12, TRUE,TRUE,FALSE,FALSE,0)	Formats the font with 12-point Helvetica in bold and italic. The TRUE and FALSE arguments correspond to selected or deselected check boxes.
ALIGNMENT(3,FALSE)	Uses the third alignment option, Center.
COLUMN.WIDTH(20)	Changes column width to 20.
ROW.HEIGHT(26)	Changes row height to 26.
RETURN( )	Ends the macro.

Each argument in a macro function reflects the option selected or text entered in the equivalent dialog box. Using the macro directory in Chapter 32, you can understand what most macro functions do and how to change them.

Edit your macro as you would edit a worksheet: select cells and use edit commands to insert or delete the cells. Use the formula bar to edit the macro function. For example, if you decide you do not want the column width to change, you can delete that command. To edit your macro, follow these steps:

1. Select cell A4, which contains the COLUMN.WIDTH function.

2. Choose the Edit Delete command. Then select the Shift Cells Up option, as shown in figure 28.9, and choose OK or press Enter.

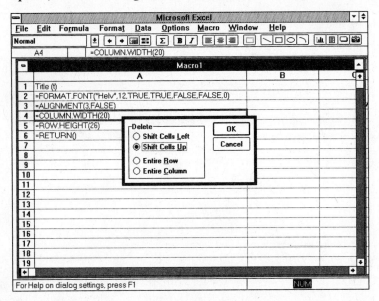

Fig. 28.9. Use on a macro sheet the same editing commands that you use on a worksheet.

Deleting the COLUMN.WIDTH function removes that command from the macro's operation. The functions in cells below A4 move up just as they would on a worksheet.

Adding a Data Entry Input Box

Inserting a cell enables you to add a macro function you forgot or to add a macro function that could not be selected as a command during the recording process. The following steps add an input box that asks the operator to enter the title.

1. Select cells A2:A3, and choose the Edit Insert command. Select the Shift Cells Down option, and choose OK or press Enter. This creates two blank cells under the macro name so that you can type in two more functions.

2. In the blank cell A2, type the following macro function:

   =INPUT("Enter the title",2,"Title Box")

3. In the blank cell A3, type the following macro function:

   =FORMULA(A2)

The INPUT function displays a data-entry input box. The text Enter the title appears in the box to prompt the operator. The only type of entry accepted is type 2, text or numbers used as text. Title Box appears in the title bar of the box. Choosing OK in the INPUT box accepts what the operator has typed and enters it in the same cell, A2, on the macro sheet. The INPUT function produces a text entry in cell A2 of the macro sheet just as the worksheet formula =2+3 produces a 5 in the worksheet cell containing the formula.

The FORMULA(A2) function takes the text in cell A2 of the macro sheet, the result of the INPUT function, and enters that text in the active cell of the active worksheet. When the operator types text into the INPUT dialog box, the text appears in the active worksheet cell.

Making Dialog Boxes Pause

Another easy but useful way you can customize your recorded macro is by making selected dialog boxes pause. For example, you can change the FORMAT.FONT function so that the macro stops, displays the Fonts dialog box, and waits for your selections. After you make selections from the Format Fonts dialog box and choose OK, the macro continues.

Using the macro directory in Chapter 32, you find that the FORMAT.FONT code takes the following forms and arguments:

FORMAT.FONT(*name_text,size_num,bold,italic,underline,strike,color...*)
FORMAT.FONT?(*name_text,size_num,bold,italic,underline,strike, color...*)

The recorded code in cell A4 is currently:

FORMAT.FONT("Helv",10,TRUE,TRUE,FALSE,FALSE,0)

This translates into the Helvetica font type (notice the quotation marks around text words), 12-point size, bold, and italic. The first two arguments are TRUE, so bold and italic check boxes are selected. The underline and strike arguments are FALSE, so those check boxes are not selected. Color is 0, or black.

The question mark (?) in the second form of FORMAT.FONT causes a dialog box to pause when the macro reaches that function. (Only commands that produce a dialog box from the menu can use this question mark format.) When the macro reaches the question mark, it stops, displays the dialog box for that command, and waits for you to make selections. The selections you made during the recording are used as default selections for the dialog box. The italicized arguments in the form of FORMAT.FONT indicate optional entries.

To add a dialog box that pauses the macro, follow these steps:

1. Select cell A4 so that the FORMAT.FONT code appears in the formula bar.

2. Select the formula bar by clicking on it or by pressing F2.

3. Enter a question mark after FORMAT.FONT and before the first parenthesis; then choose OK or press Enter.

The question mark makes the Fonts dialog box appear at this point in the function. The macro sheet now should look like figure 28.10.

Running Macros

Before you can use a macro, the macro sheet that contains the macro must be open, but it does not have to be the first or second sheet on your screen. Open macro sheets the same way you open a worksheet—with the **File Open** command. Remember that macro sheets have the XLM extension.

To display the original worksheet and run your edited macro, follow these steps:

1. Choose the Window menu, and then select the worksheet you want. Select cell B6.

2. Activate the macro with the Ctrl+t shortcut key combination. (The previous method started the macro with **Macro Run**.) A dialog box like the one shown in figure 28.11 appears so that you can "Enter the title."

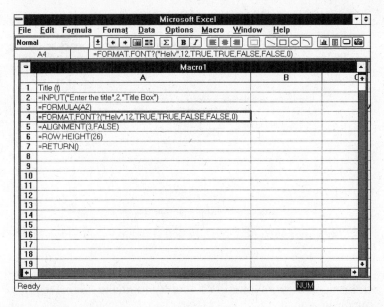

Fig. 28.10. *Adding a question mark after some functions makes the dialog box pause for operator selections.*

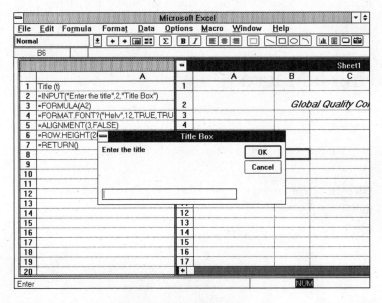

Fig. 28.11. *The data-entry dialog box used in your macro.*

3. Type the word **Sales** in the text box, and choose OK or press Enter.

As shown in figure 28.12, the Fonts dialog box appears with the options for Helvetica, 12-point, bold, and italic selected as the defaults.

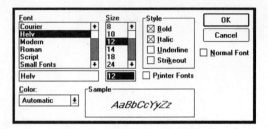

Fig. 28.12. *The question mark in the function makes the Font dialog box pause.*

4. Select Helvetica, 10-point, and Bold, thus deselecting Italic; then choose OK or press Enter. (You could not make this selection in the original macro.)

The macro then continues to run, aligning the text and changing the row height. The worksheet and macro now appear as in figure 28.13. Notice that the column width did not change, because you deleted that function from the macro.

Saving a Macro Sheet

You save a macro sheet the same way you save a worksheet. To save, follow these steps:

1. Activate the macro window, and then choose the **File Save As** command.

2. Give the sheet the name QSMACRO. Excel will add the file extension XLM.

3. Choose OK or press Enter.

> **Note:** *Recording Macros on Existing Macro Sheets*
> To record a macro on a macro sheet that has been previously saved and reopened, you need to tell Excel where on the sheet you want the recording to be placed. To do this, activate the macro sheet, select the cell where you want the recording to begin, and then choose the **Macro Set Recorder Command**. Reactivate the worksheet or chart for which you want a macro and follow the recording procedures you just learned.

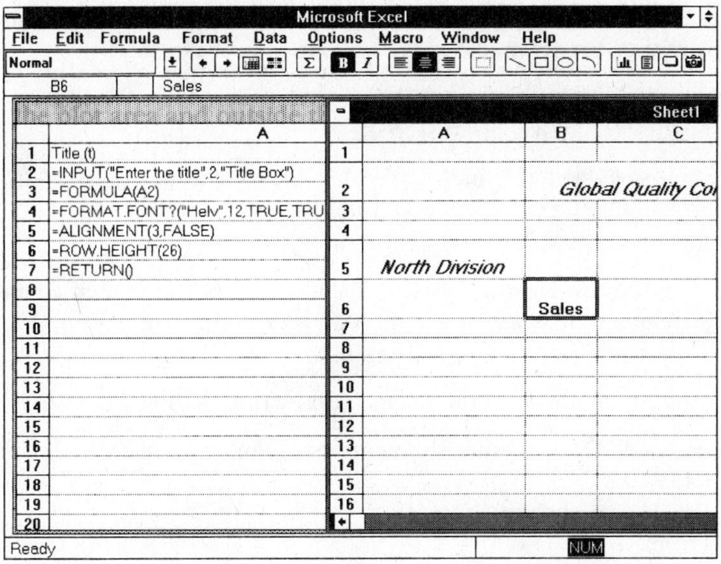

Fig. 28.13. *The edited macro sheet and the worksheet after the macro is run.*

Creating Function Macros

Excel includes 146 worksheet functions (predefined formulas), ranging from simple ones, such as SUM, to complex ones, such as MIRR and TREND. You may need functions, however, that Excel does not have. The following steps demonstrate how to create your own function using a worksheet function macro.

Because function macros use worksheet functions or formulas rather than menu commands or actions, you cannot record a function macro. Instead, you paste or type functions and arguments into your function macro. Your function macro uses the arguments that you specify in the same way that a built-in Excel function uses arguments.

In this example, you will create a function macro that calculates profit margin with the following formula:

= (Sales – Cost)/Sales

When you are finished, you can use this function macro just as if it were a built-in Excel function of the form PMARGIN(Sales,Costs).

If the QSMACRO.XLM macro sheet is open, activate it. If the macro sheet is not open, open a new macro sheet by following these steps:

1. If you are continuing from the command macro, and its macro sheet is still active, go to step 4.

2. If you saved the command macro sheet created previously, choose the **File Open** command and open the macro sheet named QSMACRO.XLM (macro sheets end with XLM).

3. If you did not do the Command Macro Quick Start, open a new, blank macro sheet. Choose the **File New** command, select Macro Sheet, then choose OK or press Enter.

Next, construct your function macro. Follow these steps:

1. Select cell C1 and enter the name of the macro function, **PMARGIN**.

2. Select cell C2 and choose Formula Paste Function.

   Figure 28.14 shows the Paste Function list.

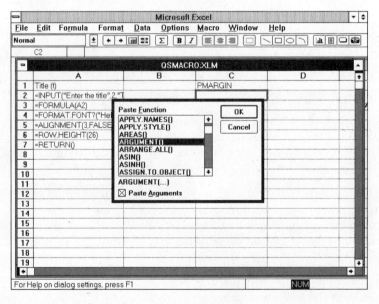

Fig. 28.14. *Select from the list the macro function you want to paste into the sheet.*

3. Select ARGUMENT( ) from the list box. Be sure that the Paste **A**rguments check box is selected. Selecting this check box pastes in a prompt that shows you what to type between the parentheses. Choose OK or press Enter.

4. In the box that appears, select the first argument type:

   name_text,data_type_num

5. Choose OK or press Enter.

   This puts the function and arguments,

   =ARGUMENT(*name_text,data_type_num*)

   in the formula bar as shown in figure 28.15. The *name_text* argument is the text name, in quotation marks, for one of the variables in your PMARGIN function macro.

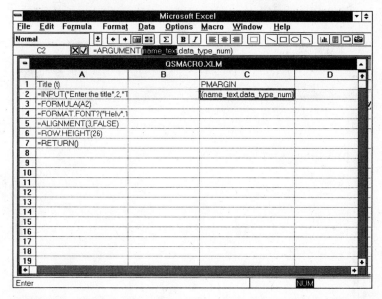

Fig. 28.15. *Pasting a function is easier than trying to remember the arguments.*

6. Edit the function to match,

   =ARGUMENT("Sales",1)

   and enter the edited formula in cell C2.

   Sales is the first variable in PMARGIN(Sales,Costs). The number 1 indicates that only numbers can be input for Sales. If a non-number is entered, an alert dialog box is displayed when the operator chooses OK or presses Enter.

7. In cell C3, enter or paste the following formula:

   =ARGUMENT("Costs",1)

Costs, another numeric argument, is the second variable used in PMARGIN.

8. Using the text names for variables, enter in cell C4 the following formula to calculate the profit margin:

=(Sales–Costs)/Sales

9. Enter the following RETURN code in cell C5:

=RETURN(C4)

The RETURN code does two things: it ends the PMARGIN macro and it returns the value in C4 on the macro sheet to the location of the PMARGIN function on the worksheet (see fig. 28.16).

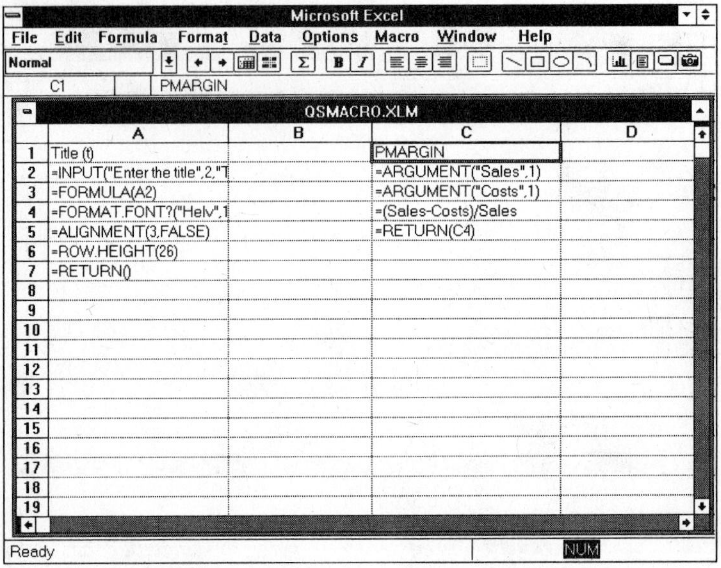

Fig. 28.16. The function macro now should appear as shown.

Now you must name the macro function so that Excel can locate it when you want to run it. Follow these steps:

1. Select cell C1.

2. Choose the Formula Define Name command.

   The function's name PMARGIN is already in the Name text box and =$C$1 shows in the Refers to box.

3. Select the Function option to designate that this name belongs to a function macro.

When you select Function, the option of choosing a Ctrl+key combination disappears. You cannot use a Ctrl+key to execute a function macro.

4. Choose OK or press Enter.

To make sure that your function macro works correctly, follow these steps:

1. Choose the File New command and select Worksheet. Choose OK or press Enter to open a new worksheet.

2. Use the Ctrl+t macro, which is also on the QSMACRO sheet, to help you enter the labels shown in figure 28.17. Enter the numbers shown in cells C6 and C7 of figure 28.18.

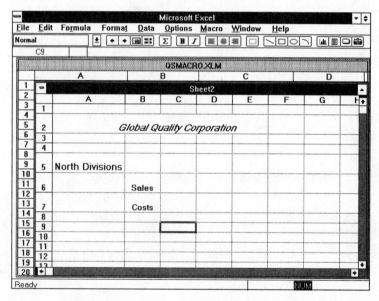

Fig. 28.17. A worksheet for testing the new function macro.

3. Select cell C9, and choose the Formula Paste Function command. Press the End key to go to the bottom of the list, and select the function you have created:

=QSMACRO.XLM!PMARGIN( )

Because the function is on a macro sheet external to the worksheet, its name must refer to that macro sheet. Your macro sheet may have a different name than QSMACRO.XLM. Choose OK or press Enter.

4. Edit the PMARGIN function in the formula bar to look like the following:

=QSMACRO.XLM!PMARGIN(C6,C7)

5. Press Enter. The answer, 0.50 or 50%, appears as shown in figure 28.18.

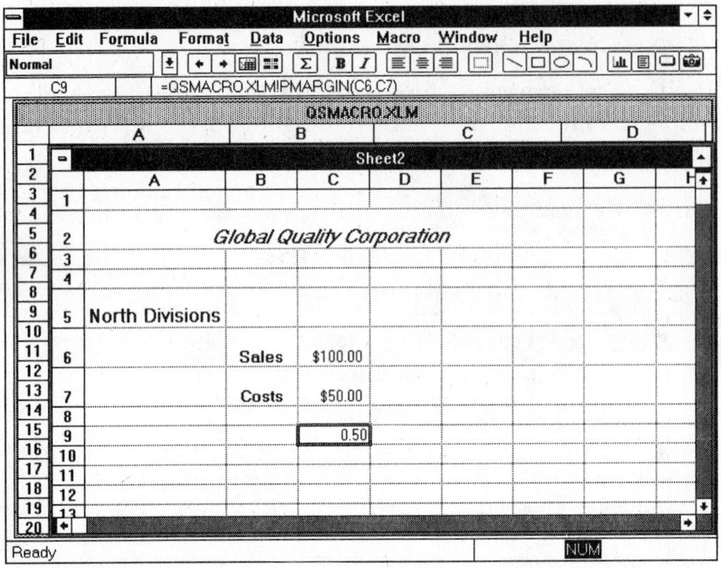

Fig. 28.18. Worksheets use your function macros in the same way they use built-in worksheet functions.

Notice that you must enter the argument values, C6 and C7, in the same order that the ARGUMENT terms appear in the column of macro code. The Sales argument is first, and the Costs argument is second.

If you want to preserve this sheet of macros to use again, you must save it. Make sure that you first save the macro sheet with File Save **As**, then save the worksheet. Saving in this order updates the external reference names used in the function macros (names like QSMACRO.XLM). The worksheet then stores the name of the macro sheet that contains the necessary functions. The macro sheet must be open for the macro functions on the worksheet to work.

From Here...

Excel's macro recorder makes it easy to record and edit command macros that save you a lot of time. Eventually, however, you will want to modify recorded macros and write command and function macros from scratch. When you reach that point, read Chapters 29–32.

The large number of macro functions available may intimidate you at first. As you work with macros, you will find that you can solve most problems by first recording the macro and then making changes to it. You can solve many business problems using only the recorder, the INPUT function, and the question mark (?)—just as you did in this Quick Start.

29

Creating Macros and Add-In Macros

M acros are sequences of commands and functions that automatically run Excel operations for you. You can create macros to replace simple repetitive keystrokes, such as setting a numeric format and selecting a font. On the other hand, you can create macros that turn Excel into a specialized program designed to perform specific, complex tasks, such as medical accounting or inventory analysis.

Macros are composed of functions similar to worksheet functions. Each function is the equivalent of a command, action, or worksheet function. The names of most macro functions make their functions easy to figure out. For example, FORMAT.FONT does the same thing as the Format Font command. Macros can also use worksheet functions to make calculations.

Many menu commands, such as Edit Copy or Formula Paste Function, work the same in a macro sheet as they do in a worksheet. You can apply everything you have already learned about editing worksheets to macros.

Macro functions run down a column in the macro sheet, one function to a cell. Each macro function performs some command or action according to the arguments found within its parentheses, much the same as a worksheet function. These arguments define the selected options, such as the font and style selected by the FORMAT.FONT function. Chapter 32, "Macro Function Directory," contains listings of the macro functions and their arguments.

Defining Macro Types

There are two types of macros: *command macros* and *function macros*. Command macros store action sequences containing commands from the menu, as well as keystrokes and mouse actions. These macros also can contain additional Excel commands not available from the menu. You activate command macros by pressing a Ctrl+key combination that you define or by choosing the macro name from a list box. You also can run command macros from custom menus that you create.

Command macros can range from the simple, such as range formatting, to the complex, such as industry-specific applications with custom menus, help windows, and dialog boxes. Excel macros can even operate and control other Windows programs. Following are some uses for command macros:

- Formatting a selected range with bold and currency format

- Printing frequently used reports in a specific order

- Accepting and cross-checking data entry

- Automating the preparation and upload of data to a mainframe

- Automating the download, analysis, charting, and printing of data from a mainframe

- Creating custom menus, help files, and alert and dialog boxes

- Linking and controlling other Windows applications

- Calling C language programs that perform specialized operations

- Building custom applications

The second type of macros are *function macros*. Function macros contain custom worksheet functions, which can be used in worksheets in the same way built-in Excel functions (such as SUM and MIRR) are used. Function macros do not use menu commands and cannot produce an action. They are used only for calculations. Function macros cannot be recorded; you must type or paste them into the macro sheet.

Running and Stopping Command Macros

If you have inherited files from someone else, purchased an Excel "template," or have run through the Quick Start, you may already have macros. To run an existing macro, you must first open the macro sheet in which the macro resides.

Opening Macro Sheets

You can use two types of macro sheets. Normal macro sheet files end with the extension XLM. These macro sheets can be visible when loaded, and the names of the macros on the sheet appear in the Macro Run dialog box. Another type of macro sheet, using the extension XLA, is used for add-in macros. These macros are designed to be invisible to the operator. When these macro sheets are opened, their macros appear to be an integral part of Excel. Excel comes with a number of XLA macros that are described in Chapter 15, "Using Excel's Add-In Macros." Chapter 30, "Modifying and Programming Macros," describes how to save your recorded or written macros so that they work as add-in macros. Both XLM and XLA sheets can contain command and function macros.

Follow these steps to open a macro sheet so that you can use the macros it contains:

1. Choose the File Open command.

2. Look in the list box for files with the extension XLM, or change the name in the file name box to *.XLM. This file-name pattern lists only macro files.

3. Press Enter to display the macro file names. Select the macro sheet you want, and then choose OK or press Enter.

You will probably want to load some of your macros with the worksheets they control. One way to load multiple documents is to save them as a group with the File Save Workspace command. To save a group of files as a workspace, open and arrange all the worksheets, charts, and macro sheets that you want to load together. Choose File Save Workspace, and then name the workspace file. When you next want all these documents loaded together, choose File Open and select that workspace file. (Workspace file names end with XLW.) A second way to automatically open a macro when you open a worksheet is to create an Auto_Open macro. This process is described in Chapter 30.

Running Command Macros

When the macro sheet is open, you can run one of the command macros it contains in three different ways. You can execute a macro by pressing its shortcut key combination—holding down the Ctrl key and pressing the macro's associated character. You also can activate a macro by choosing the **Macro Run** command, selecting the macro name from the list box (see fig. 29.1), and pressing Enter. Finally, you can choose a custom menu command that runs a macro. (Custom menus and commands are described in Chapter 31, "Adding Custom Menus and Dialog Boxes.")

Be aware that some macros are designed to work with a specific range selected or are designed to work under specific conditions. For example, if you run a worksheet macro when a chart is active, the macro will probably fail, and the STEP box used for troubleshooting will display.

If you have more than one macro sheet open, you can tell the macros apart because the name of each macro sheet precedes the macro name in the list box of the **Macro Run** command. Figure 29.1 shows the Run list box.

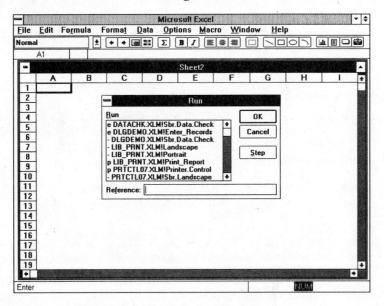

Fig. 29.1. *Run macros by name from the Run list box.*

You can assign the shortcut key, a Ctrl+key combination, to the macro when it is built. If you forget the shortcut key combination for a macro, choose **Macro Run** and look at the letter or number on the left side of the list box. The shortcut key also appears at the bottom of the **Formula Define** Name dialog box when you select a command macro.

To watch a macro operate one function at a time, choose the **Macro Run** command, select the macro name, and then choose the **Step** button. When the macro runs, a Single Step dialog box will appear. The dialog box enables you to run the macro one step at a time. This Single Step dialog box is described in the next section and in Chapter 30.

> **Note: *When Macros Have the Same Shortcut Key***
> When two macros have the same shortcut key, the macro appearing first in the list box of the Macro **Run** Command is the one that will be activated. You cannot give the same name to two macros on the same sheet; naming the second macro reassigns the name away from the first macro. Macros on different sheets, however, can have the same name.

Excel discriminates between macros named with upper- and lowercase letters. Therefore, you have 52 shortcut key combinations for running macros. If macro shortcut keys are difficult to remember, start the macro from the **Macro Run** box.

Stopping Macros

 You can stop most macros by pressing Esc. Pressing Esc stops the macro and displays a Single Step dialog box used for troubleshooting, like the one shown in figure 29.2. The box shows the cell on which the macro stopped and gives you a chance to **Halt**, single **Step** through the macro, **Evaluate** how the macro will run, or **Continue** its operation. (If a macro is displaying a dialog box, you must respond to the dialog box. The dialog box takes precedence over the Single Step box.) Troubleshooting macros with the Step dialog box and STEP function is described in the next chapter.

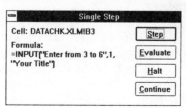

Fig. 29.2. The Single Step box appears when you stop a macro with Esc.

Many macros that create custom menus also add an Exit or Quit Macro command to the available menu commands. These macros may use a macro function that prevents the Esc key from stopping the macro. If this condition is present with a macro you are using, you must use the menu command to stop the macro.

Building Command Macros

You can build macros in three ways: recording macros, recording them and then modifying them, or programming them without the recorder.

In the first method, you record the entire macro and then the macro replays exactly as you recorded it, selecting the same menu items and dialog box options. This process works well for such simple jobs as preparing cells with frequently used formats, fonts, and borders.

The second method of creating macros is most effective for the majority of Excel users. You build the main structure of the macro with the recorder and then edit this structure to add features. For example, you can use the macro recorder to insert and format new rows in a database. You can then manually add INPUT, FORMULA, and IF macro functions that request the data for entry and cross-check the data before entering it in a database. Another valuable modification is inserting a question mark (?) after a macro function, such as FORMAT.FONT?( ), to make that macro function's dialog box pause for changes. These techniques are covered in Chapter 30.

The third method of building macros takes advantage of Excel's extensive programming language. With Excel's programming language, you can manipulate files, automate extensive data analysis and charting, add custom menus and dialog boxes, link and control other Microsoft Windows applications, and build custom application programs. In these more complex applications, a skeleton of routines is usually created with the recorder, and then these skeletons are extensively modified by hand coding. Entry-level and more in-depth programming are discussed in Chapters 30 and 31.

Understanding How Command Macros Work

Figure 29.3 shows a simple macro that has been recorded. The macro name is in the topmost cell of column A. The explanation is typed in column B. The name is created and placed there by the macro recorder, or it is named and placed there manually. The macro must be named either by the recorder or with the Formula Define Name command.

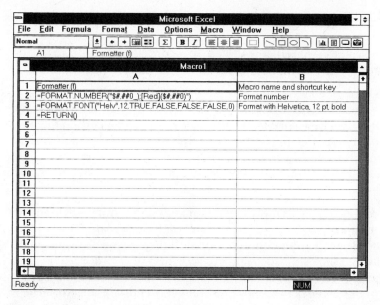

Fig. 29.3. *A simple recorded macro in column A and the typed explanation in column B.*

When you run a macro, Excel looks for the appropriate macro sheet and the name on that sheet. The macro starts in the named cell and proceeds down the column reading and calculating each cell's contents. Text or blank cells are ignored. Contents beginning with an equal sign are evaluated as macro functions. If a macro crosses multiple columns, the macro continues reading and calculating in the next column. A macro stops when it reaches a macro function such as RETURN or HALT.

The macro sheet is in one respect the reverse of a normal worksheet. On a worksheet, you see the results of hidden formulas. On a macro sheet, you see the formulas and macro functions, but the results are hidden. The results of macro functions can be either TRUE/FALSE logic results, a calculated result, or an entered result. A TRUE result indicates that a macro function operated correctly. A FALSE result can indicate that a Cancel button was chosen from a dialog box. Some functions, such as an INPUT box function, return to the cell whatever the operator typed into the Input dialog box. A function that contains syntax errors or cannot operate correctly returns an error value. Because macro functions return different values to cells, you can use these returned values to control how the program operates, check data, or take data from an Input box and put it into the active cell on the worksheet.

Recording a Command Macro

Even the newest Excel user can learn to record command macros. Command macros save time and work, yet are easy to create and use.

When you build a command macro, Excel records all your menu choices, mouse actions, and keyboard entries as functions on a macro sheet. A macro sheet looks like a worksheet with some of the commands in the menu bar disabled when the macro sheet is active; the **Options Display** command is preset to display functions, not their results. Columns in macro sheets are wider than in worksheets so that you can see the macro functions more easily.

Macro functions that represent commands and actions will seem familiar. For example, the macro equivalent of the **Format Font** command is FORMAT.FONT. The equivalent of selecting a range of cells is SELECT. Figure 29.3 shows one such simple macro that was recorded. The explanations in the adjacent cells in column B describe what each of the macro functions in column A does. The RETURN function ends the macro. (The macro recorder enters only the functions in column A; the explanations in column B were added manually afterward.)

You can use two commands to record a macro: **Macro Record** and **Macro Start Recorder**. The **Macro Record** command works best for recording and naming a new macro. The **Macro Start Recorder** works best when you want to add macro functions to an existing macro. The following sections discuss each command.

Recording a Command Macro on a New Macro Sheet

To open a macro sheet and record a new macro, follow these steps:

1. Activate the worksheet or chart on which you want to use the macro.

2. If you want to use this macro on any selected worksheet range or on a selected object in any chart, select cells or chart objects before you begin the macro recording. If you start the recorder and then select cells or objects, the macro will record the specific cells or objects that you select.

3. Choose the **Macro Record** command.

If a macro sheet is not open, the command automatically opens a
new macro sheet and asks you to name the macro and shortcut key.
The macro starts recording in the first cell of the first column. Excel
puts the macro name and shortcut key for the macro in the first cell
and then places all the recorded macro functions in cells going
down the column.

The Record Macro dialog box appears after you choose the Macro
Record command (see fig. 29.4).

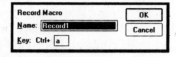

Fig. 29.4. *The Record Macro dialog box asks for the macro name and
shortcut key.*

4. Type the Name of the macro in the Record Macro dialog box.

   The name you type becomes the name of this macro. The name
   must conform to Excel's rules for names. Start with a letter; do not
   use spaces, symbols, or periods. Instead, you can use the dash (-)
   and the underscore (_).

5. Select the Key text box, and type a single character for use in the
   Ctrl+key combination. Delete the character before typing a new
   character, because only one is allowed in the box. (This step is
   optional; you do not have to assign a key combination to a command macro.)

6. Choose OK or press Enter.

   The macro name and the Ctrl+key combination give you two ways
   of activating your macro. Later you can start the macro by choosing
   the macro name from the Macro Run command's list box or by
   typing the Ctrl+key combination. For example, Ctrl+c might
   format preselected cells with your own custom currency format.

   The key character can be an upper- or a lowercase letter. Because
   Excel can distinguish between upper- and lowercase letters, you
   can have up to 52 different Ctrl+key combinations.

   Notice that the word Recording appears in the status bar at the
   bottom of the screen. From this point on, Excel records your menu
   choices and mouse or keyboard actions.

Excel records macros in either relative or absolute reference mode. A macro recorded in relative reference mode refers to the cells it acts on relative to the position of the last active cell in the worksheet. Macros using absolute reference mode move the active cell in the worksheet to exactly the same cell that was selected during the recording.

7. Choose Macro Relative Record if you want cell movements or selections to be recorded relative to the currently active cell. Choose Macro Absolute Record if you want cell movements or selections to be recorded in the same location on playback as during the recording. This command toggles between the two command names, so if the command Absolute Record is available for selection, you are currently in the Relative Record mode.

8. Make the menu choices and perform the keyboard or mouse actions that you want recorded. With each menu command chosen or action taken, the recorder adds another macro function to the column. Figure 29.5 shows macro functions extending down a column. The macro has not stopped recording yet.

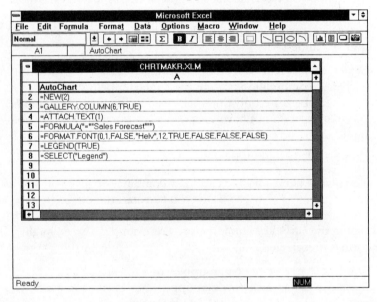

Fig. 29.5. *Macro functions are recorded in cells down a column.*

Excel ignores menu selections that you make from dialog boxes when you select the Cancel button or press Esc.

If you make a mistake while you are recording the macro, you can remove the incorrect macro function after you stop the recorder. Use the Edit commands to make the correction. Do not try to remove a macro function with the UNDO macro command while you are recording. With the recorder on, choosing Edit Undo enters the UNDO function into the macro.

9. Choose Macro Stop Recorder when you are finished recording.

    Choosing the stop command inserts a RETURN macro function at the end of the macro, as shown in figure 29.6. This marks the end of the macro. It also means that your macro is now usable.

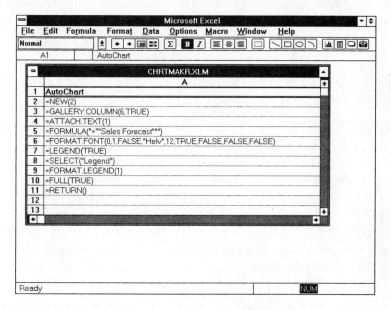

Fig. 29.6. *The RETURN function marks the end of the macro.*

10. Activate the macro sheet by selecting it from the bottom of the Window menu; then choose the File Save As command to name and save the macro sheet. Macro sheets are saved with the XLM file extension.

Use the techniques in the next section to add macros to an existing macro sheet. Don't forget to add documentation in the columns adjacent to the macro. Documentation should describe how the macro works and what each function or section of the macro does. Documentation makes a macro's operation and functions easier to remember.

To see the macro you have created, activate the macro sheet with the **Window #** command, where # is the number of the macro sheet.

Recording a New Macro on an Existing Macro Sheet

The second method of recording macros places the recorded macro on an existing macro sheet in a position that you specify. This method is used most frequently to record macros on a sheet and then modify them. It enables you to position the recorded macro where you want to.

To record a new macro on an existing macro sheet, follow these steps:

1. Choose the **File Open** command and open the macro sheet to which you want to add a macro. Macro sheets use the file extension XLM.

   Alternately, if the macro sheet is open, you can choose the **Window #** command to activate the macro sheet you want.

2. Select the cell where you want the macro name to appear. This will be the top, title cell of the macro. Normally, this cell will appear at the top of an adjacent blank column, or you can insert a few blank cells below the RETURN of an existing macro. Recorded macro functions will go in cells down the column below this name.

3. Choose the **Macro Set** Recorder command. This assigns the name Recorder to the selected cell. When a macro is recorded, it always starts in the cell assigned the range name Recorder.

4. Activate your worksheet and choose the **Macro Record** command.

5. Type the macro name and shortcut key in the Record Macro dialog box. Choose OK or press Enter.

6. Choose the **Macro Relative** Record command or the **Macro Absolute** Record command.

7. Make the menu choices and perform the keyboard or mouse actions that you want recorded.

8. Choose the **Macro Stop** Recorder command when you are finished recording.

9. Before testing the macro, save it as described previously.

Recording Changes Inside an Existing Macro

Once you have created a macro, you may find that you want to add more recorded commands or change the dialog box settings in a macro. You do not need to be a programmer to make these changes. You can record changes almost as easily as recording on an existing macro sheet.

To record additions or changes on a macro sheet, you insert cells in the existing macro to make room for the new functions you will record. Then you set the Recorder name at the top of the blank cells and record your changes so that they fill into the blank area. These are the steps to record changes or additions to an existing macro:

1. Select the cells where you want to insert new or different macro functions. Give yourself a safe margin by selecting more cells than the commands you will record. Figure 29.7 shows a macro with cells selected. If you use additional columns to contain documentation, make sure that you select cells across all columns that the macro and documentation uses.

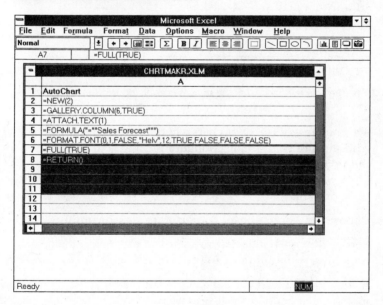

Fig. 29.7. Select cells where you want to insert additional recorded functions.

2. Choose the **Edit Insert** command, select the Shift Cells **Down** option, and then choose **OK**. The macro will open to give room to record inside.

3. Select the top cell in the opened space and choose the **Macro Set** Recorder command. This assigns the name Recorder to that cell. Recorded functions will start here. Figure 29.8 shows the macro after the new Recorder location is set.

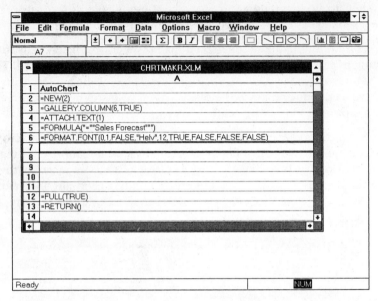

Fig. 29.8. The macro sheet after the new Recorder location is set.

4. Activate the worksheet or chart where the macro is used. Put the worksheet or chart in the configuration and settings required for this point in the macro—for example, selecting specific cells or displaying a window to duplicate the conditions the macro expects to be present.

5. Choose the **Macro Record** command to start recording.

6. Record the commands that you want to add. Select dialog box options as you want them to be recorded.

   If you did not insert enough cells in the macro you are recording in, the macro recorder will stop when there are no blank cells left. An alert box will tell you when recording stops.

7. Choose the **Macro Stop Recorder** command.

8. Activate the macro sheet and delete the RETURN macro function at the end of your added functions. Delete blank cells by selecting them, and then choose the **Edit Delete** command and select the

Shift Cells Up command. Make sure that you also delete cells in documentation columns so that documentation cells and function cells remain together.

Figure 29.9 shows the AutoChart macro after a legend is added and is formatted for the bottom position (1 represents the first option button in the Format Legend dialog box). Removing the blank cells and the unwanted RETURN in cell A9 will complete this modification. The next time the AutoChart macro runs, it will add a legend and move the legend to the bottom.

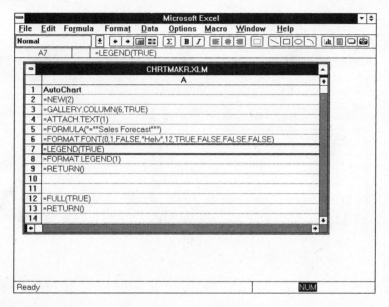

Fig. 29.9. *Recording within an existing macro is an easy way to add to a macro.*

Chapter 30 describes many easy ways to modify recorded macros. With simple changes, you can make dialog boxes pause for operator selection, input boxes request data, and have IF functions check for incorrect data.

Building Function Macros

Excel has a wide selection of built-in math, financial, logical, and text functions. But you may find yourself wishing for functions specific to your business. Imagine the time and frustration you would save if the formulas you frequently use were built-in functions.

Excel gives you the power to make that happen. You can create custom function macros that work just like Excel's built-in functions, such as SUM or LOOKUP. If you performed the exercises in Chapter 28, "Command and Function Macro Quick Start," you created a function macro that calculated profit margin.

The difference between function macros and built-in functions is that you define how the function macros work. After you define a function macro on a macro sheet, you can use it the same as you would any built-in function. You can put function macros on the same sheet as command macros.

Figure 29.10 shows a macro function that calculates calories when given the fat, carbohydrates, and protein in grams that a food contains.

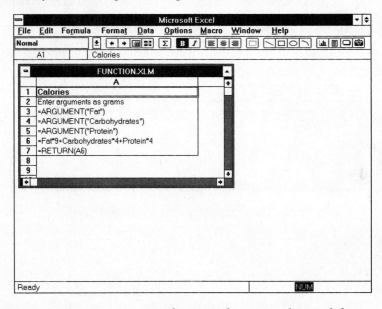

Fig. 29.10. Function macros create functions that are used in worksheets.

The function is entered in a worksheet with a format like this:

=**FUNCTION.XLM!Calories(*Fat, Carbohydrates, Protein*)**

The argument prompts, "Fat," "Carbohydrates," and "Protein," are pasted along with the function when you choose the Formula Paste Function command with the Paste Arguments check box selected. When you use the function in a worksheet, you replace these prompts with cell references or numbers. A completed macro function in a worksheet cell might look like this:

=**FUNCTION.XLM!Calories(*A12, B36, R42*)**

Building your own functions increases the accuracy of your formulas, reduces repetitive typing, hides complex formulas from novices, presents a cleaner and clearer worksheet, and ensures that the formulas used are those approved by management or an audit team.

Understanding How Function Macros Work

Function macros do calculations. They do not produce actions as command macros do.

A function macro also has a name at the top. Below that name are the *arguments*. Arguments specify what information from the worksheet will be used in the macro's calculations. On the worksheet, the arguments are the items within the parentheses of a function.

Arguments in a function macro accept information in the order it appears within parentheses in the worksheet. Each argument received is assigned to a name, such as Sales. For example, in the Quick Start function macro, PMARGIN(Sales,Costs), Sales is the first argument, and Costs is the second. These names are then used in calculations. In addition to the simple math shown in these examples, you can use all the worksheet functions to do calculations within a function macro.

The result of a function macro's calculations is returned to the macro function in the worksheet. This can produce a result in a cell or a result used within a larger worksheet formula.

The macro sheet that contains the function macros must be open for a function macro to return an answer. If the function macro sheet is not open, the worksheet cell that depends on the macro function produces a #REF! error. If you want a specific set of function macro sheets to open when Excel starts, copy those sheets into the XLSTART directory.

Function macros on open sheets appear at the bottom of the Formula Paste Function list box preceded by the name of the macro sheet. This means that you can paste in the functions without having to memorize them. Saving a function macro sheet as an XLA add-in macro adds your custom function macros to the Paste Function list just as though they were built into Excel.

Creating a Function Macro

Creating a function macro is similar to manually typing a command macro. Function macros cannot be recorded, because they cannot contain action or menu commands. You enter macro and worksheet functions in function macros by typing them or by pasting them into cells from the Formula Paste Function list box.

Function macros must be built in a specific order. The macro in figure 29.10 is an example of that order. After you open a new or existing macro sheet, the order of entries as you work down a column on the macro sheet is as follows:

1. Enter a name for the function macro in the top cell where you want the function macro.

2. Enter a RESULT function to specify the type of result returned to the worksheet. This term is optional and is not shown in the figure. If the function calculates a result of a different type, the function returns an error. (1 specifies numeric result; 2 specifies text. Others are listed in the macro directory.)

3. Enter ARGUMENT functions down the column in the same order that arguments appear between parentheses in the function macro.

4. Enter the formulas that the function macro uses to calculate its result. Use the names of the arguments as the variables in formulas.

5. Enter the RETURN function and specify which cell in the macro function contains the final calculated answer.

6. Select the cell containing the macro name at the top of the macro.

7. Choose the Formula Define Name command and select the Function option.

8. Choose OK or press Enter.

Enter an ARGUMENT function for each variable used in the calculation. Rather than typing in functions, you can paste them in using the Formula Paste Function command. A function can have up to 14 arguments. The order in which the arguments are entered between parentheses dictates the order in which you must enter variable values between parentheses in the worksheet.

There are two forms for the ARGUMENT function. The first form is as follows:

=ARGUMENT(*name_text*,*data_type_num*)

In this form, *name_text* is a text name in quotation marks that describes that argument—for example, ARGUMENT("Sales").

The second form of the ARGUMENT function is as follows:

=**ARGUMENT***(name_text,data_type_num,ref)*

This form names the cell address *ref* with the name of *name_text*. The value associated with *name_text* is entered in the *ref* cell on the macro sheet.

For both of the forms, *data_type_num* is a number specifying the type of data, such as text or numeric. If no number is specified, the argument assumes text, a number, or a logical value as the type. If a worksheet passes an incorrect argument type, the macro returns a #VALUE! error to the worksheet.

The RETURN function must reference the cell containing the final result of the calculations. This is how the answer gets back to the worksheet. For example, RETURN(C4) returns to the worksheet the contents of cell C4 from the macro sheet. (Remember, functions in the macro sheet do produce results.)

The macro sheet is formatted to show the functions and not the results. Reformat the macro sheet with **Options Display Formula** to see the results of macro function calculations. The shortcut key to switch between displaying functions and results is Ctrl+`.

Using Function Macros

Function macros work only when their macro sheet is open. Use **File Open** to open any macro sheet containing the function macro(s) you want. Remember that macro sheet names end with XLM. If you want a set of function macros always to be available, copy their XLM files into the XLSTART directory. Read the next chapter to learn how to change your function macros into add-in macros.

Once the macro sheet is open, you can paste the name of a function macro into a worksheet cell or macro sheet cell with **Formula Paste Function** just as you paste built-in worksheet functions. Function macros appear at the bottom of the Paste Function list, as shown in figure 29.11. Function macros must be preceded by the name of the macro sheet on which they reside. For this reason, it is much easier to paste in a function macro than it is to type it.

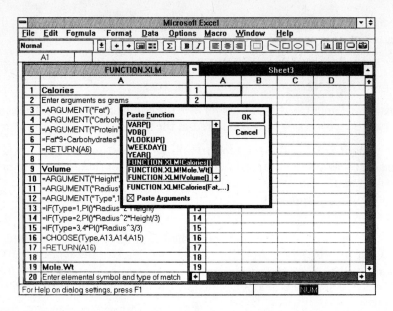

Fig. 29.11. *Function macros are easiest to use if pasted from the Paste Functions list.*

If you save your function macro sheets as add-in macros with the XLA file extension, the function macros on those sheets appear within the Paste Function list and are indistinguishable from Excel's predefined functions.

From Here...

Recorded command macros are easy to create and can save you a great deal of extra work on repetitive jobs. With a few simple modifications, you will find that your recorded macros can do even more. Chapter 30 describes simple changes that enable your macros to pause dialog boxes for changes, display data-entry boxes, and check results with IF functions.

Function macros are very powerful for companies that do a considerable amount of scientific, engineering, or financial work involving specialized formulas. Everyone in a company can use the same macro sheet containing the same functions. This practice increases the probability that worksheets use approved formulas and constants and will reduce typing errors in formulas.

The following three chapters explain how to create custom applications in Excel. Although Excel has a full programming language, you do not need to become a programmer to become more productive. As you will see in the next chapter, you easily can record macros and then make them much more powerful with simple modifications. Although you may want to eventually do some programming, you will find you can greatly increase productivity by recording and modifying macros.

30

Modifying and Programming Macros

Recorded macros can add a great deal of productivity to Excel. And modifying recorded macros can increase your productivity even further. The first part of this chapter describes how to make a few simple modifications to macros. These easy modifications enable macros to display messages, ask for data, check the data, and display dialog boxes that are normally displayed by menu commands.

Later in the chapter, you learn to enhance the capabilities of Excel by programming with macro functions. You use these functions in the same way you program with a language such as BASIC or dBASE. This chapter describes how to use control functions and subroutines within Excel. Chapter 31 describes how to create custom menus and dialog boxes. The result can be a totally customized application that looks little like the original Excel but contains all the analytical, database, and charting capabilities of Excel.

Two macro features described in this chapter make macros easier to use. The first feature turns your recorded, modified, or programmed macros into add-in macros. The macro sheet for an add-in macro is invisible to operators; the macro sheet adds commands and functions just as though they were built into Excel. (Chapter 15 describes the add-in macros that come with Excel.) With the second feature, you can assign macros to a button or a worksheet graphic object. The macro will run when you click on this assigned button or graphic object.

Editing Macros

You can use the same formula and sheet editing procedures for a macro sheet that you use in the worksheet. Select the cell to edit; then press F2 or click in the formula bar to edit the macro function argument. To copy or clear parts of a macro and to insert or delete cells, use the same **Edit** commands that you use in worksheets.

You can enter additional macro functions into an existing macro by inserting cells or rows into the macro sheet. Use the **Edit Insert** command to insert cells or rows; then use the **Formula Paste Function** command to paste the macro functions you need in the new cells.

Be careful when inserting rows: if your macros are in adjacent columns, inserting rows through one macro may insert a blank row through other macros. This blank row affects the appearance of the macro but does not stop the macro from running; however, a blank row through a menu description area spoils the appearance of the menu, and a blank row through a dialog box description causes an error.

> **Note:** *Before Editing a Macro*
> If the recorder is on while you edit a macro, all your **Edit** commands and actions appear as macro functions in the macro being edited. Make sure that the macro recorder is off. Otherwise, the result can be quite a mess.

Type your macro functions and names in lowercase characters. Then, when you press Enter, the functions that Excel recognizes as correctly spelled are converted to uppercase. You can spot mistakes in an entry when you see that a function remains in lowercase. Names defined with upper- and lowercase change to the same upper- and lowercase characters when you enter them.

Naming Macros and Shortcut Keys Manually

You may want to name a manually entered macro, rename an existing macro, or change a Ctrl+key combination. The macro must have its first cell named, or the macro does not work. Either the cell containing the text name of the macro or the first cell containing a macro function can be assigned the

macro name with the Formula Define Name command. To prevent maintenance problems later, naming the cell that contains the macro name is
preferred.

If you create a macro by using the Macro Record command, the macro is
automatically named with the name you enter in the Record dialog box. If
you manually enter the entire macro, you have to name the first cell yourself.
You can create a shortcut key at the same time that you name the macro with
the Formula Define Name command.

To create a macro name and shortcut key for a macro you created manually
instead of with the Macro Record command, follow these steps:

1. Activate the macro sheet containing the macro that is unnamed.
   The first cell in the macro should contain the name you want to use
   for this macro, as shown in figure 30.1.

2. Select the cell containing the name of the macro at the top of the
   column of macro functions (cell B1 in the figure).

3. Choose the Formula Define Name command. The Define Name
   dialog box appears, as shown in figure 30.1. Notice that this dialog
   box has more options than the Define Name dialog box in a
   worksheet.

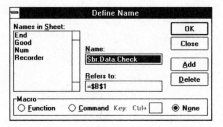

Fig. 30.1. *The Define Name dialog box on a macro sheet has options
additional to those in a worksheet.*

4. Select the Name box and type a legal Excel name (use no blank
   spaces and do not start with a number). If you selected the cell
   containing the macro title, the Name box already displays the
   name.

5. Select the Command Key option and type or edit the Ctrl+key
   character. This procedure indicates that the name belongs to a
   command macro.

6. Choose OK or press Enter.

Follow these steps to change a macro name or add a shortcut key:

1. Activate the macro sheet containing the macro you want to change.

2. Choose the Formula Define Name command. A dialog box appears (see fig. 30.2), from which you can change either the macro name or the shortcut key.

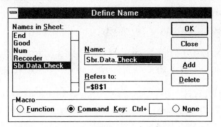

Fig. 30.2. *Edit a macro name or shortcut key with the Define Name box.*

3. Select from the list box the macro name for which you want to change the name or the shortcut key.

4. If you want to change a name, select the Name box and edit the name. Figure 30.2 shows the name of an existing macro selected for editing. The new name is entered in the Name box.

5. If you want to change a shortcut key, select the Command Key box and edit the Ctrl+key character.

6. Choose OK or press Enter.

Understanding the Values That Macros Return

The macro sheet displays functions, but these functions return results, just as the formulas return results in a worksheet. A result can be a number, text, or logical value (TRUE/FALSE). The value that a macro function returns is useful when you're performing calculations, making decisions, and controlling macro operation.

You can see the results returned by macro functions by activating the macro window, selecting the Options Display command, and deselecting the Formulas box. Figure 30.3 shows the DATACHK macro in two windows. The left window shows macro functions; the right window displays the values returned by each function. If OK is chosen in the input dialog box, cell B3 contains the value the operator typed. If the Cancel button is chosen, cell B3 contains a FALSE result.

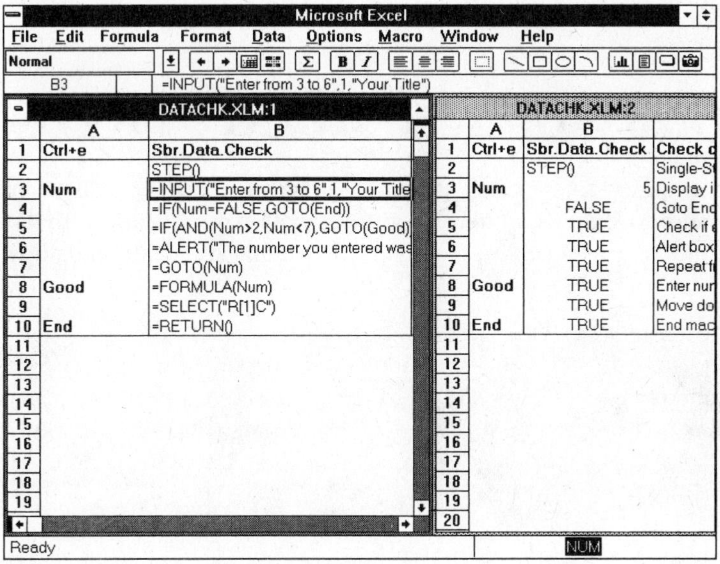

Fig. 30.3. Displaying the values returned by functions can aid you in debugging macros.

If you want to toggle a sheet quickly between displaying functions and their results, press Ctrl+`. The ` accent is on the same key with the tilde (~). Press Ctrl+` again to toggle the screen back to its previous view.

You also can see the results that functions return while the macro operates. The troubleshooting section of this chapter describes how to step through a macro one function at a time. While you are in this single-step mode, choosing the Evaluate button shows you the result of each function within a cell. If the cell contains multiple functions or nested functions, you see each term evaluated separately.

Some of the macros listed in Chapter 32, "Macro Function Directory," return values from different parts of the macro sheet or worksheet. You can find the names of worksheets and directories, the contents and format of cells, and much more. Some of the useful macros are listed here:

ACTIVE.CELL
GET.DOCUMENT
GET.CELL
GET.NAME

GET.WINDOW
GET.FORMULA
SET.VALUE
DIRECTORY

Modifying Recorded Macros

The easiest way to create custom macros is to use the recorder to create a
foundation and then add to this foundation with modifications that display
data-entry boxes, check data, or even add menus and custom dialog boxes.

> **Note: *Enclosing Text Arguments in Quotation Marks***
> Some arguments for macro functions are expected to be text. These
> arguments usually have the word *text* in the argument name, such as
> *name_text* or *style_text*. Enter text arguments within quotation
> marks as in the following example: =INPUT("Enter the title",2,"Title
> Entry Box").

The two macros in figure 30.4 are examples of how a simple recorded macro
can have power added to it. These macros create a chart from selected
worksheet cells. The macro on the left is the original recorded macro. The
macro makes bold the chart title typed during the recording. The macro on
the right is the same macro with some additions: a FORMULA and INPUT box
combination accepts any chart title, and the question marks inserted in
dialog box functions pause dialog boxes so that the operator can make
changes. The macro functions in this example are covered in following
sections.

Displaying Messages

Use the ALERT and MESSAGE functions to generate custom messages and
warnings. ALERT displays a dialog box containing a message. The user must
choose the OK button to put away the box and continue. Figure 30.5 shows
an alert box that was added to a recorded macro with the addition of the
following function:

=ALERT("The value entered is outside the acceptable range",3)

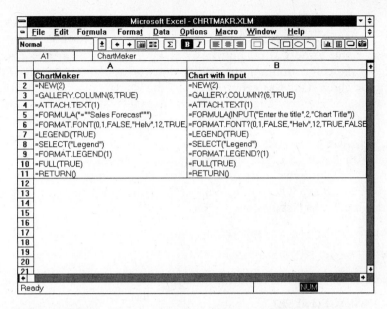

Fig. 30.4. *Recording and then modifying simple macros can produce powerful results.*

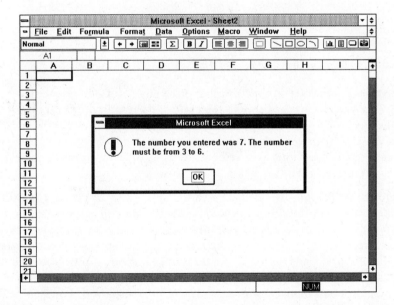

Fig. 30.5. *Use alert boxes to notify the operator of an error or to give information about an operation.*

Macro functions that display a box with OK or Cancel return the result TRUE if OK is chosen or FALSE if Cancel is chosen. You can check whether the operator chose the Cancel button by using an IF function that checks whether the cell containing the INPUT function contains a FALSE. If the operator chose OK, the cell containing the INPUT function contains the operator's entry. Dialog boxes such as FORMAT.FONT return a TRUE if they operated or return a FALSE if the Cancel button was chosen.

The MESSAGE function is more subtle and doesn't require the operator to stop and make a choice. The message appears in the status bar at the bottom of the screen and stays there until another MESSAGE function removes it. MESSAGE works well for letting the operator know what the macro is doing or how much of a task has been completed.

To display messages, use this format:

=MESSAGE(TRUE,"*message*")

To return the status bar to normal, use this format:

=MESSAGE(FALSE)

To clear the status bar, use this format:

=MESSAGE(TRUE,"")

Pausing Dialog Boxes

Normally, when you run a recorded macro, you do not get a chance to make any changes to the dialog box selections. The macro runs as recorded without letting you select different options. One easy and useful change you can make to your recorded macros causes dialog boxes to wait for your selections. The options you selected during the recording become the default settings when the dialog box opens.

Identify the dialog boxes that you want displayed by inserting a question mark (?) after the function name and before its opening parenthesis. Figure 30.6 shows formatting functions with question marks inserted. When the macro reaches these functions, the macro stops, displays the appropriate dialog box, and waits for your selections or dialog box input. Note that the selections in the dialog box you recorded become the default selections in the dialog box when it pauses. With the box displayed, you can make changes to the selections and choose OK or press Enter to continue with the macro.

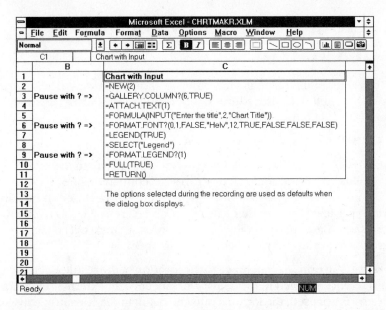

Fig. 30.6. *Put a question mark after a macro function name to make a dialog box pause for operator selections.*

The macro directory in Chapter 32 shows the format and arguments for each command that accepts a question mark. In general, any command you record that displays a dialog box can have its macro function modified with a question mark. For example, the FORMAT.FONT or PAGE.SETUP functions accept a question mark.

Macro functions that display dialog boxes accept default values for arguments. For example, FORMAT.NUMBER can use two formats, with or without a question mark. In these formats, the bold italic arguments are mandatory and the italic arguments are optional:

FORMAT.NUMBER(*format_text***)**

FORMAT.NUMBER?(*format_text***)**

Here, *format_text* is the same type of expression you see in the Format Numbers list box. If you do not enter the optional *format_text* argument in the version with a question mark, the dialog box displays standard defaults.

Entering Worksheet Values with a Macro

You can enter values through a macro just as though you typed the value into a worksheet cell. This procedure is done with the FORMULA function. The form for the FORMULA function follows:

> **FORMULA(*formula_text*,*reference*)**

Here *formula_text* is what is being entered. The argument *formula_text* is text, a value or formula, or a reference to a cell containing one of these items to be entered. The argument *formula_text* must be enclosed in quotation marks if it is text. The argument also can be a cell reference to a cell on the macro sheet that contains a value to be put into the worksheet or an external reference to any open worksheet or macro sheet.

reference is an optional reference to the location of the result; *reference* can be a reference to a cell in the active worksheet or an external reference. If *reference* is not used, the formula puts the result in the currently active cell.

> **Tip: *Until You Are Familiar with R1C1 Cell References***
> When you begin learning Excel macros, it may be difficult to type a worksheet formula within the FORMULA function. Instead, turn on the recorder, record the entry of the formula into the worksheet, and then turn off the recorder. Copy and paste that recorded FORMULA function into your macro. To see how to record the entry of the formula directly inside an existing macro, read the section "Recording Changes Inside an Existing Macro" in the next chapter.

Text or formulas must be enclosed in quotation marks. (Text or formulas that include quotes must have two quotes for each one that will appear in the cell entry.) Formulas must use the R1C1 format. Values entered with FORMULA do not need to be enclosed in quotation marks. For example, enter the number 345 in the worksheet's active cell in this way:

> =FORMULA(345)

Enter the title, Global Quality Corporation, in this way:

> =FORMULA("Global Quality Corporation")

Enter the formula A1+B2 into the active worksheet cell in this way:

> =FORMULA("=R1C1+R2C2")

Selecting Cells and Ranges in a Worksheet

The best way to specify the worksheet cells or ranges that you want a macro to work with is to use names. If you use named cells or ranges, the worksheet can be rearranged, and the macro still can find and work on the cells you want. If you want to select the cell named Data.Cell on the worksheet, for example, use a function like this one:

   =SELECT(!Data.Cell)

In this example, the ! indicates the active worksheet. To enter a value in the cell named Data.Cell on the active worksheet, use either

   =SELECT(!Data.Cell)

   =FORMULA("Title")

   OR

   =FORMULA("Title",!Data.Cell)

The first method selects the cell named Data.Cell and then enters the text into it. The second method does not change the active cell in the active worksheet. This method directly enters "Title" in the cell named Data.Cell. The second method operates faster.

Using INPUT

If you want a macro to accept data that you type and then let the macro enter it in a cell, use the INPUT function. INPUT functions produce simple dialog boxes that accept one cell's worth of data at a time.

INPUT functions work well for requesting data through a dialog box and then testing the data before entering it in a worksheet. Input boxes are much easier to use than custom dialog boxes. INPUT also checks the type of data entered—whether the data is it a number, text, formula, and so on. Use the FORMULA function to put the entered value into the worksheet.

INPUT takes the following form:

   =INPUT(*message_text*,*type*)

The *type* argument is a number specifying whether an allowable input is a formula, text, name, and so on. Refer to the macro directory in Chapter 32 for a list of types. If you enter data of the wrong type, Excel displays an alert box telling you of the mistake and then displays the input box again so that you can edit your entry. If you choose OK, INPUT returns to its cell whatever you typed. If you choose Cancel in the input dialog box, INPUT returns the value FALSE.

Figure 30.3 shows a macro that asks for an entry with an input box in cell B3. In this macro, cell names are used within functions rather than as cell references. The names shown in column A refer to the adjacent cell in column B. The IF function in cell B4 checks whether the Cancel button was chosen. If FALSE is returned to the input cell, the GOTO(END) function makes the macro operation jump to the end of the macro. If the operator chooses OK in the input box, cell B4 contains the typed entry. The FORMULA function in cell B8 enters the result from that entry into the active cell of the active worksheet.

❖ Creating Buttons That Run Macros

If you want an easy way to run a macro on a specific worksheet, assign the macro to a button or graphic object. The macro runs when you click on a button or graphic object that has a macro assigned to it. This setup can be helpful when you're creating systems for use by people with little Excel experience or for systems that operate from a graphical menu.

> **Tip: *Running Macros from the Keyboard***
> You only can run macros assigned to buttons or graphics with the mouse. If you want to run a macro quickly from the keyboard, use a shortcut key.

Figure 30.7 shows buttons for data entry, calculation, and printing down the side of the worksheet that was created in the worksheet Quick Start. Clicking on one of these buttons displays input boxes for data entry, recalculates the worksheet, prints specified reports, or sets the data-entry values back to defaults.

Figure 30.8 shows a graphical front end to a business information system that extracts information from a local or mainframe database. An operator can click on a portion of the world map in which the company does business. Then the operator can click on one of the buttons to retrieve specific information on business in that area. You can make the map selections possible by using a map as a background and overlaying it with invisible graphic circles or rectangles drawn with tools from the tool bar. After a macro is assigned to these circles or rectangles, you can make the circles or rectangles invisible by changing their border and fill patterns to a None option.

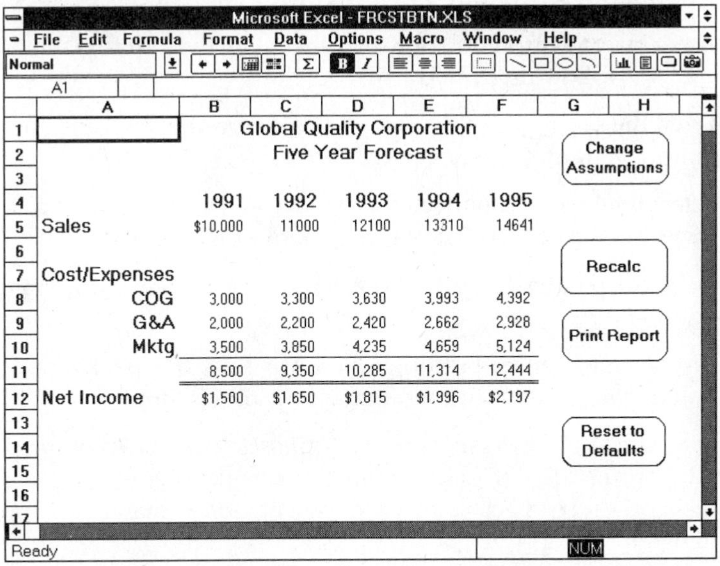

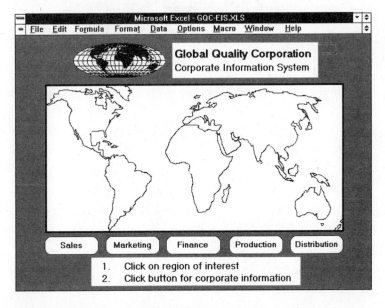

Fig. 30.7. Use macro buttons on frequently changed or printed worksheets.

Fig. 30.8. Create visual menus by assigning macros to graphics or buttons.

To run a macro from a button or graphic object, move the mouse pointer over the button or graphic object. If the button or object has a macro assigned to it, the pointer changes to the selection hand you have seen in the Help window. When the hand is over the button or object, click once.

To create a macro button on your worksheet like those across the bottom of figure 30.9, follow these steps:

1. Open the macro sheet containing the macro you want to assign to a button. Activate the worksheet.

2. Select the Button tool from the tool bar. This tool appears as a shadowed box to the left of the Camera icon.

3. Move the pointer cross hair to where you want one corner of the button.

4. If you want a square button, hold down Shift. If you want the button aligned with and the shape of gridlines, hold down Ctrl.

5. Drag across the worksheet to mark the size of a macro button. When you release the mouse button, the macro button appears on the worksheet where you have drawn it and the dialog box shown in figure 30.9 appears.

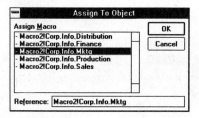

Fig. 30.9. Use this dialog box to assign macros to a button or graphic object.

6. From the Assign Macro list, select the macro you want, and then choose OK or press Enter.

7. Type the text you want to appear as a label on the button in the still-selected macro button.

Before you can run the macro assigned to the button, you must click off the button so that it is not selected.

To assign a macro to a graphic object, follow these steps:

1. Open the macro sheet containing the macro you want to run. Activate the worksheet.

2. Select the graphic object on the worksheet that you want to trigger the macro.

3. Choose the Macro Assign to Object command.

4. From the Assign Macro list, select the macro you want to run, and then choose OK or press Enter.

To change the macro assigned to a button or graphic object, follow these steps:

1. Open the macro sheet containing the macro you want to reassign. Activate the worksheet containing the button.

2. Hold down the Ctrl key and click on the button or graphic object.

3. Choose the Macro Assign to Object command.

4. Select the name of the macro you want to assign.

5. Choose OK or press Enter.

To format a macro button or graphic object that has an assigned macro, hold down the Ctrl key and select the macro button or graphic object. Select all or a portion of the text inside the macro button and use the Format Font command or the tool bar icons to format the text. To align the text, use the Format Text command to align or turn the text in the macro button in the same way that you format text boxes. If you want the macro button automatically to adjust its size for a best fit around the text, select the Automatic Size check box.

Running Macros Automatically

Run macros automatically when worksheets open or close by creating Auto_Open and Auto_Close names in the worksheet. These macros are useful for preparing worksheets as soon as they open, adding custom menus when a worksheet opens, or removing custom menus when a worksheet closes.

To create an Auto_Open or Auto_Close name, follow these steps:

1. Activate the worksheet.

2. Choose the Formula Define Name command.

3. Select the Name text box and type the name **Auto_Open** or **Auto_Close**.

4. Select the **Refers** to text box and enter the name of the macro sheet and macro you want to run automatically.

5. Choose OK, and then resave the worksheet.v

Auto macros that include the external reference to the macro open the macro sheet if it is not already opened. If the worksheet and macro sheet are in the same directory, for example, enter the macro in the **Refers** to box in this way:

=DBAID.XLM!DataEntry

If the macro is in a different directory from the worksheet, enter the macro in the Refers to box as follows:

=C:\EXCEL\CLIENTS\DBAID.XLM!DataEntry

You can open a worksheet without the automatic macro running by holding down the Shift key as you choose OK or pressing Enter from the Open dialog box.

❖ Creating Add-In Macros

Add-in command or function macros act as though they were built into Excel. Command macro names on an add-in sheet do not appear in the Macro Run list, and function macros on an add-in sheet appear in the Paste Functions list box in alphabetical order and without being preceded by their worksheet name. Add-in macro sheets are hidden, and you cannot unhide them by using the **Window Unhide** command. Add-in macros are an excellent way to add custom features to your work environment so that Excel appears to have been designed especially for your business.

You can change any Excel command or function macro into an add-in macro by saving its macro sheet with the add-in file format. To save a macro sheet as an add-in, follow these steps:

1. Activate the macro sheet.

2. Choose the **File Save As** command.

3. Type a new name if desired.

4. Choose the **O**ptions button. From the **F**ile Format list, select Add-In.

5. Choose OK twice.

Add-in macro files end with the file extension XLA. If you want the add-in macro to run when Excel starts, copy the appropriate XLA file into the XLSTART subdirectory.

Whenever an add-in macro sheet is open, function macros display within the Paste Functions list box the same as Excel's predefined macros do. You can use command macros on an add-in macro sheet as subroutines within other macro sheets without specifying the sheet name. For example, instead of using the subroutine

=REPORTS.XLM!Print_It( )

you can run the same subroutine on any other macro sheet with

=Print_It( )

If you want to open an add-in macro sheet as a normal macro that you can edit, hold down the Shift key as you choose OK or press Enter from the Open dialog box.

Writing Macros

After you become more confident with macros and more familiar with modifying recorded macros, you may want to go further into programming macros. This section of the chapter describes how you can type macro functions manually or do more extensive modifications so that macros select specific cells and ranges, test for special conditions, evaluate cell contents, and loop through repetitive procedures.

Understanding Cell References in Macros

Macros can reference cells and ranges in more than one way. Macros can use the A1 style, which you are accustomed to using on a worksheet, or the R1C1 style, which is more convenient for relative moves and macro programming. The reference type also depends on whether the macro refers to an absolute reference or a relative reference and again on whether it refers to the active sheet, the macro sheet, or a specific named sheet.

References can be either relative to the active cell or absolute. When you record a macro, you can switch between relative and absolute by choosing the **M**acro Relative Record or the **M**acro Absolute Record command. Following are the relative reference forms you should use:

Form	*Description*
R[1]C[–2]	One row down and two columns left from the active cell in the same *macro* sheet that is running
!R[1]C[–2]	One row down and two columns left from the active cell in the *active worksheet*
Sheetname!R[1]C[–2]	One row down and two columns left from the active cell in the sheet with the name *Sheetname*

Absolute references refer to a specific cell. The forms you should use for absolute references follow:

Form	*Description*
$A$1	Absolute reference to the cell A1 in the macro sheet containing the macro that is running
R1C1	Absolute reference to the cell in the first row and first column of the macro that is running
Sheetname!$A$1	Absolute reference to the cell A1 on the sheet named *Sheetname*
Sheetname!R1C1	Absolute reference to the cell in the first row and first column of the sheet named *Sheetname*

When you record the selection of a cell with the macro recorder, the cell's location is referenced in R1C1 style. Because this is a text style, the reference must be enclosed in quotation marks. For example, the following function selects cell B2 on whatever sheet is active:

=SELECT("R2C2")

Some macro arguments must have references as text. These arguments usually are listed in Chapter 32's macro directory in a form similar to *ref_text*. In these cases, the reference must use the R1C1 style and be enclosed in double quotation marks.

Some functions, such as the FORMULA function, can use either A1 or R1C1 style references. In this case, the function and its arguments are listed in the directory as

FORMULA(*formula_text*,*reference*)

This function can use the form

FORMULA("GQC",!$B$55)

OR

FORMULA("GQC",!R55C2)

When you switch the workspace between A1 and R1C1 format using the **Options Workspace** command, references in the macro without quotation marks change their style to conform to the style used in the workspace.

You can learn more about how references work by examining how recorded macros write selections and relative moves. When you're writing macros, the best procedure is to use cell and range references as little as possible; instead, use named cells or ranges. In place of using relative moves, such as R[1]C[1], use the OFFSET function described later in the section "Selecting Cells with OFFSET." Although more complex to understand, OFFSET produces macros that are much faster and more flexible.

Selecting Cells and Ranges in the Macro Sheet

Some macro functions, such as FORMULA(*formula_text,ref*), can specify that their actions affect the reference indicated by the argument *ref*. Other functions, such as FORMAT.NUMBER(*format_text*), affect whatever cell or range currently is selected. To choose the cells you want to be affected by this type of function, use the SELECT function to select the cell or range before the macro reaches the function.

Using an external cell reference that includes the document name makes the macro work with only the named document (worksheet, chart, or macro sheet). To make a cell selection specific to the ACCTRCV.XLS worksheet, for example, write the SELECT function as follows:

=SELECT("ACCTRCV.XLS!R2C5:R2C10")

This function selects the cells from row 2, column 5, to row 2, column 10, on this worksheet. This command selects that range even if that sheet is not active (it must be open). Because the sheet does not have to be activated, the macro runs faster.

If the range R2C5:R2C10 has the name Delinquent assigned to it, then the same range can be selected with the following function:

=SELECT("ACCTRCV.XLS!Delinquent")

To make the macro work with whatever sheet currently is active, precede the reference with an exclamation point (!). To select the range D15:E20 on the currently active worksheet and to make cell D15 the active cell in the range, for example, use this formula:

```
=SELECT(!D15:E20,!D15)
```

Select multiple noncontiguous ranges on a worksheet by separating the ranges or range names with commas, as in this example:

```
=SELECT("R5C2:R8C2,R7C3:R10C3","R7C3")
```

Naming Macro Cells

Using names in worksheets and macros adds a little time to their creation, but it saves much work later. The use of names in macros can be even more important than their use in worksheets.

Macros that refer to named cells or ranges on a worksheet continue to work even when that worksheet has been rearranged. And macros that reference other cells on the macro sheet are much easier to read and maintain.

If your worksheet contains cells or ranges that are named, you can select a cell or range on the active worksheet during your recording by pressing the F5 (Goto) key to select the named area and then continuing with the commands to affect that area. If you have a report that changes in size each month, for example, name the report area Month_Report. A macro to select and print this area each month would look like this one:

```
Print.Report
=FORMULA.GOTO("Month_Report")
=SET.PRINT.AREA( )
=PRINT(1,,,1,FALSE,FALSE,1,FALSE,1)
=RETURN( )
```

Names make macros significantly easier to understand and maintain. Figure 30.10 shows the DATACHK.XLM macro. The names in column A refer to the adjacent cell in column B. (The cells in column B are named; column A shows only what the names are.) Using names in this way makes it easy for the macro to look at cell contents within itself and makes it simpler for you to figure out what the macro is doing.

To use the names in column A to name the adjacent cells in column B, follow these steps:

1. Enter names down the left column. Select the range of the macro to include the names and the adjacent macro formulas, as shown in figure 30.11.

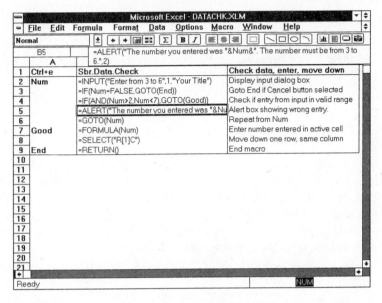

Fig. 30.10. *Use named cells to make understanding which cells a macro references easier.*

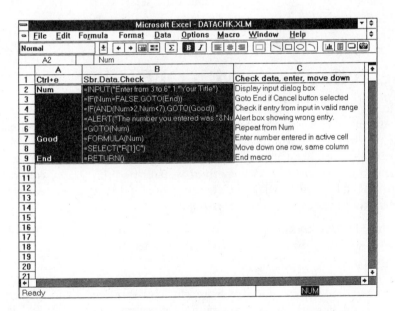

Fig. 30.11. *Select the names in column A and the cells they apply to in column B.*

2. Choose Formula Create Names; then select the Left Column option to use the names in the left column.

3. Choose OK or press Enter. You now can use the names in place of cell references.

Moving the Active Cell on a Worksheet

When you need to move the active cell in a macro, use the relative cell reference form with R1C1 style inside a SELECT formula. Remember to enclose the R1C1 reference in quotation marks. Make the movement relative to the active cell on the worksheet by enclosing the number in square brackets. If you want the active cell to move down three rows and two columns to the right, for example, use the following:

    =SELECT("R[3]C[2]")

To move up two rows in the same column, use the following:

    =SELECT("R[−2]C")

Functions such as FORMAT.FONT affect the selected cell or range. In this case, use the SELECT function as shown.

Selecting Cells with OFFSET

Although R1C1 moves are easy to understand, macros that use them for many cell selections can be slow. A method that is faster and far more flexible for use when entering data via a macro is to use the OFFSET function. OFFSET returns a cell or range reference that is offset by a specified distance from a known location. This method is like standing on one cell in the worksheet, the active cell, and throwing values at distant cells. Because the active cell is not moving, the macro operates faster.

With OFFSET, you easily can reference a cell that is a specified location from the active cell or from a named cell. OFFSET has this form:

    =OFFSET(*reference,rows,cols,height,width*)

Here, *reference* is a base location from which other references are offset. The arguments *rows* and *cols* specify the number of rows and columns that the offset is distanced from the base location. If you want an offset to specify a range, specify the height and width arguments. The top left corner of a range is the location offset from *reference* by *rows* and *cols*.

You can use the reference that OFFSET returns to enter data in cells or to select cells and ranges a known distance from the reference cell. OFFSET by itself does not work with commands that affect selected cells, such as FORMAT.FONT. To enter the number 5 two rows down and one column to the right of cell A12, use this function:

=FORMULA(5,OFFSET(A12,2,1))

Excel uses a programming construct known as a FOR-NEXT loop to repeat a set of functions. Each time the FOR-NEXT loop repeats, the value of a *counter* changes. This changing value can be used by the OFFSET function to step through a sequence of cells. Each time the value of the counter changes, the reference returned by offset changes. FOR-NEXT loops are described later in this chapter, in the "Repeating Tasks by Looping" section.

The following function enters the number 5 offset from the active cell in the worksheet:

=FORMULA(5,OFFSET(ACTIVE.CELL( ),2,1))

If you want to enter data in cells with a FOR-NEXT loop, use the counter name in the FOR argument to specify the row or column offset. The following example is useful for stepping entries across the cells in a sales history database. The value to be entered in a cell is stored in the name Sales (this name is like a variable name in BASIC.) The top left corner of the sales history database is named Sales.Hist. The row for entries is one row down from this name. The offset that moves entries across the columns in the sales history database is Sales.Month. A FOR function increases the Sales.Month from 1 through 12. As the value of Sales.Month changes, the reference returned by OFFSET changes. You can use this reference with the FORMULA functions to enter a value in each of 12 monthly columns. The FORMULA function to do this procedure follows:

=FORMULA(Sales,OFFSET(Sales.Hist,1,Sales.Month))

To do the same thing but allow an operator to type an entry into each cell, use this function:

=FORMULA(INPUT("Enter data",1),OFFSET(Sales.Hist,1,Sales.Month))

FORMULA works quickly with OFFSET because OFFSET does not actually select the cell in which the data is entered. Some functions, such as those that format, can format only a selected cell. For these types of functions, use OFFSET combined with SELECT to select cells or ranges offset from a base location. The following formula selects a cell two rows down and two columns right from the active cell:

=SELECT(OFFSET(ACTIVE.CELL( ),2,2))

If you want to select a range that is two cells wide by two cells deep with the upper left corner two cells down and two cells right from the active cell, use this formula:

=SELECT(OFFSET(ACTIVE.CELL( ),2,2,2,2))

To get information from a cell that is offset from a base location, use the INDEX function. This function retrieves the contents of an offset cell.

Finding the Right Macro Function

Excel has a large number of macro functions available for modifying macros or for use in writing new macros. The list of functions is as extensive as in most programming languages. The list of results and commands shown in table 30.1 simplifies finding basic commands that you will need in most modifications. Chapter 32, "Macro Function Directory," contains the full list of commands and descriptions.

Table 30.1
Common Macro Functions

Operation To Perform	Function or Modification
Choose from a dialog box	Add a ? before the ( ) in the recorded macro function
Select a cell or range or move the active cell	SELECT
Return the reference of displaced a distance from a base location	OFFSET
Return the value in a cell displaced within a range	INDEX
Read the current cell or range address	SELECTION
Enter a value from the keyboard	INPUT, FORMULA
Cross-check data entry	IF, INPUT, IS functions
Display a message or warning	ALERT, MESSAGE
Control macro operation by time	WAIT, ON.TIME
Activate a macro when a key	ON.KEY is pressed

Operation To Perform	*Function or Modification*
Change the direction of subroutine program flow in a macro	GOTO
Make a decision	IF
Choose from alternatives	CHOOSE
Format current selection	FORMAT.*command*
End or stop a macro	HALT, RETURN
Repeat a procedure	FOR, FOR.CELL, WHILE, NEXT, BREAK
Test if the active cell is blank, or a number, text, an error, etc.	ISBLANK, ISNUMBER, ISTEXT,...
Return information about references, formulas, windows, documents, or notes	GET.*command*

Making Decisions and Testing Conditions

The IF function is the great decision maker in Excel. Use IF to decide how a macro reacts, based on a condition in the macro or worksheet. IF works well for checking data-entry values and for branching the macro to new operations.

IF takes the following form:

=IF(*logical_test*,\ *value_if_true,value_if_false*)

When the comparison or logical condition you enter in *logical_test* is true, then the value or formula in *value_if_true* executes. If the comparison or logical condition is not met, then the value or formula in *value_if_false* executes.

Figure 30.12 shows a charting macro that checks whether the input box has been canceled. If the box has been canceled, E5 contains FALSE, so the IF statement in E6 sends macro operation to cell E10, named Title.Skip, which skips over functions related to formatting a title. Because the title does not exist if Cancel was chosen, you don't want the macro to try to format a nonexistent title. If you chose OK for the input box in E5, the value typed in the input box is returned to E5. The IF function in E6 finds that E5, Title.Input, is not FALSE, so the IF function attempts to execute the *value_if_false* argument. Because no *value_if_false* argument exists, the macro continues with cell E7.

❖ Converting Returned Values

When you begin programming, you may face the difficult proposition of a function returning a value when you want a reference. Or the function may return a reference when you want a value. You can see when this situation happens by using the single-step debugging mode and choosing the Evaluate button. When debugging, you see at what step a function returns a value rather than a cell reference. (Debugging is discussed in the "Finding Problems" section later in this chapter.)

In many cases, Excel coerces the result of the function into the correct form that is needed. When coercion is not successful, use the DEREF, TEXTREF, or REFTEXT functions to change the result of a function into the form needed by another function.

	D	E	F
		F6	If Cancel button, skip title code goto E10
1		Adv.Chrt.Mkr	
2		STEP()	Insert equal to see steps
3		=NEW(2)	Create chart from selected data
4		=GALLERY.COLUMN?(6,TRUE)	Pause Column dialog to allow selection of type
5	Title.Input	=INPUT("Enter the title",2,"Chart Title")	Ask for title, if Canceled then E5 is False
6		=IF(Title.Input=FALSE,GOTO(Title.Skip))	If Cancel button, skip title code goto E10
7		=ATTACH.TEXT(1)	Attach title
8		=FORMULA(Title.Input)	Enter results of Title.Input into chart title
9		=FORMAT.FONT?(0,1,FALSE,"Helv",12,	Pause Font dialog box
10	Title.Skip	=LEGEND(TRUE)	Create legend
11		=SELECT("Legend")	Select legend
12		=FORMAT.LEGEND?(1)	Pause Legend dialog box
13		=FULL(TRUE)	Maximize to full screen
14		=RETURN()	

Fig. 30.12. Use IF functions to test the values returned by other functions or operator entries.

Copying and Deleting Macros

You can copy and paste macros from one sheet to another. This feature is convenient when you have a library of macros or subroutines that you want to combine on other macros sheets. To transfer a macro, use **Edit Copy** and **Edit Paste** to copy the macros you need onto one sheet. Name the top cell in the copied macro with the **Formula Define Name** command and select the **Command** option at the bottom of the dialog box.

Make sure that any cell references either refer to the active sheet (showing just "R1C1" or !A1 style reference) or use external references to refer to a specific worksheet (such as "FORCAST.XLS!R1C1" or FORCAST.XLS!A1).

Clearing the macro functions from the macro sheet is not enough to get rid of a macro. You also must delete the macro name. After you clear all the functions from the macro sheet, use **Formula Define Name** to select and delete the macro names you want to remove.

Programming Macros Manually

You can enter manually all or part of the macro functions that create a macro. The macro functions and structure of the sequence can be likened to programming in an interpretive language such as BASIC. For most procedures, you will want to record sequences of commands and actions and then modify the recordings. But, for complex programming needs, you will need to write the macro or macro subroutines manually.

If you are familiar with programming, you know how important planning and documentation are. Any time you write macros manually, you can save time by designing the macro before you begin. The most important point to remember is to write your macro in subroutines and have a main macro that controls when and how each subroutine runs.

Designing the Macro

Before you begin building the macro, you should organize what you want the macro to do. Write down the steps and tasks to be done. Break these tasks into subroutines.

Macros are easier to test and troubleshoot if you can isolate problems in subroutines. Use sample data to test each subroutine; then paste together the subroutines into a larger macro or link them to a master control macro that tells each subroutine when to run. (This chapter's section "Using Subroutines" describes how to link subroutines to a main macro.)

Another advantage of programming macros from a collection of subroutines is that you can create a library of subroutines that handles frequently needed tasks. This library can be used with many worksheets.

Macros are easier to understand if you break up sections within a macro by text headings. Format the headings with italic or bold so that they are easy to see. You can even use color to define certain areas within a macro, such as an area that contains all the functions involved within one level of a FOR-NEXT loop. (Excel does not read text or blank cells in macros.)

Documenting the Macro

Documenting macros is like backing up files on your hard disk. Many people fail to do it until they have caused themselves a great amount of work and job insecurity. Many people often are tempted to create the macros, use them immediately, and leave documentation for later. Then weeks or months later, when you or someone else must modify the macro, you have forgotten how it works.

Even if you are a novice Excel user and do not understand many of the macro functions, you should put an explanation of what the macro does in the column to the right of the macro. You also can attach a note of instructions to the cell with the macro name by selecting the macro name cell and choosing Formula Note.

The sample macro in figure 30.13 shows one of the best methods for documenting macros. This method makes macros easier to read, edit, and understand. The method titles the top cells in a macro so that the macro is more organized. Borders and shading can be used for separating distinct parts.

You can separate segments of a macro by including text and blank cells as dividers. The text and blank cells do not affect macro operation but do help to show where separate tasks begin and end within a large macro. Because Excel macros ignore text and blank cells, you can enter remarks or segment headers by typing them as text. You may want to format these remarks with italic or bold so that they stand out.

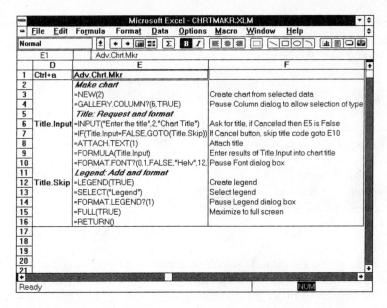

Fig. 30.13. *Document your macros in two or three columns.*

Another way of making your macros easier to read is to use Forma**t B**order to outline the column containing macro functions or the column containing documentation. Use color formatting to format areas of a macro that are similar; for example, use blue for the first level of a FOR-NEXT loop and use a red to mark a function that you need to come back to for cross-checking or replacing.

Controlling the Order of Macro Operations

Macro functions execute in the order they are listed down the column. However, you can change this flow of execution in a number of ways. A GOTO command or a subroutine call can reroute the macro to a different section of the macro. The IF function is an excellent method of controlling when branching takes place.

GOTO(*ref*) permanently branches macro operation to the cell location specified by *ref*. The macros in figures 30.10 and 30.12 show examples of the GOTO function. If the Cancel button from an input box is chosen, the cell for that input box returns FALSE. An IF function then can test for that FALSE condition and make the macro operation "go to" another cell to continue operating. This same method is used in checking for valid entries and branching back to the input box if an entry is out of limits.

> **Tip: *The GOTO and FORMULA.GOTO Functions***
> You use FORMULA.GOTO in a macro to go to and select a cell or range on the worksheet. FORMULA.GOTO is equivalent to the Formula Goto command or F5 key on the worksheet. The GOTO function directs a macro to look at macro functions in a different location. Normally, a macro reads and operates on each function in the cells down the column. GOTO can redirect macro operation so the macro begins reading and operating on functions in a different location.

Be careful when using GOTO because it makes the flow of macro logic and operation difficult to unravel. You can end up with macros that go to other macros that go to other macros that go to the original. Trying to correct problems in these entangled macros can be a nightmare. Use GOTO only to skip forward within the same macro. If you need to go outside the currently operating macro, use a subroutine.

Using Subroutines

Use subroutines to prevent snarls of GOTO commands. *Subroutines* are macros used for accomplishing specific and frequently repeated tasks. When a main macro needs the function that a subroutine performs, the main macro transfers macro operation to that subroutine. When the subroutine is finished, control returns to the original macro and continues from where it left off. Not only are subroutines easier to understand and write than GOTO statements, but often you can share subroutines among macros or paste subroutines onto other macro sheets.

Subroutines are nothing more than macros that perform a specific task for the main macro. They act as efficient subcontractors who do a special and repetitive job. For example, you may have a subroutine that sets the page layout and displays dialog boxes requesting header and footer information. This same subroutine can be used by different macros. Another example is a data extract subroutine used by different databases on the same worksheet.

Subroutine macros end with RETURN, just as normal macros do. When a subroutine macro reaches RETURN, it returns to the macro function following the one that called the subroutine.

The best way to write macros using subroutines is to write one main macro that acts as a script. This script tells the different subroutines when to run. The main macro should do little work itself; its purpose is to coordinate which subroutines run.

To get a subroutine to run, "call" it by name, where *macroname* is the cell reference or name at the beginning of the macro. Use the following form:

>**=*macroname*( )**

Suppose, for example, that you have a macro named Print_It that is designed to print any selected range. You can run this macro as a subroutine from any macro with this call:

>=Print_It( )

If the subroutine is on another macro sheet (perhaps a sheet containing a whole library of subroutines), include an external reference to the macro. Use the following form:

>**=worksheet!*macroname*( )**

>OR

>=USEFUL.XLM!Print_It( )

Macros that are used only as subroutines can include arguments specified within the parentheses. These macros are set up in the same way that function macros are set up to use arguments. If you use a subroutine macro as a normal macro, then don't set it up to accept arguments.

❖ Repeating Tasks by Looping

Use a loop when you need a macro that repeats a task numerous times. Excel can use three types of loops: FOR.CELL, FOR-NEXT, and WHILE-NEXT.

The FOR.CELL loop is a useful function that works well when you want to run commands on every cell within a range. It repeats the functions between FOR.CELL and NEXT on every cell within the range specified as an argument in FOR.CELL.

One type of loop uses FOR-NEXT functions. This loop repeats the macro segment between the FOR and NEXT macro functions "for" the number of times specified by a counter. Some uses for the FOR-NEXT loop are to repeat data-entry requests or to move across areas. You can reduce the size of your recorded programs by replacing long sequences of repeated functions with shorter FOR-NEXT loops that repeat a process.

Another type of loop, WHILE-NEXT, continues to repeat a loop "while" a condition is met. When the condition is not satisfied, the loop breaks and the macro continues. You can use a special command, BREAK, to break out of the FOR.NEXT or WHILE NEXT loop under special conditions that you define.

FOR.CELL works in conjunction with a NEXT function. All functions between the FOR.CELL and NEXT functions work on each cell in the range specified in the FOR.CELL argument. An example is in the command macro examples at the end of this chapter. Following is the form for FOR.CELL:

FOR.CELL(*ref_name*,*area_ref*,*skip_blanks*)

The *ref_name* argument is a text name that the function uses to store the cell reference of the cell currently being worked on. Enclose the *ref_name* in quotation marks. The argument *area_ref* is the range of cells that any functions following FOR.CELL will work on. You can specify multiple areas to be looped over by using an *area_ref* that looks like this one:

FOR.CELL("Checker",(Inventory,Cost))

Here, Inventory and Cost are two named columns in a database. Omitting *area_ref* runs the FOR loop over the current selection. *skip_blank* is a TRUE or FALSE argument specifying whether blank cells should be skipped. Omitting it or using FALSE runs the loop over all cells in the area.

FOR-NEXT loops use a named counter to track how many times a loop repeats. The FOR function takes this format:

=FOR(*counter_text*,*start_num*,*end_num*,*step_num*)

counter_text is a name that stores a numeric value. The *counter_text* begins counting at the *start_num*. Each time the loop runs, the *step_num* is added to the *counter_text*. When the value stored in *counter_text* finally reaches the *end_num*, the loop stops.

> **Note: *Using Quotation Marks with Counter Names***
> The *counter_text* for FOR.CELL and FOR functions must be in quotation marks. Excel stores a number or a reference in the name specified by *counter_text*. Each time through the FOR loop, the value in the name increases or decreases. Each time through the FOR.CELL loop, the name holds the reference of the cell being tested. If you want to use the value or reference stored in *counter_text*, do not put quotation marks around the name you used (see fig. 30.16).

The WHILE-NEXT loop often is easier to use than FOR-NEXT. The WHILE-NEXT loop begins with the following macro function:

=WHILE(*logical_test*)

In this function, *logical_test* is a conditional or comparative equation that results in TRUE or FALSE. WHILE-NEXT loops operate by repeating the macro between the WHILE and the NEXT functions until the *logical_test* within WHILE turns FALSE. The macro then continues through the rest of the macro when it reaches the NEXT function. If you want to set a special condition that causes looping to stop, refer to the discussion of the BREAK macro function in the macro directory. The sample command macros contain an example of the WHILE-NEXT loop.

Examining Sample Command Macros

The macros examined in this section show how simple macros can be, yet how they can save you time and work. Many of the command macros were created by the recording of a macro and then modification of it. In these macros, the names in column A are assigned to the adjacent cells in column B. An explanation of each function is in column C.

Cross-Checking Data

The macro shown in figure 30.14 cross-checks entered data. You can use it to cross-check data being entered into a database row or into entry areas of a worksheet. One IF function checks for the Cancel button selection from the input box. The other IF function checks to make sure that the value entered in the input box—stored in cell B2 (Num)—is greater than 2 and less than 7. The alert box shows any incorrect numeric value entered in the input box by including the returned input value in a concatenated (joined) text string. Text and numbers can be joined with the &. The formula bar shows the full ALERT function.

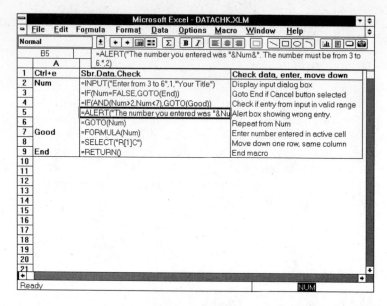

Fig. 30.14. *Use IF and GOTO functions to check returned values and to change the macro's direction of operation.*

Checking a Range of Cells with FOR.NEXT

The macro shown in figure 30.15 checks each cell in the range named Inventory to see whether the cell contents are less than 20. "Shader" is the *ref_name* that holds the cell reference of the cell being affected. If less than 20, the SELECT(Shader) function selects the cell being checked. The PATTERNS function then shades that cell red. (Some functions can be joined into a single statement with the + sign, as you see in cell B3.)

Using OFFSET To Enter Data Quickly

In the macro in figure 30.16, the FOR and NEXT functions are used for stepping a data-entry macro through a series of cells to enter sales information for six years. To run the macro, you must give a cell on the worksheet the name History.Sales. SET.NAME assigns the year 1990 to the name Year.First. The FOR function then assigns numbers incrementing by 1 to the counter name, Year; it increments from Year.First to Year.First+5. INPUT asks the operator for an entry and shows the current year being entered. The FORMULA functions combine with OFFSET to place the first year at the worksheet cell with the name History.Sales. OFFSET then uses the value of Year-Year.First to increment across six columns. The year is entered in one row, and the sales amount is entered in the cell underneath its year. Notice that when you run this macro, the active cell on the worksheet never moves.

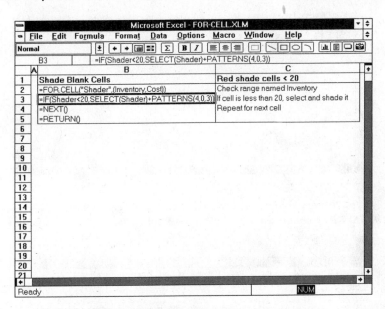

Fig. 30.15. *Use FOR.CELL to operate on every cell in a range.*

Printing with a Macro

When you have many print jobs to do, the macro shown in figure 30.17 cuts through the keystrokes. This macro shows how to use the FORMULA.GOTO macro function to select and print any named range or typed range reference. The result is as though you had programmed your own scrolling list box. Choose Cancel in the Goto box to end the macro.

The PRINT function in cell B4 illustrates how omitted optional arguments may still require commas as placeholders to position the other arguments. The PRINT function in B5 is

=PRINT(1,,,B4,FALSE,FALSE,1,FALSE,1)

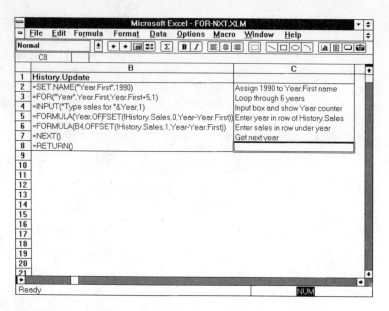

Fig. 30.16. *This macro demonstrates how to assign a value to a name and use a FOR-NEXT loop combined with OFFSET to enter values across a worksheet.*

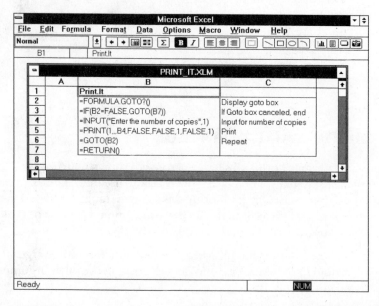

Fig. 30.17. *Use this macro to print multiple named ranges or typed references.*

Examining Sample Function Macros

As you learned in previous chapters, function macros are productive and reduce errors when you frequently use the same formulas. These examples show some methods of handling calculations where values from tables must be looked up or where one function handles more than one type of calculation.

A Calorie Function

In the Calorie function macro shown in figure 30.18, you enter the fat, carbohydrate, and protein content of a food in grams, and the function returns the number of calories in that food.

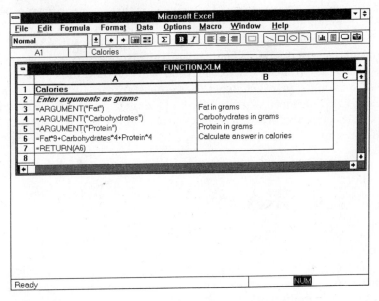

Fig. 30.18. *Some function macros may be short, but they still save you time.*

Volume Function To Choose between Solutions

In the volume function (see fig. 30.19), one of two solutions is calculated, depending on whether the type argument is a 1 or 2. If the type is a 1, then the volume of a cone is found. If the type is a 2, the volume of a cylinder is found. In this example, IF functions are used for deciding which formula calculates. A CHOOSE function then returns the result of the calculated formula. A CHOOSE function uses the value of the first argument, Type, to select from a list of arguments that follows.

Molecular Weight Lookup Function

The molecular weight function in figure 30.20 accepts a text entry of a chemical element's symbol, such as Ca for calcium. This text then can be used for looking up the molecular weight for that element from a table. However, two methods are demonstrated for looking up an answer. One method uses VLOOKUP and can produce an inaccurate result. VLOOKUP is commonly used by operators familiar with other spreadsheets; however, for exact matches, Excel has a better method. This method uses MATCH and INDEX and finds an exact match or returns an error warning. (Check Chapter 13 on advanced worksheet techniques to learn how these methods work.) Both methods are shown, but you should use only the MATCH and INDEX method because you will want a correct answer, not a close one.

Troubleshooting

Macros save a great deal of time and work. When you customize recorded macros by making small modifications, the macros become even more valuable. But when you begin to make significant changes, or when you begin to type macros directly onto the macro sheet, the probability of errors increases—especially when you are learning.

This chapter includes some tips on how to troubleshoot macros and how to deal with some of the more common difficulties. One of the most important tips is to keep your macros short and simple. If you need to accomplish more than what a short and simple macro can handle, use subroutines to join small macros.

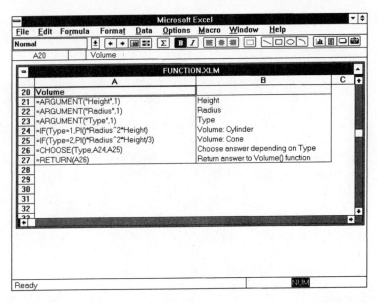

Fig. 30.19. This function macro demonstrates choosing between calculations.

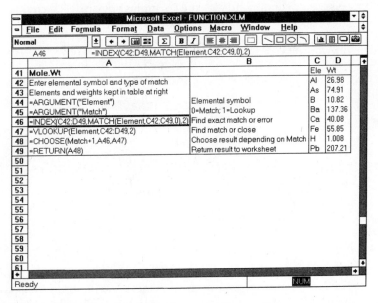

Fig. 30.20. Use a lookup table to find answers from a list.

The most important technique you will learn in troubleshooting macros is the use of the STEP function to single-step through macros as they operate. When you use the **Evaluate** button in the Step dialog box, you see the actual result returned by a function. This technique enables you to see whether the function was correctly evaluated and whether it returned an incorrect result or an error.

> **Tip: *Making Your Macros Run Faster***
> Turn off screen updating to make your macros run faster. Insert the macro function ECHO(FALSE) at the point in the macro where you want screen refreshing turned off. To turn screen refreshing back on in the middle of a macro, insert ECHO(TRUE). Screen refreshing always is turned back on when the macro is finished.

Finding Problems

Excel tries to catch errors when it runs the macros. For example, errors in macro syntax cause a Single Step alert box to be displayed on the screen. The alert box tells you which cell in the macro has a problem (see fig. 30.21).

In addition, you can monitor the values that macro functions produce. Use the Options Display command with the Formulas option deselected or press Ctrl+` (grave accent) to see values on a worksheet.

See Chapter 32, "Macro Function Directory," to see the values returned by different macro functions. Selecting a Cancel button in a dialog box, for example, results in a FALSE value in the cell that activates the dialog box.

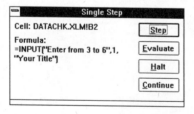

Fig. 30.21. The Single Step box enables you to watch macros operate one function at a time.

A great aid in correcting macro errors is the STEP function. You can put as many STEP functions as you want in your macro. Whenever Excel comes across the STEP formula, it presents a dialog box with four options (see fig. 30.22).

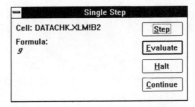

Fig. 30.22. *Use the Evaluate button to see the result that a function returns.*

The buttons in the Single Step dialog box are the following:

Button	Description
Step	Runs the current macro function and then steps to the next cell in the macro.
Halt	Exits the macro and returns to the active document.
Evaluate	Calculates the smallest term within the current macro cell and displays its results in the Single Step box. Figure 30.22 shows the INPUT function from figure 30.21 after its evaluation. The number 9 was entered.
Continue	Returns to normal macro operation until another STEP function or error is met.

Whenever you have a possible macro problem, insert a STEP function before the suspected problem with the following procedure. The STEP function should be entered as =STEP( ). When macro operation hits the STEP function, the macro goes into single-step mode. At that time, you can evaluate the result of each macro function to see where the error occurred.

Press Esc to enter single-step mode during normal macro operation. However, because you may not press Esc at just the right moment, this procedure is less accurate than inserting STEP in a macro.

Excel comes with an add-in macro that helps you troubleshoot, or "debug," your macros. This macro, named DEBUG.XLA, automates such trouble-shooting features as entering STEP formulas, setting break points, and switching the macro sheet between formula display and results display. This add-in macro is described in Chapter 15.

Reviewing Troubleshooting Approaches

The following tips include some of the more common problems faced when you're running and creating macros.

Problem:
The macro doesn't work at all.

Solution:
Go through the following steps to filter out the most common reasons for a macro not working.

1. Choose Formula Define Name or Formula Goto and verify that the top cell of the macro is named and that it is selected as a command or function type of macro (with an optional Ctrl+key combination if it is a command macro).

2. Choose Options Display and deselect the Formulas option. If you see error values displayed in macro function cells, check them out. For example, #NAME? means that the macro function cannot find one of the names used. Macro functions generally display TRUE or a value when they perform correctly.

3. Insert a STEP function as the first function below the macro name. Run the macro and use the Evaluate button to see how each function operates.

Problem:
The macro works, but not correctly.

Solution:
Go through the following checklist in order:

1. If an alert box appears, check the cell listed for the correct syntax (grammar). Common syntax errors are missing commas, leaving out mandatory arguments, and forgetting quotation marks around text items.

2. Choose Options Display and deselect the Formulas option. If you see error values displayed in macro function cells, check them out. For example, #NAME? means that the macro function cannot find one of the cell reference names. This problem is frequently a spelling or typographic problem. Macro functions generally display a value of TRUE if the macro function performs correctly.

3. Insert STEP functions prior to sections of the macro where you suspect a problem. Use the Evaluate button in the Single Step dialog box to see the result of each function. If a function shows a

FALSE because it didn't operate, a # error because the syntax or argument was wrong, or an incorrectly calculated value, you have found the function causing the problem.

Problem:
After a reasonable amount of searching and fruitless corrections, the macro still does not work correctly.

Solution:
Try these escalating approaches to inscrutable macros:

1. Leave the problem alone for a while and let your subconscious work on it.

2. Try "breaking" the macro into sections and testing the operation of each section separately. This method may isolate a section that does not work correctly. You can temporarily stop the macro at an early stage by inserting a RETURN function where you want it to stop. Move the RETURN down the macro as you work your way through.

3. Another method is to separate sections of the macro. When the sections work correctly, join them by pasting them, using GOTO formulas or subroutines. Retest the operation as you add each section to the whole.

4. Start over! On difficult bugs, you may save time by starting again from scratch; but rethink, replan, and approach the macro with a different solution. Build your new macro in small sections that each can be tested independently. Link these sections together.

Problem:
A message appears from a macro problem.

Solution:
Press F1 for help in deciphering what the message means.

Problem:
The name of the function macro does not show up in the Formula Paste Function list box.

Solution:
Check the end of the Paste Function list. Function macros appear at the end of this list. Function macro sheets saved as add-ins display their functions in alphabetic order in the list. If the function really is missing, then ensure that the macro sheet is open. If it is, name the macro with Formula Define Name.

Problem:
The macro is recorded, but the code appears at the end of another macro.

Solution:

Make sure that you reposition the starting point of the macro recorder by using the **Macro Set Recorder** command.

Problem:

Inexperienced operators enter values or make selections that "bomb" the macro.

Solution:

Use alert boxes that display instructions and error-trapping formulas to prevent errors by those unfamiliar with the program. The DATACHK macro examined in this chapter illustrates how to check for the Cancel button being selected and how to check for correct entry values.

Problem:

The active cell in the macro keeps jumping back to the same cell location used when the macro was recorded originally. The macro is unusable in different worksheets and different cell locations.

Solution:

This problem occurs when the macro is recorded in absolute reference mode. The macro replays exactly the same cell selections as the ones selected during recording.

Use relative addressing. Doing so allows the macro to work on cell locations that are in the same relative location to whatever cell is the active cell when the macro runs. To record with relative addressing when you are in absolute mode, choose **Macro Relative Record**. You can alternate between **Relative Record** and **Absolute Record** as you record the macro.

Problem:

As macro cells are inserted and deleted, the cell names and documentation in the columns left and right of the macro functions may be left in their old locations. The cell names need to be relocated so that they are adjacent to the correct cell.

Solution:

Use **Formula Goto** to pinpoint the actual cell given a particular name. Either cut and paste the name in the left column or insert and delete cells to move the names.

Problem:

On running Single Step with Evaluate, # error values appear as results for a function.

Solution:

If a macro function shows the error value #N/A when evaluated, suspect that an argument has been left out of the macro function or that the wrong type of argument has been used. For example, text that should be enclosed in quotation marks is not, or a number has been used in place of text. If #NAME ! appears, you forgot to give a name to a particular cell reference, you misspelled a name, or you forgot to enclose a text value in quotation marks.

Problem:
One macro function uses the cell reference returned by another macro function. Instead of working correctly, the result is a # error.

Solution:
Some functions return the value found in a cell and not the cell's reference. If you use one of these functions to find a reference for use by another function, you may run into trouble. In many cases, Excel coerces a result into the desired form. In some cases, the function cannot be coerced. As a result, a function receives the contents of a cell and not the cell's reference. When this situation happens, try a different function to return a cell reference or use the DEREF, REFTEXT, and TEXTREF functions to manipulate the first functions.

Problem:
The macro acts as though other macros are attached to it. The first macro works; then, when the macro should end, other macros operate.

Solution:
Make sure that your first macro ends with a RETURN( ) or HALT( ). A macro does not stop at a blank cell but continues down the column looking for further macro functions. If the macro runs into another macro, the second macro begins to execute.

From Here...

The best thing to do at this point is to record macros and modify them. Get practice working with macros and understanding how different macro functions can be used together.

After you have some experience with the fundamental functions described in this chapter, read Chapter 32, "Macro Function Directory," to learn about other functions. After you feel confident recording and modifying macros, you may want to create custom menus and commands that run your macros. Chapter 31 describes how to create custom menus and custom dialog boxes.

31

Adding Custom Menus and Dialog Boxes

W hen you build macros for yourself, often you can run macros with just the shortcut keys or from the Macro Run dialog box. But when you need to create a custom application for use by others, you will want to create custom commands and menus for your macros.

If you are building macros that accept a great deal of input or require selections of options, you may want to create custom dialog boxes. You can draw your own custom dialog boxes in the Dialog Editor, a program that comes with Excel, and then paste the new dialog boxes into your macro sheet. With the knowledge that you acquire in this chapter, you can use the data entered or options selected in custom dialog boxes to control your own Excel programs. In fact, you can use Excel's custom menus and dialog boxes to create programs specific to your business or industry.

Understanding Menus and Commands

This section is an overview of the elements required to create a system of custom menus and commands. Later sections describe the detail of adding a command to a menu, adding a menu to a menu bar, or creating an entirely new menu bar.

Excel has a menu bar that holds menu names, and each of these menus pulls down to display commands. All these menus can be customized. You can add your own menu bars, add menus to existing bars, or add commands to existing menus.

Excel has 6 built-in menu bars, with each menu bar defined numerically as 1 through 6. To these built-in menu bars, you can add up to 15 custom menu bars to display your own menus. Your custom menu bars are assigned the next available number, which is returned by the ADD.BAR function that you use to add the menu bar.

The six built-in menu bars are listed here in order:

Menu Bar	Full Menu	Short Menu
Worksheet	1	5
Chart	2	6
Null (no files)	3	
Info	4	

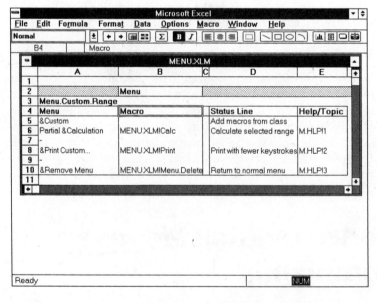

Fig. 31.1. Custom menu commands are arranged in this table on the macro sheet.

To describe the menus and commands you want to appear on a menu bar, create a table on a macro sheet like the table shown in figure 31.1. The following description explains each column in this table. Later sections of this chapter describe the actual construction and use of this table.

The first column in the menu table (column A in fig. 31.1) contains the menu name and the commands in the order you want them to appear. Menu section lines are specified by a hyphen. An ampersand precedes letters that will be the underlined (active) letters in the menu or command names. For example, because cell A7 contains a hyphen, a line in the menu will separate the commands Partial Calculation and **P**rint Custom. The ampersand (&) in front of the C in Custom in cell A5 indicates that the C will be the active (underlined) letter.

The second column in the table (column B in fig. 31.1) lists the external reference to the macro that runs when that command is chosen. Notice that the reference does not use an equal sign at the beginning. For example, if the **P**rint Custom command is chosen, the MENU.XLM! Print macro named in cell B8 will run.

The third column (column C in fig. 31.1) is blank in Excel for Windows. The column is used for shortcut keys for Excel on the Macintosh.

The fourth column (column D in fig. 31.1) contains a message that appears on the status bar when an operator selects the menu or command. An entry in this column is optional. For example, when you select the command **R**emove Menu, the corresponding message `Return to normal menu` appears in the status bar.

The fifth column indicates a custom Help file. These Help files are text files that have been compiled with the Custom Help Conversion Utility available free from Microsoft. An entry in this column is optional.

Adding Commands to Existing Menus

Adding commands to existing menus is an easy way to make macros readily accessible to all levels of users. In fact, it's a convenient way to add a professional touch to your recorded or modified macros.

Figure 31.2 shows the menu table needed to add a single command. As the previous section described, this table uses five columns. In this table, the command Down Load runs the COMMAND.XLM! Down.Load macro. (The added command and macro name do not have to be the same.) The fourth and fifth columns are optional.

Figure 31.3 shows the macros needed to add the Down Load command to the bottom of the **D**ata menu. The macro functions used to add or delete commands are the following:

=ADD.COMMAND(*bar_num,menu,command_ref,position*)

=DELETE.COMMAND(*bar_num,menu,command*)

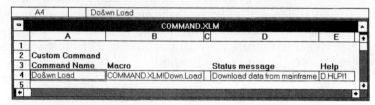

Fig. 31.2. This single-row table defines the custom command Down Load.

	A	B	C	D
1				
2	Custom Command			
3	Command Name	Macro		Status message
4	Do&wn Load	COMMAND.XLM!Down.Load		Download data from mainf
5				
6	Ctrl+a	Add.Custom.Command		
7		=ADD.COMMAND(1,"Data",A4:E4)		
8		=RETURN()		
9				
10	Ctrl+d	Delete.Custom.Command		
11		=DELETE.COMMAND(1,"Data","Down Load")		
12		=RETURN()		
13				
14				
15		Down.Load		
16		=ALERT("This command incomplete",3)		
17		=RETURN()		
18				

Fig. 31.3. Use ADD.COMMAND to add commands to existing menus and DELETE.COMMAND to remove commands.

In figure 31.3 the macro Add.Custom.Command adds the Down Load command to the **Data** menu. The command specifies that the predefined full worksheet menu bar will receive the command in the table whose range is A4:E4. This new command will appear under the **Data** menu. As no position argument is specified, the Down Load command adds to the bottom of the menu.

The macro Delete.Custom.Command uses the name of the menu and command to delete Down Load from the **Data** menu on the number 1 predefined full worksheet menu bar.

The macro Down.Load is a dummy macro. It displays an alert box saying that the macro is incomplete.

> **Note:** *Naming the Top Cell in Manually Typed Macros*
> Remember to use the Formula Define Name command to name the top cell in manually typed macros. Macros that run from a menu table, such as the Down.Load macro (see fig. 31.3), do not have to be named as a command macro. However, the top cell in the macro must be named.

Adding Menus to Existing Menu Bars

When you want to add a number of custom commands to a predefined menu bar or to add commands associated with a specific task, you will probably want to add a menu to a predefined menu bar. You can then assign your new commands to this new menu.

Figure 31.4 shows the menu table needed to define the new menu Custom. This menu name will appear to the right of the Window menu on the full worksheet menu bar (1). The Custom menu will have these commands: Partial Calculation (to run the Calc macro); Print Custom (to run the Print macro); and Remove Menu (to run the Menu.Delete macro).

A3	Menu.Custom.Range				

MENU.XLM

	A	B	C	D	E
1					
2		Menu			
3	Menu.Custom.Range				
4	Menu	Macro		Status Line	Help/Topic
5	&Custom			Add daily macros	
6	Partial &Calculation	MENU.XLM!Calc		Calculate selected range	M.HLP!1
7	-				
8	&Print Custom...	MENU.XLM!Print		Print with fewer keystrokes	M.HLP!2
9	-				
10	&Remove Menu	MENU.XLM!Menu.Delete		Return to normal menu	M.HLP!3
11					

Fig. 31.4. This menu table adds the Custom menu and its own set of commands.

The ADD.MENU and DELETE.MENU functions add and delete menus from a menu bar. These menus have their own sets of commands. The custom menu can be added to or deleted from built-in or custom menu bars. The forms for the ADD.MENU and DELETE.MENU functions are as follows:

=ADD.MENU(*bar_num,menu_ref,position*)

=DELETE.MENU(*bar_num,menu*)

The *bar_num* argument is the number of the built-in menu bar. If you are adding to a custom bar, reference the cell containing the ADD.BAR function that added the custom menu bar. The *menu_ref* argument is the range name or cell reference of the menu table. In the example in figure 31.4, this is the range Menu.Custom.Range, with the cell reference A5:E10. The *position* argument specifies where you want the menu inserted in the menu bar. Use the number or quoted text name of the menu before which you want it inserted. If you omit the position argument, the added menu is placed to the right of the rightmost menu, not including the Help menu.

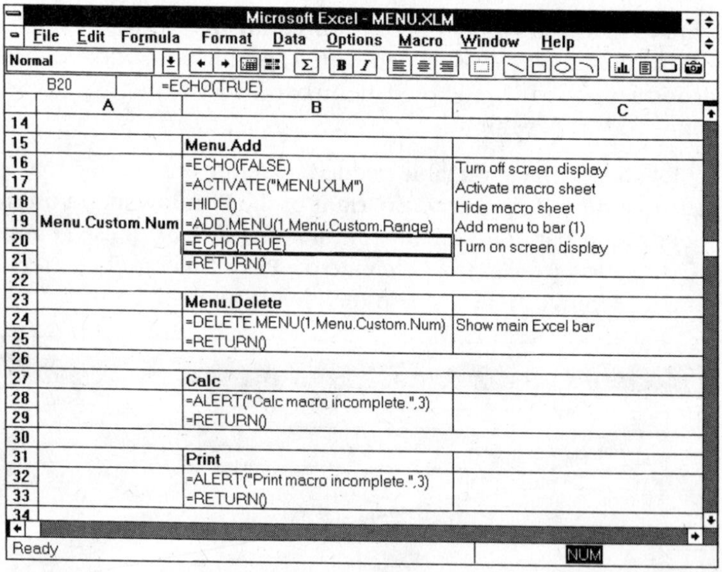

Fig. 31.5. These commands add and delete a menu in the full worksheet menu bar.

Figure 31.5 shows the ADD.MENU and DELETE.MENU functions; these functions add and delete the menu named Custom. The number that specifies the added menu is returned by the ADD.MENU function. Notice that the menu to delete is not referenced by a constant number. Instead, the name Menu.Custom.Num that refers to cell B19 is used to refer to the number of the menu being deleted. In this way, the delete function continues to work even when the menu's number changes as menus are added or rearranged. The Calc and Print macros are dummy macros that only display alert boxes.

Creating Custom Menu Bars

If you have many commands to add or if you need to build an entire custom system, you can add your own menu bars. You can use 15 custom menu bars in addition to the 6 built-in menu bars.

Menu bars require menu tables that define all the menus and commands in the bar. Figure 31.6 shows the menu tables that define the custom menu bar shown in figure 31.7.

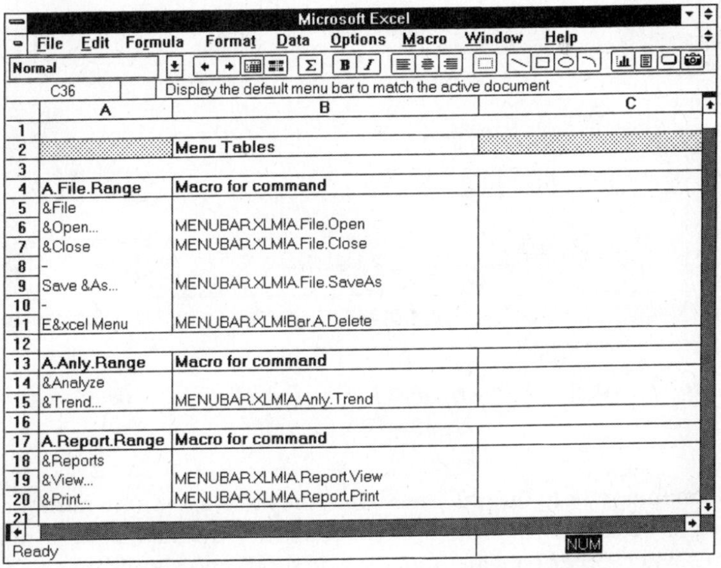

Fig. 31.6. These menu tables define the menus used in a custom menu bar.

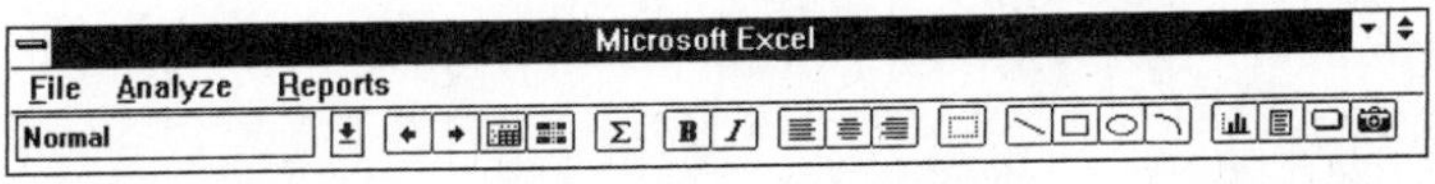

Fig. 31.7. This custom menu bar is defined in the menu tables from figure 31.6.

This is the order in which you specify, add, and show a custom menu bar:

1. Add a custom menu bar with the ADD.BAR function.

2. Add menus to this bar by referencing the bar's number and its menu table with the ADD.MENU function.

3. When you need the bar, display it with the SHOW.BAR function.

Figure 31.8 shows how this custom menu bar is added in the BAR.A.ADD macro.

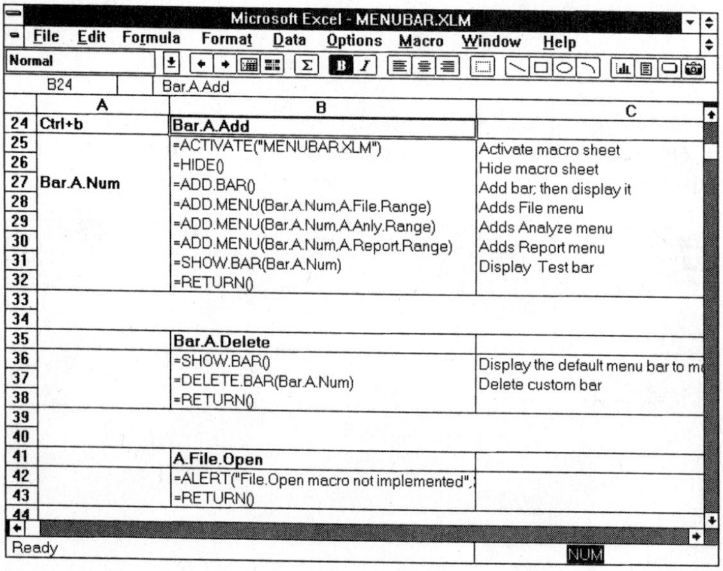

Fig. 31.8. The BAR.A.ADD macro adds the menu bar, specifies its menus, and displays the bar.

As with menus, when you add a menu bar, the bar is assigned a number. This number is returned by the ADD.BAR function. Because a bar's number changes when other bars are added or deleted, you should not refer to a custom menu bar by a specific number. Instead, when you need the number that specifies a bar, refer to the cell containing the ADD.BAR function that added the bar. For example, in figure 31.8, a bar is added with the ADD.BAR function in cell B27. This cell is named BAR.A.NUM. If you switched the display to see the result of ADD.BAR, you would see the number assigned to this bar.

To remove this added bar, use the DELETE.BAR function in cell B37. Because the bar number may be different if the macro is run in different situations, do not attempt to delete a specific bar number, such as

DELETE.BAR (12). Instead, reference the cell containing the ADD.BAR function, such as DELETE.BAR (B27) or DELETE.BAR (BAR.A.NUM).

When you are ready to delete your custom menu bar, use the functions in the order shown in the BAR.A.DELETE macro. You must show another bar before you can delete your custom bar. If you do not specify a bar in the SHOW.BAR function in cell B36, Excel automatically shows whatever bar is the default for the current mode of Excel. Notice that the DELETE.BAR function uses a reference to BAR.A.NUM to specify which menu bar to delete rather than a specific custom bar number.

Drawing Dialog Boxes with the Dialog Editor

You may want to add a custom dialog box to your macros when a command needs multiple items of information. Dialog boxes are also useful for giving an operator a choice of options that make a command operate differently. By using Excel macros, you can create custom dialog boxes that have all the features used by built-in dialog boxes. The following descriptions do not cover the most advanced features but do cover such features as groups of options, list boxes, setting defaults, and using the dialog box results to control macro operation.

Understanding a Dialog Table

To create a dialog box, you must specify the items in a dialog box and their locations in a dialog table. You can type these tables, but a far easier method is to draw the dialog box with the Dialog Editor and paste the resulting information into a table in the macro sheet.

Figure 31.9 shows the dialog box produced by the dialog table in figure 31.10. A dialog table requires seven columns of information. Figure 31.10 shows three additional columns of information on the sides of the table (columns D, L, N). These columns contain reference information or the contents of a scrolling list.

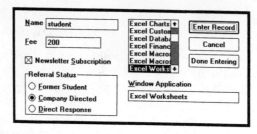

Fig. 31.9. *A dialog box like this can receive entered data and control macro operation.*

Type	Item	X	Y	Width	Height	Text	Int/Result	Result Names	List Box Contents
D — Student Data									
blank	12	0	0	552	177				1-2-3 to Excel
text	5	24	14	50	18	&Name			CorelDraw Intro
text edit	6	74	12	170	18		student	Rslt.Name	Excel Charts
text	5	24	44	90	18	&Fee			Excel Custom
number edit	8	74	42	130	18		200	Rslt.Fee	Excel Database
check box	13	24	72	220	18	Newsletter &Subscript	TRUE	Rslt.News	Excel Finance
group box	14	24	96	220	72	Referral Status			Excel Macros 1
radio group	11	24	114	180	45		2	Rslt.Referral	Excel Macros 2
radio button	12	32	114	172	15	&Former Student			Excel Worksheets
radio button	12	32	132	164	15	&Company Directed			PageMaker Intro
radio button	12	32	150	164	15	&Direct Response			PC Intro
text	5	268	108	264	12	&Window Application			Windows 3 Intro
text edit	6	268	126	264	18		Excel Wor	Rslt.WinApp	WinWord Adv
linked list box	16	268	12	120	90	=REFTEXT($N$9:$N$23)	9		WinWord Custom
default ok button	1	412	12	120	21	Enter Record		Rslt.Enter	WinWord Intro
cancel button	2	412	39	120	21	Cancel		Rslt.Cancel	
ok button	3	412	66	120	21	Done Entering		Rslt.Done	

Fig. 31.10. *The dialog table that produces the dialog box shown in figure 31.9.*

The seven columns in a dialog table control these aspects of a dialog box:

Column	Control
E	Item number
F	X position of upper left corner
G	Y position of upper left corner
H	Width of item
I	Height of item
J	Text for item
K	Initial value of item

In figure 31.10, the seven columns are in columns E through K. Column D contains text that describes what the adjacent item is. Column L contains names that refer to the dialog box results in the adjacent cell to the left. For example, the TRUE/FALSE result from the Newsletter Subscription check box in cell K14 can be referenced in a macro with the name Rslt.News. Column N contains the contents of the linked list box that is specified in cell J22.

The position of items in the box, their height, and their width are specified in columns F, G, H, and I. The top left corner of the dialog box is where X equals 0 and Y equals 0 for positioning of items in the box. The X, Y, Width, and Height measurements are in screen dots. Cells F9 and G9 specify the position of the top left corner of the dialog box. When the cells are zero, the box is centered on-screen.

In the example, row 9 describes the dialog box outline. Other rows describe a specific type of item or group. The item types that correspond to each item number in column E are listed in a following table. The numbers in columns F through I are calculated by the drawing you will create in the Dialog Editor. The text for items, such as titles or option names, are also entered in the Dialog Editor. Specify the underlined active letter for options, check boxes, and text boxes by preceding a letter in the name of that item with an ampersand (&). You can create the data for this table in the Dialog Editor, and then modify it after you have pasted it into the macro sheet in a table like the one shown here.

The linked (scrolling) list box defined in row 22 is referenced in J22 with a REFTEXT function. This cell normally must have a quoted R1C1 reference to the items in a list; however, if you add to or delete from the list, the quoted reference will not adjust. Using the REFTEXT function as shown in J22 enables you to expand or contract the list at will; the reference adjusts and REFTEXT changes the reference to the quoted R1C1 form.

Table 31.1 is a list of items available in dialog boxes. Take note that some items must be in a specific order. For example, an option button group must precede an option button.

Table 31.1
Items Available in Dialog Boxes

Item	Type	Description
1	OK button (default)	Closes the dialog box and returns results in the Init/Result column. Button is selected when box opens. Name of button is specified in Text column.
2	Cancel button (nondefault)	Closes the dialog box and does not return data. Name appears inText column.

continues

Table 13.1 *(continued)*

Item	Type	Description
3	OK button (nondefault)	Closes the dialog box and returns results in the Init/Result column. Button is not selected when box opens. Name appears in Text column.
4	Cancel button (default)	Closes the dialog box and does not return results. Button is selected when box opens. Name appears in Text column.
5	Text	Used as titles or labels.
6	Text edit box	Can be multiple lines in height; text column ignored; uses initial value in Init/Result column.
7	Integer edit box	Like text edit box; accepts –32765 to 32767.
8	Number edit box	Like text edit box; accepts only numbers.
9	Formula edit box	Like text edit box; accepts formulas; shows in Init/Result as text in R1C1 format.
10	Reference edit box	Like text edit box; shows in Init/Result as text in R1C1 format.
11	Option button group	Must immediately precede a group of option buttons; text is the name of group box; Init/Result returns the number of the option in group selected.
12	Option button	Option button; text is the name of the button; number of selected button returned to Init/Result of Option button group. Groups of option buttons must be in sequence and preceded by an option button group (11).
13	Check box	Text is the name of box. Init/Result is TRUE if selected; FALSE if deselected; #N/A if gray.

Item	Type	Description
14	Group box	An outline box that does not affect operation. Use for appearance. It can be used to create lines or boxes and does not affect the operation of other items.
15	List box	Lists items. List referenced in text column using a range name or quoted R1C1 text. See fig. 31.10 for an example of how to use REFTEXT to reference a list that changes in size. Init/Result returns number of item in list selected. Use the INDEX worksheet function to extract text item from list when giving number of item.
16	Linked list box	Same as list box, but must be preceded in dialog table by a text edit box (6). The list item selected appears in edit box. Init/Result returns number of item, but preceding text box returns text item from list.
17	Icon	One of three (1-3) icons with buttons such as ALERT. Enter 1 to 3 in text column.
18	Linked file list box	Lists files in directory. Must follow a text edit box (6) and precede a linked drive and directory list (19).
19	Linked drive and directory list box	Lists drives and directories. If item precedes a text box (5), the text box will show the current drive and directory.
20	Directory text	Shows name of current directory.
21	Drop-down list box	Shows a list of items. List is referenced like a list box (15). Init/Result contains the number of default selection from list. The height of list is in the Height column.
22	Drop-down combination box	Like a drop-down list but it must follow a text edit box (6).

Drawing Dialog Boxes

Without the Dialog Editor, creating custom dialog boxes is an incredible chore. But with the Dialog Editor it can be fun—almost like drawing in a painting program.

Figure 31.11 shows a dialog box in the Dialog Editor. You can resize and move each item in the dialog box, as well as the outline of the dialog box.

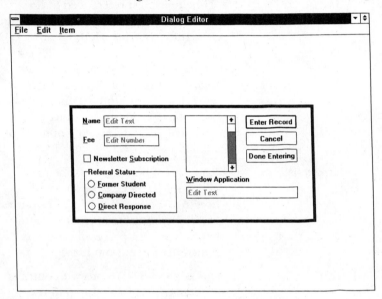

Fig. 31.11. Use the Dialog Editor to create the items you want.

Start the Dialog Editor from within Excel by selecting the Excel Control menu (press Alt, space bar) and then choosing the Run command. Select the Dialog Editor option and press Enter. The Dialog Editor will appear with a small, empty dialog box at mid-screen.

Drag the corner or edge of the empty box to change it to the size you want. Add items to the box by selecting items from the Item menu. As soon as you add an item, move it into position by dragging on its center. Resize boxes or text areas by dragging on their edges. Type text labels while an item is selected. In some cases, you may need to type a blank space at the end of text for the label to show completely.

You can save time reorganizing the dialog table later if you select items in the order prescribed in table 31.1 that lists the items. For example, add an option group, and then add the option buttons for that group as the next items. In many cases, you can press Enter after adding an item as a shortcut to get the next appropriate item or a duplicate of the item. To delete items, select them, and then choose Edit Clear or press the Delete key.

To align items precisely, change labels, or enter the Init/Result values, select an item and then choose the Edit Info command; or double-click on the item. Figure 31.12 shows the Info box for an option group box.

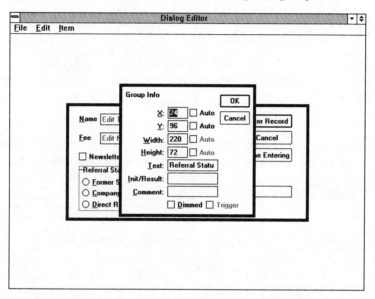

Fig. 31.12. *Choose the Edit Info command to edit or align selected items precisely.*

When you are finished adding and arranging items, select the entire dialog box by choosing the Edit Select Dialog command. Choose the Edit Copy command. Switch to Excel by pressing Alt+Tab. Next, activate the macro sheet in which you want the table. Select the cell at the top left corner of where you want the table, and choose the Edit Paste command. You may want to format the table as shown in figure 31.10 and add descriptions and named cells. Make sure that items are in the correct order as described in table 31.1. If they are not listed in the correct order, insert and delete rows; then copy and paste so that items are in the correct order. For example, option buttons (item 12) must follow an option button group (item 11).

If you need to edit a dialog box, you can make minor changes within the table on the macro sheet. To make major changes, select the same area of the dialog table that was pasted into the macro sheet, copy it with Edit Copy, and paste it into the Dialog Editor with Edit Paste. When you are finished editing, copy the dialog box and paste it back into the macro sheet.

> **Tip: *Never Leave Blank Rows in the Dialog Table***
> A blank row in the dialog table causes the DIALOG.BOX function to fail.

Using Dialog Boxes

The dialog box that you drew with the Dialog Editor appears with the single function DIALOG.BOX, as shown in cell B38 of figure 31.13. The function is as follows:

=DIALOG.BOX(E9:K25)

Here, the range E9:K25 specifies the seven columns of information required by the dialog box. Notice that there are no blank rows in this range.

	A	B
32		**Main Routines**
33		
34	Ctrl+e	**Enter Records**
35		=ECHO(FALSE)
36		*Set defaults, start dialog box*
37	Entry.Restart	=SET.VALUE($K$10:$K$25,{"";"student";"";"200";TRUE;"";"2";"";"";"";"Excel Worksheets";"9";"";"";""})
38	Entry.Dialog	=DIALOG.BOX(E9:K25)
39		*Check Cancel button*
40		=IF(Entry.Dialog=FALSE,GOTO(Entry.End))
41		*Data entry checks*
42		=Sbr.Data.Check()
43		=IF(Chk.Fees=FALSE,GOTO(Entry.Dialog))
44		*Insert Row in Database*
45		=FORMULA.GOTO("Database")
46		=SELECT("R[2]C")
47		=SELECT("R")
48		=INSERT(2)
49		*Insert Data in Row*
50		=FORMULA(Rslt.Name,OFFSET(ACTIVE.CELL(),0,0))
51		=FORMULA(IF(Rslt.News=TRUE,"Yes","No"),OFFSET(ACTIVE.CELL(),0,1))
52		=FORMULA(Rslt.Fee,OFFSET(ACTIVE.CELL(),0,2))
53		=FORMULA(CHOOSE(Rslt.Referral,"Former Student","Company Directed","Direct Response"),OFFSE
54		=FORMULA(Rslt.WinApp,OFFSET(ACTIVE.CELL(),0,4))
55		=IF(Entry.Dialog=16,GOTO(Entry.End))
56		=GOTO(Entry.Restart)
57	Entry.End	=FORMULA.GOTO(!$A$1)
58		=ECHO(TRUE)
59		=RETURN()
60		
61		**Subroutines**
62		
63		**Sbr.Data.Check**
64	Chk.Fees	=IF(AND(Rslt.Fee>=100,Rslt.Fee<=300),GOTO(Chk.Done))
65		=ALERT("You entered "&Rslt.Fee&" as the Dues Paid. Enter a number greater than 5, but less than 20.
66	Chk.Done	=RETURN()

***Fig. 31.13.** The macro that displays, updates, and uses information from the dialog box shown in figure 31.9.*

Tip: *Using Names To Refer to Returned Results*
The names in column L of the dialog table shown in figure 31.10, L9:L25, refer to the cells in the Init/Result column, K9:K25. The names in column A of the macro, shown in figure 31.13, refer to the adjacent cell to the right in column B. Using this method, your macros can use readable names to refer to the results that a dialog box or function returns. You can quickly create names, such as those in figure 31.13, by selecting the names in column A and the adjacent cells in column B and then choosing the Formula Create Names command. Select the Left column as containing the names of the macro cells in column B of figure 31.13.

Setting Dialog Default Values

Initial dialog default values, the values returned by dialog entries, and selections appear in the dialog table in the Init/Result column. Initial values that a dialog box displays are those values it finds in this column. The values must be in the correct row location as specified in the table that describes each type of item. If you want a dialog box to start with specific values, use the SET.VALUE function to put a constant value in each appropriate Init/Result cell. In the example cell in figure 31.13, B37 contains an array of values that sets all the default values in one command. This function is as follows:

```
=SET.VALUE($K$10:$K$25,{"";"student";"";"200";TRUE;"";
    "2";"";"";""; "";"Excel Worksheets";"9";"";"";""})
```

This function places each element in the array into the corresponding cell from K10 to K25. Notice that semicolons separate elements that are in different rows in the array. You can use a single SET.VALUE function to set the value in a single cell.

If you want the dialog box to redisplay with the values that were last entered or the options last selected, do not reset the values in the Init/Result column. If you want the dialog box to open the first time with the settings from the last time the macro was run, save the worksheet so that the Init/Result column is preserved; do not use a SET.VALUE function to reset the Init/Result column when the macro runs the first time.

Retrieving Dialog Input

When you choose the OK button in a dialog box, the information entered and options selected appear in the Init/Result column next to the appropriate dialog item. If you choose the Cancel button, the Init/Result column does not change.

In the Enter Records macro (see fig. 31.13), the IF function in B40 checks to see if the Cancel button was chosen. If Cancel was chosen, the DIALOG.BOX function returns FALSE. In this case, the IF function sends the macro to B57, where the macro ends.

In B42, a subroutine, shown in B63:B66, checks the value entered in the Fee text box to see that it is between 100 and 300. If it is within limits, the result is TRUE in B64, and the subroutine returns. If it is not in limits, the result is FALSE, and the alert box displays.

When the subroutine returns to the macro at cell B43, if the data check was FALSE, the IF function in B43 restarts the dialog box; the operator then can reenter correct values.

If the Fee entry is in limits, the macro continues to B45:B48, where a row is inserted into the database shown in figure 31.14. The row is inserted into the second row of the database. This row makes room for the new data. The active cell is moved to the first cell in this blank row. You will not see the row inserted on-screen because of the ECHO(FALSE) statement in B35.

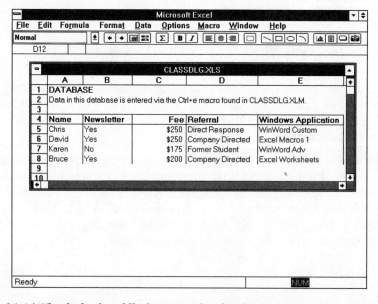

Fig. 31.14. The dialog box fills data into this database.

Information is taken from the dialog box and entered into the blank database row by the FORMULA functions in B50:B54. The FORMULA functions reference the dialog box entries by name, as for example, Rslt.Name. These names are shown in column L of the dialog table. (These are not part of the table but are there for documentation.) The FORMULA function then puts the named result into the worksheet cell specified by the OFFSET function. Each OFFSET function uses the active cell, the first cell in the blank row, as a base point and offsets the entered value by a different column position. The row argument for OFFSET is zero, so data is entered in the same row as the active worksheet cell. Again, because ECHO(FALSE) was used at the beginning, you will not see this happen.

In cell B53, a CHOOSE function is used to change the 1, 2, or 3 result from option buttons into a text answer that is stored in the database. For example, when Rslt.Referral contains 1, the choice is "Former Student."

Cell B55 checks to see whether the nondefault OK button, Done Entering, was selected in the dialog box. If it was selected, the macro goes to Entry.End, cell B57, and the macro ends. When a nondefault OK or Cancel button is selected, the number of its row in the dialog table, 16 in this case, is returned to the DIALOG.BOX function. In this case, the value returned to DIALOG.BOX is stored in the name Entry.Dialog.

When the Cancel button is chosen, cell B40 sends the macro to its end, Entry.End. When the Done Entering button is chosen, cell B55 sends the macro to its end, Entry.End. The final ECHO(TRUE) function refreshes the screen display so that you can see the additions to the database. If you wish to see the macro as it operates, remove the ECHO (FALSE) function in B35 and rerun the macro. Notice that macro operation is slower when the screen is redrawn after each change.

From Here...

Excel's macro language has a great deal of capability and flexibility. You can write attractive programs with extensive analytical, printing, and charting capabilities with far less planning, programming, and maintenance than if you programmed them in a language such as C.

This book does not touch on some more advanced macro capabilities, such as controlling other Windows programs via Excel macros, linking data with Dynamic Data Exchange, and controlling the links with DDE or linking in C-language routines with Dynamic Link Libraries. Although you can do a great deal with Excel's macro language by itself, the top end is wide open.

32

Macro Function Directory

T his chapter has three sections. The first section organizes and lists all Excel macros by type. The second section describes macros in general terms. The third section gives the syntax (grammar), the menu command if an equivalent exists, and the action the macro performs or the result it returns.

The Excel macro language is so extensive that not all the macro functions can be covered in depth in *Using Excel 3 for Windows*, Special Edition. This chapter describes important macro functions that can give you the most productivity with the least amount of programming knowledge. All Excel commands have been listed so that you can see the full power available.

Many macro functions are the equivalent of Excel menu commands or worksheet functions. To learn the most about these macros, read the menu command and worksheet descriptions as well as the macro function descriptions.

When you use a macro function, pay particular attention to its syntax or structure. You must follow the syntax exactly. A frequent cause of problems is a missing comma that separates arguments. Use periods to separate parts of a macro name, such as FILE.DELETE. Enclose in quotation marks (" ") text arguments, such as window names, R1C1 references, and messages.

Macro Functions Listed by Type

Two fundamental types of macros exist: command macros, which take actions, and function macros, which make calculations but do not take actions.

Command macros can take actions, do calculations, and make decisions. Function macros are limited to macros that do not perform actions. Both types of macros can include worksheet functions.

Before reading the macro function descriptions, you may want to read through the lists that group macro functions by the type of tasks they perform. The lists may help you keep the functions organized in your mind. You also may want to refer to the lists when you know what you want to do but do not know which macro function to use.

Menu Equivalent Commands

Some macro functions perform the same commands as those you choose from menus. These functions appear in macros you record.

Some Excel commands prompt you for more information by displaying a dialog box that you fill in. The equivalent macro function gets that information in two ways. The macro can receive the information from the macro arguments (variables inside parentheses), or the macro can display the dialog box and enable the user to select options and enter values.

An example of this situation is the Format Border command. The macro equivalent of this command is as follows:

BORDER(*outline,left,right,top,bottom,shade,outline_color,left_color,right _color,top_color,bottom_color***)**

With this macro function, you identify the options that are selected in the dialog box by entering TRUE for the appropriate arguments. A FALSE entry turns off an option's selection.

Consider this example:

BORDER(FALSE,TRUE,TRUE,FALSE,TRUE,FALSE)

This function creates borders on the left, right, and bottom sides of the selected range; the function does not outline the cells, nor does it shade the cells. The other arguments (the ones referring to color) are optional, so they have been dropped. Arguments in some macro functions accept cell references, formulas, logical values, numbers, or text enclosed in quotation marks.

> **Tip: *Omitting Optional Arguments***
> When you omit optional arguments, you may have to include commas as placeholders for arguments you may add later. You do not have to enter optional arguments within the parentheses, but if other arguments will follow an optional argument, you still must include the correct number of commas. Excel uses these commas to calculate where arguments are located between parentheses. If no optional arguments follow, you can omit unnecessary commas.

The following lists of commands and their associated macro functions can help you locate the correct macro function. After finding the function name, refer to the directory description for more information.

Application Control Menu Commands

These macro functions execute the commands found on the Application Control menu (Alt+space bar).

Maximize	APP.MAXIMIZE
Minimize	APP.MINIMIZE
Move	APP.MOVE
Restore	APP.RESTORE
Run	none
Size	APP.SIZE
Close	QUIT

Document Control Menu Commands

These macro functions execute the same commands you execute from the Document Control menu (Alt+hyphen).

Close	CLOSE
Maximize	FULL(TRUE)
Move	MOVE
Restore	FULL(FALSE)
Size	SIZE
Split	SPLIT

File Menu Commands

These macro functions execute the same commands you execute from the File menu.

File Close	FILE.CLOSE
File Close All	CLOSE.ALL
File Delete	FILE.DELETE
File Exit	QUIT
File Links	OPEN.LINKS; CHANGE.LINKS; LINKS; UPDATE.LINKS
File New	NEW
File Open	OPEN
File Page Setup	PAGE.SETUP
File Print	PRINT
File Print Preview	PRINT.PREVIEW
File Printer Setup	PRINTER.SETUP
File Save	SAVE
File Save As	SAVE.AS
File Save Workspace	SAVE.WORKSPACE

Edit Menu Commands

These macro functions execute the same commands you execute from the Edit menu.

Edit Clear	CLEAR
Edit Copy	COPY
Edit Copy Picture	COPY.PICTURE
Edit Cut	CUT
Edit Delete	EDIT.DELETE
Edit Fill Down	FILL.DOWN
Edit Fill Up (w)	FILL.UP
Edit Fill Right	FILL.RIGHT
Edit Fill Left (h)	FILL.LEFT
Edit Fill Workgroup	FILL.WORKGROUP
Edit Insert	INSERT
Edit Paste	PASTE
Edit Paste Link	PASTE.LINK
Edit Paste Picture	PASTE.PICTURE; PASTE.PICTURE.LINK
Edit Paste Special	PASTE.SPECIAL
Edit Repeat	EDIT.REPEAT
Edit Undo	UNDO

Formula Menu Commands

These macro functions execute the commands found on the Formula menu.

Formula **A**pply Names	APPLY.NAMES
Formula **C**reate Names	CREATE.NAMES
Formula **D**efine Names	DEFINE.NAME
Formula **D**elete Names	DELETE.NAME
Formula **F**ind	FORMULA.FIND; FORMULA.FIND.NEXT; FORMULA.FIND.PREV
Formula **G**oal Seek	GOAL.SEEK
Formula **G**oto	FORMULA.GOTO
Formula **N**ote	NOTE
Formula **P**aste Name	LIST.NAMES
Formula **R**eplace	FORMULA.REPLACE
Formula **S**elect Special	SELECT.SPECIAL; SELECT.LAST.CELL
Formula **S**how Active Cell	SHOW.ACTIVE.CELL

Format Menu Commands

These macro functions execute the commands found on the Format menu.

Format **A**lignment	ALIGNMENT
Format **B**order	BORDER
Format **B**ring To Front	BRING.TO.FRONT
Format **C**ell Protection	CELL.PROTECTION
Format **C**olumn Width	COLUMN.WIDTH
Format **F**ont	FORMAT.FONT
Format **G**roup	GROUP
Format **J**ustify	JUSTIFY
Format **L**egend	FORMAT.LEGEND
Format **M**ain Chart	MAIN.CHART
Format **M**ove	FORMAT.MOVE
Format **N**umber	FORMAT.NUMBER
Format **O**bject Placement	PLACEMENT
Format **O**bject Protection	OBJECT.PROTECTION
Format **O**verlay	OVERLAY
Format **P**atterns	PATTERNS
Format **R**ow Height	ROW.HEIGHT
Format **S**cale	SCALE
Format **S**end to Back	SEND.TO.BACK
Format **S**ize	FORMAT.SIZE
Format **S**tyle	DEFINE.STYLE; DELETE.STYLE; MERGE.STYLE
Format **T**ext	FORMAT.TEXT
Format **U**ngroup	UNGROUP
Format **3**-D View	VIEW.3D

Data Menu Commands

These macro functions execute the commands found on the Data menu.

Data Consolidate	CONSOLIDATE
Data Delete	DATA.DELETE
Data Extract	EXTRACT
Data Find	DATA.FIND; DATA.FIND.NEXT;
	DATA.FIND.PREV
Data Form	DATA.FORM
Data Parse	PARSE
Data Series	DATA.SERIES
Data Set Criteria	SET.CRITERIA
Data Set Database	SET.DATABASE
Data Set Extract	SET.EXTRACT
Data Sort	SORT
Data Table	TABLE

Options Menu Commands

These macro functions execute the commands found on the Options menu.

Options Calculate Document	CALCULATE.DOCUMENT
Options Calculate Now	CALCULATE.NOW
Options Calculation	CALCULATION; PRECISION
Options Color Palette	COLOR.PALETTE; EDIT.COLOR
Options Display	DISPLAY
Options Freeze Panes	FREEZE.PANES
Options Full Menus	SHORT.MENUS
Options Protect Document	PROTECT.DOCUMENT
Options Remove Page Break	REMOVE.PAGE.BREAK
Options Set Page Break	SET.PAGE.BREAK
Options Set Print Area	SET.PRINT.AREA
Options Set Print Titles	SET.PRINT.TITLES
Options Short Menus	SHORT.MENUS
Options Workspace	WORKSPACE

Window Menu Commands

These macro functions execute the commands found on the Window menu.

Window #document	ACTIVATE
Window Arrange All	ARRANGE.ALL

Window **Hide**	HIDE
Window **New Window**	NEW.WINDOW
Window **Show Info/Document**	SHOW.INFO
Window **Unhide**	UNHIDE
Window **Workgroup**	WORKGROUP

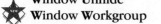

Chart Menu Commands

These macro functions execute the commands found on the Chart menu.

Chart Add **Arrow**	ADD.ARROW
Chart Add **Overlay**	ADD.OVERLAY
Chart Add **Legend**	LEGEND
Chart Attach **Text**	ATTACH.TEXT
Chart **Axes**	AXES
Chart Calculate **Now**	CALCULATE.NOW
Chart Color **Palette**	EDIT.COLOR
Chart Delete Arrow	DELETE.ARROW
Chart Delete **Overlay**	DELETE.OVERLAY
Chart Edit **Series**	EDIT.SERIES
Chart **Gridlines**	GRIDLINES
Chart **Protect** Document	PROTECT.DOCUMENT
Chart Select **Chart**	SELECT
Chart Select Plot Area	SELECT.PLOT.AREA
Chart Short **Menus**	SHORT.MENUS

Gallery and Chart Format Commands

These macro functions execute the commands found on the Gallery and
Chart Format menus.

Gallery 3-D **Area**	GALLERY.3D.AREA
Gallery 3-D **Column**	GALLERY.3D.COLUMN
Gallery 3-D **Line**	GALLERY.3D.LINE
Gallery 3-D **Pie**	GALLERY.3D.PIE
Gallery **Area**	GALLERY.AREA
Gallery **Bar**	GALLERY.BAR
Gallery **Column**	GALLERY.COLUMN
Gallery **Combination**	COMBINATION
Gallery **Line**	GALLERY.LINE
Gallery **Pie**	GALLERY.PIE
Gallery **Preferred**	PREFERRED

Gallery (XY) Scatter	GALLERY.SCATTER
Gallery Set Preferred	SET.PREFERRED
Format 3-D View	VIEW.3D
Format Font	FORMAT.FONT
Format Legend	FORMAT.LEGEND
Format Main Chart	MAIN.CHART.TYPE
Format Move	FORMAT.MOVE
Format Overlay	OVERLAY
Format Patterns	PATTERNS
Format Size	FORMAT.SIZE
Format Text	FORMAT.TEXT

Macro Menu Commands

These macro functions execute the commands from the Macro menu.

Macro Run	RUN
Macro Assign to Object	ASSIGN.TO.OBJECT

Action Commands

The action macros listed here repeat mouse and keyboard actions such as scrolling with the mouse or pressing function keys.

A1.R1C1	HLINE
ACTIVATE	HPAGE
ACTIVATE.NEXT	HSCROLL
ACTIVATE.PREV	PROMOTE
APP.ACTIVATE	SELECT
BEEP	SELECT.END
CANCEL.COPY	SET.UPDATE.STATUS
CREATE.OBJECT	SHOW.DETAIL
DELETE.FORMAT	SHOW.ACTIVE.CELL
DUPLICATE	SHOW.LEVELS
FORMULA	SHOW.CLIPBOARD
FORMULA.ARRAY	SPLIT
FORMULA.FILL	UNLOCKED.NEXT
FORMULA.CONVERT	UNLOCKED.PREV
FORMULA.FIND.NEXT	VLINE
FULL	VPAGE
HIDE.OBJECT	VSCROLL

Macro Functions for Customizing Excel

These macro functions modify Excel to give it the screen appearance, menus, dialog boxes, and help files you need.

ADD.BAR	DELETE.MENU
ADD.COMMAND	DIALOG.BOX
ADD.MENU	DISABLE.INPUT
ALERT	ECHO
CALL	ENABLE.COMMAND
CANCEL.KEY	GET.BAR
CHECK.COMMAND	HELP
CUSTOM.REPEAT	MESSAGE
CUSTOM.UNDO	RENAME.COMMAND
DELETE.BAR	SHOW.BAR
DELETE.COMMAND	

Control Macro Functions

These macro functions can start, stop, or redirect the flow of macro operation. Excel also runs subroutine macros. Functions such as FOR, FOR.CELL, WHILE, and NEXT enable you to repeat parts of macros by using a looping process.

ARGUMENT	INPUT
BREAK	NEXT
ELSE	ON.DATA
ELSE.IF	ON.KEY
END.IF	ON.RECALC
ERROR	ON.TIME
EXEC	ON.WINDOW
EXECUTE	POKE
FCLOSE	REGISTER
FOPEN	REQUEST
FOR	RESTART
FOR.CELL	RESULT
FPOS	RETURN
FREAD	SEND.KEYS
FREADLN	SET.NAME

FSIZE	SET.VALUE
FWRITE	STEP
FWRITELN	TERMINATE
GOTO	UNREGISTER
HALT	VOLATILE
IF	WAIT
INITIATE	WHILE

Macro Functions That Return Values

These macro functions return information about the worksheet environment. Information such as the names of windows, locations, or names of linked worksheets is returned in the cell that contains the macro function. To see the returned value on the macro sheet, select Options Display and deselect the Formulas option.

ABSREF	GET.NAME
ACTIVE.CELL	GET.NOTE
CALLER	GET.OBJECT
DEREF	GET.WINDOW
DIRECTORY	GET.WORKSPACE
DOCUMENTS	LAST.ERROR
FILES	NAMES
GET.CELL	REFTEXT
GET.CHART.ITEM	RELREF
GET.DEF	SELECTION
GET.DOCUMENT	TEXTREF
GET.FORMULA	WINDOWS
GET.LINK.INFO	

Worksheet Macro Functions

You can use the worksheet functions within command or function macros. Worksheet functions, which are described in Chapter 10, "Using Functions," are used in many examples in the chapters in Part II, "Excel Worksheets."

Macro Descriptions

Most macro functions have English command names and are easy to remember. Macros that duplicate commands from the menu frequently use the menu command word, a period, and then the command, such as FORMAT.FONT.

Macro functions receive information from the arguments listed between parentheses. These arguments can be values, cell references, or range references, and they must be separated by commas. Arguments that define position or movement measure locations in points, with 72 points equal to 1 inch. (Points are the same units used to measure the height of fonts.)

Here are some rules for entering and using arguments in macro functions:

- In the syntax lines in the following sections, arguments appearing in ***bold italic*** are mandatory, and those appearing in *regular italic* are optional. In the explanatory text, arguments are listed in italic.

- You do not have to enter an optional argument, but you must include the appropriate commas if commas are required as place-holders to position the arguments that follow.

- You must enter arguments in the order shown and separate them with appropriate commas.

- Text arguments and arguments that include the word "text" in the argument name must be enclosed in quotation marks ("). These arguments are often shown with the word *text* in the argument name, such as *name_text*. If an argument is described as a text argument, enclose the argument in quotation marks.

- Options in dialog boxes are turned on or off in response to a TRUE or FALSE value for that argument. If you enter TRUE as an argument, the option is selected (turned on). FALSE deselects (turns off) the option.

To make macro functions and their arguments easier to remember, use the Formula Paste Formula command with the Paste Arguments check box selected. This option pastes in the macro function and puts a named description of the arguments in the correct position between the function's parentheses.

In most cases, you will want to use the Paste Arguments check box. For example, if you paste the Alert function in a cell while the Paste Argument check box is selected, the following message appears:

```
ALERT(message_text,type_num)
```

This message shows you what two arguments you need to include.

> **Tip:** *Using Pasted Argument Names as Range Names*
> You can leave pasted argument names, such as *rate* and *nper*, in
> macro functions and use the argument names as range names.
> Beware of duplicate names, however, because other functions may
> use the same name for an argument.

Some macro functions produce results that duplicate the worksheet function with the same name, such as ABS. For these macro functions, see the
description of worksheet functions in Chapter 10 for more information.

Macro Function Directory

Refer to Chapter 10, "Using Functions," for information on worksheet
functions. All worksheet functions can be used in command and function
macros. Also remember that in syntax lines, arguments printed in **bold
italic** are mandatory; arguments printed in *regular italic* are optional. All
compound argument names are joined by underscore marks.

A1.R1C1(*logical*)

Equivalent to **Options Workspace R1C1**. Switches between A1- and R1C1-
style cell references. When the *logical* argument is TRUE, the function
results in A1 reference style. When FALSE, the function results in R1C1
reference style.

ABSREF(*ref_text,reference*)

Returns the new absolute cell reference or range that is the result of the
original cell or range location, *reference*, and the relative change, *ref_text*,
given in R1C1 style. The reference *ref_text* must be in R1C1 format and
enclosed in quotation marks. The returned reference is offset from the
upper-left corner of *ref_text* when *ref_text* is a range. If *ref_text* is a range,
a range is returned. (Also see the description of the RELREF macro function.)

Consider the following examples:

=ABSREF("R[−1]C[−1]",QTR.XLS!C2)

is $B$1 on the QTR worksheet.

=SELECT(ABSREF("R[2]C[1]",!$A$7))

selects $B$9 on the active worksheet.

ACTIVATE(*window_text,pane_num*)

Equivalent to F6 or Ctrl+F6. Activates a pane in a window when a window is split; activates another window when multiple windows are open. Be sure to enclose *window_text* (the window name) in quotation marks—for example, "QRTR1" or "QTR1:2". If a document has more than one window open and you do not specify a window in *window_text*, the first window is affected. Omitting *window_text* specifies the current document. Use one of the following numbers for the *pane_num* argument:

pane_num	*Pane Activated*
1	Top, left, top left, or only pane
2	Right or top right pane
3	Bottom or bottom left pane
4	Bottom right pane

ACTIVATE.NEXT( )

Equivalent to Ctrl+F6. Activates next window.

ACTIVATE.PREV( )

Equivalent to Shift+Ctrl+F6. Activates previous window.

ACTIVE.CELL( )

Returns the active cell reference in external reference format. Because Excel automatically evaluates this cell reference for its contents, you actually receive the value in that active cell. If you want a text string of the cell reference, use the REFTEXT function.

Consider these examples:

    =ACTIVE.CELL( )

in cell A2 of the macro sheet results in a value of 5 in cell A2 if the active cell of the worksheet contains a 5. Within another macro function, ACTIVE.CELL acts like an address.

    =SELECT(!A1:ACTIVE.CELL( ))

selects the range on the active worksheet from A1 to the active cell.

ADD.ARROW( )

Equivalent to Chart Add Arrow. Adds an arrow; takes no argument.

ADD.BAR(*bar_num*)

Adds an empty menu bar and returns its ID number if successful. See Chapter 31 for examples. Up to 15 bars can be created. SHOW.BAR displays the menu bar. Excel has six resident menu bars:

bar_num	*Menu Bar and Menu Size*
1	Worksheet and macro, full menu
2	Chart, full menu
3	Null menu, when no documents are open
4	Info window
5	Worksheet and macro, short menu
6	Chart, short menu

ADD.COMMAND(*bar_num,menu,command_ref,position*)

Adds the command found in *command_ref* to the menu defined by *bar_num*. Returns the position number of the command last added. The *position* argument specifies where the command is added. Use a number or quoted name to specify the command above which the new command is added. Omit the position to put the command at the bottom. See Chapter 31 for examples.

ADD.MENU(*bar_num,menu_ref,position*)

Adds the menu defined in *menu_ref* to the menu bar defined by *bar_num*. The menu is added to the right of existing menus on the bar with the ID *bar_num*. Returns the *position* number for the new menu. Specify the position where the menu is added by number or quoted menu name. The new menu appears before the specified position. Omit the *position* argument to put the menu last. See Chapter 31 for examples.

ADD.OVERLAY( )

Equivalent to **Chart Add Overlay.** Adds overlay to chart. If overlay already exists, TRUE is returned. No arguments.

ADDRESS(*row_num,column_num,abs_num,a1,sheet_text*)

Equivalent to the ADDRESS worksheet function. Creates a text address given a row and column. See Chapter 10 for more information.

ALERT(*message_text,type_num*)

The ALERT function is excellent for giving operators information they must respond to for warning about data-entry errors. ALERT displays your message in an alert box and waits for the operator to select a button. ALERT returns TRUE when the operator chooses OK; ALERT returns FALSE when the operator chooses Cancel. (Chapters 29 and 30 show you how to examine for OK and Cancel button selection.) Enclose the message in quotation marks. Each *type_num* produces a different icon in the alert box. Use one of the following numbers for the *type_num* argument:

type_num	Type of Alert Box	Operator Response
1	Choice of question	OK button results in TRUE; Cancel results in FALSE.
2	Information	OK button for confirmation.
3	Warning	OK button for confirmation.

Following are two examples:

    =ALERT("Choose OK to delete data",1)
    =ALERT("The number must be between 1 and 12",3)

ALIGNMENT(*type_num,wrap*)
ALIGNMENT?(*type_num,wrap*)

Equivalent to Format **Alignment**. Changes the alignment of text. Select first the text you want to align. If *wrap* is TRUE, text wraps in the cell. When FALSE or omitted, text does not wrap. Use one of the following numbers for the *type_num* argument:

type_num	Alignment
1	General
2	Left
3	Center
4	Right
5	Fill

For example,

    =SELECT("Titles")
    =ALIGNMENT(3)

centers the contents of the range named Titles.

APP.ACTIVATE(*title_text,wait_logical*)

Activates the application that has the title bar specified in *title_text*. If no *title_text* is shown, Excel activates automatically. If *wait_logical* is TRUE or omitted, you must activate Excel before the application activates. If FALSE, the application activates immediately. Make sure that the specified *title_text* exactly matches the title bar.

APP.MAXIMIZE( )

Equivalent to Application Control Maximize.

APP.MINIMIZE( )

Equivalent to Application Control Minimize.

APP.MOVE(*x_num,y_num***)**
APP.MOVE?(*x_num,y_num***)**

Equivalent to Application Control Move. Moves the application window, Excel, to a new location on-screen. The value of *x_num* specifies the horizontal position from the left edge of the window in points (72 points per inch on paper); *y_num* specifies the vertical position in points measured from the top of the screen down. Using the ? (question mark) form enables you to position the window by using the keyboard or mouse.

APP.RESTORE( )

Equivalent to Application Control Restore. Restores Excel window to its previous size and location.

APP.SIZE(*x_num,y_num***)**
APP.SIZE?(*x_num,y_num***)**

Equivalent to Application Control Size. Changes the size of the Excel application window. *x_num* and *y_num* are the horizontal and vertical size, respectively, in points (72 points per inch on paper). Using a ? enables you to size the window by keyboard or mouse.

APPLY.NAMES(*name_array,ignore,use_rowcol,omit_col,***
    order_num,append_last)**
APPLY.NAMES?(*name_array,ignore,use_rowcol,omit_col,omit_row,***
    order_num,append_last)**

Equivalent to Formula Apply Names; works the same as that command.

Argument	Description
name_array	The name or names to apply as text elements of an array
order_num	1 = Row Column
	2 = Column Row

Other arguments are TRUE or FALSE to select or deselect options in the Apply Names dialog box.

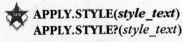 **APPLY.STYLE(***style_text***)**
APPLY.STYLE?(*style_text***)**

Equivalent to the Format Style command. The *style_text* argument is a quoted text name that is the same as the name in the Style list. Returns #VALUE! and stops the macro if the name does not exist. Use ERROR(FALSE) before APPLY.STYLE and ERROR(TRUE) after APPLY.STYLE if you want the macro to continue running when the name does not exist.

AREAS(*reference*)

Finds the number of areas in *reference*.

ARGUMENT(*name_text,data_type_num*)
ARGUMENT(*name_text,data_type_num,reference*)

Every function macro must use at least one ARGUMENT to pass values to the function macro. Chapter 29 describes how to use the ARGUMENT function.

Argument	*Description*
name_text	Name of the argument enclosed in quotation marks
data_type_num	Type of argument
	1 Number
	2 Text
	4 Logical
	8 Reference
	16 Error
	64 Array
reference	The referenced cells in the macro sheet where the value of the argument will be stored

With the exception of the numeric arguments 8 and 64, you can add together the digits for the *data_type_num* argument. For example, 3 indicates that either a text or a numeric entry is acceptable. (For more information, see the function macros in Chapters 28 and 29.)

ARRANGE.ALL( )

Equivalent to **Window Arrange All**.

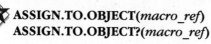 **ASSIGN.TO.OBJECT(*macro_ref*)**
ASSIGN.TO.OBJECT?(*macro_ref*)

Equivalent to the **Macro Assign to Object** command. *macro_ref* is a quoted external reference to the macro. The macro is assigned to the currently selected object. If an object is not selected, returns #VALUE, and the macro stops. One technique to prevent macro failure is to place an ERROR(FALSE) *before* ASSIGN.TO.OBJECT and an ERROR(TRUE) *after* ASSIGN.TO.OBJECT.

Here is another example:

ASSIGN.TO.OBJECT("GQC-EIS.XLM!FINANCE")

ATTACH.TEXT(*attach_to_num,series_num,point_num*)
ATTACH.TEXT?(*attach_to_num,series_num,point_num*)

Equivalent to **Chart Attach Text**. Attaches text in charts. See the command description for more information.

Argument	Description
attach_to_num	Indicates where text will attach
	For 2-D Charts
	1 Chart title
	2 Value axis (y)
	3 Category axis (x)
	4 Series or data point
	5 Overlay y-value axis
	6 Overlay x-value axis
	For 3-D Charts
	1 Chart title
	2 Value axis (z)
	3 Series axis (y)
	4 Category axis (x)
	5 Series or data point
series_num or *point_num*	Indicates to which series number or point number the text will attach

For more information, see the chart reference functions.

AXES(*(x_main,y_main,x_over,y_over)*) 2-D
AXES?(*(x_main,y_main,x_over,y_over)*) 2-D
AXES(*x_main,y_main,z_main*) 3-D
AXES?(*x_main,y_main,z_main*) 3-D

Equivalent to **Chart Axes**. Selects the axis displayed in the current chart. Arguments correspond to dialog box options. TRUE enables an option; FALSE disables an option. See the command description for more information.

BEEP(*number*)

Produces a tone depending on *number*. The *number* argument, which can be any number from 1 to 4, produces a distinctive frequency tone.

BORDER(*outline,left,right,top,bottom,shade,outline_color,*
*left_color,right_color,top_color,bottom_color***)**
BORDER?(*outline,left,right,top,bottom,shade,outline_color,*
*left_color,right_color,top_color,bottom_color***)**

Equivalent to Format Border. Arguments correspond to options. TRUE or FALSE enable or disable the first six options. Colors are numbers from 1 to 16 off the color palette. See the command description for more information. The *outline*, *left*, *right*, *top*, and *bottom* arguments are numbers 0 through 7, representing the following line characteristics:

Number	Line Characteristic
0	No border
1	Thin
2	Medium
3	Dashed
4	Dotted
5	Thick
6	Double
7	Hairline

BREAK( )

Breaks out of a FOR.CELL, FOR-NEXT, or WHILE-NEXT loop in a macro. Use an IF macro function to break when a condition is met. BREAK exits the loop. The macro continues after the NEXT statement.

 BRING.TO.FRONT( )

Equivalent to the Format Bring to Front command. It acts on the selected object. Returns an error of #VALUE! if object(s) are not selected.

CALCULATE.DOCUMENT( )

Equivalent to Options Calculate Document. Calculates the active document only. Returns #VALUE! if a chart is active.

CALCULATE.NOW( )

Equivalent to Options/Chart Calculate Now. Calculates all open documents.

CALCULATION(*type_num,iter,max_num,max_change,update,*
*precision,date_1904,calc_save,save_values***)**
CALCULATION?(*type_num,iter,max_num,max_change,update,*
*precision,date_1904,calc_save,save_values***)**

Equivalent to Options Calculation. Sets the Calculation dialog box. TRUE enables options; FALSE disables them. See the command description for more information.

Argument	Description
type_num	Type of calculation
	1 Automatic
	2 Automatic except tables
	3 Manual
iter	Iteration check box
max_num	Maximum number of iterations
max_change	Maximum change
update	Update Remote References check box
precision	Precision as Displayed check box
date_1904	1904 Date System check box
calc_save	Recalculate Before Save check box
save_value	Save External Link Values check box

CALL(*register_ref,argument1,...*)

Calls procedures from the Microsoft Windows dynamic library. Only knowledgeable programmers should use this macro function. If used incorrectly, the function can stop computer operation.

CALLER( )

Results in the reference of the cell containing the function that called the currently running function macro. If the currently running macro is a command macro, #REF! is the returned value. The function can return a range from array formulas.

CANCEL.COPY( )

Equivalent to Esc. Eliminates the marquee (dashed line) surrounding a cut or copied area.

CANCEL.KEY(*enable,macro_ref*)

Prevents macros from being stopped or tells to which macro to transfer control after interruption.

Argument	Description
enable	TRUE reactivates Esc if *macro_ref* is not given
	TRUE transfers control to *macro_ref* if the current macro is interrupted by Esc
	FALSE or omitted prevents macro interruption by the Esc key
macro_ref	Specifies where macro control will transfer

CELL(*info_type*,*reference*)

Equivalent to the CELL worksheet function. This function is used to maintain compatibility with other worksheets. In Excel, macros use GET.CELL to find information in the referenced cell.

CELL.PROTECTION(*locked*,*hidden*)
CELL.PROTECTION?(*locked*,*hidden*)

Equivalent to Format Cell Protection. TRUE enables an option; FALSE disables it. See the command description for more information.

CHANGE.LINK(*old_text*,*new_text*,*type_of_link*)
CHANGE.LINK?(*old_text*,*new_text*,*type_of_link*)

Equivalent to File Links. The arguments *old_text* and *new_text* must be linked files enclosed in quotation marks. If *type_of_link* is 1, the link is with Excel; if 2, the link is through DDE. See the command description for more information.

CHECK.COMMAND(*bar_num*,*menu*,*command*,*check*)

Adds and removes check marks alongside commands in a menu.

CLEAR(*type_num*)
CLEAR?(*type_num*)

Equivalent to Edit Clear. Sets the Clear dialog box. See the command description for more information. The number used in the *type_num* argument determines which type of items are cleared.

Use one of the following numbers for the *type_num* argument:

type_num	Result
Worksheet	
1	All
2	Formats
3	Formulas (the default)
4	Notes
Chart	
1	Selected Series
2	Format in Selected Point or Series

CLOSE(*save_logical*)

Equivalent to Document Control **Close**. Closes the active window. If *save_logical* is TRUE, the document is saved. If FALSE, the document is not saved and not entered. A message appears asking whether you want to save. If the argument is omitted, a message displays asking whether you want to save the document.

CLOSE.ALL( )

Equivalent to **File Close All** command displayed by Shift+**File**.

COLOR.PALETTE(*file_text*)
COLOR.PALETTE?(*file_text*)

Copies a color palette from the file specified by *file_text* into the active document.

COLUMN.WIDTH(*width_num,reference,standard,type_num*)
COLUMN.WIDTH?(*width_num,reference,standard,type_num*)

Equivalent to Format **Column Width**. Changes the columns in the reference argument to the width of *width_num*. See the command description for more information.

Argument	Description	
width_num	Width measured as the width of one character in the first font of the Format Font dialog box	
reference	An external reference (if omitted, function uses current selection)	
standard	TRUE selects the standard width check box	
type_num	1	Hide column
	2	Unhide column
	3	Best fit width

For example,

=COLUMN.WIDTH(12)

changes the columns of the currently selected cells to widths of 12.

=COLUMN.WIDTH(8,!$B:$E)

changes the widths of columns B through E in the active worksheet to 8.

COMBINATION(*type_num*)
COMBINATION?(*type_num*)

Equivalent to Gallery Combination. Selects a combination chart format. The value of *type_num* must be one of the available formats.

CONSOLIDATE(*source_refs,function_num,top_row,left_col,create_links*)
CONSOLIDATE?(*source_refs,function_num,top_row,left_col,create_links*)

Equivalent to the Data Consolidate command.

COPY( )

Equivalent to Edit Copy. Copies the current selection.

COPY.CHART(*size_num*)

This function is the Macintosh Excel equivalent of COPY.PICTURE. The function is included for macro compatibility.

COPY.PICTURE(*appearance_num,size_num*)

Equivalent to Shift+Edit Copy Picture. Copies the selected worksheet or picture to the clipboard to be pasted later to another picture or a different Windows application.

Argument		Description
appearance_sum	1	As shown on-screen
	2	As shown when printed
*size_sum**	1	As shown on-screen
	2	As shown when printed
*(Available only if you are copying a chart)		

CREATE.NAMES(*top,left,bottom,right*)
CREATE.NAMES?(*top,left,bottom,right*)

Equivalent to Formula Create Names. Sets the Create Names dialog box. TRUE enables an option; FALSE disables the option.

CREATE.OBJECT(*object_type,ref_1,x_offset1,y_offset1,***ref2,**
x_offset2,y_offset2,text,xy_series)**

Creates an object of the type specified.

(Other function forms are available for text, buttons, and embedded charts.)

Following are the available object types:

object_type	Object Created
1	Line
2	Rectangle
3	Oval
4	Arc
5	Embedded chart
6	Text box
7	Button
8	Picture (from camera)

The offset arguments include the following:

Argument	Description
ref_1	The cell at the upper left corner of the object.
x_offset1	Horizontal offset from ref_1 to the upper left corner in points (1/22 inch).
y_offset1	Vertical offset from ref_1 to the upper left corner in points (1/22 inch).
ref_2	The cell at the lower right corner of the object.
x_offset2	Horizontal offset from ref_2 to the lower right corner in points (1/22 inch).
y_offset	Vertical offset from ref_2 to the lower right corner in points (1/22 inch).
text	Text argument used as the last argument for text boxes or macro buttons.
xy_series	A number from 0 to 3 corresponding to options in the First Row/Columns dialog box that specifies orientation of chart data. Used as the last argument with charts.

CUSTOM.REPEAT(*macro_text,repeat_text,record_text***)**

Creates a custom **Edit Repeat** command.

 CUSTOM.UNDO(*macro_text,undo_text***)**

Creates a custom **Edit Undo** command.

CUT( )

Equivalent to **Edit Cut**. Cuts the current selection.

DATA.DELETE( )
DATA.DELETE?( )

Equivalent to **Data Delete**. The form with a question mark displays a dialog box with a warning; the other macro function immediately executes the **Data Delete** command on the database.

> **Note: *Beware of DATA.DELETE***
> Make sure that you test DATA.DELETE with a sample database. Use the COUNTA function to test for criteria in the Criteria range. If no criteria are specified, all records will be deleted.

DATA.FIND(*logical***)**

Equivalent to **Data Find**. TRUE executes the find; FALSE stops the find.

DATA.FIND.NEXT( )
DATA.FIND.PREV( )

DATA.FIND.NEXT is the same as pressing down arrow to move to the next found record. DATA.FOUND.PREV is the same as pressing up arrow to move to the previous found record. You must first execute DATA.FIND. These functions produce FALSE if nothing is found.

DATA.FORM( )

Equivalent to **Data Form**. The database range must be set, or the #VALUE! error stops the macro.

DATA.SERIES(*rowcol,type_num,date_num,step_value,stop_value***)**
DATA.SERIES?(*rowcol,type_num,date_num,step_value,stop_value***)**

Equivalent to **Data Series**. Sets the Series dialog box.

Argument		Description
rowcol	1	Rows
	2	Columns
type_num	1	Linear
	2	Growth
	3	Date
date_num	1	Day
	2	Weekday
	3	Month
	4	Year
step_value		Incremental number
stop_value		Stopping value

DEFINE.NAME(*name_text,refers_to,macro_type,shortcut_text,hidden*)
DEFINE.NAME?(*name_text,refers_to,macro_type,shortcut_text,hidden*)

Equivalent to Formula Define Name. Defines the name of *name_text* on the active worksheet.

refers_to	Meaning of name_text
Value	That value
External reference	Cells on an external worksheet
Formula	The formula
Omitted	The current cell selections

If the active document for DEFINE.NAME is a macro sheet, the *macro_type* argument, a number from 1 through 3, has the following results:

macro_type	Result
1	Function macro
2	Command macro
3	Default, not a macro

The *shortcut_text* argument gives the Ctrl+key combination for a command macro. When the hidden argument is TRUE, the defined name is hidden. When the hidden argument is FALSE or omitted, the name is normal.

DEFINE.STYLE(*style_text,number,font,alignment,border,pattern,protection***)**
DEFINE.STYLE?(*style_text,number,font,alignment,border,pattern,protection***)**

(Numerous function formats available.) Equivalent to choosing Format Style and choosing the Define button.

DELETE.ARROW( )

Equivalent to Chart Delete Arrow. Deletes the selected arrow. Produces FALSE if the selection is not an arrow.

DELETE.BAR(*bar_num***)**

Deletes the custom menu bar that has the number *bar_num*. See Chapter 31 for examples of its use.

DELETE.COMMAND(*bar_num,menu,command***)**

Deletes the commands in the specified menu command from within the bar with the specified *bar_num* ID. *bar_num* can be an original or added Excel menu bar. The *menu* argument specifies the menu the command will be deleted from. The *menu* argument can be its number or its text name. If the *command* to be deleted does not exist, #VALUE! is returned. After a command is deleted, all remaining command numbers decrease by 1. See Chapter 31 for examples.

DELETE.FORMAT(*format_text***)**

Equivalent to Format Number. Deletes the custom numeric format specified by *format_text*. The text for *format_text* must be enclosed in quotation marks and must be the same as an existing custom format in the list box. Cells having the deleted format revert to General format. You cannot delete default numeric formats.

DELETE.MENU(*bar_num,menu***)**

Deletes the menu specified by *menu* in the bar specified by *bar_num*. The *menu* argument can be the name as text or the number of the menu. See Chapter 31 for an example.

DELETE.NAME(*name_text***)**

This function does the same thing as deleting a name with the Formula Define Names command with the Delete button. Enclose the text for *name_text* in quotation marks.

DELETE.OVERLAY( )

Equivalent to Chart Delete Overlay. If the overlay chart is already deleted, TRUE is returned.

DELETE.STYLE(*style_text*)

Equivalent to choosing the Format Style command and choosing the Delete button. If the Style does not exist, #VALUE! is returned and the macro stops.

 DEMOTE(*rowcol*)
DEMOTE?(*rowcol*)

Equivalent to clicking a row and column and then clicking the demote button. For the *rowcol* argument use the following:

rowcol	What It Affects
1 (or omitted)	Row
2	Column

DEREF(*reference*)

Returns the values in the referenced location. A single *reference* returns a single value; a referenced range returns an array of values. If it refers to the active sheet, the *reference* argument must be an absolute reference. See SET.NAME for an example.

DIALOG.BOX(*dialog_ref*)

Displays the custom dialog box described in the range *dialog_ref*. DIALOG.BOX returns the item number of the button pressed. Choosing Cancel returns FALSE. See Chapter 31 for examples.

DIRECTORY(*path_text*)

Changes the drive and directory to the path name specified in *path_text*. The function results in the name of the set directory as text. You can refer back to this macro cell to find the current directory. If you do not specify *path_text*, the macro returns the current directory. For example,

=DIRECTORY( )

returns "C:\EXCEL\FORECAST" if the current drive and directory are C:\EXCEL\FORECAST.

The command

=DIRECTORY("C:\BUDGET")

changes the active drive and directory to C:\BUDGET. See Chapter 15 for additional directory macro functions that can be added in.

DISABLE.INPUT(*logical*)

Stops input from the keyboard or mouse when logical is TRUE. Enables input when logical is FALSE. Use this function to disable the keyboard during macro operations that you do not want interrupted, such as Dynamic Data Exchange (DDE). Use DISABLE.INPUT(FALSE) to turn the keyboard back on so that you can regain control.

 DISPLAY(*formulas,gridlines,headings,zeros,color_num,* *reserved,outline,page_breaks,object_num*)
DISPLAY?(*formulas,gridlines,headings,zeros,color_num,* *reserved,outline,page_breaks,object_num*)

Equivalent to **Options Display**. Sets options in the Display dialog box. TRUE enables options, and FALSE disables them. Colors are numbered from 0 to 16. 0 is automatic coloring.

A second form of this function, WINDOW.INFO.DISPLAY, replicates **Window Show Info**, setting the Info menu and formatting the Info window.

DOCUMENTS(*type_num*)

Equivalent to a horizontal array of text names listing all the open documents in alphabetical order. The *type_num* arguments include the following:

type_num	Description
1 or omitted	Names of all documents except add-ins
2	Names of add-in documents
3	Names of all documents

ECHO(*logical*)

TRUE or no entry leaves screen updating on. FALSE turns updating off. Use TRUE during troubleshooting. Use FALSE to increase macro speed.

 EDIT.COLOR(*color_num,red_value,green_value,blue_value*)
EDIT.COLOR?(*color_num,red_value,green_value,blue_value*)

Chooses new colors for the color palette. The *color_num* argument is a number from 1 to 16. Other values are the values shown when editing the color palette. These values can be from 0 to 255. Hue, saturation, and luminence settings in a recording are converted to the corresponding red, green, and blue values.

EDIT.DELETE(*shift_num*)
EDIT.DELETE?(*shift_num*)

Equivalent to **Edit Delete**. Sets the Delete cells dialog box. For the *shift_num* argument, use the following:

shift_num	Action
1	Shift cells left
2	Shift cells up
3	Delete entire row
4	Delete entire column

 EDIT.REPEAT( )

Equivalent to the **Edit R**epeat command.

 EDIT.SERIES(*series_num,name_ref,x_ref,y_ref,z_ref,plot_order***)**
EDIT.SERIES?(*series_num,name_ref,x_ref,y_ref,z_ref,plot_order***)**

Equivalent to the **C**hart **E**dit **S**eries command.

 ELSE( )

Controls the functions used in conjunction with IF, ELSE.IF, and END.IF. Use =ELSE in a cell by itself to specify that the following functions should be run if all preceding IF and ELSE.IF statements were FALSE. See the IF function for examples.

 ELSE.IF(*logical_test***)**

Used with the IF, ELSE and END.IF functions to specify different actions depending upon the result of logical tests. Most worksheet users are familiar with the IF function that tests a logical condition such as B36>5. If that condition is TRUE, one set of actions occurs. If the condition is FALSE, a different set of actions occurs.

ELSE.IF checks for additional logical conditions that follow the first IF function. The ELSE.IF function gives IF functions in a command macro more test conditions and possible results. See the IF function in this directory for further explanation and an example of IF, ELSE.IF, ELSE, and END.IF.

ENABLE.COMMAND(*bar_num,menu,command,enable***)**

Enables or disables the command specified by the command argument for the menu with the ID specified in *bar_num*. The *bar_num* argument can be a built-in menu number, or it can reference the cell containing the ADD.BAR function that added the menu. The *menu* argument can be the text name or the number. (The leftmost menu number is 1.) The *command* argument is specified as the name in text or the numeric position of the commands. The top command in a menu is numbered 1. Using a command of 0 specifies all commands in the menu.

An *enable* value of TRUE enables the command; an enable value of FALSE disables the command. If the command being disabled is a built-in Excel command or does not exist, #VALUE! is returned.

 END.IF( )

Ends the block of functions that began with an IF function. See the example listed for the IF function. In a macro, use a single END.IF in a cell to end any block IF functions.

ERROR(*enable_logical*,*macro_ref*)

Tells Excel what to do about errors that occur during macro operation. (During normal macro operation, an error displays a dialog box from which you can choose to stop the macro, single-step through it, or continue operation.)

Argument	Description	
enable_logical	TRUE	With a *macro_ref*, transfers macro control to the error-handling routine in the macro located at *macro_ref*.
		Without a *macro_ref*, turns on normal error checking.
	FALSE	Error checking is disabled. Excel continues to run regardless of errors.

ERROR(TRUE) is the only condition that gives you error conditions. In ERROR(TRUE,*macro_ref*), you must build in your own error-trapping and message routines.

You can disable function errors that interrupt a macro by putting =ERROR(FALSE) in a cell before the function and =ERROR(TRUE) in a cell following the function. This technique prevents the function error from halting the macro, but it does not resolve any syntax or logic problems that caused the error.

EXEC(*program_text*,*window_num*)

Starts the program named *program_text* in a window with a size specified by *window_num* as 1 (normal), 2 or omitted (minimized), or 3 (maximized). Use the full file name with extension. You can include any program arguments, such as /S or /R, in *program_text*. When the program starts the function, it returns the task ID number that is used in DDE communication to that program. Use SEND.KEYS to send keystrokes over a DDE channel to the program. For example, to start Microsoft Word for Windows, use the following function:

=EXEC("WINWORD.EXE")

Include the full path name if the program is not in the default path. Include any startup parameters or file names just as you would if you started the program from File Run or from the DOS prompt.

EXECUTE(*channel_num,execute_text*)

Used in conjunction with the INITIATE macro function to communicate with another application through the DDE channel. The *channel_num* should be a reference to the macro cell containing the INITIATE macro function.

EXTRACT(*unique*)
EXTRACT?(*unique*)

Equivalent to Data Extract. Use TRUE for the unique value to check the Unique option. FALSE disables the option.

FCLOSE(*file_num*)

Closes the disk file identified as *file_num*. This file must be opened by FOPEN. *file_num* is the value returned by the FOPEN function.

 FILE.CLOSE(*save_logical*)

Equivalent to File Close. TRUE saves the file. FALSE does not save. Omitting the logical value displays an alert box querying you to save if changes were made.

FILE.DELETE(*file_text*)
FILE.DELETE?(*file_text*)

Equivalent to File Delete. Enter the drive, path, and file name as text. You can use the asterisk (*) and question mark (?) wild cards for file names. If a matching file name is not found, a dialog box appears requesting that you insert the appropriate disk. See Chapter 15 for information about add-in file and directory functions.

FILES(*directory_text*)

Produces a horizontal array of up to 256 file names found in the directory you specify. You can use the asterisk (*) and question mark (?) wild cards to specify file name patterns.

To read file names for the current directory, enter **=FILES( )** as an array formula across a row for as many cells as you want names. Cells that exceed the array size return #N/A!. You also can use the INDEX function to read a specific file, as in this example:

=INDEX(FILES( ),0,1)

Determine the number of files in the FILES function with a formula such as the following:

=COLUMNS(FILES( ))

FILL.DOWN( )

Equivalent to Edit Fill Down.

FILL.LEFT( )

Equivalent to Edit Fill Left.

FILL.RIGHT( )

Equivalent to Edit Fill Right.

FILL.UP( )

Equivalent to Edit Fill Up. Corresponds to the Edit Fill commands.

 FILL.WORKGROUP(*type_num*)
FILL.WORKGROUP?(*type_num*)

Equivalent to the Edit Fill Workgroup command. Type 1 fills all information, 2 fills formulas, and 3 fills formats.

FONT(*name_text,size_num*)
FONT?(*name_text,size_num*)

Equivalent to Options Font in Excel for the Macintosh. Included for compatibility.

FOPEN(*file_text*,*access_num*)

Opens on disk a text file with the name *file_text*. The *access_num* argument controls the read/write access, with 1 for read/write access, 2 for read-only access, and 3 for creating a new file (read/write access). A file ID number results. Close the file with FCLOSE.

FOR(*counter_text,start_num,end_num*,*step_num*)

Controls a FOR-NEXT loop to repeat macro procedures. Use the BREAK macro with a conditional macro like IF to interrupt a FOR-NEXT loop before it is complete. The *counter_text* argument is a text name in quotation marks that stores the counter number that counts the times the loop is repeated. The *start_num* and *end_num* arguments specify the first and last counter numbers. The *step_num* argument is the amount by which the counter increases on each pass through the loop. When *step_num* is omitted, it is assumed to be 1. See Chapter 30 for examples.

 FOR.CELL(*ref_name,area_ref,skip_blanks***)**

Creates a loop that operates on all cells in the area specified by *area_ref* with the functions listed between FOR.CELL and NEXT. The *ref_name* argument is a name in quotation marks in which Excel stores the reference of the cell currently being worked on. The *area_ref* is the cell reference range over which the following functions will be repeated. When *skip_blanks* is TRUE, blank cells in *area_ref* are not affected. For more information, see the example in Chapter 30.

 FORMAT.FONT(*name_text,size_num,bold,italic,underline,*
     *strike,color,outline,shadow***)**
FORMAT.FONT?(*name_text,size_num,bold,italic,underline,*
     *strike,color,outline,shadow***)**

Equivalent to Format Font. Applies fonts as appropriate for the Font dialog box under a worksheet or chart. Two forms exist: one is used for worksheets and macros; the other is used for charts.

(Other forms are available for text boxes and chart items.)

FORMAT.LEGEND(*position_num***)**
FORMAT.LEGEND?(*position_num***)**

Equivalent to Format Legend. Same as the dialog box that positions a chart legend. The *position_num* argument affects legend position in the following ways:

position_num	Legend Position
1	Bottom
2	Corner
3	Top
4	Right
5	Left

FORMAT.MAIN(*type_num,view,overlap,gap_width,vary,*
     *drop,hilo,angle,gap_depth,chart_depth***)**
FORMAT.MAIN?(*type_num,view,overlap,gap_width,vary,*
     *drop,hilo,angle,gap_depth,chart_depth***)**

Equivalent to Format Main Chart. The *type_num* argument specifies the type of chart, as follows:

type_num	Type of Chart
1	Area
2	Bar
3	Column
4	Line
5	Pie
6	XY (Scatter)
7	3-D Area
8	3-D Column
9	3-D Line
10	3-D Pie

FORMAT.MOVE(*x_offset,y_offset*,*reference*) worksheet objects
FORMAT.MOVE?(*x_offset,y_offset*,*reference*) worksheet objects
FORMAT.MOVE(*x_pos,y_pos*) charts
FORMAT.MOVE?(*x_pos,y_pos*) charts

Equivalent to Format Move. Moves the object or chart item. Returns TRUE if item moved. Positions are measured in points (1/72 inch). The *reference* argument is the cell relative to which worksheet objects are positioned.

FORMAT.NUMBER(*format_text*)
FORMAT.NUMBER?(*format_text*)

Equivalent to Format Number. Use a text string enclosed in quotation marks that is the equivalent of an existing number or date format in the **Numbers** list box. For example,

    =FORMAT.NUMBER("d-mmm-yy")

**FORMAT.OVERLAY(*type_num*,*view,overlap,width,vary,*
  drop,hilo,angle,series_dist,series_num)**
**FORMAT.OVERLAY?(*type_num,view,overlap,width,vary,*
  drop,hilo,angle,series_dist,series_num)**

Equivalent to Format Overlay. See FORMAT.MAIN.

FORMAT.SIZE(*x-off,y-off*,*reference*) worksheet object, relative
FORMAT.SIZE?(*x-off,y-off*,reference) worksheet object, relative
FORMAT.SIZE(*width,height*) worksheet/chart object, absolute
FORMAT.SIZE?(*width,height*) worksheet object and chart item, absolute

Sizes a selected object.

**FORMAT.TEXT(*x_align,y_align,orient_num,auto_text,*
  auto_size,show_key,show_value)**
**FORMAT.TEXT?(*x_align,y_align,orient_num,auto_text,*
  auto_size,show_key,show_value)**

Equivalent to Format Text. Same as the dialog box for the Format Text command. Arguments are equivalent to the dialog box options and are selected by TRUE and deselected by FALSE.

Argument	Description
x_align	Horizontal alignment
	1 Left
	2 Center
	3 Right
y_align	Vertical alignment
	1 Top
	2 Center
	3 Bottom
orient_num	Text orientation
	0 Horizontal
	1 Vertical
	2 Upward
	3 Downward

FORMULA(*formula_text*,*reference*)

Enters a formula in the referenced cell. Omitting the *reference* enters the formula in the active cell. For example,

=FORMULA("=R2C3*3")

enters the formula

=$C$2*3

in the active cell of the active worksheet. (See Chapters 28, 29, 30, and 31 for additional examples.)

FORMULA.ARRAY(*formula_text*,*reference*)

Enters an array formula just as if you had pressed Shift+Ctrl while entering. Specify the range with *reference* or with the currently selected range. See FORMULA.FUNCTION.

 FORMULA.CONVERT(*formula_text*,*from_a1*,*to_a1*,*to_ref_type*,*rel_to_ref*)

Converts formulas in quoted text form by changing R1C1 style and absolute/relative reference.

FORMULA.FILL(*formula_text*,*reference*)

Fills the selected range or reference with the formula, just as if you had pressed Shift while entering a formula.

FORMULA.FIND(*text, in_num, at_num, by_num, dir_num, match_case***)**
FORMULA.FIND?(*text, in_num, at_num, by_num, dir_num, match_case***)**

Equivalent to Formula Find. Text must be enclosed in quotation marks.

Argument	Description for Dialog Box Options	
in_num	1	Formulas
	2	Values
	3	Notes
at_num	1	Whole
	2	Part
by_num	1	Rows
	2	Columns
dir_num	1 or omitted	Next occurrence
	2	Previous occurrence
match_case	TRUE	Matches upper/lowercase exactly
	FALSE or omitted	Match is case-sensitive

FORMULA.FIND.NEXT( )
FORMULA.FIND.PREV( )

Equivalent to F7 and Shift+F7, respectively. Finds the next or previous cell in the worksheet as specified in the Formula Find dialog box. These functions return FALSE if no cell is found.

 FORMULA.GOTO(*reference, corner***)**
FORMULA.GOTO?(*reference, corner***)**

Equivalent to Formula Goto. The *reference* argument should refer to a cell in the macro sheet, an R1C1 style reference as text, or an external reference to a worksheet. When the *corner* argument is TRUE, the reference scrolls to the upper left corner of the window. For example,

    =FORMULA.GOTO(!$B$3)

goes to $B$3 on the active worksheet, and

    =FORMULA.GOTO("R5C3")

goes to C5 on the active worksheet. With named ranges, use formats similar to the following:

    =FORMULA.GOTO(!Sales)

FORMULA.REPLACE(*find_text,replace_text,look_at,*
look_by,active_cell,match_case*)
FORMULA.REPLACE?(*find_text,replace_text,look_at,*
look_by,active_cell,match_case*)

Equivalent to Formula Replace. Enclose *find_text* and *replace_text* in quotation marks, or use a cell reference. You can use the asterisk (*) and question mark (?) wild cards in *find_text*.

Argument		Description
find_text		Searches for the text enclosed in quotation marks
replace_text		Replaces the text enclosed in quotation marks
look_at	1	Whole
	2	Part
look_by	1	Rows
	2	Columns
active_cell	TRUE	Replaces in current cell only
	FALSE	Replaces in selection or entire document
match_case	TRUE	Matches upper/lowercase exactly
	FALSE	Match is case-sensitive or omitted

FPOS(*file_num,position_num*)

Positions the file in preparation for reading or writing. The first position is 1. Another function, FOPEN, opens the file and returns the ID number used as *file_num*. FPOS returns `#VALUE!` if the file ID number is not valid.

FREAD(*file_num,num_chars*)

Reads the specified number of characters from the file, beginning at the current location in the file.

FREADLN(*file_num*)

Reads the current position in the file to the end of the line. FOPEN returns *file_num* when the file is opened.

FREEZE.PANES(*logical*)

Equivalent to Options Freeze Display. TRUE freezes the panes; FALSE unfreezes them.

FSIZE(*file_num*)

Returns the number of characters in the file specified by *file_num*.

FULL(*logical*)

Equivalent to Document Control Maximize/**R**estore. TRUE expands the active window to maximum size. FALSE restores it to the original size.

FWRITE(*file_num,text*)

Writes the text string to the file specified by *file_num*, beginning at the current position in the file. FWRITE returns #N/A! if the function is unable to write to the document.

FWRITELN(*file_num,text*)

Starts at the current position in the text file and writes the specified text, followed by a carriage return and line feed.

> **Note: *The GALLERY Commands***
> The following commands choose the type of chart by the number shown in the chart's gallery. In GALLERY macro functions, the *delete_overlay* argument can be TRUE, FALSE, or omitted. TRUE in *delete_overlay* deletes the overlay, if present, and applies the new format to the main chart. Using FALSE or omitting the *delete_overlay* value applies the new format to the chart that contains the currently selected chart item.

GALLERY.3D.AREA(*type_num*)
GALLERY.3D.AREA?(*number*)

Equivalent to **Gallery 3D Area**.

GALLERY.3D.COLUMN(*type_num*)
GALLERY.3D.COLUMN?(*number*)

Equivalent to **Gallery 3D Column**.

GALLERY.3D.LINE(*type_num*)
GALLERY.3D.LINE?(*number*)

Equivalent to **Gallery 3D Line**.

GALLERY.3D.PIE(*type_num*)
GALLERY.3D.PIE?(*number*)

Equivalent to **Gallery 3D Pie**.

GALLERY.AREA(*type_num,delete_overlay*)
GALLERY.AREA?(*number,delete_overlay*)

Equivalent to **Gallery Area**.

GALLERY.BAR(*type_num,delete_overlay*)
GALLERY.BAR?(*number,delete_overlay*)

Equivalent to **Gallery Bar**.

GALLERY.COLUMN(*type_num,delete_overlay*)
GALLERY.COLUMN?(*number,delete_overlay*)

Equivalent to **Gallery Column**.

GALLERY.LINE(*type_num,delete_overlay*)
GALLERY.LINE?(*number,delete_overlay*)

Equivalent to **Gallery Line**.

GALLERY.PIE(*type_num,delete_overlay*)
GALLERY.PIE?(*number,delete_overlay*)

Equivalent to **Gallery Pie**.

GALLERY.SCATTER(*type_num,delete_overlay*)
GALLERY.SCATTER?(*number,delete_overlay*)

Equivalent to **Gallery xy Scatter**.

GET.BAR( )

Returns the number of the active menu bar.

 GET.BAR(*bar_num,menu,command*)

Returns the name or position of a command where *bar_num* is the number of a built-in menu bar or the number returned by the ADD.BAR function that added a menu bar. The *menu* argument is the menu containing the command as a text name in quotation marks or as a number, with 1 the leftmost number. If *command* is the command name as text, its numeric position is returned. If *command* is a numeric position on the menu, the name is returned.

 GET.CELL(*type_num,reference*)

This function is a valuable one that finds characteristics such as formatting, location, or contents of a cell, or the upper left cell of the range specified by reference. The *type_num* argument specifies the type of cell information returned. The *type_num* argument refers to the following characteristics:

type_num	Returned Value
1	Top left cell of reference as text
2	Row of top cell in reference
3	Column of leftmost cell in reference
4	Same as TYPE(reference)
5	Contents of reference

type_num	Returned Value
6	Formula in reference as text
7	Number format of cell as text
8	Number that equals cell's alignment numbers as in ALIGNMENT( )
9	Number for type of left border

0	No border
1	Thin line
2	Medium line
3	Dashed line
4	Dotted line
5	Thick line
6	Double line
7	Hairline

type_num	Returned Value
10	Number for type of right border

0	No border
1	Thin line
2	Medium line
3	Dashed line
4	Dotted line
5	Thick line
6	Double line
7	Hairline

type_num	Returned Value
11	Number for type of top border

0	No border
1	Thin line
2	Medium line
3	Dashed line
4	Dotted line
5	Thick line
6	Double line
7	Hairline

type_num	Returned Value
12	Number for type of bottom border

0	No border
1	Thin line
2	Medium line
3	Dashed line
4	Dotted line
5	Thick line
6	Double line
7	Hairline

type_num	Returned Value
13	Number from 0 to 18 indicating pattern
14	TRUE if cell is locked
15	TRUE if cell is hidden
16	Column width in normal font characters
17	Row height in points
18	Name of font as text
19	Size of font in points
20	TRUE if cell is bold
21	TRUE if cell is italic
22	TRUE if cell is underlined
23	TRUE if cell is struck over
24	Font color (1 to 16)

Sixteen additional attributes are readable.

GET.CHART.ITEM(x_y_index,*point_index,item_text***)**

Returns the vertical or horizontal location of a point on a selected chart item.

Argument		Description
x_y_index	1	Request horizontal coordinate
	2	Request vertical coordinate
point_index	1	Lower left point of line or upper left of object
	2	Upper right point of line or upper middle of
For an object		
	3	Upper right of object
	4	Right middle of object
	5	Lower right of object
	6	Lower middle of object
	7	Lower left of object
	8	Left middle of object
For an arrow		
	1	The base
	2	The head

Argument	Description
	For a pie slice
1	Outermost counter-clockwise point
2	Outer center point
3	Outermost clockwise point
4	Midpoint of the most clockwise radius
5	Center point
6	Midpoint of the most counter-clockwise radius

If the *item_text* argument is omitted, the function uses the currently selected chart item. *item_text* options are listed in the chart version of SELECT( ).

 GET.DEF(*def_text*,*document_text*,*type_num*)

Returns the range name corresponding to the reference, *def_text*, in document. *def_text* is a reference in R1C1 style enclosed in quotation marks. If multiple names are at the address *def_text*, only the first name is returned. Use GET.NAME to return the definition of a name. Use a *type_num* of 1 (the default) to return unhidden names, 2 to return hidden names, and 3 to return all names.

GET.DOCUMENT(*type_num*,*name_text*)

Returns information about the document defined by *name_text*. There are 44 available *type_num* results:

type_num	Returned Value
1	Name of document as text. Path and window number are not included.
2	Path name corresponding to *name_text* if document has been saved. If document has not been saved, #N/A is returned.
3	1 if worksheet, 2 if chart, 3 if macro, and 4 if Info window.
4	TRUE if changes have been made since last save.
5	TRUE if file is read-only.
6	TRUE if file is protected.

type_num	Returned Value
7	TRUE if document contents are protected.
8	TRUE if document windows are protected.
9	Number of first row used in worksheet or macro (0 returned if document is blank).
10	Number of last row used in worksheet or macro (0 returned if document is blank).
11	Number of first column used (0 if sheet is blank).
12	Number of last column used (0 if sheet is blank).
13	Number of windows.
14	Calculation mode, where 1 is Automatic, 2 is Automatic Except Tables, and 3 is Manual.
15	TRUE if iteration is enabled.
16	Maximum number of iterations.
17	Maximum change between iterations.
18	TRUE if remote references update.
19	TRUE if Precision as Displayed is enabled.
20	TRUE if 1904 date numbering is enabled.
21	A text array four cells wide of the names of the four default fonts.
22	A numeric array four cells wide of the four font sizes.
23	A logical array four cells wide showing which of the four fonts are bold.
24	A logical array four cells wide showing which of the four fonts are italic.
25	A logical array four cells wide showing which of the four fonts are underlined.
26	A logical array four cells wide showing which of the four fonts are struck over.

The function can return 18 other attributes.

For charts, use the following results for the *type_num* arguments 9-12:

type_num	Returned Value
9	The type of main chart, where 1 is area, 2 is bar, 3 is column, 4 is line, 5 is pie, and 6 is scatter.
10	The type of overlay chart, using the same numbering scheme as when *type_num* equals 9 (#N/A! is returned if no overlay exists).
11	The number of series in main chart.
12	The number of series in overlay chart.

GET.FORMULA(*reference*)

Returns the formula contents of the upper left corner of the reference area (the active area if reference is not entered). Results are returned as text in R1C1 style just as the formula would appear in the formula bar.

 ### GET.LINK.INFO(*link_text,type_num,type_of_link,reference*)

Returns information about the update settings for a link.

GET.NAME(*name_text*)

Returns the definition for the range name of *name_text*. The name_text argument can define a value, a formula, or a reference. *name_text* returns the equivalent contents of the Refers To text box for the Formula Define Name command.

GET.NOTE(*cell_ref,start_char,num_chars*)

Returns a specified number of characters, *num_chars*, from the note at *cell_ref*, beginning with a specific character in the note, *start_char*. A maximum of 255 characters can be returned.

 ### GET.OBJECT(*type_num,object_id_text,start_num,count_num*)

Returns information that can be used to manipulate an object. 40 different object attributes can be examined.

 ### GET.WINDOW(*type_num,window_text*)

Returns specific types of information about the window of *window_text*. If you do not specify *window_text*, Excel assumes that you mean the active window. The function returns 22 *type_num* results.

type_num	Result Value
1	Name of document as text.
2	Number of window.
3	X position from left edge of screen to left edge of window (in points).
4	Y position from top edge of screen to top edge of window (in points).
5	Width in points.
6	Height in points.
7	TRUE if window is hidden.

The function returns 15 additional attributes.

 GET.WORKSPACE(type_num)

Returns workspace information depending on *type_num*. The function returns 29 different workspace parameters.

type_num	Result
1	Name of the environment in text.
2	Version number as text.
3	Number of decimals, if Auto_Decimal is selected.
4	TRUE in R1C1 style; FALSE in A1 style.
5	TRUE for scroll bars displayed.
6	TRUE for status bar displayed.
7	TRUE for formula bar displayed.
8	TRUE for remote requests enabled.
9	Returns alternate menu key.
10	Returns special modes: 1 is Data Find, 2 is Copy, and 3 is Cut.
11	X position of Excel from left edge.
12	Y position of Excel from top.
13	Workspace width in points.

type_num	Result
14	Workspace height in points.
15	1 if Excel is in a normal window, 2 if minimized, and 3 if maximized.
16	Free memory in kilobytes.
17	Memory available to Excel in kilobytes.
18	TRUE if math coprocessor is available.
19	TRUE if mouse is present.

10 additional attributes are returned.

 GOAL.SEEK(*target_cell,target_value,variable_cell*)
GOAL.SEEK?(*target_cell,target_value,variable_cell*)

Equivalent to the Formula Goal Seek command.

GOTO(*reference*)

Transfers macro operation to the upper left corner of the reference. Can be used to link two macros. If *reference* is an external reference to another macro sheet, control transfers to the other macro sheet. GOTO does not transfer control automatically back to the original location when the branch is complete.

 GRIDLINES(*x_major,x_minor,y_major,y_minor,z_major,z_minor*)
GRIDLINES?(*x_major,x_minor,y_major,y_minor,z_major,z_minor*)

Equivalent to Chart Gridlines. Use TRUE to enable an option in the Gridlines dialog box; use FALSE to disable an option.

 GROUP( )

Equivalent to the Format Group command. The function groups selected graphic objects on the worksheet. If no objects are selected or the objects cannot be grouped, returns #VALUE!.

HALT(*cancel_close*)

Stops a macro from running. Use with an IF macro function to stop a macro when a condition is met. You can use HALT to stop a subroutine and prevent it from returning to the macro that called it. The *cancel_close* argument is a logical value that specifies whether a macro sheet, when encountering the HALT function in the Auto_Close macro, is closed.

 HELP(*file_text!topic_num*)

Equivalent to Help. Displays help for the topic *file_text!topic_num*. HELP without a *file_text!topic_num* displays the main help index. The *file_text!topic_num* argument must refer to a valid help topic. Custom help files can contain glossary terms and jump topics just as built-in Excel help files can. This function is used to call custom help topics if *file_num!topic_num* is of the following form:

   filename!topic_num

Help files must be compiled to run with HELP. To get a free copy of the Help compiler, call Microsoft.

HIDE( )

Equivalent to **Window Hide**. Increase macro speed by hiding windows on which you are working. Functions such as FORMULA continue to work on hidden worksheets. Show the hidden windows with the ACTIVATE macro function.

 ### HIDE.OBJECT(*object_id_text,bide*)

Hides or displays an object. *object_id_text* is the object name and number. *bide* is a logical value that hides the object when it is TRUE or omitted.

HLINE(*num_cols*)

Horizontally scrolls the active window by the number of columns specified by *num_cols*.

HPAGE(*num_windows*)

Scrolls the active windows one window width to the right or left. A positive *num_windows* scrolls right; a negative scrolls left.

HSCROLL(*position,col_logical*)

Scrolls the active window horizontally. When *col_logical* is TRUE, the window scrolls to the column specified by position. When *col_logical* is FALSE, the window scrolls by the fraction of a window width specified by position. To scroll to a specific column, use a format such as the following:

   =HSCROLL(*n*,TRUE)

n is the number column you want.

 ### IF(*logical_test,value_if_true,value_if_false*)

IF functions enable you to test for certain conditions in a worksheet or macro and produce different actions or calculations based on those tests. Macros can use two forms of IF functions.

The first form of IF function is very similar to that used in a worksheet. This form is illustrated in multiple examples in Chapters 28 through 32. This form tests for calculated values, input values, or document conditions, and then changes the macro operation depending on the TRUE or FALSE result of that test.

The second form of IF function is known as a block IF function. Block IF functions use the following syntax:

IF(*logical_test*)

The function is entered in a cell by itself.

This IF function enables you to check more than one logical test and do something different based on the result of each test. Each of these different sections of the macro that check different logical tests uses additional functions that work with the IF function. These additional functions are ELSE.IF, ELSE, and END.IF.

These functions are always found in the following order in a macro:

IF(*logical_test*)
ELSE.IF(*logical_test*)
ELSE.IF(*logical_test*)
ELSE( )
END.IF( )

Enter each function in its own cell. A macro can have one or more ELSE.IF functions. However, there can be only one ELSE and END.IF for each block IF at the same level. (IF functions can be nested within other IF functions to create more complex macros.)

These functions work as follows. The IF function checks its logical test, and if TRUE, it executes the functions or formulas that follow up to the next ELSE.IF or ELSE function. If FALSE, the macro moves to the first ELSE.IF function.

If the ELSE.IF function test is TRUE, the functions and formulas up to the next ELSE.IF or ELSE function are executed. If FALSE, the macro moves to the next ELSE.IF or ELSE function.

Additional ELSE.IF functions can be inserted to check additional logical tests. If they are TRUE, the functions and formulas that follow them are executed. If they return FALSE, the macro moves to the next ELSE.IF or ELSE function.

At the final ELSE function, all functions and formulas that are between the ELSE and END.IF execute. These functions and formulas execute only if all other logical tests were FALSE.

Finally an END.IF function ends this block of logical tests and their resulting actions.

In the example in figure 32.1, a block IF function checks four different tests and produces four different responses depending on the result of those tests. At the beginning of the macro, an INPUT box asks the operator to enter a number less than 200. Depending upon the number entered, a text message is entered in the active cell of the active macro or worksheet. This message describes the entered number. An example is "Between 50 and 150". Before running this macro, make sure that the active cell is blank. The text message writes into the active cell of the active worksheet or macro sheet.

	A	B
1		**Check.Data**
2	**Data**	=INPUT("Enter a number less than 200",1)
3		=IF(Data=FALSE,GOTO(End))
4		=IF(Data<50)
5		= FORMULA("Under Fifty")
6		Run subroutines here
7		=ELSE.IF(Data<=150)
8		= FORMULA("Between 50 and 150")
9		Run subroutines here
10		=ELSE.IF(Data<=175)
11		= FORMULA("Between 151 and 175")
12		Run subroutines here
13		=ELSE()
14		= FORMULA("Your entry was greater than 175")
15		Run subroutines here
16		=END.IF()
17	**End**	=RETURN()

Fig. 32.1. An example of a block IF function.

In figure 32.1, cell B2 has been assigned the name Data by the Formula Define Name command. Cell B17 has been assigned the name End. The labels in column A are used as visual reminders. (The use of INPUT boxes is described in Chapters 28 and 29.)

Cell B3 checks whether the Cancel button has been chosen in the INPUT box from cell B2. If the Cancel button is chosen, the macro goes to the end cell, B17.

The block IF functions begin in cell B4 where the IF function checks the number stored in Data. The INPUT box stored the typed number in cell B2, the cell named Data. If Data is less than 50, the result of the IF in B4 is TRUE, so the functions between B4 and B7 are executed. The FORMULA function in B5 enters the quoted text in the active cell of the active worksheet or macro. The text remark in cell B6 illustrates that a subroutine could be called within this IF function. If Data is not less than 50, B4 is FALSE, so the macro moves to B7.

In B7 the ELSE.IF function checks if Data is less than or equal to 150. If this is TRUE, the text in the FORMULA function in B8 is entered in the active cell. If FALSE, the macro moves to the ELSE.IF in cell B10.

If the ELSE.IF in B10 is TRUE, the FORMULA in B11 enters text in the active cell. If FALSE, the macro moves to the ELSE function in B13.

An ELSE function marks the last set of actions that result from a block IF. Functions and formulas between the ELSE and END.IF function are executed only when all other IF and ELSE.IF functions have been FALSE.

The END.IF function in cell B16 finally ends the block IF function started in cell B4.

> **Tip: *Indenting IF, FOR, and WHILE Function Segments for Readability***
> You can place spaces between the equal sign and the first letter of a function to indent segments of related macro functions. This can make macros easier to read because IF and END.IF functions can be at one level of indentation; the functions they enclose can be at a deeper level. Indenting functions is also useful with FOR-NEXT and WHILE-NEXT functions and the functions they enclose.

INITIATE(*app_text,topic_text*)

Opens and initiates communication with another Windows application through the DDE channel. The *app_text* argument is the DDE name of the application you are accessing, as specified in the application manual. INITIATE returns the channel ID number for DDE communication with the application specified in *app_text. topic_text* is the name of the document, as text, being accessed. Consider this example:

=INITIATE("WINWORD","C:\LETTERS\SALES.DOC")

Use the EXEC function to start an application and load a document.

INPUT(*message_text,type_num,title_text,default,x_pos,y_pos*)

Creates a dialog box and returns the information entered into it. The prompt, title, and default arguments are text and must be enclosed in quotation marks. Other arguments are numbers. Choosing OK from the box or pressing Enter returns the entry in the box to the macro function cell. Choosing Cancel returns FALSE. Chapters 29 and 30 illustrate how to use this function for data entry.

type_num	Data Type
0	Formula, returned as R1C1 in text
1	Number
2	Text
4	Logical
8	Absolute reference
16	Error
64	Array

You can add together type numbers. For example, a type with the value 3 indicates that the function accepts number or text entries.

INSERT(*shift_num*)
INSERT?(*shift_num*)

Equivalent to Edit Insert. *shift_num* can be an argument from 1-4. Use 1 to shift cells right. Use 2 or omitted to shift cells down. 3 shifts an entire row, and 4 shifts an entire column. *shift_num* is optional if an entire row or column is selected.

JUSTIFY( )

Equivalent to Format Justify.

 LAST.ERROR( )

Returns the reference of the last error in the macro sheet.

LEGEND(*logical*)

Equivalent to Chart Add Legend. Adds a legend when *logical* is TRUE or omitted. Deletes the legend when logical is FALSE.

 LINKS(*document_text,type_num*)

Returns a horizontal array of all worksheets linked to the document specified by *document_text*. The default is the name of the active document. *type_num* specifies the type of link, where an Excel link is 1. If no links exist, the returned value is #N/A!. To open all links to the worksheet FORCAST.XLS, for example, use this form:

    =OPEN.LINKS(LINKS("FORCAST.XLS"))

LIST.NAMES( )

Equivalent to the Formula Paste Name command with the Paste List button.

**MAIN.CHART(*type_num,stack,100,vary,overlap,
drop,hilo,overlap%,cluster,angle*)**
**MAIN.CHART?(*type_num,stack,100,vary,overlap,
drop,hilo,overlap%,cluster,angle*)**

Equivalent to Format Main Chart in Excel V2.2 and earlier versions. In Excel 3.0, use the FORMAT.MAIN function. All arguments are options in the Main Chart dialog box. Enable an option with TRUE; disable with FALSE.

type_num	Chart
1	Area
2	Bar
3	Column
4	Line
5	Pie
6	Scatter

MAIN.CHART.TYPE(*type_num*)

This macro function is included for compatibility with Macintosh Excel 1.5 and earlier versions. Produces the same effect as the FORMAT.MAIN function.

 MERGE.STYLES(*document_text*)

Equivalent to choosing Format Style and choosing the Merge button. Merges styles from another sheet into the active sheet.

MESSAGE(*logical,text*)

Displays messages in status bar. When *logical* is TRUE, *text* is displayed. FALSE removes messages and returns status bar to normal. Only one message displays at a time.

MOVE(*x_pos,y_pos,window_text*)
MOVE?(*x_pos,y_pos,window_text*)

Equivalent to Window Move. Moves the entire window by repositioning the upper left corner. *window_text* is the name of the window, in quotation marks, as it appears in the title bar. The active window moves if *window_text* does not specify a different window. *x_pos* and *y_pos* are measured in points. The upper left for the active window is MOVE(1,1).

 NAMES(*document_text,type_num*)

Returns a horizontal array of names in the document defined by *document_text*. The default is the active document. A *type_num* of 1 (or omitted) returns normal names, 2 returns hidden names, and 3 returns all names.

NEW(*type_num*,*xy_series*)
NEW?(*type_num*,*xy_series*)

Equivalent to **File New**. Use a *type_num* of 1 for a worksheet; 2 for a chart; 3 for a macro sheet; 4 for an international macro sheet; and quoted text for templates. The *xy_series* argument specifies how data is oriented if a chart is opened. If *xy_series* is 0, the dialog box is displayed for operator input; 1 (default), first row/column is data; 2, first row/column is category (x) labels; and 3, first row/column is x values for a scatter chart.

NEW.WINDOW( )

Equivalent to **Window New Window**. Creates a new window.

NEXT( )

Ends a FOR, FOR.CELL, or WHILE loop. See Chapter 30 for examples.

NOT(*logical*)

Changes TRUE to FALSE and FALSE to TRUE.

NOTE(*add_text*,*cell_ref*,*start_char*,*num_chars*)
NOTE?( )

In a note attached to *cell_ref*, the *add_text* value replaces the text, beginning at *start_char* and continuing for *num_chars*. The default for *cell_ref* is the active cell. The text added (*add_text*) must be less than 255 characters. NOTE( ) deletes the note attached to the active cell.

 OBJECT.PROTECTION(*locked*,*lock_text*)

Equivalent to the **Format Protection** command.

OFFSET(*reference*,*rows*,*cols*,*height*,*width*)

A worksheet function that has much value in macros. Determines a cell reference or range that is offset from the specified reference. The upper left cell in the returned reference is rows down and cols right of *reference*. The returned reference is height tall and width wide. For example,

    =OFFSET(D4,–1,1,1,1)

is E3. For additional examples, see Chapters 30 and 31. You can use OFFSET as the reference within FORMULA to specify an offset cell where data will be entered.

ON.DATA(*document_text*,*macro_text*)

Runs the *macro_text* macro when an application sends data to the document named *document_text*. Omit *macro_text* to turn off the ON.DATA macro function.

ON.KEY(*key_text*,*macro_text*)

Runs the *macro_text* macro when the key specified by *key_text* is pressed. The *key_text* argument can indicate single keys or combination keys such as Shift+Ctrl+right arrow. Use empty text, a pair of quotation marks with nothing inside (""), as the *macro_text* for no response to a keystroke. Omit *macro_text* to return a key to normal operation, so the function is ON.KEY(*key_text*).

The value of *key_text* can be composed of the following codes:

Key	Code
Backspace	{Backspace} or {BS}
Break	{Break}
Caps Lock	{Capslock}
Clear	{Clear}
Del	{Delete} or {DEL}
Down arrow	{Down}
End	{End}
Enter	{Enter}
Esc	{Escape} or {ESC}
Help	{Help}
Home	{Home}
Ins	{Insert}
Left arrow	{Left}
Num Lock	{NumLock}
PgDn	{PgDn}
PgUp	{PgUp}
PrtSc	{PrtSc}
Right arrow	{Right}
Scroll Lock	{Scrollock}
Tab	{Tab}
Up arrow	{Up}
F1	{F1}
F2	{F2}
F3	{F3}
F4	{F4}
F5	{F5}
F6	{F6}
F7	{F7}
F8	{F8}
F9	{F9}
F10	{F10}
F11	{F11}
F12	{F12}
F13	{F13}
F14	{F14}
F15	{F15}

You can combine keys with Shift, Ctrl, and Alt.

If you want to combine with	*Precede key with*
Shift	+
Ctrl	^
Alt	%

For example,

=ON.KEY("+%{F1}","MONTHEND.XLM!Extract")

runs the macro Extract on the macro sheet MONTHEND.XLM when Shift+Alt+F1 is pressed.

=ON.KEY("+%{F1}")

returns the Shift+Alt+F1 key to its normal use.

The function

=ON.KEY("+%{F1}","")

disables the Shift+Alt+F1 key.

 ON.RECALC(*sheet_text,macro_text***)**

Runs the macro specified by *macro_text* when the document specified by *sheet_text* recalculates.

ON.TIME(*time,macro_text,tolerance,insert_logical***)**

When *insert_logical* is TRUE or omitted, Excel runs the macro named *macro_text* at the time specified by time. The *macro_text* argument must be a text reference in R1C1 style. The time can indicate only a time so that the macro runs every day, or time also can include the date. Use the time as a reference or quoted time *n* as one of the date/time formats recognized by Excel.

ON.WINDOW(*window_text,macro_text***)**

Starts the macro named *macro_text* when the window named *window_text* is activated. Turn off ON.WINDOW for a specific window by giving the macro function again without a *macro_text* argument.

 OPEN(*file_text,update_links,read_only,format,prot_pwd,***
    write_res_pwd,ignore_rorec,file_origin)
OPEN?(*file_text,update_links,read_only,format,prot_pwd,***
    write_res_pwd,ignore_rorec,file_origin)

Equivalent to **File Open**. Opens *file_text* as if it were selected manually to open a file. TRUE in any position selects the option in the appropriate dialog box. The *update_links* argument can have values of 0 to update neither external nor remote references, 1 to update external references only, 2 to update remote references only, and 3 to update both. If you use the OPEN? form, you can use the asterisk (*) and question mark (?) wild cards in the *file_text* name.

 OPEN.LINKS(*document_text1*,*doc_text2*,...,*read_only*,*type_of_link*)
OPEN.LINKS?(*document_text1*,*doc_text2*,...,*read_only*,*type_of_link*)

Equivalent to File Links. Opens files necessary for links to other documents. For *document_text*, you can use up to 13 document names. Using TRUE for the *read_only* argument enables read-only access. *type_of_link* 1 is an Excel link. *type_of_link* 2 is a DDE link.

For example, to open the links to the active worksheet, use the following:

=OPEN.LINKS(LINKS( ))

 OUTLINE(*auto_styles*,*row_dir*,*col_dir*,*create_apply*)

Equivalent to the Formula Outline command. The *auto_styles*, *row_dir*, and *col_dir* arguments correspond to check boxes in the dialog box where TRUE selects the check box, FALSE deselects the check box, and an omitted argument leaves the box the same. The *create_apply* arguments are as follows:

create_apply	Action
1	Produces an outline with the current settings
2	Applies outlining styles according to outline levels

**OVERLAY(*type_num*,*stack*,*100*,*vary*,*overlap*,*drop*,*hilo*,*overlap%*,
cluster,*angle*,*series_num*,*auto*)**
**OVERLAY?(*type*,*stack*,*100*,*vary*,*overlap*,*drop*,*hilo*,*overlap%*,
cluster,*angle*,*series*,*auto*)**

Equivalent to Format Overlay in Excel V2.2. Use the FORMAT.OVERLAY function for newer versions of Excel. Use the same argument values used in MAIN.CHART. The *series* argument is the number of the first series in the overlay. The *auto* argument represents the Automatic Series Distribution option.

OVERLAY.CHART.TYPE(*type_num*)

This macro function is included for compatibility with Macintosh Excel. It is the equivalent to the FORMAT.OVERLAY function in Excel 3 for Windows.

PAGE.SETUP(*head,foot,left,right,top,bot,heading,grid,h_center,*
 v_center,orientation,paper_size,scaling)
PAGE.SETUP?(*head,foot,left,right,top,bot,heading,grid,h_center,*
 v_center,orientation,paper_size,scaling)
PAGE.SETUP(*head,foot,left,right,top,bot,size,h_center,*
 v_center,orientation,paper_size,scaling)
PAGE.SETUP?(*head,foot,left,right,top,bot,size,h_center,*
 v_center,orientation,paper_size,scaling)

Equivalent to **File Page Setup**. Use the first two forms to set the page for worksheets or macro sheets. Use the second two forms for charts. Arguments that correspond to a check box should use TRUE to select the check box and FALSE to deselect a box.

Argument	Use the argument...
head	Header as text enclosed in quotation marks
foot	Footer as text enclosed in quotation marks
left	Left margin number
right	Right margin number
top	Top margin number
bot	Bottom margin number
heading	TRUE to check Row & Column Headings box
grid	TRUE to check Gridlines box
h_center	Center Horizontally box
v_center	Center Vertically box
size	1 Screen Size (charts only)
	2 Fit to Page (charts only)
	3 Full Page (charts only)
orientation	1 Portrait
	2 Landscape
paper_size	1 Letter
	4 Ledger
	5 Legal
	20 Envelope #10
	(26 paper sizes are available)
scaling	TRUE to fit the print area to a single page or a number for the percentage of scaling. This argument is ignored if the printer is not capable of scaling.

PARSE(*text*)
PARSE?(*text*)

Equivalent to **Data Parse**. The text argument is the parse line in the dialog box in text form. Use the recorder to create this function within your macro. This function works on a selection of cells no more than one column wide.

PASTE( )

Equivalent to **Edit Paste**.

PASTE.LINK( )

Equivalent to **Edit Paste Link**.

 PASTE.PICTURE( )

Equivalent to the **Edit Paste Picture** command.

 PASTE.PICTURE.LINK( )

Equivalent to the **Edit Paste Picture Link** command.

PASTE.SPECIAL(*paste_num,operation_num,skip_blanks,transpose*)
PASTE.SPECIAL?(*paste_num,operation_num,skip_blanks,transpose*)

Equivalent to **Edit Paste Special**. Equivalent to the Paste Special dialog box when pasting into a worksheet or macro sheet. Use TRUE to select the *skip_blanks* and *transpose* options. The *paste_num* and *operation_num* options correspond to options in the dialog box.

paste_num	Option
1	All
2	Formulas
3	Values
4	Formats
5	Notes

operation_num	Option
1	None
2	Add
3	Subtract
4	Multiply
5	Divide

PASTE.SPECIAL(*rowcol,series,categories,replace*)
PASTE.SPECIAL?(*rowcol,series,categories,replace*)

Equivalent to **Edit Paste Special**. Equivalent to the Paste Special dialog box when pasting from a worksheet into a chart. Use a value of 1 for *rowcol* to be Rows, and 2 for Columns. For other arguments, use TRUE to enable the option.

PASTE.SPECIAL(*paste_num*)
PASTE.SPECIAL?(*paste_num*)

Equivalent to **Edit Paste Special**. Equivalent to the Paste Special dialog box when pasting from a chart into another chart. For the *paste_num* argument, use one of the following numbers:

Number	Items Pasted
1	All
2	Formats Only
3	Formulas Only

 PATTERNS( )

(Eight formats available.) Equivalent to **Format Patterns**. The PATTERNS macro function has eight forms depending on what has been selected. In general, review the dialog box for each type of selection. Then use numbers as argument values where the numbers begin with 1 for the first option and increase to the right or down. To see the available arguments, paste the macro function into your macro sheet with the Paste Arguments check box selected. Record this macro function and select the options you want to make changes or additions.

 PLACEMENT(*placement_type*)

Equivalent to **Format Object Placement**. The argument is one of three numbers corresponding to the placement of the check boxes from top to bottom.

POKE(*channel_num, item_text, data_ref*)

Uses the DDE channel specified by *channel_num* to send DDE data to *item_text* from the *data_ref*. Use INITIATE to open a channel to another WINDOWS application. INITIATE returns the *channel_num*.

PRECISION(*logical*)

Equivalent to **Options Calculation Precision as Displayed**. TRUE enables Precision as Displayed.

PREFERRED( )

Equivalent to **Gallery Preferred**.

 PRINT(*range_num, from, to, copies, draft, preview, print_what, color, feed*)
PRINT?(*range, from, to, copies, draft, preview, print_what, color, feed*)

Equivalent to **File Print**. Use the PRINT macro function to print the selected area.

Argument	Description
range_num	Page range

	1	Print all
	2	Print specified range

Argument	Description
from	First page if 2 chosen in *range_num*
to	Last page if 2 chosen in *range_num*
copies	Number of copies
draft	TRUE to select Draft Quality
preview	TRUE to preview the print
print_what	Indicates what should be printed

	1	Document
	2	Notes
	3	Both

Argument	Description
color	Not available in Windows
feed	Not available in Windows

 PRINT.PREVIEW( )

Equivalent to the **File Print Preview** command.

PRINTER.SETUP(*printer_text*)
PRINTER.SETUP?(*printer_text*)

Equivalent to **File Printer Setup**. Use the name of the printer (enclosed in quotation marks) as you see it in the Printer Setup dialog box.

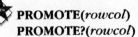 **PROMOTE(*rowcol*)**
PROMOTE?(*rowcol*)

Equivalent to selecting the promote button. Promotes the selected row or column.

rowcol	Action
1 or omitted	Promote rows
2	Promote columns

PROTECT.DOCUMENT(*contents,windows,password,objects***)**
PROTECT.DOCUMENT?(*contents,windows,password,objects***)**

Equivalent to **Options Chart Protect** Document. Use TRUE and FALSE to enable and disable the options that correspond to check boxes. *password* is a text password in quotation marks.

QUIT( )

Equivalent to **File Exit**. Quits Excel and displays a dialog box asking whether documents that have changed should be saved. You can use Quit in Auto_Close macros to close Excel when a document closes.

REFTEXT(*reference,a1*)

Converts the *reference* to an absolute reference in text form. Use REFTEXT to convert references returned by other functions into text that can be manipulated with text worksheet functions. Set a1 to TRUE for an A1 style reference. FALSE returns an R1C1 style.

 REGISTER(*module_text,procedure_text,type_text,function_text,argument_text***)**

Use with the CALL function. Because REGISTER can cause system errors, it should be used only by experienced programmers.

RELREF(*reference,rel_to_ref*)

Returns the relative location of *reference* with respect to *rel_to_ref*. The relative location is specified as text in R1C1 style, such as `R[-2]C[3]`.

REMOVE.PAGE.BREAK( )

Equivalent to **Options Remove Page Break**. No action is taken if the active cell is incorrectly positioned.

RENAME.COMMAND(*bar_num,menu,command,name_text*)

Renames the command or menu name specified by the argument command. *bar_num* is the number of the menu bar or the value returned by ADD.BAR. *menu* is the text name or number of the menu being affected. *command* is the text name or numeric position of the command being replaced. If *command* is 0, the menu name is replaced. *name_text* is the new name. Whenever possible, specify menu or commands as text rather than numbers because numeric positions may change.

REPLACE(*old_text,start_num,num_chars,new_text*)

Equivalent to REPLACE worksheet function.

REPLACE.FONT(*font_num*, *name_text*, *size_num*, *bold*, *italic*, *underline*, *strike*, *color*, *outline*, *shadow*)

Equivalent to Format Font command in Excel 2.1. Arguments are the same as the Font dialog box options. The *font* argument must be the number (from 1 to 4) of the font you want replaced. Use a *name_text* that matches an available font, such as "Courier". Use TRUE to enable.

REQUEST(*channel_num*, *item_text*)

Requests data associated with *item_text* over DDE link from the application specified by *channel_num*. REQUEST receives data as a data array.

RESTART(*level_num*)

Removes from stack *level_num* addresses for previous RETURN functions, causing a subroutine to return to a previous level of calling macro.

RESULT(*type_num*)

Used with a function macro to specify the type of data the macro returns to the worksheet. Use one of the following numbers as the *type_num* argument:

type_num	Data Type
1	Number
2	Text
4	Logical
8	Reference
16	Error
64	Array

The *type_num* can be the sum of other type numbers.

RETURN(*value*)

Stops execution of the macro if the macro has not been used as a subroutine. Control returns to whatever initiated the macro: another macro, or the keyboard if the user activated the macro. The *value* argument is the value or reference to a value that a function macro returns to the worksheet. See Chapters 28 and 29 for examples.

ROW.HEIGHT(*height_num*, *reference*, *standard_height*, *type_num*)
ROW.HEIGHT?(*height_num*, *reference*, *standard_height*, *type_num*)

Equivalent to Format Row Height. Rows specified by reference are changed to the height in points indicated by *height_num*. If you omit *reference*, the function uses the rows of the active cells. If you include the *reference* argument, it must be either an external reference to the active worksheet or an R1C1-style reference. Return to standard height rows by using a TRUE value for *standard_height*. The *type_num* argument is a number 1 to hide the row; 2 to unhide the row; and 3 to set the best fit.

 RUN(*reference,step*)
RUN?(*reference,step*)

Equivalent to **M**acro **R**un. The *reference* must be either an external reference to a macro or an R1C1-style reference in text form. When the *reference* is 1, all Auto_Open macros on the active sheet run. When *reference* is 2, all Auto_Close macros on the active sheet run. When step is TRUE, the macro runs in single-step mode.

SAVE( )

Equivalent to **F**ile **S**ave. Saves the active document under the last file name used.

 SAVE.AS(*document_text,type_num,prot_pwd,back_up,*
    write_res_pwd,read_only_rec)
SAVE.AS?(*document_text,type_num,prot_pwd,backup,*
    write_res_pwd,read_only_rec)

Equivalent to **F**ile **S**ave **A**s. Saves the active document under a new name or in a different format.

Argument	Description
document_text	Drive, path, and file name in quotation marks ("C:\EXCEL\FORCAST.XLS")
type_num	Saving format

1	Normal Excel format
2	SYLK
3	Text
4	WKS
5	WK1
6	CSV
7	DBF2
8	DBF3
9	DIF
10	Reserved
11	DBF4
12	Reserved
13	Reserved
14	Reserved
15	WK3

Argument	Description
	16 Excel 2.x
	17 Template
	18 Add-in macro
	19 Text (Macintosh)
	20 Text (Windows)
	21 Text (OS/2 or DOS)
	22 CSV (Macintosh)
	23 CSV (Windows)
	24 CSV (OS/2 or DOS)
	25 International macro
	26 International add-in macro
prot_pwd	Password in quotation marks
read_only_rec	Logical value specifies whether to save as read only recommended
write_res_pwd	Enables user to write to a file
backup	TRUE for a backup file

If your macro closes a worksheet that has had changes made to it, the operator will be prompted with a Save Changes dialog box asking whether changes should be saved. The prompt can interrupt an automatically running macro where you want to close sheets that have changed. To "clean up" a changed sheet so that it can be closed without the Save Changes dialog box, insert a SAVE.AS(,0) function before the closing function.

SAVE.WORKSPACE(*name_text***)**
SAVE.WORKSPACE?(*name_text***)**

Equivalent to File Save Workspace. Use a name enclosed in quotation marks for the workspace. Omitting the *name_text* saves the workspace as RESUME.XLW or the name of the last workspace document from the current session.

SCALE(*cross,cat_labels,cat_marks,between,max,reverse***)**
SCALE?(*cross,cat_labels,cat_marks,between,max,reverse***)**

(Form shown is for 2-D charts; five additional forms are available.) Equivalent to Format Scale. Use this function when the category axis is selected and the chart is not a scatter chart. The cross argument is the number of the category where the value axis should cross. *cat_labels* and *cat_marks* specify the number of categories between labels and marks, respectively. Use TRUE to enable options for the last three arguments.

SELECT(*selection,active_cell*)

Use this function with worksheets or macro sheets to select cells or change the active cell. The *selection* argument specifies the cells selected, and *active_cell* specifies which of those cells is active.

The selection should be either a reference to the active worksheet, such as !B3:C12, or an R1C1 style reference, such as `"R[3]C:R[5]C[4]"`. For example,

   =SELECT(,"RC[1]")

moves the active cell to the right, and

   =SELECT(!A1:ACTIVE.CELL( ))

selects the range on the active worksheet from A1 to the active cell. See Chapters 28, 29, 30, 31, and 32 for more examples.

 SELECT(*object_id_text,replace*)

Selects objects on a worksheet or macro sheet. Use a quoted text object name and number for the *object_id*. If replace is TRUE or omitted, only the named object is selected. If FALSE, existing selected objects also are selected.

SELECT(*item_text,single_point*)

This form of SELECT selects named items on a chart. An *item_text* must be enclosed in quotation marks. The text values understood for *item_text* are as follows:

   Chart
   Plot
   Legend
   Axis 1
   Axis 2
   Axis 3
   Axis 4
   Title
   Text Axis 1
   Text Axis 2
   Text Axis 3
   Text n (nth floating text)
   Arrow n (nth arrow)
   Gridline 1
   Gridline 2
   Gridline 3
   Gridline 4

Gridline 5

Gridline 6

Dropline 1

Dropline 2

Hiloline 1

Hiloline 2

Sn (entire series n)

SnPm (marker for point m in series n)

Text SnPm (text attached to point m in series n)

Text Sn (series title for series n)

Floor (base of 3D chart)

Walls (walls of 3D chart)

SELECT.CHART( )

This macro function is included for compatibility with Macintosh Excel and is the equivalent of the **Chart Select Chart** command.

SELECT.END(*direction_num*)

Moves the active cell in the direction indicated to the edge of the block. Similar to Ctrl+arrow. Use one of the following numbers for the *direction_num* argument:

direction_num	Direction
1	Left
2	Right
3	Up
4	Down

SELECT.LAST.CELL( )

Selects the cell at the lower right corner of the worksheet or macro sheet that is used or referred to.

SELECT.PLOT.AREA( )

Equivalent to **Chart Select Plot Area**. You also can use the SELECT("Plot") macro function.

SELECT.SPECIAL(*type_num,value_type,levels*)
SELECT.SPECIAL?(*type_num,value_type,levels*)

Equivalent to **Formula Select Special**. Use the following *type_num* values for SELECT.SPECIAL:

type_num	Description
1	Notes
2	Constants
3	Formulas
4	Blanks
5	Current region
6	Current array
7	Rowwise equivalents
8	Columnwise equivalents
9	Precedents
10	Dependents
11	Last cell
12	Visible cells in outline
13	All objects

If you specify a *type_num* of 2 or 3, you also must indicate the *value_type* as 1 for numbers, 2 for text, 4 for logicals, or 16 for error values. You can add *value_type* arguments together to select multiple types. When you specify a *type_num* of 9 or 10, select levels of 1 for direct only or 2 for all levels.

 SELECTION( )

Returns an external reference or object identifier of the current selection. Most macro functions use this reference as the value contained within the reference. If you want to work with the actual reference, use the REFTEXT function to convert the SELECTION reference to text. Returned values for objects are as follows:

Object	Returned Value
Imported graphic	Picture n
Linked graphic	Picture n
Chart picture	Picture n
Linked picture	Chart n
Worksheet range	Picture n
Linked worksheet range	Picture n
Text box	Text n
Button	Button n
Rectangle	Rectangle n
Oval	Oval n
Line	Line n
Arc	Arc n
Group	Group n

SEND.KEYS(*key_text*,*wait_logical*)

Transmits the keystrokes in *key_text* to the active Windows 2.0 application, just as though the keys were typed from the keyboard. The function enables you to control other Windows programs. Sends character keys such as "fas." Use the key codes in ON.KEY for additional codes. If *wait_logical* is TRUE, the macro waits while the keystrokes are processed. If FALSE or omitted, the macro continues.

 SEND.TO.BACK( )

Equivalent to the Format Send to Back command. Puts the selected object to the back.

SET.CRITERIA( )

Equivalent to Data Set Criteria.

SET.DATABASE( )

Equivalent to Data Set Database.

 SET.EXTRACT( )

Equivalent to Data Set Extract.

SET.NAME(*name_text*,*value*)

Defines the *name_text* on the macro sheet as a value. Omitting *value* deletes the name. Use SET.NAME to store values during macro operation. For example,

=SET.NAME("Rate",.12)

sets the name Rate equal to .12,

=SET.NAME("Print",B42:F54)

sets the name Print equal to the range B42:F54, and

=SET.NAME("Contents",DEREF(B16))

sets the name Contents equal to the value in cell B16. See Chapter 31 for examples of this function used with a dialog box.

SET.PAGE.BREAK( )

Equivalent to Options Set Page Break.

SET.PREFERRED( )

Equivalent to Gallery Set Preferred.

SET.PRINT.AREA( )

Equivalent to **O**ptions **S**et Print **A**rea.

SET.PRINT.TITLES( )

Equivalent to **O**ptions **S**et Print **T**itles.

 SET.UPDATE.STATUS(*link_text,status,type_of_link*)

Changes the update status to automatic or manual. *link_text* is the path name in quotation marks for the file you want to change. Use a status of 1 for automatic, 2 for manual. The *type_of_link* is 1 for not available; 2 for DDE; 3 for not available; and 4 for outgoing New Wave.

SET.VALUE(*reference,values*)

Changes the contents of the cells referred to by reference to values. If the cells contain formulas, they are not changed. Using this function is a good way to set up worksheets, dialog boxes, or data forms with initial values. For example,

> =SET.VALUE(B3,6)

puts the value 6 in B3. Worksheet ranges can be filled from arrays, as in the following example:

> =SET.VALUE(!A3:B5{2,3;4,5;6,7})

SHORT.MENUS(*logical*)

Equivalent to **O**ptions **S**hort **M**enus. When logical is TRUE or omitted, short menus are enabled.

SHOW.ACTIVE.CELL( )

Equivalent to Ctrl+Backspace. Moves the window to show the active cell.

SHOW.BAR(*bar_num*)

Displays the menu bar indicated by the ID *bar_num. bar_num* can be the ID of one of Excel's menu bars or the ID of a custom bar. A custom bar's ID is returned by the ADD.BAR macro function. See Chapter 31 for examples.

SHOW.CLIPBOARD( )

This function, which runs the clipboard, is included for compatibility with Macintosh Excel.

 SHOW.DETAIL(*rowcol,rowcol_num,expand*)

Expands or collapses detail in an outline. Use *rowcol* of 1 to affect rows; 2 to affect columns. *rowcol_num* is the number of the row or column you want to expand or collapse. You must use a number even if the worksheet is in A1 mode. Use ROW(ACTIVE.CELL( )) and COLUMN(ACTIVE.CELL( )) to determine the row or column number of the active cell. When expand is TRUE, details expand; when expand is FALSE or omitted, detail collapses.

SHOW.INFO(*logical*)

Equivalent to **W**indow **S**how **I**nfo/Document. TRUE for logical displays the Info window. If the Info window is already displayed, FALSE for logical activates the document for that Info window.

 ### SHOW.LEVELS(*row_level,col_level*)

Displays row or column levels in an outline. Numeric arguments specify the number of levels to display.

SIZE(*width,height,window_text*)

Equivalent to **D**ocument **C**ontrol **S**ize. The upper left corner of *window_text* stays fixed as the lower right corner adjusts to the requested width and height. The width and height are in points. Omitting *window_text* changes the size of the active window.

SORT(*sort_by,key1,order1,key2,order2,key3,order3*)
SORT?(*sort_by,key1,order1,key2,order2,key3,order3*)

Equivalent to **D**ata **S**ort. Use a *sort_by* of 1 to sort by rows, or 2 to sort by columns. Define the keys with an external reference in either style, with R1C1 style enclosed in quotation marks, or with a name enclosed in quotation marks. Enter 1 for ascending order or 2 for descending order.

SPLIT(*col_split,row_split*)

Equivalent to **W**indow **S**plit. The function puts a split through the window on the column or row indicated. Use the row or column number to specify the argument. The *col_split* argument splits the window into left and right, and *row_split* splits it into top and bottom. Enter a 0 for the split you want removed.

 ### STANDARD.FONT(*font_text,size_num,bold,italic,underline, strike,color,outline,shadow*)

Defines the Normal style for the active worksheet or macro sheet for previous versions of Excel. This function is included for compatibility. Use DEFINE.STYLE and APPLY.STYLE in Excel 3 for Windows.

STEP( )

Begins single-step operation through a macro. Helpful for troubleshooting. You can start single-stepping manually during macro operation by pressing the Esc key. Refer to Chapter 30 for more information on troubleshooting.

STYLE(*bold,italic*)
STYLE?(*bold,italic*)

This function is included for compatibility with Macintosh Excel. Use TRUE and FALSE to enable or disable the style on selected cells.

Subroutines
reference(*arg1,arg2,...*)

Subroutines act as subcontractors to perform tasks for the main macro. When a main macro reaches *reference*, it branches to the new macro at *reference* and begins operation at the upper left corner of *reference*. The argument *reference* can be either a cell reference or a name. You can use external references. When the subroutine macro is complete, a RETURN macro function at the end of it sends control back to the original macro. Subroutines can be either command or function macros. Command macros and function macros that are used solely as subroutines can accept arguments. Subroutines can have up to 14 arguments.

TABLE(*row_ref,column_ref*)
TABLE?(*row_ref,column_ref*)

Equivalent to **Data Table**. The *row_ref* argument specifies the row input, and *column_ref* specifies the column input. The references should be either external references, such as !$B$3 or QTR.XLS!$C$5, or R1C1 style references enclosed in quotation marks. You must select the table area before using the TABLE macro function.

TERMINATE(*channel_num*)

Closes DDE channels opened with the INITIATE macro function. Because some applications have a limited number of channels, you should close channels that are not in use. The *channel_num* is returned by the INITIATE function.

 TEXT.BOX(*add_text,object_id_text,start_num,num_chars*)

Updates the text contents of a text box. *add_text* is the text, in quotation marks, that you want to put in the box. The *object_id_text* is the quoted text and number describing the text box, such as "Text 5". *start_num* specifies the character position where text will start being replaced. If omitted, this is assumed to be 1. *num_char* is the number of characters to replace. If it is 0, there is no replacement; if omitted, all characters are replaced.

TEXTREF(*text,a1*)

Changes the argument *text* into a reference. Use this function to convert a text string into a reference that can be used by other functions. Use the function REFTEXT to change a reference into text that can be manipulated.

Use TRUE for a1 for an A1 style reference. FALSE or an omitted a1 argument produces R1C1 style.

UNDO( )

Equivalent to **Edit Undo**.

 UNGROUP( )

Equivalent to the **Format Ungroup** command. Select the group before issuing the command.

UNHIDE(*window_text*)

Equivalent to **Window Unhide**. The *window_text* argument names the window to be displayed.

UNLOCKED.NEXT( )
UNLOCKED.PREV( )

Equivalent to Tab or Shift+Tab, respectively. Moves active cell to the next or previous unlocked cell on a protected worksheet.

 UNREGISTER(*register_number*)

Removes previously registered dynamic link libraries.

 UPDATE.LINK(*link_text,type_of_link*)

Equivalent to choosing the **File Links** command and choosing the **Update** button to update from a selected file. *link_text* is the quoted text of the path for the link as shown in the File Links dialog box. Omitting *link_text* limits the update to links in the active document to other Excel documents. Use a *type_of_link* of 1 for an Excel link 2 for a DDE link, and 4 for a New Wave link. 3 is unavailable.

 VIEW.3D(*elevation,perspective,rotation,axes,height%*)
VIEW.3D?(*elevation,perspective,rotation,axes,height%*)

Equivalent to the **Format 3-D View** command and dialog box options.

VLINE(*number_rows*)

Scrolls the active window by rows. A positive *num_rows* scrolls down; a negative scrolls up.

 VOLATILE( )

Specifies that a function macro will recalculate whenever the worksheet recalculates. VOLATILE( ) must precede formulas in the function macro that you want to recalculate. If VOLATILE is not used, the function is recalculated only when one of its variables or terms changes.

VPAGE(*num_windows*)

Scrolls the active window vertically by the number of full screens specified by *num_windows*. A positive *num_windows* scrolls the window down; a negative scrolls the window up.

VSCROLL(*position,row_logical*)

Scrolls the active window vertically. When *row_logical* is TRUE, the window scrolls to the row specified in scroll. When *row_logical* is FALSE, the window scrolls a percentage of the entire window as indicated by the scroll argument. For example,

    VSCROLL(50,TRUE)

scrolls to row 50;

    =VSCROLL(.5)

scrolls to row 8192.

WAIT(*serial_number*)

Puts macro operation on hold until the time specified by *serial_number*. You can interrupt the WAIT by pressing Esc. To wait a specified period of time from the current time, use the NOW function plus the wait time as one of the time text formats Excel recognizes. For example, to put a macro on hold for 5 minutes, use the following format:

    =WAIT(NOW( )+"00:00:05")

WHILE(*logical_test*)

The WHILE function repeats formulas and functions between the WHILE and NEXT function "while" a test condition is TRUE. When the test condition becomes FALSE, the macro continues its operation at the first cell after the NEXT condition. Use a WHILE-NEXT loop when you are unsure of the number of times formulas and functions may need to repeat. Use a FOR-NEXT loop when you know the exact number of times you want certain formulas and functions repeated. The *logical_test* argument must be a value or formula that evaluates to a TRUE or FALSE result. A WHILE loop begins with a WHILE function and ends with a NEXT( ).

Figure 32.2 illustrates a WHILE-NEXT loop that repeats while increasing the number stored in Count. When the number stored in Count reaches five, the loop stops and the macro continues after the NEXT function. Each time through the loop the FORMULA function enters the number stored in Count in a cell offset from the active cell in the active worksheet or macro sheet. Because the offset changes depending upon the value stored in Count, each number is entered in a different cell. A WAIT function slows down the operation so that you can watch each repeated action.

	A
1	Put.Numbers
2	= SET.NAME("Count",0)
3	= WHILE(Count < 5)
4	= FORMULA(Count,OFFSET(ACTIVE.CELL(),Count,Count))
5	= WAIT(NOW() + "00:00:01")
6	= SET.NAME("Count",Count + 1)
7	= NEXT()
8	= RETURN()

Fig. 32.2. An example of a WHILE-NEXT loop.

The SET.NAME function in cell A2 stores the value 0 in the name Count. Notice that Count is enclosed in quotes when it is created by the SET.NAME function. Count stores a number that will be tested in the WHILE function. When the test returns FALSE, the WHILE loop will end.

The WHILE function in cell A3 tests to see if the value in Counter is less than 5. Because Count was initially set to zero in cell A2, the first time through, the macro passes the test and executes the functions in cells A4 and A5. (The spaces used to indent between the equal sign and the function name do not change the macro, but do make it easier to read what functions are within the WHILE-NEXT loop.)

The FORMULA function in cell A4 enters the value stored in Count into the cell referenced by the function,

    OFFSET(ACTIVE.CELL( ),Count,Count)

The cell referenced by this function is offset from the active cell by the number of rows and columns stored in Count. When you run the macro, you will see that as the value stored in Count changes, the cell where the number is entered also changes. Using OFFSET is much faster than first selecting a cell and then using FORMULA to enter a value in a worksheet. OFFSET is also an easy way to control data entered relative to a specific worksheet location. The use of OFFSET to enter data via a macro is described in Chapters 30 and 31.

The WAIT function pauses the macro by adding one second to the current time, NOW. This is used so that you can see the macro entering numbers more slowly.

The SET.NAME function adds 1 to the value stored in Count. This function increases Count so that it eventually reaches the value 5. Notice that the first argument, Count, is enclosed in quotes because the word Count is being redefined as a name in which to store variables. The second argument uses the existing name Count as a number in a math calculation, so it does not have Count in quotes.

Upon reaching the NEXT function, the macro returns to cell A3 and retests the value in Count. SET.NAME added 1 to the previous value in Count. The value is now 2, still less than 5, so the loop repeats. When the loop repeats enough that the value in Count reaches 5, the WHILE test returns FALSE, so the loop stops and the macro continues at the cell after the NEXT function. In this case, that next cell contains a RETURN function that ends the macro.

 WINDOWS(*type_num*)

Returns the names of all windows as a horizontal array of text values. The names are given in the order of the level on-screen. The *type_num* argument specifies the types of documents returned. 1 returns all windows (the default); 2 returns add-in documents only; and 3 returns all documents.

 WINDOW.INFO.DISPLAY(*cell,formula,value,format,protection, names,precedents,dependents,note*)

This function replicates Window Show Info, setting the Info menu and formatting the Info window. See also the DISPLAY functions.

 WORKGROUP(*name_array*)

Equivalent to the Window Workgroup command. Enclose the names in *name_array* in quotation marks and braces. Use the following format:

WORKGROUP({"FINANCE.XLS","AR.XLS"})

WORKSPACE(*fixed,decimals,r1c1,scroll,status,formula,menu_key, remote,entermove,underlines,tools,notes,nav_keys,menu_key_action*)
WORKSPACE?(*fixed,decimals,r1c1,scroll,status,formula,menu_key, remote,entermove,underlines,tools,notes,nav_keys,menu_key_action*)

Equivalent to Options Workspace. Arguments corresponding to options in the Workspace dialog box are enabled with TRUE and disabled with FALSE. The *underlines* option is available only with Macintosh Excel. *menu_key_action* should be 1 or omitted to activate Excel menus or 2 to activate Lotus 1-2-3 help.

From Here...

This directory of macro functions is intended to serve as a reference. The chapters in Part VI, "Advanced Techniques," serve as a resource for using Excel with DOS and Windows programs. Chapter 35 intoduces methods you can use to customize Excel for your needs.

Part VI

Advanced Techniques

Includes

Using Excel with Windows Programs

Using Excel with DOS Applications

Customizing Excel

Excel gains power from its synergy with other applications. Excel reads and writes files from major applications without your even knowing that a file conversion has taken place. You can also create Dynamic Data Exchange links between Excel and other Windows or OS/2 programs so that data passes between them. DDE makes programs work as though they were designed as one. Excel macros can even control other Windows and OS/2 programs. All these factors add together to produce an electronic worksheet that works in concert with other Windows, Presentation Manager, and even DOS programs.

In Chapter 33, "Using Excel with Windows Programs," you learn how easy it is to move data or charts between Excel and other Windows applications. For example, you can copy a chart or a portion of your worksheet with Excel's **Edit Copy** command, switch to a Windows or Presentation Manager word processing program, and choose the **Edit Paste** command to paste what you have copied into a report. You can even copy and paste charts. You will also see how to add graphic artist-level enhancements to Excel charts using CorelDRAW! and how to create quick training documents containing Excel screen shots using Word for Windows or Aldus PageMaker.

Chapter 34, "Using Excel with DOS Applications," shows you how to use Excel, Windows, and standard DOS programs together. Excel reads and writes many major DOS program files, such as 1-2-3 and dBASE, and different types of text files. You don't have to translate files; you just open them, work with them, and save them. Translations and conversions are all done transparently. Excel even saves files in the original format unless you tell it otherwise. Chapter 34 also describes how you can copy and paste screen data between Excel and standard DOS programs such as WordPerfect and 1-2-3.

Chapter 35, "Customizing Excel," describes ways you can increase the performance of Excel or customize Windows so that it works the way you want.

33

Using Excel with Windows Programs

E xcel is part of the new generation of software taking advantage of greater processor power and the new Windows software environment. This environment has a number of advantages when you are working with multiple programs:

- Easy learning: operating procedures in Windows, OS/2, and Macintosh programs are similar

- Capability to run multiple Windows and DOS programs

- Capability to cut and paste "static" information between Windows and DOS programs

- Capability to create "hot links" that pass live data between Windows or Presentation Manager programs

- Use of embedded objects that enable you to create a "compared document" composed of objects created in different Windows programs. You then can edit each object by using the program that originally created it

In this chapter, you learn how to use some of these features to enhance and extend the capabilities of Excel. You will see how to perform the following operations:

- Link Excel charts and tables into Word for Windows documents so that you can use Excel results in your word processing documents

- Exchange graphics with CorelDRAW! so that you can add special graphic effects to Excel charts or use CorelDRAW! art in your Excel worksheets and charts

- Embed Excel worksheets and charts into PowerPoint so that you easily can update your PowerPoint presentations

- Copy Excel screen shots into PageMaker or Word for Windows to make instant documentation or training aids

This chapter first presents the general concepts of how to use Excel with other Windows programs. The chapter then describes examples using specific Windows programs.

Transferring Information through the Windows Clipboard

Using Excel with Windows is like having a large integrated software system, even if the programs come from different vendors. With the Windows clipboard, you can cut or copy information from one Windows or DOS program and paste it into another. Chapter 34, "Using Excel with DOS Programs," explains the many ways to exchange Excel data and charts with common DOS programs. The Appendix lists some of the widely used Windows programs that relate to Excel and its use. A large catalog of Windows products is included in Que's *Using Microsoft Windows 3*.

Copying and Pasting Text between Windows Programs

To copy or cut text information from Excel and paste it into another Windows program such as Word for Windows (the Windows word processing program), follow these steps:

1. Select the range of cells that you want to transfer, and then choose the Edit Copy or Edit Cut command.

2. Activate the Windows program into which you want to paste the information by pressing Alt+Tab until the program appears or by pressing Ctrl+Esc to display the Task List. Then double-click on the Windows program, or select the program and press Enter. (If the Windows program is not running, activate the Program Manager and start Word for Windows.)

3. Move the insertion point to the location in the program where you want to insert the Excel data.

4. Choose the Edit Paste command for the receiving Windows program.

The Excel data pastes into the receiving program. The data is not linked back to Excel. Refer to "Linking Data between Programs with DDE," later in this chapter for information on linking.

Transferring an Excel Chart to Another Windows Program

You can capture an entire Excel chart, a "bit-mapped picture" of a worksheet range, or an image of the screen and paste it into other Windows programs, such as Aldus PageMaker (a page layout program), Word for Windows (a word processing program), or CorelDRAW! (a professional art package).

To copy an Excel chart into another program, follow these steps:

1. Activate the Excel chart that you want to copy.

2. Select the entire chart by clicking on the chart background or by choosing the Chart Select Chart command.

3. Activate the other Windows program.

4. Choose that program's Edit Paste or Edit Paste Link command. (Programs that do not have DDE linking capability do not have an Edit Paste Link command.)

Capturing a screen image (screen shot) can be valuable for technical documentation or training materials. If you do not have a Windows program for documents, such as Aldus PageMaker or Word for Windows, you can create short training or technical documents with Excel. Paste screen shots into Excel worksheets, and then use Excel text boxes or word-wrapped text in cells to create multicolumn text descriptions.

To capture an image of an entire Windows or Excel screen that you can paste into Windows programs, follow these steps:

1. Prepare the Windows or Excel screen the way you want it to appear in the screen shot.

2. Press the Print Screen key to copy a bit-map of the screen image into the clipboard. On computers with older ROM BIOS, you may need to press the Alt+Print Screen key combination. The Print Screen key may be shown on the key cap as PrtScrn. This keystroke may not work on Toshiba portables.

3. Activate the Windows program into which you want to paste. The program must be capable of accepting graphics from the clipboard.

4. Choose the Edit Paste command. The image now becomes an object that you can format or manipulate in the receiving program.

To copy a portion of the worksheet rather than the entire screen as a bit-mapped image that acts like a graphic, follow these steps:

1. Select the worksheet range that you want to copy.

2. Hold down the Shift key and choose the Edit Copy Picture command. (This command appears on the Edit menu only when you hold down the Shift key as you select the menu.)

3. Select the As Shown when Printed option if you want to paste into another Windows program.

4. Activate the other Windows program.

5. Select where you want the graphic image of the worksheet range, and then choose that program's Edit Paste command.

Linking Data between Programs with DDE

Many Windows programs can communicate with each other via Dynamic Data Exchange (DDE). Through DDE, a Windows program can send or receive data to other DDE-capable Windows programs.

DDE takes place in two ways: linking Excel to other programs using a remote reference formula (much as you link Excel worksheets and charts together by using external references) or using macros to control DDE. You can type a remote reference formula into a cell if you know the correct syntax, or you can paste the formula into a cell by using the Edit Paste Link command.

In DDE, there are clients and servers. A *client* receives the data sent by the *server.* Excel can act as both a client and a server and can handle multiple clients and multiple servers.

Linking Excel to Other Windows Programs

Excel can receive data from other Windows programs through DDE "hot links" to other DDE Windows programs. As data in the server program changes, the data in Excel (the client) can update automatically. Applications in which this feature is important include tracking prices in stock transactions, continuous monitoring of manufacturing line inventory, and analyzing laboratory data that is read from monitors.

DDE links also can update under manual control. This usually is done in most business situations if you need to update data in a worksheet or update a link between Excel and a word processor such as Word for Windows.

You can create DDE links through the menu, through typed formulas that duplicate the external reference formula created by the menu, or through macros. DDE control through the use of macros is beyond the scope of this book.

Excel can create DDE links through its Copy and Paste Link commands if the other Windows program also has DDE commands available on the menu. In this case, creating DDE links is no more difficult than linking two worksheets.

Follow these steps to link Excel to another DDE-capable Windows program:

1. Open Excel and the other Windows program. Activate the Windows program that will send information—the server.

2. Select the text, cell, range, value, graphic object, or data fields that you want to link.

3. Choose the Edit Copy command.

4. Activate the other Windows program and select where you want the linked data to appear.

5. Choose the Edit Paste Link command or its equivalent. You may be given a choice as to whether the linked data should update automatically or only when you manually request an update. Windows programs will operate faster if you use manually updated DDE links.

Note: *When You Can't Paste Links into Excel*
The server program may not support DDE through a Paste Link command. If Excel's Edit Paste Link command is not available (shown in gray) in the receiving program after you copy data from another Windows program, the program from which you copied does not support DDE through menus; you cannot paste the link into Excel.

Turning Excel DDE Links On and Off

If you want Excel to use the last worksheet values it received and not request remote reference updates from other programs, choose the **Options Calculation** command and deselect the Update **R**emote References option. (You can put the remote reference links back in effect by selecting the Update **R**emote Reference option.)

Excel can send information via DDE to other Windows programs just as it can initiate information requests. You can turn off Excel's capability to pass data to other programs by choosing the **Options Workspace** command and then selecting the **I**gnore Remote Requests option. To enable remote requests and allow information to pass out of Excel, deselect the **I**gnore Remote Requests option.

Linking Charts and Tables to Word for Windows

Excel and Word for Windows work side by side to create documents that combine the table and chart capabilities of Excel with the text-manipulation and layout features of a powerful word processor. Word for Windows' menus and commands are so similar to Excel's that you can start working within the hour that you install the program. Word for Windows' ribbon and ruler at the top of the screen are similar to Excel's tool bar, so you can do most of the formatting without using menu commands.

One of the advantages of using Word for Windows with Excel is the capability of Word for Windows to incorporate Excel charts and worksheets in text documents. You can paste in this incorporated data as unlinked items or link the items back to the original Excel documents. Linking to the Excel document enables you to easily update the Word document.

Pasting Unlinked Worksheet Data

To paste unlinked Excel worksheet data into Word for Windows and create a table, follow these steps:

1. Select the range in the Excel worksheet that you want to transfer.

2. Choose the **Edit Copy** command in Excel.

3. Activate Word for Windows and the document you want to paste into. Move the insertion point to where you want the table to appear.

4. Choose the **Edit Paste** command in Word for Windows.

As figure 33.1 shows, the Excel range becomes a table when pasted into Word for Windows. Character, border formatting, and column widths are preserved. The information in this table is not linked to the Excel worksheet. Each cell from the worksheet becomes a cell in the Word for Windows table.

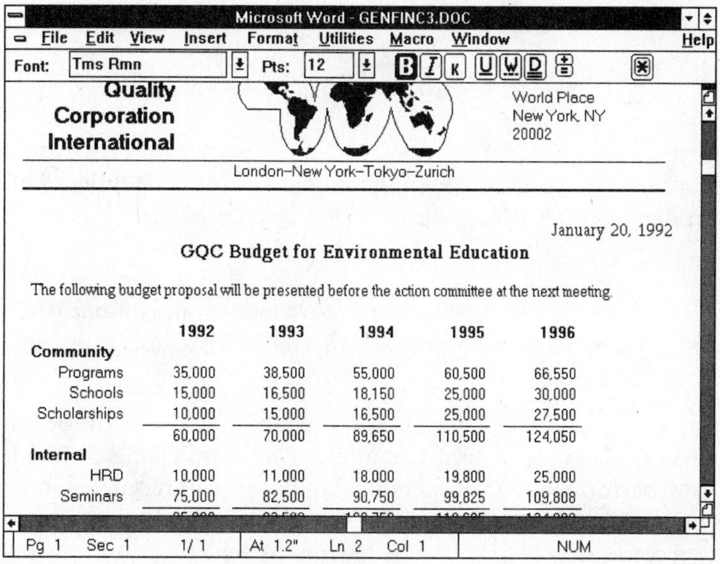

Fig. 33.1. *Data pasted from Excel into Word for Windows becomes a table.*

Pasting Linked Worksheet Data

To link an Excel worksheet range in a Word for Windows document, follow these steps:

1. Select the range in the Excel worksheet.

2. Choose the Edit Copy command in Excel.

3. Activate Word for Windows and the document that you want to paste into. Move the insertion point to where you want the data to appear.

4. Choose the Edit Paste Link command in Word for Windows. The Paste Link dialog box appears (see fig. 33.2).

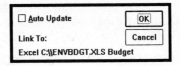

Fig. 33.2. The Paste Link dialog box.

5. Select the Auto Update check box if you want Excel data to update automatically the document when data changes. Deselect Auto Update if you want to specify when updates occur.

6. Choose OK or press Enter.

A range from Excel linked to a Word for Windows document (the one in figure 33.1, for example) also appears in a table. This table is linked back to the Excel range.

If you select the Auto Update option, the table in the Word for Windows document updates whenever data in the worksheet changes. This form of link slows performance and is needed only by systems requiring continuous updates. For most business applications, deselect the Auto Update option. You then can update the Excel table in Word by selecting the entire table and pressing the F9 key.

When you paste the linked data into Word for Windows, you actually insert a hidden field code in the document that looks similar to the following code:

```
{DDE  Excel  C:\\FINANCE\\  R5C2:R15C6  \*  mergeformat}
```

If you select automatic updating, the field code uses DDEAUTO. To see the code behind the table, select the entire table. Then press Shift-F9 or choose the View Preferences command and select the Show All * option.

> **Tip:** *Preserving Links When You Reorganize*
> Links are easier to maintain if you edit the Excel range in Word's
> field code. You can change the range R5C2:R15C6, for example, to
> an Excel range name that defines the same cells, such as BUDGET.
> Using named Excel ranges in the links enables you to rearrange the
> Excel worksheet and still preserve the link to Word.

Including a Worksheet File

You can include a disk-based worksheet file or range from a file in a Word
for Windows document without opening Excel. Position the insertion point
in the Word document, and then choose the **Insert File** command. Change
the file specification in the Insert File **Name** box to *.XLS and press Enter to
see the worksheet names. Select the worksheet file from the **Files** list and
type a range name into the **Range** box if you are importing a range. If you
want the Word document to maintain a permanent link to the Excel
worksheet, select the **Link** check box. After you press Enter, you are asked
to select from a list the type of file that you want to convert. Select the BIFF
format to convert the Excel file. This command inserts an {INCLUDE} field
code into the Word document that reads, converts, and imports the portion
of the Excel sheet that you want. If you select the Link option, you can update
the document whenever you want by selecting all the imported data and
pressing the F9 key or by choosing the Utilities Calculate command.

Pasting an Excel Chart into Word for Windows

To paste or link an Excel chart into a Word for Windows document, follow
these steps:

1. Save the Excel chart in the directory where you expect it to remain.

2. Choose the **C**hart Select **C**hart command.

3. Choose the **E**dit **C**opy command.

4. Activate the Word for Windows document and position the
   insertion point where you want the chart to appear.

5. Choose the **E**dit **P**aste command to paste a picture of the chart.

Choose the Edit Paste Link command to paste a picture that is linked to the worksheet.

6. If you choose Paste Link, select the Auto Update check box if you want the document to update whenever the chart changes. Deselect the Auto Update check box if you want to update the document only when you request.

7. Use Word for Windows techniques to move, resize, and format the chart within the document. If the frame enclosing the chart is too large to grab a right edge for resizing, choose the Format Picture command and set the height and width in the Scaling group to 50 percent. You then should be able to see and grab the chart's scaling handles.

Figure 33.3 shows a linked chart within a Word for Windows document. Pasting a chart with a link into Word for Windows creates a field code that appears like this:

```
{DDEAUTO Excel D:\\FINANCE\\FORCAST.XLC Chart \* mergeformat}
```

If you did not select the Auto Update check box, you can update the linked chart by selecting it and then pressing the F9 key to calculate.

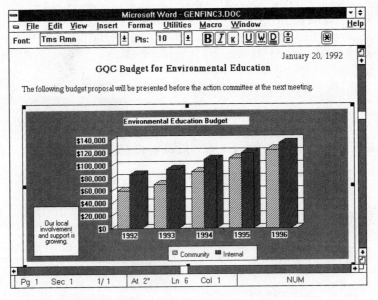

Fig. 33.3. *Link Excel charts into Word for Windows documents.*

Tip: *Preventing Size Changes in Word*

Resizing a chart's window in Excel changes the size and cropping you may have performed on the chart in Word for Windows. The chart in Word changes size the next time its link is updated. To prevent this size change, activate the chart in Excel and choose the **Chart Protect** Document command with the **W**indows check box selected. You do not need to enter a password. This procedure locks the size and position of the chart window and prevents it from changing in Excel. This procedure prevents the linked chart in Word for Windows from changing.

Exchanging and Enhancing Graphics with CorelDRAW!

CorelDRAW! is a drawing and graphics-design Windows program with the capabilities needed for professional graphic arts. It comes with 150 type styles from 56 type families that work with LaserJet and PostScript printers. The program also includes more than 3,000 symbols and a library of more than 750 pieces of clip art that you can copy, modify, and reuse in your own documents. It includes extensive capabilities to manipulate curves, fill objects or backgrounds with graduated shading, and use custom or Pantone colors.

CorelDRAW! works well with Excel for two reasons. First, although Excel creates impressive charts by itself, CorelDRAW! gives you significantly more power to modify and enhance Excel charts. (CorelDRAW! does not support DDE links.) You can add graphic details necessary for advertisements, brochures, or high-quality sales presentations. Second, you can draw pictures or cut clip art from CorelDRAW! and paste those pictures into Excel worksheets. This enables you to add logos to sheets or create picture charts with such images as stacked airplanes, trucks, or dollars. When you want to extend the chart or graphics capabilities of Excel, consider a Windows program like CorelDRAW!.

Copying an Excel Chart to CorelDRAW!

To copy an Excel chart into CorelDRAW!, follow these steps:

1. Activate Excel and the chart document. Choose the Chart Select Chart command.

2. Choose the Edit Copy command.

3. Activate CorelDRAW! and open a new or an old document.

4. Choose the Edit Paste command to paste the Excel chart into CorelDRAW!. Figure 33.4 shows an Excel chart pasted into CorelDRAW!

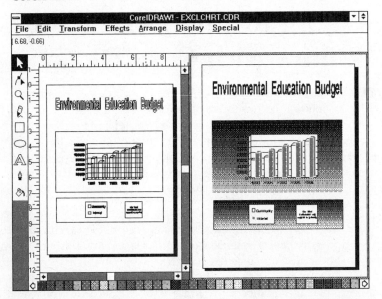

Fig. 33.4. *Modify Excel charts using the professional graphics capabilities of CorelDRAW!.*

5. Select any object within the chart, such as a part of the logo, lines, bars, and so on, and then color or modify the object.

Add color or gradient backgrounds or include logos or drawings with the chart. Use the extensive fonts available with CorelDRAW! to extend the font selection available in your printer.

Pieces of the Excel chart become individual objects when pasted into CorelDRAW!. Clicking on a bar, for example, reveals that the bar is an individual graphic object that now can be moved, sized, colored, formatted and distorted independently from the rest of the chart. You even can use CorelDRAW! to do four-color separations required by printers for color charts, annual reports, or business proposals.

Copying a CorelDRAW! Picture to Excel

CorelDRAW! also is an excellent tool for creating original art for use in your Excel worksheets or charts. You can copy from the extensive library of clip art that comes free with CorelDRAW!. You also can do freehand drawing or modify scanned images with CorelDRAW!. You then can copy these pictures from CorelDRAW! and paste them into Excel worksheets or charts.

To copy a picture from CorelDRAW! and paste it into Excel, follow these steps:

1. Select the graphic objects in CorelDRAW!.

2. Choose the Edit Copy command.

3. Activate Excel and the worksheet or chart into which you want to paste the artwork.

4. If you are pasting into a worksheet, select the cell at the upper left corner of where you want to place the artwork. If you are pasting artwork into a chart to be used as a chart marker, select the 2-D bar, column, or line where you want to place the marker.

5. Choose the Edit Paste command.

Figure 33.5 shows an Excel worksheet that has a CorelDRAW! figure pasted in as a logo. Figure 33.6 shows an Excel 2-D column chart using stacked pictures pasted from CorelDRAW!.

To learn more about graphic objects in worksheets, read Chapter 9, "Drawing and Placing Graphics in Worksheets." To learn more about creating picture charts like the ones in figures 33.5 and 33.6, read Chapter 19, "Formatting Charts."

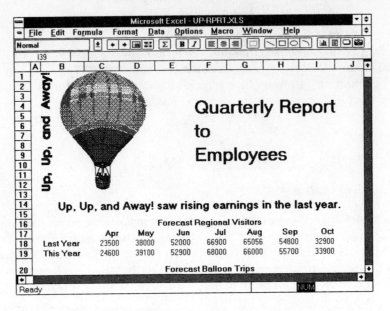

Fig. 33.5. Include your company's logo or artwork on your worksheets.

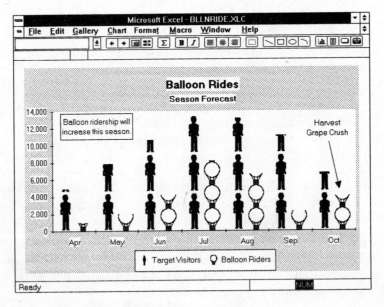

Fig. 33.6. Use figures drawn in CorelDRAW! to enliven your Excel charts.

❖ Embedding Excel Charts and Tables in PowerPoint

Microsoft PowerPoint is designed to help you plan, compose, and create presentations. With PowerPoint you can create and organize presentations for 35mm slides, overhead transparencies, or personal computer projectors, as well as print audience handouts and speaker's notes.

PowerPoint and Excel are the first two Windows programs to include the power of embedded objects. An *embedded object* is an object, such as an Excel chart, embedded into another program's document, such as a PowerPoint presentation. The object carries with it all the information needed so that you can open and edit the object using the original program's menus and commands. In the following sections you learn how to embed a chart from Excel into a PowerPoint presentation. When you need to make a change to the chart while in PowerPoint, you need only to double-click on the chart in the PowerPoint slide. This opens and activates Excel and loads the chart so that you can edit or reformat it using normal Excel procedures. After you close the chart window in Excel, you return to PowerPoint, and the updated chart appears in the slide. Excel worksheets also can be embedded in PowerPoint slides with the same process.

Embedding an Excel Chart into PowerPoint

To embed an Excel chart into a PowerPoint slide, follow these steps:

1. Activate Microsoft PowerPoint, open the presentation file, and move to the slide where you want to embed an Excel chart. Figure 33.7 shows a blank PowerPoint slide.

2. Choose the File Insert Excel Chart command (Insert is a cascading menu).

   Excel starts and activates. A PowerPoint chart document opens in Excel, as shown in figure 33.8.

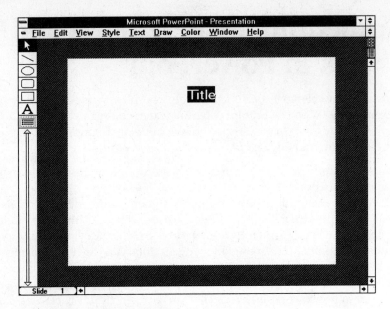

Fig. 33.7. A blank PowerPoint slide.

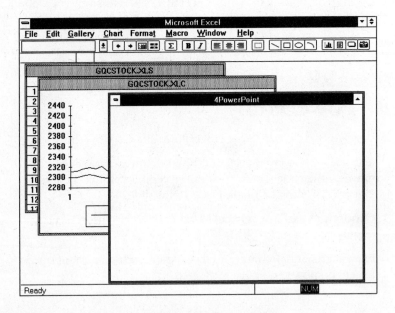

Fig. 33.8. The blank PowerPoint chart window in Excel.

3. From the Excel menus, choose the File Open command to open a chart, or choose the Window menu and activate an open chart.

4. Choose the Edit Copy command from the Excel menu to copy the Excel chart.

5. Activate the PowerPoint chart window in Excel by clicking on it or by choosing it from the Window menu.

6. Choose the Edit Paste command from Excel's menu to paste the Excel chart into the PowerPoint chart window.

7. Close the PowerPoint document by choosing the File Close command or pressing Ctrl+F4.

PowerPoint reactivates, and the chart you created appears in the PowerPoint slide (see fig. 33.9). You can format, size, and move the chart as you would other objects in PowerPoint.

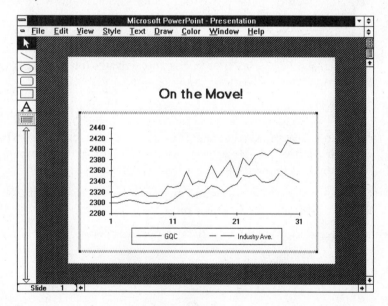

Fig. 33.9. This Excel chart is embedded into a PowerPoint slide.

The embedded PowerPoint chart refers to the same worksheet from which the chart received its data. The embedded chart does not refer to the chart that was copied. If you change the worksheet, the PowerPoint chart can be updated, but if you change the chart (outside of Powerpoint), the PowerPoint chart is not updated.

You also can create a chart in the PowerPoint chart window while in Excel without using an Excel chart as an intermediate step. To do this, open an Excel worksheet in step 3 and then select a valid worksheet range that will create a chart. Copy the range with the **Edit Copy** command, switch to the PowerPoint chart document, and choose the **Edit Paste** command. Format the new chart. Close the PowerPoint document as described in step 7.

Editing an Embedded Chart or Worksheet in PowerPoint

To edit an embedded chart or worksheet (object) in PowerPoint, follow these steps:

1. Activate PowerPoint and move to the slide containing the embedded object (chart or worksheet).

2. Double-click on the embedded object.

   Excel activates if it is open or opens and activates if it is closed. The PowerPoint chart or worksheet appears in a document window.

3. Edit the PowerPoint object by using normal Excel commands. To open a worksheet linked to the chart, choose Excel's **File Links** command, select the worksheet from the **Links** list, and then press Enter or choose OK. (PowerPoint's embedded object remembers where the data came from, just as Excel's charts remember.)

4. Choose the **File Close** command or press Ctrl+F4 to close the PowerPoint document in Excel and return to PowerPoint.

The updated or reformatted Excel chart or worksheet appears in its slide in PowerPoint.

Copying Excel Screen Shots into PageMaker

Aldus PageMaker was one of the first powerful programs written for Windows. It brought the power of extremely expensive typesetting and page layout systems to personal computers at an affordable price. PageMaker is designed to produce text-oriented materials that require graphics features beyond the ability of word processors. In PageMaker, you can mix text and graphics in any arrangement. The program's powers include the capability to place multicolumn formats on the same page; to insert, move, size, and crop graphics; to wrap text around graphics or text callouts; and to output to typesetting equipment.

By using Aldus PageMaker, you can create training or technical documents with Excel (or other Windows programs) by capturing an image of the current Windows screen, a *screen shot*, and then pasting that screen shot into the PageMaker document. You also can paste screen shots into many other Windows programs.

To capture the screen shot of any Windows program and paste it into Aldus PageMaker, Word for Windows, Windows Paintbrush, or an Excel worksheet, follow these steps:

1. Open the Windows program, such as PageMaker, into which you will paste the screen shot. Load the document that will receive the screen shot.

2. Activate Excel or another Windows program for which you need a screen shot. Display on-screen the subjects you want to capture in the screen shot.

3. Press the Print Screen key. On some computers you may need to press Alt+Print Screen. (These key combinations may not work on Toshiba portables.) This loads a bit-mapped image of the screen into the clipboard.

4. Activate the Windows program that will receive the screen shot by pressing Alt+Tab until the program is active or by pressing Ctrl+Esc and selecting the program from the Task List.

   PageMaker receives the image as a "floating object," which you can move to any location. Position the insertion point in Word for Windows or select a cell in Excel.

5. Choose the Edit Paste command.

Figure 33.10 shows an Excel screen shot pasted into the top of a training document in PageMaker. After you paste the screen shot, you can move, resize, crop, or format it by using the commands available in Aldus PageMaker, Word for Windows, or Excel.

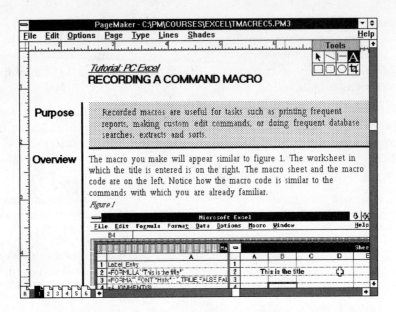

Fig. 33.10. *You can take screen shots directly from within Windows and paste them into most Windows programs that accept graphics.*

From Here...

Two of the great powers of the Windows environment are the capability to switch between programs and to transfer data easily between programs. Another advantage of Windows programs is that their menus and operating procedures operate in the same way. In the previous examples you can see how many commands—such as **Edit Copy** and **Edit Paste**—are similar between programs. In fact, many Windows programs operate so similarly that you often can perform simple tasks without training or opening the manual.

More than 400 programs are designed to take advantage of Windows 3. You can take advantage of this power by sharing data and skills between programs. The appendix lists the programs described in this chapter and others that integrate well with Word for Windows.

34

Using Excel with DOS Applications

I f you use DOS applications, such as dBASE II, dBASE III, Paradox, Lotus 1-2-3, Multiplan, WordPerfect, or Microsoft Word, sharing information with Excel will be easy for you. Excel also simplifies the exchange of ASCII files with mainframes.

Excel loads and saves many file formats, such as dBASE, Lotus 1-2-3, and Multiplan. Also, Excel loads or creates text files for information transfer with applications such as Quicken that do not use one of the common formats as an interchange. (Lotus 1-2-3 compatibility and data exchange are discussed in Chapter 5, "Making the Switch from 1-2-3 to Excel." For information on using Windows applications with Excel, refer to Chapter 33.)

Switching between DOS Programs

Windows enables you to load more than one DOS or Windows program at a time. If you are running Windows on a 386 computer with more than 2M of memory, the computer will continue to run DOS programs even when the programs are in the *background*, or not active. On a 286 computer or in Windows 3 Standard mode, DOS programs are put on hold when they are not in the *foreground*, or active.

To switch between programs that are loaded, hold down the Alt key as you press Tab. Continue to press Tab while holding down the Alt key until you see the title bar of the program you want, and then release both keys.

To see a list of the programs that are loaded and to select the program you want to switch to, press Ctrl+Esc. The Task List that appears shows you all the programs that are loaded. Double-click on the program you want to activate; or press the up- or down-arrow keys to select a program, and then press Enter.

If you are running Windows in 386 Enhanced mode, you can run DOS programs either full-screen or in a window. To switch the active DOS program between full-screen or window, press Alt+Enter.

Copying and Pasting between DOS Programs and Excel

You can copy and paste text and numbers between DOS programs (like those mentioned earlier) and Excel. You can perform this task with Windows in either Standard or 386 Enhanced mode.

Copying and Pasting in Standard Mode

When Windows runs in Standard mode, the mode for 286 computers, DOS programs must run full-screen. Therefore, you must copy an entire screen of text from DOS programs to paste into Excel. You can, however, paste selected data from Excel into DOS programs.

If you are running Windows with the minimum memory configuration of 1M, you may not be able to run a DOS program with Excel and copy and paste between the DOS program and Excel. If this is the case, you may have to add extended memory.

To copy from a full-screen DOS program when in Standard mode and paste into Excel, follow these steps:

1. Activate the DOS program and position the screen to show the data that you want.

2. Press the Print Screen key. On PCs with older ROM BIOS, you may need to press Alt+Print Screen.

3. Switch to Excel by pressing Ctrl+Esc to display the Task List. If Excel is running, select it from the list, and then press Enter. If Excel is not running, select the Program Manager, and then press Enter so that you can start Excel.

4. Select the cell in which you want the first line from the program screen.

5. Choose the **E**dit **P**aste command.

Excel places each line of text or numbers into separate cells underneath the cell that you select in step 4. A line of data is not separated into individual cells.

Remove unwanted data with Excel's editing or clearing techniques. Separate lines of data into separate cells using the parsing technique described in this chapter under "Parsing Long Text Lines into Cells."

To copy selected data from Excel and paste into a DOS program, follow these steps:

1. Select the cell or range in Excel.

2. Choose the **E**dit **C**opy command.

3. Switch to the DOS program by pressing Ctrl+Esc and selecting the program from the Task List.

4. Position the DOS program's typing cursor where you want to paste the Excel data.

5. Reduce the DOS program to an icon by pressing Alt+Esc. Continue to press Alt+Esc until you see the DOS icon selected on the Windows desktop in the lower left corner.

6. Press Alt+space bar to display the icon's pop-up menu, and then choose the **E**dit **P**aste command. The program will reactivate to full screen and paste the data at the location you selected in step 4.

You must paste data into Lotus 1-2-3 one cell at a time. Pasted lines of data end with a carriage return. Therefore, when you copy multiple lines of data and paste them into Lotus 1-2-3, all lines of data are pasted into the same cell. Programs such as WordPerfect move the cursor to the next line when they receive a carriage return. Lotus 1-2-3, however, enters the data in the cell and waits for more data. The next line of data is entered into the same cell on top of the first line.

Copying and Pasting in 386 Enhanced Mode

When Windows is in 386 Enhanced mode, you can run DOS programs full-screen or in a window. DOS programs in a window can be moved on-screen in the same way that true Windows programs can. DOS programs in a window operate with the same commands and display that the programs use when running under DOS. While you run DOS programs in a window, you can copy selected text or numbers from a DOS program screen and switch to another DOS or Windows program to paste the selected copy in.

To copy from a DOS program and paste into Excel, follow these steps:

1. If the program is not in a window, press Alt+Enter or Alt+space bar.

2. Select the data that you want copied by dragging across it with the mouse.

   If you are using a keyboard, press Alt+space bar; then select the Edit Mark command, press the movement keys to move to the corner of the data you want to select, and then press Shift+arrow keys to select the data. Press Alt+space bar again and select the Edit Copy command.

3. Switch to Excel by pressing Alt+Esc to display the Task List. If Excel is running, select it from the list, and then press Enter. If Excel is not running, select the Program Manager and press Enter so that you can start Excel.

4. Select the cell where you want to paste a single cell or a column of data.

5. Choose the Edit Paste command.

When you copy numbers from a DOS program into Excel, copy a single number or column of numbers at one time. The number or column will paste into a single cell or a column of cells. If you copy entire lines, the numbers will not separate for pasting into individual cells. (Long lines of data can be passed into cells using the technique described in the "Passing Long Text Lines into Cells" section of this chapter.)

To copy data from Excel and paste it into a DOS program, follow these steps:

1. Select the cell or range that you want to copy in Excel.

2. Choose the Edit Copy command.

3. Switch to the DOS program.

4. Position the cursor where you want the data.

5. Press Alt +space bar and select the Edit Paste command.

Data will enter the DOS program just as though you had typed it. Excel puts a tab between each cell's contents, which makes tables of data easy to align when pasted into a word processor. All you need to do is set the tabs for the area that contains Excel data so that the columns of data align. Use right or decimal alignment tabs for the best alignment of numbers.

Importing and Exporting Data and Charts Using Files

Excel can share its data and charts with other programs. When you need to transfer information between Excel and another program, you will export data from Excel to a file that the other program can read, or you will import data from the other program in a file that Excel can read. Excel reads and writes many other program file formats automatically.

Reviewing File Formats Used by Excel

Excel imports (reads) and exports (writes) many file formats used by other DOS, Macintosh, and mainframe programs. If no specific file format is available to transfer information directly, you can create a text file format that will transfer text and numbers.

The file formats that Excel can read and write are listed in table 34.1.

Table 34.1
File Formats Read by Excel

File Format	File Extension	Description
Excel 2.X	XLS	Excel 2.X
Text	TXT	Text: tabs separate cells of data; rows end with a carriage return. ANSI text for Windows; ASCII text for OS/2; Text for Macintosh.
CSV	CSV	Comma Separated Values: data is separated by commas. Text is enclosed in quotation marks ("*text*"). Numbers containing commas are enclosed in quotation marks ("*number1,number2*").
WKS	WKS	1-2-3 Release 1, 1A, and Symphony; Microsoft Works.
WK1	WK1	1-2-3 Release 2x
WK3	WK3	1-2-3 Release 3
DIF	DIF	Data Interchange Format: common low-level worksheet format (VisiCalc).
DBF 2	DBF	dBASE II
DBF 3	DBF	dBASE III.X
DBF 4	DBF	dBASE IV.X
SYLK	SLK	Symbolic Link: Multiplan, Microsoft Works.

If you are unsure of the appearance of a CSV or text file, create an Excel worksheet and save it with CSV and text file formats. Use a word processor such as the Windows Notepad to see how Excel encloses data in tabs, commas, and quotes.

If you need to export an Excel chart to a program that does not use the Windows clipboard, you can save the chart to an HPGL file (Hewlett-Packard Graphics Language). The section "Transferring Excel Charts in HPGL Format" in this chapter demonstrates how to save a chart to an HPGL file.

Exporting Data to DOS or Mainframe Programs

You can export data to many DOS or mainframe programs by saving the file in one of the many formats that Excel saves. Most DOS or mainframe applications can then translate from one of these formats into their own formats. You can use the formats from table 34.1 to exchange data between Excel and programs as small as Quicken's check register or as large as Cullinet mainframe accounting software.

To save Excel worksheets in another format, follow these steps:

1. Choose the File Save As command. Type the file name in the text box, but do not add a file extension. Do not press Enter.

2. Choose the Options button. The dialog box expands, as shown in figure 34.1.

Fig. 34.1. The Save Options dialog box enables you to save to different file formats.

3. Select from the File Format list the format in which you want to save. Table 34.1 lists these formats and their descriptions.

4. Choose OK or press Enter.

Exporting Text Files for Word Processing and Database Programs

Text files are standard media for importing new information into word processing and database programs. Saving an Excel worksheet as a text file enables you to retrieve the worksheet in your word processing program, and then include it in a report. Using a text file to pass a worksheet to a word processing program allows you to pass multiple pages. (Copying and pasting, as described at the beginning of this chapter, are limited to what is on-screen.)

When sending Excel information to a mainframe or database program, use a file format such as DIF, WK1, or DBF if the program understands one of those formats. If the program does not, use Excel's CSV format. Most database and mainframe programs can read CSV formatted text.

Transferring Files to Macintosh Excel

Newer Macintosh computers are able to read and write Windows Excel files directly from an MS-DOS disk. For older Macintosh computers, you will need to transfer the data between computers. Transfer between computers is done with a null-modem serial cable (a non-normal serial cable) and a Macintosh-to-PC communication program. A number of good programs accomplish this transfer. Because many of these programs also convert and translate programs, you may be able to leave your Excel file in its native XLS format and let the transfer software do any necessary file conversions.

If the dates are four years off after importing from or exporting to the Macintosh Excel worksheet, change Excel's date system with **Options Calculation** and select or deselect the 1904 **D**ate System as necessary.

Importing Excel Data to WordPerfect 5.1

Excel worksheets or ranges can be read directly into some programs such as WordPerfect. Instead of using a file format as an intermediary, WordPerfect (and some other word processors) has the capability to read data directly from the Excel worksheet on disk. If your version of WordPerfect does not have a file converter for Excel 3, save your Excel 3 document with an Excel 2.X format.

To import Excel data into a WordPerfect 5.1 file, follow these steps:

1. Position the cursor in your WordPerfect file where you want the data to appear.

2. Press Ctrl +F5 . Select **S** preadsheet (5).

3. Choose **I** mport.

4. Choose **F** ilename (1) and type in the full path name and file name.

5. Choose Range (2) and enter the range of data or range name. If you do not specify a range or a range name, the entire file is brought in.

6. Choose Type (3) and select either Table (1) or Text (2). You may need to reformat fonts and columns in tables in order to fit the data on the page.

7. Choose Perform Import (4).

Transferring Excel Charts in HPGL Format

Excel can export its charts to a file that can be read and imported by many DOS programs. Excel charts are "printed" to disk in an HPGL format by sending the information normally sent to an HP plotter to a disk file.

Before you can perform this procedure, you must have an Excel plotter driver installed in Windows with the plotter configured to a port called File. To install an HP plotter, press Alt+space bar from Excel. Choose the Run command, and then select the Control Panel option. When the Control Panel appears, press F1 for help on how to run the printer installation program. Install an HP plotter and configure it on the port named File. Choose the Setup button and deselect the Draft option. Plotter information will be sent to a file.

To save an Excel chart to disk, follow these steps:

1. Activate the Excel chart and set the page setup with the headers, footers, and margins you want.

2. Choose File Printer Setup, select HP Plotter on File, and choose OK.

3. Choose the File Print command and press Enter. You will be prompted for a file name. Enter the name with an HPGL file extension so that it is easy to find, and then press Enter.

The HPGL file saves to the current Excel directory.

To import the Excel chart you saved as an HPGL file into WordPerfect 5.1, follow these steps:

1. Position the WordPerfect cursor where you want the chart.

2. Press Alt+F9, and then choose Figure (1).

3. Choose Create (1).

4. Choose Filename (1) and type the full path name and file name of the chart.

5. Choose Edit (9) to see and rotate the chart.

WordPerfect displays the chart as a line box in the document. To see the chart as it will appear when printed, press Shift+F7, 6 to view the document.

Importing Data from DOS or Mainframe Programs

Excel can import (read) data files directly from DOS or mainframe programs that are in a specific format. Table 34.1 lists these formats. If your program cannot save files in one of these formats, you can save the data to a text file. Excel can read three different types of text files: CSV (comma separated values), TXT (tab separated values), and column-delimited text (values defined by their column positions).

To open a file from one of the programs Excel recognizes, follow these steps:

1. Choose the File Open command.

2. Change the file extension in the File Name text box from *.XL* to *.*, and then press Enter.

3. Select the file that you want to open. The file should be one of the file types described earlier that Excel recognizes. (A column-delimited text file can use any file extension.)

4. Choose OK or press Enter.

The file will open into a new worksheet.

When Excel loads a non-Excel file, Excel remembers the format the file came from. Unless you specify otherwise, Excel saves the file back to that same format. Saving to a non-Excel format can result in the loss of formulas, functions, special features, and formatting. If you want to save the opened file in an Excel format, choose the File Save As command, choose the Options button, and then select the Normal format from the File Format list. Next choose OK, enter a name, and choose OK again. (Normal is the Excel 3.0 format.)

> **Note: *Extracting Selective Information from Files***
> If you need to read selective information from an Excel, dBASE, or text file that is laid out in a row and column database format, you may want to use Q+E. With Q+E you can extract selective information from large files that remain on disk. Q+E is described in Chapter 26.

Importing Text Files into Excel

Use text files to pass data when Excel cannot read a program's file format. Most programs can save or print data to a text file and specify how that text file is laid out. For information on how to perform this task in your DOS or mainframe program, check the index of your program's manual under the headings "ASCII," "ANSI," "report generator," "text file," or "printing to disk."

Excel imports three types of text files: CSV, text, and column-delimited. Excel will automatically separate data fields from CSV and text files into cells. Each row of data will read into an Excel row. Each comma-separated or tab-separated segment of data will appear in its own cell.

To see how to format a text or CSV file, create an Excel worksheet with sample data in cells. Save that worksheet using the **File Save As** command, choose the **Options** button, and select the Text or CSV format from the **File Format** list. Now use Windows Notepad or a word processor to examine that file and see how commas, quotes, or tabs are placed around data. When you create a text or CSV file, use commas, tabs, and quotes in the same way.

The third type of text file that Excel will read is known as a column-delimited text file. Each data field is assigned to specific character locations in a line of text. For example, first names may be stored from position 1 to 12, last names from position 13 to 25, and so on. Unused positions are filled with space characters. Use the **Data Parse** command to separate lines of data into cells according to each cell's range of column positions. Refer to the "Parsing Long Text Lines into Cells" section in this chapter for a description of this command.

You can see, edit, print, and save text files by opening them with the Windows Notepad. Windows Notepad saves its files back into text format.

To open a text file into Excel, follow these steps:

1. Choose the **File Open** command.

2. Choose the Text button to display the Text file dialog box (see fig. 34.2).

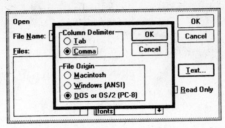

Fig. 34.2. Set the type of text file you are opening in the Text file dialog box.

3. In the Column Delimiter box, select Tab if your data is separated by tabs; select Comma if your data is separated by commas.

4. Select the type of program or system from which the data came. Select Macintosh, Windows, or DOS or OS/2 to tell Excel the type of character set being used. Windows programs use ANSI; DOS and OS/2 programs use PC–8; and Macintosh programs use Text.

5. Choose OK.

6. Select the file that you want to open and choose OK or press Enter.

If the file has a TXT or CSV file extension and is in the format described in table 34.1, you do not have to tell Excel the format as described in steps 3 and 4. If the file does not separate into individual cells, the file may be column-delimited or you may have selected the wrong type of column delimiter. If you need to separate data fields from a long line of text into individual cells, read the section "Parsing Long Text Lines into Cells."

Reading Quicken Data into Excel

Quicken is a popular check register and money manager program that runs in DOS. Although Quicken does not save a file directly to Excel format, it is easy to send any of Quicken's financial and budget reports to a text file that Excel will import. You can use this method with many DOS-based accounting programs.

To create a text file from Quicken, follow these steps:

1. Activate Quicken and open the account you want to work with.

2. Select the type of report that you want to print either from the Main menu (3 Reports) or from the register (F5 - Reports). Enter the requested printing data, such as titles, date range, and filter.

3. Choose F8 to print. Select the printing option for Disk (1-2-3 File). Although this option says 1-2-3 File, it is actually a CSV file.

4. When prompted for the file name, enter the path name and file name. If no path name is used, the file saves to the current Quicken directory. Use any file extension.

To open the Quicken report into Excel, follow these steps:

1. Choose the File Open command from Excel, type *.* in the File Name box, and choose OK or press Enter. Change to the directory containing the Quicken CSV file. Select the file.

   If you used a CSV or TXT extension on the file, Excel recognizes the file and separates the values into cells. If you used a different file extension, follow steps 2 and 3 to tell Excel the type of text file.

2. Choose the Text box from the File Open dialog box.

3. Select the Comma Column Delimiter and the DOS File Origin. (Quicken is a DOS program.)

4. Choose OK twice to open the file into a new worksheet.

The Quicken report will enter into a new worksheet with data in separate cells. If necessary, widen column widths to see the data.

Parsing Long Text Lines into Cells

Column-delimited text files load into a new worksheet in column A. Each row of the text file enters a cell in column A. Each entire row is in a cell of column A. Data is not separated into cells. To separate these long lines into cells you must *parse*, or segment, them.

Before you can parse a long line of text, you need to tell Excel where to divide the text lines. Square brackets are used around data in a sample line to show Excel where data should be segmented. You can type these square brackets into a sample line yourself or let Excel guess where to put the brackets, and then edit Excel's guess as necessary. The sample line used for these brackets appears in the Data Parse dialog box (see fig. 34.4).

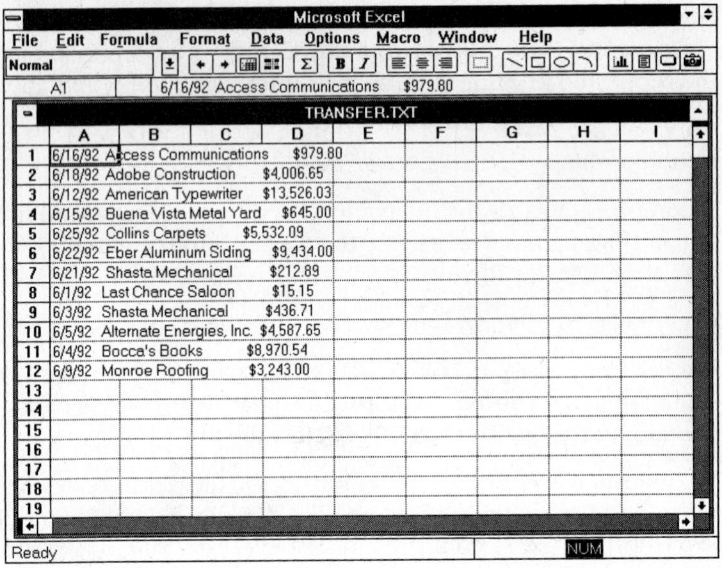

Fig. 34.3. *Excel uses the first line of text as a sample for how to parse (divide) the line into cells.*

To parse the column of text shown in figure 34.3, follow these steps:

1. Open the text file, and then use the File Save As command with the Options button to save the file in Normal format so that it will be in Excel format.

2. Select column A and format it with a nonproportional font, such as Courier or Line Printer, enabling you to see how data aligns in columns. Make sure that there are sufficient blank columns to the right of column A to hold the data after parsing. Parsed data will overwrite cells to the right.

3. Select the cells in column A that you want to parse. Excel will use the text in the first cell you select as the sample line that determines how all selected lines will be parsed. If the column positions vary throughout the file, you may need to divide the files into rows with similar column positions and parse each of these groups separately.

4. Choose the Data Parse command. The Parse dialog box displays the first selected row and shows a ruler of character positions (see fig. 34.4).

5. Choose the Guess button. Excel puts square brackets around the data in the first line to show you how it thinks you want the data parsed.

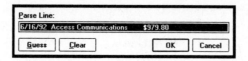

Fig. 34.4. The Parse dialog box.

6. Enter or edit square brackets ([]) as you would edit in the formula bar. Enclose data that you want in a cell within square brackets.

7. Choose OK or press Enter.

The square brackets define the left and right edges of what will be placed in separate cells. Use the left and right arrows, the left and right square bracket keys, Del, and Backspace to edit the **Parse** Line. Using the arrow keys, move to the extreme right in the parse box to see the full line of data. Excel beeps if you attempt to delete a character or space.

Make sure that the brackets are wide enough to include the full width of all characters in a field of data. For example, after selecting the **Guess** button, brackets appear around the first dollar amount as [$979.80]. Leaving this field with only seven characters between the brackets will leave out the leading parts of large numbers, such as $13,526.50. The brackets must be edited to allow for three more leading spaces, as shown in figure 34.5.

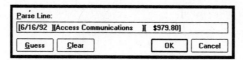

Fig. 34.5. Edit the Parse Line to show Excel how you want text lines divided into cells.

Figure 34.5 shows the right portion of the **Parse** Line dialog box set for a correct parse. Notice how the brackets are placed back-to-back (][) to ensure that all data is included. You can skip data by not including its character positions within brackets.

Figure 34.6 shows the results of the parse in the selected range. The data in each line has been segmented into cells. Columns have been widened after parsing to show the full cell's content.

Always cross-check the serial date numbers between different programs; some programs use different starting dates in the century. As a result, all dates may be offset by a corresponding amount. To correct this problem, follow these steps:

1. Insert a new column (B).

2. Fill the new column with a formula that adds the necessary number of days to the imported dates in the original column (A). (For example, if the imported dates in column A are offset by one day, insert a blank column B and fill it with a formula such as =A1+1.)

3. Format column B to appear as dates.

4. Change the formulas in column B to values by copying the dates, and then paste over the original column B using Edit Paste Special with the Values option selected.

5. Delete the original column A.

	A	B	C	D	E	F	G
1	6/16/92	Access Communications	$979.80				
2	6/18/92	Adobe Construction	$4,006.65				
3	6/12/92	American Typewriter	$13,526.03				
4	6/15/92	Buena Vista Metal Yard	$645.00				
5	6/25/92	Collins Carpets	$5,532.09				
6	6/22/92	Eber Aluminum Siding	$9,434.00				
7	6/21/92	Shasta Mechanical	$212.89				
8	6/1/92	Last Chance Saloon	$15.15				
9	6/3/92	Shasta Mechanical	$436.71				
10	6/5/92	Alternate Energies, Inc.	$4,587.65				
11	6/4/92	Bocca's Books	$8,970.54				
12	6/9/92	Monroe Roofing	$3,243.00				
13							
14							
15							
16							
17							
18							
19							

Fig. 34.6. *Parsing divides a long line of text into cells.*

From Here...

Using Windows 3 and Excel with your existing DOS programs offers many advantages. Excel coexists well with character-based systems such as WordPerfect and Lotus 1-2-3. Excel can read files from programs such as dBASE to do charting and analysis—tasks that are impossible or difficult in dBASE. And if dBASE files are too large to fit into a worksheet, you can link Excel to the dBASE files on disk using Q+E, a free program that comes with Excel. Many corporations maintain corporate and division sales, marketing, and financial data on their mainframe computers, and then download the data as text files to Excel for analysis, charting, and reports.

Customizing Excel

E xcel by itself is the best computerized worksheet available. With Windows, Excel is even more powerful and versatile. You can customize both Excel and Windows to fit your workplace and style. In this chapter, you learn how to access Excel customization features, change the colors and backgrounds used by Windows, use international character sets in your worksheets, and even change how the mouse operates.

Customizing Features in Excel

This chapter describes ways of customizing Excel that have not yet been covered in this book. You might want to go back and explore previously discussed topics. The following features and topics are covered in other chapters:

- *Ten-key accounting pad.* Use the **Options Workspace** command with the **Fixed Decimal** option so that you can type numbers on the numeric pad and have the decimal automatically entered.

- *Automatic rounding of formatted numbers.* Use the **Options Calculation** command with the **Precision as Displayed** option to make Excel calculate with the formatted number you see on-screen.

- *Worksheet templates.* Create templates for tasks that you perform frequently. Templates are quick to get to in the **File Open** box and can be set up with the macros and workspace settings needed for specific jobs.

- *File loading on start-up.* Load worksheets, charts, and macros on start-up by storing them in the XLSTART directory. When you use the same tools and add-ins frequently, this setup enables you to get to your work quickly and easily.

- *Add-in macros.* Create macros that are invisible when opened and act like built-in Excel features.

- *Function macros.* Create predefined functions that act the same as built-in worksheet functions.

- *Custom menus.* Use custom menu bars, menus, and commands to change the control system of Excel completely. You use macros to change the menu structure.

- *Custom dialog boxes.* Use the Dialog Editor to draw custom dialog boxes; then display those boxes and retrieve information from them under macro control.

- *Worksheet background colors.* Use the **Options Display** command to change gridline and heading colors.

- *Workspace tools.* Use the **Options Workspace** command to add or remove workspace tools, such as the formula bar, tool bar, scrolling bars, status bars, and so on.

- *Hidden elements.* Use the **Windows Hide** command to hide worksheets, charts, and macro sheets. Use the **Format Cell** Protection command to hide cell contents from the formula bar.

- *Protection.* Use the **Options Protect** Document command to protect worksheets from being opened without a password. Use a Read-Only specification to protect worksheets from being written over.

Creating Your Own Colors

Excel has a palette of 16 colors available for your use in worksheet and chart patterns. Although this palette is filled with a standardized set of colors when you get Excel, you can change the palette to use 16 colors that you choose. After you define a set of colors, you can copy those colors to other worksheets or save a worksheet as a template so that you can reuse the palette.

If you have a monochrome video driver installed, your colors appear in color lists as color names. You are not able to edit the colors in the palette.

Be careful! Before you change colors on the palette, realize that your changes may affect objects you have already colored. For example, if you have created a text box with the fourth color on the palette as the background color, changing the fourth color on the palette also changes the background color of your text box.

To choose your own colors for the color palette, follow these steps:

1. Open the worksheet or chart on which you want custom colors.

2. Choose the Options Color Palette command for worksheets or Chart Color Palette for charts. Figure 35.1 shows the color palette with names. On a color monitor, you can see the actual colors.

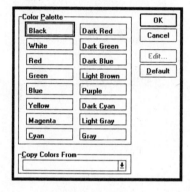

Fig. 35.1. *The color palette contains 16 colors that you can change.*

3. Select on the palette the color you want to change. Click on that color box, or press the arrow keys to select the color.

4. Choose the Edit button to display the Color Edit box shown in figure 35.2. (The Edit button is unavailable if you are using a monochrome monitor; you cannot change colors on a mono- chrome screen.)

5. Select the new color you want for the selection you made in step 3:

 Click in the large box on the color you want. To change the lumi- nance, drag the pointer up or down along the right column. Watch the sample color in the Color/Solid box below the large box.

 Choose mixtures of red, green, and blue. To mix these colors, select the Red, Green, and Blue boxes and enter a number from 0 to 255; 255 represents the greatest amount of the color. To change the hue of a color, select Hue and enter a number from 0 to 239; in the large box, 0 hue is the color at the left edge and 239 hue is the color at the right edge. Use the same method to change the saturation (Sat); 0 saturation is the color at the bottom edge of the large box and 240 saturation is the color at the top edge. To change the luminance (Lum), enter a number from 0 to 240; 240 is the maximum luminance at the top of the right column.

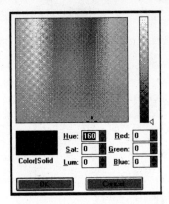

Fig. 35.2. Choose a custom color for the new color on your palette.

6. Choose OK or press Enter.

7. Choose OK or press Enter to accept your color change.

If you want to return the palette to its original set of 16 colors, choose the **Options** (or **Chart**) **Color Palette** command. Then choose the **Default** button.

When you copy a colored object from one document to another, the object carries with it the palette number of its color. When the object is pasted into the new document, the object uses the color assigned to that number on the palette of the new document. In other words, objects may change color when copied between documents that have different palettes.

If you want to copy the color palette from one document to another, follow these steps:

1. Open both the document from which you want to copy and the document to which you are copying. Activate the document that should receive the new palette.

2. Choose the **Options Color Palette** command (or **Chart Color Palette** for charts).

3. In the Copy Colors From list box, select the name of the document from which you are copying colors.

4. Choose OK or press Enter.

Colored objects in the document receiving the new palette change to reflect the new palette.

Customizing Excel with the Control Panel

You can customize Excel's features and appearance with the Control Panel. The Control Panel runs from Excel or from the Windows Program Manager. In the Control Panel, you can set the computer's date and time, install or delete printers and fonts, change colors used in Windows borders and backgrounds, select international date and currency formats, and more.

For information on how to use customizing programs found in the Control Panel, activate the Control Panel window—even if you are already in a customizing program such as the Color dialog box. Press F1 or choose the **Help Index** command. To display the topic you want information about, click on the appropriate underlined name; or press Tab to select the name, and then press Enter.

To start the Control Panel from the Program Manager, do the following:

1. Activate the Main group window in the Program Manager by pressing Ctrl+F6, clicking on the Main group window, or double-clicking on its icon. The Main window is shown in figure 35.3.

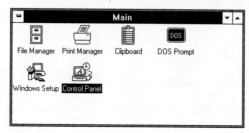

Fig. 35.3. *The Main group window contains the Control Panel program item.*

2. Choose the Control Panel icon to start the Control Panel. Double-click on the icon; or press the arrow keys to select the Control Panel, and then press Enter. Figure 35.4 shows the open Control Panel.

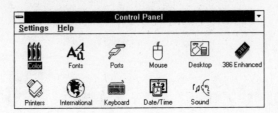

Fig. 35.4. The Control Panel contains utilities that customize Windows.

To start the Control Panel from within Excel, do the following:

1. Activate the Excel Control menu by pressing Alt+ space bar or by clicking on the Excel Control menu icon to the far left of the Excel title bar.

2. Choose the Run command. The Run Application dialog box appears, as shown in figure 35.5.

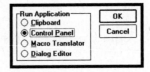

Fig. 35.5. The Run Application dialog box enables you to run four programs from within Excel.

3. Select the Control Panel option, and choose OK or press Enter. The Control Panel window appears (see fig. 35.4).

Changing the Screen Appearance

You can change the color or gray scale for most portions of the Excel screen. You can select from predefined color combinations or create your own color combinations for different screen parts in Windows and Windows programs. To choose from the predefined color combinations, follow these steps:

1. Choose the Color icon from the Control Panel by double-clicking on the icon or pressing the arrow keys to select the color and then pressing Enter. Figure 35.6 shows the Color dialog box.

2. Select Color Schemes, and select a color combination from the pull-down list. Figure 35.7 shows some of the names of color combinations.

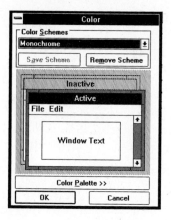

Fig. 35.6. *Choose predefined or custom colors for screen elements from the Color dialog box.*

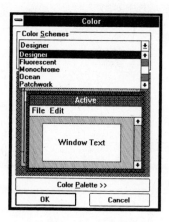

Fig. 35.7. *Choose a predefined color combination for window screen elements.*

3. Check the appearance of this color combination in the sample window in the Color dialog box. Select a different color to fit your mood or environment. Monochrome is best for monochrome screens. The default Windows color combination has the name Windows Default.

4. Choose OK or press Enter to accept the new colors.

Changing the Pattern and Wallpaper behind Windows

All Windows programs and the Program Manager reside on a desktop. You can customize Windows to show the patterns or pictures you want on this desktop. Excel comes with a number of patterns and pictures you can use; or you can draw your own desktop background pictures, using the Windows Paintbrush program that comes free with Windows.

To change the pattern or *wallpaper* (desktop background) do the following:

1. Choose the Desktop icon from the Control Panel by double-clicking on the icon or pressing the arrow keys to select the icon and then pressing Enter. Figure 35.8 shows the Desktop dialog box that appears.

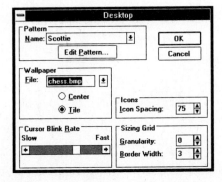

Fig. 35.8. Choose the background (wallpaper) you want from the Desktop dialog box.

2. Select Name and select a pattern from the pull-down list. Patterns are two-color patterns that fill the background behind a Window.

   OR

   Select File and select a wallpaper (picture) from the pull-down list. Wallpapers are pictures or digitized images stored in a BMP (bit-map) file.

3. Choose OK or press Enter.

If the wallpaper is centered on-screen and does not fill the screen background, repeat the preceding steps and choose the Tile option. This option repeats the bit-mapped image to fill the screen. Figures 35.9 and 35.10 show two of the wallpapers that come with Windows.

Fig. 35.9. *The Chess wallpaper is one of the wallpapers you can use behind Windows programs.*

Fig. 35.10. *The Ribbons wallpaper is one of the more carefree-looking Windows wallpapers.*

You can create your own wallpapers by drawing pictures in the Windows Paintbrush accessory and saving the picture to the Windows directory with the BMP format. Reopen the Desktop dialog box, and your drawing is one of the listed wallpapers.

Changing Mouse Speed and Button Selection

Typically, only one button on the mouse is used—normally the left button. If you are left-handed and want the right button to work instead, you can use the Control Panel to switch. You also can use the Control Panel to control the rate of motion and the click speed for the mouse. To start the Mouse program, double-click on the Mouse icon on the Control Panel; or press the arrow keys until the icon is selected, and then press Enter. Figure 35.11 shows the Mouse dialog box that appears.

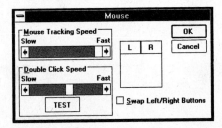

Fig. 35.11. You can change mouse performance with the Mouse dialog box.

Adjust how quickly the mouse moves across the screen by selecting the Mouse Tracking Speed scroll bar and dragging the scroll box to the Slow or Fast side. If you are a Windows beginner, you may want to start on the Slow side.

Adjust how quickly you must press the mouse buttons for a double-click by selecting Double Click Speed and dragging the scroll box to the Slow or Fast side. Use a slower rate if you are new to Windows. Test the double-click rate by double-clicking on the TEST square. The TEST square changes color when it recognizes a double-click.

If you want to swap the active mouse button to the right side, select the Swap Left/Right Buttons check box.

Changing International Character Sets

When you work in Windows, you can switch among different international character sets, time and date displays, and numeric formats. The international settings you choose show up in new formatting within your Excel worksheets. For example, the Format Numbers list shows number and date/time formats for the country you have selected.

To specify the international settings you want to use, choose the International icon from the Control Panel by double-clicking on the icon or by pressing the arrow keys to select the icon and then pressing Enter. Figure 35.12 shows the International dialog box from which you can select country, language, date, currency, and other formats. Windows may need your original installation disks to change some settings.

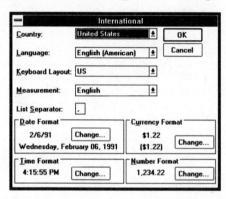

Fig. 35.12. Select the international formatting options you need from the International dialog box.

Select from the Country, Language, and Keyboard Layout lists the format you need to use. Review the contents of the format text boxes in the lower part of the dialog box to ensure that they show the format you want.

> **Tip: *Changing Individual Country Settings***
> If you need country settings that are not in the Country or Language lists, select each formatting group, choose the Change button, and make changes to individual formats as needed. (Select Change buttons from the keyboard by tabbing to them and then pressing the space bar.)

Defining a New Start-Up Directory

When Excel starts, it opens all files found in the XLSTART subdirectory. This feature is useful for automatically starting templates, macro-driven applications, and macro add-ins. If you want a separate start-up directory, either for temporary working files or as a private start-up directory on a network, follow these steps to specify one additional start-up directory:

1. With the File Manager, create the directory you want to use as a start-up directory.

2. Activate Excel and choose the File Open command.

3. Select the ALTSTART.XLA add-in macro from the LIBRARY directory. The LIBRARY directory is a subdirectory under the directory containing EXCEL.EXE.

4. Type in the text box the path name of the directory you want as an additional start-up directory.

5. Choose OK or press Enter.

From Here...

Windows and Excel are flexible work environments that make customizing your workspace easy. By changing some features, you can modify Windows and Excel to suit your needs and comfort level. You can create your own color palettes, change the screen colors and patterns, control the mouse operation and speed, change the international character set, and add start-up directories. Take advantage of Windows by setting it up the way you want it.

Excel Support and Add-Ins

This directory represents only some of the products and resources designed to work with Excel. However, the directory will give you an idea of the many available products and services.

Resources, Consulting, and Support

CompuServe

CompuServe
5000 Arlington Centre Boulevard
P.O. Box 20212
Columbus, OH 43220
800-848-8199

CompuServe is an on-line database containing databases, data files, and question and answer forums on hundreds of topics and industries. CompuServe contains multiple forums and libraries of macros and data available for Excel and other Windows applications. To access the many Windows forums and libraries, type **GO MSOFT** at any menu prompt. To directly access the Excel forums and libraries, type **GO MSEXCEL** at any menu prompt.

Microsoft Corporation   Microsoft Corporation
One Microsoft Way
Redmond, WA 98052-6399
800-426-9400 nontechnical
206-454-2030 Excel technical;
6AM-6PM, M-F, Pacific time zone

Microsoft maintains a telephone support line for technical questions on Windows, Excel, and Word for Windows.

Que Corporation   Que Corporation
11711 N. College Avenue
Carmel, IN 46032
317-573-2500
800-428-5331 outside Indiana

Que Corporation is the leading publisher of computer books in the world. Other books available on Windows topics include *Using Microsoft Windows 3*, 2nd Ed., *Windows 3 QuickStart*, *Using Word for Windows*, and many more. Call Que for a free catalog. Corporate and volume discounts are available.

Ron Person & Co.   Ron Person & Co.
P.O. Box 5647
Santa Rosa, CA 95402
415-989-7508
707-539-1525

Ron Person & Co., based in San Francisco, is one of 14 firms that have attained Microsoft's highest rating for Excel consultants, Microsoft Consulting Partner. The firm is also a Microsoft Registered Developer for Excel and Word for Windows. In addition to consulting, Ron Person & Co. delivers training and licenses training materials to corporate clients in Windows, Excel, and Word for Windows.

Windows Applications

Access for Windows   Eicon Technology Corporation
2196 32nd Avenue
Montreal, Quebec H8T 3H7
Canada
514-631-2592

Eicon Technology provides Windows compatible communication for micro-to-mainframe, micro-to-mini, and LAN-to-LAN. Access for Windows is a 3270 emulation package that runs under Windows.

Amí Pro   Lotus Development Corporation
Word Processing Division
5600 Glenridge Drive
Atlanta, GA 30342
404-851-0007

Amí Pro is a professional level word processor that works well with Excel. Amí Pro includes tools for drawing over documents.

BrainCel®   Promised Land Technologies, Inc.
900 Chapel Street, Suite 300
New Haven, CT 06510
203-562-7335

BrainCel gives Excel worksheets the pattern recognition and forecasting capabilities of neural network software. BrainCel is taught using real data and real outcomes that you enter into Excel worksheets. Once taught, BrainCel predicts outcomes from raw data entered in the worksheet. BrainCel is useful for risk analysis, stock trading, and pattern recognition of data that is too difficult to analyze using standard statistical methods.

CICERO   Micro Modeling Associates, Inc.
Word Financial Center
North Tower, 18th Floor
New York, NY 101281-1318
212-432-4245

CICERO retrieves data from business and financial databases, such as Lotus One Source U.S. Equities, and brings the data directly into Excel for analysis and reporting. CICERO contains built-in financial models, charts, and report templates.

CorelDRAW!   Corel Systems Corporation
1600 Carling Avenue
Ottawa, Ontario K12 8R7
Canada
613-728-8200

CorelDRAW! is a drawing and art program capable of producing professional graphics. Gradient shading, stretching, fitting text to curves and Bezier curves are a few of the features available. When Excel charts are copied into CorelDRAW!, each object in the chart can be manipulated separately. CorelDRAW! includes an extensive collection of fonts and clip art. Some of the drawings used in this book are taken from CorelDRAW! clip art.

DynaComm
Future Soft Engineering, Inc.
1001 S. Dairy Ashford, Suite 101
Houston, TX 77077
713-496-9400

DynaComm is a family of cross-platform communication programs that run in Windows, OS/2, and Macintosh environments. DynaComm products include a high-level scripting language compatible across platforms. Many asynch and bisynch protocols as well as networks are supported.

EXTRA! for Windows
Attachmate Corporation
13231 S.E. 36th Street
Bellevue, WA 98006
206-644-4010

EXTRA! for Windows gives Windows applications mainframe connectivity including concurrency, background file transfer, remote, LAN, and Token Ring connections.

FAXit! for Windows™
Alien Computing
37919 50th Street East
Palmdale, CA 93550
805-947-1310

FAXit! enables you to send a facsimile of any Windows document from within the Windows application. For example, from within Excel you can print a worksheet or chart to FAXit! instead of printing it to a printer; the worksheet or chart is faxed to the destination phone you specify. FAXit! can send and receive in the background. A number of major hardware fax boards are supported.

Heizer Software
Heizer Software
1941 Oak Park Boulevard, Suite 30
P.O. Box 232019
Pleasant Hill, CA 94523
800-888-7667

Heizer Software distributes hundreds of Excel worksheets, templates, and macros designed for many different purposes and industries. You can use these products as they are, as a base for customization, or you can use them to learn tricks and techniques. Stock market data and the tax template used in this book came from Heizer Software. Call for a free catalog.

IRMA Workstation
for Windows
Windowlink for IRMA
Crosstalk for Windows
DCA, Inc.
1000 Alderman Drive
Alpharetta, GA 30202
404-442-4000

Workstation for Windows offers a variety of connectivity options and hardware adapters for connection to mainframes, as well as asynchronous connectivity. Windowlink for IRMA enables the use of DCA or IBM coax for single-session PC-to-mainframe communications. Crosstalk provides asynchronous communication software.

ObjectVision   Borland
  for Windows™   1800 Green Hills Road
                           P.O. Box 660001
                           Scotts Valley, CA 95067-0001

ObjectVision enables you to quickly create forms for data entry, retrieval, and editing in Paradox, Btrieve, dBASE, and ASCII files. DDE links can be created to Excel worksheets. Forms, boxes, lists, and buttons are drawn on screen. Data-entry checking and decision logic are created using graphical decision trees and functions familiar to Excel users.

OPTIONS XL   Montgomery Investment Group
                           1455 Roman Drive
                           Rohnert Park, CA 94928
                           707-795-5673

OPTIONS enables you to calculate option theoretical values, volatilities, and sensitivities in custom spreadsheets. You can use seven models for pricing options on equities, bonds, futures, and more. OPTIONS is compatible with many real-time quote services and uses custom financial functions and models written in high performance Dynamic Link Libraries.

Pack*Rat*™   Polaris Software
                           1820 S. Escondido Boulevard
                           Escondido, CA 92025
                           619-743-7800

Pack*Rat* is an information manager that keeps track of names and addresses, schedules, contact lists, phone logs, expenses, and file logging. Pack*Rat* comes with macros for Excel and Word for Windows that add new commands to the menus. These commands enable Excel users to link expense data into Excel worksheets and track worksheet versions with file logging. Word for Windows users can look up addresses from within Word for Windows or print Word for Windows documents merged with name and address lists from Pack*Rat*.

PowerPoint   Microsoft Corporation
                           One Microsoft Way
                           Redmond, WA 98052-6399
                           206-882-8080

PowerPoint helps a speaker develop slide presentations, speaker notes, and audience handouts. Master templates can be used for consistency. PowerPoint uses OLÉ so that Excel charts and tables can be embedded into slides and handouts.

Q+E   Pioneer Software
               5540 Centerview Drive, Suite 324
               Raleigh, NC 27606
               919-859-2220

A version of Q+E comes free with Excel. Q+E is one of the best tools available for linking Excel to databases. Q+E can work as a separate Windows program through which you can can directly query, edit, join, or build databases. Q+E also enables Windows programs such as Excel and Word for Windows to integrate with databases. Q+E supports dBASE, Excel, and text files as well as Standard Query Language and DDE links. Contact Pioneer Software for information regarding drivers for additional databases.

@RISK   Palisades Corporation
               31 Decker Road
               New Field, NY 14867-9988
               607-277-8000

@RISK adds risk analysis capabilities to your worksheets. Input values can be defined as probability distributions for far better analysis through what-if or sensitivity analysis. The distribution of outputs for up to 1,000 points in the worksheet can be analyzed for each input distribution.

Rumba   Wall Data Inc.
               17769 N.E. 78th Place
               Redmond, WA 98052-4992
               206-883-4777

Rumba is a 3270 emulation package with development tools for Windows. Use Rumba to link data in Excel to mainframe applications.

Solver   Frontline Systems, Inc.
               140 University Avenue, Suite 100
               Palo Alto, CA 94301
               415-327-7296

Frontline Systems, Inc., developed the Solver add-in for Excel. Contact Frontline Systems for more advanced versions of Solver and for powerful forecasting and decision support add-ins for Excel. Frontline Systems maintains a computer bulletin board for developers; the bulletin board contains information on advanced uses and automation of Solver and its other products.

Word for Windows   Microsoft Corporation
                             One Microsoft Way
                             Redmond, WA 98052-6399
                             206-882-8080

Word for Windows is a professional level word processor designed to integrate with Excel. The menus and dialog boxes are similar to Excel's. Through menus, you can copy or link data and charts from Excel to Word documents. Word for Windows includes an extensive built-in programming language, WordBASIC, that you can use to customize Word for Windows or build complete document-oriented solutions, such as fax and EMail front-ends. Word for Windows was developed by Microsoft, the developer of Excel.

Index

P

X

Y

Z

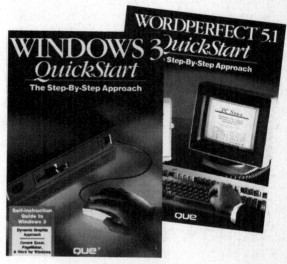

BUSINESS REPLY MAIL

First Class Permit No. 9918   Indianapolis, IN

Postage will be paid by addressee

11711 N. College
Carmel, IN 46032

BUSINESS REPLY MAIL

First Class Permit No. 9918   Indianapolis, IN

Postage will be paid by addressee

11711 N. College
Carmel, IN 46032

Editing Cells

Description	Command
Change relative/absolute reference	Formula Reference
Delete cell contents	Edit Clear

Editing Worksheets

Description	Command
Change row height	Format Row Height
Change column width	Format Column Width
Copy selected cell(s)	Edit Copy, then paste
Fill selected cells	Edit Fill Right/Fill Down
Insert cells, rows, or columns	Edit Insert
Move selected cell(s)	Edit Cut, then paste
Paste last copy or cut	Edit Paste
Paste selected contents	Edit Paste Special
Remove cells, rows, or columns	Edit Delete

Entering Data

Description	Command
Use accountant's ten-key pad	Options Workspace, Fixed Decimal
Paste functions in formulas	Formula Paste Function
Paste names in formulas	Formula Paste Name
Use numbers with auto decimals	Options Workspace, Fixed Decimal

Exit Excel

Description	Command
Exit Excel	File Exit

Files

Description	Command
Close active document	File Close
Close all documents	Shift+File Close All
Create new document	File New, worksheet/chart/macro
Create document from template	File New, template name
Create template from document	File Save As, Options button, File Format, Template
Delete file from disk	File Delete
Open existing document	File Open
Open nonExcel file	File Open, change file extension in box, OK
Save with a new name	File Save As
Save with same name	File Save
Save to a nonExcel format	File Save As, Options button, File Format
Save files as a group	File Save Workspace

Finding/Replacing Contents

Description	Command
Find cell address or range	Formula Goto
Replace text or formulas	Formula Replace
Select cells with special characteristics	Formula Select Special
Select cells with specific text	Formula Find

Formatting Cell Contents

Description	Command
Align text, dates, numbers	Format Alignment
Apply formatting style	Format Style
Create border or line; shade cells	Format Border
Calculate with displayed number	Options Calculation, Precision as Displayed
Change character fonts	Format Font
Use custom color palette	Options Color Palette
Change default format	Format Style, redefine Normal
Format numbers/dates	Format Number
Create custom number/date format	Format Number, Format
Hide zero values	Options Display, Zero Values
Redefine style	Format Style, Define button
Word wrap text across range	Format Justify
Word wrap text in single cell	Format Alignment, Wrap Text

Formulas

Description	Command
Prevent rounding errors	Options Calculation, Precision as Displayed
Paste functions in formulas	Formula Paste Function

Linking and Consolidating

Description	Command
Change/update links	File Links, Change/Update button
Create link	Edit Copy, then Edit Paste Link
Open files that feed a sheet	File Links, Links list
Transfer static data	Edit Copy, then Edit Paste Special, Values
Consolidate worksheets	Data Consolidate

Lotus 1-2-3

Description	Command
Save Excel as Lotus	File Save As, Options, File Format, WKS/WK1/WK3
Save Lotus as Excel	File Save As, Options, File Format, Normal
Lotus 1-2-3 movement keys	Options Workspace, Alternate Navigation Keys
Lotus 1-2-3 commands to Excel commands tutor	Options Workspace, Alternate Menu or Help Key (/), Lotus 1-2-3 Help option
Lotus 1-2-3 Help	Help Index, Switching from Lotus 1-2-3
Paste Excel Help notes	Help Lotus, Instructions, Lotus command
Remove Excel Help notes	Escape key
Accept 1-2-3 keys, demo in Excel	Help Lotus, Demo, Lotus command

Macros

Description	Command
Assign macro to object	Macro Object
Record new macro on new sheet	Macro Record
Record and name macro on existing macro sheet	Macro Set Recorder, then Macro Record
Record functions only on an existing macrosheet	Macro Set Recorder, then Macro Start Recorder
Stop macro recording	Macro Stop Recorder
Stop macro running	Esc
Run macro assigned to object	Click on object
Run macro	Macro Run
Record with relative/absolute reference	Macro Relative Record/Absolute Record

Naming

Description	Command
Define name	Formula Define Name
Delete name	Formula Define Name, Delete
List names and cells	Formula Paste Name, Paste List
Create names from text in cells	Formula Create Names
Paste name in formula	Formula Paste Name
Replace formula references with names	Formula Apply Names

Outlining

Description	Command
Create outline	Formula Outline, Create
Apply outline styles	Formula Outline, Apply Styles

Print

Description	Command
Change default printers or printer settings	File Printer Setup
Change margins in preview	File Print Preview, Margins
Set page layout, margins, orientation for sheet	File Page Setup
Preview document	File Print Preview
Print document	File Print
Set manual page break	Options Set Page Break
Delete manual page break	Select adjacent to page break, Options Remove Page Break
Set area to print	Options Set Print Area
Remove printing area	Formula Define Name, Select Print Area, Delete
Set rows/columns for titles	Options Set Print Titles

Protection

Description	Command
Format changeable/hidden cells	Format Cell Protection
Restrict document access	File Save As, Options, Protection Password
Turn worksheet protection on/off	Options Protect Document

Q+E

Description	Command
Activate the Q+E window	Data Activate Q+E*
Connect to external database	Data Set Database, External Database
Paste field names into worksheet	Data Paste Fieldnames
Set criteria range	Data Set Criteria
Set extract range	Data Set Extract
Extract data meeting criteria	Data Extract
Delete data meeting criteria	Data Delete
Extract using SQL SELECT	Data SQL Query

*Q+E must be loaded with the QE.XLS add-in before the Data Activate command is available.

Solver

Description	Command
Back solve for single solution	Formula Goal Seek
Solve for best solution*	Formula Solver, **S**olve
Change constraints*	Formula Solver, Add/Change/Delete

*Solver must be installed before the Formula Solver command is available.

Undo

Description	Command
Back out of menu or dialog box	Escape key/Cancel button
Back out of formula bar edits	Escape key/X box
Undo last change in worksheet	Edit Undo

Window Changes

Description	Command
Excel Control menu	Alt, space bar
Document Control menu	Alt, - (hyphen)
Change Excel to icon	Alt, space bar, Minimize
Change size	Control menu, Size, arrow
Close window	Control menu, Close
Define Windows defaults	Alt, space bar, Run, Control Panel
Enlarge window to full screen	Control menu, Maximize
Restore to previous size	Control menu, Restore
Move window location	Control menu, Move, arrow

Workgroups

Description	Command
Group windows	Window Workgroup
Ungroup windows	Activate other window
Fill workgroup	Edit Fill Workgroup

Worksheet Windows

Description	Command
Activate document window	Window # (Document number)
Arrange windows	Window Arrange All
Freeze/unfreeze panes	Options Freeze Panes/Unfreeze Panes
Hide/unhide window	Window Hide/Unhide
New window on document	Window New Window
Split window panes	Alt, - (hyphen), Split, arrow, Enter

Function Keys

If your computer has only ten function keys, you can use these combinations:

    Alt+F1 for F11

    Alt+F2 for F12

Function Key	Description
F1	Help
Shift+F1	Context Help
F2	Activate Formula Bar
Shift+F2	Formula Note
Ctrl+F2	Window Show Info
F3	Formula Paste Name
Shift+F3	Formula Paste Function
Ctrl+F3	Formula Define Name
Ctrl+Shift+F3	Formula Create Names
F4	Formula Reference
Ctrl+F4	Control Close (document window)
Alt+F4	File Exit (Close Excel)
F5	Formula Goto
Shift+F5	Formula Find (cell contents)
Ctrl+F5	Control Restore (document window)
F6	Next pane
Shift+F6	Previous pane
Ctrl+F6	Next document window
Ctrl+Shift+F6	Previous document window
F7	Formula Find (next)
Shift+F7	Formula Find (previous)
Ctrl+F7	Control Move (document window)
F8	Extend mode (on/off)
Shift+F8	Add mode (on/off)
Ctrl+F8	Control Size (document window)
F9	Options Calculate Now
Shift+F9	Options Calculate Document
F10	Activate menu bar
Ctrl+F10	Control Maximize (document window)
F11	File New (chart)
Shift+F11	File New (worksheet)
Ctrl+F11	File New (macro sheet)
F12	File Save As
Shift+F12	File Save
Ctrl+F12	File Open
Ctrl+Shift+F12	File Print

QUE® CORPORATION

LEADING COMPUTER KNOWLEDGE